Author: Vanina Mangano, PMP, PMI-RMP, PMI-SP, ITIL, Project+

Co-Author: Al Smith, Jr. PMI-ACP, CRISC, Lean/Six Sigma Black Belt, SCJP

Technical Editor: Gabriela Spindola, PMP

The PM Instructors™

A Never Limited Publishing Book

ISBN 978-1490588704

Printed in the United States of America 070813.

First Printing 2009
Never Limited Publishing books may be purchased for educational, business, or sales promotional use. For more information contact 888-687-6629.

Table of Contents

Chapter 1: PMP Exam Preparation Overview

Course Objectives:

- ☐ Describe the application process
- ☐ Identify the PMP® exam requirements, format, blueprint, costs
- ☐ Explain exam day

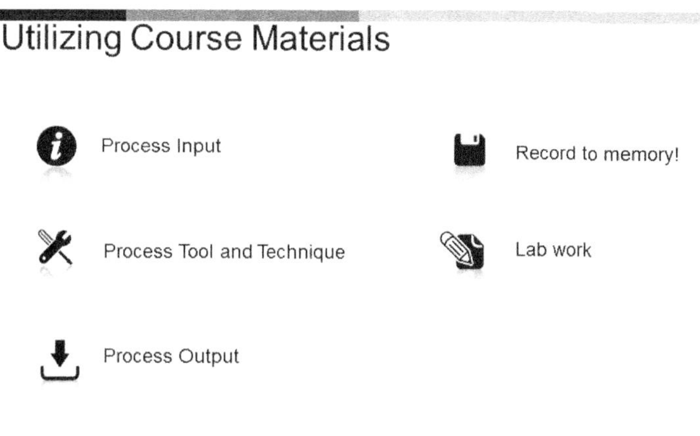

Understanding and Utilizing Course Materials

Process Input

This symbol indicates that an input belonging to a process within *A Guide to the Project Management Body of Knowledge (PMBOK® Guide)* has been referenced.

Process Tool and Technique

This symbol indicates that a tool and technique belonging to a process within the *PMBOK® Guide* has been referenced.

Process Output

This symbol indicates that an output belonging to a process within the *PMBOK® Guide* has been referenced.

Record to memory!

Some terms and concepts require a higher level of understanding or recall than others. This symbol is an indicator of those items.

Lab work

This symbol is a recommendation of when to complete given lab work. Lab exercises can be found at the end of each chapter.

The Project Management Institute

- Snapshot of background
  - Founded in 1969
  - Not-for-Profit member based organization
  - Over 650,000+ members worldwide, in 185+ countries
  - www.PMI.org

Project Management Institute

PMI offers a variety of credentials. Credential aspirants may pursue one or earn multiple credentials throughout their career. As with the PMP® credential, the PMI-RMP®, PMI-SP®, PMI-ACP®, and PgMP® credentials have application requirements that must be met, such as a minimum number of hands-on experience in the topic related to the credential. The CAPM® is considered to be an entry-level credential into the project management profession, and is meant for those that do not yet have sufficient experience to pursue the PMP® credential.

The Project Management Institute

- *A Guide to the Project Management Body of Knowledge* (*PMBOK® Guide*), 5th Edition
- The "de facto global standard" for the project management profession
- Certification exams largely based on its contents
  - Program Management Professional (PgMP)®
  - **Project Management Professional (PMP)®**
  - **Certified Associate in Project Management (CAPM)®**
  - PMI Risk Management Professional (PMI-RMP)®
  - PMI Scheduling Professional (PMI-SP)®
  - PMI Agile Certified Practitioner (PMI-ACP)®

The Project Management Institute

- PMI Code of Ethics and Professional Conduct

  "As practitioners of project management, we are committed to doing what is right and honorable. We set high standards for ourselves and we aspire to meet these standards in all aspects of our lives—at work, at home, and in service to our profession."

  - Applicable to: *PMI members, PMI credential holders, credential applicants, PMI volunteers.*
  - Aspirational vs. Mandatory Conduct
  - Values:
    - Responsibility
    - Respect
    - Fairness
    - Honesty

*PMI.org 2012. Project Management Institute. 31 Jan 2012 Inc http://www.pmi.org/en/About-Us/Ethics/Code-of-Ethics.aspx

PMI Code of Ethics and Professional Conduct

Audience

The *PMI Code of Ethics and Professional Conduct* is applicable to all PMI members, active PMI credential holders (including those that are not active PMI members), credential applicants, and those that serve in a volunteer capacity for PMI.

Aspirational vs. Mandatory Conduct

The *PMI Code of Ethics and Professional Conduct* contains four values. Each value is described in the context of aspirational and mandatory conduct. **Aspirational** conduct refers to the conduct that practitioners strive to uphold. Although they are aspirational in nature, they are not considered optional. **Mandatory** conduct refers to conduct that is measurable and is held to a firm requirement.

Not upholding these values may mean disciplinary actions will be taken against an individual, who will need to come before the PMI Ethics Review Committee. Violators of the code may lose their membership and/or credential status.

Values[1]

- **Responsibility**: *"Responsibility is our duty to take ownership for the decisions we make or fail to make, the actions we take or fail to take, and the consequences that result."*
- **Respect**: *"Respect is our duty to show a high regard for ourselves, others, and the resources entrusted to us."*
- **Fairness**: *"Fairness is our duty to make decisions and act impartially and objectively. Our conduct must be free from competing self interest, prejudice, and favoritism."*
- **Honesty**: *"Honesty is our duty to understand the truth and act in a truthful manner both in our communications and in our conduct."*

[1] *PMI.org. 2012. Project Management Institute. 31 Jan. 2012, http://www.pmi.org/en/About-Us/Ethics/Code-of-Ethics.aspx

International Organization for Standardization

- Network of national standards institutes across 160+ countries
- Published >18,000 global standards
  - ISO 9000
  - ISO 21500
- Non-governmental organization that serves as a bridge between public and private sectors
- Maintains library of standards
- www.iso.org

International Organization for Standardization

About ISO

The International Organization for Standardization (ISO) is an international standard-setting body that is comprised of volunteer representatives across 160 countries. Since 1926, ISO (originally International Federation of the National Standardizing Associations (ISA)) has published industrial and commercial standards, several of which have become law. ISO itself is a non-governmental organization, instead serving as a bridge between the public and private sectors. As of December 2010, ISO has published over 18,000 standards.

ISO 9000 Series

According to ISO, the ISO 9000 series contains a generic set of requirements for implementing a quality management system, which can be applied to any organization. The purpose of this family of standards is to ensure that customer and stakeholder needs are met. ISO 9000 is based on the fundamentals of quality management systems, including the eight management principles. ISO 9001 deals with the requirements that organizations must meet in order to claim compliance with the standard. The quality management section of the *PMBOK® Guide* specifies that the quality section is "intended to be compatible with" ISO, referencing ISO 9000 and ISO 8402.

ISO 21500

In 2012, ISO published a project management standard – ISO 21500. This standard focuses on providing high level concepts and processes considered to form good practices in project management.

How this Applies to the Exam

Students should expect to see 1-3 questions on the exam relating to ISO.

PMP Exam Blueprint

Initiating	13%
Planning	24%
Executing	30%
Monitoring & Controlling	25%
Closing	8%

About the PMP Exam

PMP Exam Blueprint

The PMP certification exam covers five domains, all of which are addressed within this book:

1. Initiating
2. Planning
3. Executing
4. Monitoring and Controlling
5. Closing

Exam Objectives

The following exam objectives are covered within each of the domains shown above:

Initiating – 13%

- Conduct project selection methods
- Define scope
- Document project risks, assumptions, and constraints
- Identify and perform stakeholder analysis
- Develop project charter
- Obtain project charter approval

Planning – 24%

- Define and record requirements, constraints, and assumptions
- Identify project team and define roles and responsibilities
- Create the WBS
- Develop change management plan
- Identify risks and define risk strategies
- Obtain plan approval
- Conduct kick-off meeting

Executing – 30%

- Execute tasks defined in project management plan
- Ensure common understanding and set expectations
- Implement the procurement of project resources
- Manage resource allocation
- Implement quality management plan
- Implement approved changes
- Implement approved actions and workarounds

Monitoring and Controlling – 25%

- Measure project performance
- Verify and manage changes to the project
- Ensure project deliverables conform to quality standards
- Monitor all risks

Closing – 8%

- Obtain final acceptance for the project
- Obtain financial, legal, and administrative closure
- Release project resources
- Identify, document and communicate lessons learned
- Create and distribute final project report
- Archive and retain project records

PMP Exam Format

- 200 multiple choice questions
  - 175 scored, 25 pre-test
  - Pass / Fail exam
    - *Proficient*
    - *Moderately Proficient*
    - *Below Proficient*
- 4 hour exam + 15 minute tutorial
- Computer-based testing (CBT) vs. paper-based testing (PBT)

PMP Exam Format

Exam Questions

The exam contains a cumulative total of 200 multiple choice questions, broken out as follows:

- 175 scored questions
- 25 pre-test questions. Pre-test questions are *anonymously* mixed in with the scored questions. Pre-test questions allow PMI to first analyze questions before deciding on whether to absorb them as part of the official database of scored questions.

Exam Scoring

This is a pass or fail exam. Those taking a computer-based exam will receive an immediate score. Applicants do not see the total number of correct / incorrect questions. Instead, each exam domain receives the following result:

- **Proficient:** *above average level of knowledge*
- **Moderately proficient:** *average level of knowledge*
- **Below proficient:** *below average level of knowledge*

PMI does not publish a passing / failing percentage.

Computer Based Testing

Computer-based testing is the primary method of taking the exam. In order to qualify to take a paper-based test, applicants must reside 186.5+ miles from the nearest computer-based testing center. Paper-based testing may be administered by an employer who has a minimum of 10 employees taking the exam (distance is not a factor in this case).

PMP Exam Costs*

	Member	Non-Member
Computer-Based Testing	$405	$555
Paper-Based Testing	$250	$400
Computer-Based Re-examination	$275	$375
Paper-Based Re-examination	$150	$300
CCR Credential Renewal	$60	$150

* Visit www.PMI.org for updated exam costs

PMP Exam Pricing and Costs[2]

Eligibility Window

An applicant has a one-year window to take the certification exam once their application has been approved. If an applicant fails, they may re-take the exam up to two times within the one-year eligibility window.

CCR

After achieving a credential, credential holders must meet Continuing Credential Requirements (CCR). Every three years, credential holders must earn a specified number of Professional Development Units (PDUs) in order to maintain their credential status as active.

---

[2] Applicants should visit PMI.org for updated exam pricing. Prices shown on the material are current as of February 2013, and are subject to change.

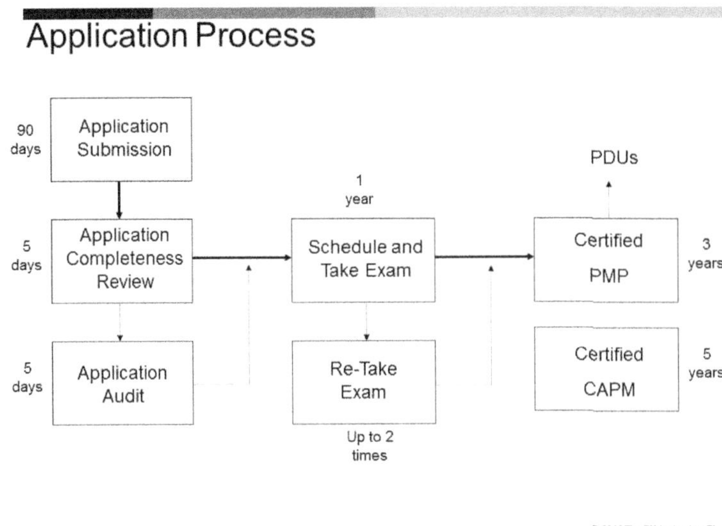

Application Process

1. After submitting the credential application to PMI, the application will be checked to make sure it is complete. The application will be processed within 3-5 business days. Once an applicant begins an application, they will have up to 90 days to submit it.
2. If the application is found to be complete, applicant will be asked to submit payment.
3. (If audited only) Applications are selected to participate in the audit process at random, although PMI reserves the right to audit applications at any time. Approximately 12% of applications are selected for a random audit. If an application is selected, the applicant will be required to show documented proof of meeting eligibility requirements. If audited, applicants have up to 90 days to complete the audit process.
4. After payment (or passing the audit), the applicant may schedule and take the exam. The eligibility window of 1 year begins on the day that the application (or audit) is approved. Applicants may take the exam up to three times within the eligibility window. Computer-based exam results are provided immediately.
5. The CCR cycle is every 3 years on the anniversary of passing the exam. Requirements for PMP® credential holders include 60 project management related PDUs. PDUs are not applicable to CAPM credential holders, since this credential does not renew.

PMP Exam Requirements

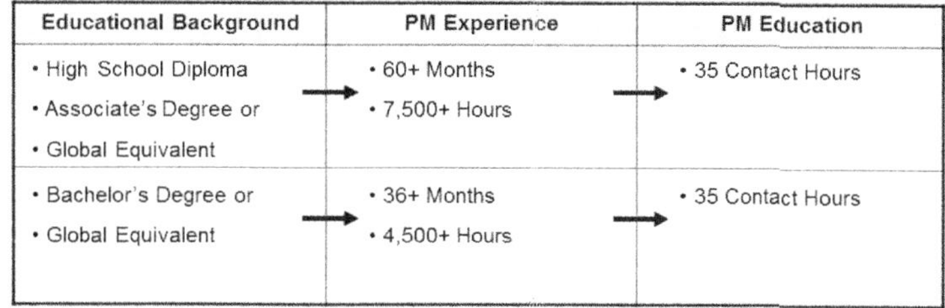

Educational Background	PM Experience	PM Education
• High School Diploma • Associate's Degree or • Global Equivalent	→ • 60+ Months • 7,500+ Hours	→ • 35 Contact Hours
• Bachelor's Degree or • Global Equivalent	→ • 36+ Months • 4,500+ Hours	→ • 35 Contact Hours

- Must be accrued within the past 8 consecutive years
- Months may not overlap

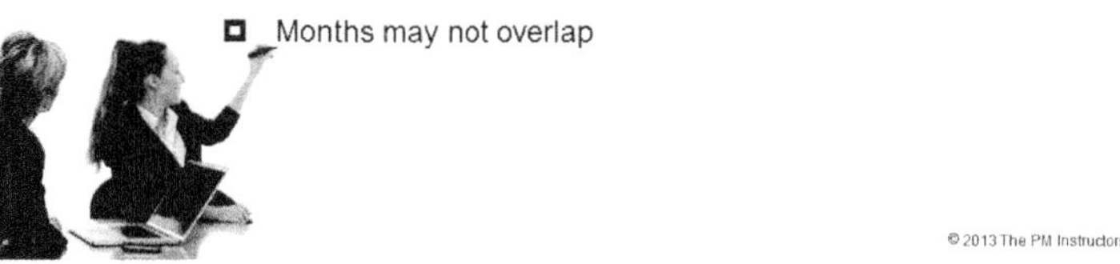

© 2013 The PM Instructors™

PMP Exam Requirements and Qualifications

Educational Background Requirements

PMI has two different levels of requirements, according to an applicant's highest level of education attained. Project management work experience refers only to hours spent working on project management related activities within the past 8 consecutive years; education "contact" hours refers specifically to project related training / education. Note: there is no specific timeframe that contact hours must have been earned.

> **A high school diploma or associate's degree or the global equivalent** requires a minimum of 60 months of hands-on project management experience totaling 7,500+ hours, and 35 educational "contact" hours earned in the area of project management.
>
> **A bachelor's degree, or the global equivalent** requires a minimum of 36 months of hands-on project management experience totaling 4,500+ hours, and 35 educational "contact" hours earned in the area of project management.

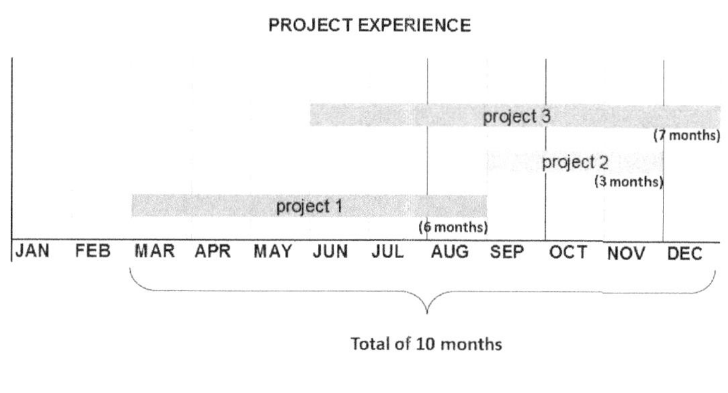

© 2013 The PM Instructors™

As noted in the requirements, the PMP application requires documentation of total hours of project management experience, and also total number of non-overlapping months of experience. In the sample image reflecting project experience, three projects are shown, some of which overlap. Note that in documenting experience, a month may not be counted twice. For example, project 1 and project 3 overlap during the months of June, July, and August. This would therefore count as 3 months of experience (versus 6). The total number of hours, on the other hand, may overlap. All hours worked on projects 1, 2, and 3 would count towards your total number of hours.

Training Providers

Training providers may include Registered Education Providers (REP), PMI component organizations, training companies or consultants, company sponsored-programs, distance learning companies that include an end of course assessment, and university/college courses.

Question Characteristics & Components

- Noise
- Common Terminology
- Too Much Information
- Select the BEST answer
- Inaccurate / Not
- Situational
- Calculation

Question Format

Format of Questions

All questions will be delivered in multiple-choice format with one correct answer. However, there are many formats within the scope of a multiple-choice question that one can see on the exam. The bullets above describe the various ways that a question may be asked.

The Challenge

What makes PMI exams challenging is that there may be more than one right answer. You must select the BEST answer from a PMI perspective. This means that during the preparation process, you will need to train yourself to answer questions from a PMI standpoint, and not your own. Many organizations follow different processes and use various terms differently. This is not only what makes the exam challenging, but what also presents a benefit, as it promotes a common understanding of terms and processes.

Sample Question

1. Which of the following is not a characteristic of a project?
   A. Repetitive and ongoing
   B. Temporary
   C. Have a definite beginning and end
   D. Result in a unique product or result

The question above shows a common question format that uses the key word "not". All questions will contain four potential options: A, B, C, or D. There is only one correct answer.

The correct answer for the question above is A.

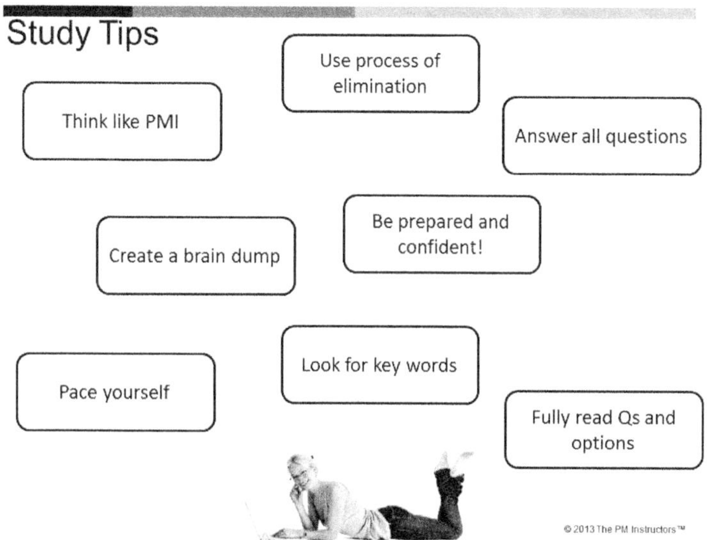

Study Tips and Preparation

Study Tips

There are a few tips to consider before fully diving into the content. Keep in mind that knowing the content does not necessarily guarantee that you will pass the exam. You also need to practice and build effective test taking skills. Here are a few tips to keep in mind as you study:

1. Make sure that you fully read through the questions and every option. If option A looks good, read through the remaining options before selecting it. Remember that there can be more than one right answer, and you need to pick the best one.
2. Look for key words within the questions, such as except, best, not. For the options, look for words that signify proactive behavior, since this is often a sign that it is a good choice.

3. Think like PMI. By this I mean the standards and content that PMI publishes. Every organization has a slightly different approach to managing projects, and the exam will be based on the *PMBOK® Guide*, so you will need to answer based on the *PMBOK® Guide* content, not necessarily how your organization does it.
4. Use the process of elimination. If you aren't sure about the answer, begin by eliminating the options that you know aren't right. This increases the likelihood of selecting the correct option.
5. Come to the exam prepared and confident. Don't second guess yourself. Many students say that when they changed an answer in completing a practice exam, their first choice was typically the correct one.
6. Pace yourself through the exam. This is a timed exam, so you can't spend 5 or 10 minutes digesting a question. If you spend too much time on one, take a guess, mark it for review, and come back to it at the end before submitting the exam. You will have an opportunity to do this. Set milestones for yourself, such as being 50% complete by the time you reach 1 ½ hours into the exam.
7. Make sure that you answer all questions. A blank question is a wrong one.
8. Create a brain dump! Use your extra tutorial time effectively by jotting down formulas and other key pieces of information when you are mentally fresh at the beginning of the exam time.

Brain Dump
What you write down on the scratch sheet of paper provided the moment you sit down at your test station.
Maximum time: 15 min.
What is a "brain dump" list?

- You must return ALL scratch paper to the test center representative after your exam, including your brain dump sheet.
- Examples: All formulas, process names, name of theorists and theories, types of power, conflict management techniques, etc.

Brain Dump

It is often advised to create a brain dump list at the beginning of the exam, provided that you are given scratch sheet of paper to work with. This will be the case for the PMP exam, and you can use the remaining time left over from your 15 minute computer-based tutorial to start your brain dump.

Using your scratch sheet of paper, write down key pieces of information that you may forget as you move through the exam. When you first sit down at the beginning of the exam, you will be mentally fresh, and remembering things like formulas will be easier. But two hours into the exam, it is easy to forget this information as you become mentally tired. Creating a brain dump list is perfectly legal, although you need to memorize this information, as you can't bring it into the exam with you.

Before exam day, strategize what will go on to your brain dump list, and practice creating it. Ideally, it would take no more than 10 minutes to create, as you don't want to take up too much of your exam time.

Exam Day

- Schedule your exam strategically
  - ✓ Alert
  - ✓ Rested
  - ✓ Prepared
- Arrive up to 1 hour early
- Bring all required items to the test center
  - ✓ 2 forms of ID
  - ✓ Eligibility letter
- Bring all recommended items to the test center
  - ✓ Dress in layers
  - ✓ Bring a snack
  - ✓ Brain dump list for pre-test review

Exam Day

There are additional information and tips about exam day to review, to clarify what you can expect on the big day. It always helps to go in prepared and comfortable with what will take place.

Consider the following:

- Schedule the exam at a time that is convenient for you, and when your performance will be at an optimum level. Be sure to get plenty of rest the night before. Avoid cramming at the last minute, since this is likely to exhaust you mentally.
- Arrive up to 1 hour early for your exam. Arriving early also helps to avoid a stressful drive if you hit traffic unexpectedly when in route.
- Bring two forms of ID with you and your confirmation letter showing the exam date and time.
- It can get quite cold in the testing rooms, so dress in layers if possible. Typically, testing centers do not allow you to take a jacket with you into the room unless you are wearing it, but you can always leave a sweater within your locker if needed.
- Bring a snack for your break if needed.
- If you arrive early, you can also review your brain dump list while you wait, although you will need to leave this in your locker before going into the test room.

Module Summary

In this module we:

- Described the application process
- Identified the PMP® exam requirements, format, blueprint, costs
- Explained exam day

Individual Assessment

Self-Assessment Exam Questions

1. Which of the following is not a formal process of the Project Time Management Knowledge Area?
    A. Estimate Activity Resources
    B. Create Schedule Management Plan
    C. Develop Schedule
    D. Control Schedule

2. Which of the following BEST describes the purpose of the procurement management plan?
    A. A plan that defines the portion of the project scope that is to be included within the related contract
    B. A plan that describes how the procurement processes will be managed from developing procurement documents through contract closure
    C. A plan that integrates and consolidates all the subsidiary management plans and baselines from the planning processes through closure
    D. A plan that describes the criteria that will be used to rate or score seller proposals

3. The purpose of the process improvement plan is:
    A. to document process-related lessons learned after carrying out quality audits
    B. to define how quality assurance activities are to be carried out
    C. to describe how the project team will implement the company's quality policy
    D. to outline how the team will assess and analyze the effectiveness of the processes

4. A project manager is working through potential options by performing decision tree analysis. Scenario A has a failure impact of -$5,000 with a probability of 25% and no impact if successful, and scenario B has a failure impact of -$3,500 with a probability of 65% and no impact if successful. Which scenario should the project manager choose?
    A. Scenario A
    B. Scenario B
    C. Neither scenario
    D. Insufficient information provided

5. You are the project manager of a project building a new product for a local government agency. Currently, you are preparing to identify the list of activities with the close participation of the project team members that will be performing the work. As a starting point, you gather the descriptions of the work to be carried out. Where will you obtain this information?
    A. Activity attributes
    B. WBS dictionary
    C. Activity list
    D. Work breakdown structure

6. The purpose of work performance data is:
    A. to provide information on the activities that must be executed
    B. to notify the sponsor of what work remains
    C. to provide information on the status of project work
    D. to identify the variance between work planned and work performed

7. Immediately after a planning meeting concluded, a project manager and the development lead held an ad hoc discussion about the schedule for a project they are working on. During their discussion, they uncover that each thought a set of deliverables were going to be completed at different points in the schedule. In light of this new revelation, they agree to update the schedule and share the information with the rest of the team. What is the BEST type of communication to use when dealing with complex issues, such as this one?
    A. Informal written
    B. Formal written
    C. Informal verbal
    D. Formal verbal

8. After carrying out the Control Schedule process, typical results include the creation of change requests, updates to various project documents, and:
   A. calculated schedule variance and schedule performance index
   B. creation of the schedule baseline, which is a component of the project management plan
   C. identification of the critical chain
   D. leads and lags added to the schedule for the first time

9. Which of the following is an inaccurate statement?
   A. The risk register is a part of the project documents.
   B. The risk register is first created during the Identify Risks process.
   C. The contents of the risk register are updated during project planning.
   D. After its creation, the risk register becomes an input and output of the remaining risk management processes.

10. The project manager has just determined that a stakeholder meeting is warranted to discuss the current status of time reserves. Which of the following would be the most effective means of meeting with the stakeholders?
    A. Hold a group meeting in the conference room
    B. Schedule individual one-on-one conference calls
    C. Schedule a group conference call
    D. Send an email to all stakeholders and request single responses to the project manager

11. Nubs and Bits is a Seattle based company that produces healthy snacks for dogs of all sizes. Its latest project involves creating a snack for large breeds that takes up to one hour to consume. The project manager, who has managed multiple projects for Nubs and Bits over the past five years, begins to work with a team of experts to decompose the project's deliverables. What process is the project manager performing?
    A. Collect Requirements
    B. Define Scope
    C. Create WBS
    D. Validate Scope

12. Which of the following is a project manager likely to use when attempting to show the pattern of relationship between two different variables?
    A. Scatter diagram
    B. Cause and effect diagram
    C. Control chart
    D. Histogram

13. Which of the following provides additional details of the activity cost estimates?
    A. Basis of estimates
    B. Activity cost estimates dictionary
    C. Cost estimate definitions
    D. WBS dictionary

14. A project management team is faced with a lack of resources due to several competing projects labeled as high priority. None of the three senior developers within the company would be available as needed for the project, and the project sponsor rejected the possibility of acquiring resources externally. What will the project management team be forced to do?
    A. Abandon the project, since the necessary resources are unavailable
    B. Alter the resource requirements by accepting a lower skill level for the tasks lacking resources
    C. Place the project on hold until the necessary resources are available to complete the tasks in question
    D. Insist that the project sponsor allow the project management team to acquire the resources externally

15. Activity A has a probability of 10% and an impact of $4,000. What is the expected monetary value of Activity A?
    A. $4,000
    B. $4,400
    C. $400
    D. $3,600

16. Stakeholder analysis, which is a tool and technique that analyzes the influences and interests of stakeholders, is utilized by which of the following processes:
    A. Identify Stakeholders
    B. Communications Planning
    C. Plan Risk Management
    D. Information Distribution

17. Rosco Enterprises is currently working on a large commercial fencing project that will construct a custom-built fence around a 10,000 square foot property. To deliver by the committed date, the company will need to hire a sub-contactor to produce the custom maple wood post end-caps. After the request for proposal (RFP) was sent out to prospective sellers, Rosco Enterprises scheduled an event where they would answer questions from the prospective sellers to help clarify the details of the work. What is this event called?
    A. Bidder conferences
    B. Question and answer sessions
    C. Seller sessions
    D. Seller conferences

18. Which of the following processes is concerned with identifying and documenting the relationships among the project activities?
    A. Define Activities
    B. Sequence Activities
    C. Develop Schedule
    D. Control Schedule

19. Before generating the first release of the schedule baseline, the project manager shared the information with the functional manager of the primary department that the project was involved with. Although the functional manager's approval was not required for project documents, the project manager made a regular practice of keeping them informed of the project. What type of organizational structure do the project manager and functional manager most likely work within?
    A. Projectized
    B. Functional
    C. Matrix
    D. Traditional

20. Nubs and Bits is a Seattle based company that produces healthy snacks for dogs of all sizes. Its latest project involves creating a snack for large breeds that takes up to one hour to consume. The project manager, who has managed multiple projects for Nubs and Bits over the past five years, decides to build a prototype. What value do prototypes provide?
    A. Allow for early feedback on the requirements
    B. Provide customers with a preview of the product
    C. Allow the marketing team to showcase the product
    D. None. The project manager made a poor choice

21. The Monte Carlo technique is a type of:
    A. what-if scenario analysis
    B. risk management tool
    C. schedule compression
    D. waste of management funds

22. Which of the following statements is inaccurate?
    A. Precedence Diagramming Method (PDM) uses dummy activities
    B. Precedence Diagramming Method (PDM) displays activities on the node
    C. Arrow Diagramming Method (ADM) uses only one type of logical relationship
    D. Both Precedence Diagramming Method (PDM) and Arrow Diagramming Method (ADM) use the finish-to-start dependency

23. Which of the following is not a component of the project management plan?
    A. Scope management plan
    B. Schedule baseline
    C. Project scope statement
    D. Risk register

24. A project team member called the project manager to notify him that there seemed to be confusion about the resources needed to complete her activity. The project manager, who was running late for a meeting, told the team member not to worry about it and ended the conversation by telling her to have a good day, and that they would touch base in the coming weeks. The project team member was left wondering whether or not the project manager understood the severity of the situation, since without the resources, her activity could not proceed and the deadline would be missed. In this scenario, what was the communication role of the project manager?
    A. Sender
    B. Encoder
    C. Receiver
    D. Decoder

25. Corporate Sublime is a software development company with headquarters in Australia, and a remote office based out of the USA. After determining that the latest project required a specialized expertise in creating and managing the project schedule, a full-time scheduler was brought on board. While estimating the resource requirements, the scheduler discovers that several activities require a specialized skill-set not currently available within the company. In order to determine the next step, what is the scheduler most likely to do?
    A. Acquire the resources externally
    B. Double check the resource calendars
    C. Wait to see if the company hires the resources
    D. Perform alternative analysis

26. Small, incremental improvements within a product or process is known as:
    A. Halo effect
    B. Kaizen
    C. Kanban
    D. Muda

27. A project manager looking to show how requirements link to business needs is likely to use what?
    A. Requirements management plan
    B. Requirements traceability matrix
    C. Requirements documentation
    D. Requirements accountability matrix

28. A project manager has just estimated the cost of individual activities. What process will the project manager carry out next?
    A. Estimate Costs
    B. Determine Budget
    C. Manage Budget
    D. Control Costs

29. A Recreational Vehicle rental company is launching a consignment program for private owners to participate in, who are looking to rent out their vehicles. The project manager has just begun estimating the durations of the project activities. It was clear early on that a high level of uncertainty existed in four activities that were considered very important. Based on this information, what is the project manager most likely to do?
    A. Insert a lag in front of the four activities
    B. Add a feeding buffer to the four activities
    C. Add a reserve to the four activities
    D. Insert a lead in front of the four activities

30. Which of the following BEST defines resource breakdown structures?
    A. Availability of various types of resources, including human, equipment, and material resources
    B. Subcategories of resource categories, including labor and material
    C. A hierarchical view of the resource categories and resource types used in a project
    D. A hierarchical view of the project deliverables broken down into smaller components

31. Which quality theorist defined quality as fitness for use, with fitness being defined by the customer?
    A. Phillip Crosby
    B. Vilfredo Pareto
    C. Joseph Juran
    D. W. Edwards Deming

32. A collection of related activities that result in the completion of a major deliverable describes what?
    A. Project life cycle
    B. Project management life cycle
    C. Phase
    D. Process Group

33. Nicolas is the sponsor of a project that will replace all equipment that has already surpassed their end of life time span. He decides to assign this project to Carina, his top performing project manager. Carina's first task will be to write the project charter. Who will be responsible for signing the project charter document, thereby approving the project?
    A. Carina
    B. Nicolas
    C. Project management team
    D. Both Carina and Nicolas

34. Rosco Enterprises is currently working on a large commercial fencing project that will construct a custom-built fence around a 10,000 square foot property. To deliver by the committed date, the company will need to hire a sub-contactor to produce the custom maple wood post end-caps. So far, the procurement statement of work has been clearly outlined, as well as the delivery date for the end caps. Based on the information provided, what type of contract will Rosco Enterprises likely use for the work carried out by the sub-contractor?
    A. Fixed price
    B. Cost reimbursable
    C. Cost plus
    D. Time and materials

35. Which of the following is not an input to the Manage Communications process?
    A. Communications management plan
    B. Work performance reports
    C. Organizational process assets
    D. Communication methods

36. Taquitos R Us is a trendy fast food restaurant preparing to open two new restaurants within the same county. To launch this effort, the company hires a full-time project manager. After officially kicking off the project and documenting the detailed scope and high-level schedule, the project manager begins working on determining what the overall budget will be. Which of the following refers to the activity cost estimates, plus the contingency and management reserves?
    A. Cost performance baseline
    B. Project funding requirements
    C. Project budget
    D. Program budget

37. Which of the following statements is inaccurate?
    A. There are three tools and techniques used to develop the risk management plan.
    B. The result of holding planning meetings within the Plan Risk Management process are documented and summarized within the risk management plan.
    C. Tracking risk activities will be defined based on the risk management plan.
    D. Funds set aside for risk activities are discussed as part of the risk management plan.

38. You are the scheduler of a project responsible for the development of a new housing community with a budget of 50 million US dollars, making it the largest project you have participated in. Currently, you are in the process of estimating the resources needed to carry out the project's activities, along with the close efforts of the project manager. During the early stages of your efforts, the project manager requests the availability of the five critical resources attached to the project. What document will you use to obtain this information?
    A. Resource breakdown structure
    B. Resource calendars
    C. Project schedule
    D. Schedule management plan

39. The purpose of the Validate Scope process is:
    A. To define and document the needs of the stakeholders, and meet the project objectives
    B. To develop a detailed description of the project and product
    C. To formalize acceptance of the completed project deliverables
    D. To monitor the status of the project and product scope and manage changes to the scope baseline

40. In which process are change requests reviewed, approved, and / or rejected?
    A. Direct and Manage Project Work
    B. Perform Integrated Change Control
    C. Manage Project Work
    D. Approve Project Work

41. You are the project manager of a project with a budget at completion (BAC) value of $40,000. Based on current reports, the project has an earned value (EV) of $15,000, an actual cost (AC) of $18,000, and a planned value (PV) of $16,500. Assuming that the project will continue to perform at a steady rate, what is the to-complete performance index?
    A. 1.0
    B. .83
    C. .90
    D. 1.14

42. During a planning meeting, the project manager informed the scheduler that a potential change to the scope of the project was currently under consideration. The scheduler was concerned that altering the scope in any way would likely result in a change to an already aggressive and tight schedule. The scheduler's concern was based on the concept of:
    A. Schedule compression
    B. Triple constraints
    C. Schedule modeling
    D. Proper schedule management

43. Which of the following is not used as an input to the Conduct Procurements process?
    A. Source selection criteria
    B. Make or buy decisions
    C. Procurement documents
    D. Selected sellers

44. Which of the following BEST defines a control account?
    A. The account managed by the accounting team, where funds for the project are allocated and managed
    B. The account managed by the project management team, where funds for the project are allocated and managed
    C. A management control point placed after a work package within a work breakdown structure (WBS)
    D. A management control point placed between a deliverable and work package within a work breakdown structure (WBS)

45. Giving customers extras, such as adding in functionality or increasing performance, not included in the project scope is known as:
    A. Voice of the Customer (VOC)
    B. Halo effect
    C. Customer service
    D. Gold plating

46. Which of the following is not considered to be a component of the project management plan?
    A. Procurement management plan
    B. Scope baseline
    C. Project scope statement
    D. Milestone list

47. Nicolas is the sponsor of a project that will replace all equipment that has already surpassed their end of life time span. He has assigned this project to Carina, his top performing project manager. Carina is in the process of managing the work that is being carried out by the project team. What process is she performing?
    A. Perform Project Work
    B. Develop Project Management Plan
    C. Execute Project Management Plan
    D. Direct and Manage Project Work

48. Where will the project manager look to determine how the project team will be acquired?
    A. Schedule management plan
    B. Resource breakdown structure
    C. Staffing management plan
    D. Project management plan

49. Source selection criteria allows:
    A. the organization to document and archive criteria used to select sellers.
    B. the organization to document lessons learned from selecting sellers.
    C. the buyer to rate and evaluate all prospective sellers.
    D. the potential sellers to determine whether they are qualified to bid on the work.

50. You are the project manager of a $40,000 project. Based on current reports, the project has an earned value (EV) of $15,000, an actual cost (AC) of $14,000, and a planned value (PV) of $16,500. Based on the schedule performance index (SPI), how is the project performing?
    A. On schedule
    B. Under budget
    C. Behind schedule
    D. Ahead of schedule

Individual Assessment

Self-Assessment Exam Answers

1. Answer: B
Explanation: Create Schedule Management Plan is not an official process. The schedule management plan is created as part of the Plan Schedule Management process, the first process of the Project Time Management Knowledge Area.

2. Answer: B
Explanation: The procurement management plan describes how the procurement-related processes will be managed and carried out, from the initiation of the procurement contract life cycle to the closure of the contract. Other options describe the procurement statement of work, project management plan, and source selection criteria.

3. Answer: D
Explanation: The process improvement plan maps out how the team will assess and analyze the effectiveness of the processes. The idea is to enhance the value of the processes, and increase customer value. The plan should also address targets for improved performance, process metrics and configuration. This plan will be executed as part of performing quality assurance activities.

4. Answer: A
Explanation: To solve a decision tree, calculate the expected monetary value of each scenario. Expected monetary value can be calculated by multiplying the impact by the probability. Scenario A has a potential implication of -$1,250, and scenario B has a potential implication of -$2,275. Therefore, scenario A is the best choice.

5. Answer: B
Explanation: The WBS dictionary contains the description of the work for each component within the work breakdown structure, along with several other pieces of information that will be invaluable to the project manager, such as the responsible organization. At this stage, the activity list or the activity attributes have not been developed yet, so those aren't viable options to choose from. If you chose the WBS, you were close, but it does not contain the descriptions of the components within it.

6. Answer: C
Explanation: Work performance data refers to the raw data, observations, and measurements of the data identified during execution of the work performed. It therefore provides information on the status of work, such as which activities have started and finished, how much has been spent to date, including actual costs and durations of activities.

7. Answer: B
Explanation: All of the options listed are types of communication. When dealing with complex issues, it is best to use a written format that is formal. Formal written is also the best choice when working with team members across other cultures, communicating through long distances, updating a plan, or dealing with legal matters.

8. Answer: A
Explanation: Work performance information is an output of the Control Schedule process, which includes EVM results, such as schedule variance (SV), schedule performance index (SPI), as well as other performance measurements generated out of the process.

9. Answer: C
Explanation: The contents of the risk register continue to be updated after the project moves out of the Planning processes. This is reflected within the updates made as a result of the Control Risks process, which is part of the Monitoring and Controlling Process Group. If the risk register were only updated during the Planning processes of the project, it could not contain actual outcomes of risks and the outcomes of risk response plans.

10. Answer: A
Explanation: The best and preferred method for dealing with stakeholders is face-to-face – when feasible. Meeting one-on-one with stakeholders is not necessary or time efficient, unless the situation warrants it.

11. Answer: C
Explanation: The question describes the Create WBS process. This process is responsible for the creation of the work breakdown structure (WBS), which is a decomposition of the project deliverables.

12. Answer: A
Explanation: A scatter diagram shows the pattern of relationship between two different variables. The purpose is to analyze the relationship between identified changes within the two variables. Dependent and independent variables are plotted on a graph, with a diagonal line passing through -- the closer the variables are to each other, the more closely they are related.

13. Answer: A
Explanation: The basis of estimates provides additional details of the cost estimates, such as assumptions made, known constraints, estimate ranges, and confidence level of the estimates. This is an output of the Estimate Costs process.

14. Answer: B
Explanation: Abandoning the project or placing it on hold doesn't seem like the best option, although we don't necessarily have all of the information required to make this decision. This decision is typically made by the project sponsor. Altering the resource requirements by accepting a lower skill level for the tasks lacking resources would be the best option, if it is feasible, as opposed to abandoning or closing out the project.

15. Answer: C
Explanation: The formula for calculating expected monetary value is probability x impact. Therefore, multiply $4,000 by 10% to get $400.

16. Answer: A
Explanation: According to the *PMBOK® Guide, 5th edition,* stakeholder analysis occurs as part of the Identify Stakeholders process. Here, the influences, interests, needs, wants, and expectations of stakeholders are identified and documented.

17. Answer: A
Explanation: Bidder conferences are held by the buyer and provide a venue for all potential sellers to come together and have their questions answered in an open and fair platform. The buyer has the responsibility of making sure that all potential sellers receive the same opportunity (no preferential treatment) and receive answers to questions asked.

18. Answer: B
Explanation: The question is defining the purpose of the Sequence Activities process, which is part of the Project Time Management Knowledge Area. This process uncovers activity dependencies and places the activities in the proper sequence.

19. Answer: C
Explanation: Notice that the functional manager's authorization or signature is not necessary for project documents. This means that we can rule out functional, where the project manager has no authority. In this case, it is clear that the project manager *does* have authority, although the existence of the functional manager's role allows us to also rule out projectized as an option. Since traditional is not an official type of organizational structure, that leaves matrix as the best choice.

20. Answer: A
Explanation: Prototypes allow for early feedback on the requirements for further refinement and clarification. They are a technique used as part of the Collect Requirements process.

21. Answer: A
Explanation: The Monte Carlo technique is a commonly used type of what-if scenario analysis that simulates hundreds to thousands of potential outcomes (such as schedule outcomes). While this is frequently used as a risk management tool, "what-if scenario analysis" is a more specific description of the technique, and therefore a better choice.

22. Answer: A

Explanation: Only the Arrow Diagramming Method (ADM) uses dummy activities, which are not real activities, but instead are meant to show that a relationship between two activities exists. All of the other statements are accurate.

23. Answer: D
Explanation: The project management plan contains several plans and baselines. Risk register is neither a plan or a baseline, and is therefore the correct answer. Instead, the risk register is considered to be part of the project documents. On the other hand, the project scope statement is part of the scope baseline, which is part of the project management plan.

24. Answer: C
Explanation: The sender, who initiated the communication, is the project team member; the receiver of the information is the project manager.

25. Answer: D
Explanation: Alternative analysis includes the consideration of what other options exist in carrying out an activity. In this case, specialized resources are not available in-house. The team will need to consider various options, including accepting a less-specialized resource (if possible), or acquiring the resource externally.
Before this decision can be made, the options will need to be identified and assessed. In regards to the other options, we do not have enough information yet to move forward with hiring resources externally, although this may wind up being the case later on; double checking the resource calendars won't alter the result, and waiting is not the PMI-way of doing things (always go for the proactive option).

26. Answer: B
Explanation: The concept of continuous improvement centers around the idea that small or incremental improvements within a product or processes has the ability to reduce cost and keep consistency of performance. The word Kaizen in Japan translates to "alter and make better".

27. Answer: B
Explanation: The requirements traceability matrix is a table that traces the life of the requirements – from their origin and how they link to the business needs, to their acceptance and delivery.

28. Answer: B
Explanation: In this scenario, the project manager has just completed the Estimate Costs process. The process that follows is Determine Budget.

29. Answer: C
Explanation: A reserve is a provision in the project management plan that is inserted as a way of mitigating cost and / or schedule risk. Through reserve analysis, a time reserve can be added to those activities that have a high level of uncertainty, which is the case in the project described within the question

30. Answer: C
Explanation: A resource breakdown structure (RBS) is a graphical, hierarchical view of the resource categories and types used within a project.

31. Answer: C
Explanation: Juran defined quality as fitness for use, with fitness being defined by the customer. He also advocated the involvement of top management in regards to quality.

32. Answer: C
Explanation: What you are being provided with is the definition of a phase. Frequently, a project's life cycle will be divided into phases in order to manage the project more effectively. At a minimum, you'll find a starting, middle, and closing phase, which occur sequentially. But how these phases are structured, the number, and so forth, will vary across organizations, industries, and even by project.

33. Answer: B
Explanation: The project charter is typically signed off by the project's sponsor, who is responsible for approving the project. In this case, Nicolas is identified as the sponsor, and is therefore the correct answer.

34. Answer: A

Explanation: A fixed price contract, also known as lump sum, is where the seller provides an estimate for the work, negotiates with the buyer, and commits to doing the work at that price. The seller has the greatest risk, because if the estimate was not good, they may end up with little to no profit.

35. Answer: D
Explanation: Inputs to the Manage Communications process include the communications management plan, work performance reports, enterprise environmental factors, and organizational process assets. Communication methods is a tool and technique of the process.

36. Answer: B
Explanation: The project funding requirements come from the cost baseline and are adjusted to reflect early progress or cost overruns. Aside from the cost baseline, which itself includes the activity cost estimates and contingency reserves, project funding requirements also include the management reserve amount.

37. Answer: C
Explanation: Tracking risk activities is defined *within* the risk management plan. A minor change to one or a few words can alter the validity of a statement, as is the case here. As an exam tip, be sure to read through the questions and responses carefully; avoid skimming.

38. Answer: B
Explanation: Resource calendars include the availability of various types of resources, including human, material, and equipment, which may contain their own respective resource calendars, with a master resource calendar typing them all together.

39. Answer: C
Explanation: The purpose of the Validate Scope process is to formalize acceptance of the completed project deliverables.

40. Answer: B
Explanation: The purpose of the Perform Integrated Change Control process is to review change requests, approve or deny them, and control changes to the deliverables.

41. Answer: D
Explanation: The formula for calculating TCPI when based on the BAC is: (BAC – EV) / (BAC – AC). Plug in the values to get the following calculation: ($40,000 - $15,000) / ($40,000 - $18,000) = 1.14

42. Answer: B
Explanation: Triple constraints, now often called the "classic triple constraints", refer to the connection between cost, time, and scope. The idea is that any time any one of these is changed, the other two will experience some type of impact. The fifth edition of the *PMBOK® Guide* expanded this concept to include other factors, such as risk, resources, and quality.

43. Answer: D
Explanation: Selected sellers is an output of the Conduct Procurements process, not an input. Inputs of the Conduct Procurements process includes: procurement management plan, procurement documents, source selection criteria, seller proposals, project documents, make-or-buy decisions, procurement statement of work, and organizational process assets.

44. Answer: D
Explanation: A control account is a management control point, often placed somewhere between a deliverable and a work package, where management would like to see reporting on scope, cost, resource, and schedule information for the summary of all items below it.

45. Answer: D
Explanation: Gold plating is a term often tied to quality. It involves giving customers extras that are not included in the project scope, meaning that it is a form of scope creep. This can include things like extra features, increasing performance, and adjusting components.

46. Answer: D
Explanation: The milestone list is not a component of the project management plan, and is therefore the correct option. The project scope statement is not a component of the project management plan on its own. It is,

however, part of scope baseline. The scope baseline is a component of the project management plan, and consists of the project scope statement, WBS, and WBS dictionary.

47. Answer: D
Explanation: The purpose of the Direct and Manage Project Work process is to lead and perform the work defined in the project management plan and implement approved changes to achieve the project's objectives.

48. Answer: C
Explanation: The staffing management plan is a component of the human resource management plan, and provides details of how the project team will be acquired, trained, managed, developed, and released. While project management plan was also technically correct, staffing management plan was the *best* choice, since it was a more specific choice.

49. Answer: C
Explanation: Source selection criteria refers to the criteria used to select the sellers. This criteria allows the buyer to rate and evaluate all the prospective sellers. The criteria used can be objective or subjective, and is sometimes included within the procurement documents.

50. Answer: C
Explanation: SPI is calculated by dividing the earned value and planned value (EV / PV). Plug in the values provided to get the following calculation and result: $15,000 - $16,500 = 0.91. An SPI of greater than one is an indicator of good performance (ahead of schedule); below 1 is an indicator that the project is behind schedule, and an SPI equal to one means that the project is on schedule.

Chapter 2: Project Management Foundation

Learning Objectives:

- ☐ Define key project management terms
- ☐ Recognize the various project life cycles
- ☐ Explain the project environment
- ☐ Describe the project constraints

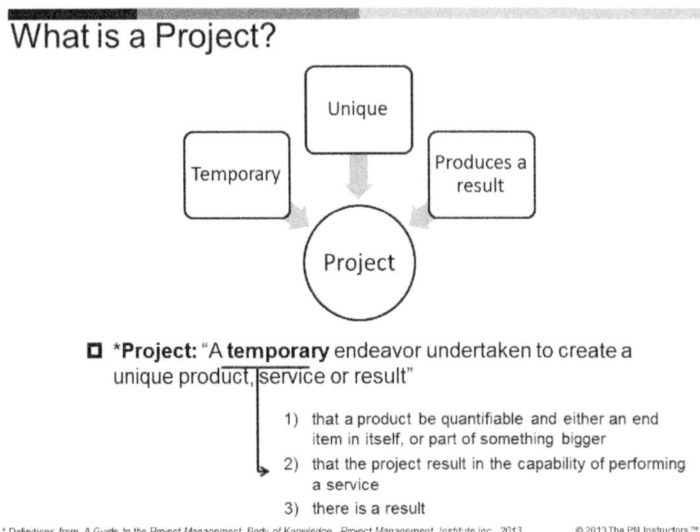

What is a Project?
Unique
Temporary
Produces a result
Project
*Project: "A temporary endeavor undertaken to create a unique product, service or result"
1) that a product be quantifiable and either an end item in itself, or part of something bigger
2) that the project result in the capability of performing a service
3) there is a result
* Definitions from A Guide to the Project Management Body of Knowledge, Project Management Institute Inc., 2013
© 2013 The PM Instructors™

Project versus Operations

Project

The *PMBOK® Guide* defines a project as "A temporary endeavor undertaken to create a unique product, service or result." By temporary, it's referring to a definite beginning and a definite end. So how exactly is the end defined? There are 3 possible ways:

1) Reaching a project's objective

2) Discovering that the objective cannot be reached

3) The project is terminated early

In these three scenarios, there is a closing moment as opposed to the project being ongoing. It should be noted that temporary does not signify duration.

Additional characteristics outlined by the *PMBOK® Guide* also specify that a product should be quantifiable and either an end item in itself, or a part of something bigger; the project should result in the capability of performing a service; and that there is some type of end result at the conclusion of the project.

To determine whether or not you a project, answer the following questions:

Is it temporary?

Is it unique?

Will the end of the project coincide with achieving project objectives?

If the answer to these questions is yes, you have yourself a project! If no, you may be dealing with ongoing operations.

What is Operations?

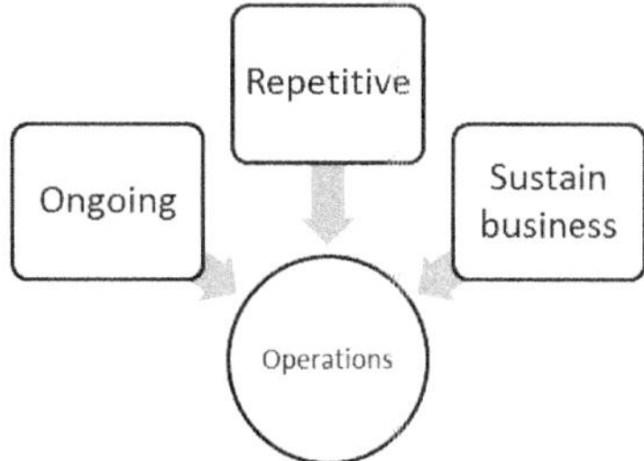

- **Operations:** Work that is ongoing and repetitive, meant to sustain the business
- Shared characteristics (Projects / Operations):
  - ✓ Performed by people
  - ✓ Constrained by limited resources
  - ✓ Planned, executed, and controlled

Operations

Operations refer to work that is ongoing (versus temporary) and repetitive (versus unique). While the purpose of a project is to achieve it's objective and end, the purpose of operational work is to sustain the business.

They seem to be opposites, yet they are often confused for one another. The reason for this confusion is that they do share characteristics. Both projects and operations are:

Performed by people

Constrained by limited resources

Planned, executed and controlled

The reason that it's important to differentiate between a project and operational work is that you can't manage operational work in the format of a project, because a project is managed in a way that is meant to achieve closing objectives.

Key Definitions

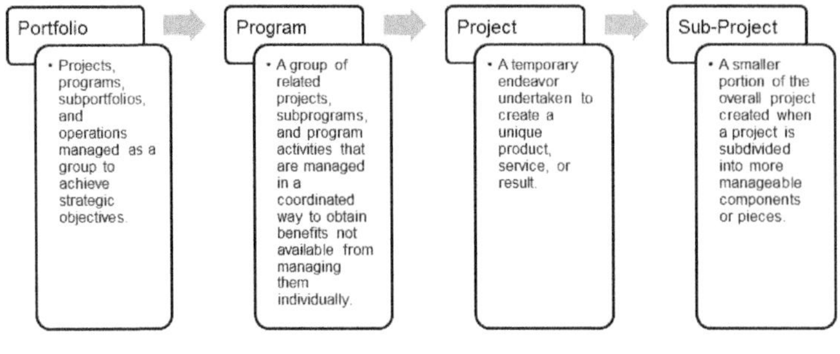

* Definitions from *A Guide to the Project Management Body of Knowledge, Project Management Institute Inc., 2013*

Key Definitions

Portfolio

A portfolio is a group of projects, programs, subportfolios, and operations managed as a group to achieve *strategic* objectives. All of the projects and programs falling under a portfolio share a similar purpose, which is to meet the objective of the portfolio.

Program

A program refers to a group of related projects, subprograms, and program activities that are managed in a coordinated way to obtain benefits not available from managing them individually. Program management is the central management of these projects with the purpose of meeting the objectives of the program. As you'd imagine, a program manager is the individual that manages one or more programs. They may also manage multiple project managers, who are each assigned to an individual project within the program.

The purpose of a program is to benefit from managing projects together rather than individually. Here are some reasons that projects may be grouped together:

1) They can be sub-projects of a larger project; 2) Some of the projects may utilize the same resources; 3) One project may have a dependency on another; 4) They can mirror each other or a previous project.

There are also strategic and business benefits to program management, such as

Improved management

A higher chance of success

Cost savings

Sub-Project

A sub-project refers to a smaller portion of a larger project, created when a project is broken up into smaller, more manageable pieces.

Progressive Elaboration

- ***Progressive Elaboration:** The iterative process of increasing the level of detail in a project management plan as greater amounts of information and more accurate estimates become available.
  - A characteristic of projects that means to develop in increments as the project moves forward.
  - Is planned
  - Not considered scope creep

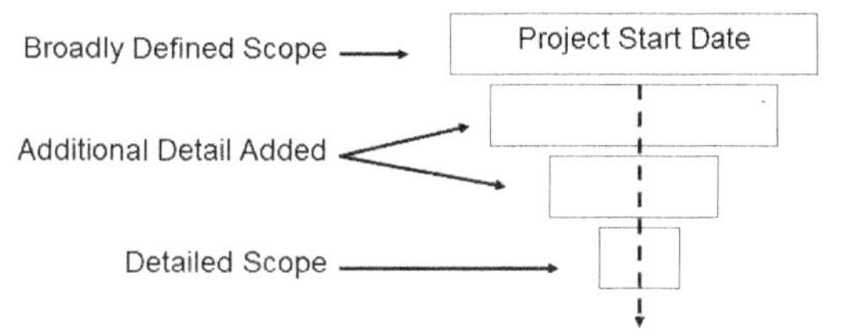

* Definitions from *A Guide to the Project Management Body of Knowledge*, Project Management Institute Inc., 2013

Progressive Elaboration

Projects often follow the concept of progressive elaboration. Progressive elaboration is defined as the iterative process of increasing the level of detail in a project management plan as greater amounts of information and more accurate estimates become available. This means that a project may begin with a broad scope that is further elaborated as the project moves forward, when more detail is revealed. The project team will elaborate on the project's scope as they receive additional requirements and objectives to be accomplished.

Progressive elaboration is something that is planned and coordinated. This is different from something known as scope creep. Scope creep is where additional features and functionality are added without approval, and without addressing the effects it has on time, costs, or resources.

Key Definitions

- ***Project Management**: The application of knowledge, skills, tools, and techniques to project activities to meet the project requirements.
  - Identifying the requirements and establishing clear objectives
  - Managing competing priorities
  - Meeting stakeholder expectations
- ***Stakeholders**: An individual, group, or organization who may affect, be affected by, or perceive itself to be affected by a decision, activity, or outcome of a project. Examples:
  - Project manager / project team
  - Customer
  - Sponsor
  - End-users
  - Project Management Office (PMO)

* Definitions from *A Guide to the Project Management Body of Knowledge*, Project Management Institute Inc., 2013

Project Management

The *PMBOK® Guide* defines project management as "the application of knowledge, skills, tools and techniques to project activities to meet project requirements." In other words, it involves planning, organizing, monitoring and controlling the project activities, in order to meet the requirements. The project manager is like the conductor of a large orchestra, making sure that each section plays its part at the right time, in the right way, and that everything flows together and is in sync.

As you can see, project management is far more than managing a project schedule, which is what many people think that project managers do, when in actuality, the project schedule is just one of the many components that exist as part of project management. Managing a project involves:

- Identifying the requirements and establishing clear objectives
- Managing competing priorities
- Meeting stakeholder expectations

Stakeholders

The term stakeholder is a broad one, representing several groups and individuals connected to the project at hand. It is formally defined as an individual, group, or organization who may affect, be affected by, or perceive itself to be affected by a decision, activity, or outcome of a project. To put it in simpler terms, a stakeholder is anyone that can *impact* the project, or be impacted *by* the project.

The following are just some examples of stakeholders:

- Project manager
- Sponsor
- Customer
- Department heads / functional managers
- Executive team
- Project team
- Project Management Office

This is not meant to be a complete list. Stakeholders can also expand to include vendors, government agencies, and others that can influence the project.

The responsibility falls on the shoulders of the project manager to make sure that stakeholders fully understand the decisions to be made, are kept informed, and that overall, their needs in regards to the project are met. This is why stakeholders must be identified early on in the project, in order to ensure that the project requirements are fully specified.

Key Definitions

- ***Project Management Office**: An organizational structure that standardizes the project-related governance processes and facilitates the sharing of resources, methodologies, tools, and techniques.

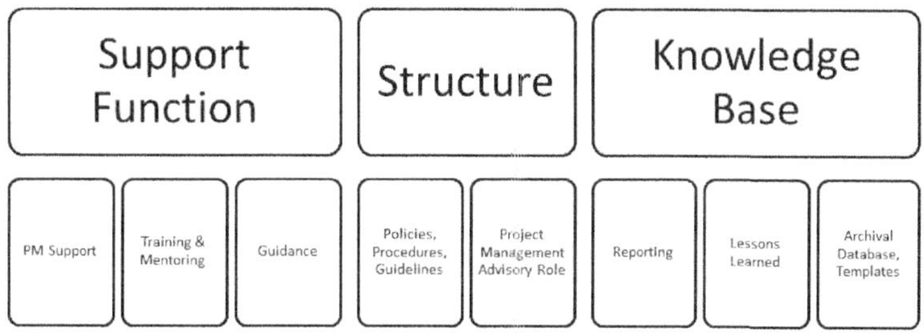

* Definitions from *A Guide to the Project Management Body of Knowledge*, Project Management Institute Inc., 2013

Project Management Office

A Project Management Office, or PMO, is established as a centralized unit within an organization to provide management of projects and programs. PMOs refer to an organizational structure that standardizes the project-related governance processes and facilitate the sharing of resources, methodologies, tools, and techniques. They are often likened to a department within a company, and their job is to coordinate and oversee the company's projects, although the magnitude of what a PMO does within an organization varies.

There is a difference between what a project manager does and the role of a PMO. Oftentimes, project manager reports directly to the PMO, if it exists. The PMO and project manager have different objectives, as follows:

Project Manager Objectives:

- Focused on the requirements driven by the project; Deliver project objectives
- Controls resources within the project in accordance to the project objectives (although to an extent)
- Report on the project they are working on

PMO Objectives:

- View the project from an enterprise-wide perspective
- Pursues organizational objectives
- Concerned with optimizing the shared resources across the organization
- Report on the overall progress of all projects, typically through consolidated reporting

As you can see, the project manager is focused on their own given projects while the PMO focuses on a broader level. The PMO is also concerned about future improvement and compiling best practices – things that will benefit future projects. This can include archiving project reference materials, best practices, templates – all the things that are considered organizational process assets. This can also include suggesting corrective action.

PMOs can exist in any type of organizational structure. One of the many benefits of a PMO, from a project manager's perspective, is the fact that it provides room for advancement and growth because it offers an advancement within their specific profession. When creating a PMO it's important to devote the necessary time to creating a strong foundation, because if not set up correctly, it can damage an organization's perception of what a PMO is about, and also the magnitude of what they can accomplish.

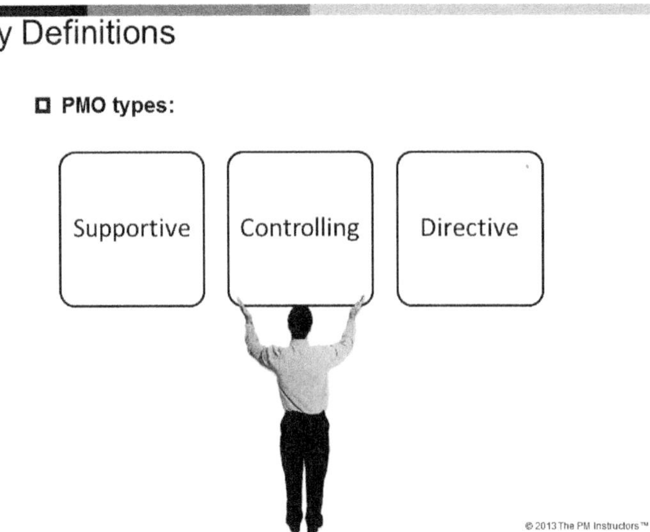

There are three types of PMO structures commonly seen in organizations. The difference among the various types is the amount of control and influence that the PMO has within the organization.

Supportive PMO Type

Supportive PMOs often have a low degree of control and influence within an organization. They serve as consultants to projects, often times providing resources such as templates, training, best practices, and lessons learned.

Controlling PMO Type

Controlling PMOs often have a moderate degree of control and influence within an organization. They not only provide support, but also may drive compliance to a project management framework, methodologies, and prescribed practices.

Directive PMO Type

Directive PMOs often have a high degree of control and influence within an organization. They drive and control projects, directly managing projects and also compliance of prescribed practices.

Key Definitions

- ❑ ***Project Based Organizations**: A variety of organizational forms that involve the creation of temporary systems for the performance of projects.
- ❑ **Business Value:** The entire value of the business, including the tangible and intangible elements.

* Definitions from *A Guide to the Project Management Body of Knowledge, Project Management Institute Inc., 2013*

Project Based Organizations

Project based organizations (PBO) refer to the various organizational forms that create temporary systems for carrying out their work. PBOs focus primarily on project work, and eliminate the functional approach to structuring the organization. This can aid in removing much of the existing bureaucracy within an organization.

Business Value

Business value refers to the entire value of the business, including the tangible and intangible elements. This is unique to every organization.

- Examples of tangible elements: *monetary assets, fixtures, stockholder equity, utility.*
- Examples of intangible elements: *good will, brand recognition, public benefit, trademarks.*

Various Life Cycles

- ❑ ***Project Life Cycle:** The series of phases that a project passes through from its initiation to its closure. It defines the project from beginning to end, connected by various **phases**.
- ❑ **Project Management Life Cycle:** The management of phases within the project life cycle using the five Process Groups:
  - Initiating
  - Planning
  - Executing
  - Monitoring and Controlling
  - Closing
- ❑ ***Product Life Cycle:** The series of phases that represent the evolution of a product, from concept through delivery, growth, maturity, and to retirement. It defines the product from beginning to end, connected by various product phases.

* Definitions from *A Guide to the Project Management Body of Knowledge, Project Management Institute Inc., 2013*

Life Cycles

Project Life Cycle

All projects contain a project life cycle, which literally refers to the life of a project. A project life cycle defines the project from beginning to end, connected by various phases. A project life cycle can vary by industry, organization, and even by project.

Phase

A project phase is a collection of logically related project activities that accumulates in the completion of one or more deliverables; it is what projects are generally divided into in order to manage them more effectively. Usually, phases define technical work, deliverables, who is involved, and monitoring and approval. A project may contain various numbers of phases – it can vary by company, project size and complexity, and even industry. There is no set number of phases that a project may contain, although it is common to see standardization of phases.

A common, more generic group of phases comes together to form the *project management life cycle*, which includes an initiating, planning, executing, and closing phase. All of these phases together encompass the project life cycle.

A *product life cycle* refers to the life of a product, from beginning to the end, connected by various product phases.

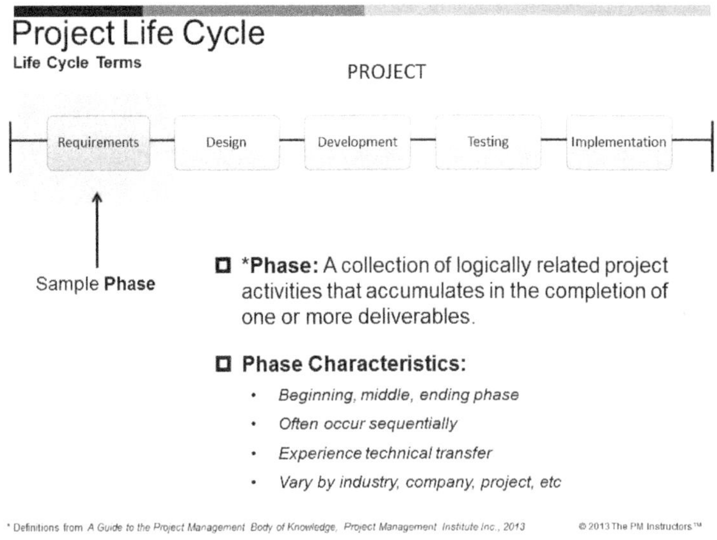

The following are common characteristics of project phases:

- They normally include some type of initial or beginning period, an intermediary period, and finally an ending or closing phase;
- Phases are often sequential, but may occur in parallel;
- Phases transition to the next through a technical transfer, also known as a hand-off. There are formal procedures that occur when moving on to the next phase, as opposed to occurring automatically;
- There is no set number of phases that a project must have, since it can vary depending on the complexity of the project itself.

The image shown above displays a sample software development project broken out into five phases: requirements phase, design phase, development phase, testing phase, and implementation phase.

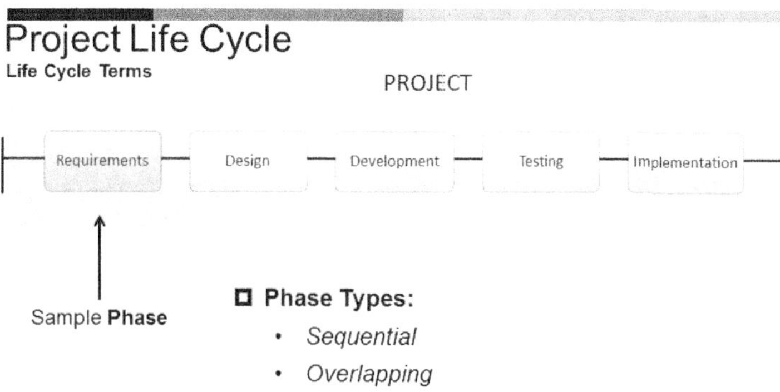

There are two primary phase relationship types: sequential and overlapping phases.

- **Sequential relationship**: A sequential relationship is where a phase begins after the previous phase has formally ended.
- **Overlapping relationship**: An overlapping phase may begin before the previous phase has formally ended.

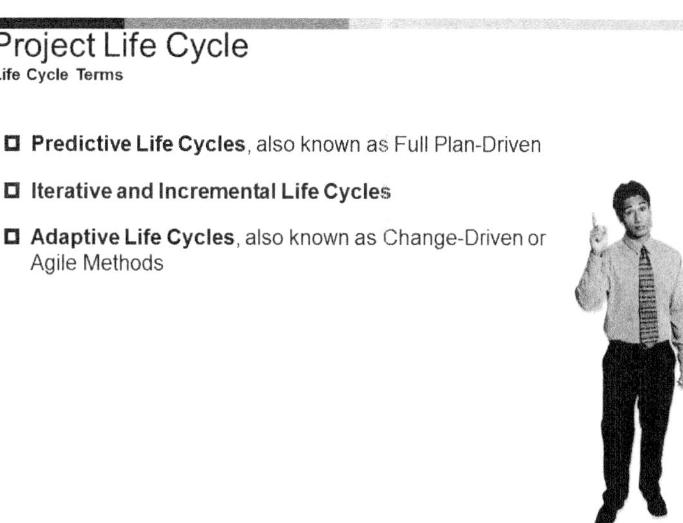

Additional types of life cycles can exist within a project. This includes predictive life cycles, iterative and incremental life cycles, and adaptive life cycles.

- **Predictive Life Cycles:** Also known as fully plan-driven, these life cycles contain a clear scope, schedule, and cost early on within the life of a project. Projects containing this type of life cycle typically include a heavy planning period at the onset of the project, followed by execution of the plan.
- **Iterative and Incremental Life Cycles:** These types of life cycles contain iterations (phases) that are repeated as the project team elaborates on the project scope. Through these iterations, a product can be built incrementally through the life of the project.

- **Adaptive Life Cycles:** Also known as change-driven or agile methods, these life cycles focus on responding to high levels of change and ongoing involvement with project stakeholders. Like incremental life cycles, adaptive life cycles also focus on iterations, although the iterations occur far more rapidly through shorter durations of the cycles.

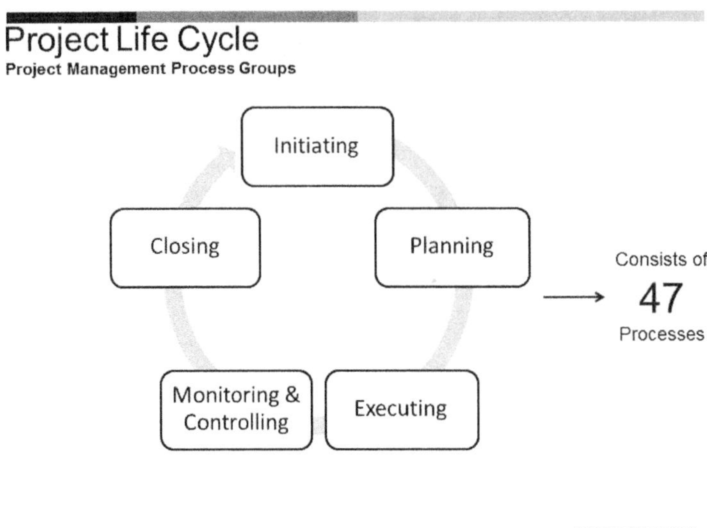

Project Management Process Groups

The management of a project consists of 47 processes, and these processes can be categorized either by Process Group or by Knowledge Area. The processes within a phase are dynamic, overlap, and are iterative. The project manager is responsible for determining which processes are needed according to the project's unique set of needs. The processes that make up each Process Group may be used multiple times throughout the project, oftentimes repeated by phase as needed.

Initiating Process Group

The purpose of the Initiating Process Group is to authorize, start, and define a new project or phase. This is the very first thing to occur within a project. There are two processes that occur within this Process Group:

Develop Project Charter

Identify Stakeholders

Planning Process Group

The purpose of the Planning Process Group is to define the project objectives and to develop the course of action required to attain those objectives. The planning Process Group is where the project management plan is created, which consists of several subsidiary plans and baselines. This Process Group consists of 24 processes:

Develop Project Management Plan

Plan Scope Management

Collect Requirements

Define Scope

Create WBS

Plan Schedule Management

Define Activities

Sequence Activities

Estimate Activity Resources

Estimate Activity Durations

Develop Schedule

Plan Cost Management

Estimate Costs

Determine Budget

Plan Quality Management

Plan Human Resource Management

Plan Communications Management

Plan Risk Management

Identify Risks

Perform Qualitative Risk Analysis

Perform Quantitative Risk Analysis

Plan Risk Responses

Plan Procurement Management

Plan Stakeholder Management

Executing Process Group

The purpose of the executing Process Group is to complete the work defined in the project management plan, which is developed during the planning Process Group. There are other things that will take place, such as coordinating and managing resources (this includes people, equipment, and material resources), distributing information, and implementing approved changes. There are 8 processes that make up the executing Process Group:

Direct and Manage Project Work

Perform Quality Assurance

Acquire Project Team

Develop Project Team

Manage Project Team

Manage Communications

Conduct Procurements

Manage Stakeholder Engagement

Monitoring and Controlling Process Group

The purpose of the monitoring and controlling Process Group is to track, review, and regulate the project performance, and identify any necessary changes. There are eleven processes that fall within monitoring and controlling:

Monitor and Control Project Work

Perform Integrated Change Control

Validate Scope

Control Scope

Control Schedule

Control Costs

Control Quality

Control Communications

Control Risks

Control Procurements

Control Stakeholder Engagement

Closing Process Group

The purpose of the closing Process Group is to finalize all activities in order to *formally* complete the project, a phase, or a contract. There are two processes within this Process Group:

Close Project or Phase

Close Procurements

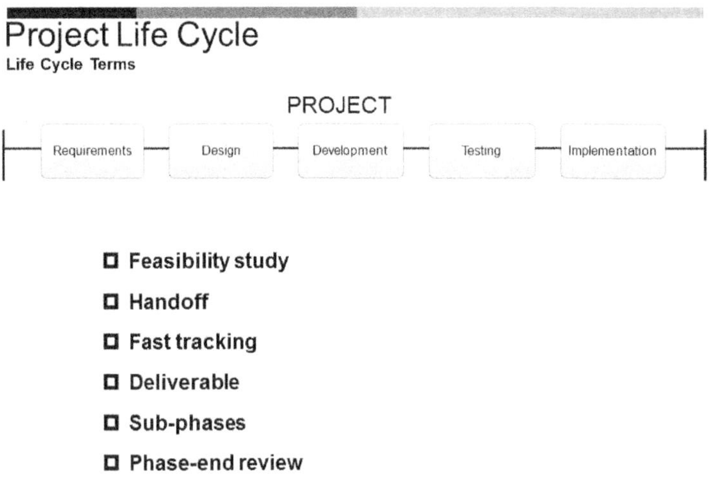

Additional Life Cycle Terms

Additional life cycle terms to be familiar with include:

Feasibility Study: The initial study conducted to assess the potential project, and to determine whether or not it will be accepted. Sometimes, you will have competing projects and the results of the feasibility study are used to determine which project to move forward with. A feasibility study can be treated as its own project, or it can be a part of the first phase. A feasibility study may also be conducted at other points, throughout the project's life.

Hand-Off: A phase transition, where a new phase formally begins after the previous phase has been closed and approved. Also known as a technical transfer.

Fast Tracking: A schedule compression technique in which activities or phases that were originally planned to be completed in sequence are completed in parallel for at least part of their duration.

Deliverable: A unique and verifiable product, result, or capability to perform a service that is required to be produced in order to complete a process, phase, or project.

Sub-Phases: A phase that has been further broken up for more efficient management. This may occur for the same reasons that a project life cycle is broken up into phases in the first place: because of the project size, complexity, constraints, and the level of risk involved. A sub-phase may have the same deliverable as its parent phase, or it may have a related deliverable.

Phase-End Review: The process conducted at the end of a phase to determine whether authorization to close out that phase may be obtained. Phase end reviews are also called by other various names, such as: phase exits, phase gates, and kill points.

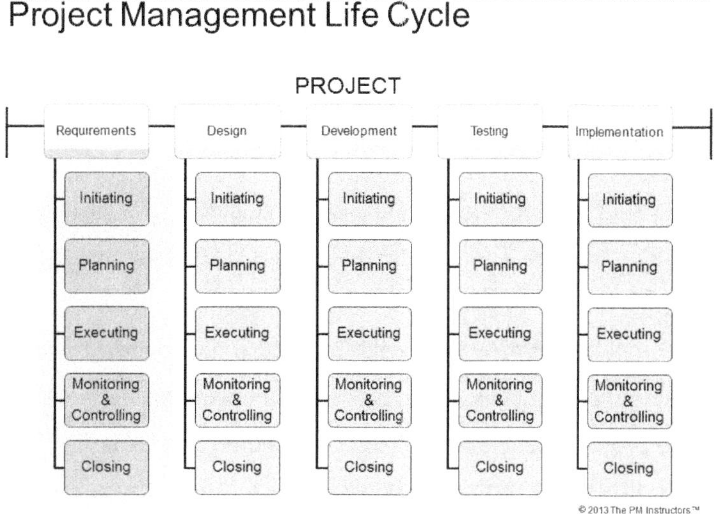

Project Management Life Cycle

The project management life cycle refers to the management of the phases within a project, as well as the high-level management of the overall project. The diagram above shows a generic group of phases for a software development project. Each of the phases shown is managed using the five Process Groups, and the various processes that fall within the groups. *Note: This does not mean that all 47 project management processes must be performed for each phase (or for each project) - that remains up to the project manager to determine, based on the needs of the project.*

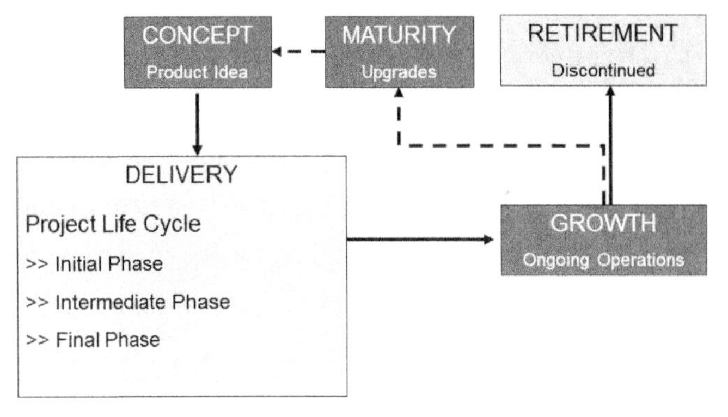

Product Life Cycle

The *product* life cycle is something that exists even before the project life cycle. In fact, the *project* life cycle is just one of the parts that make up the product life cycle. Oftentimes, the product life cycle experiences the following stages:

- CONCEPT: Oftentimes, a product begins with a business plan, which leads to the formalization of a concept. The product idea takes life, oftentimes moving into a feasibility study.
- DELIVERY: The project idea is where the project life cycle itself begins
- GROWTH: Once the project life cycle comes to a close and the product has been delivered or created, the product shifts into ongoing operations, and experiences growth. From there, there are two paths that a product may take:
  - MATURITY: The product may experience upgrades, in which case it moves back into the product idea stage and becomes a new project. Once the upgrade has been completed, it cycles back into ongoing operations; or
  - RETIREMENT: The product may be discontinued and retired.

Project Life Cycle

Trends

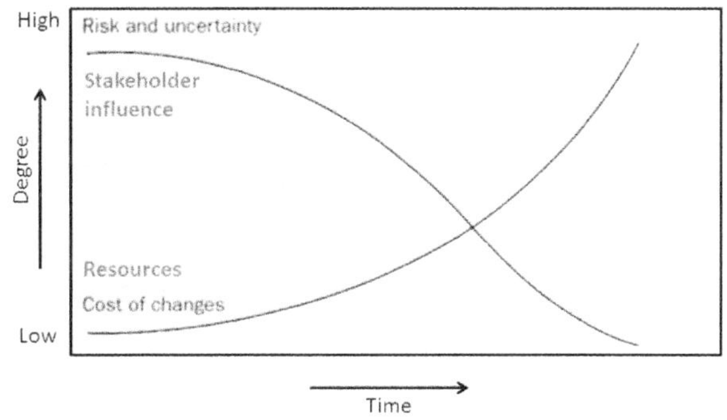

* Project Management Institute, *A Guide to the Project Management Body of Knowledge*, (*PMBOK® Guide*) – Fifth Edition, Project Management Institute, Inc. 2013, Figure 2-9, Page 40.

Life Cycle Trends

One common element that project life cycles experience is a trend in resources, costs, risks, and stakeholder influence.

There's a connection between the peak period experienced in resources and costs. Costs tend to be low at the beginning and peak during the execution stage of the project, since that is the point where the majority of resources are used. Costs and resource used decline rapidly toward closing.

Stakeholder influence, amount of risks, and cost of change also experience similar trends: they are high at the beginning of a project, and low at the end. At the onset of a project, uncertainty is at its peak, and therefore, the amount of active risks and stakeholder influence is high. When uncertainty is high, stakeholders oftentimes have an increased level of influence over decisions, and the likelihood of their requested changes being approved is high. Changes to a project can cause added costs, and as the work begins, the cost of changes increases as a result of rework.

Overview of trends:

- Costs and resources are lowest at the beginning of the project, and peak at the middle where a concentration of work is carried out
- Stakeholder influence is greatest at the beginning of the project, when their needs are still being clarified, and steadily drops as the project moves forward
- Cost of change is lowest at the beginning of a project, and increases as work is carried out
- Risk is highest at the beginning of the project, when a lot of uncertainty exists, and steadily decreases as project successes are reached and risks are managed and planned for
- The likelihood of project success is lowest at the beginning of a project, and increases over time

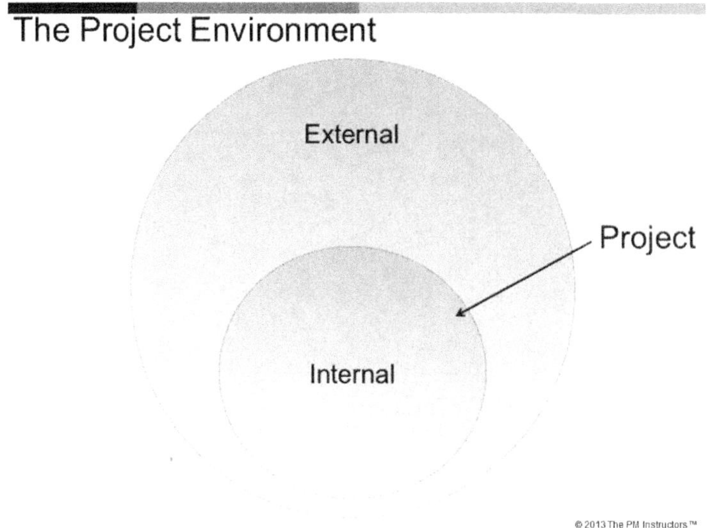

Project Environment

In order to manage a project, it's important to understand the environment that a project functions within. The project environment (and therefore the project) is influenced by external and internal factors. Organizations and various sources identify certain factors as internal, while others identify the same factors as external. The important thing to understand in the midst of these discrepancies is that these factors (whether internal or external) influence the overall project.

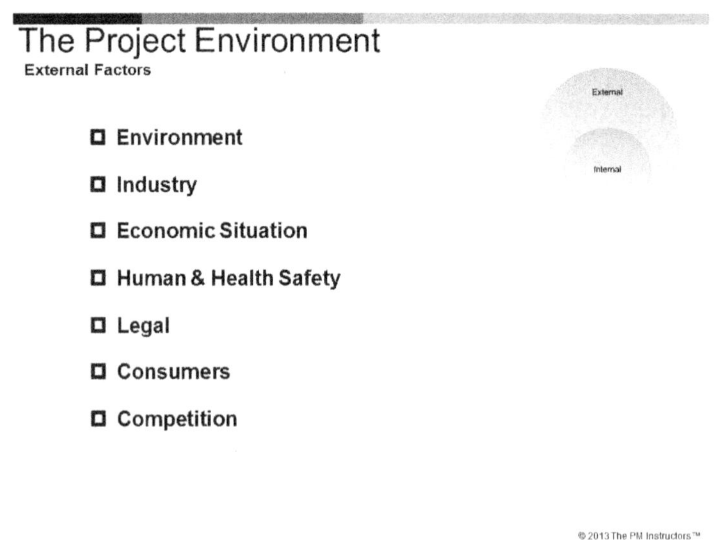

External Factors

For purposes of this course, the following are shown as external factors:

- Environment, such as weather, natural disasters, and other obstacles resulting from weather occurrences. If the location that the project is being conducted is susceptible to certain environmental conditions, the conditions need to be accounted for within the project. This also involves taking into consideration the local ecology, the physical geography, and understanding existing restrictions, such as protected areas.
- Industry, such as anything occurring within the industry that may impact the project.

- Economic Situation, such as an upward or downward turn in the economy (i.e. recession).
- Human & Healthy Safety, such as human and heath regulations (e.g. FDA); this can also include existing conditions, such as health and safety conditions within certain countries or regions.
- Legal, such as intellectual property rights.
- Consumers, which includes knowing the consumer expectations.
- Competition (self-explanatory), which can also be considered an external factor.

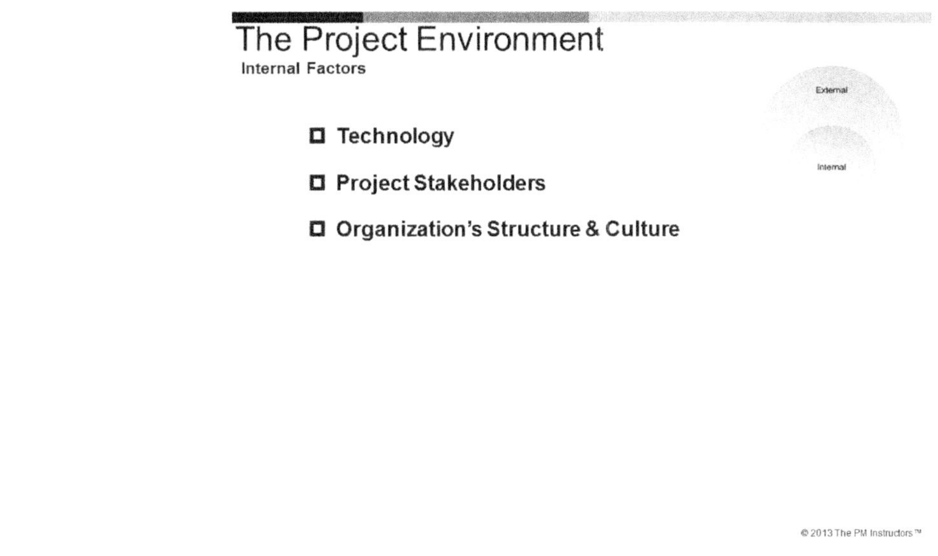

Internal Factors

For purposes of this course, the following are shown as internal factors:

- Technology, including the technology that the project relies on, the technology currently available for use by the project, and the technology that the project is creating.
- Project stakeholders, such as their varying levels of interest and expectations. *A stakeholder is any individual or organization that is impacted by the project, or who can impact the project.*
- Organization's structure and culture, which includes the organizational type that the project exists within. It also includes different layers within a cultural aspect, such as considering the company culture, ethnic culture; religious and economic cultures. These cultural aspects must be considered, since they heavily influence the project. The various organizational types, including functional, projectized, and matrix, will be covered next.

Organizational Structures

Overview

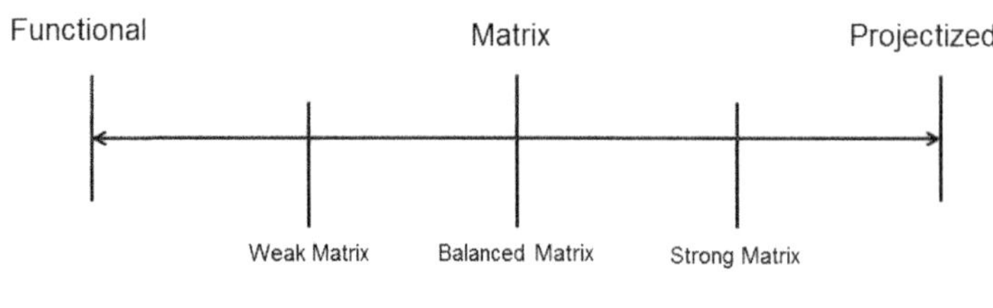

Composite

Organizational Structures

There are three types of organizational structures:

Functional

Projectized

Matrix

A matrix organization contains a blend of functional and projectized. The diagram above shows an additional visual of where the weak matrix, balanced matrix, and strong matrix fall in relation to a functional and projectized organization.

Composite indicates that there is more than one organizational structure. For instance, a functional organization may have a department dedicated to projects, or a department that is managed as a matrix organization. The diagram below shows this overlapping of structures:

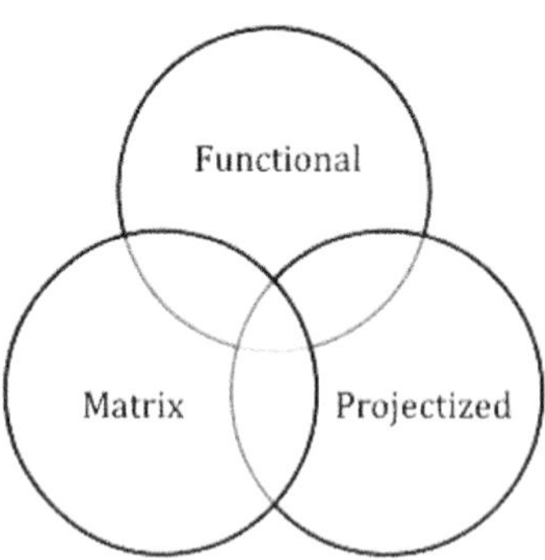

Organizational Structures
Functional Organization

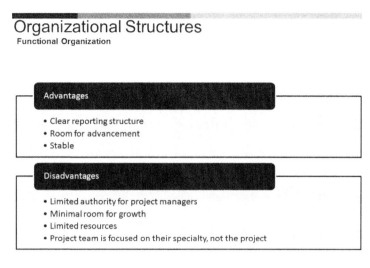

Advantages
- Clear reporting structure
- Room for advancement
- Stable

Disadvantages
- Limited authority for project managers
- Minimal room for growth
- Limited resources
- Project team is focused on their specialty, not the project

Functional Organization Overview

A functional organization is the more traditional type of organization, where a company is divided into departments, and each department is led by a functional / department manager, who reports to either the president or CEO. There is a clear chain of command – it's structured as a hierarchy. Typically, the project manager reports to a functional manager who is responsible for the project coordination, and many times, the project manager has other job functions. In these cases, the project manager typically manages projects within their functional department.

Additional notes:

Project Manager's Level of authority: minimal to none

Availability of resources: minimal to none

Control of project budget: functional manager

Role of project manager: part-time

Project manager's reporting manager: functional manager

Project administrative staff: part-time

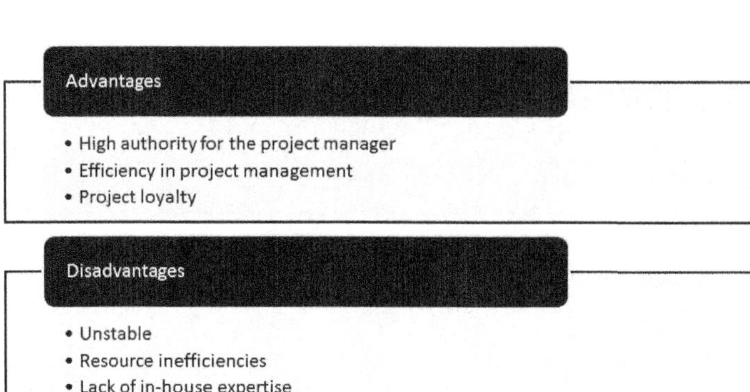

Organizational Structures
Projectized Organization
Advantages
• High authority for the project manager
• Efficiency in project management
• Project loyalty
Disadvantages
• Unstable
• Resource inefficiencies
• Lack of in-house expertise
© 2013 The PM Instructors™

Projectized Organization Overview

A projectized organization is nearly the opposite of functional. This organization revolves around the projects it manages, and the project managers are the ones with the authority, reporting directly to the CEO. The concept of this type of organization is to center around the project. Those working on the project typically have loyalty to that project, removing the barrier of competing priorities between the project and a functional department. A project manager has the authority to obtain resources.

Additional Notes:

Project Manager's Level of authority: high

Availability of resources: high

Control of project budget: project manager

Role of project manager: full-time

Project manager's reporting manager: CEO

Project administrative staff: full-time

Organizational Structures

Matrix Organization

Advantages

- **Weak Matrix:** Project coordination and better project communication
- **Balanced Matrix:** Efficient project management and strong project communication
- **Strong Matrix:** Efficient project communication and staff not disbanded after project

Disadvantages (All Matrix Types)

- Dual reporting relationship
- Complex management
- Potential conflict between management

Matrix Organization Overview

There are three types of Matrix organizations, which are a blend of functional and projectized. The whole idea is to benefit from the advantages of both. One difference that exists within Matrix organizations is that staff working on projects report to both a functional manager and project manager.

Matrix Types

- Weak matrix, that leans towards a functional organization
- Balanced matrix, that involves a balanced blend of both functional and projectized
- Strong matrix, that leans more towards the projectized organization

Additional Notes – Weak Matrix:

Project Manager's Level of authority: limited

Availability of resources: limited

Control of project budget: functional manager

Role of project manager: part-time

Project manager's reporting manager: functional manager

Project administrative staff: part-time

Additional Notes – Balanced Matrix:

Project Manager's Level of authority: low to moderate

Availability of resources: low to moderate

Control of project budget: project and functional manager

Role of project manager: full-time

Project manager's reporting manager: functional manager

Project administrative staff: part-time

Additional Notes – Strong Matrix:

Project Manager's Level of authority: moderate to high

Availability of resources: moderate to high

Control of project budget: project manager

Role of project manager: full-time

Project manager's reporting manager: manager of projects

Project administrative staff: full-time

The table below illustrates the important highlights of each organizational structure:

Organizational Structures

Matrix Organization

Org Structure / Project Characteristics	Functional	Matrix: Weak	Matrix: Balanced	Matrix: Strong	Projectized
Project Manager's Authority	Little or None	Low	Low to Moderate	Moderate to High	High to Almost Total
Resource Availability	Little or None	Low	Low to Moderate	Moderate to High	High to Almost Total
Who Manages the Project Budget	Functional Manager	Functional Manager	Mixed	Project Manager	Project Manger
Project Manager's Role	Part-Time	Part-Time	Full-Time	Full-Time	Full-Time
Project Management Administrative Staff	Part-Time	Part-Time	Part-Time	Full-Time	Full-Time

* Project Management Institute. *A Guide to the Project Management Body of Knowledge*, (*PMBOK® Guide*) – Fifth Edition. Project Management Institute, Inc. 2013. Table 2-1. Page 22.

Project Constraints

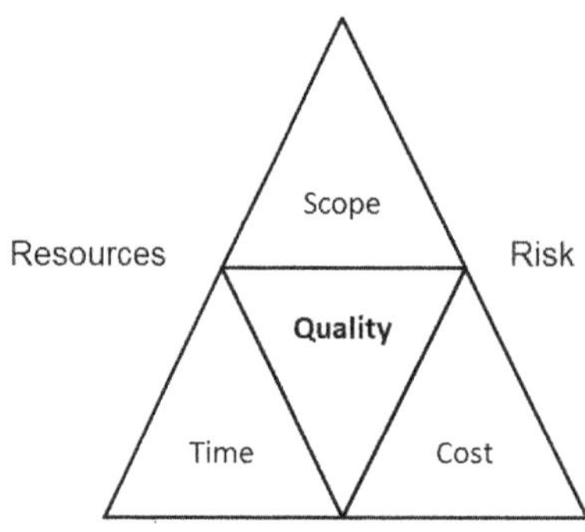

Project Constraints

Triple Constraints

The triple constraints consist of time, cost and scope. The idea is that they are tied to each other; when one of the constraints is changed, probability is high that at least one of the other two constraints will be affected by that change. For instance, if additional scope is added to the project, there is a high probability that it will impact the schedule and / or the budget.

Expanded Constraints Model

The 5th edition of the *PMBOK® Guide* expanded the triple constraints model to include quality, risk, and resources as part of the project constraints. This provides a more realistic look at the various project constraints that are connected together and that can impact one another.

Module Summary

In this module we:

- Understood / recognized project management terminology
- Recognized the various project life cycles
- Explained the project environment
- Described the project constraints

Chapter Quiz

Exam Practice Questions

1. A project manager working for a mid-level software company is in the process of executing the project work. During risk management planning, the team had discovered 42 risks that require some form of action or response. Over the coming weeks, the time to implement these actions would take place. During which stage of this project would the impact of risk be at its highest?
   A. Initiating
   B. Planning
   C. Executing
   D. Closing

2. Which of the following does not represent a type of organizational structure?
   A. Projectized
   B. Functional matrix
   C. Strong matrix
   D. Balanced matrix

3. Ab-O-Matic is a growing company based out of Seattle, Washington. The company's latest undertaking involves rolling out a series of consumer products targeted towards athletes looking for a dynamic way of working out indoors. The senior program manager of the company is conducting a program kick-off meeting with the project managers that will each lead the development of the new product. As part of this meeting, the senior program manager cautioned her team to keep a close watch on risks, particularly when they were most prone to materialize. The probability of risk occurring is highest during which stage of project management?
   A. Initiating
   B. Planning
   C. Executing
   D. Closing

4. A project manager working on a mid-level pharmaceutical project was in the process of developing risk responses. A project team member approached her to let her know that a new risk was identified that had been missed during the initial process of risk identification. After documenting the risk, the project manager had to get approval from her manager before moving further. This was the standard practice for any changes or additions made within the process. What organizational type does the project manager most likely work in?
   A. Functional organization
   B. Projectized organization
   C. Matrix organization
   D. Strong matrix organization

5. Which of the following is not a characteristic of a project?
   A. A temporary endeavor
   B. Meant to sustain the business
   C. Performed by people
   D. Is planned, executed, and controlled

6. During a scope planning meeting, the project manager stated that the project would be developed in increments as testing results are made available. This is an example of:
   A. Progressive elaboration
   B. Scope creep
   C. Operational work
   D. Milestone

7. Which of the following are considered part of the triple constraints?
   A. Scope, cost, risk
   B. Time, cost, quality
   C. Contract, time, cost
   D. Scope, time, cost

8. A company is currently rolling out a time management software that will be developed in 5 different language versions to be marketed globally. The rollout of the product will be developed, released and marketed within three months of each other. This can BEST be described as a:
   A. Project
   B. Portfolio
   C. Program
   D. Work package

9. Within his company, Eric is known as a top performer because of his outstanding communication skills and ability to problem solve as a software developer. His team of developers has encouraged him to apply for the new opening in the company as a project manager because they believe his firsthand experience will have greater influence within the business, and motivate the organization to include developers in critical discussions. Which of the following is NOT a required skill-set that a project manager should have?
   A. Problem solving skills
   B. Communication skills
   C. Motivating skills
   D. Development skills

10. The project has been going well until you recently discovered that the site of the offshore development team has just conducted an emergency evacuation due to a political rally that has become violent. This comes as a shock to the local project team. How could this have been avoided?
   A. By being aware of the project environment
   B. By not working with an offshore team
   C. Creating policies that require employees to continue working during political rallies
   D. The situation could not have been avoided

11. One of your colleagues is experiencing trouble managing his project, which is already showing signs of poor performance. He feels that the project is too complex and has asked for your advice. Where should you direct him?
    A. Offer to help him manage the project, even though you are currently at max capacity
    B. Direct him to his functional manager, since it is his manager's job to provide him with training
    C. Direct him to the project management office (PMO)
    D. Explain that he must take responsibility for his own project, since you are dealing with your own project issues

12. Sally is currently assigned to a project dealing with the construction of a new luxury condominium. A project team member has just asked Sally if their assignment could be delayed by one day. Sally has offered to pass on the request to the functional manager. What is Sally's role?
    A. Project expeditor
    B. Project manager
    C. Functional manager
    D. Project coordinator

13. Who has the MOST power within a Strong Matrix organization?
    A. The functional manager
    B. The project manager
    C. The project team collectively
    D. The project staff

14. Which of the following is not considered to be an advantage of a functional organization?
    A. Grouped by specialization
    B. Unstable
    C. Clear reporting structure
    D. Room for advancement

15. The project is coming to a successful close. While attending the milestone celebration party you notice that one of your colleagues looks upset. After asking if something is wrong she explains that she is concerned about her job, now that the project is coming to a close. What organizational type is this?
    A. Projectized
    B. Weak matrix
    C. Functional
    D. Strong matrix

16. Which of the following is not considered to be an advantage of a projectized organization?
    A. The project manager has a high level of authority
    B. Loyalties to the project are strong
    C. There is efficient project management
    D. In-house expertise is readily available

17. Stakeholder influence is highest within a project during which phase?
    A. Initial Phase
    B. Intermediate Phase
    C. Final Phase
    D. All Phases

18. The CFO of Blazing Broadband Internet Solutions needs to assess the value of the corporate portfolio for a presentation that he is going to provide to the board members next week. He asks the senior project manager to provide him with a chart that will allow him to visually explain the hierarchical structure of the organization, arranged by company units. What type of chart can be arranged by company units?
    A. Organizational breakdown structure (OBS)
    B. Resource breakdown structure (RBS)
    C. Responsibility assignment matrix (RAM)
    D. RACI chart

19. Which of the following BEST describes how enterprise environmental factors are utilized as an input to the Estimate Activity Resources process?
    A. Enterprise environmental factors can reveal the availability of various types of resources, including human and equipment.
    B. Enterprise environmental factors can reveal policies and procedures relating to staffing, rental, or purchase of supplies.
    C. Enterprise environmental factors can reveal factors that impact or influence resource availability and skills.
    D. Enterprise environmental factors are NOT an input of the Estimate Activity Resources process.

20. A good project manager understands that:
    A. Change is inevitable
    B. A well-constructed schedule requires no changes
    C. The baseline is fixed
    D. Each project is unlike no other

Chapter Quiz

Exam Practice Answers

1. Answer: D
   Explanation: Although the amount of active risk is highest during the beginning of the project, the impact of active risk is the greatest towards the end of the project. Typically, it's at this time that funds, resources, and time have been spent on the project, meaning that if a negative risk were to materialize, it would likely result in rework or added costs and greater delays to the project.
2. Answer: B
   Explanation: There are three types of organizational structures: functional, matrix, and projectized.
3. Answer: A
   Explanation: The probability of risk occurring is highest at the beginning of a project, when a greater amount of uncertainty exists.
4. Answer: A
   Explanation: Based on the need to obtain approval for any and all changes, the project manager most likely works within a functional organization. Within a functional organization, the project manager has little to no influence or authority.
5. Answer: B
   Explanation: The definition of a project, as defined by the *PMBOK® Guide,* is "a temporary endeavor undertaken to create a unique product, service or result". What the question is testing is whether you recognize the difference between a project and operational work. The definition of operational work is work that is ongoing, repetitive, and meant to sustain a business.
6. Answer: A
   Explanation: Progressive elaboration means to develop in increments as the project moves forward. Scope creep, on the other hand, refers to additional unplanned scope that is added to the project as the project moves forward. Scope creep is unplanned, whereas progressive elaboration is something that is planned and done for a specific reason. In this case, the project is being progressively elaborated due to testing results, which as they come to light will signal the course of the project. A milestone is a significant event or point in the project.
7. Answer: D
   Explanation: The triple constraints refer to scope, time, and cost. When any of these are changed or affected, chances are that the other two will be affected as well. For example, a change to scope will likely impact the schedule and budget; A change in budget will alter time and scope, and so on..
8. Answer: C
   Explanation: This is a great example of where multiple options appear correct. For example, you can argue that "project" is correct, since the description fits a project. However, the best answer is a "program". A program is defined as a group of related projects coordinated together. A portfolio also contains a group of projects that have been grouped in such a way to meet a specific and strategic business objective, but not necessarily because the projects are related. Work package is incorrect, since it refers to a deliverable within a work breakdown structure.
9. Answer: D
   Explanation: A project manager must have several skill-sets in order to be successful, which fall within general management skills and interpersonal skills. All of the options except for "development skills" fall within these two categories. In general, a project manager does not need to have development skills in order to manage projects. There may be special circumstances or roles within companies that may require this, but overall, it is not a requirement or necessity, while the others are.
10. Answer: A

Explanation: When managing a project, you should always be aware of the local laws affecting the project, as well as the political climate. By being aware of the political climate, the project team would have planned and taken preventive actions. The question is not necessarily asking you how to avoid the rally, but instead, how to prevent it from affecting the project.

11. Answer: C
Explanation: Of the options provided, the project management office (PMO) would be the best choice. The PMO is responsible for providing project managers with training and resources. They also have archived organizational process assets, which would help in this scenario, along with training. Offering to manage the project with him is implying that you will take on part of his project and responsibility, which is an incorrect answer. Not offering any type of assistance is a poor choice, since part of our responsibility as project managers is to encourage and educate other project managers, although not at the expense of your own projects.

12. Answer: A
Explanation: In order to answer this question, you would need to understand the responsibilities of each role within the options. Based on Sally's actions, it is clear that she does not have authority. Instead, what she's done is simply passed on information. But because a project team member came to her with a project request, we can deduce that she does play a central role within the project. A project manager, even in a functional organization, has some level of authority, so "project manager" is incorrect. Since Sally is passing on the information to the functional manager, she cannot be a functional manager herself. A project expeditor servers more as an assistant and coordinator to project communications and has no decision-making authority; whereas the project coordinator has some authority on project decisions. Based on this information, the correct answer would be project expeditor.

13. Answer: B
Explanation: Within a matrix organization, power/authority is shared between the functional manager and the project manager. So far, we can cancel out "project team" and "project staff". A strong matrix leans more towards a projectized organization where the project manager has the highest authority. In a strong matrix, although the power is shared, typically the project manager has the final decision making authority, making "project manager" the best choice.

14. Answer: B
Explanation: A functional organization is grouped within an organization chart by specialization, a structure that has been around for many decades (a traditional organization). In fact, the functional organization is the most stable out of the various types, which is why "unstable" is inaccurate, and the correct choice.

15. Answer: A
Explanation: Based on the scenario, the colleague's concern appears to be that the team will be disbanded at the closing of the project. This is common in a project-centric organization, where the team is hired specifically for a project. This rules out weak matrix and functional. Both projectized and strong matrix are organizations that are project-centric. However, a strong matrix still shares some qualities of a functional, even though it leans more towards projectized. In a strong matrix organization, resources are not disbanded after a project is completed, whereas this is the case in many projectized organization. Therefore, projectized is the correct answer.

16. Answer: D
Explanation: In a projectized organization, the project manager has the greatest amount of authority. Since the project staff is hired primarily for the project, their loyalties are tied *to* that project. An organization that is structured around managing projects would have a very efficient level of project management, therefore making that option true. Within a projectized organization, in-house expertise is not available, making this a disadvantage of this organizational structure type. If expertise is needed, that expertise must either be hired or a consulting company be brought in to provide the expertise.

17. Answer: A

Explanation: At the beginning of a project the requirements and scope are typically developed. Stakeholders have a great deal of input into this. As the project progresses and work is underway, the cost of changes increases and the amount of changes that are approved will decrease. As this is the case, stakeholders are most likely to get their requests for inclusion and changes approved during the initial phase of the project.

18. Answer: A
Explanation: Organizational breakdown structures resemble the traditional organizational chart (often referred to as an "org chart"). The OBS represents a hierarchical depiction of the organization, arranged by company units, department, or specialty.

19. Answer: C
Explanation: Resource availability is supplied through resource calendars. Enterprise environmental factors do not contain policies and procedures relating to staffing, rental or purchase of supplies – that refers to organizational process assets. Personnel related items tend to fall within the enterprise environmental factors, and they therefore contain the information that reveal any factors that may impact or influence resource availability and / or skills.

20. Answer: A
Explanation: It is impossible to plan out a project to perfection. There are too many moving parts and factors, regardless of the similarity that projects may have to others managed in the past. A good project manager understands that change is inevitable, which is why project maintenance, control, and overall close management is so important. That's not to say that this should be an excuse for poor planning. This is simply an aspect of overall project control. All other statements made within the remaining options are false.

Chapter 3: Project Management Framework

Learning Objectives:

- ☐ Recognize the project management Process Groups and Knowledge Areas
- ☐ Understand the relationships between Process Groups and Knowledge Areas
- ☐ Recognize where outputs from one process become inputs into another
- ☐ Identify the various project management processes

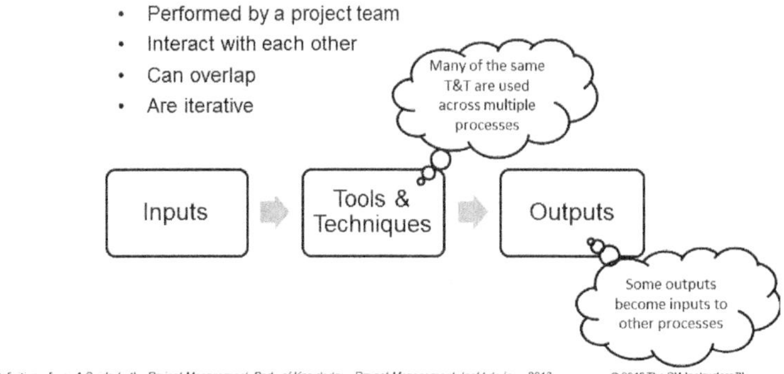

Project Management Process
*Process: "A systematic series of activities directed towards causing an end result such that one or more inputs will be acted upon to create one or more outputs."
Performed by a project team
Interact with each other
Can overlap
Are iterative
Many of the same T&T are used across multiple processes
Inputs
Tools & Techniques
Outputs
Some outputs become inputs to other processes
* Definitions from A Guide to the Project Management Body of Knowledge, Project Management Institute Inc., 2013
© 2013 The PM Instructors™

Project Management Processes

There are a total of 47 project management processes used to manage a project. A process is a set of interrelated actions and activities performed by the project team to achieve a pre-specified product, service, or result. The project manager uses their knowledge and expertise to determine which processes are relevant to the project at hand, and how often they must be iterated. Because each project is unique, not all processes must be carried out.

Each process has a series of inputs, tools and techniques, and outputs. The *PMBOK® Guide* defines input, tool, technique, and output as follows:

- **Input:** *"Any item, whether internal or external to the project that is required by a process before that process proceeds. May be an output from a predecessor process."*
- **Tool:** *"Something tangible, such as a template or software program, used in performing an activity to produce a product or result."*
- **Technique:** *"A defined systematic procedure employed by a human resource to perform an activity to produce a product or result or delver a service, and that may employ one or more tools."*
- **Output:** *"A product, result, or service generated by a process. May be an input to a successor process.*

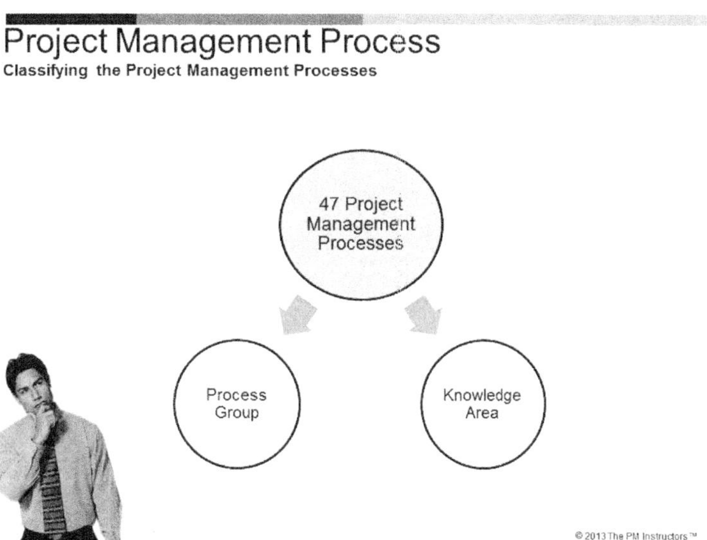
Project Management Process
Classifying the Project Management Processes
47 Project Management Processes
Process Group
Knowledge Area
© 2013 The PM Instructors™

Classifying the Processes

A process can be classified in two ways: by Process Group or by Knowledge Area.

Process Group

There are five Project Management Process Groups, typically performed in the same sequence within a project. The processes that fall within each Process Group are dynamic in nature, and interact in many ways that vary per project. Process Groups should not be confused as phases.

Knowledge Area

There are ten Knowledge Areas. Knowledge Areas can be thought of as categories or subject areas. For example, all scope related processes belong to the Project Scope Management Knowledge Area. Projects do not occur in sequence by Knowledge Area, since the processes within each Knowledge Area interact in many different ways with one another.

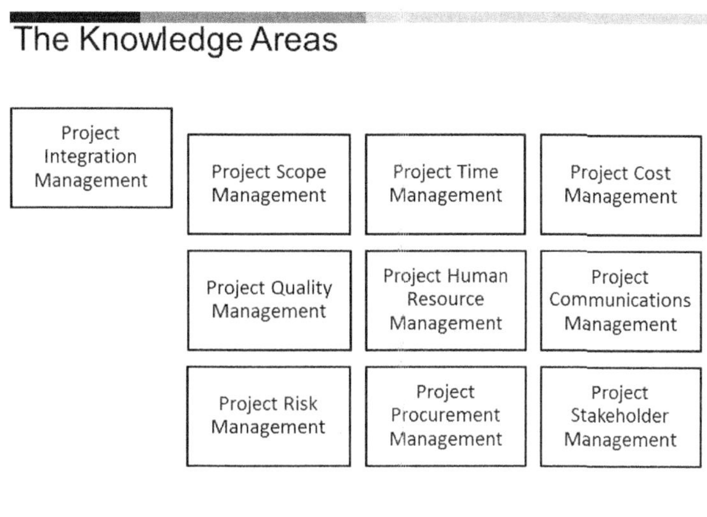
The Knowledge Areas
Project Integration Management
Project Scope Management
Project Time Management
Project Cost Management
Project Quality Management
Project Human Resource Management
Project Communications Management
Project Risk Management
Project Procurement Management
Project Stakeholder Management
© 2013 The PM Instructors™

As mentioned previously, the 47 project management processes can be categorized by Process Group and also by Knowledge Area. There are ten Knowledge Areas total, as shown in the diagram above.

Project Integration Management is the Knowledge Area that ties all of the others together; the other nine Knowledge Areas are titled according to the subject of the processes grouped within them.

Process Groups

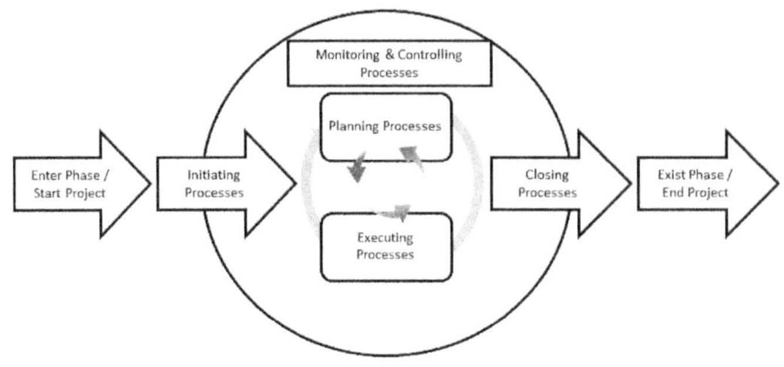

* Project Management Institute, A Guide to the Project Management Body of Knowledge, (*PMBOK® Guide*) – Fifth Edition, Project Management Institute, Inc. 2013, Figure 3-1, Page 50

Process Groups

There are a total of five Process Groups:

- Initiating
- Planning
- Executing
- Monitoring and Controlling
- Closing

The five Process Groups can be described as the project management life cycle. The processes that fall in each can be used to describe the management of the overall project (on a macro level) or the management of a phase (on a micro level). The image above reflects how the processes within each Process Group are iterative in nature, meaning that they may occur multiple times as needed.

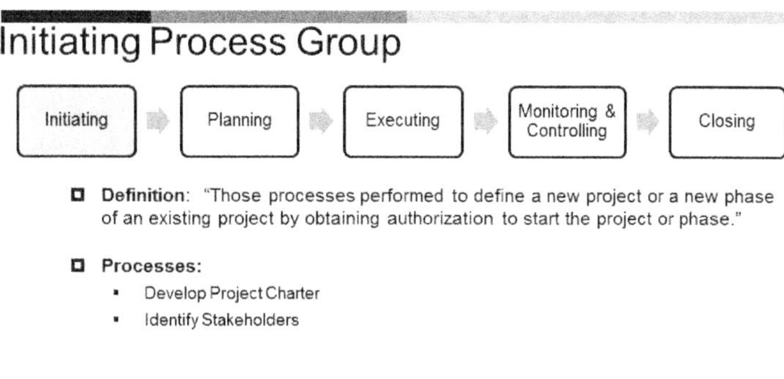
Initiating Process Group
Initiating
Planning
Executing
Monitoring & Controlling
Closing
Definition: "Those processes performed to define a new project or a new phase of an existing project by obtaining authorization to start the project or phase."
Processes:
Develop Project Charter
Identify Stakeholders
* Definitions from A Guide to the Project Management Body of Knowledge, Project Management Institute Inc., 2013
© 2013 The PM Instructors™

Initiating

The Initiating Process Group is concerned with those processes performed to define a new project or a new phase of an existing project by obtaining authorization to start the project or phase. There are a total of two processes within this Process Group:

- Develop Project Charter
- Identify Stakeholders

The key outputs produced include the project charter document and the stakeholder register.

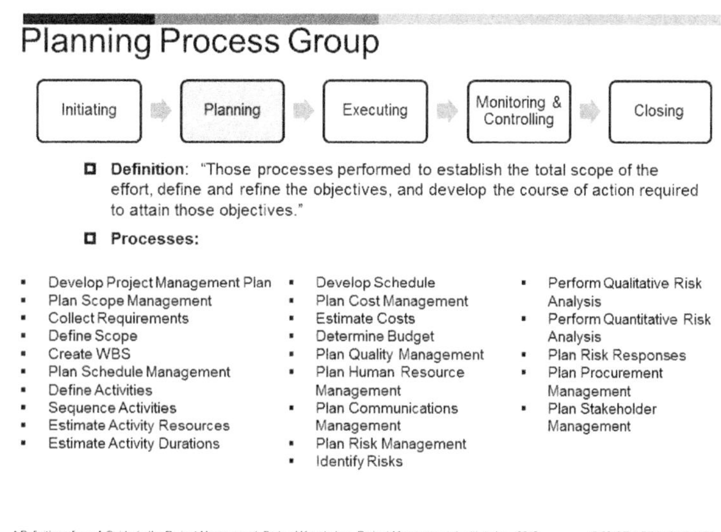
Planning Process Group
Initiating
Planning
Executing
Monitoring & Controlling
Closing
Definition: "Those processes performed to establish the total scope of the effort, define and refine the objectives, and develop the course of action required to attain those objectives."
Processes:
Develop Project Management Plan
Plan Scope Management
Collect Requirements
Define Scope
Create WBS
Plan Schedule Management
Define Activities
Sequence Activities
Estimate Activity Resources
Estimate Activity Durations
Develop Schedule
Plan Cost Management
Estimate Costs
Determine Budget
Plan Quality Management
Plan Human Resource Management
Plan Communications Management
Plan Risk Management
Identify Risks
Perform Qualitative Risk Analysis
Perform Quantitative Risk Analysis
Plan Risk Responses
Plan Procurement Management
Plan Stakeholder Management
* Definitions from A Guide to the Project Management Body of Knowledge, Project Management Institute Inc., 2013
© 2013 The PM Instructors™

Planning

The Planning Process Group is concerned with those processes performed to establish the total scope of the effort, define and refine the objectives, and develop the course of action required to attain those objectives. There are a total of 24 processes within this Process Group:

- Develop Project Management Plan
- Plan Scope Management

- Collect Requirements
- Define Scope
- Create WBS
- Plan Schedule Management
- Define Activities
- Sequence Activities
- Estimate Activity Resources
- Estimate Activity Durations
- Develop Schedule
- Plan Cost Management
- Estimate Costs
- Determine Budget
- Plan Quality Management
- Plan Human Resource Management
- Plan Communications Management
- Plan Risk Management
- Identify Risks
- Perform Qualitative Risk Analysis
- Perform Quantitative Risk Analysis
- Plan Risk Responses
- Plan Procurement Management
- Plan Stakeholder Management

The key output of this Process Group is the project management plan, which is a compilation of multiple sub-plans and project baselines (scope baseline, schedule baseline, cost baseline).

The project management plan is a culmination of all the Planning processes and their documented results. The project management plan consists of several subsidiary plans, component plans, and three baselines. The performance measurement baseline will be used to monitor actual project performance and determine whether the project is performing according to plan.

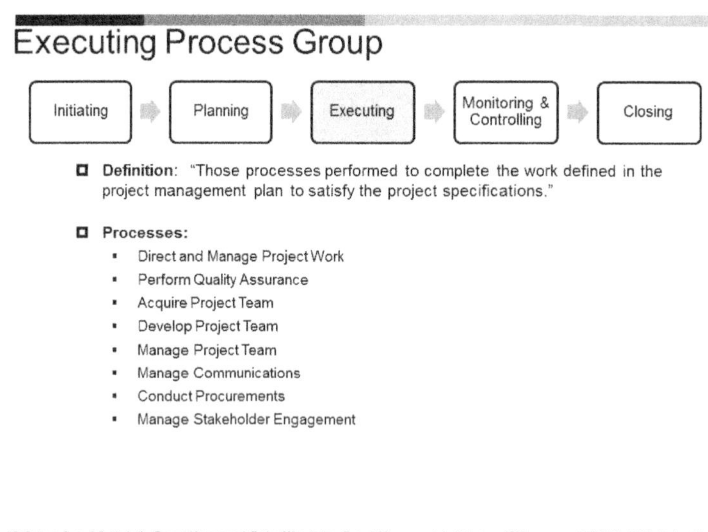
Executing Process Group
Initiating
Planning
Executing
Monitoring & Controlling
Closing
Definition: "Those processes performed to complete the work defined in the project management plan to satisfy the project specifications."
Processes:
Direct and Manage Project Work
Perform Quality Assurance
Acquire Project Team
Develop Project Team
Manage Project Team
Manage Communications
Conduct Procurements
Manage Stakeholder Engagement
* Definitions from A Guide to the Project Management Body of Knowledge, Project Management Institute Inc., 2013
© 2013 The PM Instructors™

Executing

The Executing Process Group is concerned with those processes performed to complete the work defined in the project management plan to satisfy the project specifications. This Process Group acquires and manages the project team. There are 8 processes within this Process Group:

- Direct and Manage Project Work
- Perform Quality Assurance
- Acquire Project Team
- Develop Project Team
- Manage Project Team
- Manage Communications
- Conduct Procurements
- Manage Stakeholder Engagement

The key outputs produced include the deliverables and the documentation of work performance data.

Monitoring & Controlling Process Group
Initiating
Planning
Executing
Monitoring & Controlling
Closing
Definition: "Those processes required to track, review, and orchestrate the progress and performance of the project; identify any areas in which changes to the plan are required; and initiate the corresponding changes."
Processes:
Monitor and Control Project Work
Perform Integrated Change Control
Validate Scope
Control Scope
Control Schedule
Control Costs
Control Quality
Control Communications
Control Risks
Control Procurements
Control Stakeholder Engagement
* Definitions from A Guide to the Project Management Body of Knowledge, Project Management Institute Inc., 2013
© 2013 The PM Instructors™

Monitoring and Controlling

The Monitoring and Controlling Process Group is concerned with those processes required to track, review, and orchestrate the progress and performance of the project; identify any areas in which changes to the plan are required; and initiate the corresponding changes. As part of these efforts, areas requiring necessary change are identified (such as where performance has deviated from the plan or is expected to deviate from the plan) and actions are taken to correct existing or potential variances. There are 11 processes within this Process Group:

- Monitor and Control Project Work
- Perform Integrated Change Control
- Validate Scope
- Control Scope
- Control Schedule
- Control Costs
- Control Quality
- Control Communications
- Control Risks
- Control Procurements
- Control Stakeholder Engagement

The key outputs produced as a result of monitoring and controlling efforts are performance reports, change requests, and resolution of change requests.

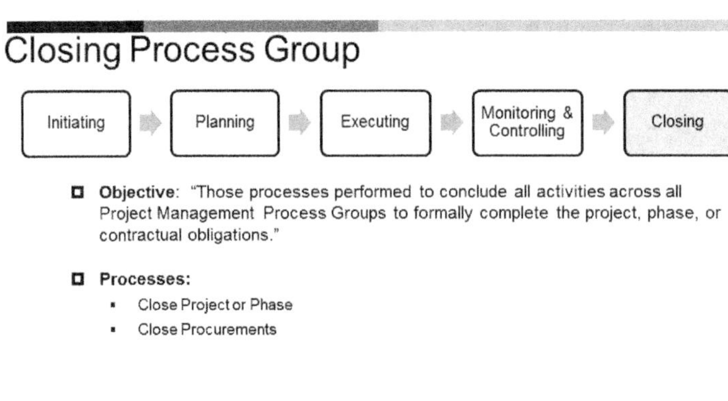
Closing Process Group
Initiating
Planning
Executing
Monitoring & Controlling
Closing
Objective: "Those processes performed to conclude all activities across all Project Management Process Groups to formally complete the project, phase, or contractual obligations."
Processes:
Close Project or Phase
Close Procurements
* Definitions from A Guide to the Project Management Body of Knowledge, Project Management Institute Inc., 2013
© 2013 The PM Instructors™

Closing

The Closing Process Group is concerned with those processes performed to conclude all activities across all Project Management Process Groups to formally complete the project, phase, or contractual obligations. There are 2 processes within this Process Group:

- Close Project or Phase
- Close Procurements

The key outputs resulting from this Process Group include the transition of the final product, service, or result, closed procurements, and the collection and archival of lessons learned.

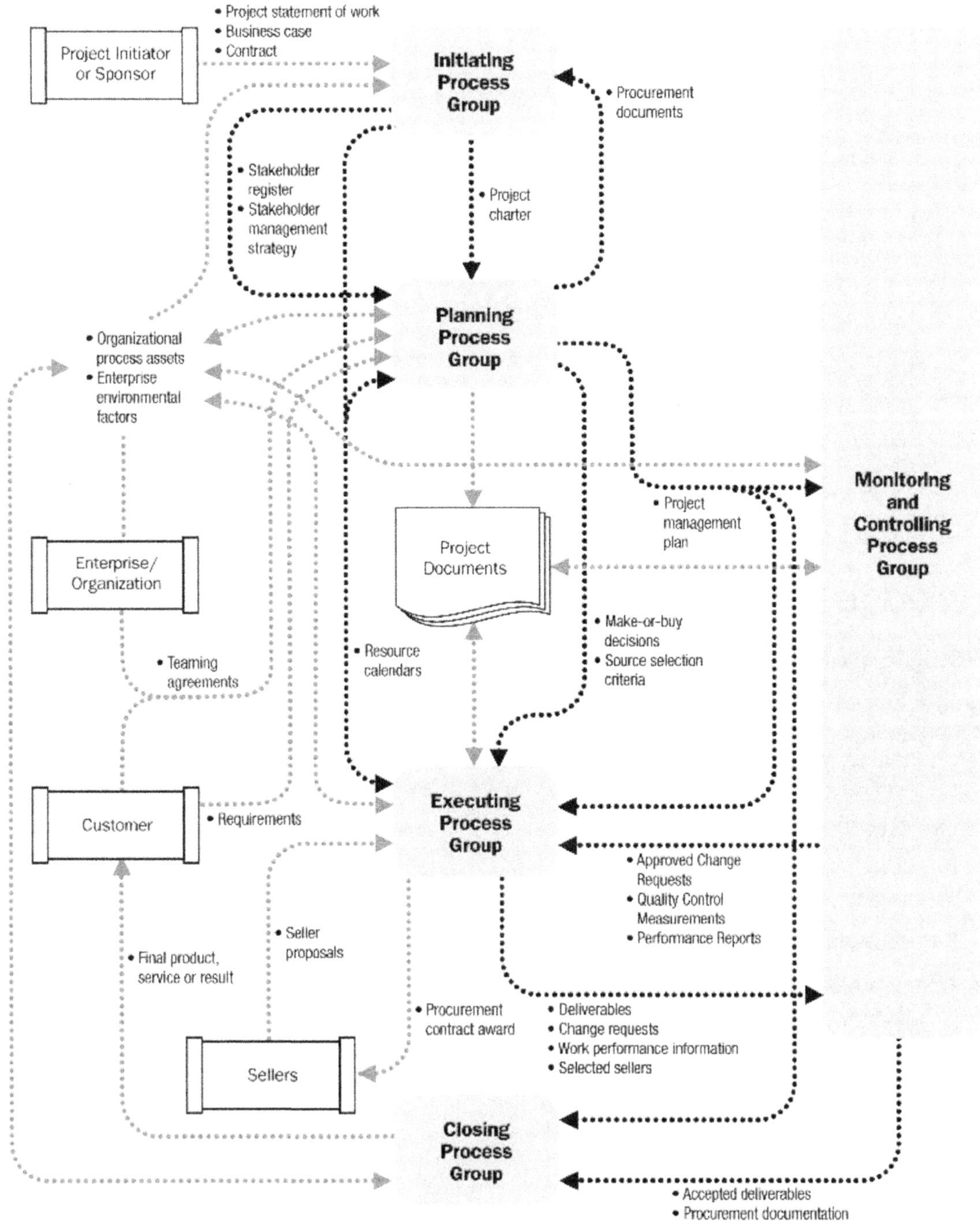

[3]

Process Interactions

As mentioned previously, the 47 project management processes within the five Process Groups are dynamic, iterative, and interact in many ways. The diagram below provides an illustration of this

---

[3] Project Management Institute, *A Guide to the Project Management Body of Knowledge*, (*PMBOK® Guide*) – Fifth Edition, Project Management Institute, Inc. 2013, Figure 3-3, Page 53.

interaction, but does not display all possible interactions that take place among the processes, since all projects are unique and have varying needs.

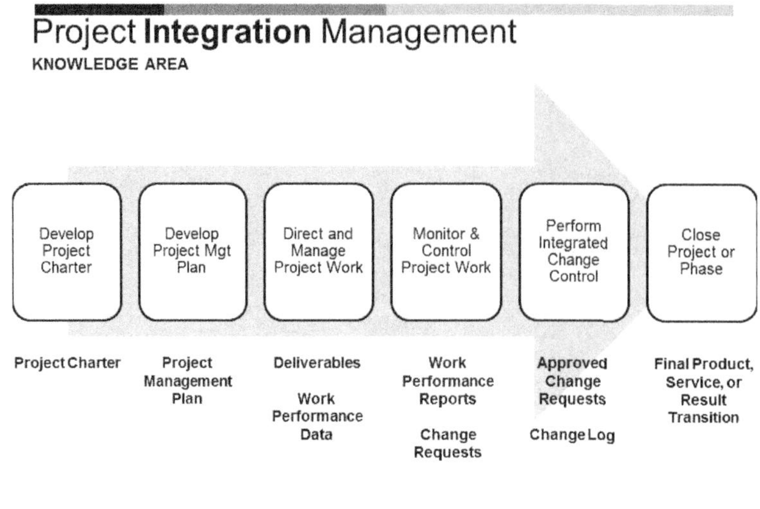

Knowledge Areas

Project Integration Management

The purpose of the Project Integration Management Knowledge Area is to coordinate all aspects of the project management plan in order to accomplish the project objectives. It includes the processes and activities to identify, define, combine, unify and coordinate the various processes and project management activities within the Project Management Process Groups. There are six processes total:

Develop Project Charter

Purpose: To develop a document that formally authorizes the existence of a project and provides the project manager with the authority to apply organizational resources to project activities.

Key outputs: Project charter

Develop Project Management Plan

Purpose: To document the actions necessary to define, prepare, and coordinate all subsidiary plans and integrate them into a comprehensive project management plan. The project's integrated baselines and subsidiary plans may be included within the project management plan.

Key outputs: Project management plan

Direct and Manage Project Work

Purpose: To lead and perform the work defined in the project management plan and implement approved changes to achieve the project's objectives.

Key outputs: Deliverables, work performance data

Monitor and Control Project Work

Purpose: To track, review, and report project progress against the performance objectives defined in the project management plan.

Key outputs: Work performance reports, change requests

Perform Integrated Change Control

Purpose: To review all change requests;, approve changes, and manage changes to deliverables, organizational process assets, project documents, and the project management plan; and communicate their disposition.

Key outputs: Approved change requests, change log

Close Project or Phase

Purpose: To finalize all activities across the Project Management Process Groups in order to formally complete the project or phase.

Key outputs: Final product, service, or result transition

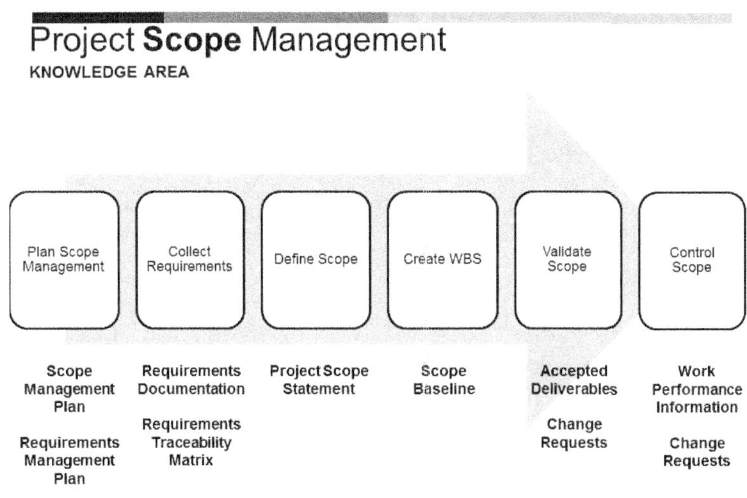

Project Scope Management

The Project Scope Management Knowledge Area is concerned with the processes required to ensure that the project includes all the work required, and only the work required, to complete the project successfully. It manages the project scope to avoid scope creep by defining and controlling what is and isn't included in the project. There are 6 processes:

Plan Scope Management:

Purpose: To create a scope management plan that documents how the project scope will be defined, validated, and controlled.

Key outputs: Scope management plan, requirements management plan

Collect Requirements:

Purpose: To determine, document, and manage stakeholder needs and requirements to meet project objectives.

Key outputs: Requirements documentation, requirements traceability matrix

Define Scope:

Purpose: To develop a detailed description of the project and product.

Key outputs: Project scope statement

Create WBS:

Purpose: To subdivide the project deliverables and project work into smaller, more manageable components.

Key outputs: Scope baseline

Validate Scope:

Purpose: To formalize acceptance of the completed project deliverables.

Key outputs: Accepted deliverables, change requests

Control Scope:

Purpose: To monitor the status of the project and product scope and manage changes to the scope baseline.

Key outputs: Work performance information, change requests

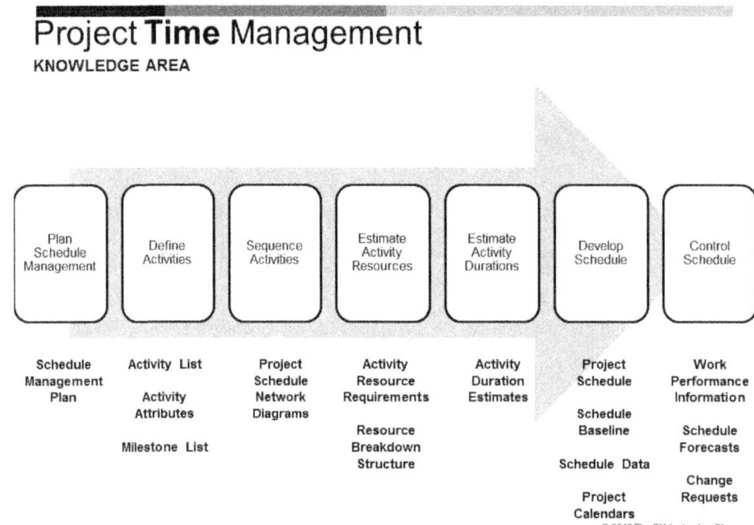

Project Time Management

The Project Time Management Knowledge Area is concerned with the processes required to manage the timely completion of the project. There are seven processes:

Plan Schedule Management

Purpose: To establish the policies, procedures, and documentation for planning, developing, managing, executing, and controlling the project schedule.

Key outputs: Schedule management plan

Define Activities

Purpose: To identify and document the specific actions to be performed to produce the project deliverables.

Key outputs: Activity list, activity attributes, milestone list

Sequence Activities

Purpose: To identify and document relationships among the project activities.

Key outputs: Project schedule network diagrams

Estimate Activity Resources

Purpose: To estimate the type and quantities of material, human resources, equipment, or supplies required to perform each activity.

Key outputs: Activity resource requirements, resource breakdown structure

Estimate Activity Durations

Purpose: To estimate the number of work periods needed to complete individual activities with estimated resources.

Key outputs: Activity duration estimates

Develop Schedule

Purpose: To analyze activity sequences, durations, resource requirements, and schedule constraints to create the project schedule model.

Key outputs: Project schedule, schedule baseline, schedule data, project calendars

Control Schedule

Purpose: To monitor the status of project activities to update project progress and manage changes to the schedule baseline to achieve the plan.

Key outputs: Work performance information, schedule forecasts, change requests

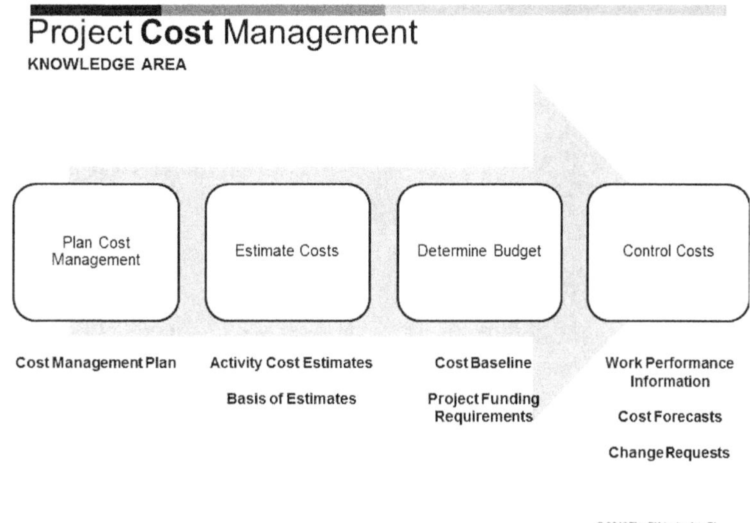

Project Cost Management

The Project Cost Management Knowledge Area is concerned with planning, estimating, budgeting, financing, funding, managing, and controlling costs so that the project can be completed within the approved budget. There are four processes:

Plan Cost Management

Purpose: To establish the policies, procedures, and documentation for planning, managing, expending, and controlling project costs.

Key outputs: Cost management plan

Estimate Costs

Purpose: To develop an approximation of the monetary resources needed to complete the project activities.

Key outputs: Activity cost estimates, basis of estimates

Determine Budget

Purpose: To aggregate the estimated costs of individual activities or work packages to establish an authorized cost baseline.

Key outputs: Cost baseline, project funding requirements

Control Costs

Purpose: To monitor the status of the project to update the project costs and manage changes to the cost baseline.

Key outputs: Work performance information, cost forecasts, change requests

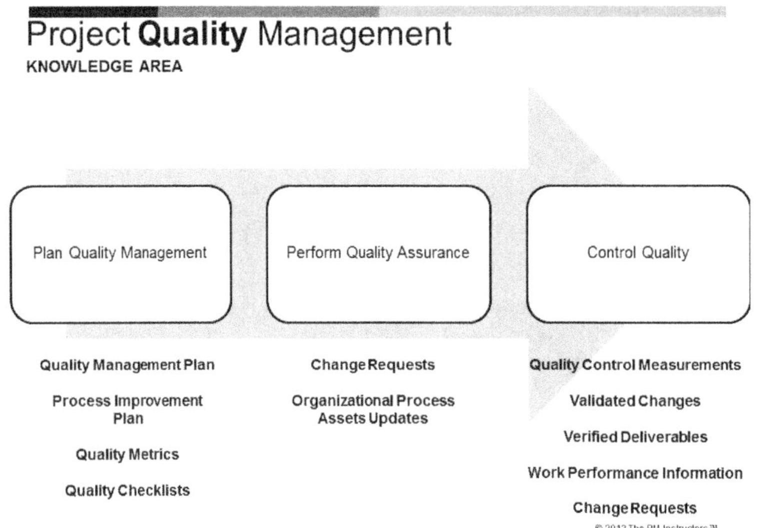

Project Quality Management

The Project Quality Management Knowledge Area is concerned with the processes and activities of the performing organization that determine quality policies, objectives, and responsibilities so that the project satisfies the needs for which it was undertaken. A focus of this area is also to prevent defects and rework through preventive measures taken as part of quality management. This process contains three processes:

Plan Quality Management

Purpose: To identify quality requirements and / or standards for the project and its deliverables and document how the project will demonstrate compliance with quality requirements.

Key outputs: Quality management plan, quality metrics, quality checklists, process improvement plan

Perform Quality Assurance

Purpose: To audit the quality requirements and the results from quality control measurements to ensure appropriate quality standards and operational definitions are used.

Key outputs: Change requests, organizational process assets updates

Control Quality

Purpose: To monitor and record results of executing the quality activities to assess performance and recommend necessary changes.

Key outputs: Quality control measurements, validated changes, verified deliverables, work performance information, change requests

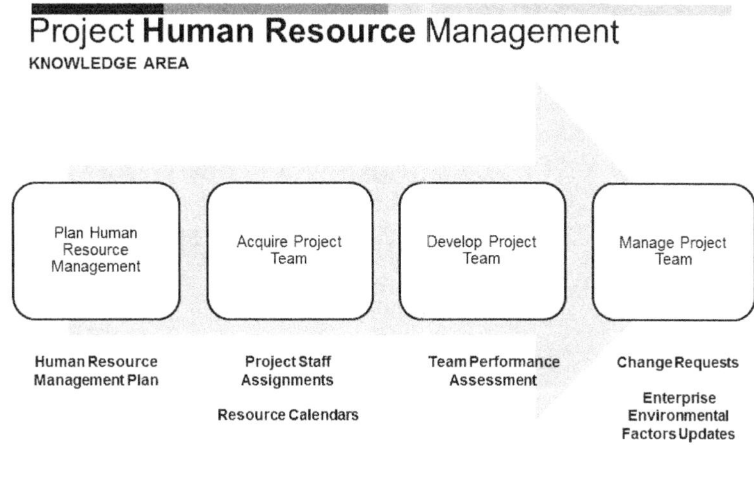

Project Human Resource Management

The Project Human Resource Management Knowledge Area is responsible for organizing, managing, and leading the project team. This includes acquiring and releasing the team members. There are four processes:

Plan Human Resource Management

Purpose: To identify and document the project roles, responsibilities, required skills, reporting relationships and create a staffing management plan.

Key outputs: Human resource management plan (contains staffing management plan)

Acquire Project Team

Purpose: To confirm human resource availability and obtain the team necessary to complete the project activities.

Key outputs: Project staff assignments, resource calendars

Develop Project Team

Purpose: To improve the competencies, team interaction, and the overall team environment to enhance project performance.

Key outputs: Team performance assessments

Manage Project Team

Purpose: To track team member performance, provide feedback, resolve issues, and manage changes to optimize project performance.

Key outputs: Change requests, enterprise environmental factors updates

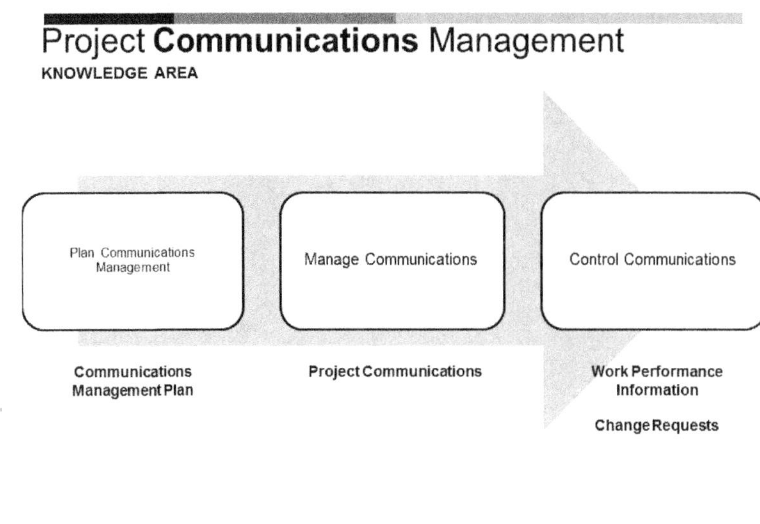

Project Communications Management

The Project Communications Management Knowledge Area is concerned with the processes that are required to ensure timely and appropriate planning, collection, creation, distribution, storage, retrieval, management, control, monitoring, and the ultimate disposition of project information. There are three processes:

Plan Communications Management

Purpose: To develop an appropriate approach and plan for project communications based on stakeholder's information needs and requirements, and available organizational assets.

Key outputs: Communications management plan

Manage Communications

Purpose: To create, collect, distribute, store, retrieve and ultimately dispose of project information in accordance with the communications management plan.

Key outputs: Project communications

Control Communications

Purpose: To monitor and control communications throughout the entire project life cycle to ensure the information needs of the project stakeholders are met.

Key outputs: Work performance information, change requests

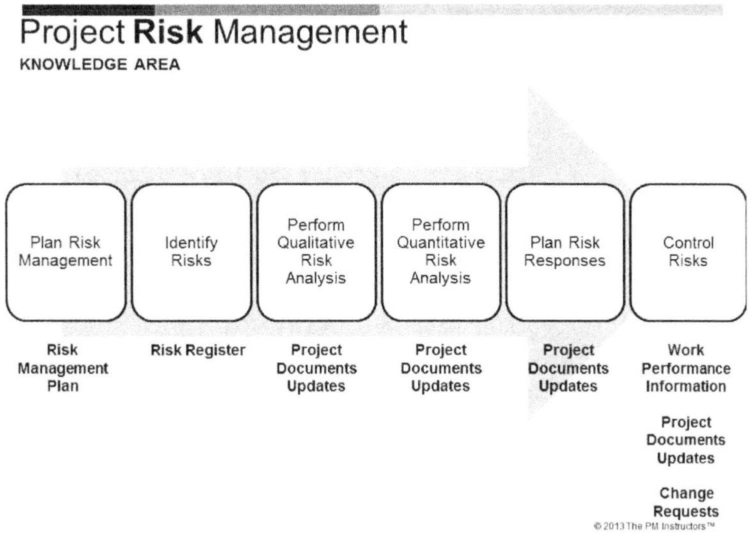

Project **Risk** Management

KNOWLEDGE AREA

Plan Risk Management	Identify Risks	Perform Qualitative Risk Analysis	Perform Quantitative Risk Analysis	Plan Risk Responses	Control Risks
Risk Management Plan	**Risk Register**	**Project Documents Updates**	**Project Documents Updates**	**Project Documents Updates**	**Work Performance Information** **Project Documents Updates** **Change Requests**

Project Risk Management

The Project Risk Management Knowledge Area is concerned with the processes necessary to conduct risk management planning, identification, analysis, response planning, and controlling of risk on a project. It is responsible for increasing the probability and impact of positive events, and decreasing the probability and impact of adverse events. There are six processes:

Plan Risk Management

Purpose: To define how to conduct risk management activities for a project.

Key outputs: Risk management plan

Identify Risks

Purpose: To determine which risks may affect the project and document their characteristics.

Key outputs: Risk register

Perform Qualitative Risk Analysis

Purpose: To prioritize risks for further analysis or action by assessing and combining their probability of occurrence and impact.

Key outputs: Project documents updates

Perform Quantitative Risk Analysis

Purpose: To numerically analyze the effect of identified risks on overall project objectives.

Key outputs: Project documents updates

Plan Risk Responses

Purpose: To develop options and actions to enhance opportunities and reduce threats to the project objectives.

Key outputs: Project documents updates

Control Risks

Purpose: To implement risk response plans, track identified risks, monitor residual risks, identify new risks, and evaluate risk process effectiveness throughout the project.

Key outputs: Work performance information, project documents updates, change requests

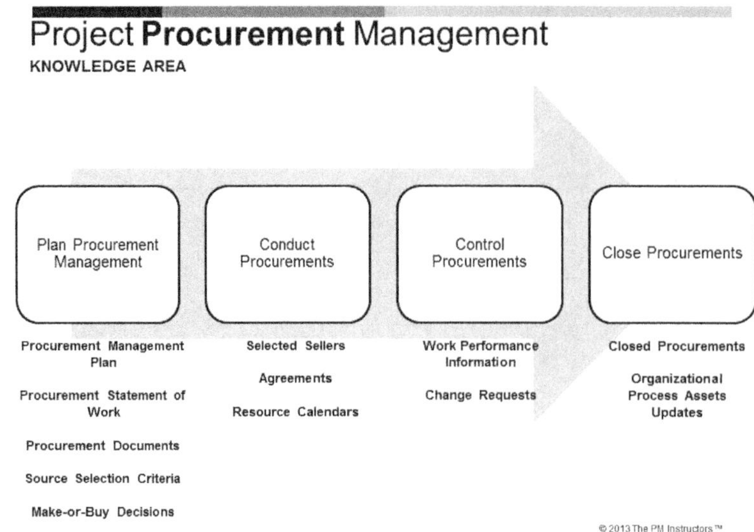

Project Procurement Management

The Project Procurement Management Knowledge Area is responsible for the life cycle of the procurement contracts. The purpose is to purchase or acquire products, services or results needed from outside the project team. There are four processes:

Plan Procurement Management:

> **Purpose:** To document project-purchasing decisions, specify approach, and identify potential sellers.
>
> **Key outputs:** Procurement management plan, procurement statement of work, make-or-buy decisions, procurement documents, source selection criteria

Conduct Procurements

> **Purpose:** To obtain seller responses, select a seller, and award a contract.
>
> **Key outputs:** Selected sellers, agreements, resource calendars

Control Procurements

> **Purpose:** To manage procurement relationships, monitor contract performance, and make changes and corrections as appropriate.
>
> **Key outputs:** Work performance information, change requests

Close Procurements

> **Purpose:** To complete each project procurement.
>
> **Key outputs:** Closed procurements, organizational process assets updates

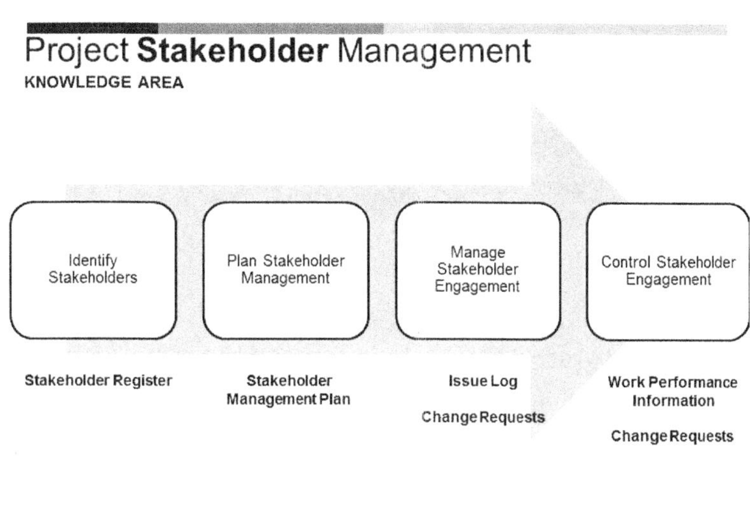

Project Stakeholder Management

The Project Stakeholder Management Knowledge Area is responsible for identifying the people, groups, or organizations that could impact or be impacted by the project, to analyze stakeholder expectations and their impact on the project, and to develop appropriate management strategies for effectively engaging stakeholders in project decisions and execution. There are four processes:

Identify Stakeholders:

> **Purpose:** To identify the people, groups, or organizations that could impact or be impacted by a decision, activity, or outcome of the project; and analyze and document relevant information regarding their interests, involvement, interdependencies, influence, and potential impact on project success.
>
> **Key outputs:** Stakeholder register

Plan Stakeholder Management:

> **Purpose:** To develop appropriate management strategies to effectively engage stakeholders throughout the project life cycle, based on the analysis of their needs, interests, and potential impact on project success.
>
> **Key outputs:** Stakeholder management plan

Manage Stakeholder Engagement:

> **Purpose:** To communicate and work with stakeholders to meet their needs/expectations, address issues as they occur, and foster appropriate stakeholder engagement in project activities throughout the project life cycle.
>
> **Key outputs:** Issue log, change requests

Control Stakeholder Engagement:

> **Purpose:** To monitor overall project stakeholder relationships and adjust strategies and plans for engaging stakeholders.
>
> **Key outputs:** Work performance information, change requests

Module Summary

In this module we:

- Understood / recognized the project management Process Groups and Knowledge Areas
- Understood the relationships between Process Groups and Knowledge Areas
- Recognized where outputs from one process become inputs into another
- Recognized that the same techniques and tools are used in several places
- Identified the various project management processes

Project Management Process Groups and Knowledge Areas Mapping[4]

Knowledge Areas (# of Processes)	**Process Groups** (# of Processes)				
	Initiating (2)	**Planning** (24)	**Executing** (8)	**Monitoring & Controlling** (11)	**Closing** (2)
Integration Management (6)	Develop Project Charter	Develop Project Management Plan	Direct and Manage Project Work	Monitor and Control Project Work Perform Integrated Change Control	Close Project or Phase
Scope Management (6)		Plan Scope Management Collect Requirements Define Scope Create WBS		Validate Scope Control Scope	
Time Management (7)		Plan Schedule Management Define Activities Sequence Activities Estimate Activity Resources Estimate Activity Durations Develop Schedule		Control Schedule	
Cost Management (4)		Plan Cost Management Estimate Costs Determine Budget		Control Costs	
Quality Management (3)		Plan Quality Management	Perform Quality Assurance	Control Quality	
Human Resource Management (4)		Plan Human Resource Management	Acquire Project Team Develop Project Team Manage Project Team		
Communications Management (3)		Plan Communications Management	Manage Communications	Control Communications	
Risk Management (6)		Plan Risk Management Identify Risks Perform Qualitative Risk Analysis Perform Quantitative Risk Analysis Plan Risk Responses		Control Risks	
Procurement Management (4)		Plan Procurement Management	Conduct Procurements	Control Procurements	Close Procurements
Stakeholder Management (4)	Identify Stakeholders	Plan Stakeholder Management	Manage Stakeholder Engagement	Control Stakeholder Engagement	

[4] Project Management Institute, *A Guide to the Project Management Body of Knowledge, (PMBOK® Guide)* – Fifth Edition, Project Management Institute, Inc. 2013, Table 3-1, Page 61.

Chapter Quiz

Exam Practice Questions

1. A project manager has requested an increase to her project budget based on a confident belief that developers would be needed to assist Help Desk with technical support calls, once the project has been released. Based on the complexity of the new application, and current experience of the existing Help Desk staff, she believes the project's success would be at risk due to poor customer satisfaction. The executive team denied her request, since they believed that her concern fell outside the scope of the project. This was an important lesson for the project manager, after she realized that they were correct. Which of the following does not accurately represent what is involved in managing a project?
   A. Meeting Stakeholder expectations
   B. Managing competing priorities
   C. Identifying the requirements and establishing clear objectives
   D. Supporting the product after completion

2. Last year, Janet successfully managed a 4.5 million dollar project for her company from beginning to end using a compressed schedule. This project was based on an inordinate amount of risk, and held a high level of visibility amongst the executive team. Part of her strategy was to ensure that the project lifecycle did not extend beyond 3 project phases, to easily track progress on the project. Which of the following statements is inaccurate, in regards to the project life cycle?
   A. It contains 3 project phases
   B. It connects the project from beginning to end
   C. Risk is highest at the beginning of the project
   D. Defines the life of the project

3. Your manager has just informed you that a new project is under consideration. In order to assist in making the decision on whether the project is a go, you have been tasked with conducting a study on the existing potential of the project. What is this type of research called?
   A. Monte Carlo analysis
   B. Cost performance index
   C. Feasibility study
   D. Cost plus fee

4. In order to maintain accountability between the business team, the development team, the testing team and the release team, the Strike First software development company requires each team to submit their required artifacts at each phase-end review. Which of the following does not represent another name used for phase-end reviews?
   A. Kill points
   B. Phase gates
   C. Hand-off
   D. Phase exits

5. After a phase-end review occurs, what comes next within a project life cycle?
   A. A feasibility study is conducted
   B. Work on the next phase begins
   C. A hand-off occurs
   D. A kick-off meeting

6. Which of the following is generated as part of the Initiating Process Group?
   A. Agreement
   B. Statement of work
   C. Organizational process assets
   D. Project charter

7. The following make up the Project Management Process Groups:
   A. Integration, Planning, Monitoring & Controlling, Closing
   B. Initiating, Planning, Executing, Monitoring & Controlling, Closing
   C. Initiating, Planning, Executing, Check, Closing
   D. Integration, Initiating, Planning, Monitoring & Controlling, Closing

8. Which of the following is not a characteristic of a process?
   A. They can overlap
   B. They are iterative
   C. They occur individually
   D. They are performed by a project team

9. The Plan-Do-Check-Act Cycle is known by which other name?
   A. Shewhart Cycle
   B. Deming Process
   C. Scientific Cycle
   D. Quality Cycle

10. The risk register has just been created. What Project Management Process Group are you in?
    A. Initiating
    B. Executing
    C. Monitoring & Controlling
    D. Planning

11. Happy Holiday Cruise Ships, Inc. is looking to modernize their IT applications. Part of their plan is to formalize how projects are managed, and how information is shared between teams in order to improve the return on investment from each of their specialized Discount Travel portfolios. They have already begun the work of setting up a Governance Board and Center of Excellence, with their next task being to create a project management office (PMO). A PMO can BEST be described as:
    A. A collection of project managers within a company
    B. A centralized unit within an organization to provide management of projects and programs
    C. A collection of company executives within an organization who provide management of projects and programs
    D. A centralized unit within an organization to provide portfolio management

12. Erica has been working on the same project for one of her largest clients for the past 2 years. Of that, she has spent the last year coordinating and managing resources, implementing approved changes and distributing information about the project requested to stakeholders. Which Process Group is responsible for the distribution of project information?
    A. Initiating
    B. Planning
    C. Executing
    D. Closing

13. Which of the following are not considered to be components of the project management plan?
    A. Procurement management plan
    B. Scope baseline
    C. Project scope statement
    D. Milestone list

14. Martha has just been told that she will be assigned as the project manager for the new office expansion project that will begin during the next quarter. Martha's assignment was identified within the project charter. During which Process Group did her assignment occur?
    A. Initiating
    B. Planning
    C. Monitoring and Controlling
    D. Executing

15. A collection of related activities that result in the completion of a major deliverable describes what?
    A. Project life cycle
    B. Project management life cycle
    C. Phase
    D. Process Group

Chapter Quiz

Exam Practice Answers

1. Answer: D

   Explanation: "Supporting the product after completion" refers to work that occurs after the project is complete and the end result transitioned over to the customer and/or operations. This refers to an ongoing activity, and is therefore outside of the project management realm and is the correct answer. All other options are a part of project management.

2. Answer: A

   Explanation: Project phases vary according to industry, project and even company. So there really is no concrete number of phases.

3. Answer: C

   Explanation: The study that the question refers to is something done *before* a project begins. Monte Carlo analysis is an analysis conducted that takes into account project risk. This is irrelevant, since the project has not yet begun. The same applies to cost performance index, which is a measure of cost efficiency on a project. Cost Plus Fee is related to the procurement activities. A feasibility study is a preliminary study conducted to determine a project's viability, which is a match and the correct answer.

4. Answer: C

   Explanation: Phase-end reviews are known by several different names -- this include kill points, phase gates, and phase exits. Hand-offs are technical transfers from one project phase to the next.

5. Answer: C

   Explanation: The answer is hand-off, which are technical transfers from one project phase to the next.

6. Answer: D

   Explanation: The question asks for the documents and information available before the project begins. The project charter is something that is drafted as part of initiation (it formally authorizes the project's existence), making this the correct answer.

7. Answer: B

   Explanation: The correct answer is Initiating, Planning, Executing, Monitoring & Controlling, and Closing.

8. Answer: C

   Explanation: Processes do overlap, making the option that states "they occur individually" inaccurate, and therefore the correct answer. The other options are all correct: processes are iterative, and they are performed by the project team.

9. Answer: A

   Explanation: The Plan-Do-Check-Act Cycle (PDCA) is known by two other names: the Shewhart cycle, after the gentleman that invented it, and the Deming Cycle, after the gentleman that popularized it. This means that the correct answer is "Shewhart Cycle".

10. Answer: D

    Explanation: The risk register contains the list of identified risks and information about them. The risk register is created during the Planning Process Group.

11. Answer: B

Explanation: A project management office (PMO) can best be described as a centralized unit within an organization that provides management and / or support of projects and programs.

12. Answer: C

    Explanation: The Executing Process Group coordinates and manages resources, implements approved changes, completes the work defined in the project management plan, and distributes information, such as reports and other information outlined and required by stakeholders.

13. Answer: D

    Explanation: The milestone list is not a component of the project management plan, and is therefore the correct option. While not a plan or baseline, the project scope statement is a part of the scope baseline, and is therefore technically part of the plan. The scope baseline is a component of the project management plan, and includes the project scope statement, WBS, WBS dictionary.

14. Answer: A

    Explanation: There are only two processes within the Initiating Process Group: Develop Project Charter, and Identify Stakeholders. The project charter is therefore created as part of the Initiating Process Group, which is when Martha's assignment occurred.

15. Answer: C

    Explanation: The correct answer is Phase. Frequently, a project's life cycle will be divided into phases in order to manage the project more effectively. At a minimum, you'll find a starting, middle, and closing phase, which often occur sequentially.

Chapter 4: Project Integration Management

Learning Objectives:

- ☐ Define the purpose of the Project Integration Management Knowledge Area
- ☐ Identify the processes of the Project Integration Management Knowledge Area
- ☐ Recall the key outputs of the Project Integration Management processes
- ☐ Differentiate between the inputs, tools and techniques, and outputs of the Project Integration Management processes
- ☐ Explain how Project Integration Management interacts with other Knowledge Areas of the *PMBOK® Guide*

Exam Domain Tasks:

- Perform project assessment based upon available information and meetings with the sponsor, customer, and other subject matter experts, in order to evaluate the feasibility of new products or services within the given assumptions and/or constraints.
- Define the high-level scope of the project based on the business and compliance requirements, in order to meet the customer's project expectations.
- Identify and document high-level risks, assumptions, and constraints based on current environment, historical data, and/or expert judgment, in order to identify project limitations and propose an implementation approach.
- Develop the project charter by further gathering and analyzing stakeholder requirements, in order to document project scope, milestones, and deliverables.
- Obtain approval for the project charter from the sponsor and customer (if required), in order to formalize the authority assigned to the project manager and gain commitment and acceptance for the project.

- Develop a change management plan by defining how changes will be handled, in order to track and manage changes.
- Present the project plan to the key stakeholders (if required), in order to obtain approval to execute the project.
- Conduct a kick-off meeting with all key stakeholders, in order to announce the start of the project, communicate the project milestones, and share other relevant information.
- Execute the tasks as defined in the project plan, in order to achieve the project deliverables within budget and schedule.
- Implement approved changes according to the change management plan, in order to meet project requirements.
- Measure project performance using appropriate tools and techniques, in order to identify and quantify any variances, perform approved corrective actions, and communicate with relevant stakeholders.
- Manage changes to the project scope, schedule, and costs by updating the project plan and communicating approved changes to the team, in order to ensure that revised project goals are met.
- Assess corrective actions on the issue register and determine next steps for unresolved issues by using appropriate tools and techniques in order to minimize the impact on project schedule, cost, and resources.
- Obtain final acceptance of the project deliverables by working with the sponsor and/or customer, in order to confirm that project scope and deliverables were met.
- Transfer the ownership of deliverables to the assigned stakeholders in accordance with the project plan, in order to facilitate project closure.
- Obtain financial, legal, and administrative closure using generally accepted practices, in order to communicate formal project closure and ensure no further liability.
- Distribute the final project report including all project closure-related information, project variances, and any issues, in order to provide the final project status to all stakeholders.
- Collate lessons learned through comprehensive project review, in order to create and/or update the organization's knowledge base.
- Archive project documents and material in order to retain organizational knowledge, comply with statutory requirements, and ensure availability of data for potential use in future projects and internal/external audits.
- Measure customer satisfaction at the end of the project by capturing customer feedback, in order to assist in project evaluation and enhance customer relationships.

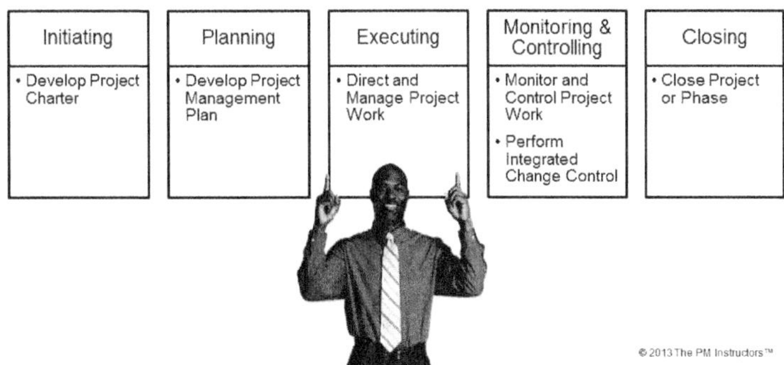
Project Integration Management
Purpose: To identify, define, combine, unify, and coordinate the various processes and project management activities within the Project Management Process Groups.
6 Project Management Processes:
Initiating
• Develop Project Charter
Planning
• Develop Project Management Plan
Executing
• Direct and Manage Project Work
Monitoring & Controlling
• Monitor and Control Project Work
• Perform Integrated Change Control
Closing
• Close Project or Phase
© 2013 The PM Instructors™

Project Integration Management Overview

The purpose of the Project Integration Management Knowledge Area is to identify, define, combine, unify, and coordinate the various processes and project management activities within the Project Management Process Groups, in order to accomplish the project objectives. It's the largest Knowledge Area of the ten, and the only one that has processes across all 5 of the Process Groups.

In the context of project management and the *PMBOK® Guide*, "Integration" refers to making choices on where to concentrate resources and efforts, anticipating and dealing with issues affecting the project, and coordinating the project work. In a sense, it creates the core structure of the project. For example, it creates the project management plan, coordinates the efforts of the change control board, and determines and documents the project management guidelines, which controls and monitors the changes throughout the project. Integration management is where the project begins and ends; it includes the execution, monitoring and controlling of the project work.

Project Integration Management is the responsibility of the project manager.

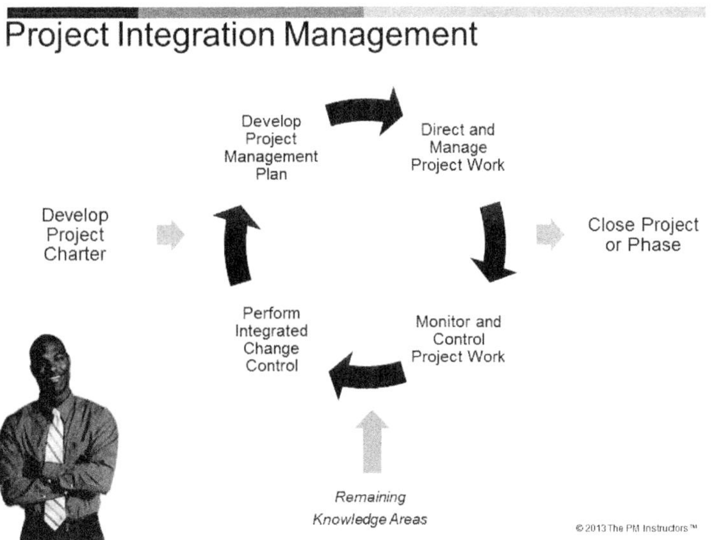
Project Integration Management
Develop Project Management Plan
Direct and Manage Project Work
Develop Project Charter
Close Project or Phase
Perform Integrated Change Control
Monitor and Control Project Work
Remaining Knowledge Areas
© 2013 The PM Instructors™

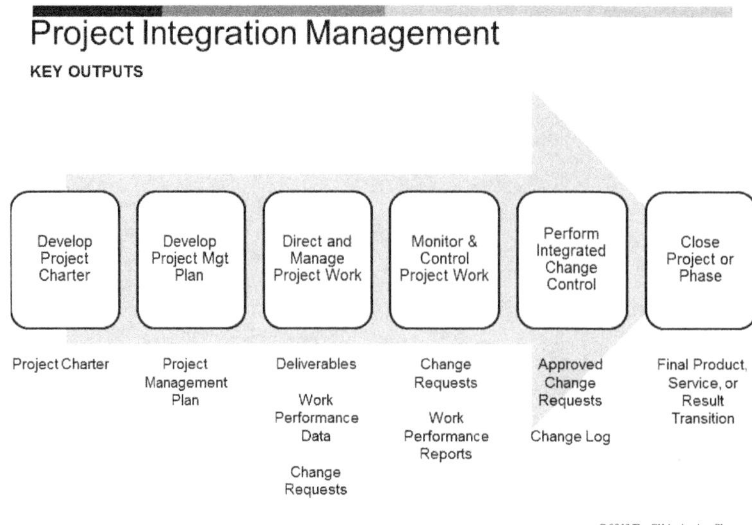

Project Integration Management contains six project management processes. They are:

- **Develop Project Charter** (Initiating Process Group): Responsible for formally authorizing a project or phase, and documenting the initial requirements to satisfy the stakeholders' needs and expectations.
- **Develop Project Management Plan** (Planning Process Group): Responsible for documenting the actions necessary to define, prepare, integrate, and coordinate all subsidiary plans.
- **Direct and Manage Project Work** (Executing Process Group): Responsible for performing the work defined in the project management plan to achieve the project's objectives.
- **Monitor and Control Project Work** (Monitoring and Controlling Process Group): Responsible for tracking, reviewing, and reporting the progress to meet the performance objectives defined in the project management plan.
- **Perform Integrated Change Control** (Monitoring and Controlling Process Group): Responsible for reviewing all change requests, approving changes, and managing changes to the deliverables, organizational process assets, project documents, and the project management plan, and communicate their disposition.
- **Close Project or Phase** (Closing Process Group): Responsible for finalizing all activities across all of the project management process groups to formally complete the project or phase.

These six processes not only *interact with one another, but also with the processes from the other nine Knowledge Areas*. They are responsible for integrating the results of the other Knowledge Areas, in order to manage the overall project.

When preparing for the certification exam, it is important to memorize the key outputs of the project management processes. Key outputs refer to the primary results generated as a result of carrying out a process, and are typically those that exclude updates made to existing documents.

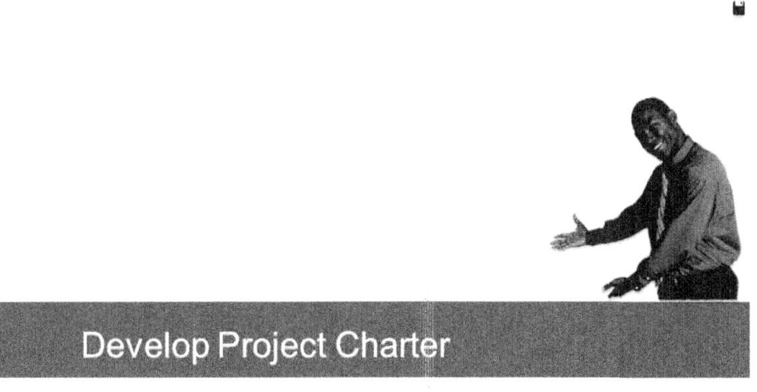
Develop Project Charter
Purpose: To develop a document that formally authorizes the existence of a project and provides the project manager with the authority to apply organizational resources to project activities.

Develop Project Charter Process Overview

The Develop Project Charter process is responsible for doing just what the name implies: *creating the project charter*. The project charter formally authorizes the existence of the project, and documents the initial requirements necessary to satisfy the stakeholders' needs and expectations. Once the project charter is approved by the project initiator or sponsor, the project is officially initiated and can move forward. Oftentimes, the project manager is formally assigned within the project charter and even assists in creating the document, although they are not approvers of the charter. It should be authored by the sponsoring organization, and initiated by an entity external to the project (such as a sponsor, program, or PMO). Through the project charter, the project manager receives authority to begin applying resources to project activities.

At a high level, the project charter accomplishes the following:

- Formally authorizes a project
- Identifies the project manager, if one is already designated
- Provides the project manager with authority to apply organizational resources to the project activities

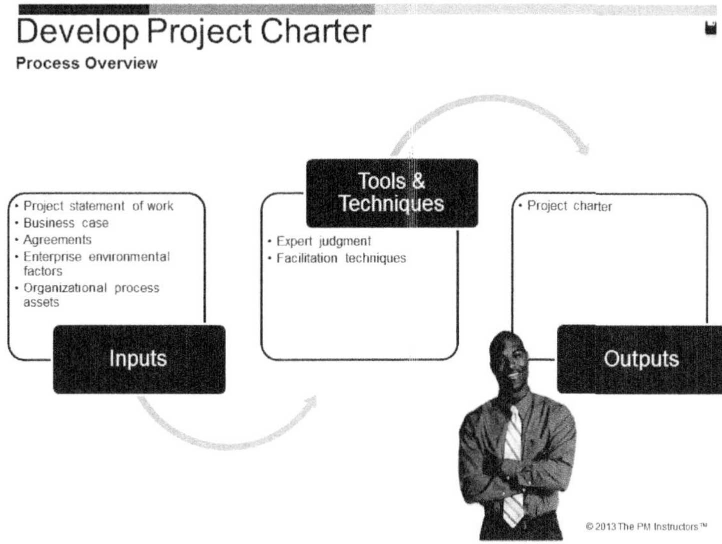
Develop Project Charter
Process Overview
• Project statement of work
• Business case
• Agreements
• Enterprise environmental factors
• Organizational process assets
Inputs
Tools & Techniques
• Expert judgment
• Facilitation techniques
• Project charter
Outputs
© 2013 The PM Instructors™

Develop Project Charter

*Project Statement of Work	Business Case	Agreements
• A narrative description of products, services, or results to be delivered by a project. • Business need • Product scope description • Strategic plan	• Justification for the project. • Need for the project • Cost-benefit analysis	• Applicable when a project is completed for an external customer.

* Definition from A Guide to the Project Management Body of Knowledge, Project Management Institute Inc., 2013

Develop Project Charter Inputs

The Develop Project Charter process contains a total of five inputs, some of which are generated externally. This includes: *project statement of work, business case, agreements, enterprise environmental factors, and organizational process assets.*

Project Statement of Work

There are 3 primary things that the project statement of work covers:

1. **The business need of the project.** This is where the reasons for a project being chartered are described. For example, it could be due to market demand, customer request, legal requirement, and so on.
2. **Project or product scope description.** The product scope description includes documentation of the product requirements and the characteristics of the service or product. It may include a high-level description of the scope, detailed enough to understand the high-level purpose of the project, and also as a base for use in future project planning.
3. **Strategic plan.** This plan is responsible for ensuring that the project supports the organization's strategic vision, goals, and objectives.

Business Case

The business case, if one has been completed, justifies the need for the project. It oftentimes includes the results of performing a cost-benefit analysis, and a description of the business need. It may also document the objectives of the project, and known risks.

According to the *PMBOK® Guide*, the business case is created as a result of one or more of the following:

- Market demand
- Organizational need
- Customer request
- Technological advance
- Legal requirement
- Ecological impacts
- Social need

Agreements

Agreements are applicable as an input when the project is completed for an external customer. The agreement, also sometimes referred to as a contract, is full of critical information, such as the terms and conditions of the work to be done, what is necessary in order for the work to be accepted, cost or schedule constraints, etc.

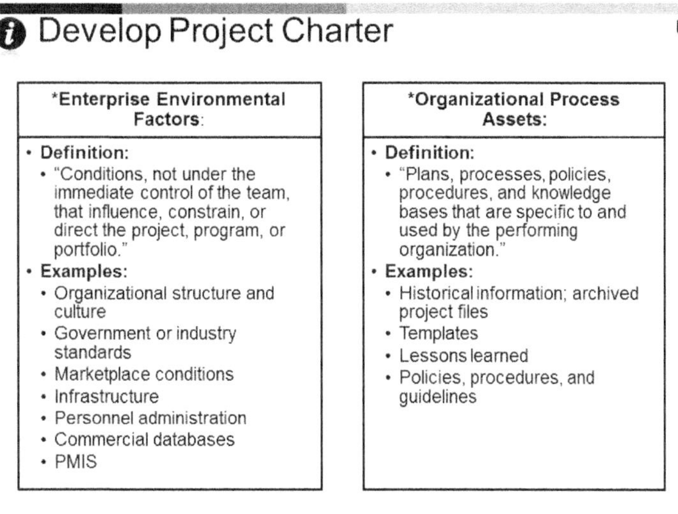
Develop Project Charter
*Enterprise Environmental Factors:
• Definition:
• "Conditions, not under the immediate control of the team, that influence, constrain, or direct the project, program, or portfolio."
• Examples:
• Organizational structure and culture
• Government or industry standards
• Marketplace conditions
• Infrastructure
• Personnel administration
• Commercial databases
• PMIS
*Organizational Process Assets:
• Definition:
• "Plans, processes, policies, procedures, and knowledge bases that are specific to and used by the performing organization."
• Examples:
• Historical information; archived project files
• Templates
• Lessons learned
• Policies, procedures, and guidelines
* Definition from A Guide to the Project Management Body of Knowledge, Project Management Institute Inc., 2013
© 2013 The PM Instructors™

Enterprise Environmental Factors

Enterprise environmental factors refer to any or all external environmental factors and internal organizational environmental factors that surround or influence the project's success. Some examples of enterprise environmental factors are:

- Organizational structure and culture
- Standards – industry or governmental
- Infrastructure
- Human resources, such as the existing resources and departments, the personnel administration policies, guidelines and approved company practices as well as a work authorization system
- Marketplace conditions
- Stakeholder risk tolerances
- Commercial databases, such as industry studies, risk databases
- Project management information system (PMIS)

Enterprise environmental factors and organizational process assets are both frequent inputs to the project management processes, although each process may utilize different aspects of each. In this case, there are several enterprise environmental factors used to create the project charter, and the *PMBOK® Guide* names many. The reason there are so many is that, at this point, the project management team takes into consideration everything affecting and surrounding the project.

Organizational Process Assets

Organizational process assets are any or all process related assets, from any or all of the organizations involved in the project that are or can be used to influence the project's success. There are two categories that organizational process assets can be divided into: organization's processes and procedures for conducting work; the corporate knowledge base for storing and retrieving information. Some examples of organizational process assets are:

- Company standards, policies, the product and project life cycle standards, and all policies and procedures

- Standardized guidelines, including guidelines for tailoring the company standards to the project needs
- Work instructions and performance and evaluation criteria
- Project templates
- Company requirements, including communication requirements, and requirements for closing out a project
- Company procedures, such as financial controls procedures, issue and defect management procedures, risk control procedures, and work authorization approval procedures
- Process measurement database, which is where measurement data is made available on processes and products
- Project files from previous company projects
- Historical information
- Lessons learned, which saves the project manager hours of work from repeating past mistakes, picking up best practices and information from past similar projects
- Issue and defect management database containing summary, status and information on issues and defects
- Configuration management knowledge base, which contains baseline information on the company standards, policies, procedures, and project documents.
- Financial database containing financial data, such as labor hours, costs, budgets, and project cost overruns.

Organizational process assets provide a way to utilize previous information, avoid making the same mistakes, and it makes referencing company information quick and easy.

Develop Project Charter

Project Selection Methods

- Used by organizations to determine which projects they will move forward

Constrained Optimization Methods	Benefit Measurement Methods
• Used to calculate the value of the projects being considered • Also known as mathematical models or calculation methods • Types: • *linear* • *nonlinear* • *dynamic* • *integer* • *multi-objective programming algorithms*	• Determine the value of a project, based on various criteria chosen • Also known as decision models • Types: • Cost-benefit analysis • Scoring models • Economic models

Project Selection Methods

Project selection methods are used by organizations to determine which projects they will move forward. Some organizations place a high degree of effort in the process used to select projects, since projects can require a large investment, or the outcome of projects chosen may have a high impact on the organization itself. Those involved in the project selection process may include a formal project selection committee or simply involve the management team. The size of the selection committee can vary, depending on the size of the organization and projects considered. If an organization has a project management office (PMO), then this may be considered part of the PMO's function

There are generally two categories of project selection methods: constrained optimization methods and benefit measurement methods.

Constrained Optimization Methods

Constrained optimization methods, also known as mathematical models or calculation methods, are used to calculate the value of the projects being considered. A purely mathematical approach is taken to selecting which projects the organization will move forward with.

For the exam, know that the following are types of constrained optimization methods:

- *linear*
- *nonlinear*
- *dynamic*
- *integer*
- *multi-objective programming algorithms*

These methods are very technical and involve complex calculations that are out of scope for this course material. For those taking the exam, all that you must know is the list of constrained optimization methods noted above.

Develop Project Charter

Project Selection Methods

- Benefit Measurement Methods

Cost-Benefit Analysis	Scoring Models	Economic Models
• Compares the cost of the project to the benefit of the outcome • Utilizes benefit-cost-ratio • A benefit cost ratio greater than 1 is good	• Takes the projects under consideration and scores them using a series of criteria chosen	• There are three types of economic models • Net present value • Internal rate of return • Payback period

Benefit Measurement Methods

Benefit measurement methods, also known as decision models, determine the value of a project, based on various criteria chosen by the project selection committee.

For the exam, know the following three types of benefit measurement methods:

- Cost-benefit analysis
- Scoring models
- Economic models

Unlike constrained optimization methods, you will need to know more about each of these three types, and other sub-types that fall under economic models.

Cost-Benefit Analysis

The cost-benefit analysis approach compares the cost of the project to the benefit of the outcome. Basically, what is the overall financial benefit of the product or service that the project would produce? Things like the development, marketing, and ongoing cost within the life of the product or service are taken into account, versus the project costs alone. One way to analyze this would be through benefit-cost-ratio. Anything with a benefit cost ratio greater than 1 is viewed as a good investment, since it means that the benefit is greater than the cost. The greater the value, the better.

In the context of cost-benefit analysis, *benefit* refers to revenue. For example, if a project selection committee is evaluating two projects, where project A had a benefit-cost-ratio of 1.5 and project B had a benefit-cost-ratio of 2.8, they would select project B. In this example, project B had a greater benefit-cost-ratio than project A.

Develop Project Charter

Project Selection Methods

- Benefit Measurement Methods

Scoring Models

- Follows a multi-step process:
  - Create a list of criteria
  - Assign each criteria a weight
  - Rate each project based on a scale agreed to by the committed
  - Generate a weighted score
  - Select the project(s) with the highest overall score

Example:

Project Criteria / Weight		Project Ratings		
Criteria	Weight	Project A	Project B	Project C
Potential Revenue	5.0	5 (25)	2 (10)	3 (15)
Alignment to Strategy	4.0	2 (8)	5 (20)	3 (12)
Ease to Market	1.0	3 (3)	1 (1)	4 (4)
Weighted Score		36	31	31

Scoring Models

A scoring model approach takes the projects under consideration and scores them using a series of criteria chosen by the organization or project selection committee. The projects with the highest score(s) are then selected.

This technique typically follows a multi-step process, such as the following:

1. Create a list of criteria that will be used in selecting projects (for example, ease to market, costs, potential revenue, alignment to strategy, etc)
2. Assign each criteria a weight, according to importance based on a scale agreed to by the committee. Some organizations use a value, while others assign %.
3. Rate each project based on a scale agreed to by the committed (for example, between 1-5) for each listed criteria
4. Generate a weighted score by multiplying the project's rating by the criteria weight, and then add up the score for each of the criteria considered within the project
5. Select the project(s) with the highest overall score

The following is an example of three projects that are scored against a set of criteria:

Project Criteria / Weight		Project Ratings		
Criteria	Weight	Project A	Project B	Project C
Potential Revenue	5.0	5 (25)	2 (10)	3 (15)
Alignment to Strategy	4.0	2 (8)	5 (20)	3 (12)
Ease to Market	1.0	3 (3)	1 (1)	4 (4)
Weighted Score		**36**	**31**	**31**

**Rating scale used: 1-5.*

Based on the example provided on the previous page, the project selected is Project A, since it contains the highest weighted score.

Develop Project Charter

Project Selection Methods

- Benefit Measurement Methods

Economic Models

- There are three types of economic models
  - Net present value
  - Internal rate of return
  - Payback period

Net Present Value (NPV)

- Refers to the present value of total revenue, minus the costs over several time periods

Internal Rate of Return (IRR)

- Refers to the rate at which the project revenue and project investment are equal

Payback Period

- Calculates the number of time periods that it takes for the organization to recover the project investment

Economic Models

There are three types of economic models you must be familiar with for the exam:

- Net present value
- Internal rate of return
- And payback period

Net Present Value (NPV)

Present value refers to today's value of future cash flows. For the exam, it will not be necessary to know how to calculate present or future value. Instead, you will need to know the definitions and how to determine the best project choice based on the values.

Net Present Value refers to the present value of total revenue, minus the costs over several time periods. For example, a company may have invested $10,000 into a project, receiving a revenue of $5,000 in the first year, and $7,000 of revenue in the second year, totaling $12,000. In this example, the net present value in two years will be $2,000; if they make an additional $3,000 in year 3, then the net present value becomes $5,000. A positive net present value is good. The higher the net present value, the better, so always select the project with the highest net present value for purposes of the exam.

Internal Rate of Return (IRR)

Internal rate of return refers to the rate at which the project revenue and project investment are equal. You don't need to know the calculations for this – it is quite complex and typically not calculated manually. For purposes of the exam, look for the highest internal rate of return when selecting a project.

Payback Period

Payback period calculates the number of time periods that it takes for the organization to recover the project investment. A shorter payback period is preferred, since it means that a profit will be achieved sooner. For the exam, look for the project with the lowest payback period. This is the simplest, and least precise project selection method.

Summary Table

The following is a table that summarizes the various benefit measurement methods:

Method	Description	Which Project to Select
Benefit-Cost-Ratio	Compares the cost of the project to the benefit of the outcome	Select the project with the *highest* number.
Weighted Scoring Model	Takes the projects under consideration and scores them using a series of criteria chosen by the organization or project selection committee	Select the project with the *highest* weighted score.
Net Present Value (NPV)	Refers to the present value of total revenue, minus the costs over several time periods	Select the project with the *highest* NPV
Internal Rate of Return (IRR)	Refers to the rate at which the project revenue and project investment are equal	Select the project with the *highest* IRR
Payback Period	Calculates the number of time periods that it takes for the organization to recover the project investment.	Select the project with the *lowest* payback period

Develop Project Charter

- **Expert Judgment**
  - Stakeholders
  - Subject matter experts
  - PMO
  - Professional and technical associations
  - Industry groups
  - Consultants
  - Other organizational units
- **Facilitation Techniques**

Develop Project Charter Tools and Techniques

The Develop Project Charter process has two tools and techniques: *expert judgment and facilitation techniques*. Note that expert judgment appears as a tool and technique across all six of the Project Integration Management Knowledge Area processes.

Expert Judgment

Expert judgment refers to the expertise provided by any group or person that has specialized education, knowledge, skill, experience, or training within the topic at hand (in this case, the creation of the project charter).

Example of expert judgment includes other departments or units within the company, consultants, stakeholders, subject matter experts, and professional or industry associations and groups. In this process, expert judgment is used to assess the inputs needed to develop the project charter, particularly in relation to technical and management details that exist within the project.

Facilitation Techniques

Developing the project charter is not typically something completed by a single individual. It may take several iterations and a joint effort by a group of individuals to bring the information together into a single document that defines the high-level goals and intended outcomes of a project. This is where facilitation techniques come in. Examples of facilitation techniques include brainstorming, problem solving, conflict resolution, and meeting management.

Develop Project Charter

Project Charter

- Formally authorizes a project
- Issued by the project initiator or sponsor
- Identifies the project manager if already designated
- Provides the project manager with authority to apply organizational resources to the project activities

Projects are chartered as a result of:
• Market demand • Organizational need • Customer request • Technological advance • Legal requirement • Ecological impacts • Social need

Develop Project Charter Outputs

The Develop Project Charter process has one output: the *project charter*.

Project Charter Contents

The project charter addresses several items, and the *PMBOK® Guide* specifies 12 of them. It is not necessary to memorize this list for the exam, but important to be familiar with them. Keep in mind that the project charter is a high-level document, and does not contain all of the finite details of the project. These details will later be refined within the project management plan.

Develop Project Charter

Project Charter Contents:

- Purpose or justification of project
- Project objectives
- High-level requirements
- High-level scope and description
- High-level risks
- Summary budget
- Summary milestone schedule
- Approval requirements
- Assigned project manager and authority level
- Sponsor

What is in a project charter?

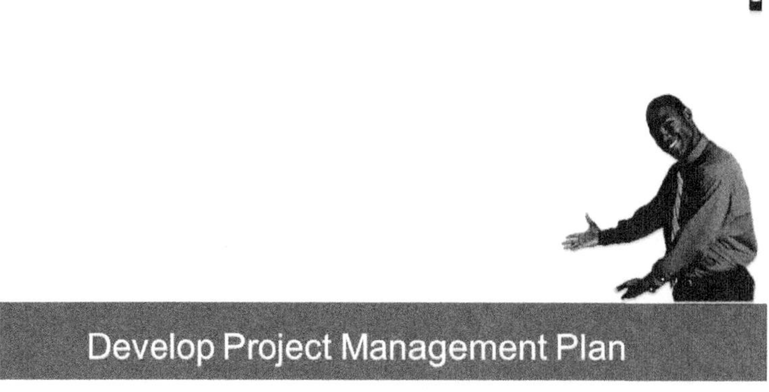
Develop Project Management Plan

Purpose: To define, prepare, and coordinate all subsidiary plans and integrate them into a comprehensive project management plan.

Develop Project Management Plan Process Overview

The Develop Project Management Plan process produces a key document that is at the center of the project itself: the project management plan. The project management plan documents the necessary actions to define, prepare, integrate, and coordinate the subsidiary plans. It consists of all sub-plans and baselines. As these sub-documents are created, they are passed on to this process to be integrated into the primary plan itself. This process also integrates the approved updates and changes to the plan, which are often a result of carrying out the other project management processes.

According to the *PMBOK® Guide*, the project management plan is a formal, approved document that defines how the project is executed, monitored and controlled, and closed. It can be either one plan, or a collection of several plans, as described above.

Plans + Baselines = Project Management Plan

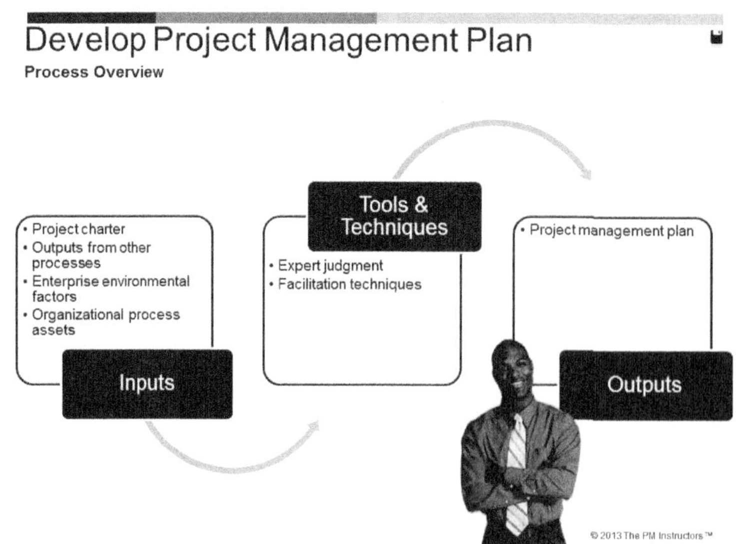
Develop Project Management Plan
Process Overview
• Project charter
• Outputs from other processes
• Enterprise environmental factors
• Organizational process assets
Inputs
Tools & Techniques
• Expert judgment
• Facilitation techniques
• Project management plan
Outputs
© 2013 The PM Instructors™

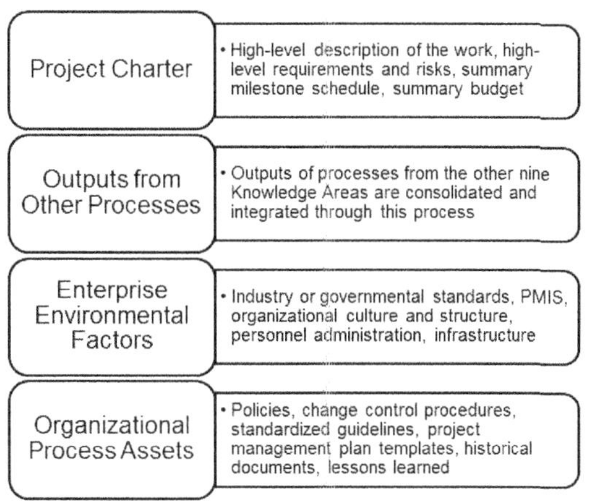
Develop Project Management Plan
Project Charter
• High-level description of the work, high-level requirements and risks, summary milestone schedule, summary budget
Outputs from Other Processes
• Outputs of processes from the other nine Knowledge Areas are consolidated and integrated through this process
Enterprise Environmental Factors
• Industry or governmental standards, PMIS, organizational culture and structure, personnel administration, infrastructure
Organizational Process Assets
• Policies, change control procedures, standardized guidelines, project management plan templates, historical documents, lessons learned
© 2013 The PM Instructors™

Develop Project Management Plan Inputs

The Develop Project Management Plan process has four inputs, one of which is produced through the other project management processes. The inputs are as follows: *project charter, outputs from other processes, enterprise environmental factors, and organizational process assets.*

It is helpful to note that all six of the Project Integration Management Knowledge Area processes use organizational process assets as an input.

Project Charter

The project charter provides the authorization for the project to move forward. It also contains a high-level description of the project and product scope, summary schedule and budget, high-level risks, and additional information that will further be detailed and refined within the project management plan.

Outputs from Other Processes

Outputs from the remaining processes of the other Knowledge Areas are fed into this process as an input, in order to be integrated into the master plan (project management plan).

Enterprise Environmental Factors

All enterprise environmental factors are used and considered when creating the project management plan, including: standards, the PMIS, infrastructure, personnel administration, and the organization's structure and culture.

Organizational Process Assets

All organizational process assets are used to create the project management plan, including: existing templates, historical documents from past projects, lessons learned, processes, procedures, and guidelines.

Imagine the time saved from using an approved template, or refining and tailoring a plan from a past similar project!

Develop Project Management Plan Tools and Techniques

Like the process before it, the Develop Project Management Plan process has two tools and techniques: *expert judgment and facilitation techniques*.

Develop Project Management Plan

- **Expert Judgment** is used to:
  - Tailor the processes according to the project needs
  - Determine the approach
  - Determine document and resource needs
  - Develop details needed

Expert Judgment

Expert judgment is used to develop the technical and management details of the project management plan, as well as determine the approach required to successfully complete the project, to determine the resources and skill levels needed to perform the project work, and to determine how to tailor the processes to meet the project needs.

Develop Project Management Plan

- **Facilitation Techniques** are used to achieve agreement to accomplish project activities. Examples of facilitation techniques include:
  - Brainstorming
  - Conflict Resolution
  - Problem Solving
  - Meeting Management

Facilitation Techniques

Facilitation techniques is used to achieve agreement between project team members in order to accomplish project activities. Examples of some key facilitation techniques used are similar to those that were used to develop the charter: *brainstorming, conflict resolution, problem solving, and meeting management.*

Develop Project Management Plan

Project Management Plan

- Integrates and consolidates all subsidiary plans and baselines from planning processes
- Tailors the processes according to the project needs
- Determines how work will be executed and baselines maintained

Plans

- Scope management plan
- Schedule management plan
- Cost management plan
- Quality management plan
- Process improvement plan
- Human resource management plan
- Communications management plan
- Risk management plan
- Procurement management plan
- Stakeholder management plan
- Change management plan
- Configuration management plan
- Requirements management plan

Baselines

- Schedule baseline
- Scope baseline
- Cost baseline

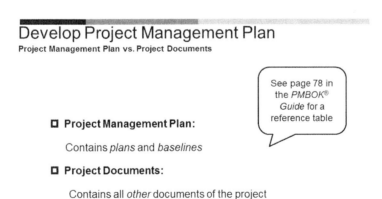

Develop Project Management Plan Outputs

As the name implies, the Develop Project Management Plan process generates the *project management plan as the output*, which itself is a compilation of several subsidiary plans and baselines.

Project Management Plan Contents

The project management plan contains several plans and baselines. How detailed it needs to be depends on the project itself; it should be tailored according to the level of complexity of the project. The table included within the next page reflects a list of some of the subsidiary plans and baselines contained within the project management plan.

Notice that the three baselines included within the plan map to the triple constraints of scope, time, and cost. Also note that this is not a comprehensive list. Any sub-plan and baseline should be absorbed as part of the project management plan.

Develop Project Management Plan

Project Management Plan vs. Project Documents

See page 78 in the *PMBOK®* *Guide* for a reference table

- **Project Management Plan:**

  Contains *plans* and *baselines*

- **Project Documents:**

  Contains all *other* documents of the project

Project Management Plan versus Project Documents

The *project management plan* contains all project plans and baselines, while the *project documents* consists of all *other* documents of the project.

Think of them as two separate buckets, and all documents created within a project must fall into either one or the other.

Key Project Management Plan Contents

Scope management plan documents how the project and product scope will be defined, managed and controlled, as well as how the work will be verified.
Schedule management plan establishes the approach and criteria for developing, managing, and controlling the project schedule.
Cost management plan establishes the criteria for planning, structuring, estimating, budgeting and controlling project costs.
Quality management plan reflects the organization's quality policy and applies it to the project. It addresses quality control, quality assurance, and continuous process improvement.
Process improvement plan is created within the same process as the quality management plan. It provides detailed steps for analyzing the processes that are meant to identify waste and non-value added activity in the project in order to increase customer value.
Human resource management plan describes how human resources will be acquired, developed, managed, and released.
Communications management plan covers all communication aspects of the project, such as the communication needs of stakeholders, how information will be collected and disseminated. It can include the items to be communicated, the purpose of the communication, the frequency, start and end dates of information distribution, the distribution format, and the communication responsibilities.
Risk management plan describes how risk management will be structured and carried out. It includes the risk methodology, roles and responsibilities, budgeting, timing, risk categories, and the definitions of risk probability and impact.
Procurement management plan describes how the procurement activities will be carried out and managed, and the procedures for closing contracts.
Stakeholder management plan describes how stakeholders will be effectively engaged.
Scope baseline contains the approved and signed off project scope statement, work breakdown structure (WBS), and WBS dictionary.
Schedule baseline contains the approved and signed off version of the project schedule.
Cost baseline contains the approved and signed off version of the project budget.

Direct and Manage Project Work

Purpose: To lead and perform the work defined in the project management plan and implement approved changes to achieve the project's objectives.

Direct and Manage Project Work Process Overview

The purpose of the Direct and Manage Project Work process is just as it sounds – to lead and perform the work defined in the project management plan and implement approved changes to achieve the project's objectives. In other words, this process executes the project management plan (which was created in the previous process) in order to accomplish the project's objectives and documented scope. This makes the process group that this process falls into easy to remember, which happens to be the Executing Process Group, given its purpose. This process is also responsible for executing the changes that are approved by the project's change control board.

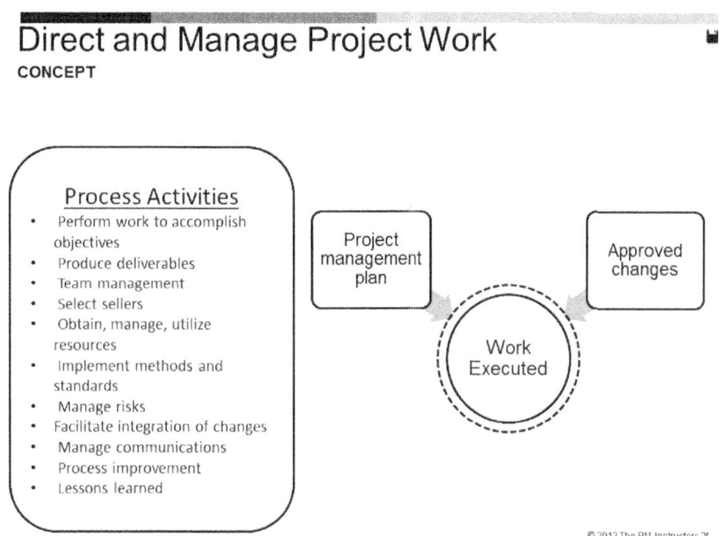

Process Concept

The *PMBOK® Guide* lists several actions managed as part of this process, which covers a wide spectrum of Executing activities. The following is an example of what occurs through this process, and is not meant to be a comprehensive list:

- Perform work towards accomplishing project objectives by performing the project activities, expending effort and funds
- Create project deliverables

- Manage the project team which includes – among other management activities – staffing and training
- Obtain quotes, bids, offers and proposals, and then select and manage the sellers used for activities obtained from outside of the internal project team
- Obtain, manage, and use resources. This includes human resources, materials, tools, equipment and facilities
- Implement methods and standards
- Manage the project deliverables by creating, controlling, verifying and validating them
- Manage risks, including implementation of risk response activities
- Integrate approved changes
- Manage communications, including the reporting of project analysis and data
- Implement approved process improvement activities
- Collect and report lessons learned

The above reads more like a list of project-execution activities, which is an accurate reflection of its overarching purpose. Keep in mind that processes that fall within the Project Integration Management Knowledge Area are broad and meant to coordinate work from across the remaining Knowledge Areas.

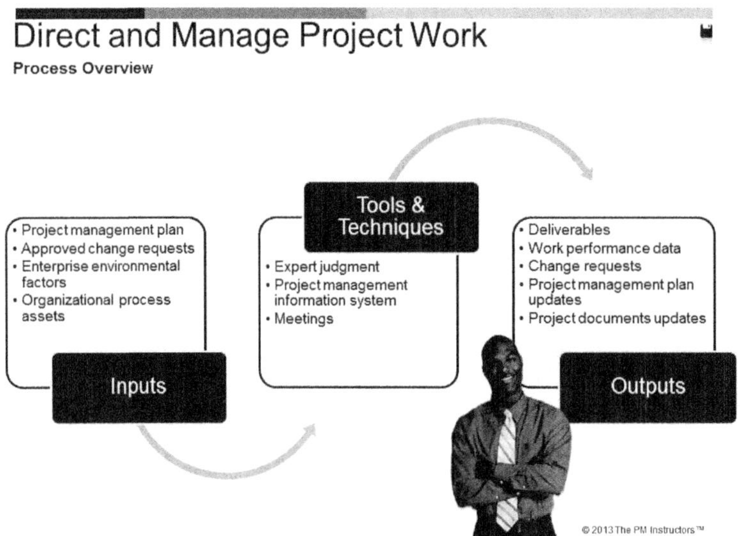
Direct and Manage Project Work
Process Overview
• Project management plan
• Approved change requests
• Enterprise environmental factors
• Organizational process assets
Inputs
Tools & Techniques
• Expert judgment
• Project management information system
• Meetings
• Deliverables
• Work performance data
• Change requests
• Project management plan updates
• Project documents updates
Outputs
© 2013 The PM Instructors™

Key outputs of this process include the following:

- Deliverables, which results from performing the work of the project;
- Work performance data, which refers to the raw data of the project;
- And change requests.

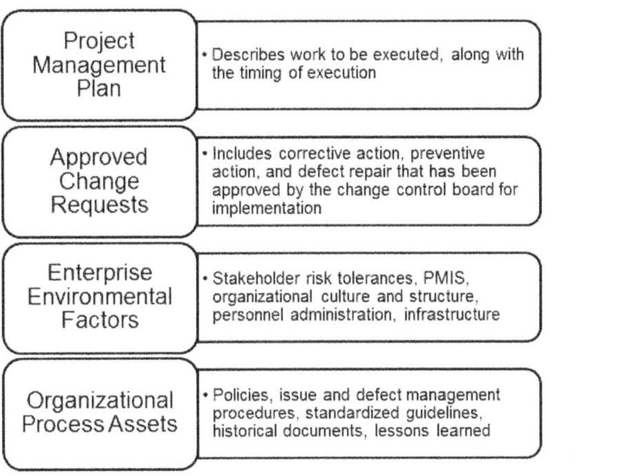

Direct and Manage Project Work
Project Management Plan
• Describes work to be executed, along with the timing of execution
Approved Change Requests
• Includes corrective action, preventive action, and defect repair that has been approved by the change control board for implementation
Enterprise Environmental Factors
• Stakeholder risk tolerances, PMIS, organizational culture and structure, personnel administration, infrastructure
Organizational Process Assets
• Policies, issue and defect management procedures, standardized guidelines, historical documents, lessons learned
© 2013 The PM Instructors™

Direct and Manage Project Work Inputs

The Direct and Manage Project work process contains a total of four inputs, three of which have already appeared in previous processes. The inputs are as follows: *project management plan, approved change requests, enterprise environmental factors, and organizational process assets.*

Project Management Plan

The project management plan includes the work to be executed, as well as the detailed schedule and budget. This plan is executed through this process.

Approved Change Requests

Change requests that were approved by the change control board, through the Perform Integrated Change Control process, are implemented through this process. These changes may fall into one of three categories:

- Corrective action
- Preventive action
- Defect repair

Enterprise Environmental Factors

Key enterprise environmental factors considered include: organizational structure and culture, infrastructure, personnel administration, the PMIS, and stakeholder risk tolerances.

Organizational Process Assets

Key organizational process assets used include: guidelines and work instructions, communication requirements, historical documents, policies and procedures, and lessons learned.

Direct and Manage Project Work

- **Expert Judgment**
- **Project Management Information System (PMIS)**: An information system consisting of tools and techniques used to gather, integrate, and disseminate the outputs of project management processes.

  Examples:

  - *Scheduling software tool*
  - *Configuration management system*
  - *SharePoint and other web interfaces*
  - *Automated systems*
- **Meetings**

Direct and Manage Project Work Tools and Techniques

The Direct and Manage Project Work process contains the following three tools and techniques, two of which have not been mentioned previously: *expert judgment, project management information system, and meetings.*

Expert Judgment

Expert judgment is used to assess the information needed to execute the work of the project. This may include the feedback and input of consultants, other units within the organization, and stakeholders.

Project Management Information System (PMIS)

The PMIS is an information system that consists of tools and techniques used to gather, integrate, and disseminate the outputs of the project management processes. It may include automated and manual systems, and is used to manage the large amount of information that typically exists within a project. Although it's an enterprise environmental factor, it's highlighted as a tool in this process, since it is very important during the execution of the work.

Meetings

Meetings is a technique that is used by several of the project management processes, and provides a means of discussing and addressing project-related topics with the project team. This is essential to executing the project work.

The *PMBOK® Guide* notes three meeting types:

1. Information exchange
2. Brainstorming, option evaluation, or design
3. Decision making

Direct and Manage Project Work Outputs

The Direct and Manage Project Work process contains the following five outputs: *deliverables, work performance data, change requests, project management plan updates, and project documents updates*. Although all of the outputs are important, the deliverables output is considered to be key. Deliverables become the result of executing the project work – it is the result that the project team worked towards. Keep in mind that, like many other processes, this process is iterative, meaning that it is performed many times throughout the project's life and necessary in order to produce deliverables.

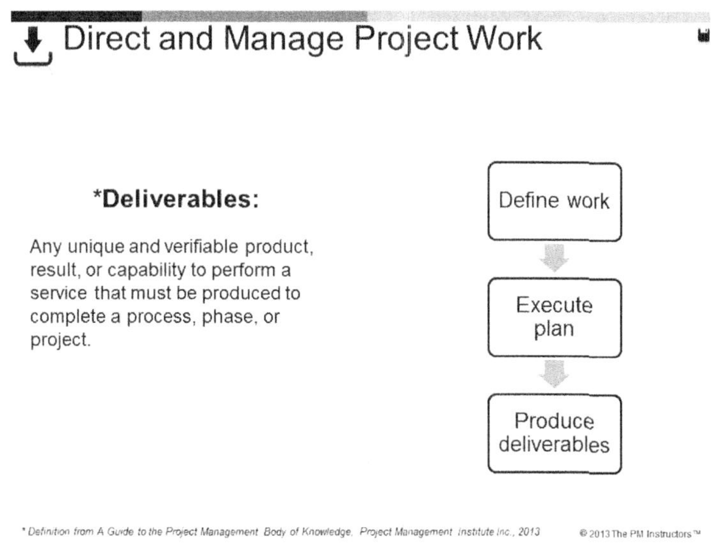

Direct and Manage Project Work
*Deliverables:
Any unique and verifiable product, result, or capability to perform a service that must be produced to complete a process, phase, or project.
Define work
Execute plan
Produce deliverables
* Definition from A Guide to the Project Management Body of Knowledge, Project Management Institute Inc., 2013
© 2013 The PM Instructors™

Deliverables

A deliverable is any unique and verifiable product, result, or capability to perform a service that is required to be produced to complete a process, phase, or project. A deliverable is often a tangible and measurable result – although this is not always the case.

After performing the work through the Direct and Manage Project Work process, the deliverables become the tangible results of that work.

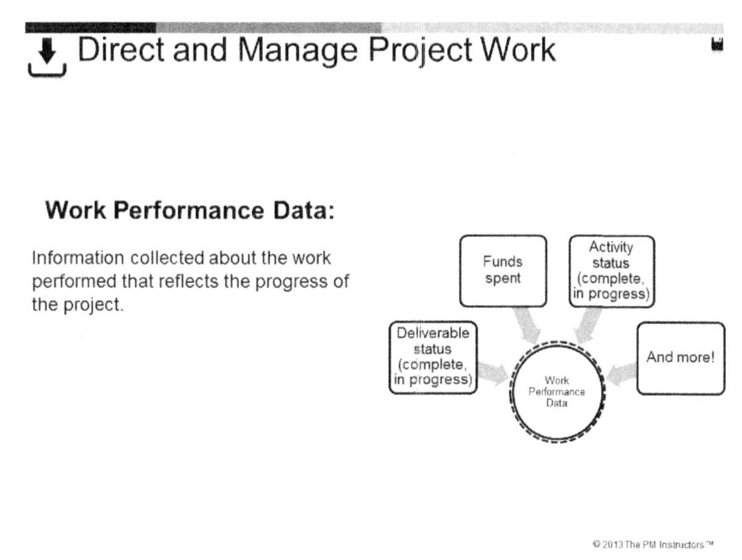

Direct and Manage Project Work
Work Performance Data:
Information collected about the work performed that reflects the progress of the project.
Funds spent
Activity status (complete, in progress)
Deliverable status (complete, in progress)
And more!
Work Performance Data
© 2013 The PM Instructors™

Work Performance Data

As part of executing the work through this process, information on the status of project activities is collected. Here is an example of the type of information collected:

- Schedule progress, started / finished activities, % of physically completed and in-progress activities, and estimated time of completion for activities not finished
- Completed / non-completed deliverables
- Quality standards update – such as the extent to which they are being met
- Authorized / incurred costs
- Resource utilization detail

Think of *work performance data* as the raw data of work performed to-date. This is in contrast to another output that will be generated through the Monitoring and Controlling processes called *work performance information.* Unlike work performance data, work performance information included results of analyzing the data / information.

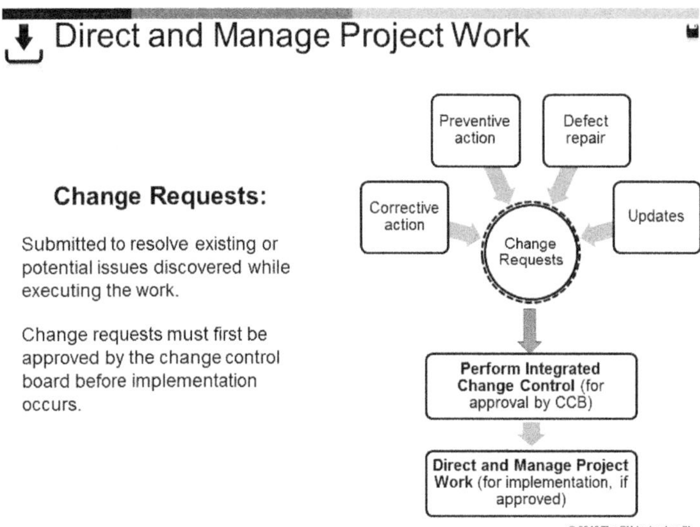

Change Requests

As the work of the project is performed, changes to the plan or approach may become necessary and evident. Change requests may take the form of:

- **Corrective actions:** Actions taken to bring the performance of the work back in line with the project management plan.
- **Preventive actions:** Actions taken to ensure project work is in alignment with the project management plan..
- **Defect repairs:** Actions taken to repair defects discovered as the work is being executed, or to replace a component due to defects.
- **Updates:** Changes to project documents that have been approved, including any document within the "project documents" list, and those considered to be a sub-component of the project management plan

Direct and Manage Project Work

Project Management Plan Updates	• Updates made to the project management plan as a result of carrying out the process
Project Documents Updates	• Updates made to the project documents as a result of carrying out the process

Project Management Plan Updates

Updates to the project management plan and project documents may be necessary as a result of carrying out this process. Typically, updates occur as a result of approved change requests. In terms of the project management plan, these updates may include changes to any of the subsidiary plans and baselines included.

Project Documents Updates

As a result of carrying out this process, any one of the project documents may require an update. However, the *PMBOK® Guide* notes that typical updates may include requirements documentation, any one of the project logs or registers.

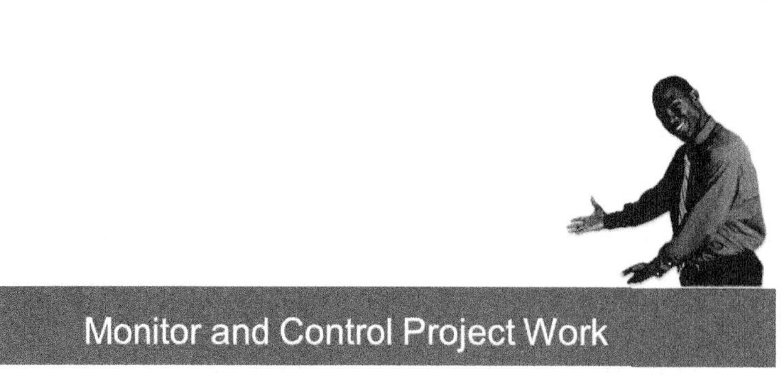

Purpose: To track, review, and report project progress against the performance objectives defined in the project management plan.

Monitor and Control Project Work Process Overview

The purpose of this process is to track, review, and report the progress of the project to meet the performance objectives defined in the project management plan. The purpose of monitoring a project is to make sure it is on track and moving along as it should be. Specifically, monitoring involves collecting, measuring, and disseminating performance information. The project manager should utilize this information to assess whether the project is on track, and if not, bring it to conformance with the project management plan. Much of these efforts involve comparing actual performance to planned performance in order to identify existing variance. The following is a list of items that the process is concerned with:

- Comparing the actual performance data collected against the project management plan
- Assessing whether any corrective or preventive actions are necessary by evaluating performance information, and making recommendations based on the outcome
- Analyzing, tracking and monitoring project risks and ensuring that appropriate actions concerning previously identified and new risks are taken
- Maintaining an ongoing information base of the project's products and documentation
- Providing information for use of reporting, progress measurement and forecasting
- Monitoring implemented changes as they occur

Monitor and Control Project Work

CONCEPT

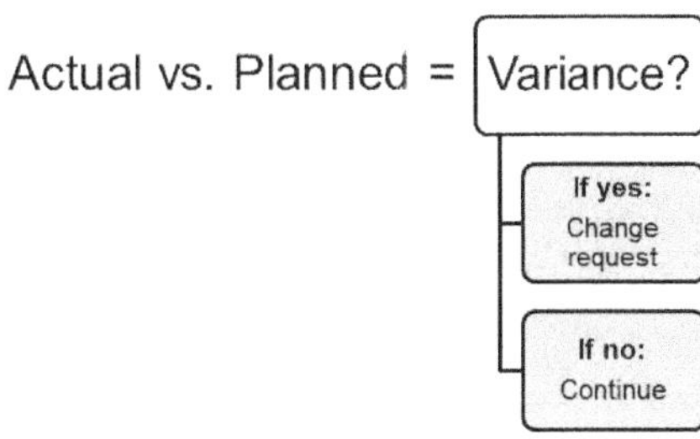

Concept

As mentioned within the introduction to the process, monitoring and controlling efforts often include a comparison of actual performance to planned performance. The idea is to identify any variances that exist. If there is potential variance or if variance is present, then the next action should be proactive – submit a change request to resolve or prevent it from occurring. If variance is not present, then no further action is necessary.

The concept described above is applicable to all processes that fall within the Monitoring and Controlling Process Group. Understanding this concept helps to simplify the purpose and outcome of the processes that fall within this specific process group.

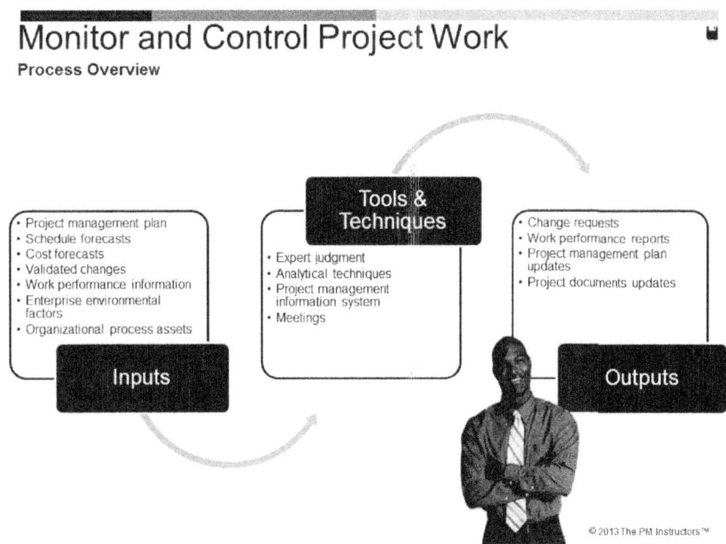

Monitor and Control Project Work
Process Overview
• Project management plan
• Schedule forecasts
• Cost forecasts
• Validated changes
• Work performance information
• Enterprise environmental factors
• Organizational process assets
Inputs
Tools & Techniques
• Expert judgment
• Analytical techniques
• Project management information system
• Meetings
• Change requests
• Work performance reports
• Project management plan updates
• Project documents updates
Outputs
© 2013 The PM Instructors™

Monitor and Control Project Work

Project Management Plan	• Planned progress
Schedule Forecasts	• Progress against the schedule baseline • May contain schedule variance and schedule performance index
Cost Forecasts	• Progress against the cost baseline • May contain cost variance and cost performance index
Validated Changes	• Approved changes that were confirmed to have been implemented correctly

Monitor and Control Project Work Inputs

The Monitor and Control Project Work process contains the following seven inputs: *project management plan, schedule forecasts, cost forecasts, validated changes, work performance information, enterprise environmental factors, and organizational process assets*. Several of these inputs have not been reviewed yet, since they are produced from processes outside of this Knowledge Area.

Project Management Plan

The project management plan is necessary in order to understand where the project should be and to compare it against the current status of the project to assess whether any requested changes are necessary.

Schedule Forecasts

Schedule forecasts are calculated through the Control Schedule process, and reflect the progress against the schedule baseline. There are multiple ways of expressing these forecasts, including using earned value management (EVM) calculations, such as schedule variance (SV) and schedule performance index (SPI). This information allows the project manager and team to determine whether the project contains variance from the approved baseline that is outside of the defined tolerance levels. If this is the case, a change request will be submitted to correct the variance.

Cost Forecasts

Cost forecasts are calculated through the Control Costs process, and reflect the progress against the cost baseline. As with schedule forecasts, there are multiple ways of expressing cost forecasts, including using earned value management (EVM) calculations. Common EVM calculations used to determine cost forecasts include cost variance (CV) and cost performance index (CPI). This information allows the project manager and team to determine whether the project contains variance from the approved budget that is outside of the defined tolerance levels. If this is the case, a change request will be submitted to correct the variance.

Validated Changes

Once a change request has been approved by the change control board, and implemented through the Direct and Manage Project Work process, the quality control team (through the Control Quality process) validates that the change has been implemented correctly. All of these validated changes are then handed over to the Monitor and Control Project Work process, which monitors to ensure that all changes have been validated.

Monitor and Control Project Work

Work Performance Information	• Work performance data that has been analyzed for decision-making purposes
Enterprise Environmental Factors	• Work authorization system, PMIS, standards, stakeholder risk tolerances
Organizational Process Assets	• Policies, procedures, organization communication requirements, lessons learned

Work Performance Information

Work performance information refers to the work performance data that has been analyzed for decision-making purposes. This includes calculated and analyzed variances of the project against the approved baselines.

Enterprise Environmental Factors

Enterprise environmental factors considered when monitoring and controlling the work of the project typically include: standards, work authorization system, stakeholder risk tolerances, and the PMIS.

Organizational Process Assets

Organizational process assets considered typically include: policies, procedures, and guidelines, as well as historical documents and lessons learned.

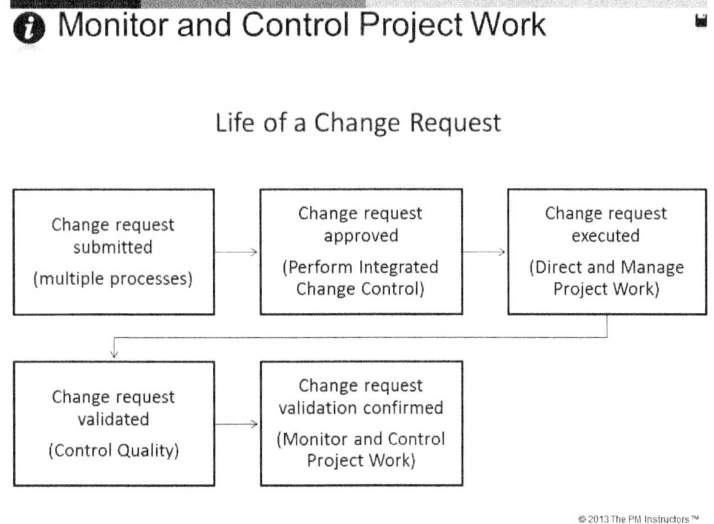

Concept

In attempting to understand and digest all of the inputs, tools and techniques, and outputs of the various processes, it helps to take a step back and begin making the connections amongst the processes. This can be done in the case of change requests, and what can be called the *life of a change request.*

The following are steps that occur throughout the life of a change request:

1. Change requests are submitted through multiple processes as outputs, particularly the processes that fall in the Executing and Monitoring and Controlling Process Groups.
2. These changes are fed into the Perform Integrated Change Control process as inputs, which is where the change control board meets and reviews them to decide which to accept or reject.
3. The decision is updated in the change log, and for those that are accepted, they are fed into the Direct and Manage Project Work process as inputs to be implemented.
4. Once changes are implemented, the Control Quality process is responsible for reviewing them to validate that they have been implemented correctly, and that the results are as expected.
5. Validated changes are then fed into the Monitor and Control Project Work process, where progress is evaluated and reporting is compiled.

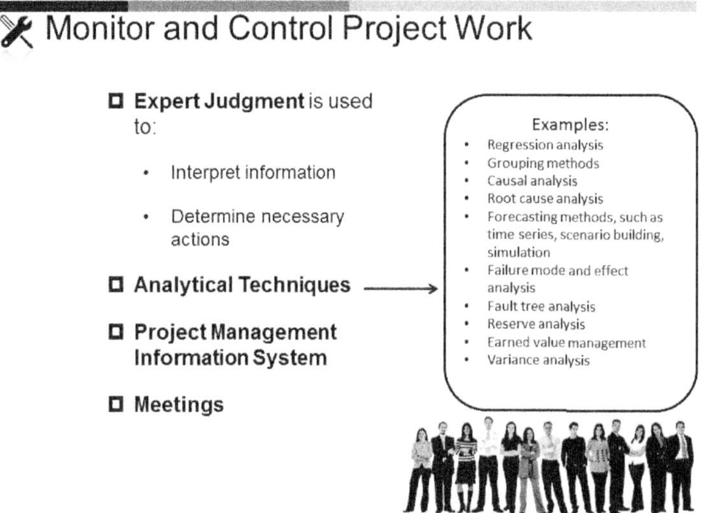

Monitor and Control Project Work Tools and Techniques

There are four tools and techniques, three of which have appeared in previous processes: *expert judgment, analytical techniques, project management information system, and meetings.*

Expert Judgment

When monitoring performance, expert judgment is used to interpret the information that comes into the process as an input, and make recommendations on how to resolve potential or existing variances. These variances refer to performance deviations from the baseline.

Analytical Techniques

Analytical techniques are used to forecast the potential outcomes of the project, based on current information available, such as through the work performance information input. This information is further analyzed through the use of various analytical techniques. The *PMBOK® Guide* notes the following as examples of analytical techniques used:

- Regression analysis
- Grouping methods
- Causal analysis
- Root cause analysis

- Forecasting methods, such as time series, scenario building, simulation
- Failure mode and effect analysis
- Fault tree analysis
- Reserve analysis
- Trend analysis
- Earned value management
- Variance analysis

The results of this analysis, in conjunction with other tools and techniques used within this process, will be summarized within performance reports.

Project Management Information System (PMIS)

When tracking project performance and compiling performance reports, the PMIS becomes central to collecting and compiling this information. This includes automated tools, resourcing tools, databases, and more.

Meetings

Meetings held as part of carrying out this process may include review meetings and user group meetings, and may be held in a variety of formats, such as face-to-face or virtual.

Monitor and Control Project Work Outputs

The Monitor and Control Project Work process contains a total of four outputs, which are as follow: *change requests, work performance reports, project management plan updates, and project documents updates.*

Change Requests

As existing and potential performance variances are identified, so are actions meant to bring the performance back in line with the project management plan. These actions are initiated through change requests, which will be reviewed by the change control board for approval before moving forward. A change request is a broader description representing one of the following:

- Recommended corrective action
- Recommended preventive action
- Defect repair

Work Performance Reports

The *PMBOK® Guide* defines work performance reports as "physical or electronic representation of work performance information compiled in project documents, intended to generated decisions, actions, or awareness". Although that sounds like a mouthful, it simply refers to all of those reports that project managers often distribute to stakeholders. Reports must be compiled in such a way that they may be archived as part of the project records.

Work performance reports adds another layer to how project information is assembled and used. The following is a summary of the various terminology used, along with a visual that shows the various stages that project information passes through:

- **Work performance data:** The raw data measured and gathered throughout the life of a project. Examples include actual start dates of activities, % complete of activities, total amount of funds spent, quality and technical performance measurements, total change requests submitted and approved, etc.
- **Work performance information:** The work performance data that has been analyzed and brought into context according to the relationships across the various areas measured throughout the project (such as cost, scope, schedule, quality, etc). Examples include status of deliverables, implementation status of change requests approved, and forecasts.
- **Work performance reports:** The physical or electronic representation of analyzed data that has been compiled in project documents, and generated for decision-making purposes or to raise awareness, raise issues, and incentivize action.

Project Management Plan Updates

As change requests are approved by the change control board, the project management team will need to update the documents impacted by the changes. This is documented within the list of outputs as project management plan updates and project documents updates. In terms of project management plan updates, any one of the plans and baselines impacted by this process may result in an update, if approved.

Project Documents Updates

Project documents updated as a result of carrying out this process include forecasts, performance reports, and issue log. This is a typical list, but the list can vary, depending on what is discovered through monitoring and controlling efforts.

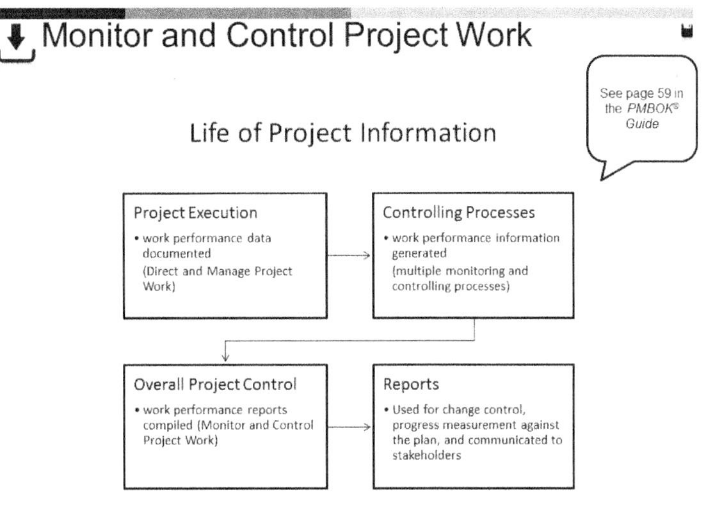

Monitor and Control Project Work
See page 59 in the PMBOK® Guide
Life of Project Information
Project Execution
• work performance data documented (Direct and Manage Project Work)
Controlling Processes
• work performance information generated (multiple monitoring and controlling processes)
Overall Project Control
• work performance reports compiled (Monitor and Control Project Work)
Reports
• Used for change control, progress measurement against the plan, and communicated to stakeholders
©2013 The PM Instructors™

Concept

Let's go back for a moment to work performance reports, and look closer into the various stages that information flows through. Work performance reports adds another layer to how project information is assembled and used. The following is a summary of the various terminology used, along with a visual that shows the various stages that project information passes through:

1. Work performance data is generated out of the Direct and Manage Project Work process, upon execution of the plan: Work performance data refers to the raw data measured and gathered throughout the life of a project. Examples include actual start dates of activities, % complete of activities, total amount of funds spent, quality and technical performance measurements, total change requests submitted and approved, etc.
2. Work performance information is generated through many of the controlling processes, which take the work performance data and compare it against the plan: Work performance information refers to the work performance data that has been analyzed and brought into context according to the relationships across the various areas measured throughout the project (such as cost, scope, schedule, quality, etc). Examples include status of deliverables, implementation status of change requests approved, and forecasts.
3. Work performance information is then fed into the Monitor and Control Project Work process as an input, to produce the work performance reports: these reports refer to the physical or electronic representation of analyzed data that has been compiled in project documents, and generated for decision-making purposes or to raise awareness, raise issues, and incentivize action.

To view another visual of how these three outputs tie together, take a look at page 59 of the *PMBOK® Guide*, where you will see the terms defined, and a flow chart of how they interrelate.

Perform Integrated Change Control
Purpose: To review all change requests; approve changes and manage changes to deliverables, organizational process assets, project documents, and the project management plan; communicate their disposition.

Perform Integrated Change Control Process Overview

The purpose of the Perform Integrated Change Control process is to review change requests, approve or deny them, control changes to the deliverables, organizational process assets, project documents, and the project management plan, and communicate their disposition. This process is important because projects rarely go exactly as planned, therefore, changes will emerge and they must be managed carefully. This process is performed from the beginning to the end of the project, and is concerned with ensuring the effectiveness of the project, managing the integrity of the baselines, and communicating changes.

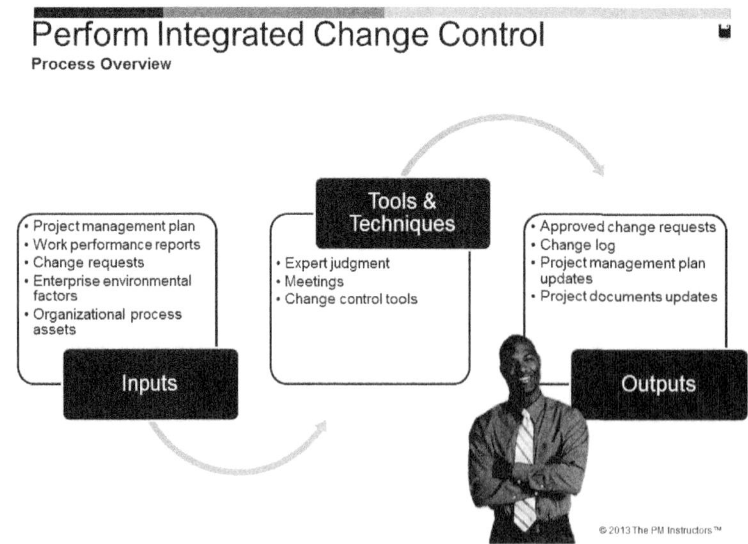
Perform Integrated Change Control
Process Overview
• Project management plan
• Work performance reports
• Change requests
• Enterprise environmental factors
• Organizational process assets
Inputs
Tools & Techniques
• Expert judgment
• Meetings
• Change control tools
• Approved change requests
• Change log
• Project management plan updates
• Project documents updates
Outputs
© 2013 The PM Instructors™

The following is an example of change management activities that typically occur through this process:

- Identify necessary or occurring changes
- Ensure that only approved changes take place
- Review and approve requested changes
- Manage approved changes
- Maintain the integrity of baselines by altering baselines only if a change has been approved
- Review and approve recommended corrective and preventive actions
- Control and update scope, cost, budget, schedule, and quality requirements based on approved changes
- Integrate approved changes across the entire project
- Document the impact of requested changes
- Validate defect repair
- Control project quality based on quality reports

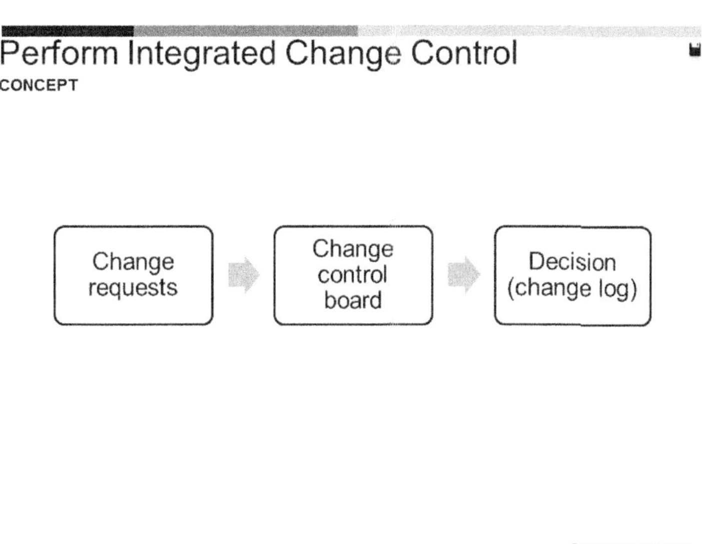

Concept

Although each organization and project is unique, for the exam, imagine that all change requests MUST filter through this process before being executed. This is the process where the change control board (CCB) that has been formed reviews change requests and determines whether or not to accept them. If the change request is accepted, it is sent to the Direct and Manage Project Work process for execution. If the change is rejected, then the requestor is notified, and a change log is updated.

Perform Integrated Change Control

CONCEPT

Configuration Management System:

- A subsystem of the overall project management system
- Contains formal documented procedures
- Contains a change control system
- Performs 3 specific activities:

Configuration Identification	Configuration Status Accounting	Configuration Verification and Audit
• Provides the basis for identifying, verifying, documenting, and labeling of the configuration of the products • Where changes are managed and accountability maintained	• Captures, stores, and accesses the configuration information necessary to manage products and product information effectively	• Makes sure that the deliverables meet the requirements as defined in the configuration documentation

Configuration Management System

Naturally, changes can impact other areas of the project. It's important that the project management team control these changes. This is done through the **configuration management system**, which is the administrative side of this process. A **change control system**, which is a sub-set of the configuration management system, is a formal documented system for handling changes. There are 3 main objectives of the configuration management system within this process:

1. It establishes an evolutionary method to identify and request changes to existing baselines that is consistent, and then used to assess the value and effectiveness of these changes
2. It provides opportunities to continuously validate and improve the project by looking at the impact of the changes
3. It provides a standard approach for the project management team to communicate changes to the stakeholders

The configuration management system has 3 specific activities within this process:

1. **Configuration Identification**, which provides the basis for identifying, verifying, documenting, and labeling of the configuration of the products, and where changes are managed and accountability is maintained.
2. **Configuration Status Accounting**, which captures, stores, and accesses the configuration information necessary to manage products and product information effectively.
3. **Configuration Verification and Audit**, which makes sure that the deliverables meet the requirements as defined in the configuration documentation.

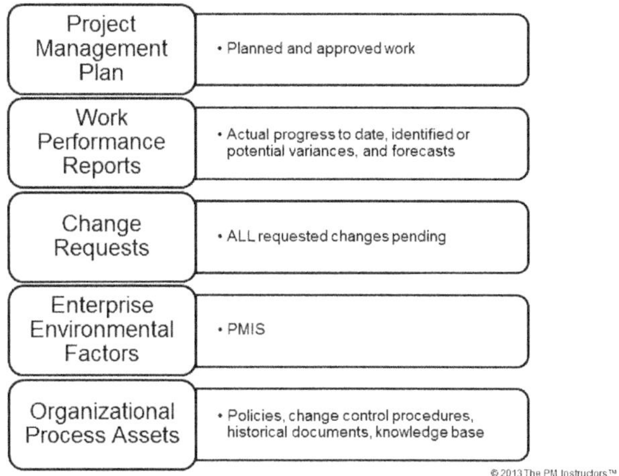

Perform Integrated Change Control
Project Management Plan
• Planned and approved work
Work Performance Reports
• Actual progress to date, identified or potential variances, and forecasts
Change Requests
• ALL requested changes pending
Enterprise Environmental Factors
• PMIS
Organizational Process Assets
• Policies, change control procedures, historical documents, knowledge base
© 2013 The PM Instructors™

Perform Integrated Change Control Inputs

The Perform Integrated Change Control process consists of the following five inputs: *project management plan, work performance repots, change requests, enterprise environmental factors, and organizational process assets.*

Project Management Plan

The project management plan provides a detailed overview of where the project is expected to be. This information will be needed to determine how and if a change request impacts the plan.

Work Performance Reports

Work performance reports provide a review of where the project currently is (status), what variances either exist or have the potential to occur, and any forecasts that have been calculated and analyzed to date. This will be evaluated against the plan, which will provide key information needed by the change control board to make a decision on the various requests being reviewed.

Change Requests

All change requests must feed into this process for review by the change control board, which will make a decision on whether to approve or deny the request. This is a critical input, since it is at the center of the process.

Enterprise Environmental Factors

The primary enterprise environmental factor considered is the PMIS.

Organizational Process Assets

The primary organizational process assets used are: change control procedures, policies and procedures for authorizing changes, project files, and the configuration management knowledge base.

Perform Integrated Change Control

- **Expert Judgment**
- **Meetings**
  - Held by the change control board (CCB)
  - Make and document decisions regarding change requests
  - Are held according to the needs of the project
  - Described within a change management plan
- **Change Control Tools**

Perform Integrated Change Control Tools and Techniques

The Perform Integrated Change Control process contains the following tools and techniques: *expert judgment, meetings, and change control tools.*

Expert Judgment

Expert judgment used by this process includes the project management team's feedback, expertise and feedback by the change control board, the PMO, and other stakeholders, as appropriate. The individuals that make up the change control board are determined early on in the project, and usually consist of specific stakeholders, and at times, the project manager. A set of roles and responsibilities of the board are determined, and this can vary by project and organization.

Meetings

Change control meetings are held by the change control board to review requested changes. Change requests are either approved or rejected during these meetings, and decisions are documented and communicated to the appropriate stakeholders.

Change Control Tools

Manual or automated tools may be needed to conduct configuration and change management activities. Tools are frequently used to track and record decisions made to change requests. Often times, project logs are maintained within these tools.

Perform Integrated Change Control

- **Approved Change Requests**
- **Change Log**
  - Approved changes
  - Rejected changes
- **Project Management Plan Updates**
- **Project Documents Updates**

Perform Integrated Change Control Outputs

The Perform Integrated Change Control process produces the following four outputs: *approved change requests, change log, project management plan updates, and project documents updates.*

Approved Change Requests

Those requested changes that have been approved will be implemented through the Direct and Manage Project Work process and are noted as "approved change requests". Status of all changes should be documented within a change log, which is included as a separate output of this process.

Change Log

The decision to approve a change or deny a change request is made by the change control board and recorded within a change log, which becomes a project artifact added to the list of project documents.

Project Management Plan Updates

Updates to various documents may occur as a result of carrying out this process, including the project management plan. This may include any of the subsidiary plan and / or baselines.

Project Documents Updates

Project documents updated as a result of carrying out this process include those documents that are subject to the formal change control process.

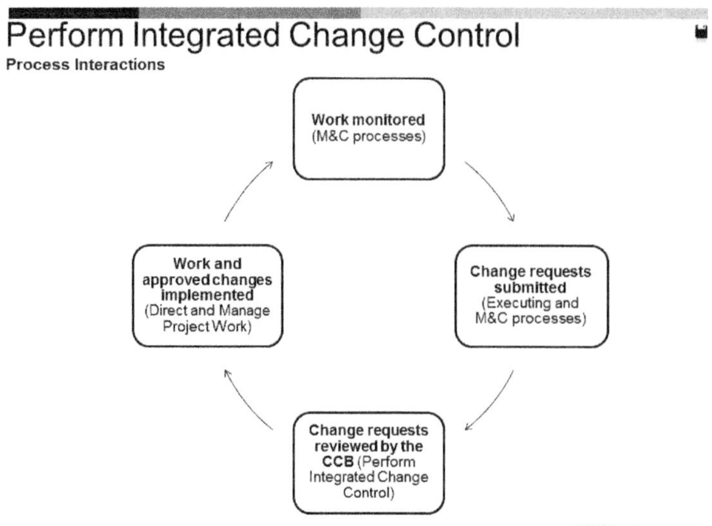
Perform Integrated Change Control
Process Interactions
Work monitored (M&C processes)
Change requests submitted (Executing and M&C processes)
Change requests reviewed by the CCB (Perform Integrated Change Control)
Work and approved changes implemented (Direct and Manage Project Work)
© 2013 The PM Instructors™

Process Interactions

Several processes interact with one another throughout the *PMBOK® Guide*. The image above reflects this level of interaction. As work is implemented, monitored, and controlled, necessary changes will emerge. Those changes will either be approved or rejected by the change control board. If approved, changes are then implemented, beginning the entire cycle all over again.

Understanding these interactions is important for the exam. Many of the exam questions are scenario based and are meant to measure whether you comprehend the purpose and interactions of the processes.

Close Project or Phase
Purpose: To finalize all activities across all of the Project Management Process Groups to formally complete the project or phase.

Close Project or Phase Process Overview

The purpose of the Close Project or Phase process is to finalize all activities across all of the Project Management Process Groups to formally complete the project or phase. In other words, this process ties all loose ends that remain by finalizing the project activities, with the intent of formally closing out the project or the phase. This process is something that must be done to close out a project, even if the project is cancelled. Note that *closing is always a formal activity*.

This process is concerned with establishing procedures that do the following:

- Coordinate the activities needed to verify and document the project deliverables
- Coordinate and formalize the acceptance of the deliverables by the customer or sponsor
- If a project is terminated without completion: investigate and document the reasons for early termination

If a project has procured goods or services, the agreements must be fully closed prior to formally closing out the overall project.

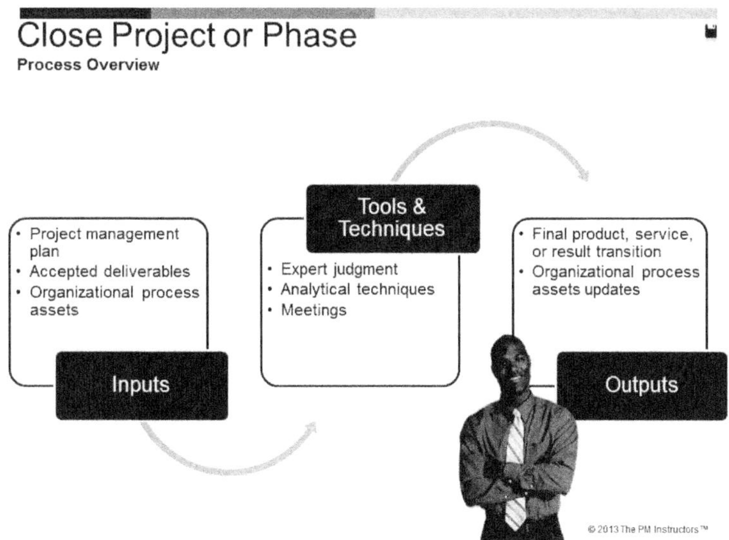
Close Project or Phase
Process Overview
Tools & Techniques
• Project management plan
• Accepted deliverables
• Organizational process assets
Inputs
• Expert judgment
• Analytical techniques
• Meetings
• Final product, service, or result transition
• Organizational process assets updates
Outputs
© 2013 The PM Instructors™

Administrative Closure Procedures

Administrative Closure Procedures: Define the activities, interactions, and related role and responsibilities of those involved in executing closure procedures.

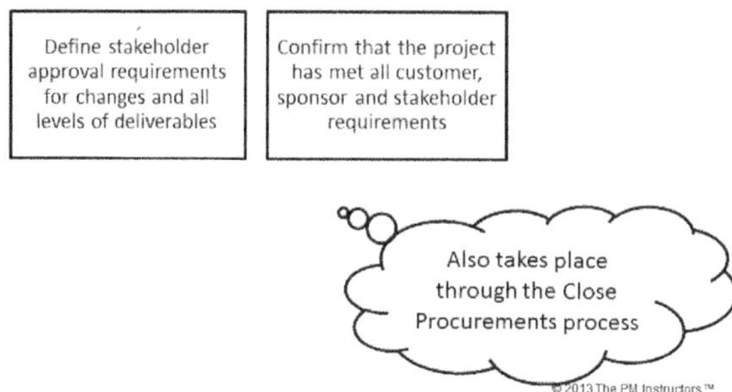

Administrative Closure

Administrative closure occurs through this process as well. Administrative closing procedures define the activities, interactions, and related roles and responsibilities of the project team members and other stakeholders that are involved in executing the project's administrative closure procedure. It also involves the collection of project records, analyzing the project success and failure rate, gathering of lessons learned, and archiving project information for future use. It transfers the project's products or services to production and establishes operations if applicable. Specifically, the administrative closuring procedures address the following actions and activities:

- Define stakeholder approval requirements for changes and all levels of deliverables
- Confirm that the project has met all customer, sponsor and stakeholder requirements; this includes:
    - Verifying that the deliverables have all been delivered and accepted;
    - Validating that completion and exit criteria have been met
    - Confirm that project completion or exit criteria have been fully satisfied

Administrative closure also takes place through another closing process: Close Procurements. In this process, the contract closure procedure includes the activities and interactions that are necessary in order to settle and close any contract agreement that was established for the project, and also to define the activities supporting the formal administrative closure of the project that relate to these contracts. The procedure involves the following: product verification to make sure all project work was completed correctly; administrative closure that involves the updating of contract records to reflect the final results; archiving of this information for future use.

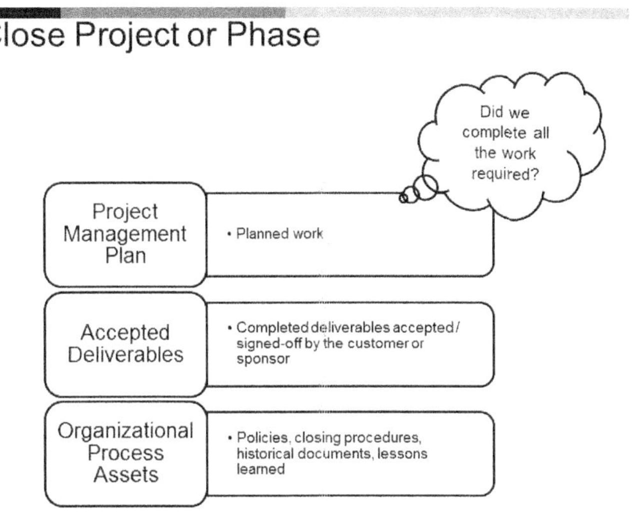
Close Project or Phase
Did we complete all the work required?
Project Management Plan
• Planned work
Accepted Deliverables
• Completed deliverables accepted/ signed-off by the customer or sponsor
Organizational Process Assets
• Policies, closing procedures, historical documents, lessons learned
© 2013 The PM Instructors™

Close Project or Phase Inputs

The Close Project or Phase process utilizes the following three inputs: *project management plan, accepted deliverables, and organizational process assets.*

Project Management Plan

As part of the closing activities, the project management team will need to ensure that all of the required work has been completed. The project management plan provides the necessary documentation to do this.

Accepted Deliverables

The work described and outlined within the project management plan will be compared to the accepted deliverables. Completed deliverables that have been verified are accepted through the Validate Scope process. An accepted deliverable means that the customer or sponsor has signed off on the completed deliverable.

Organizational Process Assets

Organizational process assets important to this process include: guidelines for closing out a project or phase, historical information, and lessons learned.

Close Project or Phase

- **Expert Judgment** is used to:
  - Perform administrative closure
  - Facilitate gathering of lessons learned
- **Analytical Techniques**
- **Meetings**

Close Project or Phase Tools and Techniques

The Close Project or Phase process has a total of three tools and techniques, which are as follow: *expert judgment, analytical techniques, and meetings.*

Expert Judgment

Expert judgment is used to perform administrative closure activities and to facilitate the gathering of lessons learned. Experts also ensure that appropriate standards are followed.

Analytical Techniques

The *PMBOK® Guide* notes two examples of analytical techniques typically used to carry out closing activities: *regression analysis* and *trend analysis.*

Meetings

In order to facilitate the gathering of lessons learned, and to review whether the project has produced all of the required outcomes, meetings are often held. In addition to lessons learned meetings, other meeting types often held include closeout, user group, and review meetings.

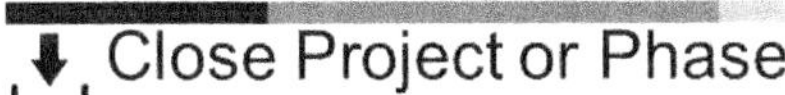

- **Final Product, Service, or Result Transition**
  - End of phase: transitioned to the next phase
  - End of project: transitioned to the customer or to operations
- **Organizational Process Assets Updates**
  - Archival of project files and documents
  - Archival of finalized closing documents
  - Archival of lessons learned

Close Project or Phase Outputs

The Close Project or Phase process produces the following two outputs: *final product, service, or result transition, and organizational process assets updates.*

Final Product, Service, or Result Transition

The final product, service, or result transition output involves the formal acceptance and handover of the final product service or result of the project to the customer or into operations. Something important to know is that this acceptance includes a formal statement indicating that the contract terms have been met. If simply closing out a phase, then this output refers to the formal transition from one phase to the next.

Organizational Process Assets Updates

Using the configuration management system, the project team will properly file the project documents by creating an index with the location of the project's documentation. Organizational process assets updated include:

- Formal acceptance documentation, which is the formal confirmation received from the customer or project sponsor stating that the project requirements and deliverables have been met
- The project files that include all the documentation and plans generated through the project activities
- Project closure documents, which includes all the documents from the closing of the project and transfer of the product, service, or result to the customer or to the operations group. If the project was closed prematurely then the reason for the early termination is documented here
- Historical information, which includes the lessons learned information, which is transferred to the lessons learned knowledge base so that it can be used by future projects

Module Summary

In this module we:

- Defined the purpose of the Project Integration Management Knowledge Area
- Identified the processes of the Project Integration Management Knowledge Area
- Recalled the key outputs of the Project Integration Management processes
- Differentiated between the inputs, tools and techniques, and outputs of the Project Integration Management processes
- Explained how Project Integration Management interacts with other Knowledge Areas of the *PMBOK® Guide*

Chapter Quiz

Exam Practice Questions

1. Sonya is a project manager for the Optical Performance Consulting Company. During her final visit with the CEO and business development team they agree to hire her company to assist them with the release of their new product. To get the project moving, Sonya asks them to provide her with a formal statement of work. A statement of work can BEST be described as?
   A. A document that formally authorizes a project
   B. The documented characteristics and boundaries of the project
   C. A plan defining how the project work will be done
   D. The initial description of the work to be done

2. The project charter has just been issued. What comes next?
   A. Development of the project management plan
   B. A kick-off meeting is held
   C. Identification of stakeholders
   D. Creation of the work breakdown structure

3. Jane has just shared with Joe that she received her new project assignment on the latest biotech research study that promises exciting breakthroughs. She is excited about this opportunity, since it will be the first project of its complexity that she will manage, and the fact that she was pre-selected for the assignment. What Process Group is Jane's project currently in?
   A. Initiating
   B. Planning
   C. Executing
   D. Monitoring & Controlling

4. Which of the following is not considered to be a component of the project management plan?
   A. Procurement management plan
   B. Scope baseline
   C. Project scope statement
   D. Milestone list

5. Which of the following is not an input of the Direct and Manage Project Work process?
   A. Approved change requests
   B. Organizational process assets
   C. Implemented change requests
   D. Project management plan

6. Martha has just been told that she will be assigned as the project manager for the new office expansion project that will begin during the next quarter. Martha's assignment was identified within the project charter. During which Process Group did her assignment occur?
   A. Planning Process Group
   B. Initiating Process Group
   C. Monitoring and Controlling Process Group
   D. Executing Process Group

7. Which of the following is a formal documented system for handling changes?
   A. Integrated change control board
   B. Configuration management system
   C. Project management information system (PMIS)
   D. Project management methodology

8. Tony is the CEO of a new startup company called Power Cloud Stock Trading Online. In his excitement to make the company public, he considers a project that could be implemented in the next 12 months, and which would potentially increase the revenue of the business by 496%. He reviews the project charter provided carefully. As a result of his excitement, he makes his first business goal of the following morning to approve the project charter. Who is typically responsible for approving the project charter?
   A. Project manager
   B. Project management team
   C. Project sponsor
   D. CEO

9. A project manager working on a mid-level pharmaceutical project is currently in the process of making project assignments. After working through a few negotiations with functional managers, he contacted the senior designer directly, who was promised to the project by contract. This is an example of:
   A. Acquisition
   B. Negotiation
   C. Pre-assignment
   D. Strategy

10. The project management information system is an example of a(n):
    A. company work authorization system
    B. corporate knowledge base
    C. organizational process asset
    D. enterprise environmental factor

11. A small project team is in the process of performing a feasibility study on the potential build out of an offshore data center. Several team members have expressed excitement about the project, since early indications from the study show that this may be a cost effective solution that can save the organization millions of dollars in annual expenses. After managing the project for three months, the project manager discovers that the executive team has just killed the project. What should the project manager do next?
    A. Express concerns regarding the project's termination
    B. Request a meeting with executive management
    C. Release the project team
    D. Perform closure activities

12. Which of the following refers to a unique and verifiable product, result or capability to perform a service that is required to be produced to complete a process, phase, or project?
    A. Change request
    B. Work performance data
    C. Project charter
    D. Deliverable

13. Bertol is in the process of monitoring and controlling the project work, and has just completed a weekly review of project status. As part of analyzing the progress reflected in the status, he identifies several areas where unacceptable variance from the plan has occurred. What should Bertol, who is the project manager of this project, do in response to the identified variance?
    A. Identify and execute corrective action
    B. Identify corrective action and submit a change request
    C. Identify preventive action and share them with the team
    D. He should do nothing in response

14. Bertol is in the process of monitoring and controlling the project work, and has just completed a weekly review of project status. As part of this review, Bertol compiles an assessment of the project's status and sends it out to the project team by email, as he does each week. What has Bertol just generated?
    A. Work performance information
    B. Work performance data
    C. Work performance report
    D. Change request

15. Gabriela has just finished facilitating a change control board meeting for the Network Optimization project. Several decisions were made regarding new change requests that were submitted over the past week. Through which process will the changes that were approved during this meeting be implemented?
    A. Direct and Manage Project Work
    B. Perform Integrated Change Control
    C. Monitor and Control Project Work
    D. Manage Project Team

16. Which of the following is not produced as a result of carrying out the Direct and Manage Project Work process?
    A. Work performance reports
    B. Deliverables
    C. Change requests
    D. Work performance data

17. Regression analysis, root cause analysis, and fault tree analysis are all examples of:
    A. Change control tools
    B. Facilitation techniques
    C. Analytical techniques
    D. Expert judgment

18. Work performance information can BEST be described as:
    A. The raw observations and measurements identified during activities performed to carry out the project work
    B. The physical or electronic representation of work performance information compiled in project documents, intended to generate decisions or raise issues, actions, or awareness
    C. Any unique or verifiable product, result or capability to perform a service that is required to be produced to complete a process, phase, or project
    D. The performance data collected from various controlling processes, analyzed in context and integrated based on relationships across areas

19. Brainstorming, problem solving, and conflict resolution are examples of:
    A. Change control tools
    B. Facilitation techniques
    C. Analytical techniques
    D. Expert judgment

20. Gabriela has just finished facilitating a change control board meeting for the Network Optimization project. Several decisions were made regarding new change requests that were submitted over the past week. Where will Gabriela document the decisions made by the change control board?
    A. Decision log
    B. Change log
    C. Project documents updates
    D. Approved change requests

Chapter Quiz

Exam Practice Answers

1. Answer: D

   Explanation: The statement of work is the initial description of the work to be done. Other options describe the project charter, the project scope statement, and the project management plan.

2. Answer: C

   Explanation: Remember that the project charter is the very first thing that the project creates, and that's because it is needed in order to formally authorize the project. Now that the project has been authorized, it is time to identify who the stakeholders are. Although this is an iterative process, efforts to identify stakeholders should begin as early as possible within a project's lifecycle.

3. Answer: A

   Explanation: The core portion of this question is that Jane has just received a project assignment, and that this assignment involves her managing the project. This would put her in the role of project manager. A project manager is usually assigned after the project charter has been created and preferably before the project management plan is developed. This would put her either in the Initiating Process Group or Planning Process Group. We receive further clarification in that Jane was *pre-selected* for the project, which can occur within the project charter. Therefore, we can safely assume that she is involved as early on as the Initiating Process Group.

4. Answer: D

   Explanation: The project management plan contains several subsidiary plans and baselines. Any document that has the word "plan" or "baseline" in it becomes a sub-component of the project management plan. Although "project scope statement" is neither, it is a component of the scope baseline, which itself contains the project scope statement, work breakdown structure, and WBS dictionary. The milestone list, on the other hand, belongs to the "project documents" grouping of artifacts, and not the project management plan, making it the correct answer.

5. Answer: C

   Explanation: Aside from executing the project management plan, the Direct and Manage Project Work process implements changes and actions that have been approved. In order to implement them, the approved items (which come through the Perform Integrated Change Control process) must be submitted as an input, leaving the implementation of the items as the result, or output, of the process, and not an input.

6. Answer: B

   Explanation: The Initiating Process Group only contains two processes: Develop Project Charter and Identify Stakeholders. Initiating is therefore the accurate choice, since the project charter is an output of this Process Group.

7. Answer: B

   Explanation: If using the process of elimination as a strategy, "project management methodology" can comfortably be eliminated first, since this is a methodology and not a documented system for handling changes. The PMIS refers to a system and / or tools used to manage projects, including the use of applications, such as SharePoint. This can also be eliminated. Integrated change control board is not a system, so this can be eliminated as well, leaving configuration management system as the correct answer. The configuration management system is a method that identifies and manages changes to existing baselines and then assesses the value and effectiveness of these changes, among several other things.

8. Answer: C

   Explanation: Many times, the project manager is not assigned before the creation of the project charter, and is sometimes identified *within* the charter, if already selected. It is typical for the project manager (if pre-selected) to assist in writing the project charter, but it is the sponsor who formally signs-off on it. In this scenario, the CEO is in the role of sponsor.

9. Answer: C

   Explanation: Pre-assignments refer to individuals formally assigned as a resource to a project during the early project stages, such as within the project charter, or within the project contract. In this particular case, the senior designer was already committed to the project, even before it began.

10. Answer: D

    Explanation: There are internal and external factors that make up the enterprise environmental factors, including tools and systems, like the PMIS. The question is referring to the system itself, not the data or procedures within it. The data and procedures are instead a part of the organizational process assets. The *PMBOK® Guide* defines enterprise environmental factors as internal and external environmental factors that influence the project's success.

11. Answer: D

    Explanation: The Close Project or Phase process should always be performed on a project, even if the project is terminated early.

12. Answer: D

    Explanation: This describes a deliverable. A deliverable, which is produced as a result of carrying out the Direct and Manage Project Work process, is defined as a unique and verifiable product, result or capability to perform a service that is required to be produced to complete a process, phase, or project.

13. Answer: B

    Explanation: As part of monitoring and controlling activities, the project management team should identify whether any existing or potential variance from the plan exists. If unacceptable variance is discovered, then corrective or preventive actions should be identified, and a change request submitted. Change request is an output of the Monitor and Control Project Work process, which is the process that Bertol is carrying out within the question's scenario.

14. Answer: C

    Explanation: A work performance report is a physical or electronic representation of work performance information compiled in project documents, which is intended to generate decisions, actions, or awareness. An example of work performance report includes status reports, which is what Bertol has just compiled.

15. Answer: A

    Explanation: The Direct and Manage Project Work process is responsible for leading and performing the work defined in the project management plan and for implementing approved changes to achieve the project's objectives. As a result, approved change requests are fed into this process as an input for implementation.

16. Answer: A

    Explanation: The outputs of the Direct and Manage Project Work process are: deliverables, work performance data, change requests, project management plan updates, and project documents updates. Work performance reports are an output of the Monitor and Control Project work process.

17. Answer: C

    Explanation: Analytical techniques forecast potential outcomes based on possible variations of project or environmental variables and their relationships with other variables. Examples of analytical techniques, as noted within the *PMBOK® Guide*, include: regression analysis, grouping methods, causal analysis, root cause analysis, forecasting methods, failure mode and effect analysis, fault tree analysis, reserve analysis, trend analysis, earned vale management, and variance analysis.

18. Answer: D

    Explanation: The *PMBOK® Guide* defines work performance information as performance data collected from various controlling processes, analyzed in context and integrated based on relationships across areas.

19. Answer: B

    Explanation: Facilitation techniques are used to guide the development of the project management plan, within the Develop Project Management Plan process. Examples of facilitation techniques include brainstorming, conflict resolution, problem solving, and meeting management.

20. Answer: B

    Explanation: The change log is where change requests of the project are documented, including status of changes, the decisions made to accept or reject the change.

Chapter 5: Project Scope Management

Learning Objectives:

- ☐ Define the purpose of the Project Scope Management Knowledge Area
- ☐ Identify the processes of the Project Scope Management Knowledge Area
- ☐ Recall the key outputs of the scope management processes
- ☐ Differentiate between the inputs, tools and techniques, and outputs of the scope management processes
- ☐ Describe the elements of the work breakdown structure

Exam Domain Tasks:

- Assess detailed project requirements, constraints, and assumptions with stakeholders based on the project charter, lessons learned from previous projects, and the use of requirement-gathering techniques (e.g., planning sessions, brainstorming, focus groups), in order to establish the project deliverables.
- Create the work breakdown structure with the team by deconstructing the scope, in order to manage the scope of the project.

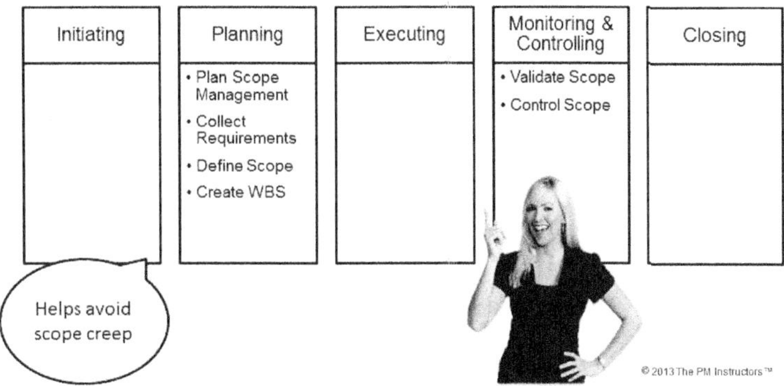

Project Scope Management
Purpose: "To ensure that the project includes all the work required, and only the work required, to complete the project successfully."
6 Project Management Processes:
Initiating
Planning
Executing
Monitoring & Controlling
Closing
• Plan Scope Management
• Collect Requirements
• Define Scope
• Create WBS
• Validate Scope
• Control Scope
Helps avoid scope creep
© 2013 The PM Instructors™

Project Scope Management Overview

Scope is critical to a project because it ensures that our focus remains on what the project set out to accomplish in the first place. The Project Scope Management Knowledge Area is concerned with ensuring that all the work required is completed within the project. This includes managing the project scope and avoiding scope creep.

Scope creep refers to new features and functionality added to the project scope as the project is under way without first addressing the effects on time, costs, and resources, or even in some cases, without customer approval -- basically, going out of the project's scope boundaries. *The goal is to do no more and no less than the approved scope.*

The scope management plan, produced out of the first scope management process, guides the remaining five scope-related project management processes. It is created early on within the life of a project, and is a component of the project management plan.

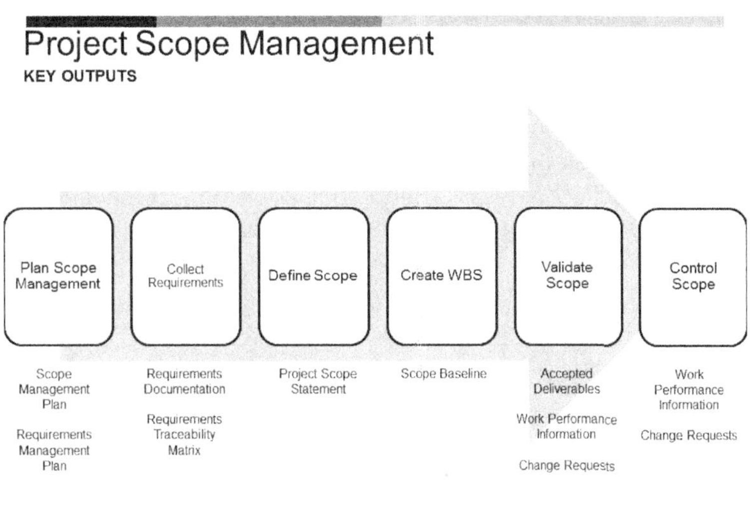

Project Scope Management
KEY OUTPUTS
Plan Scope Management
Collect Requirements
Define Scope
Create WBS
Validate Scope
Control Scope
Scope Management Plan
Requirements Management Plan
Requirements Documentation
Requirements Traceability Matrix
Project Scope Statement
Scope Baseline
Accepted Deliverables
Work Performance Information
Change Requests
Work Performance Information
Change Requests
© 2013 The PM Instructors™

The Project Scope Management Knowledge Area ensures that the project includes all the work, and only the work, required to complete the project successfully. It manages the project scope to avoid scope creep by defining and controlling what is and isn't included in the project. There are 6 processes:

- **Plan Scope Management (Planning Process Group).** Purpose: To create a scope management plan that documents how the project scope will be defined, validated, and controlled.
- **Collect Requirements (Planning Process Group).** Purpose: To determine, document, and manage stakeholder needs and requirements, to meet the project objectives.
- **Define Scope (Planning Process Group).** Purpose: To develop a detailed description of the project and product.
- **Create WBS (Planning Process Group).** Purpose: To subdivide the project deliverables and work into smaller, more manageable components.
- **Validate Scope (Monitoring and Controlling Process Group).** Purpose: To formalize acceptance of the completed project deliverables.
- **Control Scope (Monitoring and Controlling Process Group).** Purpose: To monitor the status of the project and product scope and manage changes to the scope baseline.

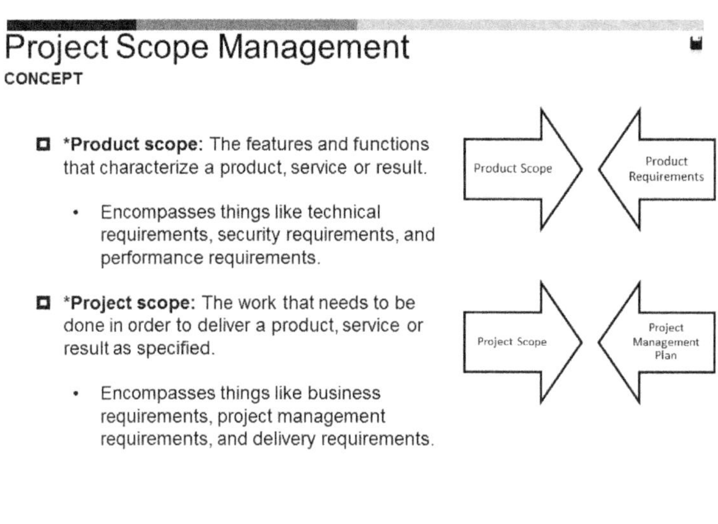

Product versus Project Scope

At the completion of a project phase, the scope of the deliverables are verified and confirmed that they meet scope requirements. Project scope is measured against the project management plan, while the product scope, on the other hand, is measured against the defined product requirements. To further clarify:

- **Product scope** refers to the features and functions that characterize a product, service or result. Generally, this encompasses things like technical requirements, security requirements, and performance requirements.
- **Project scope** refers to the work that needs to be done in order to deliver a product, service or result as specified. This generally encompasses things like business requirements, project management requirements, and delivery requirements.

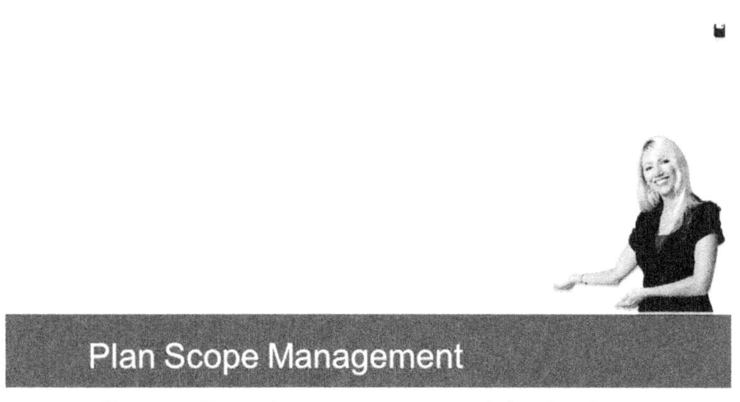
Plan Scope Management
Purpose: To create a scope management plan that documents how the project scope will be defined, validated, and controlled.

Plan Scope Management Process Overview

The purpose of the Plan Scope Management process is to create a scope management plan that documents how the project scope will be defined, validated, and controlled. This process will guide the remaining scope management processes, and reduces the likelihood that scope creep will occur. In addition to the scope management plan, this process also generates a requirements management plan, which documents how requirements will be identified, tracked, and managed.

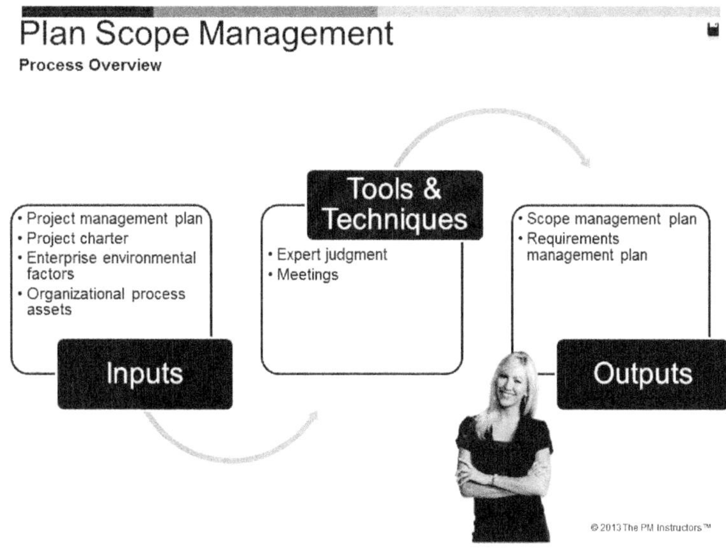
Plan Scope Management
Process Overview
• Project management plan
• Project charter
• Enterprise environmental factors
• Organizational process assets
Inputs
Tools & Techniques
• Expert judgment
• Meetings
• Scope management plan
• Requirements management plan
Outputs
© 2013 The PM Instructors™

Plan Scope Management

Project Management Plan	• Project approach, and existing subsidiary plans
Project Charter	• Contains high-level project scope and requirements, and context
Enterprise Environmental Factors	• Organizational culture, infrastructure, personnel administration, and marketplace conditions
Organizational Process Assets	• Policies, procedures, historical information, templates, and lessons learned

Plan Scope Management Inputs

The Plan Scope Management process has a total of four inputs, which are as follow: *project management plan, project charter, enterprise environmental factors, and organizational process assets.*

Project Management Plan

In any instance that a subsidiary plan is created, the project management plan is included as an input in order to influence the approach used to create additional subsidiary plans. In this instance, the project management plan is used to influence the approach taken to plan and manage scope.

Project Charter

Because the subsidiary plans are created early on within the life of the project, the project charter becomes a necessary input. It provides the high level information (in this case the high level scope and requirements) known at the beginning of the project's initiation. The project charter also provides context needed to define how scope will be managed moving forward.

Enterprise Environmental Factors

Key enterprise environmental factors used within this process include the organization's culture, infrastructure, personnel administration, and marketplace conditions.

Organizational Process Assets

Organizational process assets typically used when developing the scope and requirements management plans include policies and procedures, historical information, templates, and lessons learned.

Plan Scope Management

- **Expert Judgment:** Individuals with specialized knowledge, skills, experience, and training.
- **Meetings:** Typically includes the following individuals:
  - Project manager
  - Sponsor
  - Project management team members
  - Other key stakeholders

Plan Scope Management Tools and Techniques

There are two tools and techniques used within this process, both of which have appeared in past processes: expert judgment and meetings. The tools and techniques of the process are as follow: *expert judgment and meetings.*

Expert Judgment

Expert judgment is used when developing any subsidiary plan, such as the scope and requirements management plans. Examples of expert judgment used include those with specialized education, experience, knowledge, skills and training in developing project plans.

Meetings

Meetings are often held to bring together the required individuals that can define the necessary elements of a plan. Typical attendees include the project manager, sponsor, project management team members, and other key stakeholders that can provide input as to how scope will be defined and managed.

Plan Scope Management

Scope Management Plan	Requirements Management Plan
• Process for preparing a project scope statement • Process for creating a WBS, and describing how it will be maintained and approved • Process that defines how deliverables will be accepted • Process for how requests to change scope will be processed, and how this aligns to the change management processes of the project	• How requirements will be planned, tracked, and reported • Configuration management activities • How requirements will be prioritized • Metrics used to measure product requirements • Traceability structure, and how requirement attributes will be captured and tracked within the requirements traceability matrix

Plan Scope Management Outputs

There are two outputs of this process, both of which become components of the project management plan: *scope management plan and requirements management plan*.

Scope Management Plan

The scope management plan is oftentimes created early on within the planning stages of a project. It outlines how scope will be defined, documented, validated, managed and controlled. Basically, how the other five scope management processes will be carried out. As with all plans, how detailed it is depends on the unique needs of every project.

According to the *PMBOK® Guide*, the scope management plan contains the following elements:

- Process for preparing a project scope statement
- Process for creating a WBS, and describing how it will be maintained and approved
- Process that defines how deliverables will be accepted
- Process for how requests to change scope will be processed, and how this aligns to the change management processes of the project

Requirements Management Plan

The requirements management plan is a how-to plan and guide for analyzing, documenting, and managing requirements.

According to the *PMBOK® Guide*, the requirements management plan defines the following:

- How requirements will be planned, tracked, and reported
- Configuration management activities
- How requirements will be prioritized
- Metrics used to measure product requirements
- Traceability structure, and how requirement attributes will be captured and tracked within the requirements traceability matrix

Collect Requirements
Purpose: To determine, document, and manage stakeholder needs and requirements to meet the project objectives.

Collect Requirements Process Overview

The purpose of the Collect Requirements process is to determine, document, and manage stakeholder needs and requirements to meet the project objectives. In short, that means collecting the requirements of the project. A requirement[5] refers to "a condition or capability that is required to be present in a product, service, or result to satisfy a contract or other formally imposed specification."

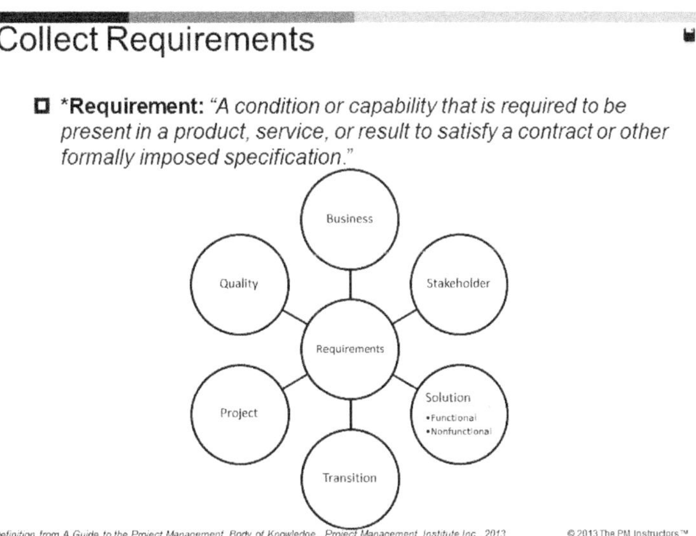
Collect Requirements
*Requirement: "A condition or capability that is required to be present in a product, service, or result to satisfy a contract or other formally imposed specification."
Business
Quality
Stakeholder
Requirements
Project
Solution
•Functional
•Nonfunctional
Transition
* Definition from A Guide to the Project Management Body of Knowledge, Project Management Institute Inc., 2013
© 2013 The PM Instructors™

There are many types, categories, and classifications of requirements, and the *PMBOK® Guide* points out the following six classifications:

- **Business requirements:** *Higher level needs of the organization*
- **Stakeholder requirements:** *Stakeholder needs*
- **Solution requirements:** *Describe features, functions, and characteristics of the product, service, or result that meet business and stakeholder requirements*
    - **Functional requirements:** *Behaviors of the product*

[5] * Definition from A Guide to the Project Management Body of Knowledge, Project Management Institute Inc., 2013

- **Nonfunctional:** *Describe the environmental conditions or qualities required for the product to be effective*

- **Transition requirements:** *Temporary capabilities*
- **Project requirements:** *Actions, processes, or other conditions that need to be met by the project*
- **Quality requirements:** *Condition or criteria needed to validate that a deliverable has been successfully completed*

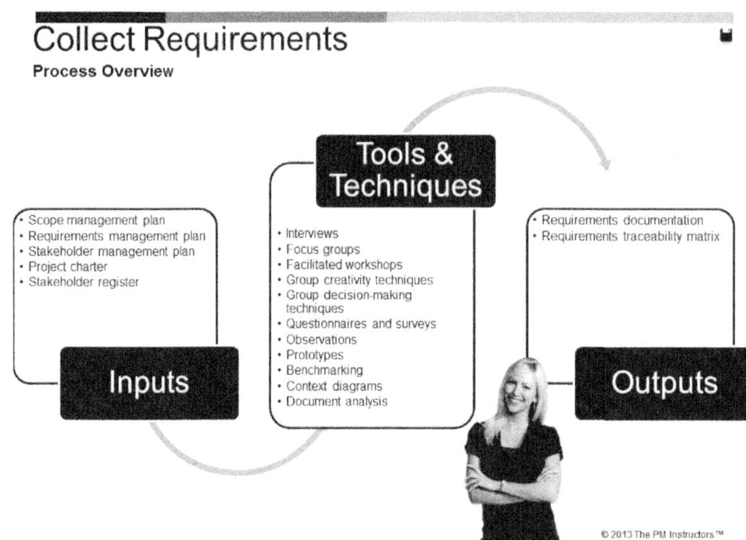

Like many project management processes, Collect Requirements is one that will need to be performed multiple times throughout the project's life. This may include refining existing requirements gathered, or further drilling down on the requirements, and gathering additional requirements as more information is known.

Key outputs (and the only two of the process) include the requirements documentation and requirements traceability matrix.

Collect Requirements

Input	Description
Scope Management Plan	• Documents the type of requirements to be collected, and how the process is to be carried out
Requirements Management Plan	• Documents how requirements will be defined and documented
Stakeholder Management Plan	• Documents the level at which stakeholders want to be engaged
Project Charter	• Contains high-level project and product requirements
Stakeholder Register	• Identifies stakeholders that should be contacted for information that would assist in gathering requirements

Collect Requirements Inputs

The Collect Requirements process utilizes the following five inputs: *scope management plan, requirements management plan, stakeholder management plan, project charter, and stakeholder register.*

Scope Management Plan

The scope management plan documents the type of requirements that will be collected for the project. This, along with the requirements management plan, captures *how* this process is to be carried out.

Requirements Management Plan

The requirements management plan is central to this process, as it defines how requirements will be defined and documented. This includes any processes that exist that define how *this* process is to be carried out.

Stakeholder Management Plan

The stakeholder management plan, which is created early on within the Planning processes of the project, provides information that is necessary to understand the communication requirements related to stakeholders. This includes how much stakeholders would like to be engaged.

Project Charter

Collecting requirements occurs very early on in the planning stages of a project. During the initial wave of planning, it is important to gather and document these requirements, and the project charter is one of few documents available at this point. Remember that the project charter contains high-level requirements documented, as well as a high-level product description. This will become an important source of information.

Stakeholder Register

The stakeholder register is the other document (aside from subsidiary plans) generated during the early stages of project planning. The stakeholder register, which will be covered in greater detail within the Project Stakeholder Management section, contains a list of identified and documented stakeholders, as well as information about them. Knowing who the stakeholders are, and whose needs you must satisfy is important to identifying and documenting requirements.

Collect Requirements

- **Interviews:** May occur one-on-one, or in groups, with the purpose of obtaining information from them.
- **Focus Groups:** Moderated by an experienced facilitator and includes the participation of prequalified stakeholders and subject matter experts.
- **Facilitated Workshops:** Also known as requirements workshops. Includes the participation of cross-functional stakeholders who actively document the requirements as a group.
  - Joint application design/development (JAD)
  - Quality function deployment (QFD)

Collect Requirements Tools and Techniques

The Collect Requirements process has a total of eleven tools and techniques, which are as follow: *interviews, focus groups, facilitated workshops, group creativity techniques, group decision-making techniques, questionnaires and surveys, observations, prototypes, benchmarking, context diagrams, and document analysis.*

Interviews

Interviewing stakeholders may occur one-on-one, or in groups, and is just as it implies: talking directly with the stakeholders to obtain information from them. This is a common method of gathering requirements.

Focus Groups

Focus groups are moderated by an experienced facilitator and include the participation of prequalified stakeholders and subject matter experts. The group participates in an interactive discussion about the requirements that goes beyond standard conversation. Compared to facilitated workshops, focus groups are more informal and are often used as a primary method of gathering feedback.

Facilitated Workshops

Facilitated workshops are also commonly referred to as requirements workshops. This includes the participation of cross-functional stakeholders who actively document the requirements as a group. This is a primary technique used that provides a good communication platform amongst stakeholders.

Some examples of facilitated workshops, which are often linked to quality management, are:

- Joint application design/development (JAD): Common in the software industry, JAD sessions focus on improving the software development process.
- Quality function deployment (QFD): Focuses on identifying critical characteristics of new product development. The process begins by gathering customer needs, prioritizing them, and developing user stories. Centralizing efforts around collecting customer needs in this manner is referred to as voice of the customer (VOC).

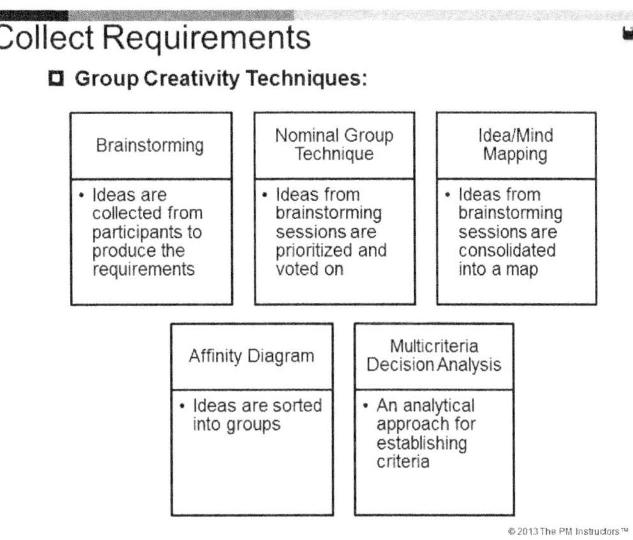

Group Creativity Techniques

Group creativity techniques consists of five techniques:

- **Brainstorming**;
- **Nominal group technique**, where ideas from brainstorming sessions are prioritized and voted on;
- **Idea / mind mapping**, where the ideas from brainstorming sessions are consolidated into a map; and
- **Affinity diagrams**, where ideas are sorted into groups
- **Multicriteria decision analysis**, which provides an analytical approach for establishing criteria.

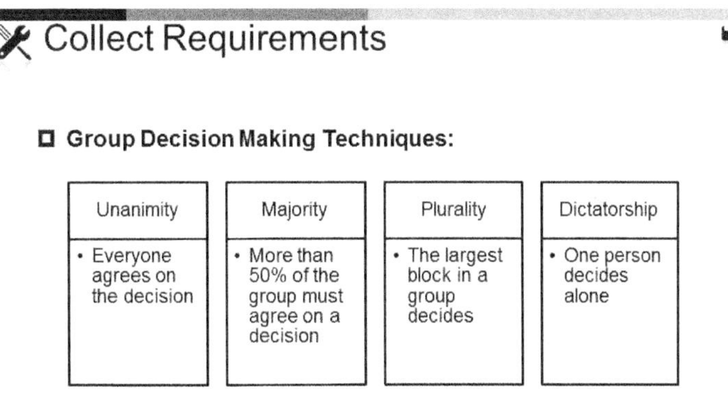

Group Decision-Making Techniques

Group decision-making techniques consist of four sub-techniques:

- **Unanimity**, where everyone agrees on the decision;
- **Majority**, where more than 50% of the group must agree on a decision;

- **Plurality**, where the largest block in a group decides; and
- **Dictatorship**, where one person decides alone.

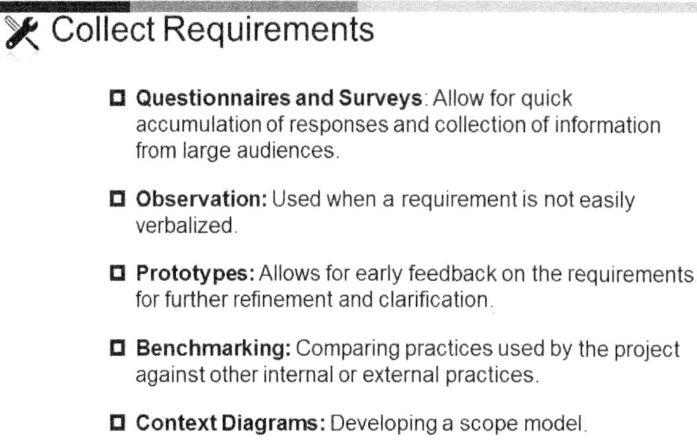

Questionnaires and Surveys

Questionnaires and surveys provide a quick means for the project manager to gather new requirements or obtain feedback about requirements collected. These are best used when the group of stakeholders providing information is large and spread out physically.

Observations

In some instances, stakeholders are not able to easily verbalize requirements. This is where observations become key, and where the project manager and others can observe an expert performing some type of activity, which demonstrates a needed requirement. Think of a time where a stakeholder says "let me show you what I mean…". Observations are often compared to job shadowing.

Prototypes

Prototypes provide a means of refining requirements early on within a project. It produces a tangible version (such as a model or user interface) of a deliverable that stakeholders can play with and experiment to determine whether it meets their needs.

There are many forms of prototypes, including small detailed models of what the end product will look like; an interface that lacks the back end of an application but allows stakeholders to view how users will interact with a product; and also storyboards.

Benchmarking

Benchmarking allows the project team to compare practices that are being used within a project against industry best practices, or even practices used by the competition. Comparisons can be internal, such as comparing practices used by other teams across a company, as well as external.

Context Diagrams

Context diagrams focus on a business system, generating a model from it that allows stakeholders to agree on scope. A business system can refer to processes, equipment, computer systems, etc. The context diagrams visually show the relationship of how entities outside of the system interact with it.

Document Analysis

Document analysis refers to analyzing documentation that already exists, and extracting requirements from them. Think of all existing documents that are relevant to the project, including standards, software documentation, business plans, agreements, business processes, and so on.

Collect Requirements

- **Requirements Documentation:** Where the requirements are documented and prioritized. May contain information such as:
  - Brief description
  - Prioritized list
  - Business need of a requirement
  - Type of requirement (such as functional, nonfunctional, quality, etc)
  - Acceptance criteria
  - How the requirement impacts the organization
  - Assumptions and constraints of the requirements

Collect Requirements Outputs

The Collect Requirements process produces the following two outputs: *requirements documentation and requirements traceability matrix.*

Requirements Documentation

The first output of the process is requirements documentation. This key document contains a great deal of information about the requirements gathered to-date, typically organized by type of requirements. The following is an example of information that may be included for each requirement within this artifact:

- A brief description
- Prioritized list
- Business needs
- Type of requirement (such as functional, nonfunctional, quality, etc)
- Acceptance criteria
- How the requirement impacts the organization
- Assumptions
- Constraints

Collect Requirements

- **Requirements Traceability Matrix:** A table that traces the life of the requirements, from their origin and how they link to the business needs, to their acceptance and delivery.

Example of what requirements may be traced to:

- Business needs, opportunities, goals, and objectives
- Project objectives
- Project scope
- Product design and development
- Test scenarios
- High-level requirements

Requirements Traceability Matrix

The requirements traceability matrix is a table that traces the life of the requirements – from their origin and how they link to the business needs, to their acceptance and delivery. For this reason, the matrix reflects current status of a requirement.

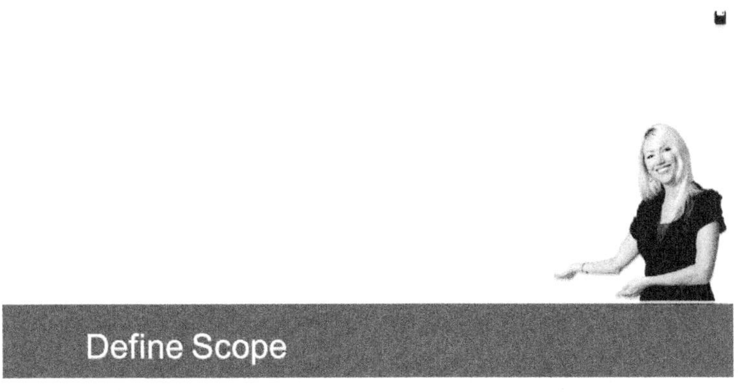
Define Scope
Purpose: To develop a detailed description of the project and product.

Define Scope Process Overview

The purpose of the Define Scope process is to develop a detailed description of the project and product, which is documented within a project scope statement document. As you can imagine, the main output of this process would therefore be the project scope statement.

Knowing the contents of the project scope statement is important for the exam.

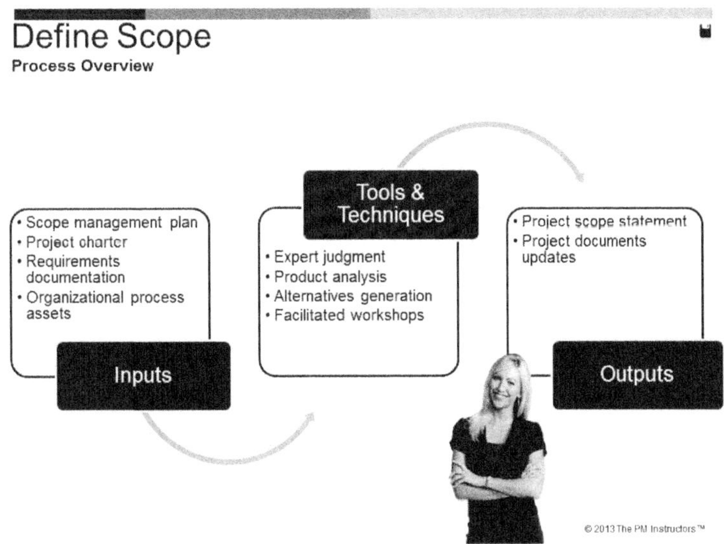
Define Scope
Process Overview
• Scope management plan
• Project charter
• Requirements documentation
• Organizational process assets
Inputs
Tools & Techniques
• Expert judgment
• Product analysis
• Alternatives generation
• Facilitated workshops
• Project scope statement
• Project documents updates
Outputs
© 2013 The PM Instructors™

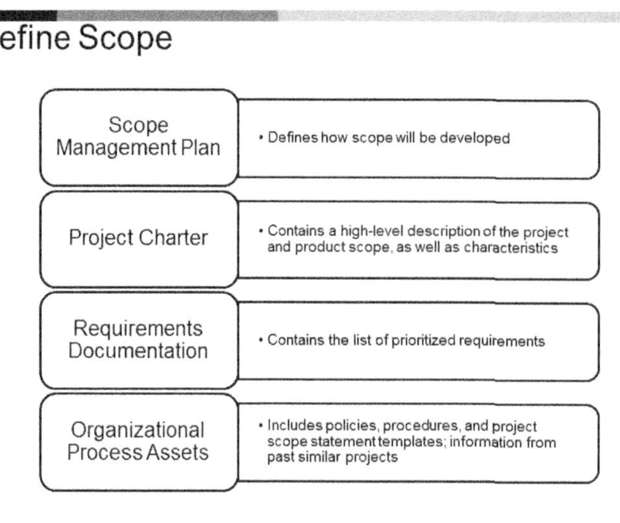

Define Scope
Scope Management Plan
• Defines how scope will be developed
Project Charter
• Contains a high-level description of the project and product scope, as well as characteristics
Requirements Documentation
• Contains the list of prioritized requirements
Organizational Process Assets
• Includes policies, procedures, and project scope statement templates; information from past similar projects
© 2013 The PM Instructors™

Define Scope Inputs

The Define Scope process has a total of four inputs – all of which have been reviewed through previous processes: *scope management plan, project charter, requirements documentation and organizational process assets.*

Scope Management Plan

The scope management plan provides the documented approach for how the Define Scope process is to be carried out. In other words, it defines how scope will be developed.

Project Charter

The project charter contains several high-level items within it, including a high-level description of the project and product scope, as well as known characteristics, deliverables, assumptions, and constraints. This information is further expanded within this process.

Requirements Documentation

The requirements documentation was created out of the previous process, Collect Requirements. After its creation, it becomes an input to all the other scope related processes the follow, including this one (Define Scope). Note that not all requirements gathered through the previous process will be selected for the project; it is through this process that a decision is made on which requirements to move forward with.

Organizational Process Assets

Organizational process assets are used to define scope. They contain the policies, procedures, and templates used to create a project scope statement. We'll also be interested in historical information from similar projects. The idea is not to re-invent the wheel, but instead, to improve it and become more efficient.

Define Scope

- **Expert Judgment:** Includes those individuals who have the expertise needed to analyze the inputs to develop the project scope statement.
- **Product Analysis:** To translate high-level product descriptions into deliverables.
- **Alternatives Generation:** Explores the various approaches and ways of executing the project.
- **Facilitated Workshops:** Includes the participation of cross-functional stakeholders who actively document the project and product scope.

Define Scope Tools and Techniques

The Define Scope process utilizes the following four tools and techniques: *expert judgment, product analysis, alternatives generation, and facilitated workshops.*

Expert Judgment

Expert judgment includes those individuals who have the expertise needed to analyze the inputs to develop the project scope statement, which itself includes documenting the deliverables of the project, as well as constraints and assumptions.

Product Analysis

Product analysis applies to projects that are developing a product (versus a service or result), and it means to translate high-level product descriptions into deliverables. Examples of techniques used as part of product analysis include: product breakdown, systems analysis, requirements analysis, systems engineering, value engineering, and value analysis.

Alternatives Generation

Alternatives generation explores the various approaches and ways of executing the work of the project. The *PMBOK® Guide* notes that various general management techniques may be used, such as brainstorming, lateral thinking, and analysis of alternatives. This technique is used by combining it with other techniques included within this process, such as expert judgment and facilitated workshops.

Facilitated Workshops

Facilitated workshops are used in the same manner as the previous process (Collect Requirements). The result of holding facilitated workshops will be documented within the project scope statement. These sessions become critical in getting the team stakeholders on the same page, in terms of project objectives.

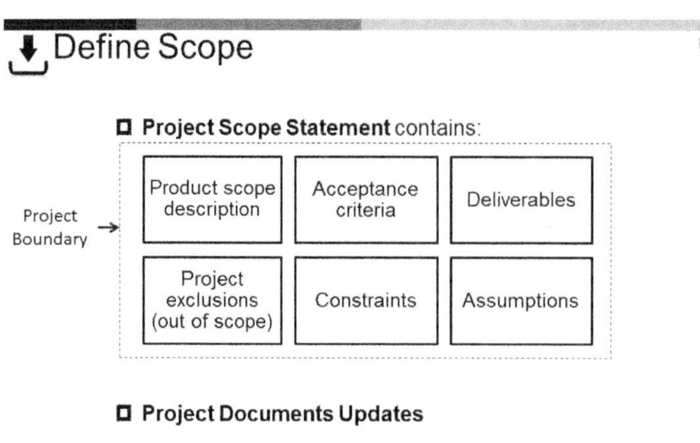
Define Scope
Project Scope Statement contains:
Project Boundary
Product scope description
Acceptance criteria
Deliverables
Project exclusions (out of scope)
Constraints
Assumptions
Project Documents Updates
© 2013 The PM Instructors™

Define Scope Outputs

The Define Scope process produces two outputs: *project scope statement and project documents updates.*

Project Scope Statement

The first and primary output of the Define Scope process is the project scope statement, a very important scope document that contains several key components that will be used by several other processes. The project scope statement contains detailed information about the work required to successfully complete the project, as well as a description of the project and product's scope to result in a clear understanding among the stakeholders about what the project aims to accomplish. The project scope statement creates the project boundaries and describes the work necessary to complete the project's deliverables. Deliverables are documented within the project scope statement, providing the work boundaries so that the project team completes no more and no less than the intended scope resulting in customer satisfaction.

Generally, the project scope statement includes the following:

- A description of the product scope and its characteristics
- Acceptance criteria
- Deliverables
- Constraints
- Assumptions
- Project exclusions, meaning what is out of scope

These are important components of the document, and you should remember and feel comfortable with them for the exam.

Project Documents Updates

Any one of the project documents impacted by carrying out this process will need to be updated. This includes the requirements documentation, which will be updated to reflect the requirements selected to move forward with the project, as well as the requirements traceability matrix and stakeholder register.

Purpose: To subdivide deliverables and project work into smaller, more manageable components.

Create WBS Process Overview

The purpose of the Create WBS process is to subdivide the project deliverables into smaller, more manageable components. For this reason, it is a process that must take place after Define Scope, which produced the project scope statement.

- ***Work Breakdown Structure (WBS):**
  - A hierarchical decomposition of the total scope of work to be carried out by the project team to accomplish the project objectives and create the required deliverables.
  - 100% Rule

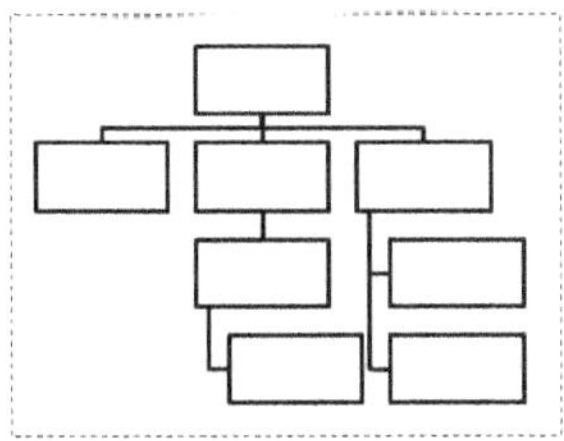

* Definition from *A Guide to the Project Management Body of Knowledge*, Project Management Institute Inc., 2013

The work breakdown structure[6] (WBS) is defined as a hierarchical decomposition of the total scope of work to be carried out by the project team to accomplish the project objectives and create the required deliverables. After its creation, the WBS will represent 100% of the project's scope, thereby outlining the project boundaries, and becoming an important communication tool among the project team and other stakeholders. This is sometimes referred to as the *100% Rule*.

[6] * Definition from *A Guide to the Project Management Body of Knowledge*, Project Management Institute Inc., 2013

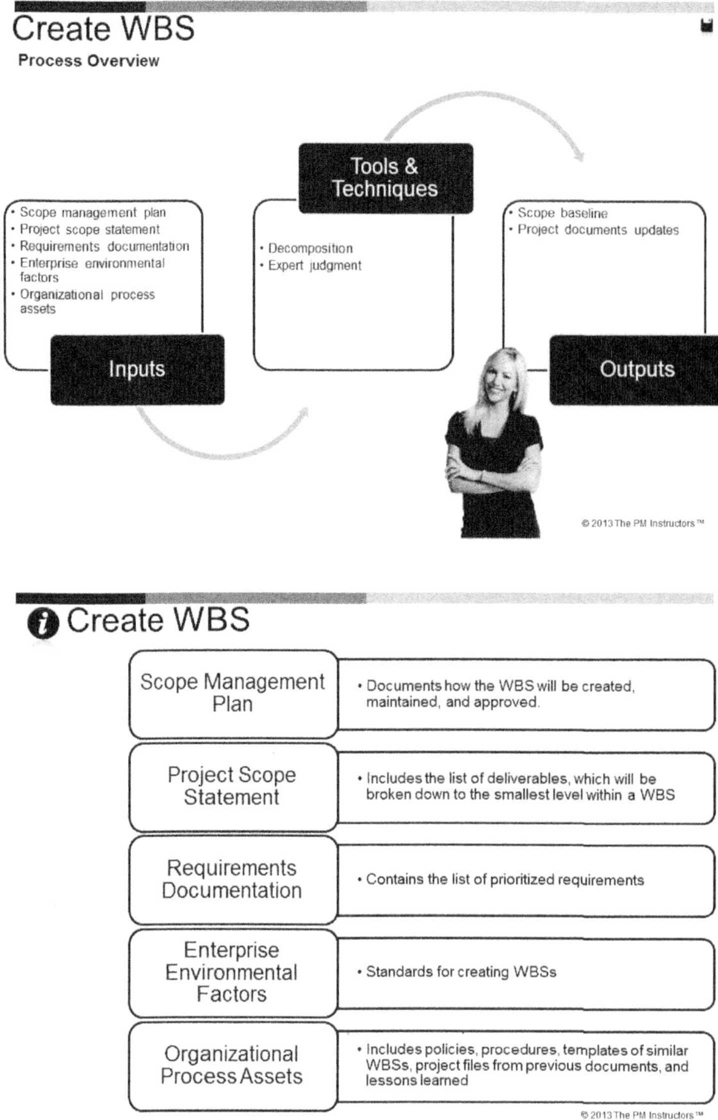
Create WBS
Process Overview
Tools & Techniques
• Scope management plan
• Project scope statement
• Requirements documentation
• Enterprise environmental factors
• Organizational process assets
Inputs
• Decomposition
• Expert judgment
• Scope baseline
• Project documents updates
Outputs
© 2013 The PM Instructors™
Create WBS
Scope Management Plan
• Documents how the WBS will be created, maintained, and approved.
Project Scope Statement
• Includes the list of deliverables, which will be broken down to the smallest level within a WBS
Requirements Documentation
• Contains the list of prioritized requirements
Enterprise Environmental Factors
• Standards for creating WBSs
Organizational Process Assets
• Includes policies, procedures, templates of similar WBSs, project files from previous documents, and lessons learned
© 2013 The PM Instructors™

Create WBS Inputs

The Create WBS process utilizes the following five inputs: *scope management plan, project scope statement, requirements documentation, enterprise environmental factors, and organizational process assets.*

Scope Management Plan

The scope management plan documents how the WBS will be created, maintained, and approved. Remember that this plan provides information on how the scope management processes are to be carried out.

Project Scope Statement

The project scope statement contains several important components used to create the WBS. Among them is the list of deliverables. It's these deliverables that will be broken down to the smallest level within a WBS, which is referred to as the work package level.

Requirements Documentation

Requirements documentation contains the list of prioritized requirements, among several other details about them, that become key to decomposing deliverables.

Enterprise Environmental Factors

Enterprise environmental factors provides standards for creating WBSs that are industry-specific, and may also serve as a reference for the project management team.

Organizational Process Assets

In this case, the primary items provided through the organizational process assets input includes policies, procedures, WBS templates from similar projects, project files from previous projects, and lessons learned. This allows project managers to become more efficient in the approach, since sub-dividing deliverables typically requires expertise.

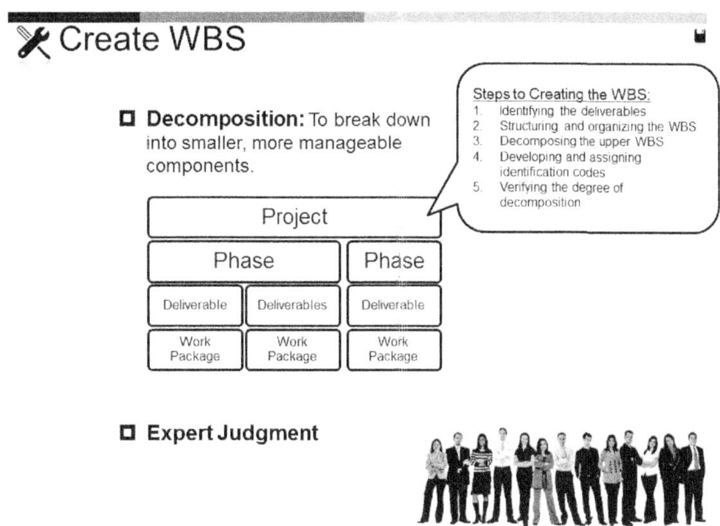

Create WBS Tools and Techniques

The Create WBS process uses the following two tools and techniques: *decomposition and expert judgment.*

Decomposition

Decomposition means to break down into smaller, more manageable components. The lowest level of a WBS is the work package level, which is the extent that deliverables are decomposed to within the WBS itself (they will be further decomposed within the first time management-related process). One level lower than the work package is the activities. That is too detailed for this hierarchical structure.

According to the *PMBOK® Guide*, there are generally five steps to creating a WBS:

1. Identifying the deliverables and related work
2. Structuring and organizing the WBS
3. Decomposing the upper WBS levels into lower level detailed components
4. Developing and assigning identification codes to the WBS components
5. Verifying that the degree of decomposition of the work is appropriate

Expert Judgment

Decomposition of the deliverables is not typically performed by a single individual. Rather, it is a joint effort performed by several subject matter experts (SME), and those with experience in work decomposition (often facilitated by the project manager).

In addition to collaborating with SMEs and project team members, project managers also tap into expert judgment by leveraging existing templates, a part of the organizational process assets input.

Create WBS

- **Work Breakdown Structure (WBS):**
  - *A deliverable-oriented hierarchical decomposition of the work to be executed by the project team, to accomplish the project objectives and create the required deliverables.*
  - Hierarchical representation of the project work; decomposes deliverables into smaller, more manageable pieces
  - Represents 100% of the project scope (called the "**100% Rule**")
  - Lowest level is called a **work package**
  - Each component contains a unique identifier and shows the relationship to its parent component

Create WBS Outputs

Create WBS has two outputs: *scope baseline and project documents updates*. However, before a review of the scope baseline can be provided, there are certain elements that must be reviewed first, including the WBS and the WBS dictionary.

Work Breakdown Structure (WBS)

The *PMBOK® Guide* defines the WBS as the following: "*a deliverable-oriented hierarchical decomposition of the work to be executed by the project team, to accomplish the project objectives and create the required deliverables*". Each level lower contains a greater amount of detail. Further in this chapter, you can view a generic example of a WBS, although it is not shown as fully decomposed. Notice that each component contains a unique identifier and shows the relationship to its parent component. Also included within the example is a control account.

A work breakdown structure (WBS) is a hierarchical representation of the deliverable-oriented project work to be executed by the project team. As a whole, the WBS represents *100% of the project work*. This is sometimes referred to as the **100% Rule**.

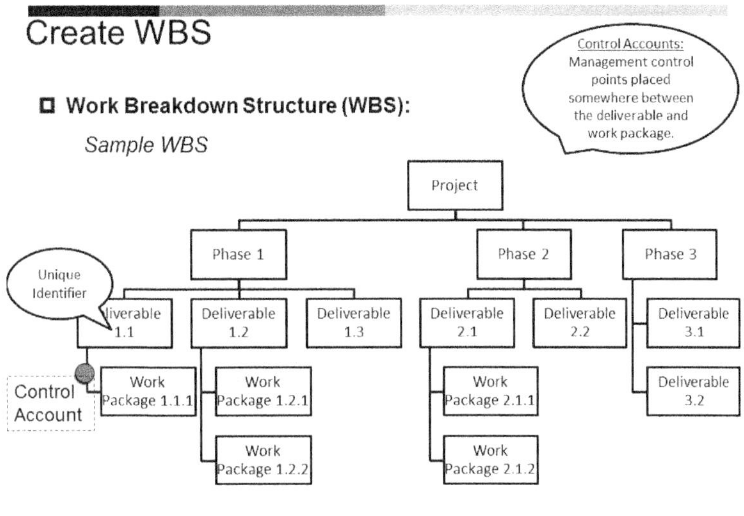

Control Account

A control account is a management control point, often placed somewhere between a deliverable and a work package, where management would like to see reporting on scope, cost, resource, and schedule information for the summary of all items below it.

Control accounts will once again surface within the Project Cost Management Knowledge Area. In many cases, earned value management is applied at the control account level for reporting purposes.

Create WBS

- **WBS Dictionary:** Provides a reference of all the WBS components. As the work progresses, the dictionary gets larger and larger. Example of contents:
  - Code of account identifier
  - Description of work
  - Responsible organization
  - Schedule milestones
  - Associated schedule activities
  - Resources required
  - Cost estimates
  - Quality requirements
  - Acceptance criteria
  - Technical references
  - Contract information

Levels of a WBS

The basic sample of a WBS shown above contains the following levels:

Level 1: project name

Level 2: project phase (first level of decomposition)

Level 3: project deliverables

It is not required that the second level include phases, and is simply dependent on the structure of the project itself. Therefore, level two may jump directly to the project deliverables. All other levels are decompositions of the deliverables themselves.

Unique Identifier

Notice that a numbering system within the WBS is in place. Each component within the WBS is assigned a unique identifier that can be traced back to a Level 2 component.

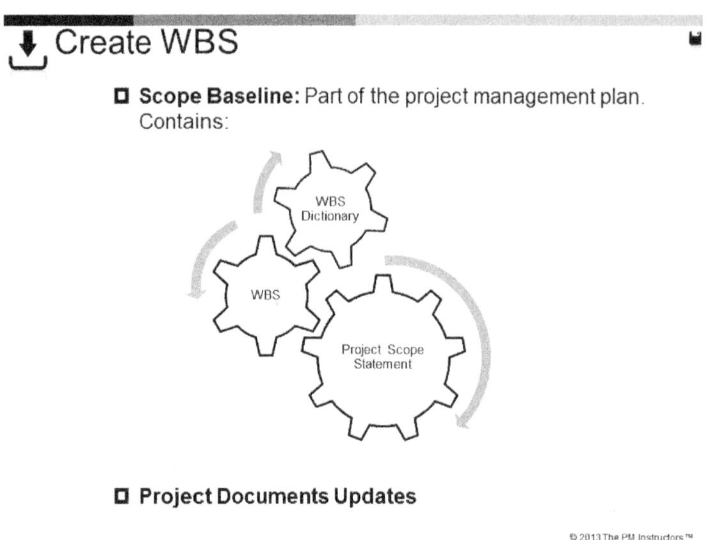
Create WBS
Scope Baseline: Part of the project management plan. Contains:
WBS Dictionary
WBS
Project Scope Statement
Project Documents Updates
© 2013 The PM Instructors™

WBS Dictionary

The WBS dictionary provides a reference of all the WBS components. As the work progresses, the dictionary gets larger and larger. For instance, it may contain the unique identifier of the components, a description of the work, who is responsible for it, milestones, activities, resources required, cost and schedule estimates, quality requirements, acceptance criteria, and more. Naturally, when you first create it, all of this information will not be available.

The WBS dictionary provides additional information about each WBS component, including all of the elements listed above. As more information is known, it is continuously documented and updated within the WBS dictionary as well, providing an important source of reference.

Scope Baseline

The scope baseline is the approved detailed project scope statement and its associated WBS and WBS dictionary. It is part of the project management plan. It is not until this point (within the Create WBS process) that all three of these items are created, which is why we see the scope baseline officially created here.

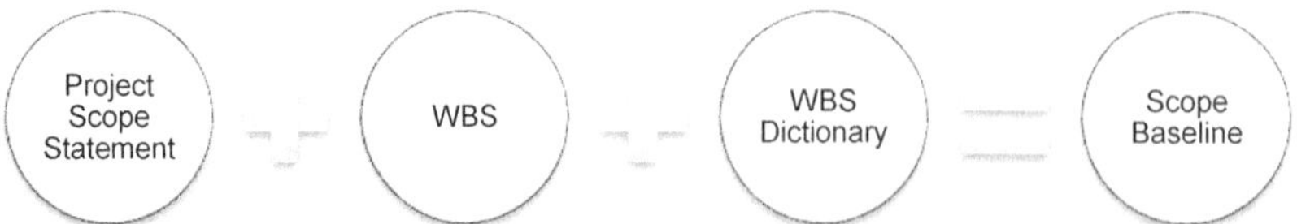
Project Scope Statement
WBS
WBS Dictionary
Scope Baseline

Project Documents Updates

Project documents that are updated as a result of this process may include the requirements documentation, or any other document impacted by the results of the process.

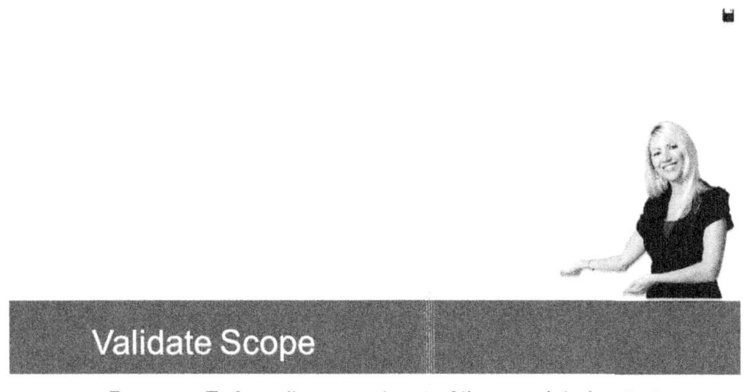
Validate Scope
Purpose: To formalize acceptance of the completed project deliverables.

Validate Scope Process Overview

The formal purpose of the Validate Scope process is to formalize the acceptance of the completed project deliverables by obtaining sign off by the customer or sponsor. By this point, the deliverables in question that are being further inspected are already complete and they've already been verified through quality control efforts. To quickly clarify, the difference between this process's role and quality control's role, is that quality is concerned with whether the completed deliverable is correct and meets the quality requirements, while scope validation measures the verified deliverables against the project and product requirements.

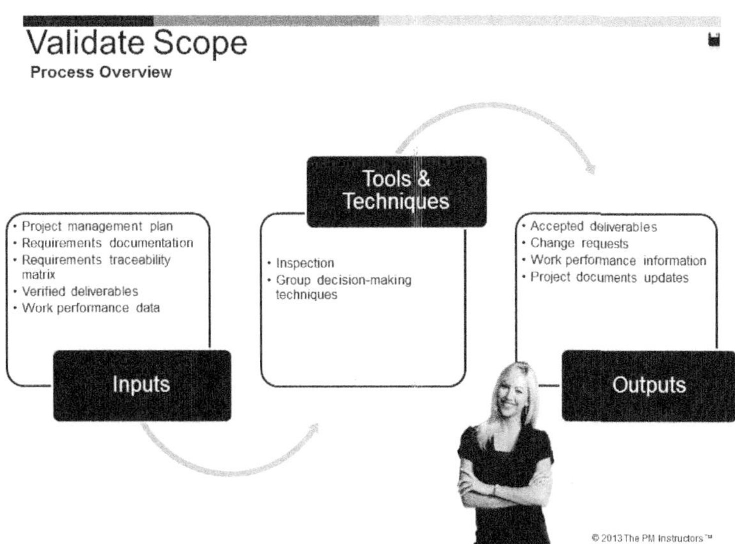
Validate Scope
Process Overview
Tools & Techniques
• Project management plan
• Requirements documentation
• Requirements traceability matrix
• Verified deliverables
• Work performance data
• Inspection
• Group decision-making techniques
• Accepted deliverables
• Change requests
• Work performance information
• Project documents updates
Inputs
Outputs
© 2013 The PM Instructors™

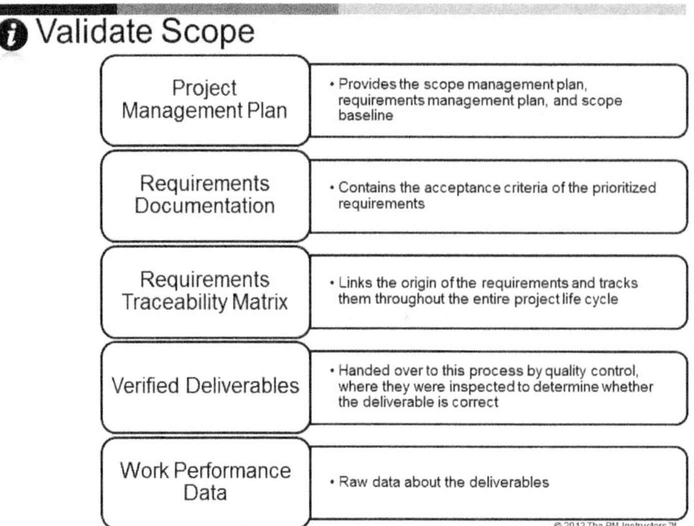
Validate Scope
Project Management Plan
• Provides the scope management plan, requirements management plan, and scope baseline
Requirements Documentation
• Contains the acceptance criteria of the prioritized requirements
Requirements Traceability Matrix
• Links the origin of the requirements and tracks them throughout the entire project life cycle
Verified Deliverables
• Handed over to this process by quality control, where they were inspected to determine whether the deliverable is correct
Work Performance Data
• Raw data about the deliverables
© 2013 The PM Instructors™

Validate Scope Inputs

The Validate Scope process uses the following five inputs: *project management plan, requirements documentation, requirements traceability matrix, verified deliverables, and work performance data.*

Project Management Plan

The project management plan contains the scope baseline, which is an important input to this process, as well as the scope management plan and requirements management plan. As a refresher, the scope baseline itself contains the project scope statement, WBS, and WBS dictionary. Remember that the project scope statement itself contains the acceptance criteria of the product, which is critical to this process.

The project management plan input itself is broad, since any other plan or baseline may also be used, which is why the entire project management plan is referenced.

Requirements Documentation

Requirements documentation is an important inclusion as an input, because it contains the acceptance criteria of the individual prioritized requirements.

Requirements Traceability Matrix

This matrix links the origin of the requirements and tracks them throughout the entire project life cycle. The signed off deliverable(s) will require this document to be updated at the end of this process.

Verified Deliverables

Verified deliverables are handed over to this process by quality control (through the Control Quality process). At this point, the quality control team has already inspected the completed deliverable for correctness.

The figure included on the next page displays how this process interacts with other processes when it comes to the various stages that deliverables pass through.

Work Performance Data

Work performance data contains raw data about the deliverables and requirements. Relevant examples include the degree of compliance with requirements, number of nonconformities, number of validation cycles, etc.

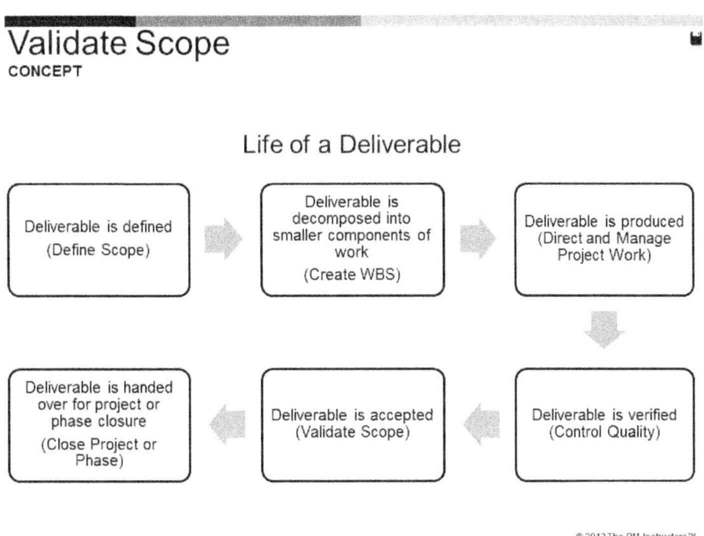

Concept

In the image above, you are taken through the series of steps that a deliverable goes through, from beginning to end, including the process where the action occurs.

1. First, the deliverable must be identified, defined, and documented with the help of the experts. This is documented within the project scope statement, which is created through the Define Scope process.
2. Next, the deliverables are further decomposed into smaller components of work, which will later be decomposed into activities. The initial decomposition of the deliverables is done within the WBS, through the Create WBS process.
3. Now it's time for the work to be executed, so that the deliverables can be produced / generated. This occurs as part of the Direct and Manage Project Work process.
4. The next step involves quality control efforts. The quality control team verifies the deliverables to ensure that they are correct. They are measured against predetermined quality requirements through the Control Quality process.
5. If deliverables pass quality control inspection, they are handed over to the Validate Scope process for inspection against the product requirements. If they pass, they will be accepted by the customer and / or sponsor.
6. Once deliverables have been verified and validated / accepted, they are handed over to the Close Project or Phase process for official phase or project closure.

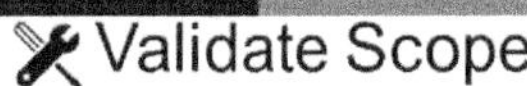
The PM Instructors

Validate Scope

- **Inspection:**
  - Often referred to as a review, audit, walkthrough, and product review.
  - The validated deliverables are inspected against the requirements and product acceptance criteria.
- **Group Decision-Making Techniques:** Used to determine whether deliverables pass inspection.

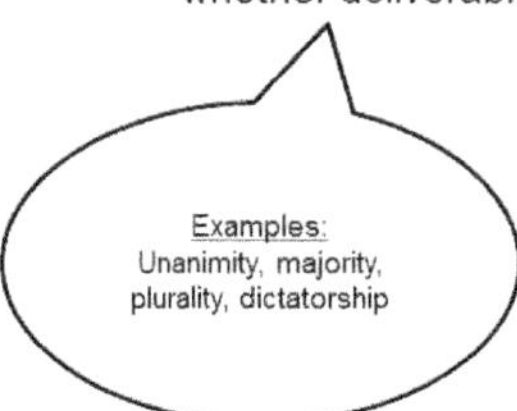
Examples:
Unanimity, majority, plurality, dictatorship

Validate Scope Tools and Techniques

The Validate Scope process utilizes the following two tools and techniques: *inspection and group decision-making techniques.*

Inspection

Inspection is also often referred to as a review, audit, walkthrough, and product review. The verified deliverables are inspected against the requirements and product acceptance criteria.

Group Decision-Making Techniques

Group decision-making techniques are used to determine whether or not a verified deliverable passes inspection. The types of techniques used are similar to those described within the Collect Requirements process.

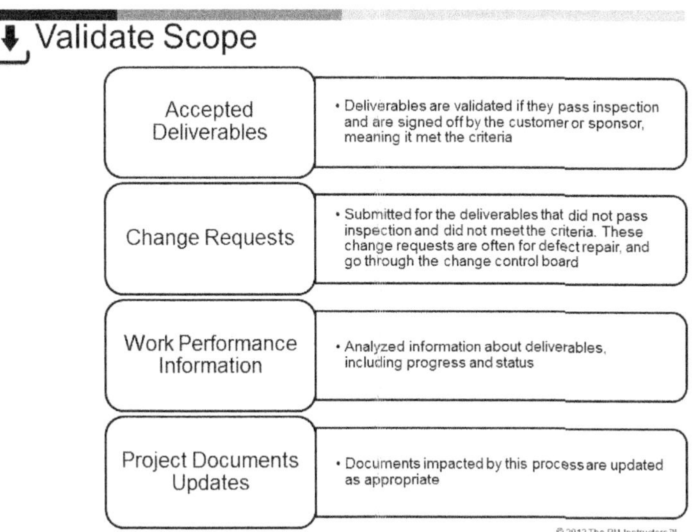

Validate Scope Outputs

There are four outputs produced as a result of carrying out the Validate Scope process, which are as follow: *accepted deliverables, change requests, work performance information, and project documents updates.*

Accepted Deliverables

If the verified deliverable passed the inspection performed within this process, and sign off by the customer or sponsor was achieved, meaning it met the criteria, then the deliverable is considered accepted. This should be documented.

Change Requests

For the deliverables that did not pass inspection and did not meet the criteria, the reason for non-acceptance should be documented. And as a result, a change request will need to be submitted. These change requests are often for defect repair. All change requests go through the change control board, who come together to review the requests through the Perform Integrated Change Control process within the Project Integration Management Knowledge Area.

Work Performance Information

Work performance information refers to the analyzed work performance data about the deliverables, including their progress and status.

Project Documents Updates

Project document updates occur as a result of carrying out the process. Any document impacted will need to be updated, such as the requirements traceability matrix.

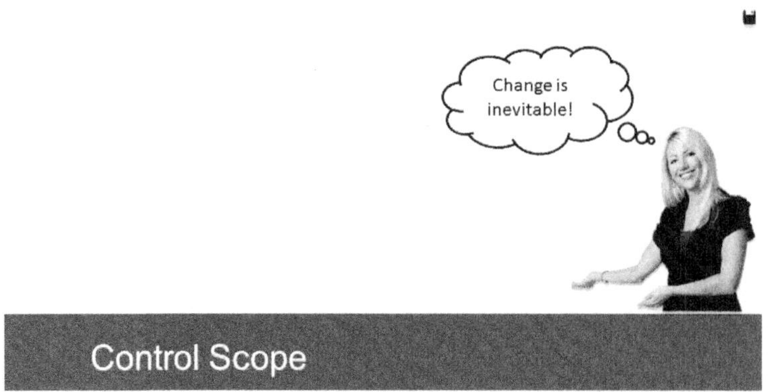

Change is inevitable!
Control Scope
Purpose: To monitor the status of the project and product scope and manage changes to the scope baseline.

Control Scope Process Overview

The Control Scope process is concerned with influencing the factors that create project scope changes and controlling the impact of those changes. This doesn't necessarily mean preventing changes, but simply controlling them to ensure that they are for the benefit of the project. This process also helps to prevent scope creep. Scope creep typically occurs when there is weak project management or a missing scope baseline. Aside from preventing scope creep, this process ensures that requested changes and recommended corrective actions are processed through the change control process. It also manages changes as they occur.

As implied above, the Control Scope process is critical to ensuring that no more and no less is created as documented within the project scope statement. *Note that change is inevitable – the purpose is not to avoid changes, but to ensure that those changes are approved and controlled.*

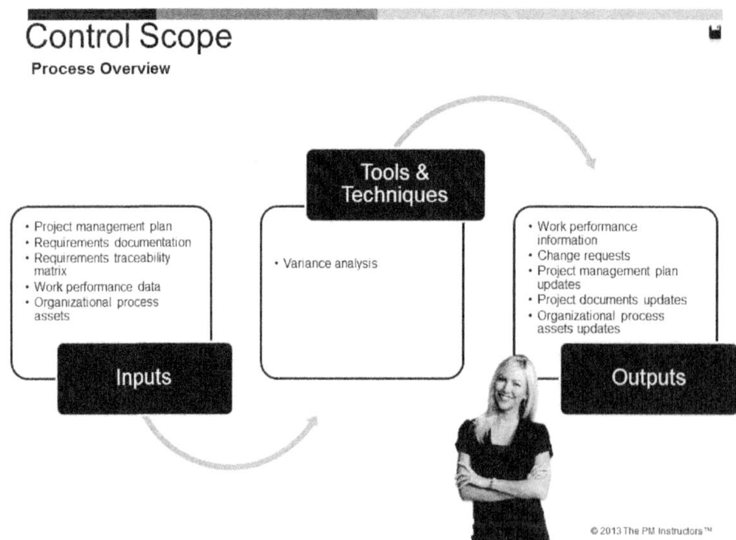

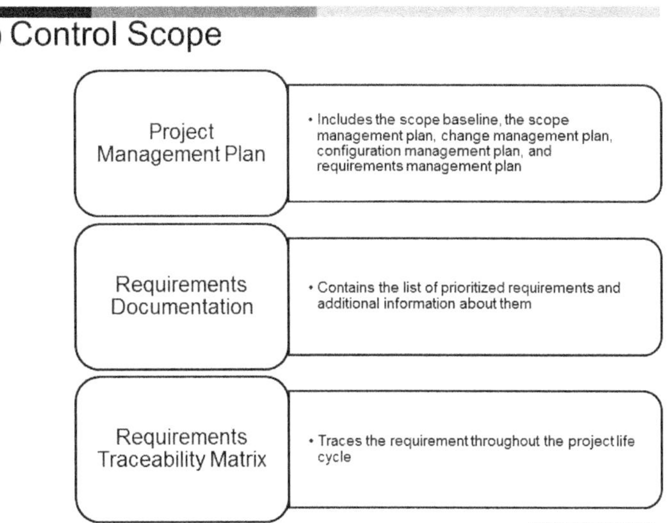
Control Scope
Project Management Plan
• Includes the scope baseline, the scope management plan, change management plan, configuration management plan, and requirements management plan
Requirements Documentation
• Contains the list of prioritized requirements and additional information about them
Requirements Traceability Matrix
• Traces the requirement throughout the project life cycle
© 2013 The PM Instructors™

Control Scope Inputs

The Control Scope process utilizes the following five inputs: *project management plan, requirements documentation, requirements traceability matrix, work performance data, and organizational process assets.*

Project Management Plan

The project management plan contains all of the subsidiary plans and baselines. Our primary interest here would be the scope baseline, the scope management plan, change management plan, configuration management plan, and requirements management plan. Although a process has not been called out that generates the change management and configuration management plans, they are considered to be created as a result of the Develop Project Management Plan process, early on within the planning stages of the project.

Requirements Documentation

Requirements documentation is an input to every scope management process after it's created. It has a list of the prioritized requirements and additional information about them.

Requirements Traceability Matrix

The requirements traceability matrix traces the requirement throughout the project life cycle. It contains the link to how the requirements being met connect to the business needs being addressed.

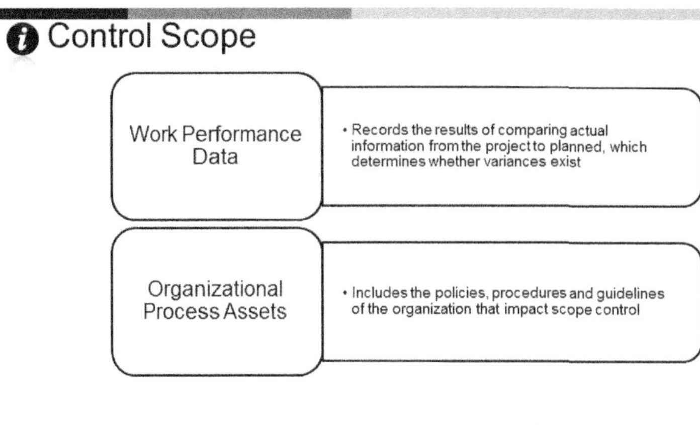

Work Performance Data

Work performance data, created as a result of the Direct and Manage Project Work process, is used to compare actual work completed against the project management plan. The purpose is to ensure that no more and no less has been completed than planned and approved.

Organizational Process Assets

Organizational process assets provide the policies, procedures and guidelines of the organization that impact scope control.

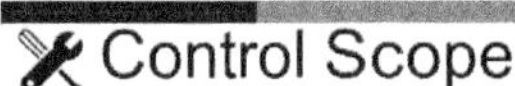

- **Variance Analysis:** Analyzes the results of comparing actual to planned.
  - It pinpoints where there are variances or deviations from the plan, and looks to determine why – what caused the variance?
  - Determines what recommended corrective or preventive actions are necessary.

Control Scope Tools and Techniques

The Control Scope process contains a single tool and techniques: *variance analysis*.

Variance Analysis

Variance analysis analyzes the results of comparing actual to planned performance. It pinpoints where there are variances or deviations from the plan, and looks to determine why. This will then allow for recommended corrective or preventive actions, which will come through in the form of change requests.

Control Scope

- **Work Performance Information:** This includes the documented results of variance analysis
- **Change Requests:** Recommended corrective or preventive actions or needed defect repairs are submitted
- **Project Management Plan Updates:** Potentially updates to the scope baseline or other baselines
- **Project Documents Updates:** Potentially updates to the requirements documentation and requirements traceability matrix
- **Organizational Process Assets Updates:** Documents what caused variances, what corrective action were taken, and whether it worked

Control Scope Outputs

The Control Scope process produces five outputs: *work performance information, change requests, project management plan updates, project documents updates, and organizational process assets updates.*

Work Performance Information

Work performance information are the documented results of variance analysis. It documents the findings of the analysis, and it will later be handed over to a reporting process that will further analyze the information and generate reports.

Change Requests

It is important that variances are resolved as needed, and this is how the recommended corrective or preventive actions or needed defect repairs are submitted – through the form of change requests. This is the case for all Monitoring and Controlling processes.

Project Management Plan Updates

As a result of carrying out this process, updates to the scope baseline or other baselines may occur. These updates would be performed if approved.

Project Document Updates

Project documents often updated as a result of this process include the requirements documentation and the requirements traceability matrix.

Organizational Process Assets Updates

Any time project managers document variances, they will want to also document the findings within the organizational process assets, including what the cause of the variances were, so that they can use this information later within this project and also in future projects. Project managers should also consider documenting the corrective action taken, and whether the actions worked. In essence, this is considered recording lessons learned.

Module Summary

In this module we:

- Defined the purpose of the Project Scope Management Knowledge Area
- Identified the processes of the Project Scope Management Knowledge Area
- Recalled the key outputs of the scope management processes
- Differentiated between the inputs, tools and techniques, and outputs of the scope management processes
- Described the elements of the work breakdown structure

Chapter Quiz

Exam Practice Questions

1. A project manager of a new construction project is in the process of putting together the project schedule. While preparing for a planning meeting, the project manager asked the project coordinator to obtain the project constraints and assumptions. Which of the following documents will the team member reference?
   A. Risk management plan
   B. Risk register
   C. Project scope statement
   D. Project management plan

2. The project work has just been completed, with the final deliverable verified and approved. What comes next?
   A. End of project celebration
   B. Archive project documents within the organizational process assets
   C. Receive customer sign-off that the product has been approved
   D. Close all contracts

3. The project scope has just been defined. What comes next?
   A. Create the project schedule
   B. Estimate the activities
   C. Issue the project scope statement
   D. Create the work breakdown structure

4. Big Food Co. is wholesale distributer of food products available to the public. They have recently decided to take on a modernization program that would bring their legacy systems into the current standards of web based applications. During their weekly planning meeting, the CIO has requested to see the WBS created by the project manager so that it can be shared with the executive board members. During what Process Group is the work breakdown structure created?
   A. Initiating
   B. Planning
   C. Executing
   D. Monitoring and Controlling

5. Which of the following does not represent an activity performed as part of the product analysis technique?
   A. Subtract product breakdown
   B. Value analysis
   C. Brainstorming
   D. Systems engineering

6. Jason works for Blazing Broadband Internet Solutions and has just completed a project that required installing 8,000 feet of new cable to improve the bandwidth for a client located in a remote location of the company's coverage area. Upon completing the project, the customer informs Jason that the service to his remote station is still at an unacceptable level. Jason verifies that the new cabling is working properly, and discovers that the problem is because of the customer's routers. As a result, he cannot resolve the problem because the issue is beyond the project's defined scope, as documented within the project scope statement. The project scope statement can BEST be described as:
   A. A detailed description of the project's deliverables and the work required to create those deliverables
   B. A document that defines, documents, verifies, manages, and controls the project scope
   C. A decomposition of the work to be executed by the project team
   D. A document that defines how the project is executed, monitored and controlled, and closed

7. The Validate Scope process is concerned with:
   A. The approval of the project scope statement
   B. Ensuring that requested changes are processed through the integrated change control process
   C. The acceptance of the deliverables
   D. Meeting the quality requirements

8. Deliverable 2.3.1 has just been assigned. What is the identifying number assigned to the next deliverable located on the same branch and level as the previous deliverable?
   A. 2.3.2
   B. 2.4.1
   C. 2.4
   D. 2.3.1.1

9. Alfred is holding a brainstorming meeting with select members of the project team to help generate different approaches and ideas of executing the project work. This is an example of:
   A. Lateral Thinking
   B. Expert Judgment
   C. Product Analysis
   D. Alternatives generation

10. Which of the following is not a tool and technique of the Define Scope process?
   A. Product analysis
   B. Alternatives generation
   C. Variance analysis
   D. Expert judgment

11. Decomposition of project deliverables occurs when?
   A. Once the code of accounts have been assigned
   B. When the deliverables reach the work package level
   C. Once the deliverables or subprojects are clarified
   D. After deliverables have been accepted

12. As the project manager of a project developing the latest product in wireless technology, you've been tasked with heading the creation of the work breakdown structure. What is the BEST way to get started?
   A. Consult with other project managers to utilize their expertise
   B. Delegate the task to the project team member with the greatest expertise in the product
   C. Obtain the most downloaded template offered through industry sources
   D. Utilize templates from previous similar projects

13. Product analysis can best be described as:
    A. A general management technique used to generate different approaches to execute and perform the project work
    B. Identifying the influences and interests of the identified stakeholders, and documents their needs, wants, and expectations
    C. The methods for translating project objectives into tangible deliverables and requirements
    D. Utilizing the expertise of those with experience in each application area of the project scope statement

14. While performing the Validate Scope process, a stakeholder voices a concern because a key feature was not identified as part of the project scope statement. Who is responsible for this oversight?
    A. The stakeholder, since it is their responsibility to voice their needs, wants and expectations to the project team
    B. The project sponsor, who did not include the feature within the project charter
    C. The project manager, who is responsible for ensuring that all needs, wants and expectations of stakeholders are identified
    D. The project team collectively for not communicating properly with all stakeholders

15. Deliverables are an output of the following process:
    A. Perform Integrated Change Control
    B. Develop Project Management Plan
    C. Direct and Manage Project Work
    D. Close Project or Phase

16. Which of the following does not represent an example of a group creativity technique?
    A. Brainstorming
    B. Multicriteria decision analysis
    C. Idea/mind mapping
    D. Root cause identification

17. Thomas is a project manager that has received an incomplete set of requirements from his customer. His development team insists that they cannot begin working on the project until they have a complete set of requirements provided. However, Thomas suggests that they begin working on the requirements using the amount of information they have, and as the scope of the project expands and the client learns more about their own needs, he can actively engage the customer to continue adding more detail to the requirements. Developing the scope in increments as the project occurs is called:
    A. Operational work
    B. Project management
    C. Scope management
    D. Progressive elaboration

18. You are the project manager of a software development company and have just received the first set of requirements from your customers. Unfortunately, the customer only provided you with detailed descriptions that explain how they take raw material and convert it into a product for consumption. In order to assist them with automating their operation and moving it online, you give the requirements to your solutions architect and ask him to decompose the requirements into more specific components of work. Decomposition refers to:
    A. An activity that has missed the scheduled finish date
    B. The breaking down of the project management plan into components
    C. The breaking down of WBS components into smaller, more manageable pieces
    D. The breaking down of work packages into activity attributes

19. Upon receiving an updated set of artifacts from your business analysts, the system architect and the testing lead, you are able to begin assigning team members to very specific tasks. This was made possible because the new level of detailed work provided in the artifacts allowed you to create a more comprehensive hierarchical decomposition of the work. Which of the following refers to a hierarchical decomposition of the work to be executed by the project team?
    A. Resource breakdown structure
    B. Organizational breakdown structure
    C. Work breakdown structure
    D. Bill of material

20. As the project manager of a software development company, you've created a work breakdown structure that shows low level transition of work moving from your developers once they have completed Unit Testing, on to the testing team to complete the System Testing. The work will then move to the customer to assist with the acceptance testing. The lowest level of this work breakdown structure (WBS) referenced is called:
    A. Work package
    B. Schedule activity
    C. Deliverable
    D. WBS component

Chapter Quiz

Exam Practice Answers

1. Answer: C

   Explanation: The project scope statement contains the project constraints and assumptions, which is what the project manager is looking to utilize, as well as the deliverables. This document also contains what is in and out of scope, and the product acceptance criteria.

2. Answer: C

   Explanation: While an end of project celebration is common, it is not part of a set process. The archival of project documents should be one of the very last tasks completed within a project's life, so it is also not the correct choice, and it would definitely come after the closing of the contracts. Before contracts can be closed, the customer must first sign-off on the final project deliverable(s).

3. Answer: D

   Explanation: If the project scope has just been defined this means that the project scope statement has already been issued / created. If scope has just been defined this would mean that project details have not been planned to the extent that activities can be estimated or a project schedule be created. The next step would be to further decompose the scope by creating a work breakdown structure (WBS). The work break down structure takes the major project deliverables defined within the project scope statement and breaks them down into smaller, more manageable pieces.

4. Answer: B

   Explanation: The WBS is created within the Project Scope Management Knowledge Area, through the Create WBS process. The WBS is created early on in the project, and will be used to create the project schedule. This cannot be an Executing or Monitoring and Controlling process. Remember that Initiating Process Group contains only two processes - Develop Project Charter and Identify Stakeholders, leaving only Planning as the correct option.

5. Answer: C

   Explanation: There are 6 methods included within product analysis: product breakdown, systems analysis, systems engineering, value engineering, value analysis, and functional analysis. Not mentioned was brainstorming, which is a part of alternatives generation, also listed as a tool and technique of the Define Scope process. The correct answer is therefore brainstorming.

6. Answer: A

   Explanation: The project scope statement includes the project objectives, the scope description, what is out of scope, deliverables, constraints, and assumptions.

7. Answer: C

   Explanation: The options included here all describe the purpose of a process. The Validate Scope process is responsible for the acceptance of deliverables. Other options describe the purpose of Define Scope, Control Scope, Control Quality processes.

8. Answer: A

   Explanation: When a deliverable is located on the same branch and level, the end number continues to increase. One level up would be 2.3, and if it would have asked you for the next sub-deliverable on the same branch, but one level down, then the answer would have been 2.4.1; if the question would have asked for the next sub-deliverable on the same branch but one sub-level down, then the answer would have been 2.3.1.1.

9. Answer: D

Explanation: Product analysis can quickly be eliminated, since this one is not related to the topic of the question. A brainstorming meeting is mentioned, so it is valuable to think back to what technique utilizes it. This would be alternatives generation, which is a technique of the Define Scope process. Lateral thinking, is also a type of alternatives generation.

10. Answer: C

    Explanation: All of the options listed are tools and techniques, so you must rely on your knowledge of what they mean and do to determine which process they belong to. Of the four listed, it is variance analysis that belongs to another process. The tools and techniques of the Define Scope process are expert judgment, product analysis, alternatives generation, and facilitated workshops.

11. Answer: C

    Explanation: Decomposition first occurs within the Create WBS process, where deliverables are decomposed into smaller components of work. The second round of decomposition occurs through the Define Activities process, where work packages (lowest level of the WBS) are broken out into activities that will be assigned to the project team for execution. The best answer is therefore "once the deliverables or subprojects are clarified", meaning that deliverables are now ready to be decomposed.

12. Answer: D

    Explanation: This question is a good practice at noticing the inclusion of the word BEST, since several answers may be correct. In this case, the best answer is to utilize information from past similar projects of the organization, since it is the most proactive choice. This would occur through the organizational process assets input of the Create WBS process.

13. Answer: C

    Explanation: Product analysis can be described as methods used for translating project objectives into tangible deliverables. Other options describe expert judgment, stakeholder analysis, and alternatives analysis.

14. Answer: C

    Explanation: It is the project manager's responsibility to ensure that all needs, wants, and expectations of stakeholders are identified. This does not imply that all stakeholders will get what they want as part of approved scope. Instead, this implies that expectations will be addressed. If, in this scenario, the project manager had identified the expectations of the stakeholder that was described early on during scope definition, it could have been addressed early and a decision communicated to that stakeholder.

15. Answer: C

    Explanation: Deliverables are generated during the Executing Process Group, as a result of executing the work reflected in the project management plan. Knowing this allows you to eliminate all options except for Direct and Manage Project Work, which is the correct answer.

16. Answer: D

    Explanation: There are several types of group creativity techniques, such as brainstorming, nominal group technique, idea/mind mapping, affinity diagram, and multicriteria decision analysis. Group creativity techniques are used as part of the Collect Requirements process to identify project and product requirements. The only technique not mentioned is root cause identification, which is the correct answer.

17. Answer: D

    Explanation: Developing the scope in increments as the project moves is called progressive elaboration. Progressive elaboration is when the project begins and the scope continues to increase and become more detailed as the project is underway. This, however, is planned, and many times occurs because information from the project's results will determine the rest of the scope or direction that the project will take.

18. Answer: C

    Explanation: Decomposition means to break something down into smaller more manageable pieces. Of the options provided, the best answer is the break-down of the WBS components (which refer to deliverables) into smaller, more manageable pieces.

19. Answer: C

    Explanation: The work breakdown structure (WBS) contains a decomposition of the work to be completed by the project team. The primary focus is on decomposing deliverables identified within the project scope statement. The WBS should reflect 100% of the project scope. Other options describe other types of breakdown structures.

20. Answer: A

    Explanation: Deliverables are at the top of the WBS. A WBS component can refer to any item within the WBS, and is therefore too broad of an answer. That leaves work package and schedule activity. Although schedule activity is a further decomposition of work packages, they are not included within the WBS. Therefore, the lowest level of the WBS is a work package.

Chapter 6: Project Time Management

Learning Objectives:

- ☐ Define the purpose of the Project Time Management Knowledge Area
- ☐ Identify the processes of the Project Time Management Knowledge Area
- ☐ Recall the key outputs of the time management processes
- ☐ Differentiate between the inputs, tools and techniques, and outputs of the time management processes
- ☐ Perform a forward pass and backward pass calculation
- ☐ Interpret various types of network diagrams to identify critical path activities

Exam Domain Tasks:

- Develop a project schedule based on the project timeline, scope, and resource plan, in order to manage timely completion of the project.

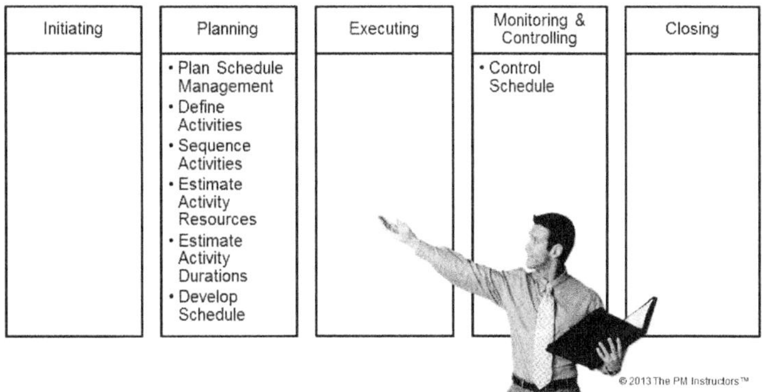
Project Time Management
*Purpose: "To manage the timely completion of the project."
7 Project Management Processes:
Initiating
Planning
Executing
Monitoring & Controlling
Closing
• Plan Schedule Management
• Define Activities
• Sequence Activities
• Estimate Activity Resources
• Estimate Activity Durations
• Develop Schedule
• Control Schedule
© 2013 The PM Instructors™

Project Time Management Overview

Completing a project on time is critical, since missing schedule milestones and deadlines often leads to a project that is over budget, or if pressed to complete a project prematurely, then the scope is not fully met. This is why such a thing as the triple constraints exists, where project time, cost and scope are related in that they impact one another.

The purpose of the Project Time Management Knowledge Area is to complete the project on time. This is done by creating a realistic project schedule, obtaining approval of that schedule to form a baseline, and monitoring deviations from the baseline.

The Project Time Management Knowledge Area consists of seven formal processes:

- Plan Schedule Management
- Define Activities
- Sequence Activities
- Estimate Activity Resources
- Estimate Activity Durations
- Develop Schedule
- Control Schedule

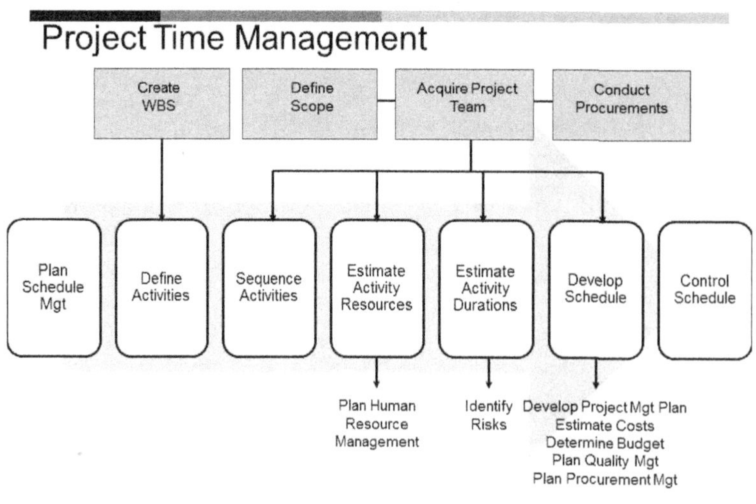

Process Interactions

Typically, the second to fifth management processes occur in parallel (*Define Activities, Sequence Activities, Estimate Activity Resources, Estimate Activity Durations, and Develop Schedule*). These processes are dynamic and interact with processes outside of this Knowledge Area. The Define Activities process creates the activity list and the milestone list. Before this can be done, the work breakdown structure (WBS) must be created through the Create WBS process. The WBS contains the deliverables that have been decomposed down to the work package level.

There are three processes that feed information to the four processes that follow defining the activities. These processes are:

- Define Scope: creates the project scope statement
- Acquire Project Team: obtains the human resources needed to perform the activities
- Conduct Procurements: contains the procured resources and information needed for the procurement activities

Likewise, the outputs of the Project Time Management processes also interact with other processes that fall outside of this Knowledge Area. For instance, once the activity resource requirements have been determined, this information will be fed into the Plan Human Resource Management process. Similarly, this information will be used within the Plan Procurement Management process. When the duration of the activities are estimated, they will interact with the Identify Risks process. We'll use this information to build our list of risks and their characteristics.

There are several processes that use the project schedule, which is an output of the **Develop Schedule** process. This includes:

- Develop Project Management Plan
- Estimate Costs
- Determine Budget
- Plan Quality Management
- Plan Procurement Management

Next, the schedule must be managed. There are two primary processes that will provide information to the Control Schedule process, which are external to this Knowledge Area:

- Direct and Manage Project Work: provides work performance data
- Develop Project Management Plan: provides the project management plan, which will contain the schedule management plan and schedule baseline

As we control and manage the schedule, there will be recommended changes made and reports generated. This will call into play two processes: Monitor and Control Project Work and Perform Integrated Change Control. Remember that all changes must first be approved before they are implemented.

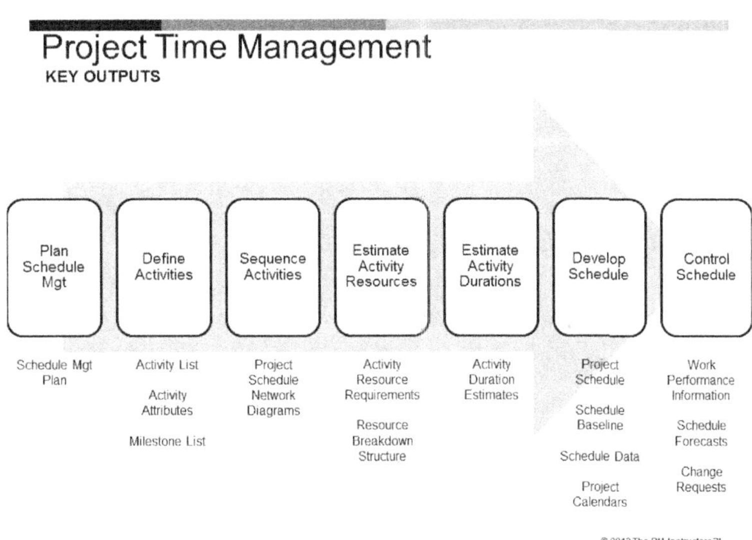

The Project Time Management Knowledge Area is concerned with completing the project on time by developing the project schedule and monitoring deviations from that schedule. There are seven processes:

- **Plan Schedule Management (Planning Process Group).** Purpose: To establish the policies, procedures, and documentation for planning, developing, managing, executing, and controlling the project schedule.
- **Define Activities (Planning Process Group).** Purpose: To identify and document the specific actions to be performed to produce the project deliverables.
- **Sequence Activities (Planning Process Group).** Purpose: To identify and document relationships among the project activities.
- **Estimate Activity Resources (Planning Process Group).** Purpose: To estimate the type and quantities of material, human resources, equipment, or supplies required to perform each activity.
- **Estimate Activity Durations (Planning Process Group).** Purpose: To estimate the number of work periods needed to complete individual activities with estimated resources.
- **Develop Schedule (Planning Process Group). Purpose:** To analyze activity sequences, durations, resource requirements, and schedule constraints to create the project schedule model.
- **Control Schedule (Monitoring and Controlling Process Group).** Purpose: To monitor the status of project activities to update project progress and mange changes to the schedule baseline to achieve the plan.

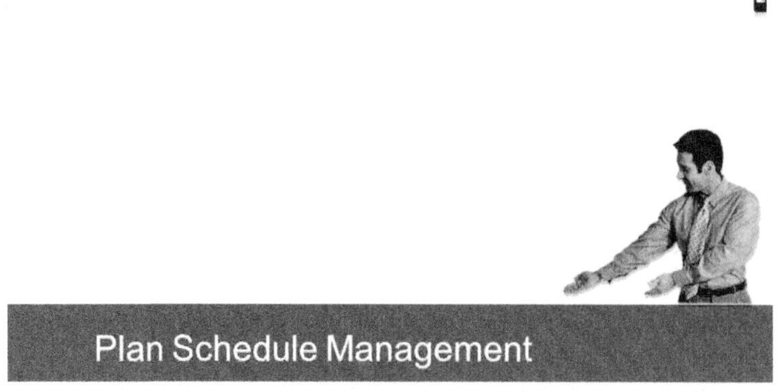
Plan Schedule Management
Purpose: To establish the policies, procedures, and documentation for planning, developing, managing, executing, and controlling the project schedule.

Plan Schedule Management Process Overview

The Plan Schedule Management Process is typically carried out early on within the life cycle of a project, as it produces the schedule management plan. This plan will define how the schedule will be created, managed, and controlled, and it becomes a key input of the Develop Project Management Plan process.

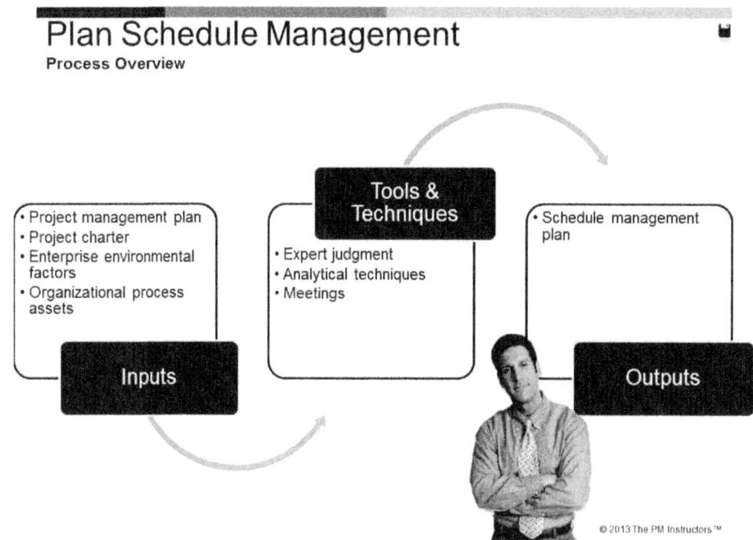
Plan Schedule Management
Process Overview
• Project management plan
• Project charter
• Enterprise environmental factors
• Organizational process assets
Inputs
Tools & Techniques
• Expert judgment
• Analytical techniques
• Meetings
• Schedule management plan
Outputs
© 2013 The PM Instructors™

Plan Schedule Management

Project Management Plan	• Contains subsidiary plans and baselines
Project Charter	• Contains a summary milestone schedule, project approval requirements, high level constraints and assumptions, and project approach
Enterprise Environmental Factors	• Organizational culture and structure, software, resource availability and skills, published commercial information, and work authorization systems
Organizational Process Assets	• Templates, historical information, lessons learned, schedule control tools, policies, procedures, and guidelines

Plan Schedule Management Inputs

Like other processes that produce management plans which touch the triple constraints, the Plan Schedule Management process contains the following four inputs: *project management plan, project charter, enterprise environmental factors,* and *organizational process assets.*

Project Management Plan

As the Planning processes continue to be iterated, the project management plan itself will continue to evolve. During the early stages of the project, it will contain other subsidiary plans, as well as the scope baseline. Any information available through the plan will be referenced when developing the schedule management plan.

Project Charter

The project charter may contain elements that impact the schedule management plan, such as summary milestone schedule, project approval requirements, constraints and assumptions, and a description of the project approach.

Enterprise Environmental Factors

There are several enterprise environmental factors that may be used to develop the schedule management plan. Common factors used include:

- Organizational culture and structure
- Software
- Resource availability and skills
- Published commercial information
- Organizational work authorization systems

Organizational Process Assets

Organizational process assets is a key input to the creation of management plans. Common assets used include:

- Templates
- Historical information
- Lessons learned
- Scheduling policies, procedures, and guidelines

Plan Schedule Management

- Expert Judgment
- Analytical Techniques
- Meetings

Techniques
- rolling wave planning
- Leads and lags
- Alternatives analysis
- Earned value management

Plan Schedule Management Tools and Techniques

The Plan Schedule Management process utilizes the following three tools and techniques: *expert judgment, analytical techniques, and meetings.*

Expert Judgment

Expert judgment involves tapping into the knowledge and expertise of those that can provide insight about the scheduling approach that would best fit the project. This insight may come from experience working in similar projects, or knowledge about scheduling methodologies.

Analytical Techniques

Analytical techniques used to create the schedule management plan may be used. The *PMBOK® Guide* notes the following examples:

- Scheduling methodology
- Scheduling tools and techniques
- Estimating approaches
- Schedule formats
- Project management software

These techniques become important to identifying the appropriate tools and techniques that will be used to perform the remaining time management processes.

Meetings

Meetings are a means of getting the right individuals in a room to work through the contents of the schedule management plan (used in combination with expert judgment). Facilitated by the project manager, these meetings often include the sponsor, project management team members, and other key stakeholders that have input into the plan.

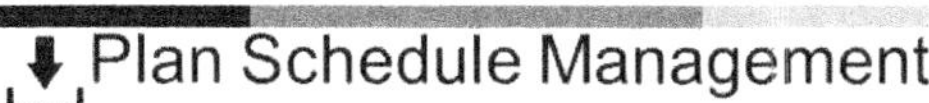
Plan Schedule Management
Schedule Management Plan:
A component of the project management plan
May be high level or detailed, depending on the needs of the project
Defines how the remaining time management processes will be performed
Schedule Management Plan Contents
Project schedule model development
Level of accuracy
Units of measure
Organizational procedure links
Project schedule model maintenance
Control thresholds
Rules of performance measurement
Reporting formats
Process descriptions
© 2013 The PM Instructors™

Plan Schedule Management Outputs

The Plan Schedule Management process produces a single output: the *schedule management plan.*

Schedule Management Plan

The only output of the Plan Schedule Management process is the schedule management plan, a component of the project management plan. Depending on the needs and complexity of the project, this plan may be high level or detailed. The exact contents of the schedule management plan will vary by organization and project, but in general, most plans will contain the following, as specified by the *PMBOK® Guide*:

- **Project schedule model development:** Documents the scheduling methodology and tools to be used.
- **Level of accuracy:** Defines the ranges used for activity duration estimates, and how contingencies are incorporated.
- **Units of measure:** Defines the rules used in measurements, such as hours, weeks, months, etc.
- **Organizational procedures links:** Provides a framework for the schedule management plan, tied to the WBS.
- **Project schedule model maintenance:** Defines the process for updating the schedule status and recording progress.
- **Control thresholds:** Documents the variance thresholds that are agreed-upon, such as what variance is considered to be acceptable before action must be taken.
- **Rules of performance measurement:** Includes earned value management rules, such as rules for establishing percent complete for activities, control accounts, EVM techniques, and schedule performance measurements.
- **Reporting formats:** Documents the reporting frequency and format of schedule reports.
- **Process descriptions:** Defines how the remaining Time Management processes will be performed.

When considering and creating the schedule management plan, one thing to keep in mind is that project managers are not meant to recreate the wheel. Using templates and plans from past similar projects is common and encouraged.

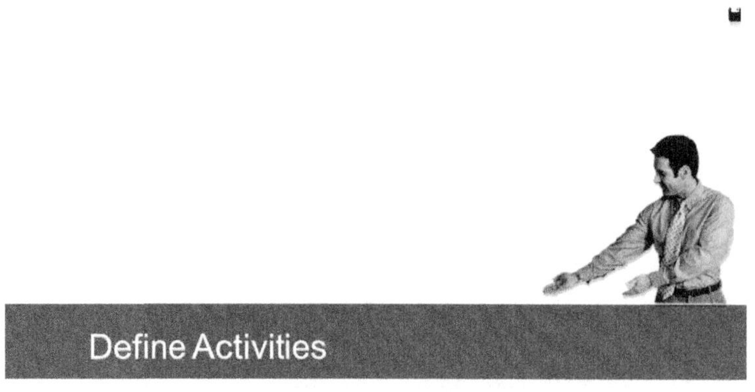
Define Activities
Purpose: To identify and document the specific actions to be performed to produce the project deliverables.

Define Activities Process Overview

The purpose of the Define Activities process is to identify and document the specific actions to be performed to produce the project deliverables. The primary result will be the decomposition of the work packages into the activity list, which includes the tasks necessary to produce the project's deliverables.

Define Activities is the second Planning process of the Project Time Management Knowledge Area.

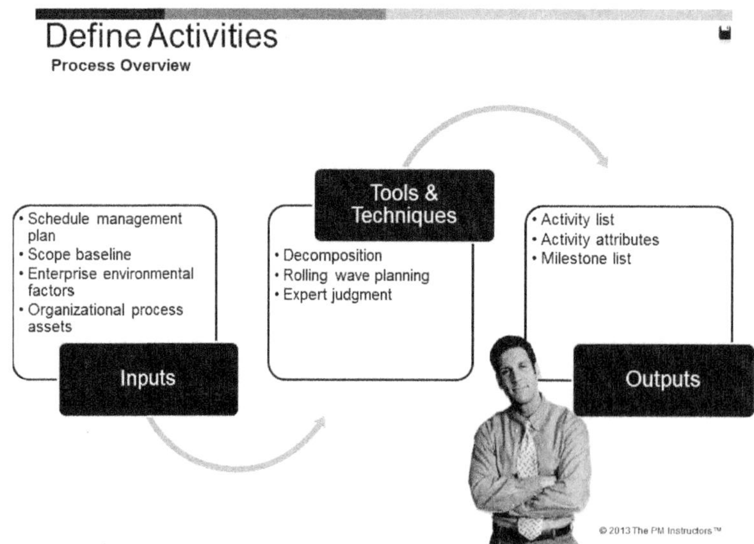
Define Activities
Process Overview
• Schedule management plan
• Scope baseline
• Enterprise environmental factors
• Organizational process assets
Inputs
Tools & Techniques
• Decomposition
• Rolling wave planning
• Expert judgment
• Activity list
• Activity attributes
• Milestone list
Outputs
© 2013 The PM Instructors™

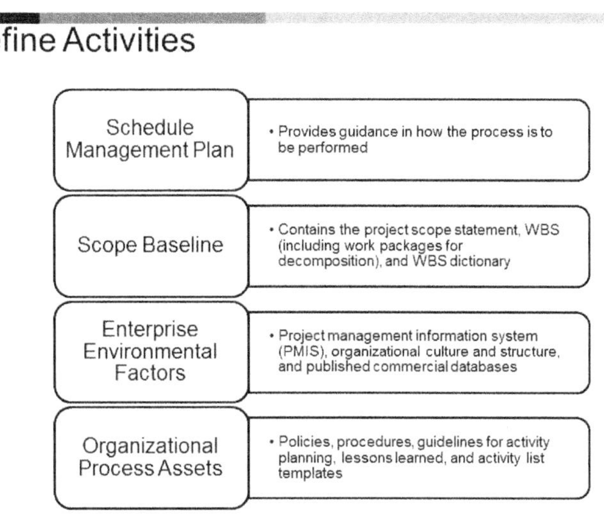
Define Activities
Schedule Management Plan
• Provides guidance in how the process is to be performed
Scope Baseline
• Contains the project scope statement, WBS (including work packages for decomposition), and WBS dictionary
Enterprise Environmental Factors
• Project management information system (PMIS), organizational culture and structure, and published commercial databases
Organizational Process Assets
• Policies, procedures, guidelines for activity planning, lessons learned, and activity list templates
© 2013 The PM Instructors™

Define Activities Inputs

The Define Activities process utilizes the following four inputs: *schedule management plan, scope baseline, enterprise environmental factors, and organizational process assets.*

Schedule Management Plan

The schedule management plan defines how the decomposition process of the work packages will be performed.

Scope Baseline

The scope baseline is a primary input for review of the Define Activities process. It contains three important components:

1. **Project Scope Statement –** a result of the Define Scope process
2. **Work Breakdown Structure (WBS)** – a result of the Create WBS process
3. **WBS Dictionary** – a result of the Create WBS process

The scope baseline is often used for change control and in making project decisions. As an input, the scope baseline primarily provides the **deliverables and their associated work packages, constraints, and assumptions of the project.**

Enterprise Environmental Factors

Enterprise environmental factors often used to create the activity lists include, but are not limited to, the PMIS, organizational culture and structure, and published commercial databases.

Organizational Process Assets

Organizational process assets used by this process include policies, procedures, and guidelines for activity planning, lessons learned, and activity list templates.

As mentioned above, templates can be used in creating the activity list by using previous activity lists from past, similar projects. This may include part or all of an activity list. The project manager and the project team members familiar with the work will then tailor the list to the current project. Using templates is considered to be an efficient practice. It not only reduces the amount of time required to generate an activity list, but it also creates consistent and more accurate results.

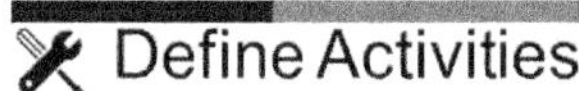

- **Decomposition:** To break down into smaller, more manageable components.

Decomposition steps:

- Step 1: Subdivide scope and deliverables down to the work package level (Create WBS process)
- Step 2: Subdivide work packages down to the activity lists (Define Activities process)

Activities are not part of the WBS

Activity = A distinct, scheduled portion of work performed during the course of a project

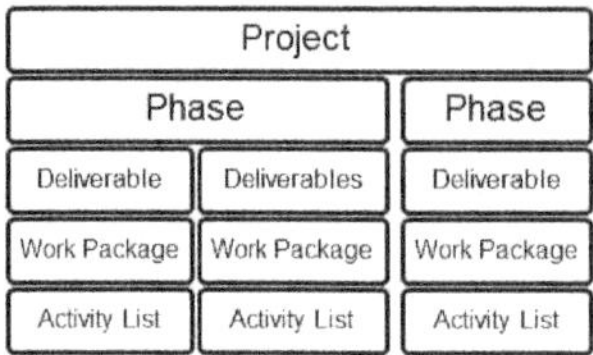

Define Activities Tools and Techniques

The Define Activities process contains three tools and techniques: *decomposition, rolling wave planning, and expert judgment.*

Decomposition

Decomposition is a tool and technique of the Define Activities process that means to subdivide scope and deliverables into smaller, more manageable components. In creating the WBS, the deliverables were decomposed down to the work package level. The Define Activities process then takes the work packages and decomposes them down further to the activity level.

Activities are the effort that is necessary to complete a work package. Many organizations have different rules in defining the total minimum and maximum amount of time that an activity may take. Some organizations have an 8-hour rule (no task should be less than 8 hours) while others require that they be a minimum of one week.

Decomposition occurs with the assistance of those that have a strong understanding of the work itself. If possible, it is always a good idea to involve the team members who will be doing the work.

The image below provides yet another visual of decomposition that takes place within a project:

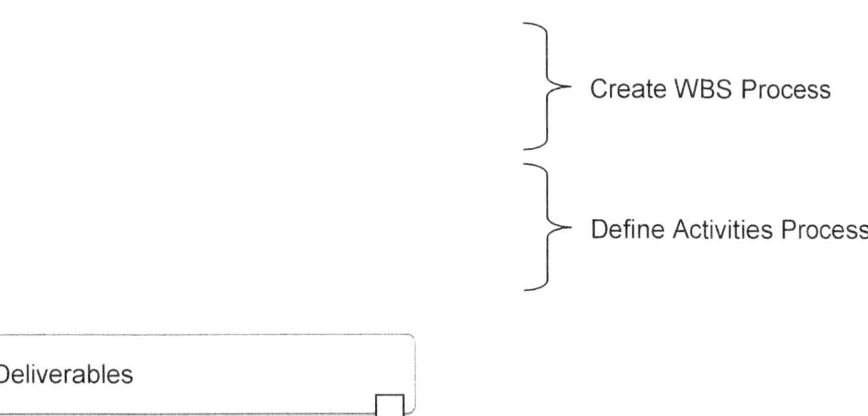
Create WBS Process
Define Activities Process

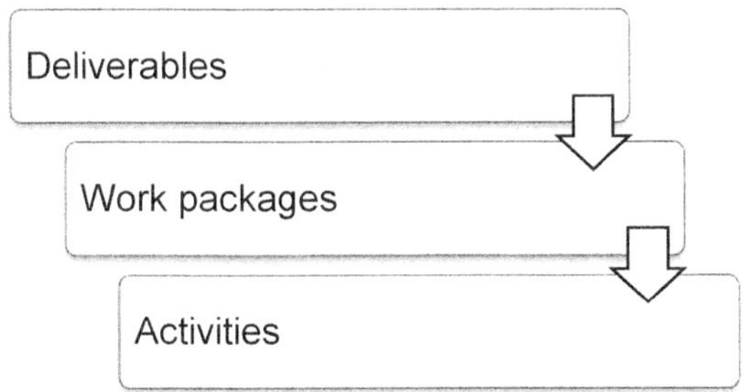
Deliverables
Work packages
Activities

Define Activities

Rolling Wave Planning:

- Work in the **near term** is planned out in detail
- Work in the **future** is planned out at higher levels of the WBS
- Using this technique is planned

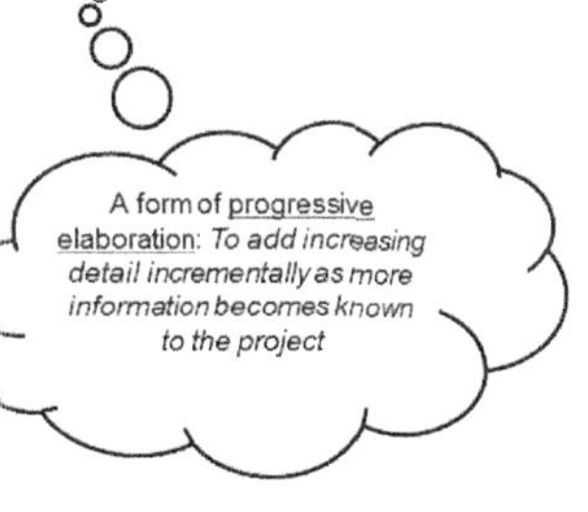
A form of progressive elaboration: *To add increasing detail incrementally as more information becomes known to the project*

Rolling Wave Planning

Rolling wave planning means that as the project moves forward, work can exist at different levels within the WBS. With rolling wave planning, the work that can be done in the near term is planned out in great detail, while the work that will take place further in the future, is only planned at these higher levels of the WBS, typically decomposed to the milestone level. This technique is often used when there isn't sufficient information available to decompose all WBS components down to the activity level. In some cases, a planning package may be added within the WBS when a deliverable cannot be decomposed down to the work package level either. This means that the deliverable has been decomposed down to the lowest level possible based on the amount of information available at that given time. As additional information becomes available, the component is further decomposed.

Rolling wave planning is a form of **progressive elaboration**. Progressive elaboration refers to adding increasing detail incrementally as more information becomes known to the project.

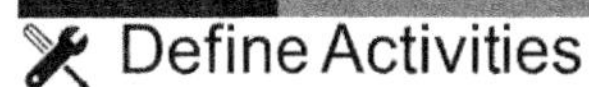

Define Activities

- **Expert Judgment:** Refers to those with **experience of the work**, such as:
  - Project team members
  - Subject matter experts
  - Project manager
  - Scheduler

Expert Judgment

Expert judgment is an important technique for establishing the work required to complete the project deliverables. Experts are those that have knowledge or experience of the work to be accomplished. These individuals may be internal or external to the organization.

The goal of expert judgment is to utilize the skills and expertise of these individuals, groups, or organizations to create an accurate and realistic list of activities.

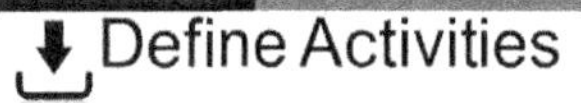

Define Activities

- **Activity List:**
  - **Definition:** comprehensive list of all schedule activities that describe the work of the project
  - **Includes:** 1) activity identifier, 2) scope of work description

Characteristics of an activity:

- Performed by a single person
- Describes the work to be accomplished
- A discrete element of work that is a tangible element of the project scope
- Experiences no interruptions while it is being performed
- Is less than two times the length of the update cycle

Define Activities Outputs

The Define Activities process produces three outputs: *activity list, activity attributes, and milestone list.*

Activity List

The activity list is a key output of the Define Activities process. It is a comprehensive list of all schedule activities required on the project. There are two key components of an activity list:

1. An activity identifier – *a reference number assigned to the activity.*

2. A scope of work description – *a description of the activity that includes enough detail so that the project team members performing the work understand what is required of them.*

According to the *Practice Standard for Scheduling*, project activities that are well constructed should contain the following characteristics:

- That a single person be responsible for performing the activity and reporting on its progress
- That it describe the work to be accomplished in a clear and understandable manner. The description should begin with a verb and contain a unique element
- That it be a discrete element of work that is a tangible element of the project scope
- Once an activity begins, there should be no interruptions within the work being performed, with the exception of non-working days within the calendar (if existing interruptions or large gaps exist, the activity may need to be broken down into two activities)
- Is less than two times the length of the update cycle

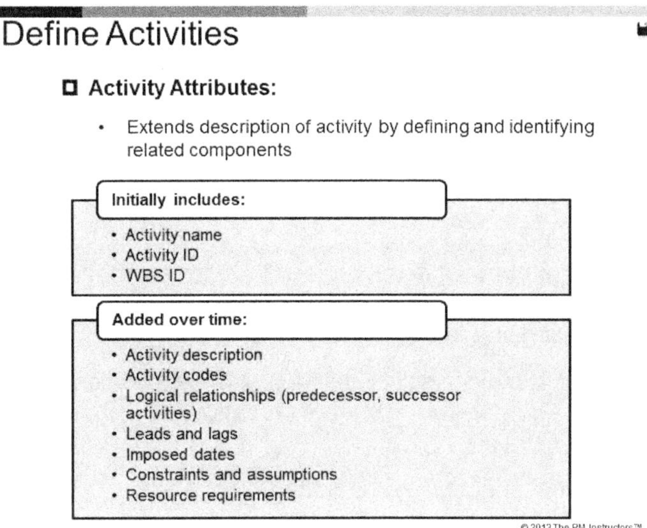

Activity Attributes

The activity attributes contain more detailed information about each activity. As project planning progresses, more information is added to the attributes as it becomes available. The attributes are very similar to the activity list, as the WBS dictionary is to the WBS. This is the activity's version of the dictionary.

In addition to being a great reference, activity attributes identify who is responsible for performing the work, and the type of activity (such as: level of effort, discrete effort, and apportioned effort). They can be used to develop the schedule, and for selecting, ordering, and sorting the planned schedule activities within the reports.

Milestone List:

- A list of all milestones within the project
- Documents whether the milestone is mandatory or optional
- Can be used to measure progress against

Milestone:	Milestone Requirements
• A significant point or event in the project (zero duration)	• Minimum of a start and finish milestone • Milestone duration = 0 • No resources should be associated to a milestone

Milestone List

A milestone list identifies all of the milestones within a project. It documents whether the milestone is mandatory or optional. A *mandatory milestone* is one that is required within a contract, whereas an optional milestone is discretionary, based on historical information or from management.

Milestone

A milestone is a significant point or event in the project. The project manager will typically define the milestones once they have an understanding of the overall structure of the project data. A milestone is commonly depicted as a diamond shape within the schedule and associated reports.

A milestone is usually inserted at major points within the schedule, such as the completion of a deliverable. They represent the completion or start of an important point within the project. They can also be associated with external constraints.

Examples of milestones within a product development project:

- Project charter signed off
- Contract approved
- Test results complete
- Stakeholder approval
- Project closed out

Milestone Requirements

- Every project must have a start milestone and a finish milestone
- The duration of a milestone is zero
- There are no resources associated with a milestone

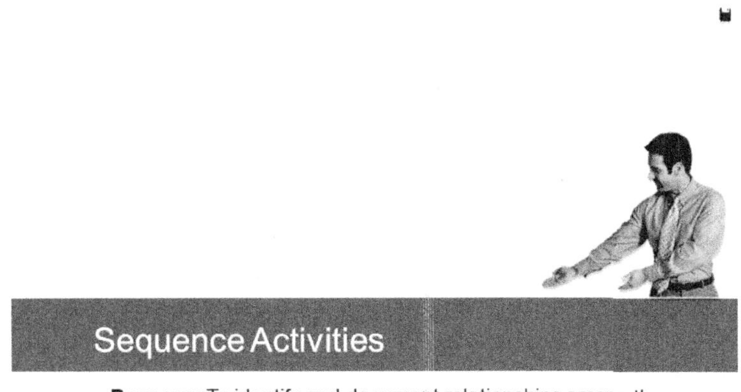
Sequence Activities
Purpose: To identify and document relationships among the project activities.

Sequence Activities Process Overview

Sequence Activities is the third process of the Project Time Management Knowledge Area. The purpose of the process is to identify and document relationships among the project activities. This allows for sequencing activities in the most logical order, according to their existing dependencies. Aside from the first and last activity, all activities will be connected to at least one predecessor and one successor activity.

The primary result of the Sequence Activities process is the creation of project schedule network diagrams, which visually show the relationship and sequencing among the activities.

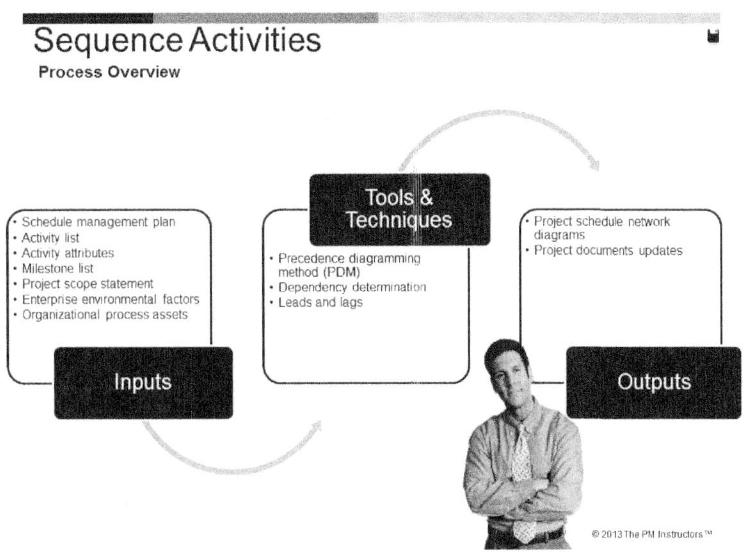
Sequence Activities
Process Overview
• Schedule management plan
• Activity list
• Activity attributes
• Milestone list
• Project scope statement
• Enterprise environmental factors
• Organizational process assets
Inputs
Tools & Techniques
• Precedence diagramming method (PDM)
• Dependency determination
• Leads and lags
• Project schedule network diagrams
• Project documents updates
Outputs
© 2013 The PM Instructors™

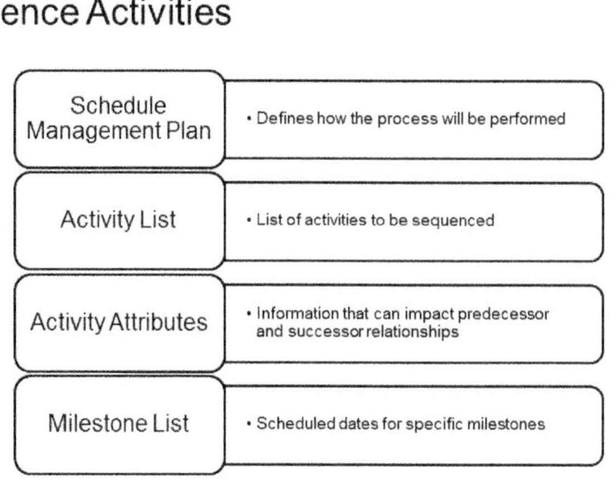

Sequence Activities Inputs

In order to determine existing dependencies and generate project schedule network diagrams, there are several inputs needed, including: *schedule management plan, activity list, activity attributes, milestone list, project scope statement, enterprise environmental factors, and organizational process assets.*

Schedule Management Plan

The schedule management plan defines how the process will be performed. This includes any tools and techniques that will be used to sequence the activities.

Activity list

The activity list provides a comprehensive list of all project activities identified, including a scope of work description per activity and an activity identifier.

Activity Attributes

Activity attributes include detailed information about each activity documented to date, such as activity ID, WBS ID, predecessor/successor activities, etc.

Milestone List

The milestone list includes a list of all identified milestones.

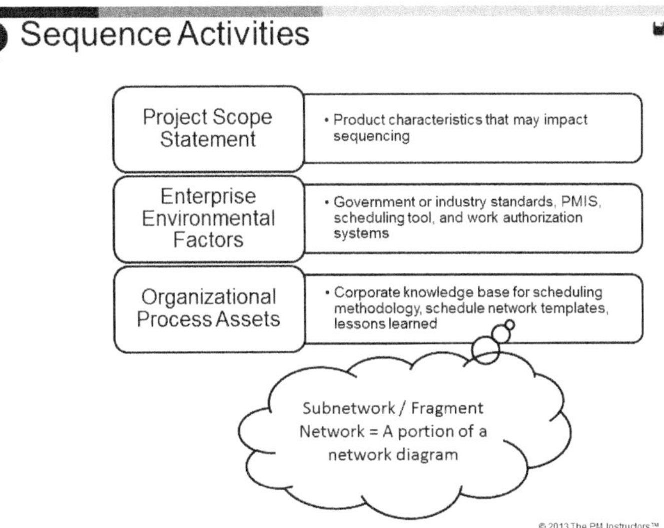

Project Scope Statement

The project scope statement contains the product scope description, and provides the documented constraints of the project that may affect activity sequencing.

Enterprise Environmental Factors

Enterprise environmental factors that may influence the sequencing of activities include government or industry standards, the PMIS, scheduling tool, and work authorization systems.

Organizational Process Assets

Organizational process assets include project files used for scheduling methodology. Notice that the first three inputs were generated out of the previous processes (Plan Schedule Management and Define Activities). Generally, this is a recurring pattern, where outputs of one process become inputs to the next.

Organizational process assets also provide templates. Specifically, schedule network templates are generally used, which involves using templates from previous similar projects. Template version of network diagrams are then taken and tailored to the current project. This applies the concept of making efficient the assets that already exist, as well as taking into account the experience and knowledge gained from previous projects. As we did in building the activity lists, project managers may either take an entire network diagram from a previous project, or use portions of it, depending on the needs of the current project. A portion of the network diagram is referred to as a **subnetwork** or **fragment networ**k. These subnetwork templates are extremely valuable when a deliverable of the current project is identical or nearly identical to the deliverable of the previous project being used as a template. Using templates helps achieve consistency of results.

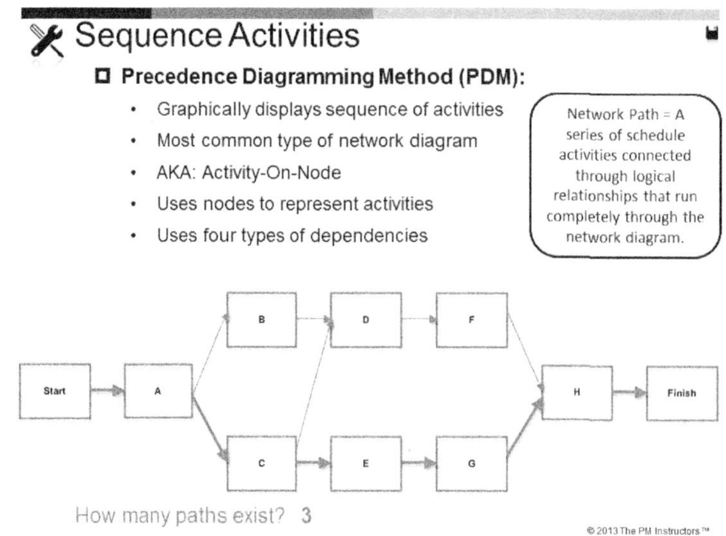

Sequence Activities Tools and Techniques

The Sequence Activities process contains three tools and techniques: *precedence diagramming method (PDM), dependency determination, and leads and lags.*

There are two network diagramming methods used: **Precedence Diagramming Method** (PDM) and **Arrow Diagramming Method** (ADM). Both types of network diagrams graphically show the sequence of activities from start to finish.

Out of the two, Precedence Diagramming Method is the most commonly used today and is the formal tool and technique of the Sequence Activities process. While they share some characteristics, there are existing differences between them, all of which you must know for exam purposes. In practice, network diagrams are compiled automatically using software, based on the information input into the program.

Precedence Diagramming Method

Precedence Diagramming Method (PDM), also known as **Activity-On-Node** (AON), identifies where the activity is shown on the diagram itself. Since this is the most commonly used type of network diagram, most modern software scheduling programs today use it to display project schedule network diagrams.

PDM uses boxes or nodes to represent the activities and connects these activities with arrows to show the logical relationships among them. Within the PDM sample diagram provided, notice that there is a start and finish to the diagram. Each box, or node, represents an activity, and by following the arrows, you can visually see the predecessor and successor activities for each individual activity. To complete the project, the project team works from left to right through the various paths of the network diagram.

Network Paths

A network path refers to a series of schedule activities that are connected through logical relationships and that run completely through the network diagram.

The sample network diagram provided contains a total of three network paths:

A-B-D-F-H　　A-C-D-F-H　　A-C-E-G-H

Dependency Types

PDM uses the following four types of dependencies, which will be discussed later within this chapter:

Finish-to-Start　　Start-to-Start　　Finish-to Finish　　Start-to-Finish

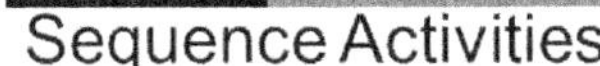

- **Arrow Diagramming Method (ADM):**
  - AKA: Activity-On-Arrow, Activity-On-Line
  - Graphically displays sequence of activities
  - Least common type of network diagram used
  - Arrows represent activities
  - Uses one type of dependency
  - Uses dummy activities

Not a tool & technique, but must know for the exam

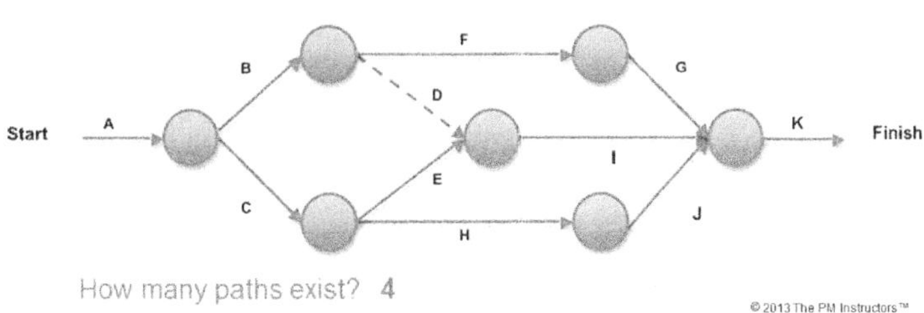

How many paths exist? 4

Arrow Diagramming Method

The Arrow Diagramming Method (ADM), also known as Activity-On-Arrow (AOA) and Activity-On-Line (AOL), identifies where the activity lies within the network diagram.

ADM is an older, less commonly used type of network diagram. It uses arrows to represent activities, and the arrows are connected by circular nodes. Within the sample ADM provided, the tail end of the arrow represents the start of the activity, while the head of the arrow represents the end of the activity. How long the arrow is has nothing to do with the duration of the activity itself.

Network Paths

The sample network diagram provided contains a total of four network paths:

A-B-F-G-K   A-B-D-I-K   A-C-E-I-K   A-C-H-J-K

Dependency Types

ADM uses only one type of dependency: Finish-to-Start.

Dummy Activities

Notice that within the sample ADM provided, there exists a dotted arrow. This is called a ***dummy* activity**. Dummy activities are not real activities, but instead, are used to show multiple dependencies between activities, and they always have a duration of zero. Dummy activities are considered when determining network paths.

Sequence Activities

Dependency Determination:

Mandatory (hard logic)	Discretionary (soft logic, preferred logic, preferential)
• Contractually or physically required. Inherent in the nature of the work	• Desired sequence based on knowledge of best practices or unusual aspect of the project
External	**Internal**
• Relationship between project activities and non-project activities from external factors	• Involve a precedence relationship between project activities and are generally inside the project team's control.

Dependency Determination

Dependency determination defines the sequence used among the activities. In some cases, this sequence is chosen by the project team, while in other cases, the sequence is required. There are three types of dependencies: mandatory, discretionary, and external.

- **Mandatory:** *Contractually or physically required. Inherent in the nature of the work.*
  Mandatory dependencies are those that are inherent in the nature of the work being done. That means that they are typically contractually required or physically required. There is no way of getting around these types of dependencies, since they are not optional. An example of a mandatory physical dependency is laying the foundation of a building before constructing the walls. *Mandatory dependencies are also known as hard logic.*

- **Discretionary:** *Desired sequence based on knowledge of best practices or unusual aspect of the project.*
  Discretionary dependencies are used when a specific sequence is desired, but is not required. This means that other sequences are acceptable. This is typically a preference of the project team, usually based on knowledge, best practices, or historical information. It can also be based on an unusual aspect of the project that calls for a specific sequence. *Discretionary dependencies are also known as soft logic, preferential logic, or preferred logic.*

- **External:** *Relationship between project activities and non-project activities from external factors.*
  External dependencies involve a relationship between project activities and non-project activities that come from external factors. These external factors are imposed outside of the project team's control. An example of this would be a law or regulation that requires a permit be obtained before the building plans can be approved. Another example is an external dependency on the shipment of parts that must arrive before another activity can begin.

- **Internal:** *Involve a precedence relationship between project activities and are generally inside the project team's control.*

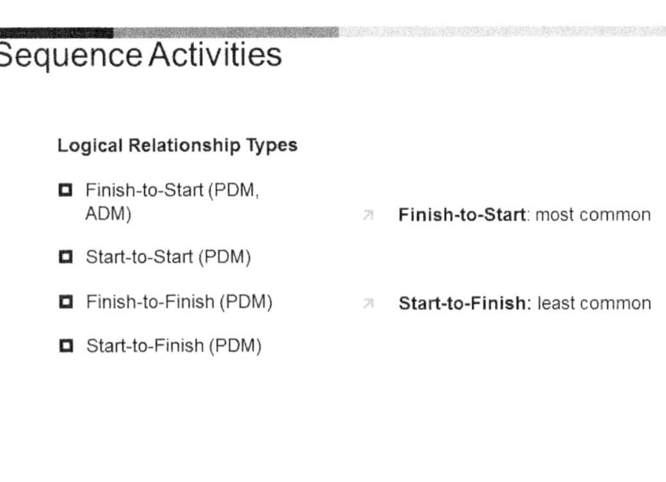

Logical Relationships

There are several logical relationships that can exist between activities, including:

- Finish-to-Start (PDM, ADM)
- Start-to-Start (PDM)
- Finish-to-Finish (PDM)
- Start-to-Finish (PDM)

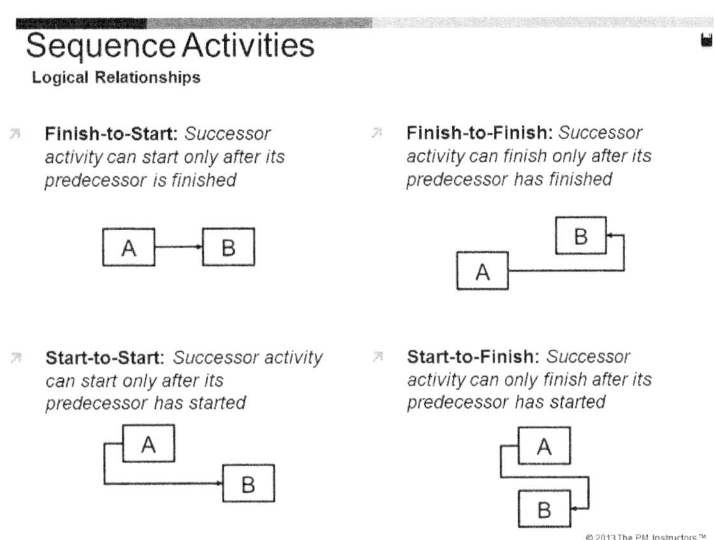

Finish-to-Start (PDM, ADM)

- *Successor activity can start only after its predecessor is finished*
- This is the **most common type** of logical relationship type, and is the only one used by both diagramming methods (PDM and ADM)

Start-to-Start (PDM)

- *Successor activity can start only after its predecessor has started*

Finish-to-Finish (PDM)

- *Successor activity can finish only after its predecessor has finished*

Start-to-Finish (PDM)

- *Successor activity can only finish after its predecessor has started*
- This is the **least used type** of logical relationship

Leads and Lags:

- **Lead:** an acceleration of the successor activity
- **Lag:** a delay in the successor activity

Leads and Lags

Lead

A lead is an acceleration of the successor activity, meaning that it begins early. The project management team determines which activities require a lead or a lag. In the example provided on the next page, activities A and B have a finish-to-start relationship, with a combined duration of 15 days. Upon adding a 4 day lead, the combined duration of both activities becomes 11.

Lag

A lag is a delay in the start of the successor activity, meaning it must wait a given amount of time before it may start. In the example provided on the next page, activities A and B have a finish-to-start relationship, with a combined duration of 11 days. Upon adding a 2 day lag, the combined duration of both activities becomes 13.

Sequence Activities

Leads and Lags:

- **Lead:** an acceleration of the successor activity
- **Lag:** a delay in the successor activity

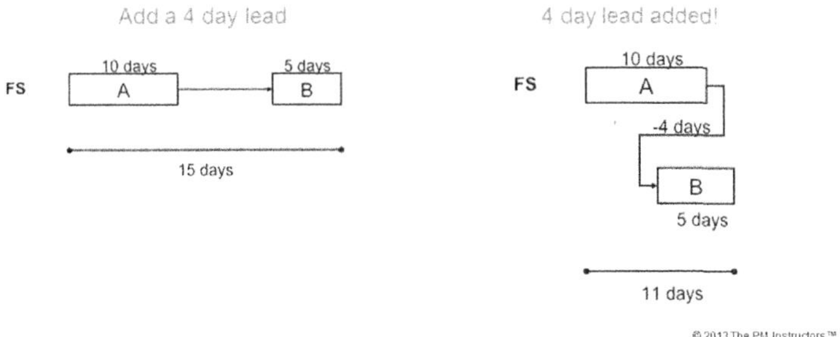

Example of Applying a Lead

In the example provided above, activities A and B have a finish-to-start relationship, with a combined duration of 15 days. Upon adding a 4 day lead, the combined duration of both activities becomes 11.

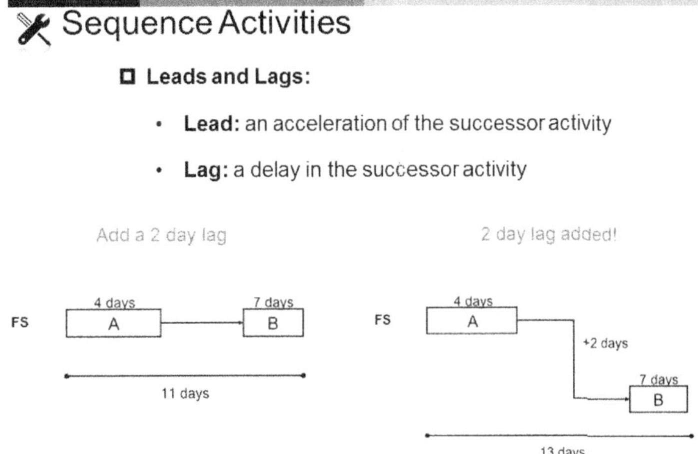

Example of Applying a Lag

In the example provided above, activities A and B have a finish-to-start relationship, with a combined duration of 11 days. Upon adding a 2 day lag, the combined duration of both activities becomes 13.

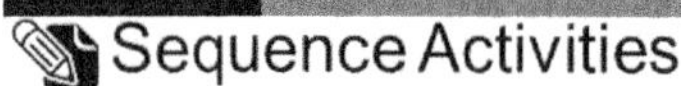
Sequence Activities

Exercise: Draw out the network diagram and identify the network paths

Activity Name	Predecessor
Activity A	Start
Activity B	A
Activity C	A
Activity D	B, C
Activity E	C
Activity F	D, E
Activity G	F

Network Diagram Exercise

Take a moment to draw out the network diagram using the table provided in the image above. The answer has been provided below.

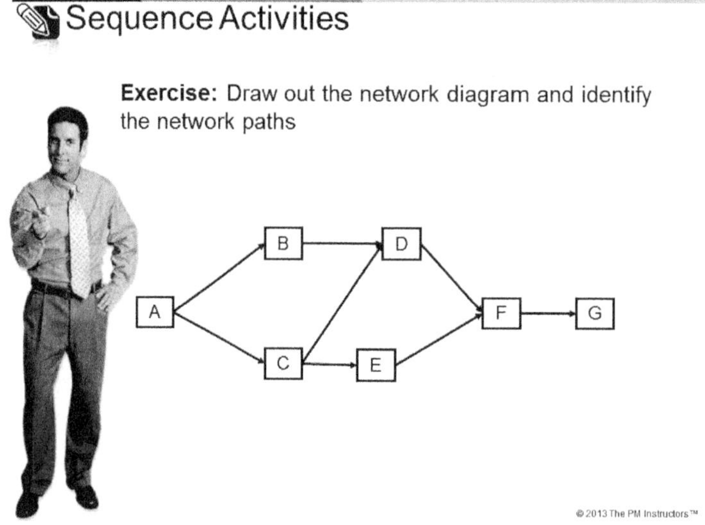
Sequence Activities
Exercise: Draw out the network diagram and identify the network paths
A
B
C
D
E
F
G
© 2013 The PM Instructors™

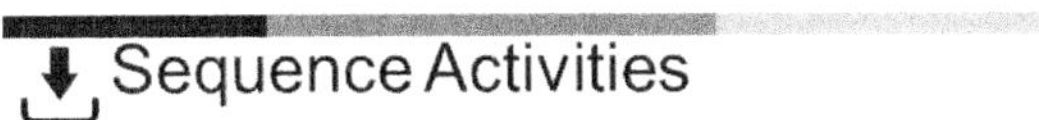

Project Schedule Network Diagrams

- Graphical graphical representation of the logical relationships among the project schedule activities
- Displays sequence of activities, dependencies, logical relationships, leads, and lags

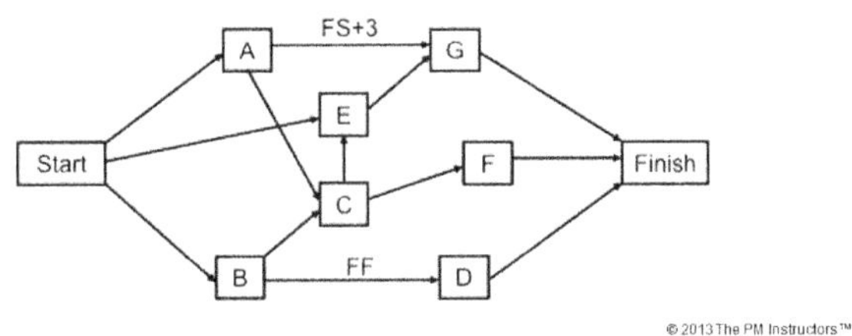

Sequence Activities Outputs

The Sequence Activities process produces the following two outputs: *project schedule network diagrams and project documents updates.*

Project Schedule Network Diagrams

The project schedule network diagram is the primary result of the Sequence Activities process. According to the *PMBOK® Guide*, the official definition of a project schedule network diagram is "a graphical representation of the logical relationships among the project schedule activities" (also referred to as dependencies).

Network diagrams can be generated manually or by using software. These network diagrams can be for the entire project, or they may summarize activities. Remember to document everything, so if there is anything unusual about the activities within the diagram to take note of, it will be recorded (including a brief description of the approach used to sequence the activities within the diagram).

Project schedule network diagram highlights:

- There are two network diagramming methods: precedence diagramming method and arrow diagramming method. PDM is the most commonly used one, and only ADM uses dummy activities.
- They are drawn from left to right and contain logical relationships among the activities, which are used to put them in the proper sequence.
- Most activities will have a finish-to-start relationship, but it's possible to have three other types in a PDM: finish-to-finish, start-to-start, and start-to-finish.
- Leads and lags should be depicted in the network diagram.
- Know how many paths exist within a network diagram, meaning how many ways you can get from the start to the finish of the diagram. In the example above, there are seven network paths.

Sequence Activities

Project Documents Updates:	• Activity list • Activity attributes • Risk register • Milestone list

Project Documents Updates

After completing a process, updated may be required to project documents. The documents impacted will be fairly intuitive.

Generally, project documents refer to all documents created within a project that is not considered to be a part of the project management plan (the project management plan primarily consists of management plans and baselines).

Of the project documents, the ones most likely to require updates after carrying out the Sequence Activities process includes:

1. The activity lists
2. The activity attributes (which document the predecessor and successor relationships, constraints, and other details about the activities)
3. Risk register (contains the list of project risks that have been identified, and all information accrued about them to date)
4. Milestone list

Estimate Activity Resources
Purpose: To estimate the type and quantities of material, human resources, equipment, or supplies required to perform each activity.

Estimate Activity Resources Process Overview

The purpose of the Estimate Activity Resources process is to estimate the type and quantities of material, human resources, equipment, or supplies required to perform each activity. While pre-assignments may exist, staff assignments are not added into the schedule within this process. Along the same lines, the type and quantity of resources may be impacted by the availability of existing resource (for example: if a senior developer is needed, but not available, you may settle for two junior developers). The same applies to equipment.

Note that multiple project management processes may occur in parallel. For instance, this process works hand-in-hand with the Estimate Costs process, since the two processes may influence each other.

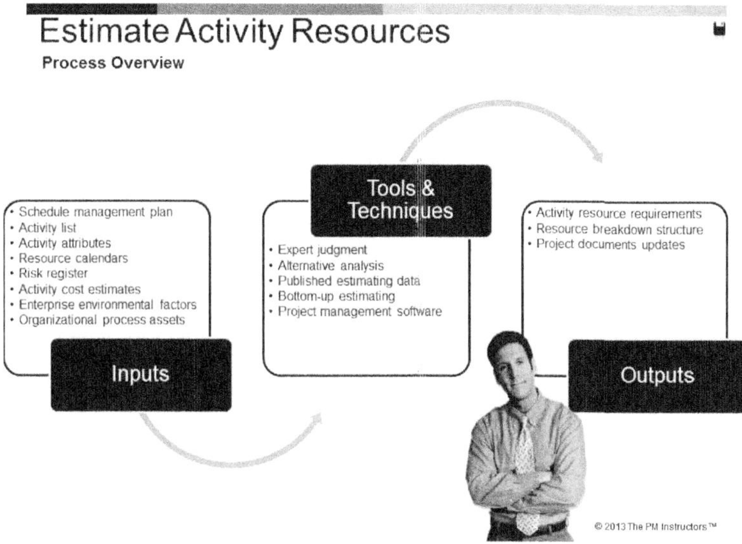
Estimate Activity Resources
Process Overview
• Schedule management plan
• Activity list
• Activity attributes
• Resource calendars
• Risk register
• Activity cost estimates
• Enterprise environmental factors
• Organizational process assets
Inputs
Tools & Techniques
• Expert judgment
• Alternative analysis
• Published estimating data
• Bottom-up estimating
• Project management software
• Activity resource requirements
• Resource breakdown structure
• Project documents updates
Outputs
© 2013 The PM Instructors™

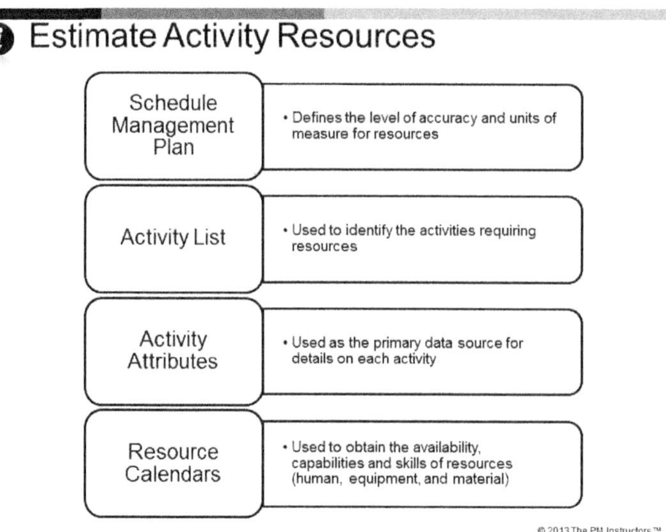

Estimate Activity Resources Inputs

The Estimate Activity Resources process contains the following eight inputs: *schedule management plan, activity list, activity attributes, resource calendars, risk register, activity cost estimates, enterprise environmental factors, and organizational process assets.*

Schedule Management Plan

The schedule management plan defines how the process will be carried out. It also documents the level of accuracy and units of measure for resources to be estimated.

Activity List

The activity list provides the list of activities (or effort) needed to result in the project deliverables, and represents 100% of the work (unless rolling wave planning is used).

Activity Attributes

Activity attributes extends the description of the activities by defining and identifying all of the components that are related to each activity. It includes specific information that continues to be added about the activities. Each time management related process will continue to add information to the activity attributes.

Resource Calendars

Resource calendars include availability of various types of resources, such as people, equipment, and material resources. This may refer to the use of a master calendar or multiple resource calendars. Although listed separately, resource calendars are tied into enterprise environmental factors.

A *composite resource calendar* includes the following:

- Availability
- Capabilities
- Skills of human resources

When considering people resources, the resource calendars should take into account the geography of the individuals, any vacation scheduled, holidays, company non-working days, etc.

Estimate Activity Resources

Risk Register	• Provides the list of identified risks, which may impact the type and quantity of resources selected
Activity Cost Estimates	• Provides the cost estimates of activities, which may impact the type and quantity of resources selected
Enterprise Environmental Factors	• Used to determine what may impact or influence resource availability and skills
Organizational Process Assets	• Used to obtain historical project information, as well as policies and procedures relating to staffing, rentals, and purchasing

Risk Register

The risk register contains the list of risks identified throughout the project, and is created through the Identify Risks process. Risks may impact the type and quantity of resources selected.

Activity Cost Estimates

The Estimate Activity Resources process works in conjunction with the Estimate Costs process, which produces the activity cost estimates. The cost estimates may impact the type and quantity of resources selected to perform the activities *Keep in mind that these are iterative processes.*

Enterprise Environmental Factors

Enterprise environmental factors refer to internal and external environmental factors that influence the success of the project. Specifically, our focus will be on anything that may impact or influence resource availability and skills.

Organizational Process Assets

Organizational process assets are assets belonging to the organizations involved in the project that influence the project's success. Specifically for this process, our focus will be the policies and procedures in relation to staffing, policies and procedures regarding rental and purchase of supplies and equipment, and any historical information that we can use, particularly for past similar projects.

Estimate Activity Resources

- **Expert Judgment:**
  - The application of expertise and knowledge provided within a specific knowledge area, discipline, or industry
  - Information comes from those with experience and knowledge of the work
- **Alternative Analysis:**
  - The consideration of what other options exist in carrying out an activity

Estimate Activity Resources Tools and Techniques

The Estimate Activity Resources process utilizes the following five tools and techniques: *expert judgment, alternative analysis, published estimating data, bottom-up estimating, and project management software.*

Expert Judgment

Expert judgment refers to the application of expertise provided by an organization, team members, consultants, subject matter experts, etc, within a specific knowledge area, discipline, or industry. In relation to this process, the focus is on individuals or groups with experience in resource planning or estimating.

Alternative Analysis

Alternatives analysis considers what other options exist in carrying out an activity. For instance, if the activity consists of writing code, what programming language will be used and should the resource include a junior or a senior developer? If considering equipment, you may ask yourself whether it makes more sense to lease, rent, or buy.

In some cases, these decisions can be bigger than the project itself. For instance, perhaps the purchase of a machine will benefit multiple projects, as opposed to renting the equipment for this project alone. In this case, the cost of the machine is allocated in a different way, so as to not weight the full burden of the cost to the project.

Estimate Activity Resources

- **Published Estimating Data:**
  - Published data that can be used to estimate resource types and quantities needed
  - Typical data used: production rates or unit costs of resources
- **Bottom-Up Estimating:**
  - The further decomposition of an activity for estimating purposes
  - Used when there is not enough information available to confidently estimate

Published Estimating Data

Published estimating data, such as results of research, can be used in estimating the type and quantities of resources. This may include production rates or unit costs of resources that relate to the project activities. This will provide an idea of how long an activity may take or how much you can expect to pay resources. Be wary of using information that is not current or authentic data.

Bottom-Up Estimating

Bottom-up estimating is an estimating technique that is considered to be fairly high in accuracy, but time consuming and costly to perform. In some cases, there will not be sufficient information available to confidently estimate an activity. When this occurs, you may choose to further decompose an activity in order to more accurately estimate the resources needed. Once this is done, the decomposed components of the activity will be aggregated to the original activity level in order to determine the resources needed.

Using bottom-up estimating requires collecting a significant amount of detail about the decomposed components. This type of technique may also be used when a definitive estimate is required, which involves a high level of accuracy. Naturally, the more detailed the activity is broken into, the more accurate the overall estimate will be.

This technique is also used in the Estimate Costs process.

Estimate Activity Resources

Project Management Software: Used to plan, organize, and manage:

- Resource calendars
- Resource breakdown structures
- Resource rates

Increases:
accuracy
organization
accessibility

Project Management Software

The use of software simplifies and expedites our work. Many times, it also increases the level of accuracy, organization, and data accessibility. Coordinating the resource type and quantities requires the use of several pieces of information in conjunction with each other, so the software will help to plan, organize, and manage resource calendars, resource breakdown structures, resource rates, and other resource elements in real-time.

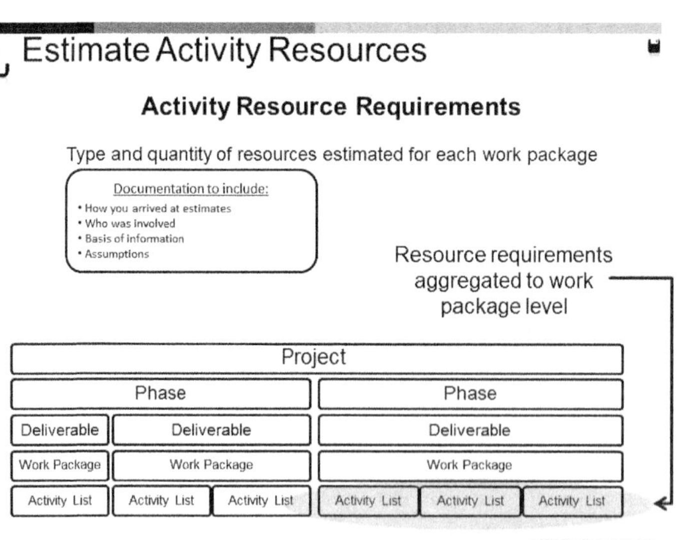
Estimate Activity Resources
Activity Resource Requirements
Type and quantity of resources estimated for each work package
Documentation to include:
• How you arrived at estimates
• Who was involved
• Basis of information
• Assumptions
Resource requirements aggregated to work package level
Project
Phase
Phase
Deliverable
Deliverable
Deliverable
Work Package
Work Package
Work Package
Activity List
Activity List
Activity List
Activity List
Activity List
Activity List
© 2013 The PM Instructors™

Estimate Activity Resources Outputs

The Estimate Activity Resources process produces three outputs: *activity resource requirements, resource breakdown structure, project documents updates.*

Activity Resource Requirements

Activity resource requirements is the primary output of the Estimate Activity Resources process. Among the most important elements of this output are the types and the quantities of resources that are required for each activity in a work package. These requirements can either be presented individually per activity, or aggregated per work package. The amount of detail needed depends on the project.

Documentation as part of this output should include things such as: how you arrived at the type and quantity of resource estimates, who was involved, and the basis for the information used to arrive at the estimates. The basis for assumptions should also be documented, including the types of resources, the availability of resources, and the quantities needed that are based on assumptions.

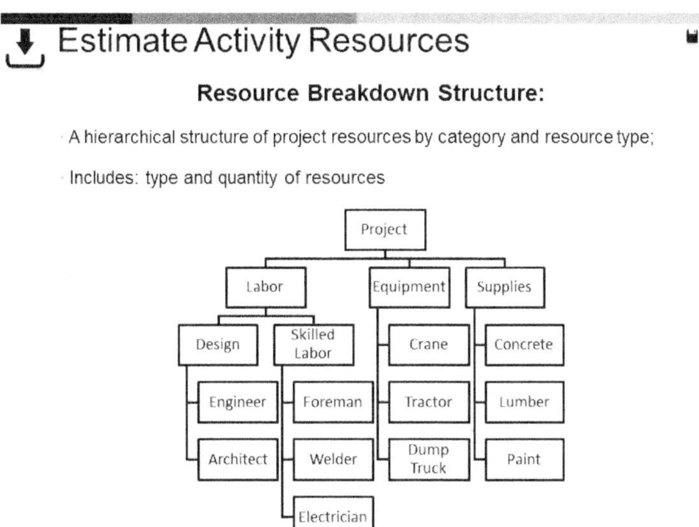

Resource Breakdown Structure

Resource breakdown structures provide a graphical, hierarchical view of the resource categories used in the project, as well as the number of resources. It reflects the type and quantities of resources outlined in the first output of this process.

Common categories used include labor, material, equipment and supplies. Within each of these categories, you can then elaborate on the type of resources needed, such as by skill level, grade level, or in a type that applies to your specific project.

Estimate Activity Resources

Project Documents Updates

Typical updates include:
- Activity list
- Activity attributes
- Resource calendars

Project Documents Updates

According to the *PMBOK® Guide*, the project documents that will most likely require updates as a result of carrying out the process, include:

- **Activity List:** After determining the type and quantity of resources, there can be a change to one or several of the identified activities.
- **Activity Attributes:** Activity attributes would require the greatest amount of updates. Resource requirements for each activity would be updated within the attributes.
- **Resource Calendars:** A resource calendar is defined as a calendar that reflects the working days and nonworking days of resources. This feeds into the project calendar. Although in this process we're not making resource-specific assignments, there will be many cases where there is only one of a specific resource, particularly if it is a resource with a specialized skill. The same for equipment. In these cases, you may need to update the resource calendars to reflect their use in the project. This may occur concurrently with actual resource assignments, which is a process that takes place in the human resource knowledge area and that we'll cover next.

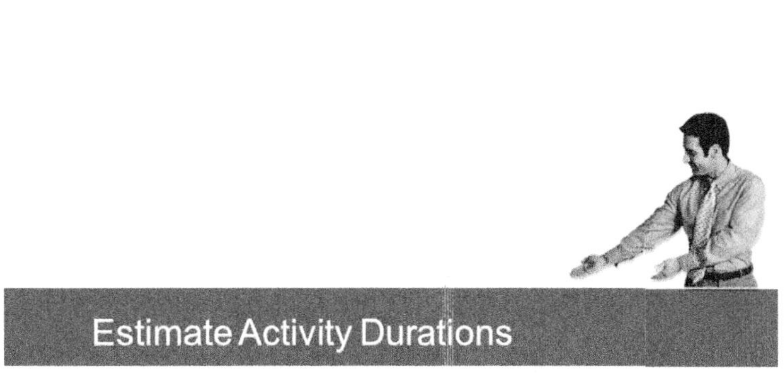
Estimate Activity Durations
Purpose: To estimate the number of work periods needed to complete individual activities with estimated resources.

Estimate Activity Durations Process Overview

Estimate Activity Durations is the fifth process of the Project Time Management Knowledge Area. The purpose of the process is to estimate the number of work periods needed to complete individual activities with the estimated resources (estimate durations). Estimating the activity durations is the final piece of information needed to begin generating the project schedule. Information used to estimate durations includes:

- The activity scope of work
- The required resource types
- The estimated resource quantities
- And the resource calendars

Much of this information is derived through feedback from experts that have knowledge of the work being performed, which should be carefully documented. There are two things to consider throughout this process:

1. Quality of the data available
2. Estimates can be progressively elaborated

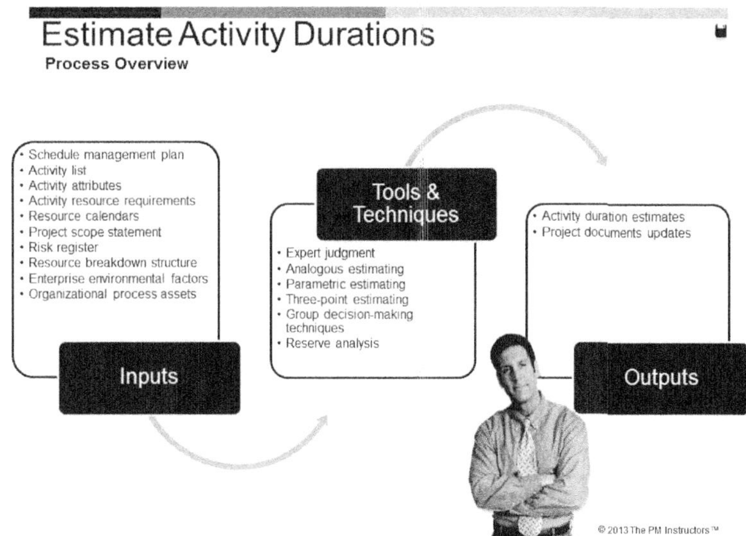
Estimate Activity Durations
Process Overview
• Schedule management plan
• Activity list
• Activity attributes
• Activity resource requirements
• Resource calendars
• Project scope statement
• Risk register
• Resource breakdown structure
• Enterprise environmental factors
• Organizational process assets
Inputs
Tools & Techniques
• Expert judgment
• Analogous estimating
• Parametric estimating
• Three-point estimating
• Group decision-making techniques
• Reserve analysis
• Activity duration estimates
• Project documents updates
Outputs
© 2013 The PM Instructors™

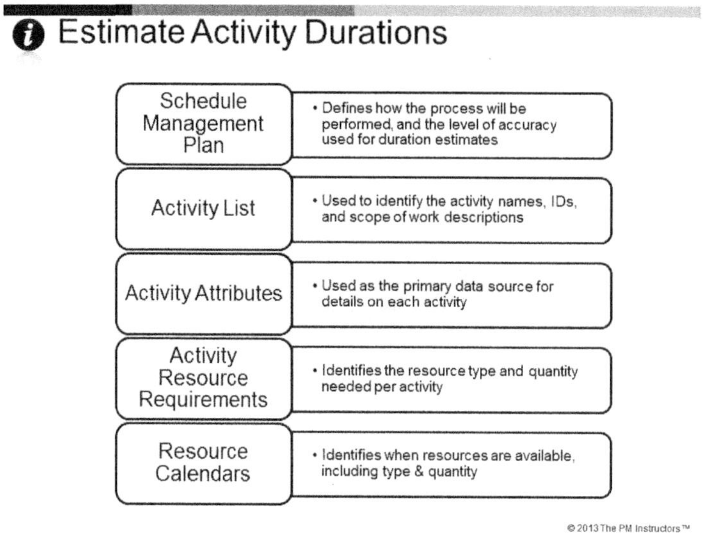

Estimate Activity Durations

Schedule Management Plan	• Defines how the process will be performed, and the level of accuracy used for duration estimates
Activity List	• Used to identify the activity names, IDs, and scope of work descriptions
Activity Attributes	• Used as the primary data source for details on each activity
Activity Resource Requirements	• Identifies the resource type and quantity needed per activity
Resource Calendars	• Identifies when resources are available, including type & quantity

Estimate Activity Durations Inputs

The Estimate Activity Durations process utilizes ten inputs: *schedule management plan, activity list, activity attributes, activity resource requirements, resource calendars, project scope statement, risk register, resource breakdown structure, enterprise environmental factors, and organizational process assets.*

Schedule Management Plan

The schedule management plan defines how the process will be carried out, and the level of accuracy that is to be used when estimating activity durations.

Activity List

The activity list contains the name, ID, and scope of work description for each activity.

Activity Attributes

The activity attributes contain all the documented information about each activity to date. Information of interest to this process includes: resource requirements, constraints, assumptions, leads and lags.

Activity Resource Requirements

Activity resource requirements include the resource type and quantity needed per activity.

Resource Calendars

Resource calendars detail when resources are available, including the type and capabilities of the human resources, and the type, quantity and capability of equipment and materials resources.

Estimate Activity Durations

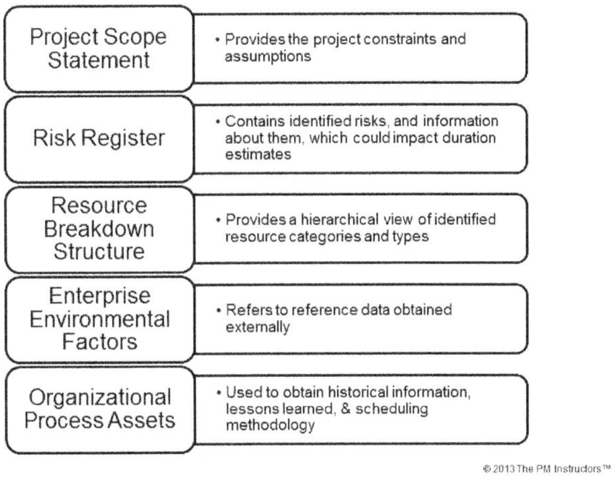

Input	Description
Project Scope Statement	• Provides the project constraints and assumptions
Risk Register	• Contains identified risks, and information about them, which could impact duration estimates
Resource Breakdown Structure	• Provides a hierarchical view of identified resource categories and types
Enterprise Environmental Factors	• Refers to reference data obtained externally
Organizational Process Assets	• Used to obtain historical information, lessons learned, & scheduling methodology

Project Scope Statement

The project scope statement contains a description of the project's scope of work, the list of deliverables, and the constraints and assumptions. In estimating the activity durations, our primary interest is the constraints and assumptions of the project, which can impact the duration estimates.

Risk Register

The risk register contains the list of risks identified to date, and all the information documented about them. This information may impact the duration estimates of activities.

Resource Breakdown Structure

The resource breakdown structure provides a hierarchical view of the resource categories and resource types, which were determined in the previous process – Estimate Activity Resources.

Enterprise Environmental Factors

Enterprise environmental factors include reference data that can be obtained externally, such as through information published commercially, reference databases that include duration estimates, and productivity metrics. Previous reference data is very useful in conjunction with expert judgment.

Organizational Process Assets

Organizational process assets provide historical information pertaining to durations, lessons learned, the scheduling methodology, and project calendars. Project calendars identify the days that activities are being worked on, and also non-working days.

Estimate Activity Durations

Expert Judgment:

- The application of expertise and knowledge provided within a specific knowledge area, discipline, or industry
- Information comes from those with experience and knowledge of the work

- What estimating technique works best?
- Which combination of techniques should be used?
- Who are the ideal individuals that will be involved in calculating the duration estimates?

Estimate Activity Durations Tools and Techniques

The Estimate Activity Durations process has a total of six tools and techniques, which are as follow: *expert judgment, analogous estimating, parametric estimating, three-point estimating, group decision-making techniques, and reserve analysis.*

Expert Judgment

Expert judgment refers to feedback and input from those familiar with the work, which is necessary to compile duration estimates that are usable and as accurate as possible.

The use of historical information is guided by experts to determine the duration estimates. Typically, historical information is used by experts and the project manager in combination with several estimating techniques.

In addition to feedback from experts familiar with the work, expert judgment also includes experts that understand the estimating process itself. These individuals (which may include only the project manager) answer questions such as:

- What estimating technique works best?
- Which combination of techniques should be used?
- Who are the ideal individuals that will be involved in calculating the duration estimates?

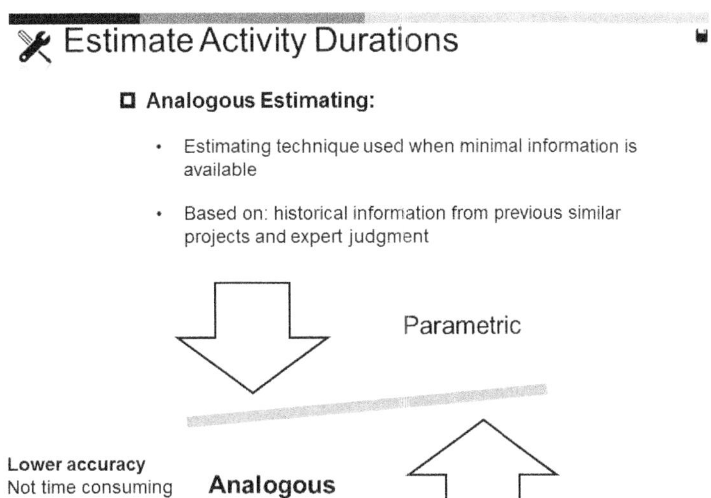

There are several estimating techniques that can be used to estimate activity durations. Each of these estimating techniques offers varying accuracy levels, benefits, and timing as to when they can be used.

Analogous Estimating

Analogous estimating is an estimating technique that can be used early on within a project (even as early as the initiating phase) and requires that only minimal information be known about the activities. Analogous estimating is based primarily on historical information from past *similar* projects used in combination with expert judgment. How reliable these estimates are is based strictly on how similar the past project information is to the current project.

Because analogous estimating is based on information from project archives, it is not considered to be a time consuming technique (this technique assumes that archives exist). As a result of this, it is also not considered to be costly.

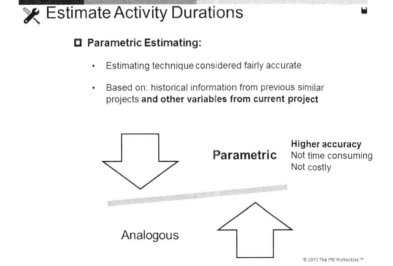

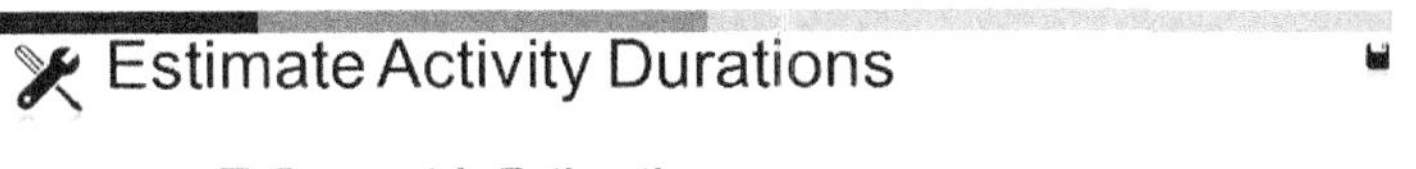

Parametric Estimating:

- Estimating technique considered fairly accurate
- Based on: historical information from previous similar projects **and other variables from current project**

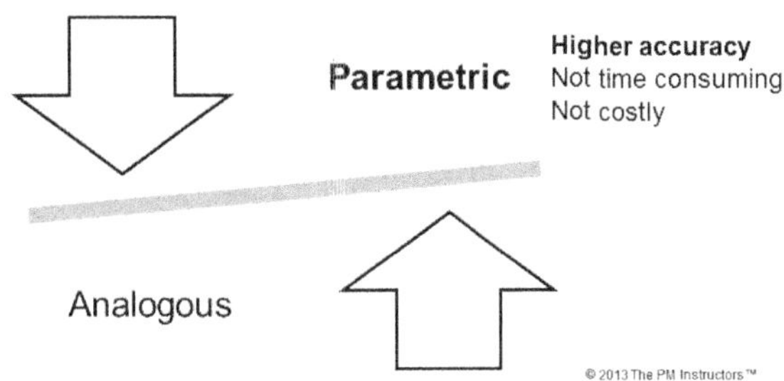

Parametric Estimating

Parametric estimating is an estimating technique that is considered to be fairly accurate, time-efficient, and low cost. Like analogous estimating, it uses historical information from past similar projects, but it also adds in the use of other variables taken from the current project. These other variables may include details such as actual square footage, labor hours, and so forth.

Like analogous estimating, the true level of accuracy lies with the quality of the data being used – and that will be impacted by the similarity of the historical projects. Parametric estimates can be used to estimate durations on an activity level, a segment of the project, or the entire project as a whole.

Because of its level of efficiency and accuracy, parametric estimating is a desirable technique to use when possible, but one that may not be viable during the very early stages of a project when specific project variables are unknown.

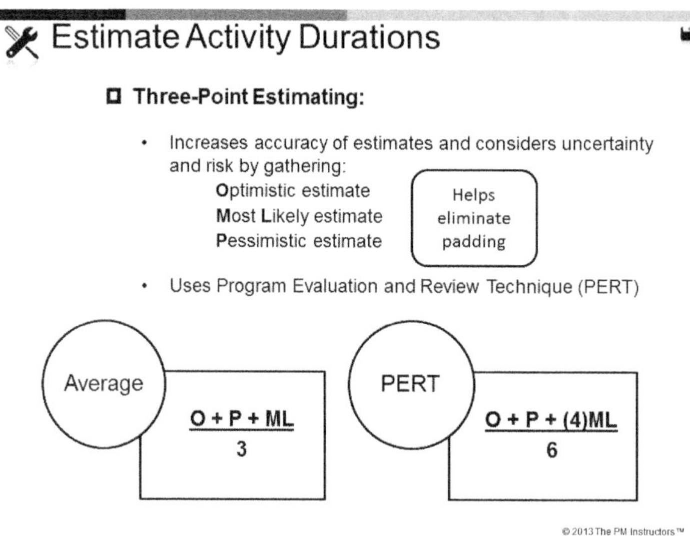

Three-Point Estimating

Three point estimates is an estimating technique used that helps increase the accuracy of duration estimates by considering two things: uncertainty and risk. Three point estimates involve obtaining three types of estimates for an activity's duration:

- **Optimistic** estimate: the fastest an activity can take to complete; a best-case scenario.
- **Most likely** estimate: a realistic estimate; literally the "likely" estimate based on the assigned resources, their productivity, and realistic expectations.
- **Pessimistic** estimate: the longest that an activity can take to complete; a worst-case scenario.

These three estimates show the potential range of an activity's duration. The wider the range, the bigger the uncertainty, and therefore the higher risk involved with that activity. The idea is that we are incorporating uncertainty into the duration estimate.

There are two ways of using this information:

1. As a simple average, where the three estimates are added together and divided by three. *Using three-point estimates helps eliminate padding* (padding estimates is not considered positive). Padding is when an expert inflates an estimate.

2. As a weighted average using the Program Evaluation and Review Technique (PERT). This technique generates an approximate range for an activity's duration by using a weighted average, and giving a higher weight to the "most likely" estimate. The PERT formula is:

   Optimistic + Pessimistic + (4 x Most Likely) / 6

   PERT calculates an estimate with higher accuracy by considering all three scenarios (optimistic, pessimistic, and most likely), but giving a higher weight to the most realistic scenario.

Estimate Activity Durations

Group Decision-Making Techniques

- Involves team-based approaches
- Examples: *brainstorming, Delphi, nominal group techniques*
- Involving experts gets their buy-in and commitment

Group Decision-Making Techniques

When estimating durations, decision techniques will be used often. The *PMBOK® Guide* references team-based approaches as those used most often for duration estimating, including brainstorming, Delphi or nominal group techniques.

A key idea in using these techniques is to incorporate the feedback of the experts that will be performing the work. This gets their buy-in and commitment to achieving work within the estimates.

Estimate Activity Durations
Reserve Analysis:
*Reserve: "A provision in the project management plan to mitigate cost and / or schedule risk."; Time Reserve / Buffer
Reserve Analysis: Adding contingency reserves into the duration estimates to account for existing uncertainty
Tend to be higher at the beginning of the project
Contingency Reserve vs. Management Reserve
Amount of time or cost needed above an estimate to reduce risk of project objective overruns.
Meant to deal with known-unknown scenarios.
Budgets set aside for unplanned changes to scope and cost.
Meant to deal with unknown-unknown scenarios.
* Definition from A Guide to the Project Management Body of Knowledge. Project Management Institute Inc., 2013
© 2013 The PM Instructors™

Reserve Analysis

There are two types of reserves, although only one pertains to the schedule: contingency reserves and management reserves.

A contingency reserve is the amount of funds or time needed above an estimate to reduce the risk of project objectives overrun – the reserve brings that risk down to a level that is acceptable by the organization. A management reserve is relevant to the budget only, and includes cost reserves set aside for unplanned changes to scope and cost.

As duration estimates are compiled, there may be a need to add in contingency reserves into the project schedule to account for existing uncertainty (uncertainty will be further addressed later on within this book). How contingency reserves are calculated vary by company, but may include:

- as a percentage of the durations
- as a fixed number of work periods
- through quantitative calculations

Because contingencies are tied into uncertainty and risk, they tend to be higher towards the beginning of the project. As more information becomes available, or as the number of active risks within the risk register gets smaller, contingency reserve will also be reduced or eliminated – this is because either they have been used, or information has become more precise and the reserves are no longer needed.

Remember to document everything!

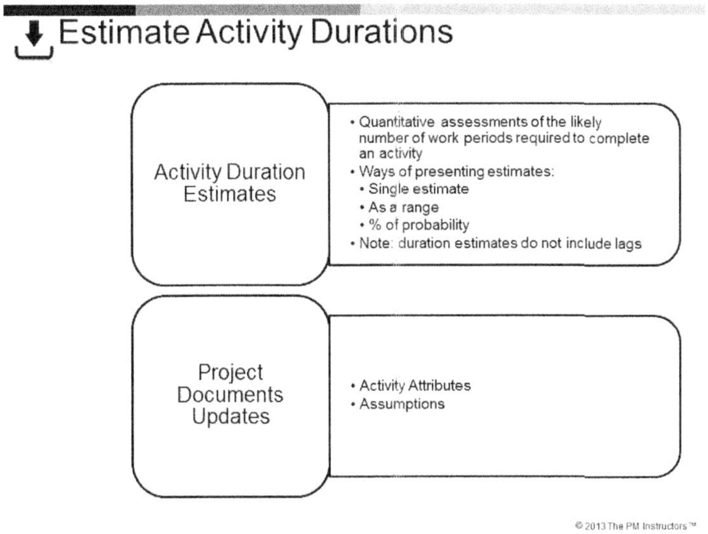

Estimate Activity Durations

Activity Duration Estimates	• Quantitative assessments of the likely number of work periods required to complete an activity • Ways of presenting estimates: • Single estimate • As a range • % of probability • Note: duration estimates do not include lags
Project Documents Updates	• Activity Attributes • Assumptions

Estimate Activity Durations Outputs

The Estimate Activity Durations process produces two outputs: *activity duration estimates and project documents updates.*

Activity Duration Estimates

According to the *PMBOK® Guide*, activity duration estimates are considered to be quantitative assessments of the likely number of work periods required to complete an activity. Literally, it is the duration estimate of each activity.

There are various ways of presenting duration estimates. One way is by providing a single duration estimate per activity. There will be times where a range is appropriate instead, which is another way of presenting durations. In this case, a duration may be presented with the addition of a + / - (example: duration of 10 days +/- 2 days). Another way of presenting duration estimates is by using percentage of probability (example: activity A has a 20% probability of finishing greater than 10 days, and 80% probability of finishing in 10 days or less).

The *PMBOK® Guide* specifically notes that lags are not included within duration estimates. So while they will be taken into account in the overall duration of the project when the schedule is developed, they are not reflected within the individual activity durations as part of this output.

Project Documents Updates

According to the *PMBOK® Guide*, project documents that are most likely to require updates as a result of carrying out the Estimate Activity Durations process include: Activity Attributes: updated to reflect the duration estimates per activity; Assumptions: updated to reflect any assumptions made about the activity when compiling duration estimates, such as skill levels and availability.

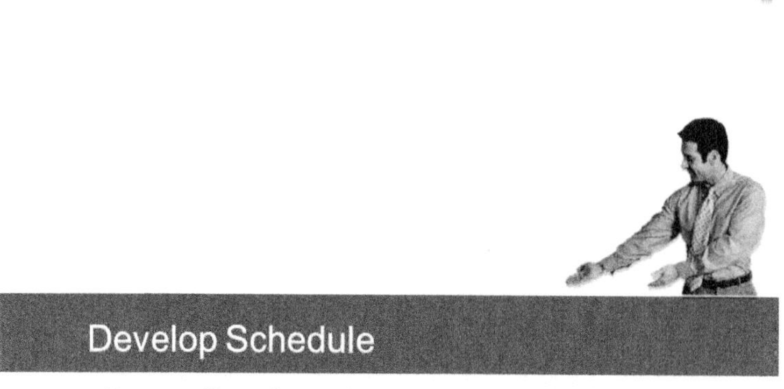
Develop Schedule

Purpose: To analyze activity sequences, durations, resource requirements, and schedule constraints to create the project schedule model.

Develop Schedule Process Overview

The Develop Schedule process is the sixth Planning related process of the Project Time Management Knowledge Area. In this process, the primary result will be the creation of the project schedule, making use of everything created to-date within this Knowledge Area. In order to do this, the process will analyze activity sequences, durations, resource requirements, and schedule constraints.

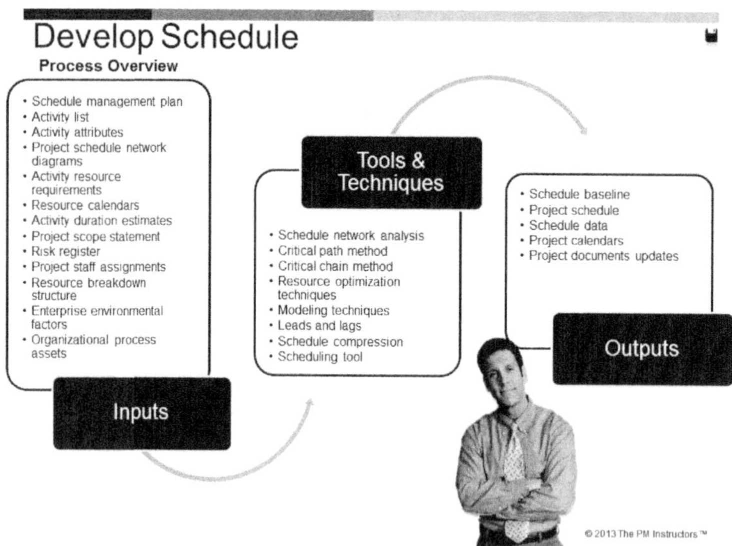
Develop Schedule
Process Overview
• Schedule management plan
• Activity list
• Activity attributes
• Project schedule network diagrams
• Activity resource requirements
• Resource calendars
• Activity duration estimates
• Project scope statement
• Risk register
• Project staff assignments
• Resource breakdown structure
• Enterprise environmental factors
• Organizational process assets
Inputs
Tools & Techniques
• Schedule network analysis
• Critical path method
• Critical chain method
• Resource optimization techniques
• Modeling techniques
• Leads and lags
• Schedule compression
• Scheduling tool
• Schedule baseline
• Project schedule
• Schedule data
• Project calendars
• Project documents updates
Outputs
© 2013 The PM Instructors ™

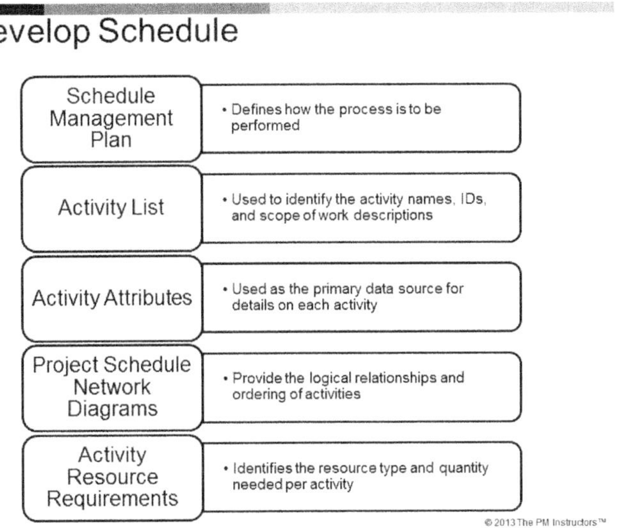

Develop Schedule Inputs

The Develop Schedule process utilizes the following thirteen inputs: *schedule management plan, activity list, activity attributes, project schedule network diagrams, activity resource requirements, resource calendars, activity duration estimates, project scope statement, risk register, project staff assignments, resource breakdown structure, enterprise environmental factors, and organizational process assets.*

Schedule Management Plan

The schedule management plan guides the team in performing the process.

Activity List

The activity list provides the activity name, ID, and brief description of the scope of work for each activity identified.

Activity Attributes

Activity attributes contains all of the documented details and information about each activity. The attributes continue to evolve as more information about each activity is known and documented.

Project Schedule Network Diagrams

Project schedule network diagrams were created out of the Sequence Activities process, and contain the logical relationships and ordering of activities. The activity dependencies are noted here, although for discretionary dependencies, this order may change as the schedule is developed.

Activity Resource Requirements

Activity resource requirements provides the type and quantity of resources needed to complete each individual activity. This was created out of the Estimate Activity Resources process.

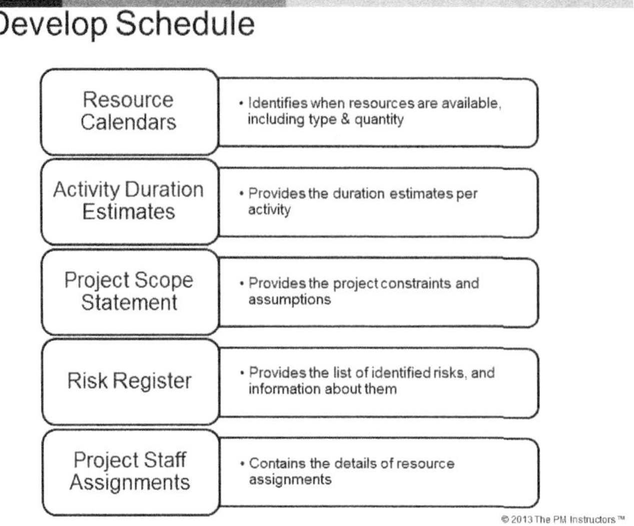

Resource Calendars

Resource calendars include the type, availability and capabilities of human resources, and type, quantity, availability, and capability of equipment and material resources.

Activity Duration Estimates

Activity duration estimates are created out of the Estimate Activity Durations process. This input contains the duration estimates for each activity, which can be presented in a number of ways: as exact durations per activity, as ranges, or as percentage of probability.

Project Scope Statement

The project scope statement contains several key project details. To develop the schedule, the primary interest will be in the constraints and assumptions of the project, which may impact the development of the project schedule.

Risk Register

The risk register contains the identified risks, and the information about them. This becomes a valuable input that allows the project management team to account for risks within the schedule model, and is used when performing schedule simulations.

Project Staff Assignments

Project staff assignments are made through the Project Human Resource Management Knowledge Area. As resources are assigned, they are fed into this process as an input, so that they may be accounted for within the schedule.

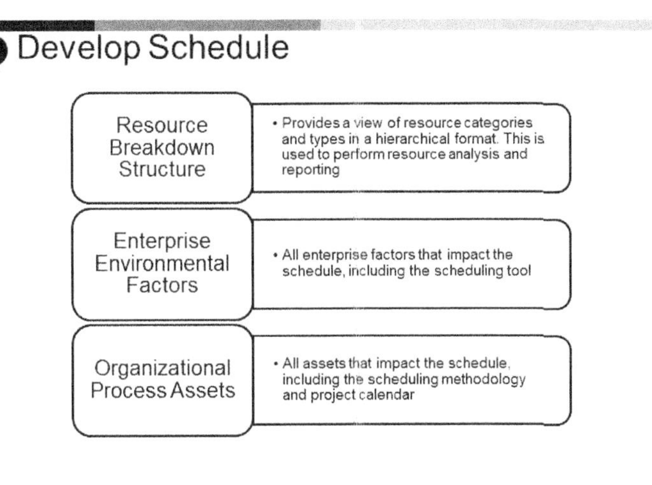

Resource Breakdown Structure

The resource breakdown structure contains the resource categories and resource types, displayed in a hierarchical format. This allows the team to perform resource analysis and reporting.

Enterprise Environmental Factors

Enterprise environmental factors used in this process include those factors that impact the creation of the schedule, particularly a scheduling tool that can be used to put together all of these inputs in order to generate the schedule.

Organizational Process Assets

Organizational process assets used in this process include: lessons learned and historical information, with a special interest in the scheduling methodology and the project calendar.

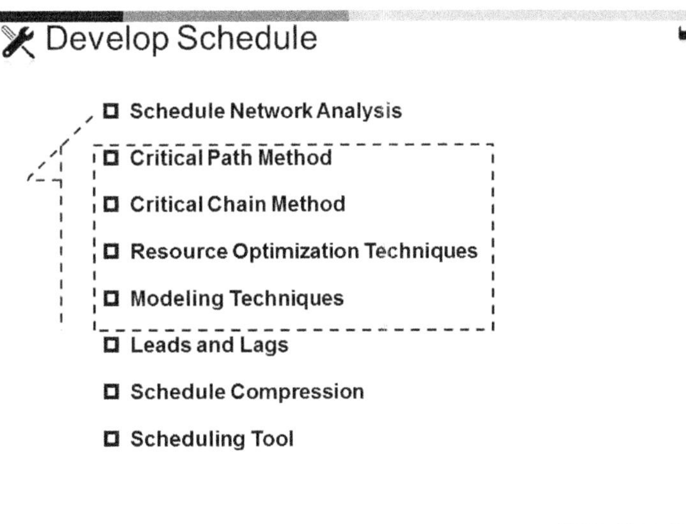

Develop Schedule Tools and Techniques

The Develop Schedule process consists of the following eight tools and techniques: *schedule network analysis, critical path method, critical chain method, resource optimization techniques, modeling techniques, leads and lags, schedule compression, and scheduling tool.*

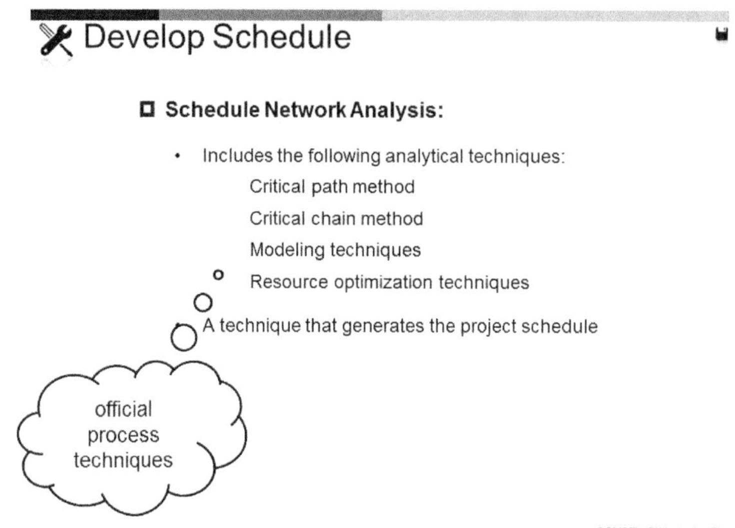

Schedule Network Analysis

Schedule network analysis, consists of the four tools and techniques listed directly below it within the process's introduction: critical path method, critical chain method, resource leveling, and what-if scenario analysis.

This single tool and technique, which encompasses these other analytical techniques, is *what generates the project schedule*.

Develop Schedule

Critical Path Method:

- **Critical Path:** the longest path through the project schedule
- **Near Critical Path:** the second longest path through the project schedule
- **Critical Activity:** activities that fall on the critical path
- **Critical Path Methodology:** calculates the amount of scheduling flexibility using a **forward pass** and **backward pass**

Critical Path Method

The *critical path* is the longest path through the project schedule network diagram. Since it is also the longest path through the project, it typically represents the overall project duration. The critical path is important because it contains zero flexibility within the activities that lie on the critical path itself. It is possible to have more than one critical path. This occurs when there are multiple network paths that share the longest duration.

Critical activities refer to activities that fall on the critical path. These activities are important to identify – when a critical activity is delayed, the entire project is delayed.

In order to understand the critical path and how to calculate it, you must first feel comfortable drawing out a network diagram by hand. Complete the following exercise, which requires that you draw out a network diagram from the information provided.

Develop Schedule

Exercise: Draw out the network diagram and identify the network paths

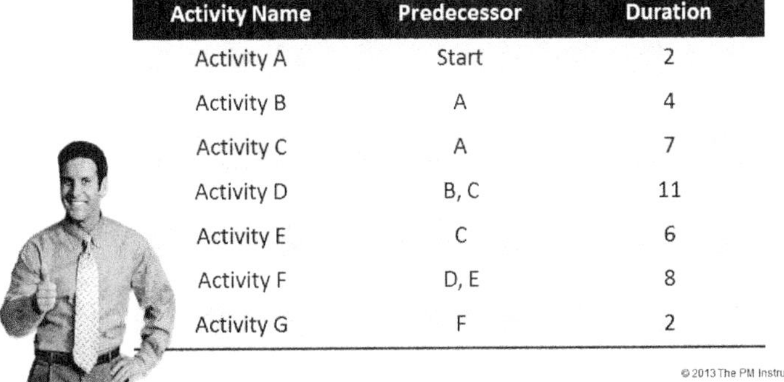

Activity Name	Predecessor	Duration
Activity A	Start	2
Activity B	A	4
Activity C	A	7
Activity D	B, C	11
Activity E	C	6
Activity F	D, E	8
Activity G	F	2

To draw out the network diagram, begin with a "start" node and connect each activity according to its predecessor listed in the chart above. Use the Precedence Diagramming Method (PDM) unless instructed otherwise. While the PMP exam contains a multiple choice question exam, you will be required to draw out network diagrams on your scratch sheet of paper to answer some questions.

In the exam, you may be presented with something that looks like the chart provided previously, or this information may instead be embedded within an exam question through a text description.

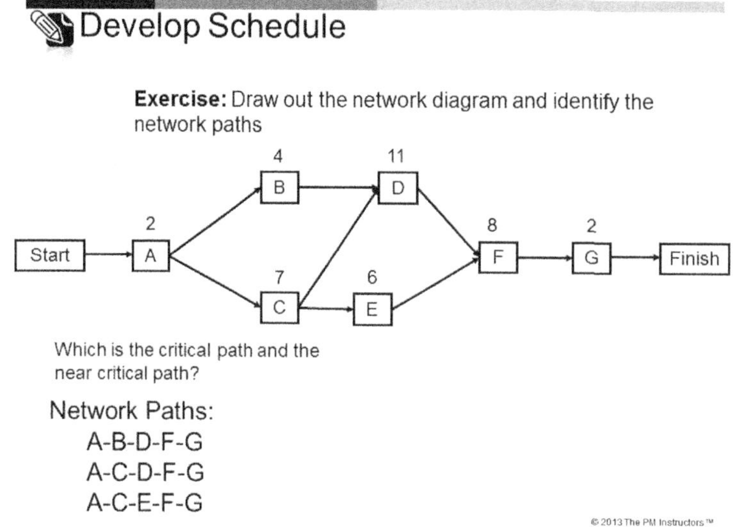

Which is the critical path? A-C-D-F-G

Which is the near-critical path? A-B-D-F-G

Note that your diagram may appear slightly differently. This is normal, as long as the logical relationships are the same. After drawing out the network diagram, notice that there are three network paths, which refers to the number of paths or ways to get through the network diagram, from start to finish. To calculate the critical path, you will need to first add the duration of each activity that falls within a path to get the total duration of each individual path. Network path durations have been provided above. The critical path will be the network path with the highest (longest) duration, which in the case of the example provided, is the path that runs through activities A-C-D-F-G.

The near critical path is the *second* longest path through the network diagram. The near critical path is important to know since at any time, the schedule may change, making the near-critical path escalate to status of critical path.

Caution: While calculating the number of network paths, critical path, and near critical path may appear simplistic, it is easy to miss a path when the network diagram is large. Be sure to check your work.

Develop Schedule

Critical Path Method:

- **Total Float**: the amount of time that a schedule activity can be delayed without delaying the project.
- **Free Float**: the amount of time that a schedule activity can be delayed without delaying the early start date of any immediate successor activity within the network path.
- CPM does not account for resource limitations
- Float is also known as slack

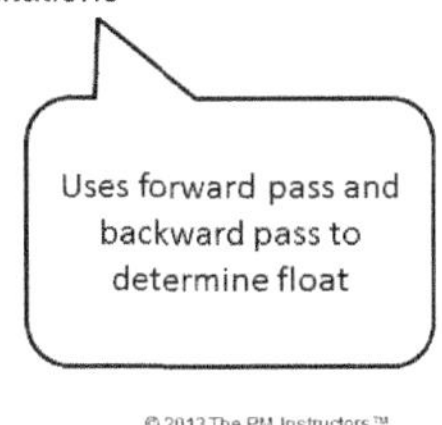

Uses forward pass and backward pass to determine float

Critical Path Method (CPM) allows the project manager to calculate the amount of scheduling flexibility that exists – whether by network path or by activity. This can be achieved by calculating how much *float* exists, which reveals the total flexibility. For instance, an activity with a 2-day float has a 2-day flexibility built into it. So if it finishes 2 days behind schedule, there is no impact to its successor activity or the project.

CPM calculates float using a *forward pass* to determine the early start and early finish dates of an activity, and using a *backward pass* to calculate the late start and late finish of an activity. At the same time, it should be noted that CPM does not account for resource limitations. Resource limitations are taken into account through the *critical chain* method. However, it does take into account activity durations, logical relationships, leads, lags, and any other known constraint that exists.

Since the critical path has zero flexibility, all critical activities that fall on the path will automatically have a float of zero as well. Note that the critical path can also have a negative float. That means that the project is behind schedule.

Float, as a general term, refers to an activity's flexibility in relation to time. It is often referred to as "slack". For instance, if an activity is delayed by one day, is there existing flexibility that allows for this scenario? Or will the delay impact the next activity or the overall project?

There are two types of float: total float and free float, whose definitions have been provided above.

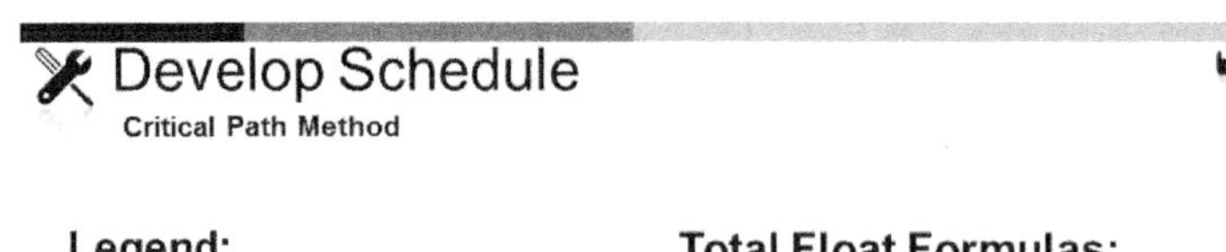

Legend:

ES	Duration	EF
	Activity Name	
LS	Float	LF

Total Float Formulas:

LS – ES
or
LF – EF

Forward Pass: Calculates Early Start (ES) and Early Finish (EF)
Backward Pass: Calculates Late Start (LS) and Late Finish (LF)

In order to calculate total float and free float, we will need to assign a general legend to use for the activities within a network diagram, so that we may identify what each number within the activity represents. For purposes of this book, the legend included in the image above will be used (this legend is not hard-coded).

In order to calculate total float and free float of an activity, we will use the critical path method, which involves performing a forward pass and a backward pass. A **forward pass** is used to determine the early start and early finish dates of each activity in a network diagram, while a **backward pass** is used to determine the late start and late finish dates of the activities.

Once early start, early finish, late start, and late finish dates are calculated, you may use one of two formulas to calculate total float. Both formulas will result in the same float value.

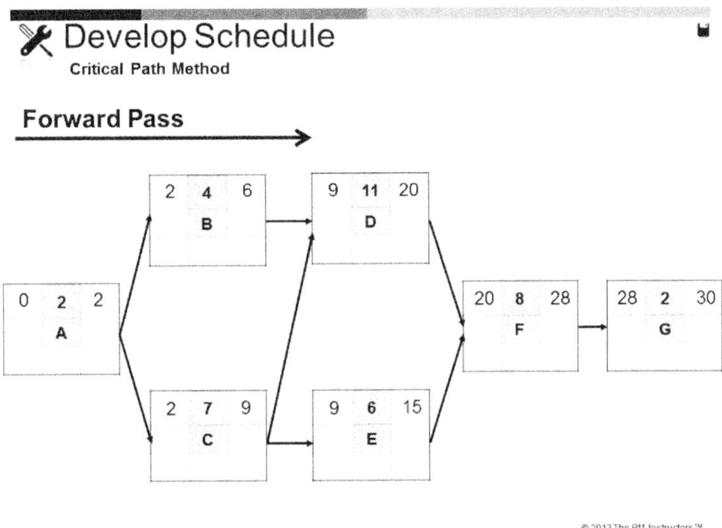

Forward Pass

There are five steps to performing a forward pass:

1. Begin with the first activity within a network diagram and work forward within the diagram, meaning from left to right.
2. Add a zero as the early start of the first activity. This means that we are not working with calendar days, but instead with durations
3. Add the duration of the first activity to the ES of zero to calculate the EF.
4. To calculate the ES of the successor activity, simply carry over the EF (the ES of an activity is the EF of its predecessor).
5. Continue calculating the ES and EF of each activity within the network diagram. In the instance where an activity has more than one predecessor, carry over the highest EF number.

Develop Schedule

Critical Path Method

Backward Pass

2 4 6 B 5 9

9 11 20 D 9 20

0 2 2 A 0 2

20 8 28 F 20 28

28 2 30 G 28 30

2 7 9 C 2 9

9 6 15 E 14 20

Backward Pass

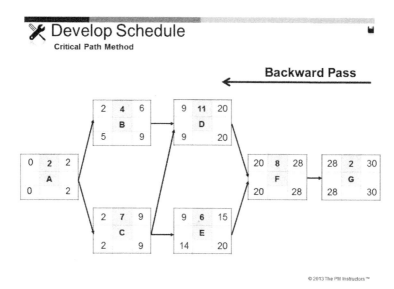

There are five steps to performing a backward pass:

1. Begin with the last activity within a network diagram and work backward within the diagram, meaning from right to left.
2. The LF of the final activity will be the activity's EF (this activity will automatically fall on the critical path, and therefore represents the duration of the project).
3. Subtract the duration of the last activity from its LF to calculate the LS.
4. To calculate the LF of the predecessor activity, simply carry over the LS (the LF of an activity is the LS of its successor).
5. Continue calculating the LS and LF of each activity within the network diagram. In the instance where an activity has more than one successor, carry over the lowest LF number.

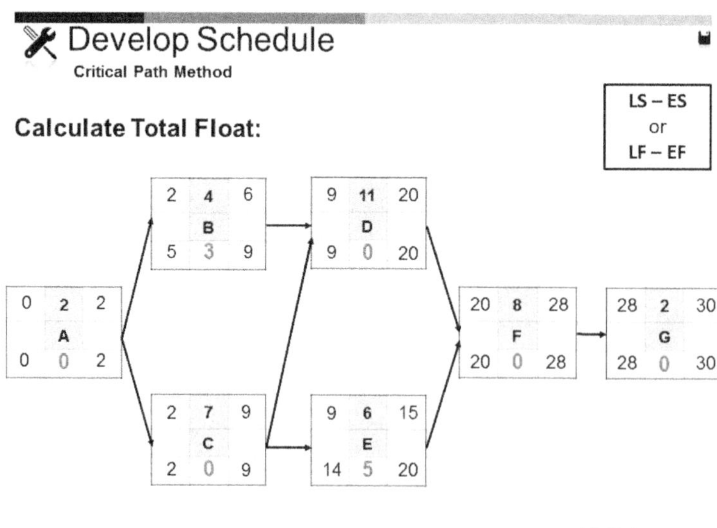

After performing a forward pass and a backward pass for the sample network diagram, you can now calculate total float. Use the legend and total float formulas provided. Answers have been included in the image above.

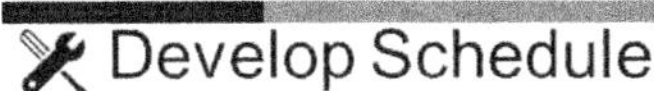
Develop Schedule

Critical Chain Method:

- Modifies the schedule to account for limited resources
- Another approach to developing the schedule, based on activity and resource dependencies
- Adds a project buffer after the final critical chain activity to prevent schedule slippage; adds feeding buffers at points within the network diagram that feed into the critical chain
- Planned activities are scheduled to start at their latest possible planned start and planned finish dates

Critical Chain:
the resource
constrained path

Critical Chain Method

Lack of resources is a common problem that project managers must deal with. When resource limitation occurs within a project, project managers may choose to use the critical chain method, which modifies the project schedule to account for limited resources.

Steps to performing CCM

As a starting point, the network diagram is generated, including any constraints built in.

The critical path is then defined, and resource availability is included. This will reveal the *resource-limited* schedule, which may reflect a different critical path than the schedule began with. This resource-constrained path is known as the *critical chain.*

In order to manage the critical chain, duration buffers may be added to account for uncertainty that exists as a result of limited resources. Remember that duration buffers are not actual working days, but are instead non-work scheduled activities.

When a buffer is placed at the end of the critical chain to protect the target finish date from slipping, it is known as a *project buffer.* Another term related to buffers is called the *feeding buffer.* This buffer is placed at points where an activity not on the critical chain path feeds into the critical chain – this is to prevent schedule slippage from occurring within the critical chain path.

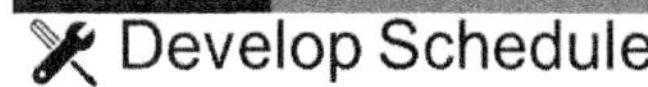

Develop Schedule

Resource Optimization Techniques:

1. Resource Leveling
   - Often completed using project management software
   - Keeps resource usage levels at a constant rate
   - Leveling out the peaks and valleys within a resource histogram
   - Criteria to leveling should be established
2. Resource Smoothing
   - Resources are adjusted to not exceed predefined limits
   - Critical path is unchanged

Reasons to use resource leveling:
• Shared or critical resource has limited availability • To keep resource usage levels at a constant rate • Spread out costs • Resources have been over-allocated • Shared or critical resources are available only at specific times

Resource Optimization Techniques

There are two types of resource optimization techniques: *Resource Leveling* and *Resource Smoothing.*

Resource Leveling

There are various reasons to level out resource usage. The following are the most common reasons to use resource leveling:

- A shared or critical resource has limited availability
- To keep the resource usage levels at a constant rate, as opposed to having heavy resource usage during some periods, and low usage in others
- To spread usage of funds (costs)

In other cases, resource leveling becomes a requirement. This is typically for the following reasons:

- Resources have been over-allocated, meaning that their time has been over extended
- A critical or shared resource is available only at specific times

Resource leveling can often be done using project management software. The idea is to level out erratic patterns and eliminate peaks and valleys by smoothing them out. One key note to know is that resource leveling often alters the critical path, oftentimes increasing the duration of the project.

Criteria should be established for prioritizing resource leveling in order to resolve existing resource conflicts. The most common criteria used is total float. This is one reason why network diagrams should already have been analyzed using the critical path method, prior to resource leveling. Other common factors in prioritizing the resolution of resource conflicts include financial considerations and physical limitations of resources.

Resource Smoothing

With resource smoothing, resources are adjusted so that they do not exceed predefined limits. A major difference between resource smoothing and leveling, is that smoothing out resources does not alter the critical path. This occurs by working with the free float and total float that exists.

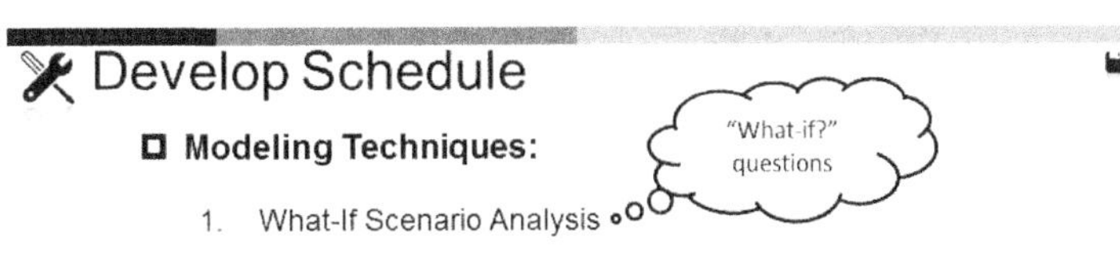

Develop Schedule
Modeling Techniques:
1. What-If Scenario Analysis
2. Simulation
"What-if?" questions

Monte Carlo Technique

The most commonly used technique that uses a software program to run a simulation of hundreds of possible scenarios.

Randomizes data and uses multiple activity assumptions.

- Likely critical paths
- Feasibility of the schedule under adverse conditions
- Schedule risk
- **Likelihood of when the project will complete**

Modeling Techniques

There are two types of modeling techniques: *What-If Scenario Analysis*, and *Simulation*.

What-If Scenario Analysis

What-if scenario analysis involves going through multiple scenarios to consider all possibilities. It translates uncertainties into potential impacts on the schedule, and can be specified at a detailed level of the project. The project team goes through several scenarios driven by "What if?" questions.

Probability	Date Complete
100%	06/01/10
95%	05/30/10
90%	05/28/10
85%	05/26/10
80%	05/24/10
75%	05/22/10
70%	05/20/10
65%	05/18/10
60%	05/16/10
55%	05/14/10
50%	05/12/10
45%	05/10/10
40%	05/08/10
35%	05/06/10

Simulation

The most common simulation technique is called **Monte Carlo analysis**. This is carried out using a software program that runs through hundreds of possible scenarios to result in likely schedule outcomes. These simulations use algorithms to determine possible outcomes. The data inputted is then randomized (typically the network diagrams and activity durations) to determine a range of possible outcomes. To do this, the program uses multiple activity assumptions. When including the duration estimates, the three types of duration estimates collected can be used (optimistic, pessimistic, and most likely duration estimates). Possible results include:

- What the likely critical path will be and the probability of an activity falling on a critical path
- Determine the feasibility of the schedule under adverse conditions
- Schedule risk
- **The likelihood of when the project will finish** (Activity Cumulative Probability Risk Distribution)

The output of the simulation is typically plotted as a probability distribution, and may be displayed in chart format. This information can be used to generate time reserves.

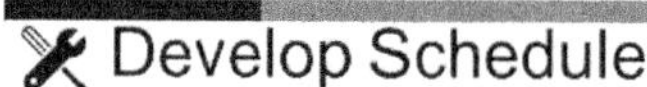

Leads and Lags

- Are refinements to adjust the start time of successor activities
- Additional leads and lags may be added in limited circumstances

Leads and Lags

Leads and lags were originally added as part of sequencing activities. Through the Develop Schedule process, they are further refined. Additional leads and lags may also be added as part of this process.

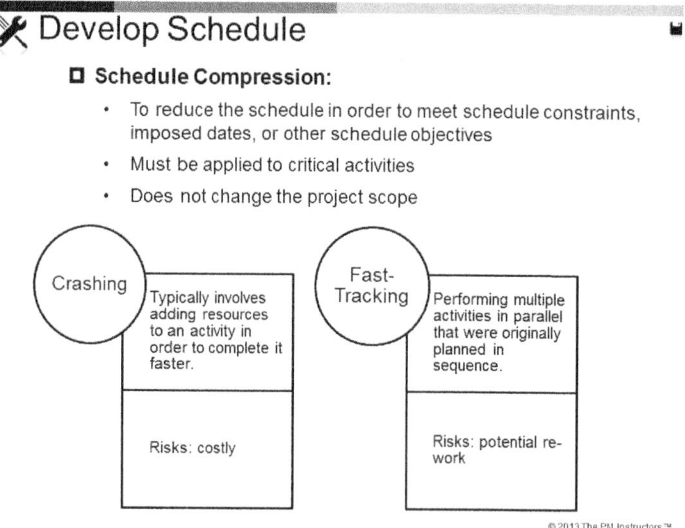

Schedule Compression

Schedule compression consists of two techniques: *crashing*, and *fast-tracking*. The purpose of both is literally to shorten the duration of the schedule. There may be a variety of reasons that this is needed, and there are different benefits and reasons to select either of these two methods.

The only way to shorten the duration of the project is to crash or fast-track an activity that falls on the critical path. Remember that critical activities have zero flexibility. If a critical path activity finishes early, the project itself may also finish early.

While schedule compression shortens the duration of the project, it is not meant to alter the project scope.

The following are common reasons to compress a schedule:

- To meet schedule constraints (a common reason)

- To meet imposed dates
- To meet other schedule objectives

Crashing

- Crashing the schedule typically means to add resources to an activity in order to complete the activity faster. This may occur through a resource working overtime or bringing on board additional resources. The idea is that effort placed into completing an activity is increased. An activity may also be crashed in other ways, such as by paying to expedite delivery of a package or to expedite other services rendered.
- Notice that all methods mentioned used to crash the schedule incur additional costs. **Before selecting a schedule compression technique, cost and schedule tradeoffs must be analyzed**. You'll need to perform this type of analysis to determine the best ways of obtaining the most compression for the least incremental cost.
- Crashing is a solution for those activities that can be shortened by adding resources or expediting services. In several cases, adding resources does not shorten the schedule. Funds must also be available for this technique to work. According to the *PMBOK® Guide*, crashing may increase risk in addition to cost.

Fast-Tracking

- While crashing involves adding effort placed into completing an activity, fast-tracking compresses the schedule by performing activities in parallel, which were originally scheduled to occur in sequence. An example of this would be beginning the development process of a software application before the design is fully complete; or beginning the editing process of a book, before the writing process is complete.
- Fast-tracking contains a higher risk than crashing, although it does not require the addition of funds. The majority of the risk in crashing is the clear cost of a resource, but with fast-tracking, the increased risk may come from potential rework.
- Generally, it is best to select the least costly technique when possible.

Develop Schedule

Scheduling Tool:

- *Automated tool meant to expedite the scheduling process of generating the start and finish dates based on the data inputted into the system
- Part of schedule model
- Data typically inputted:
    - Network diagrams
    - Resources
    - Activity durations

* Definition from A Guide to the Project Management Body of Knowledge, Project Management Institute Inc., 2013

Scheduling Tool

The *PMBOK® Guide* describes the scheduling tool as an automated tool meant to expedite the scheduling process by generating the start and finish dates based on the data inputted into the system. This data may include network diagrams, resources, and activity durations.

The scheduling tool is part of the schedule model and can be used together with other project management software, as well as manual methods (if applicable).

A popular scheduling tool used is Microsoft Project. There are other tools available in the marketplace that can be purchased, and there are also open source tools available, such as Open Workbench.

The scheduling tool is covered in detail during the early chapters of this book.

Develop Schedule

Schedule Baseline:

- The accepted and approved version of the project schedule
- A component of the project management plan

Things to note about the schedule baseline:

- Contains baseline start dates and baseline finish dates
- Is an important element to controlling the schedule
- Can be changed through the formal change control process
- Should be managed carefully

Develop Schedule Outputs

The Develop Schedule process produces six outputs, which are as follow: *schedule baseline, project schedule, schedule data, project calendars, project management plan updates, and project documents updates.*

Schedule Baseline

The schedule baseline is the accepted and approved version of the schedule, and contains baseline start dates and baseline finish dates. It is a component of the project management plan, as all baselines are.

The schedule baseline becomes an important element to controlling the schedule. In the Control Schedule process, the schedule baseline is used as a benchmark to measuring progress. Baseline planned dates will be compared with actual dates, and this will reveal the schedule's progress (for instance, are we ahead or behind schedule?). The scheduling tool will be used to baseline the schedule.

Careful attention and management should be taken to schedule baseline changes. All changes should be approved through the change control board, which occurs within the official change control process. Finishing a project on time is a measure of success, and the schedule baseline is a means of controlling and measuring that success from a scheduling standpoint.

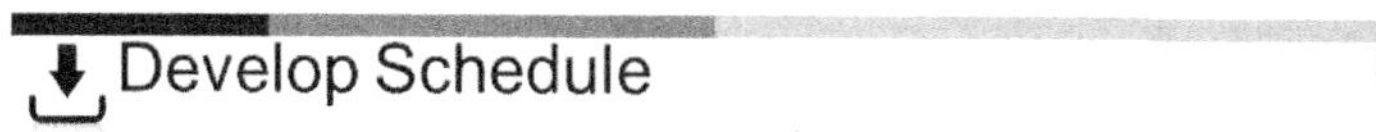

Project Schedule

- Considered preliminary until resource assignments are confirmed and schedule start and finish dates are firm
- Contains (at a minimum): planned start date and planned finish date for each activity

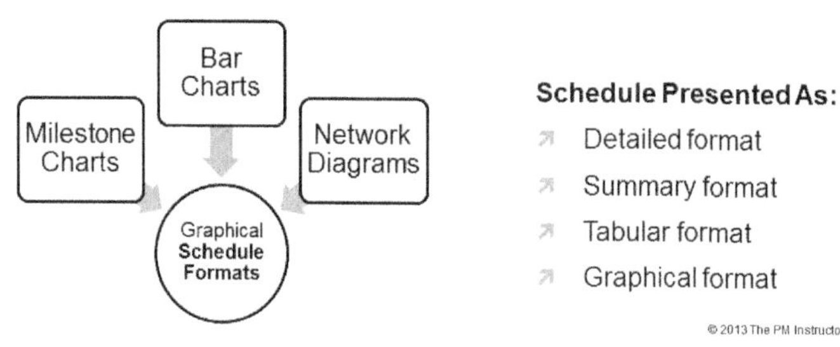

Project Schedule

Although they can vary to some degree, the basics of a schedule are fairly standard.

It is possible to have a preliminary schedule early on, assuming that resource planning is already complete. When this is the case, the schedule remains preliminary until the resource assignments are confirmed, and the schedule start and finish dates become firm. A schedule should be set no later than the completion of the project management plan.

According to the *PMBOK® Guide*, a project schedule contains (at a minimum) the following:

- A planned start date for each activity
- A planned finish date for each activity

There are various ways of presenting a schedule: it can be shown in detail, in summary form, by milestone, etc. Common formats used include: a milestone chart, bar chart, or project schedule network diagram.

When selecting the schedule format to present, always consider your audience. Should the schedule be displayed in a high-level format, or do the recipients require specific schedule details?

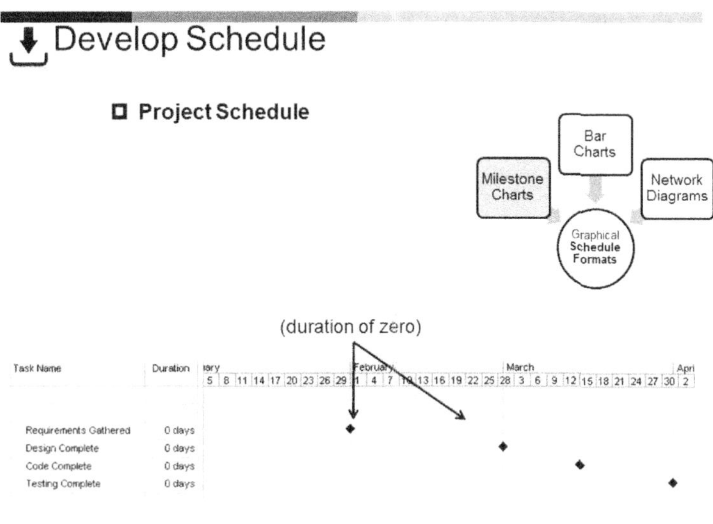

Milestone charts are similar to bar charts, except that they only identify the scheduled start or completion of major deliverables. This is commonly referred to as a *milestone schedule*. Because of its high-level nature, it becomes ideal when presenting the schedule to an executive team, project sponsor, and key stakeholders.

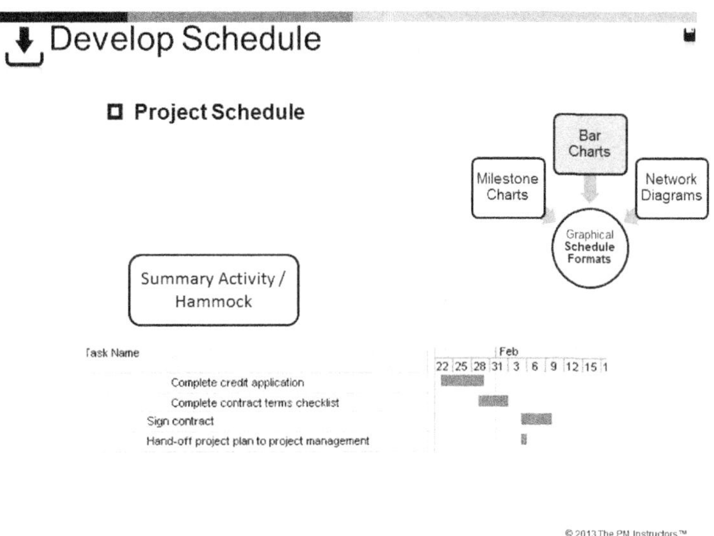

Bar charts display the start and end dates of activities, with the bar representing an activity, and the length of the bar representing its duration. A bar chart does not show dependencies between the activities or assigned resources.

Bar charts are ideal when presenting the schedule to management, or in management reports, since they often include summary activities (also referred to as hammock activities). Summary activities are groupings of related activities. Bar Charts are typically compiled after network diagrams, and are not necessarily used for planning purposes.

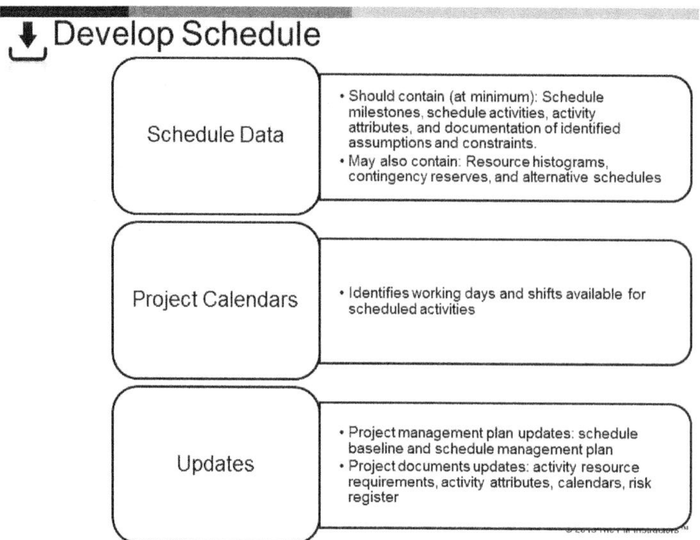

Schedule Data

According to the *PMBOK® Guide*, the schedule data contains, at a minimum, the following: schedule milestones, schedule activities, activity attributes, and documentation of the identified assumptions and constraints.

In addition to this, other supporting information may be included, such as: resource histograms that show resource requirements by time frame, contingency reserves, and alternative schedules. Alternative schedules may be versions that cover a best-case scenario, worst-case scenario, a schedule that has not gone through resource leveling, and another that can include or not include imposed dates.

Project Calendars

Project calendars define working days and shift available for scheduled activities. Work periods are therefore identified through one or more project calendars created through this process.

Project Management Plan Updates

Updates to the project management plan typically include updates to the schedule baseline (as the process is iterated) and schedule management plan.

Project Documents Updates

As a result of carrying out the Develop Schedule process, the following documents may need to be updated:

- Activity resource requirements. Resource leveling will affect resource types and quantities needed for impacted activities.
- Activity attributes. New activity information must be added, such as start and finish dates, float, resource-leveling, etc.
- Calendars. Any changes that impact the calendars should be updated, including availability of resources.
- Risk register. Any opportunities or threats uncovered should be updated in the risk register.

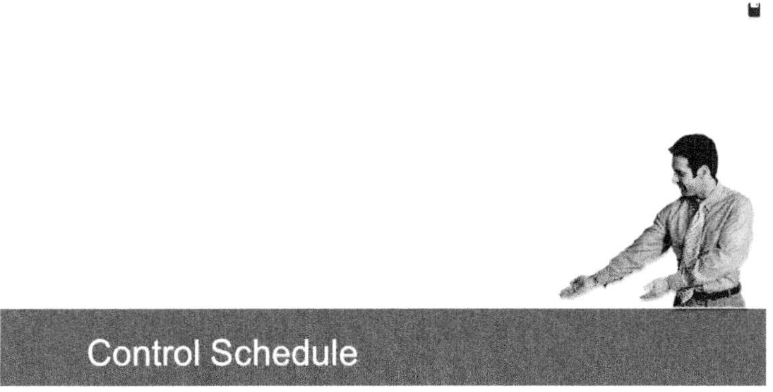

Purpose: To monitor the status of project activities to update project progress and manage changes to the schedule baseline to achieve the plan.

Control Schedule Process Overview

Control Schedule is the seventh and final process of the Project Time Management Knowledge Area, and the only process of the seven that falls within the Monitoring and Controlling Process Group. The purpose of this process is to monitor the status of the project in order to update project progress and manage changes to the schedule baseline. In order to maintain this purpose, the process:

- Determines the current schedule status
- Works to influence factors that would change the schedule
- Determines whether the schedule has changed
- Manages schedule changes as they take place

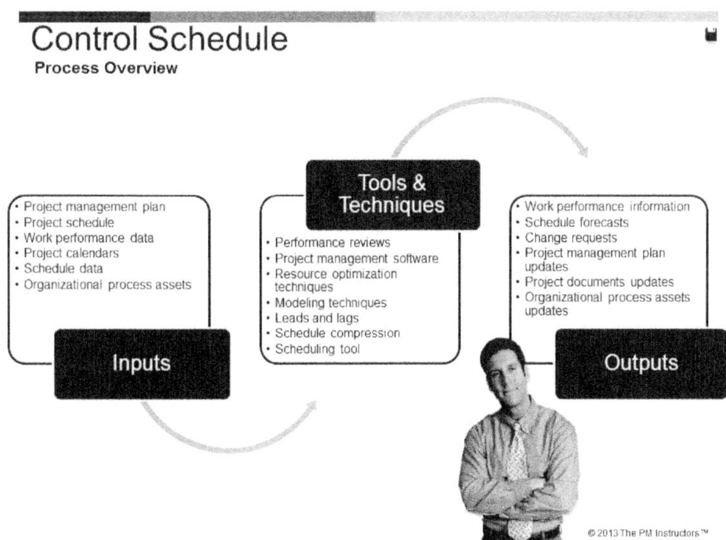

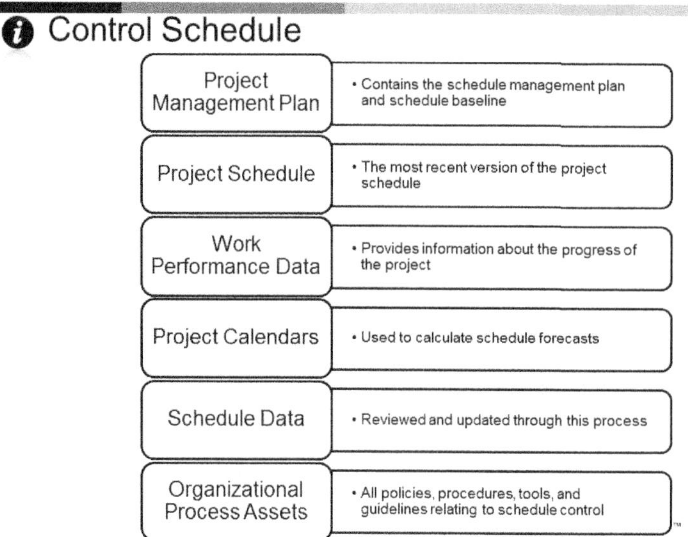
Control Schedule
Project Management Plan
• Contains the schedule management plan and schedule baseline
Project Schedule
• The most recent version of the project schedule
Work Performance Data
• Provides information about the progress of the project
Project Calendars
• Used to calculate schedule forecasts
Schedule Data
• Reviewed and updated through this process
Organizational Process Assets
• All policies, procedures, tools, and guidelines relating to schedule control

Control Schedule Inputs

The Control Schedule process utilizes the following six inputs: *project management plan, project schedule, work performance data, project calendars, schedule data, and organizational process assets.*

Project Management Plan

The project management plan contains two key documents used within this process: the schedule management plan and the schedule baseline. The schedule management plan provides the guidance as to how the schedule will be managed and controlled. This serves as the processes "how to" plan, and identifies what tools and techniques will be used, among other valuable information. The schedule baseline is the original project schedule, plus approved changes (the approved and accepted version of the schedule), which will be used to compare with the current project schedule to identify any existing variances.

Project Schedule

The project schedule is the actual version of the schedule, containing updated information – such as the activity actual start and finish dates.

Work Performance Data

Work performance data is another input that provides "actual" data regarding the project's progress. This is sometimes referred to as the project's raw data, which includes which activities have started, which have completed, as well as current progress for those that have not completed.

Project Calendars

Project calendars define the work periods available, and are created through the previous process (Develop Schedule). Project calendars are used to calculate schedule forecasts.

Schedule Data

Schedule data will be reviewed and updated through the Control Schedule process. It also contains alternative schedules that may be leveraged through this process.

Organizational Process Assets

Organizational process assets used by the process include policies, procedures, and guidelines in relation to controlling the schedule. Also typically used are schedule control tools and any monitoring and reporting methods that have been documented.

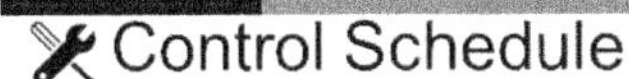

Control Schedule

Is corrective action necessary?

Performance Reviews:

- Measures, compares, and analyzes schedule performance

  Evaluates: actual start and finish dates, % complete, and remaining duration

- Techniques used:
  - Earned Value Management, such as schedule variance (SV), schedule performance index (SPI)
  - Trend Analysis
  - Critical Path Method
  - Critical Chain Method

Control Schedule Tools and Techniques

The Control Schedule process contains seven tools and techniques: *performance reviews, project management software, resource optimization techniques, modeling techniques, leads and lags, schedule compression, and scheduling tool.*

Performance Reviews

Processes that belong to the Monitoring and Controlling Process Group are typically concerned with detecting any variances that exists within their respective knowledge areas. The Control Schedule process is concerned with monitoring the progress of the project schedule, as well as controlling changes. In this respect, the *performance reviews* tool and technique measures and analyzes existing schedule performance to determine whether any variances exist, including measuring, comparing, and analyzing overall schedule performance. The project manager will evaluate actual start and finish dates, percent complete, and the remaining duration.

There are various techniques that can be performed as part of this tool and technique. The *PMBOK® Guide* points out the following:

- Trend analysis
- Critical path method
- Critical chain method
- Earned value management

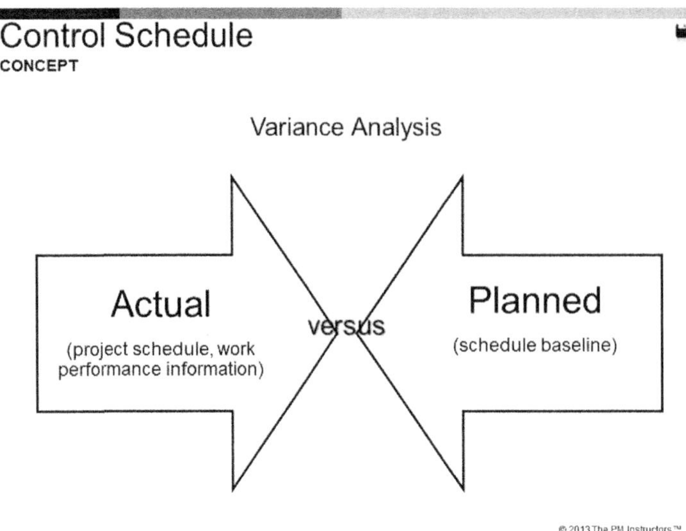

Variance Analysis

Variance analysis compares "actual" versus "planned" to determine whether any variances exist, and is performed as part of conducting performance reviews. In this case, the schedule baseline is compared to the actual project schedule and the project's Work Performance Data. When variances are discovered, the causes are identified and the degree of variance is assessed in order to determine whether corrective action is needed.

Schedule variance (SV) and Schedule Performance Index (SPI), which are calculated as part of the earned value management technique, are used to assess variations. *An explanation of SV and SPI can be found within the Project Cost Management Knowledge Area chapter.*

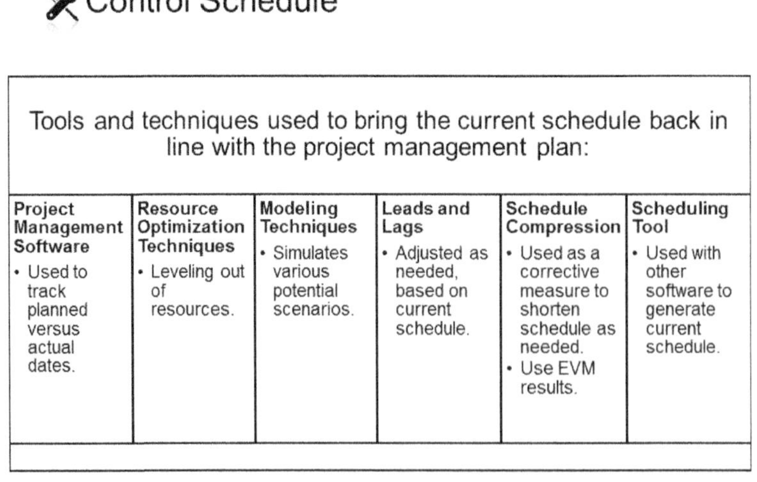

Project Management Software

Project management software, which is part of the enterprise environmental factors, is used to track planned dates versus actual dates. It's also used to forecast the impact of changes to the project schedule.

Resource Optimization Techniques

Based on the current project schedule, resources may need to be leveled. Resource leveling was discussed previously as part of the Develop Schedule process.

Modeling Techniques

Using the Monte Carlo technique, project information is input into a modeling and simulation program to run through various potential scenarios based on current data. This information assists in bringing the actual schedule back in line with the schedule baseline. What-if scenario analysis was discussed previously as part of the Develop Schedule process.

Leads and Lags

Leads and lags are adjusted as needed. The purpose of this is to bring those project activities that are currently behind schedule back in line with the schedule baseline.

Schedule Compression

Schedule compression is used as a corrective measure to bring those activities that are currently behind schedule back in line with the schedule baseline. After analyzing the schedule progress, including the SPI, SV, Cost Performance Index (CPI) and Cost Variance (CV), a schedule compression technique is chosen. If the project is behind schedule, but under budget, crashing may be a viable option to compression the schedule. If the project is behind schedule, but also over budget, then fast-tracking may be the only viable option. In all cases, only critical activities are compressed. Schedule compression was discussed within the Develop Schedule process.

Scheduling Tool

Schedule data is input into the scheduling tool in order to generate a current schedule that reflects the actual progress of the project, as well as what work remains to be completed. The scheduling tool is used along with the project management software to perform schedule network analysis.

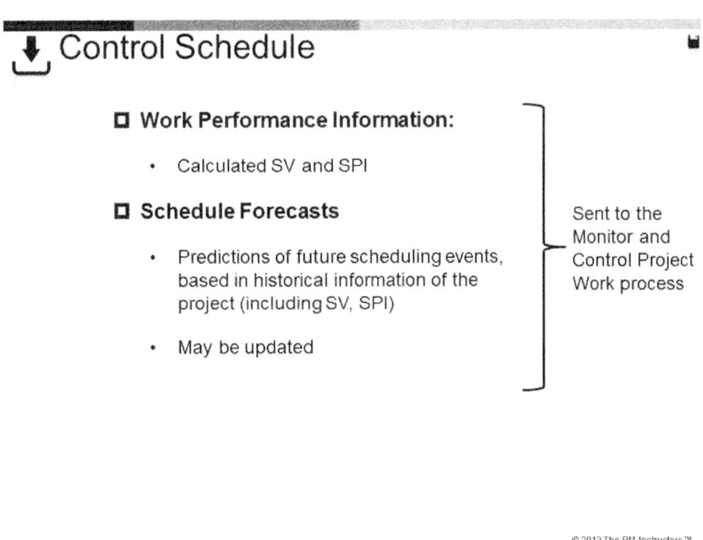

Control Schedule Outputs

The Control Schedule process produces six outputs: *work performance information, schedule forecasts, change requests, project management plan updates, project documents updates, and organizational process assets updates.*

Work Performance Information

Work performance information includes the calculated SV and SPI for WBS components, such as at the work package level and / or the control account level. This information is documented and sent to the

Monitor and Control Project Work process within the Project Integration Management Knowledge Area, which compiles the official project reports. At this stage, the project manager analyzes and determines how SV and SPI impact the overall project. This information is then communicated to the appropriate stakeholders, based on the communications management plan.

Schedule Forecasts

Like work performance information, schedule forecasts are also utilized by the Monitor and Control Project Work process, for reporting purposes. Schedule forecasts contain predictions of future events, in terms of the schedule. Forecasts are compiled and updated based on historical information of the project, including the calculated SV and SPI.

- **Change Requests:**
  - Recommended corrective and preventive actions

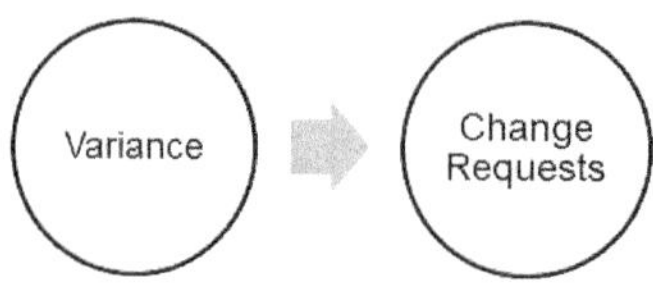

- **Updates:**
  - **Project Management Plan Updates**
  - **Project Documents Updates**
  - **Organizational Process Assets Updates**

Change Requests

Whenever variance is present, some form of corrective action is needed. This is to bring the project schedule back in line with the project management plan (specifically, the schedule baseline). In addition to corrective action, analysis of the project's performance may require that preventive actions be taken as well. An example of this is forecasting schedule slippage – rather than wait for the slippage to occur, preventive measures may be taken to reduce the probability that it will occur.

In addition to corrective and preventive actions, change requests may be necessary to alter the schedule baseline as a result of performance measures, changes made to the project schedule, and analysis of progress reports.

After carrying through the Control Schedule process, several project updates may be required, including from within the organizational process assets, project management plan, and project documents.

Project Management Plan Updates

The project management plan itself consists of several subsidiary and component plans. Typical updates include:

- **Schedule baseline:** Since all changes to the baseline must be approved, baseline changes do not occur until change requests have gone through the proper control process and received approval to be executed. Once approved, then the schedule baseline may be updated. These updates may consist of scope changes, activity resources, or activity duration estimates.
- **Schedule management plan:** Because lessons learned are being noted and officially documented, there may be changes in the way that the schedule is managed. This may be a result of many reasons, such as keeping pace with the dynamics of the schedule itself.
- **Cost baseline:** Compressing the schedule may reflect a change to the cost baseline, particularly the crashing technique, which often uses additional resources as a way of shortening the

schedule. Once this is approved through the change control process, the project budget (cost performance baseline) should reflect this change.

Project Documents Updates

Project documents typically impacted by the Control Schedule process include:

- **Schedule data:** In some cases, the project schedule will vary significantly from the baseline and it becomes inefficient to manage the schedule this way. In these instances, a new target schedule may be needed, which includes more realistic data for the project manager to manage the schedule through. In general, schedule data is updated throughout the Control Schedule process with remaining durations and changes to the schedule.
- **Project schedule:** After updating the schedule data, an updated version of the project schedule may be generated.
- **Risk Register:** As the schedule is managed, changes may occur that could impact existing risks, thereby creating a need for the risk register to be updated. As work in the schedule is performed, schedule risks will also materialize, and new risks may be created as a result of performing certain scheduling techniques (such as schedule compression).

Organizational Process Assets Updates

Whenever corrective or preventive actions are taken, the project manager should document a detailed description of the action and also why that particular course was taken. This specifically includes:

- The causes of variances
- The corrective action that was selected, and why that particular path was chosen
- Any type of lessons learned from carrying through the process. As part of lessons learned, it should be noted whether the corrective action or preventive action produced the desired result (when known)

Module Summary

In this module we:

- Defined the purpose of the Project Time Management Knowledge Area
- Identified the processes of the Project Time Management Knowledge Area
- Recalled the key outputs of the time management processes
- Differentiated between the inputs, tools and techniques, and outputs of the time management processes
- Performed a forward pass and backward pass calculation
- Interpreted various types of network diagrams to identify critical path activities

Chapter Quiz

Exam Practice Questions

1. Ronald Pierce is a high-end furniture store chain. The company is in the process of developing a new renaissance style edition for release in six months. The project manager leading the development of the new edition has just contacted the design team for an estimate on their assignments. The lead designer notified the project manager that the most likely estimate of completion is 19 days, the pessimistic estimate is 28 days, and the optimistic estimate is 15 days. What is the PERT estimate, rounded to the nearest whole number, of this assignment?
   A. 20
   B. 19
   C. 13
   D. 21

2. Ronald Pierce is a high-end furniture store chain. The company is in the process of developing a new renaissance style edition for release in six months. The project manager leading the development of the new edition has just contacted the design team for an estimate on their assignments. The lead designer notified the project manager that the most likely estimate of completion is 19 days, the pessimistic estimate is 28 days, and the optimistic estimate is 15 days. What is the standard deviation, based on the estimates provided?
   A. 6.5
   B. 2.17
   C. 21.5
   D. 20

3. Susan and David are both project managers for Blazing Broadband Internet Solutions, but they work in different divisions of the company, each having led numerous successful projects for the organization. They have been teamed together in order to find innovative solutions to problems on a new project. Using their experience from previous projects, they agree to use parametric estimating as a way of leveraging known factors of the project and both of their experiences to solve problems relating to keeping the project on schedule. Parametric estimating can BEST be described as:
   A. An estimating technique meant to improve the accuracy of an activity duration estimate
   B. An estimating technique that uses actual duration of the previous similar schedule activity to come up with the estimate
   C. A scatter diagram that tracks two variables to determine whether a relation exists
   D. An estimating technique that uses a mathematical model to calculate durations

4. Which of the following is the most common type of dependency between activities?
   A. Start-to-Start
   B. Finish-to-Finish
   C. Finish-to-Start
   D. Start-to-Finish

5. Which of the following is not an output of the Estimate Activity Resources process?
    A. Schedule data
    B. Activity resource requirements
    C. Resource breakdown structure
    D. Project documents updates

6. An activity that has an optimistic estimate of 11 days, a pessimistic estimate of 19 days, and a most likely estimate of 15 has an expected duration of:
    A. 19
    B. 14
    C. 11
    D. 15

7. Based on the following, what is the duration of the critical path?

Activity	Duration
Start-A	7
Start-B	3
A-C	3
B-C	1
B-D	4
C-D	8
C-E	6
E-End	2
D-End	11

    A. 18
    B. 29
    C. 23
    D. 12

8. If an activity has an early start of 15, a late start of 20, and a late finish of 32, what is the total float?
    A. 15
    B. 17
    C. 12
    D. 5

9. Mary Beth has been called into a meeting to assess the status and progress of her schedule activity, along with other project team members whose activities fall within the critical path. This is an example of:
    A. Variance analysis
    B. Earned value management
    C. Forecasting
    D. Performance review

10. Ron, who is the project manager, has just discovered that an important activity on the critical path will be 10 days behind schedule. The project sponsor has made it clear that the project must be completed on time, without going over budget. After analyzing the project schedule, Ron determines that performing two of the activities on the critical path in parallel will place the project back on track. What is this technique called?
    A. Fast-tracking
    B. Crashing
    C. Schedule compression
    D. Resource leveling

11. Based on the following networking diagram, what is the duration of the near-critical path?

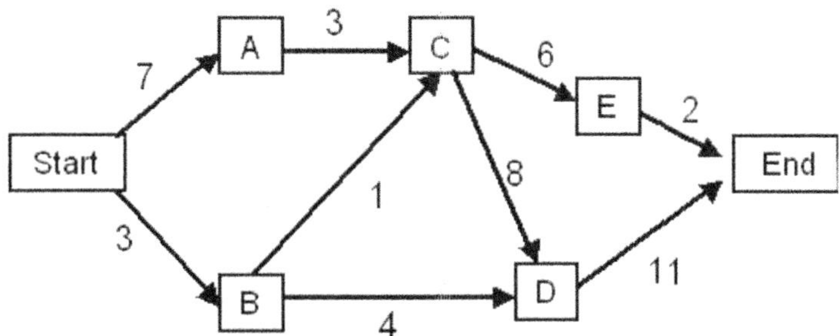

A. 18
B. 29
C. 23
D. 12

12. What is the standard deviation of an activity that has an optimistic estimate of 21 days and a pessimistic estimate of 28 days?
    A. 7
    B. 23
    C. 1.167
    D. 11.667

13. What is the range of estimate for an activity that has an optimistic estimate of 17, a most likely estimate of 22, and a pessimistic estimate of 29?
    A. 17 to 19
    B. 20.333 to 24.333
    C. 22.333 to 26.333
    D. 18.333 to 26.333

14. Which Of the following is not a type of project schedule network diagramming method?
    A. Precedence Diagramming Method
    B. Activity-on-Node
    C. Schedule Comparison Bar Chart
    D. Arrow Diagramming Method

15. As part of performing reserve analysis, Jane has added a time reserve to one of the project's network paths. What is this additional time added called?
    A. Contingency reserve
    B. Padding
    C. Buffer
    D. Management reserve

16. The following diagram is an example of which type of diagramming method?

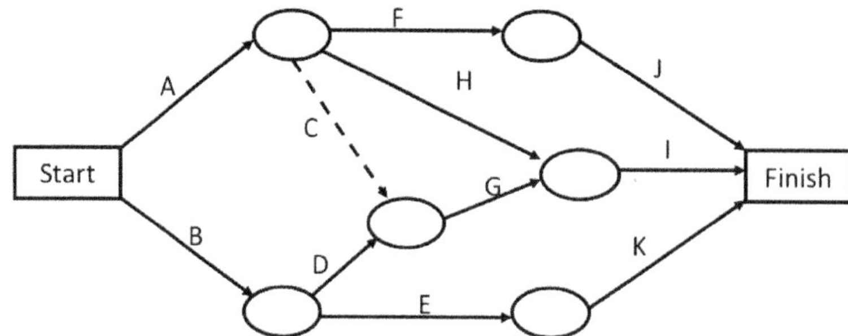

A. Activity-On-Node
B. Precedence Diagramming Method
C. Activity-On-Arrow
D. Precedence Arrow Diagramming Method

17. A pharmaceutical company is working on a new product that will revolutionize the drug industry. Currently, the project manager of the project is estimating the type and quantity of resources needed for the list of project activities. For a group of activities, the project manager purchased access to published data to use in calculating the estimates. Published estimating data can BEST be described as:
    A. An enterprise environmental factor frequently used for project purposes
    B. Data obtained through the organizational process assets to estimate resource types and quantities needed
    C. A tool and technique of the Estimate Activity Durations process
    D. Information that can be obtained externally in order to estimate resource types and quantities needed

18. Purse Centric is a clothing retail company with eleven stores throughout Europe. The company is planning to expand to North America, beginning with two stores opening concurrently. The project manager heading the opening of the west region store has been working diligently with the scheduler to generate a project schedule. While estimating the number of resources needed for phase one of the project, the scheduler had a difficult time coming up with confident estimates to provide the project manager for 2 critical activities. What should the scheduler do?
    A. Perform bottom-up estimating
    B. Use analogous estimating
    C. Base the estimates on past projects
    D. Use relevant published data

19. In order to measure the performance of the schedule, the project manager compares actual project performance to planned performance as part of regular schedule maintenance. What is the project manager looking for?
    A. Existing variances
    B. Information to report to management
    C. Communication breakdown
    D. The revised baseline

20. In what process is the resource breakdown structure created?
    A. Sequence Activities
    B. Estimate Activity Durations
    C. Estimate Activity Resources
    D. Develop Schedule

Chapter Quiz

Exam Practice Answers

1. Answer: A
   Explanation: This question requires that you use the PERT formula, which is as follows:

   (Optimistic + Pessimistic + 4(Most Likely)) / 6

   Plugging in the estimates provided by the lead designer gives you the following formula to work out: (15 + 28 + 4(19)) / 6. The answer is 19.83; when rounded to the nearest whole number, the correct answer becomes 20.
2. Answer: B
   Explanation: The formula for calculating the standard deviation of an activity is: Pessimistic – Optimistic, divided by six or ((P-O)/6). By plugging in the numbers provided by the question, you result in the following: (28 – 15) / 6. The answer is 2.17.
3. Answer: D
   Explanation: Parametric estimating is a mathematical model that results in a fairly accurate estimate, taking into account a known factor of the existing project coupled with historical information. Also described within the options are the 3-point estimating technique, analogous estimating, and regression analysis.
4. Answer: C
   Explanation: Finish to start is also the most common logical relationship used between activities. This is where the initiation of the successor activity depends on the completion of the predecessor activity. As a quick refresher, start-to-start is where the initiation of the successor activity depends on the initiation of the predecessor activity; finish-to-finish is where the completion of the successor activity depends on the completion of the predecessor activity; and start-to-finish is where the completion of the successor activity depends on the initiation of the predecessor activity.
5. Answer: A
   Explanation: In many instances, options provided make up another part of the process or related Knowledge Area, such as the input if the question asks for the outputs. In this case, schedule data is an output of the Develop Schedule process and not the Estimate Activity Resources process.
6. Answer: D
   Explanation: Selecting the correct answer for this question simply involves knowing the correct formula to use. To calculate the answer, you'll need the PERT formula (the clue in the question is "expected" duration). The formula is (Optimistic + Pessimistic + (4 x Most Likely)), all divided by 6. When you plug in the numbers given within the question, you result in 15.
7. Answer: B
   Explanation: Using the chart, draw out the network diagram, taking into account the dependencies noted in the chart. Next, add up the duration of each network path. The critical path is the path with the longest duration, which in this case is 29.
8. Answer: D
   Explanation: For calculating total float, you can use one of two formulas: either late start minus early start (LS – ES) or late finish minus early finish (LF – EF). Either formula will give you the total float. Note that an activity that falls on the critical path has a total float of zero. In this question we were provided with the early start, late start, and late finish, leaving us with only one formula to work with (LS – ES). Plug in the numbers and you get 5.
9. Answer: D

Explanation: To answer this question, you must decipher what meeting is referenced. Notice that the purpose of the meeting is to assess the status and progress of schedule activities. This type of meeting specifically describes a performance review.

10. Answer: A
Explanation: What Ron has done is compress the schedule. Notice that schedule compression is one of the options. Also notice that fast-tracking and crashing, both schedule compression techniques, are also included. Although schedule compression is a good choice (and accurate), Ron is specifically using the fast-tracking schedule compression technique, making this a better answer. Fast tracking is where multiple activities are performed in parallel, as opposed to in sequence, and crashing usually involves adding resources in order to complete the activity faster.

11. Answer: C
Explanation: The near-critical path is the second longest path within the network diagram. The near critical path is important, because at any time, a change may occur that causes the near-critical path to become the critical path. In this case, the duration of the critical path is 29. The second longest path (called the near critical path) contains a duration of 23.

12. Answer: C
Explanation: To calculate standard deviation, subtract Pessimistic and Optimistic, then divide by 6. Calculation: (28 – 21) / 6 = 1.167

13. Answer: B
Explanation: This question requires that you calculate PERT, along with standard deviation. The PERT formula is (Optimistic + Pessimistic + 4(Most Likely) / 6). The standard deviation formula is ((Pessimistic – Optimistic) / 6). When plugging in the numbers, the PERT estimate is 22.333, and the standard deviation is 2. The answer is 22.333 +/- 2, which can also be displayed as the following range: 20.333 – 24.333

14. Answer: C
Explanation: There are two types of network diagrams: Precedence Diagramming Method (PDM) and Arrow Diagramming Method (ADM). PDM is also known as activity on node, and arrow diagramming method is also known as activity on arrow. That leaves schedule comparison bar chart as the correct answer.

15. Answer: C
Explanation: This additional time reserve added to the network path is called a "buffer". Time reserves / buffers are a type of schedule contingency added to the schedule. The use of buffers is more efficient than padding estimates, since padding becomes a hidden reserve that cannot be managed.

16. Answer: C
Explanation: From simply looking at the diagram, you can immediately determine that it uses the Arrow Diagramming Method, also known as Activity-On-Arrow. The biggest clue is that a dummy activity exists within the diagram, which is the dotted line representing activity C. Only ADM uses dummy activities.

17. Answer: D
Explanation: Published estimating data is a tool and technique of the Estimate Activity Resources process, and includes published data and information that can be used to estimate resource types and quantities needed for project activities. This often includes production rates or unit costs of resources. While this is indeed considered to be an enterprise environmental factor, the question asks for the BEST description, which involves selecting the most descriptive and relevant option.

18. Answer: A
Explanation: When a confident estimate cannot be determined for an activity's resource type and quantity, the project manager and scheduler may use bottom-up estimating. This is assuming that the time and funds to determine a more accurate estimate exist. Bottom-up estimating involves further decomposing the activity to more accurately estimate each smaller component, and then sum up these smaller estimates to the original activity level.

19. Answer: A

Explanation: The project manager uses the schedule baseline to compare to the actual project schedule. The idea is to uncover any variances that may exist, and fix them. The schedule baseline is the approved and accepted version of the schedule. Think of the baseline as the original schedule, plus any approved changes.

20. Answer: C
Explanation: Resource breakdown structures are created in the Estimate Activity Resources process. They are graphical, hierarchical views of the resource categories used in a project. Common resource categories include: labor, material, equipment, and supplies.

Time Management Exercises

Network Diagram Exercise

Instructions: For each of the following network diagrams, calculate the following (use the legend presented within the Project Time Management chapter):

1. Early start, early finish, late start, and late finish for each activity
2. Identify the critical path
3. Total float for each activity

Network Diagram #1

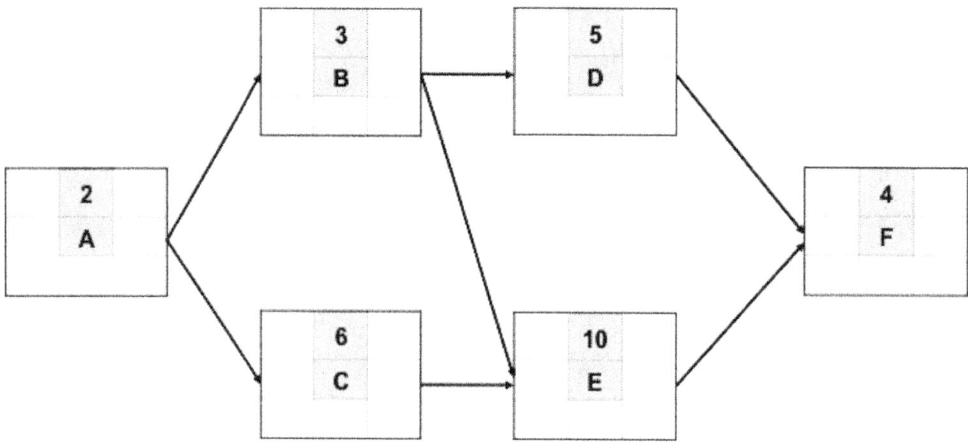

Network Diagram #2

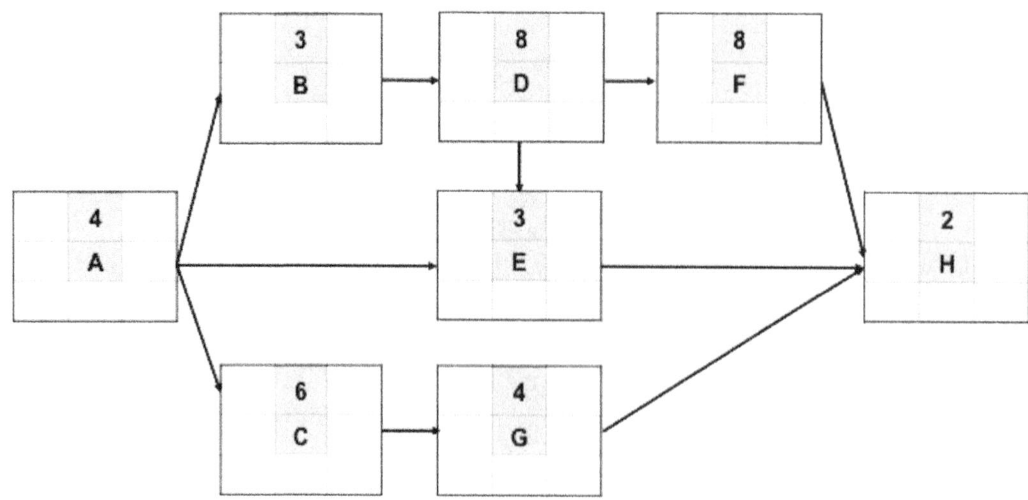

Network Diagram #3

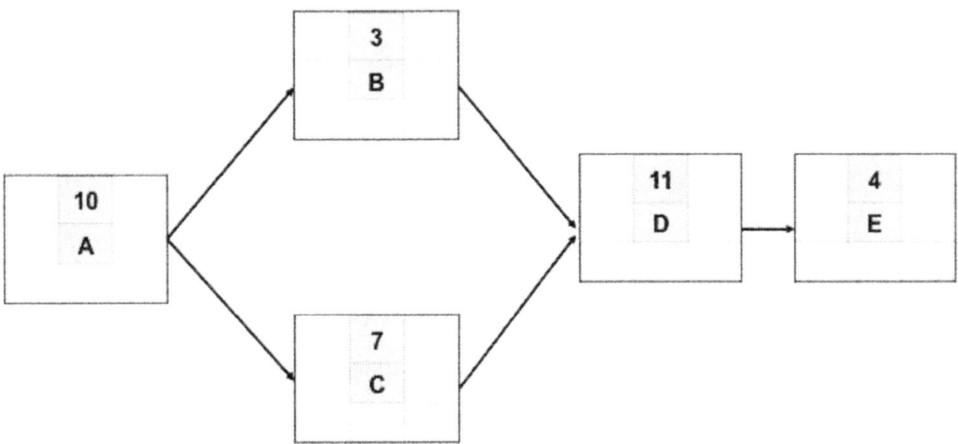

Network Diagram #4

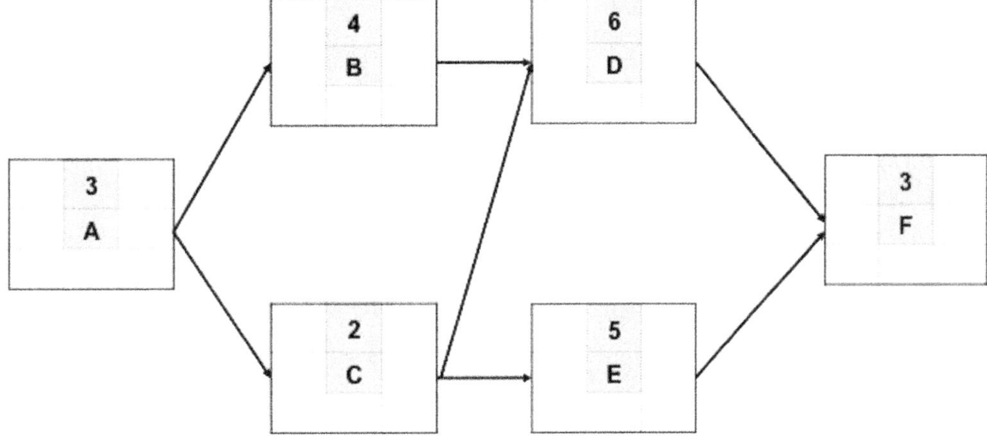

Network Diagram #5

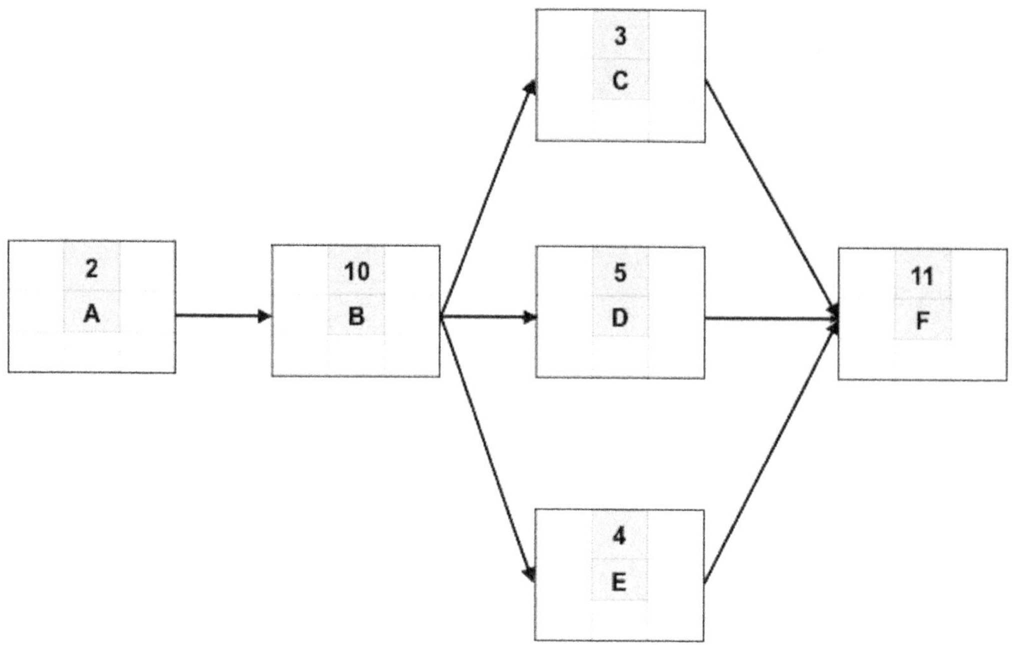

Network Diagram #6

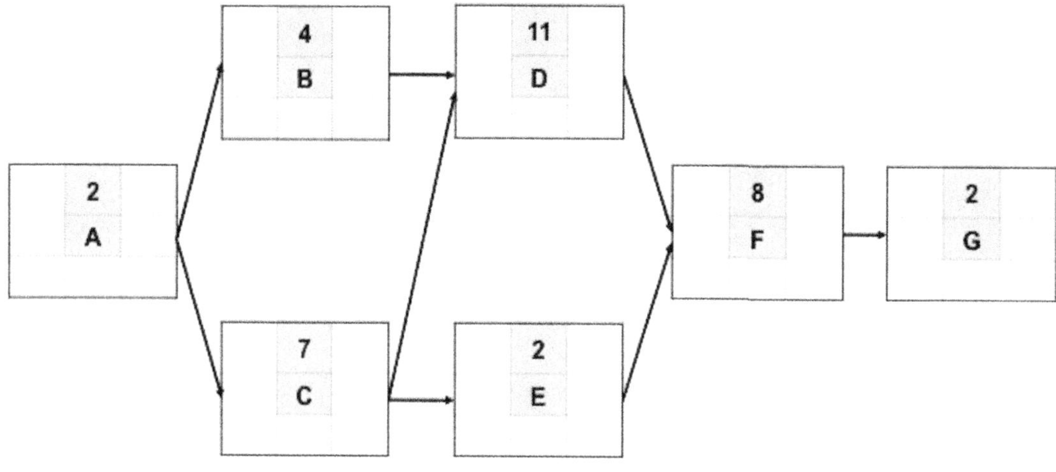

Network Diagram Exercise Answer Key

Network Diagram #1

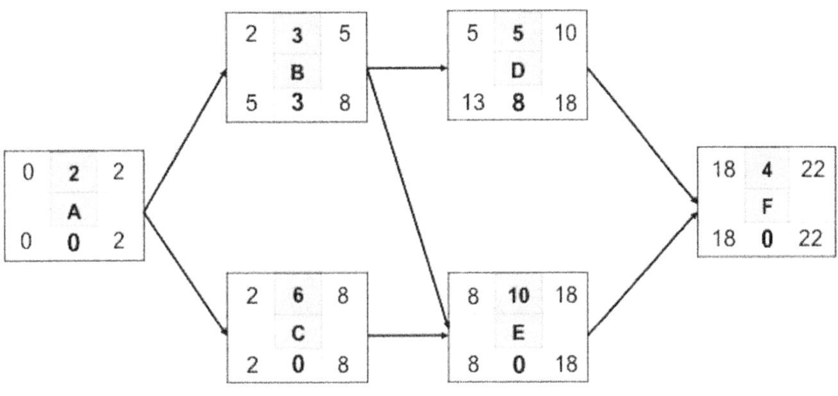

Critical Path: A-C-E-F

Network Diagram #2

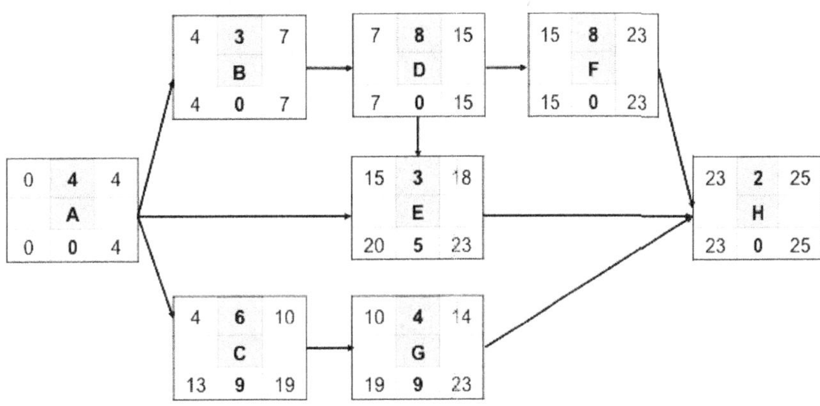

Critical Path: A-B-D-F-H

Network Diagram #3

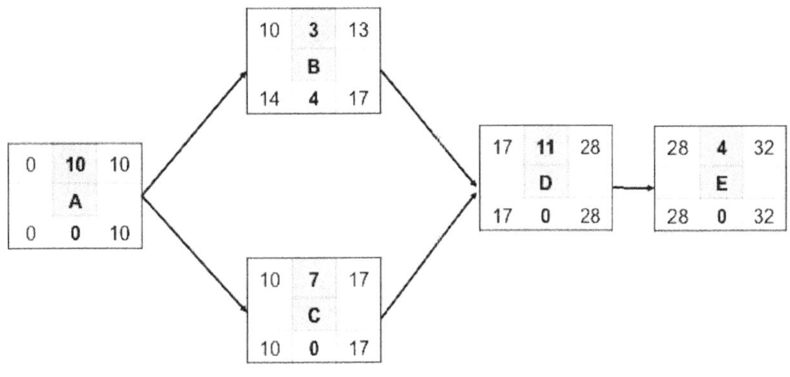

Critical Path: A-C-D-E

Network Diagram #4

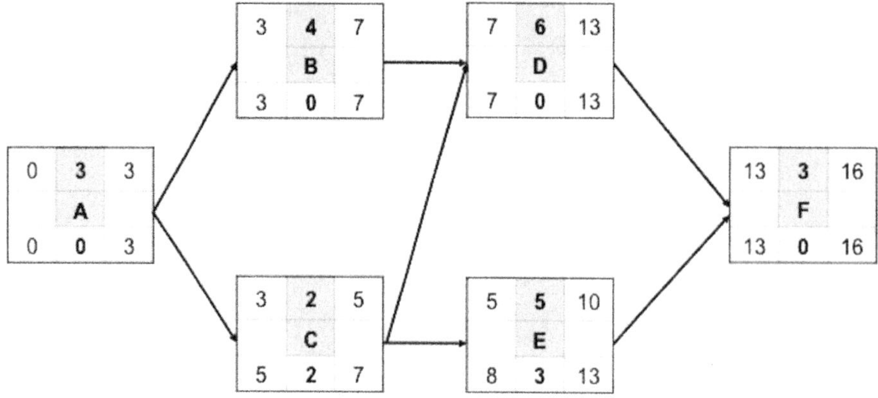

Critical Path: A-B-D-F

Network Diagram #5

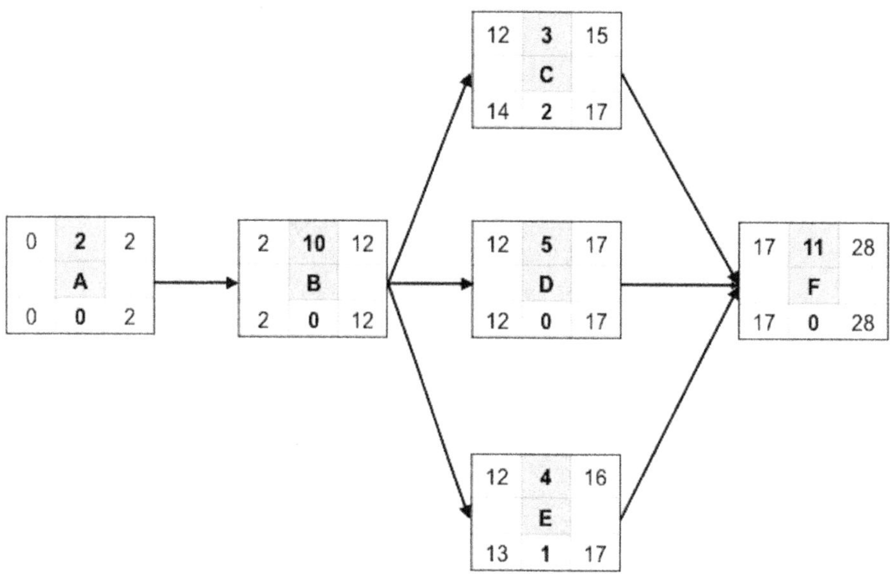

Critical Path: A-B-D-F

Network Diagram #6

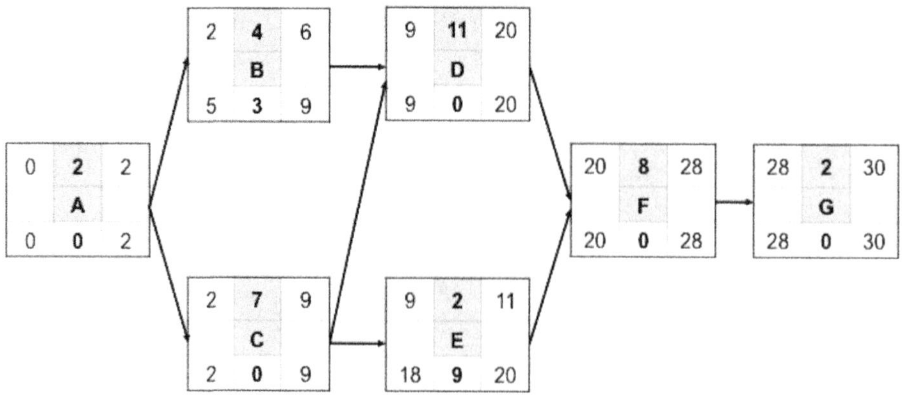

Critical Path: A-C-D-F-G

Chapter 7: Project Cost Management

Learning Objectives:

- ☐ Define the purpose of the Project Cost Management Knowledge Area
- ☐ Identify the processes of the Project Cost Management Knowledge Area
- ☐ Recall the key outputs of the cost management processes
- ☐ Differentiate between the inputs, tools and techniques, and outputs of the cost management processes
- ☐ Understand the concept of Earned Value Management (EVM)
- ☐ Solve EVM calculations

Exam Domain Tasks:

- Develop a budget plan based on the project scope using estimating techniques, in order to manage project cost.

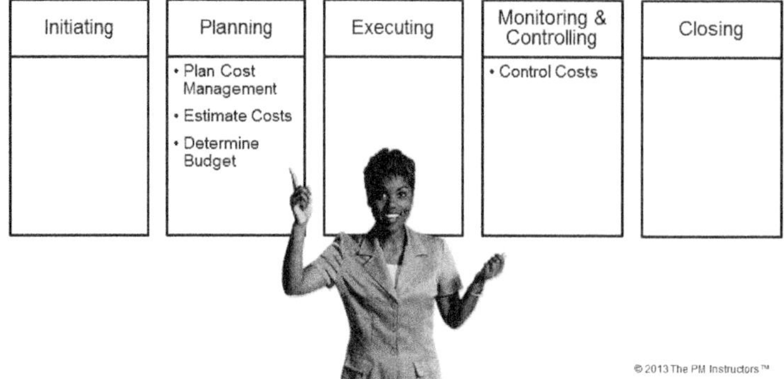

Project Cost Management Overview

The purpose of the Project Cost Management Knowledge Area is to plan, estimate, budget, finance, fund, manage, and control costs so that the project can be completed within the approved budget. In this Knowledge Area, the project budget is created, and as the work begins and moves forward, the budget is monitored and controlled, and overall performance measured and forecasted. As a result, there are several status and forecasting calculations that are contained within this Knowledge Area. For those taking the PMP or CAPM exams, this is usually an area that many are concerned with, but it can become the easiest area within the exam. And if you are merely looking to understand this section to integrate into your project management practices, the calculations and understanding of earned value management will be very insightful and rewarding to your projects.

Aside from the overall purpose stated above, this Knowledge Area is concerned with the cost of resources needed to complete the schedule activities. It considers the effects of project decisions on the budget and overall costs, including those decisions that affect using, maintaining and supporting the product or service that the project is creating.

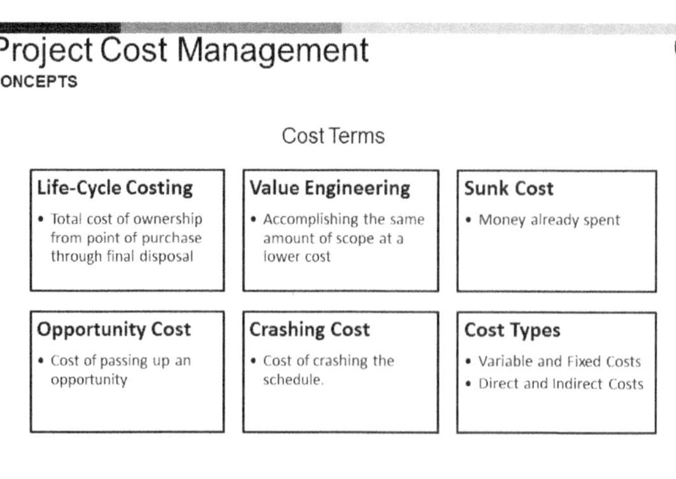

Cost Terms

There are a few cost-related terms that you will need to be familiar with for the exam:

- **Life-cycle costing** considers the overall costs of the product, not just the project costs. This includes maintenance of the product after it has been released. So if a design element saved the company a certain amount of money during the building of the product, but resulted in higher maintenance or operations cost, then the design element was a poor choice, since it cost the company more in the long run.
- **Value engineering**, also known as value analysis, refers to finding a less costly way of doing the work (achieving the same scope at a lower cost).
- **Sunk cost**, which is money already spent, and which should not be considered when determining whether or not to continue on with the project.
- **Opportunity cost** refers to money lost (or opportunity "lost") when selecting one project over another. For example, let's say you have one project with a value of 5 million dollars, and another with a value of 2 million dollars. In this example, the company has selected the first project, with a higher value. The sunk cost would therefore be the value of the project that was not selected, which in this case is 2 million dollars.
- **Crashing cost** is the cost of crashing the schedule – something discussed in the Project Time Management Knowledge Area.
- **Cost types** refer to the four ways of classifying costs: as variable or fixed costs, and as direct or indirect costs.

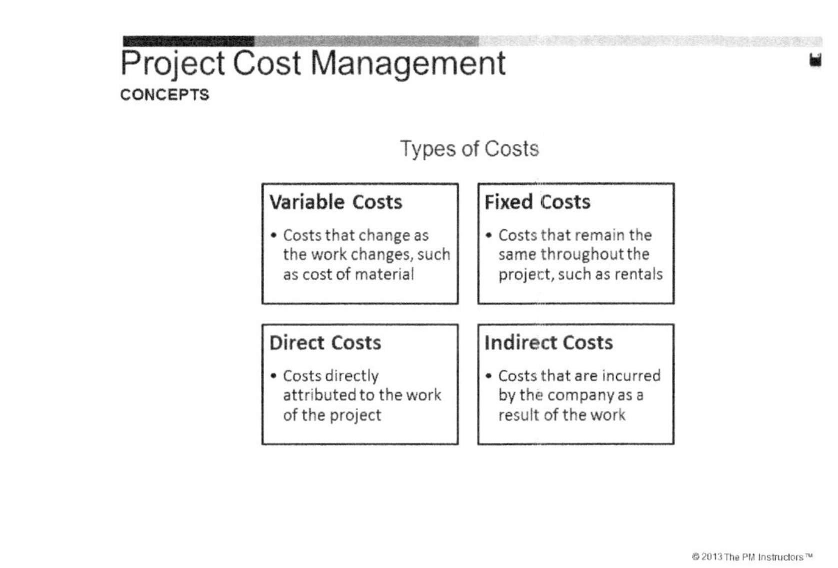

Type of Costs

There are four types of costs:

- Variable Costs – the costs that change as the work changes, such as cost of material.
- Fixed Costs, which are the costs that remain the same throughout the project, such as rentals.
- Direct Costs, which are costs directly attributed to the work of the project.
- Indirect Costs are those costs that are incurred by the company as a result of the work. An example of this would be taxes, overhead costs, and rent – just to name a few.

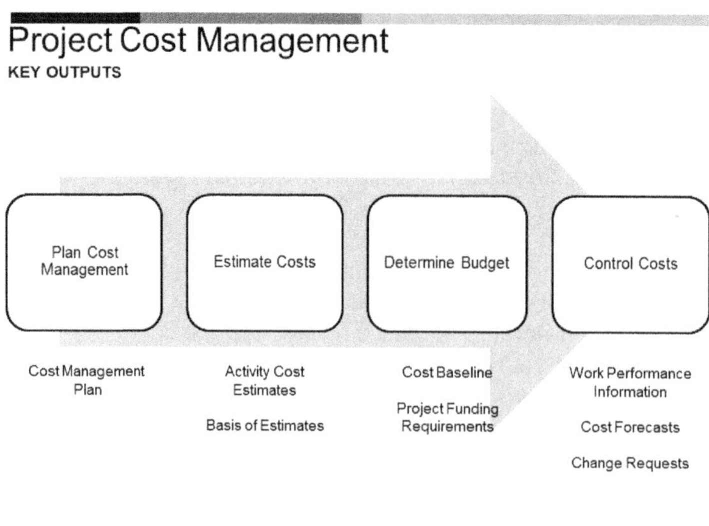

The purpose of the Project Cost Management Knowledge Area is to estimate, budget, and control costs in order to complete the project within budget. There are four processes:

- **Plan Cost Management (Planning Process Group).** Purpose: To establish the policies, procedures, and documentation for planning, managing, expending, and controlling project costs.
- **Estimate Costs (Planning Process Group).** Purpose: To develop an approximation of the monetary resources needed to complete project activities.
- **Determine Budget (Planning Process Group).** Purpose: To aggregate the estimated costs of individual activities or work packages to establish an authorized cost baseline.
- **Control Costs (Monitoring and Controlling Process Group).** Purpose: To monitor the status of the project to update the project costs and manage changes to the cost baseline.

Plan Cost Management
Purpose: To establish the policies, procedures, and documentation for planning, managing, expending, and controlling project costs.

Plan Cost Management Process Overview

The Plan Cost Management process is responsible for establishing the policies, procedures, and documentation for planning, managing, expending, and controlling project costs. The end result of this process is the creation of the cost management plan, which will dictate how the remaining cost management processes are to be carried out, and what the overall cost management approach will be for the project. When developing the cost management approach, it is important to always take into account the cost management requirements extracted from stakeholders.

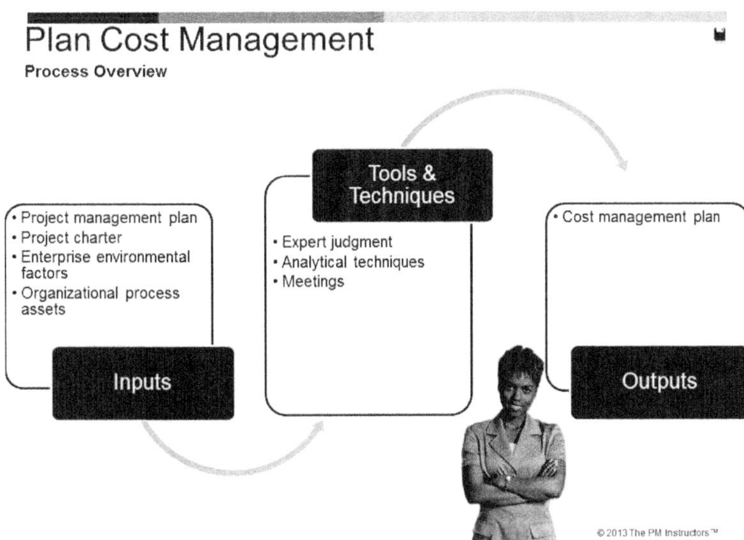
Plan Cost Management
Process Overview
• Project management plan
• Project charter
• Enterprise environmental factors
• Organizational process assets
Inputs
Tools & Techniques
• Expert judgment
• Analytical techniques
• Meetings
• Cost management plan
Outputs
© 2013 The PM Instructors™

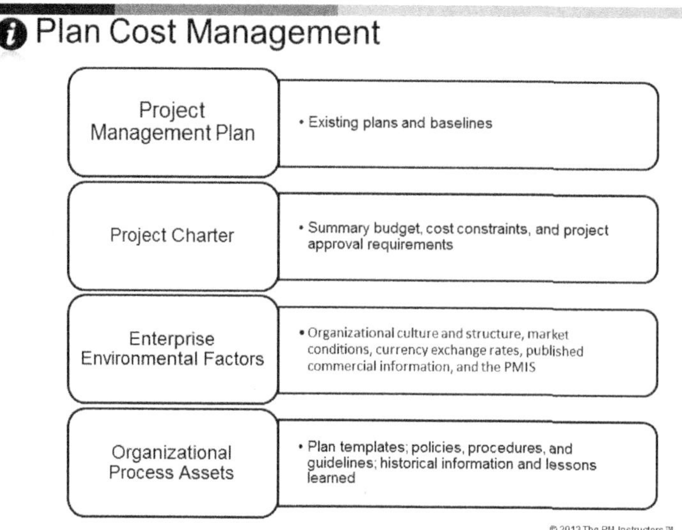
Plan Cost Management
Project Management Plan
• Existing plans and baselines
Project Charter
• Summary budget, cost constraints, and project approval requirements
Enterprise Environmental Factors
• Organizational culture and structure, market conditions, currency exchange rates, published commercial information, and the PMIS
Organizational Process Assets
• Plan templates; policies, procedures, and guidelines; historical information and lessons learned
© 2013 The PM Instructors™

Plan Cost Management Inputs

The Plan Cost Management process utilizes the following four inputs: *project management plan, project charter, enterprise environmental factors, and organizational process assets.*

Project Management Plan

The project management plan is an input to all processes that produce a subsidiary plan. It is important to consider existing plans and baselines when developing a new plan. In creating the cost management plan, the scope baseline and schedule baseline should be referenced, as well as other existing information that is relevant to managing costs.

Project Charter

Like the project management plan, the project charter is a common input to processes that produce a subsidiary plan. In many instances, the project charter will contain a summary budget and / or cost constraints. The project charter often times defines approval requirements that should be considered in managing project costs.

Enterprise Environmental Factors

There are many enterprise environmental factors that should be considered when developing the cost management plan, and other subsidiary plans. Examples of factors include the organizational culture and structure, market conditions, currency exchange rates, published commercial information, and the project management information system.

Organizational Process Assets

Typical organizational process assets considered in developing the cost management plan include cost management plan templates, historical information from past projects, lessons learned, cost estimating processes and procedures, financial and budget management policies, procedures, and guidelines.

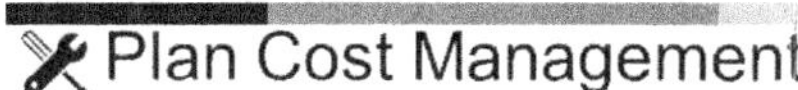

Plan Cost Management

- **Expert Judgment:** This includes information from subject matter experts, combined with historical information.
- **Analytical Techniques:**

Strategic funding options	Financial techniques
• Self-funding • Funding with Equity • Funding with debt	• Payback period • Return on investment • Internal rate of return • Discounted cash flow • Net present value

- **Meetings:** Planning meetings to develop the cost management plan.

Plan Cost Management Tools and Techniques

The Plan Cost Management process uses three tools and techniques: *expert judgment, analytical techniques, and meetings.*

Expert Judgment

Expert judgment involves the use of experts to develop the cost management approach, to be detailed within the cost management plan. Experts typically leverage historical information (obtained through the organizational process assets) to design the approach to managing costs.

Analytical Techniques

Analytical techniques used to develop the contents of the cost management plan typically consist of those that evaluate various strategic funding options. This may include analyzing whether self-funding is the right approach, funding with equity, or funding with debt.

Analytical techniques also encompass the use of various financial techniques, such as payback period, return on investment, internal rate of return, discounted cash flow, and net present value.

Meetings

Meetings are used in combination with the other two techniques. A project manager facilitates one or more planning meetings with the project management team and other subject matter experts to develop the plan.

Plan Cost Management

- **Cost Management Plan:** Describes how project costs will be planned, structured, and controlled.

Contents:
- Level of accuracy that the cost estimates will be based on
- Units of measure used in measurements
- Level of precision
- Organizational procedures
- Control thresholds
- Rules of performance measurement, which covers earned value management rules
- Cost reporting formats
- Process descriptions

Plan Cost Management Outputs

Plan Cost Management has a single output: the *cost management plan*.

Cost Management Plan

Just like the Project Scope and Time Management Knowledge Areas, there is a management plan that plays an important role within its respective Knowledge Area. The cost management plan becomes a component of the project management plan, and will be referenced as the cost management processes are carried out, and as other plans are created.

The cost management plan contains the following information:

- The level of accuracy that the cost estimates will be based on
- The units of measure used in measurements (such as staff hours, days, and weeks)
- Level of precision
- Organizational procedures links (which ties in costs to the WBS control accounts)
- Control thresholds, which outlines how much variation is acceptable before action must be taken
- Rules of performance measurement, which covers EVM rules of performance measurement
- Cost reporting formats
- And process descriptions, which outlines the tools and techniques used to carry out the three cost related processes

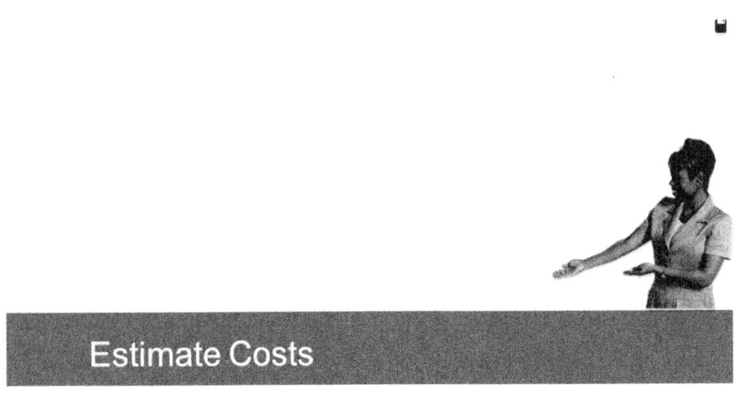

Estimate Costs
Purpose: To develop an approximation of the monetary resources needed to complete project activities.

Estimate Costs Process Overview

The Estimate Costs process is responsible for generating the cost estimates of the individual schedule activities. This is the first step to creating the project budget. The Estimate Activity Resources process works closely with this process, since costs is a big consideration in determining which resources are available for use.

Another important note regarding this process is that cost estimates are determined based on the information known at given points in time. As additional information becomes available, cost estimates can be updated to reflect a more accurate measurement.

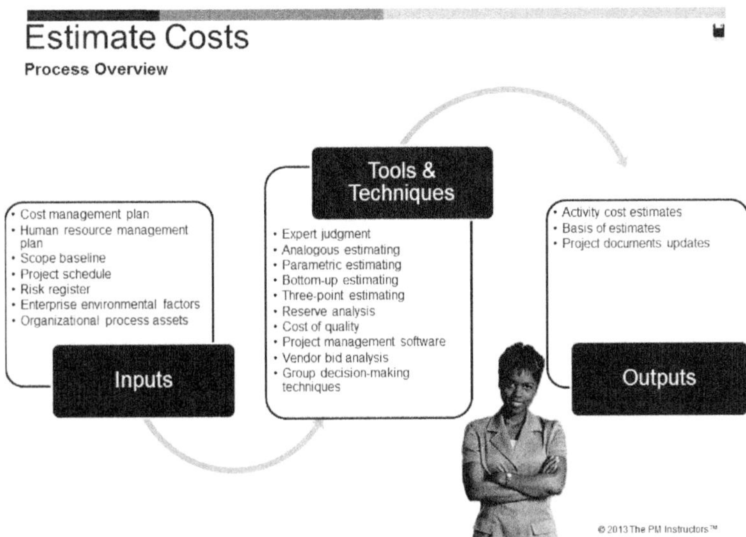

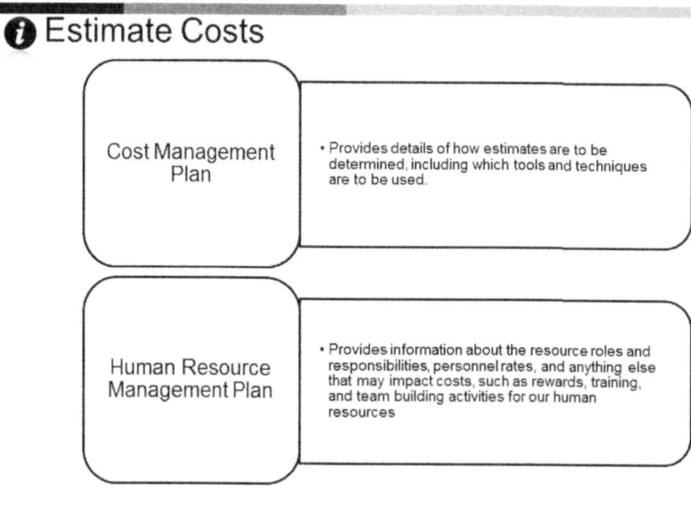

Estimate Costs Inputs

The Estimate Costs process utilizes the following seven inputs: *cost management plan, human resource management plan, scope baseline, project schedule, risk register, enterprise environmental factors, and organizational process assets.*

Cost Management Plan

The cost management plan is key to this process, since it dictates how estimates are to be approached and derived. This includes specifying which tools and techniques should be used, and to what level of precision the estimates should be at given points within the planning process.

Human Resource Management Plan

The human resource management plan provides information about the resource roles and responsibilities, as well as the personnel rates and anything else that may impact costs, such as rewards, training, and team building activities for our human resources.

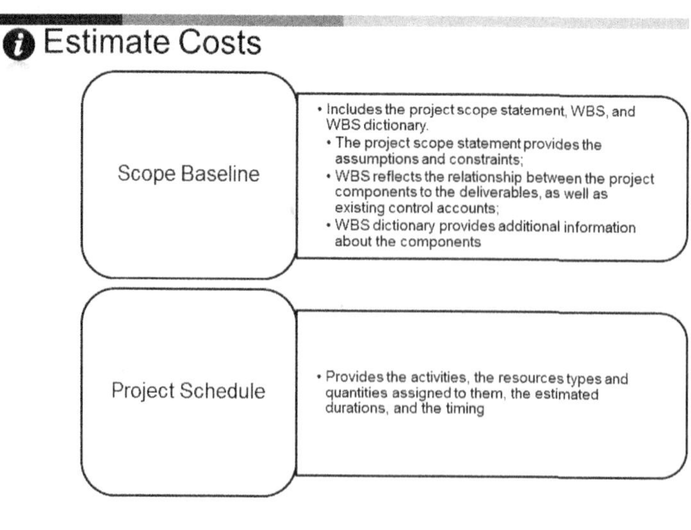

Scope Baseline

The scope baseline provides the project scope statement, WBS, and WBS dictionary. Our interests within the project scope statement lies with the assumptions and constraints; the WBS reflects the relationship between the project components to the deliverables, as well as existing control accounts; and the WBS dictionary provides additional information about each of the components.

Project Schedule

The project schedule will provide the following for use within this process: the activities, the resource types and quantities assigned to them, the estimated durations, and the timing. All of this is important to estimating costs.

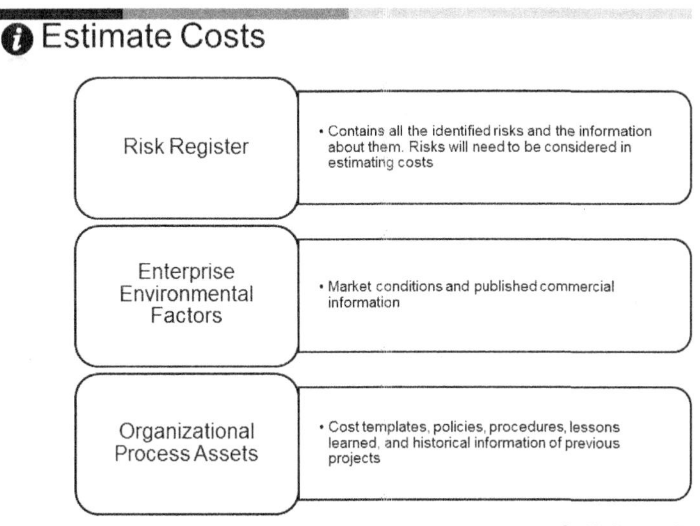

Risk Register

The risk register contains all of the identified risks and the information about them. Risks will need to be considered in estimating costs, as well as the response plans that may involve contingency funds.

Enterprise Environmental Factors

Enterprise environmental factors takes into account market conditions and published commercial information, among other things.

Organizational Process Assets

It's through organizational process assets that cost templates are obtained, as well as cost-related policies, procedures, lessons learned, and historical information of previous projects.

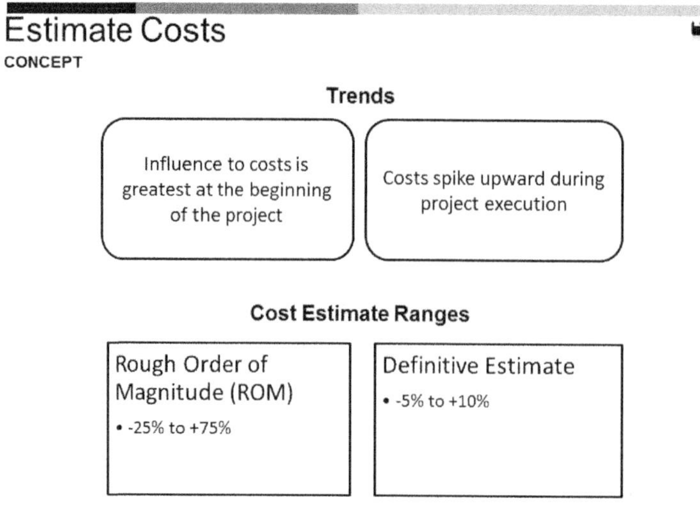

Estimate Costs
CONCEPT
Trends
Influence to costs is greatest at the beginning of the project
Costs spike upward during project execution
Cost Estimate Ranges
Rough Order of Magnitude (ROM)
• -25% to +75%
Definitive Estimate
• -5% to +10%
© 2013 The PM Instructors™

Life Cycle Trends and Budget Estimates

Influence to project costs is greatest at the beginning of the project, since that is when stakeholders have the greatest amount of influence, when there is greater uncertainty and the work has not yet begun. It is during the Executing phase that costs spike upward, since this is when resources are mostly used.

During the initiation phase it is typical that only a rough order of magnitude (ROM) estimate may be calculated, which is a range of -25% to +75%; while later, when more information is known and available, the range may be narrowed down to a definitive estimate of -5% to +10%.

- **Expert Judgment:** This includes information from subject matter experts, combined with historical information.

Helps to get buy-in
© 2013 The PM Instructors™

Estimate Costs Tools and Techniques

The Estimate Costs process uses the following ten tools and techniques: *expert judgment, analogous estimating, parametric estimating, bottom-up estimating, three-point estimating, reserve analysis, cost of quality, project management software, vendor bid analysis, and group decision-making techniques.*

Expert Judgment

Whenever estimating is involved, expert judgment is typically used. This includes information from subject matter experts, combined with historical information. Note that the project manager should not estimate time and costs alone – it is *essential* that subject matter experts be involved.

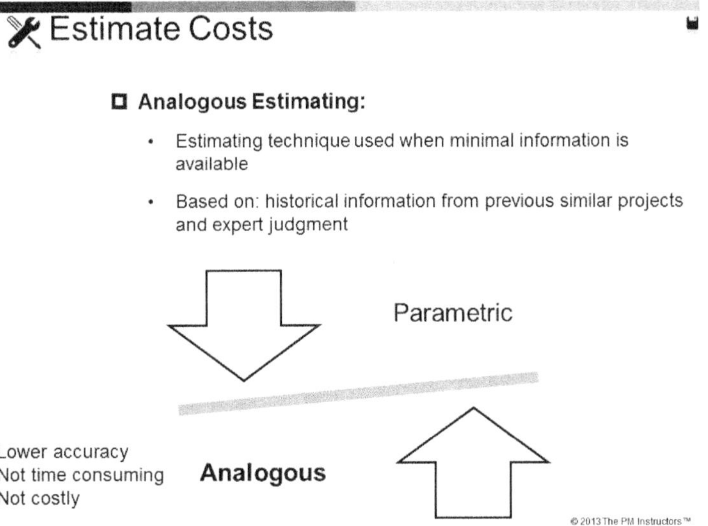

Analogous Estimating

Analogous estimating is a technique used when not much information is available to perform cost estimating activities. In this case, the project team uses actual costs of previous similar projects in combination with their own experiences. Primarily, this type of technique relies on expert judgment.

Analogous estimating is considered to be less costly than other methods, but it is also less accurate. The data of the previous project you are utilizing would need to be from a very similar project for accuracy, and this is where the expert judgment comes in – to understand when the estimates need to be adjusted to make sense for the current project, and when the previous data does not make sense to apply.

Parametric Estimating:

- Estimating technique considered fairly accurate
- Uses mathematical models to calculate cost estimates
- Based on: historical information from previous similar projects and other variables from current project

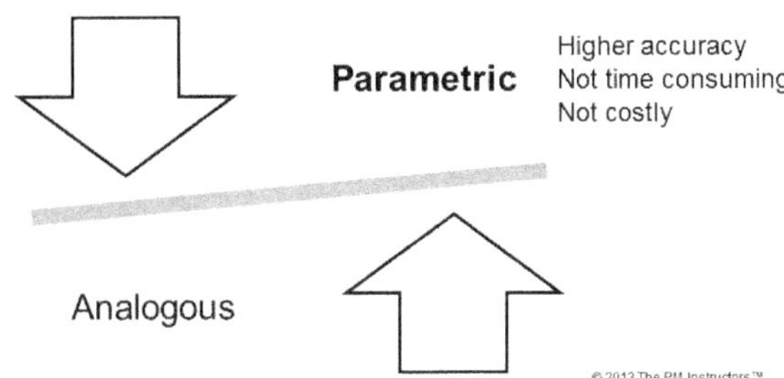

Parametric Estimating

Parametric estimating is a technique that uses mathematical models to calculate cost estimates. Historical data is used along with other variables of the current project, such as labor hours, lines of code, etc.

For example, let's look at multiplying the quantity of work with a historical unit: a software developer is tasked with completing a project that requires 50 hours of work. If the developer is paid $50 per hour, and the project task takes an estimate of 50 hours to complete, the estimated cost is $2,500. This technique can be highly accurate.

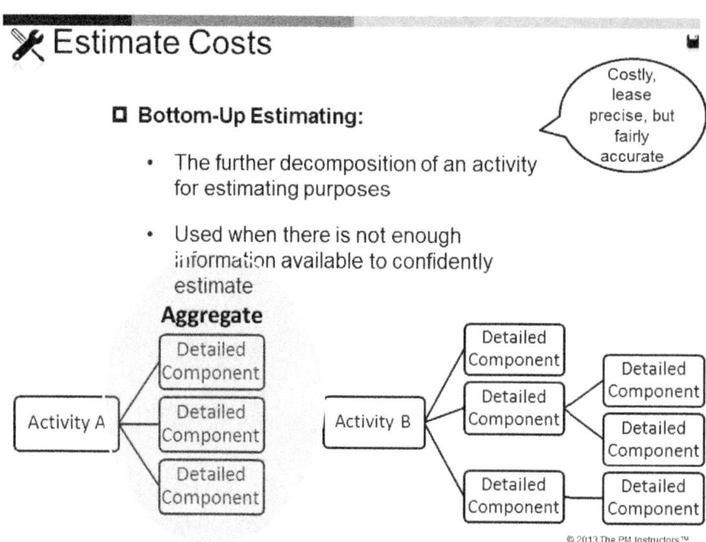

Bottom-Up Estimating

Remember that analogous is the least precise, but least costly, while bottom-up estimating is the most accurate estimate of the three, but the most costly and time consuming to perform.

In bottom-up estimating, it is possible to get a precise estimate by estimating individual work packages or schedule activities. Experts are the key to further decomposing these activities into smaller more detailed components of work. The detailed costs are then "rolled up" to higher levels for an accurate estimate. This is extremely helpful when the schedule activity or work package is large and complex, the activity cannot be estimated otherwise, or an accurate estimate is needed. This is a more costly technique to utilize.

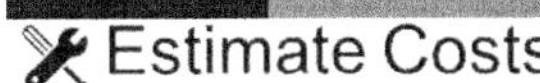

Three-Point Estimating:

- Increases accuracy of estimates and considers uncertainty and risk by gathering an Optimistic, Pessimistic, and Most Likely estimate
- Uses Program Evaluation and Review Technique (PERT)

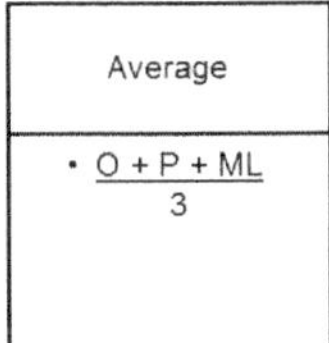

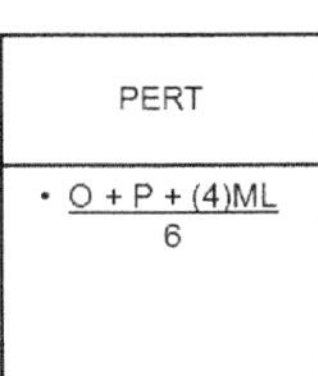

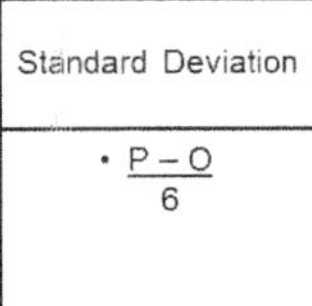

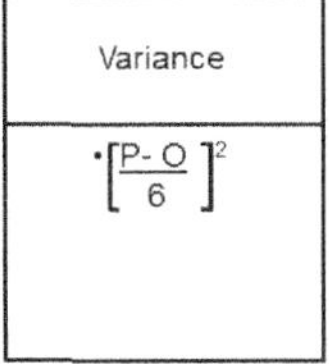

Three-Point Estimating

Three-point estimating involves gathering an optimistic, pessimistic, and most likely estimate for an activity. With these estimates, we can take a straight average and use that estimate, or we can assign a higher weight to the most likely estimate by using the Program Evaluation and Review Technique (PERT), where the most likely estimate is given a weight of four. The purpose of using PERT is to achieve an expected duration (an estimate with a higher accuracy).

The formula for PERT is:

$$\frac{O + P + 4\,(ML)}{6}$$

You can also calculate standard deviation to determine the probable range. The formula for calculating standard deviation is: P - O ÷ 6

The formula for calculating variance is standard deviation squared:

$$\left[\frac{O + P + 4\,(ML)}{6}\right]^2$$

Estimate Costs

- **Reserve Analysis:** Estimating the amount of reserve needed (contingency reserve), which accounts for uncertainty and risk
- **Cost of Quality:** Looks at the cost of quality efforts
- **Project Management Software:** The use of estimating software, which comes from the enterprise environmental factors
- **Vendor Bid Analysis:** Looks at the incoming bids from potential vendors to help estimate costs for activities that are being procured
- **Group Decision-Making Techniques:** The use of team-based approaches are used to improve accuracy in estimates

Reserve Analysis

Reserve analysis involves calculating how much cost reserve is needed. Reserves are a form of buffer. This is a type of contingency reserve that accounts for uncertainty (or risk). This is where the risk register also becomes important, since reserves allow for the project management team to account for risk.

Cost of Quality

Cost of quality looks at the cost of quality efforts. Notice that we must consider all aspects of the project that impact costs.

Project Management Software

Project management estimating software means just as it sounds – the use of software for cost estimating purposes. Software comes from the enterprise environmental factors input.

Vendor Bid Analysis

Vendor bid analysis looks at the incoming bids from potential vendors to help estimate costs for activities that are being procured.

Group Decision-Making Techniques

The use of group decision-making techniques involves team-based approaches to estimating. This may involve getting a group of experts together to develop or improve estimates. Examples of team-based approaches include brainstorming, Delphi technique, and nominal group technique. These techniques not only produce better estimates, but also help to get team-buy in.

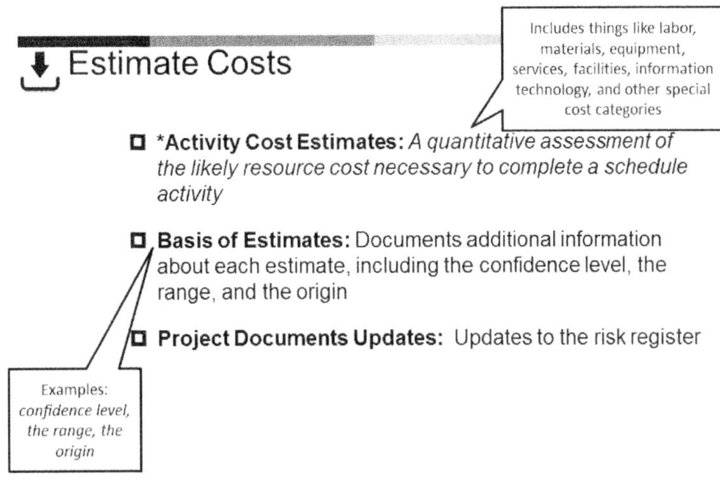
Estimate Costs
Includes things like labor, materials, equipment, services, facilities, information technology, and other special cost categories
*Activity Cost Estimates: A quantitative assessment of the likely resource cost necessary to complete a schedule activity
Basis of Estimates: Documents additional information about each estimate, including the confidence level, the range, and the origin
Project Documents Updates: Updates to the risk register
Examples: confidence level, the range, the origin
* Definition from A Guide to the Project Management Body of Knowledge, Project Management Institute Inc., 2013
© 2013 The PM Instructors™

Estimate Costs Outputs

The Estimate Costs process produces the following three outputs: *activity cost estimates, basis of estimates, and project documents updates.*

Activity Cost Estimates

Activity cost estimates is a quantitative assessment of the likely resource cost necessary to complete the schedule activity. It can either be displayed as a summary or in detail. It typically includes things like labor, materials, equipment, services, facilities, information technology, and other special cost categories. In its simplest definition, activity cost estimates refer to the cost estimate per activity.

Basis of Estimates

Along with the cost estimates for each activity, another output generated is basis of estimates. Basis of estimates documents additional information about each estimate, including the confidence level, the range, the origin; so literally, what the estimate is based on. Notice a recurring theme of documentation throughout the processes.

Project Documents Updates

Project documents updates resulting from this process typically include updates made to the risk register.

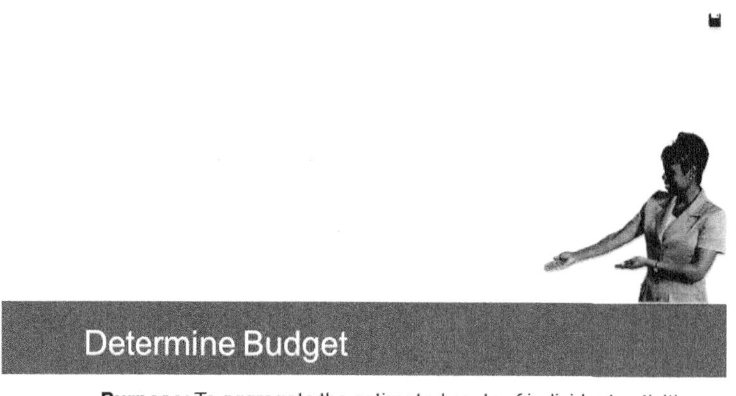
Determine Budget
Purpose: To aggregate the estimated costs of individual activities or work packages to establish an authorized cost baseline.

Determine Budget Process Overview

The purpose of the Determine Budget process is to aggregate the estimated costs of individual activities or work packages to establish an authorized cost baseline. In other words, this process calculates an overall project budget. This involves creating a cost baseline by aggregating the individual cost estimates determined in the previous process, or by aggregating the cost estimates of work packages. This allows for measurement of the project performance, which is something that will be done in the next process.

The project budget is defined as all the funds authorized to execute the project, while the cost baseline represents the approved version of the time-phased project budget, excluding management reserves.

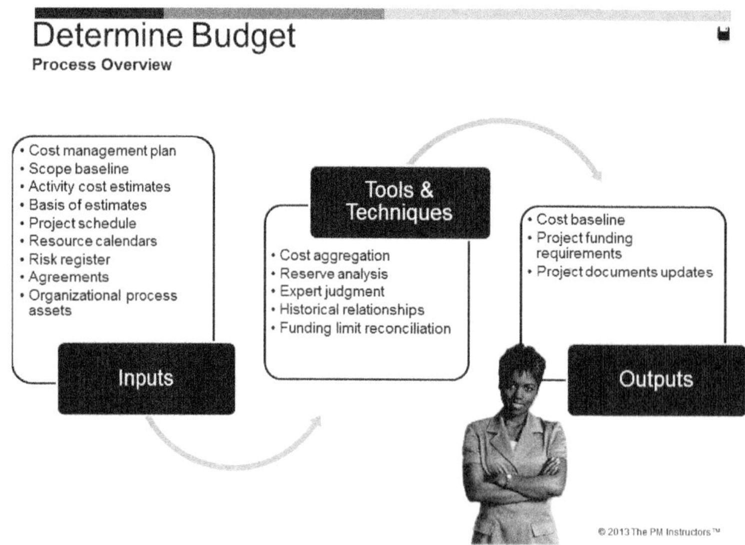
Determine Budget
Process Overview
• Cost management plan
• Scope baseline
• Activity cost estimates
• Basis of estimates
• Project schedule
• Resource calendars
• Risk register
• Agreements
• Organizational process assets
Inputs
Tools & Techniques
• Cost aggregation
• Reserve analysis
• Expert judgment
• Historical relationships
• Funding limit reconciliation
• Cost baseline
• Project funding requirements
• Project documents updates
Outputs
© 2013 The PM Instructors™

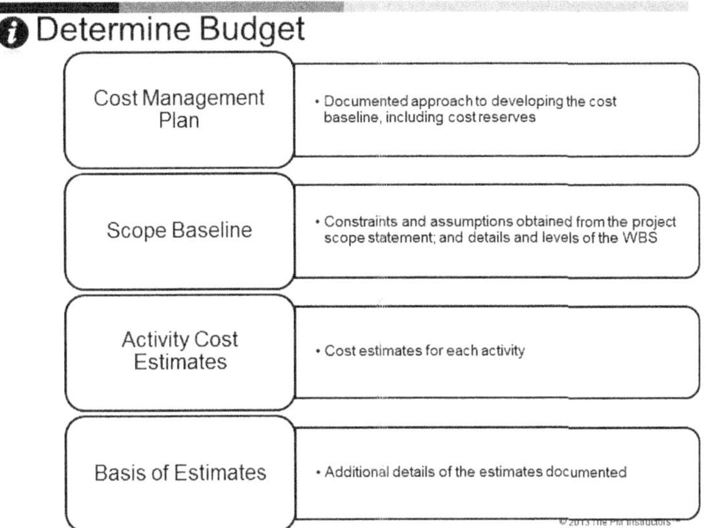
Determine Budget
Cost Management Plan
• Documented approach to developing the cost baseline, including cost reserves
Scope Baseline
• Constraints and assumptions obtained from the project scope statement; and details and levels of the WBS
Activity Cost Estimates
• Cost estimates for each activity
Basis of Estimates
• Additional details of the estimates documented

Determine Budget Inputs

The Determine Budget process has a total of 9 inputs, with three of them produced by other cost management processes. The inputs used by the process are as follow: *cost management plan, scope baseline, activity cost estimates, basis of estimates, project schedule, resource calendars, risk register, agreements, and organizational process assets.*

Cost Management Plan

The cost management plan provides documented information on how the budget is to be developed. This includes the approach to developing and getting sign-off of the budget to form the cost baseline, as well as identifying cost reserves (contingency and management reserves).

Scope Baseline

The scope baseline contains the project scope statement, WBS, and WBS dictionary. We'll need the constraints and assumptions out of the project scope statement, but also the details and levels of the WBS, including: the work packages, control accounts, and overall project levels.

Activity Cost Estimates

Activity cost estimates provide the costs of each individual schedule activity. These individual estimates will be rolled up to various levels to produce the overall project estimate.

Basis of Estimates

The basis of estimates provides additional details of the cost estimates, which were documented in the previous process.

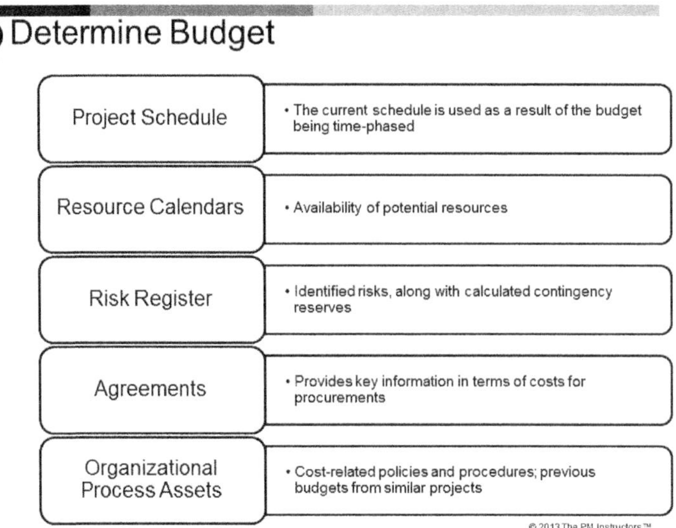

Project Schedule

The project schedule is an important input to this process due to the timing of when funds are needed. The reason being that the project budget is time-phased, as opposed to funds being disbursed all at once.

Resource Calendars

Resource calendars provide the availability of potential resources. Resource calendars are created out of the Acquire Project Team process, and the Conduct Procurements process.

Risk Register

The risk register contains the list of identified risks, including all of the information known and documented about them. This includes the identified risk responses, as well as contingency reserves. Risk responses and contingency reserves set aside to address risks typically have associated costs, making this an important input to the process.

Agreements

Agreements, also known as contracts, provide key information in terms of costs for procurements. A contract should detail the cost of products, services, or results that have been purchased, and also when payment for these items will be due.

Organizational Process Assets

Organizational process assets often utilized as part of this process includes cost-related policies, procedures, and guidelines, as well as budgeting tools. Lessons learned and historical information also provide valuable insight into how the budget is to be developed.

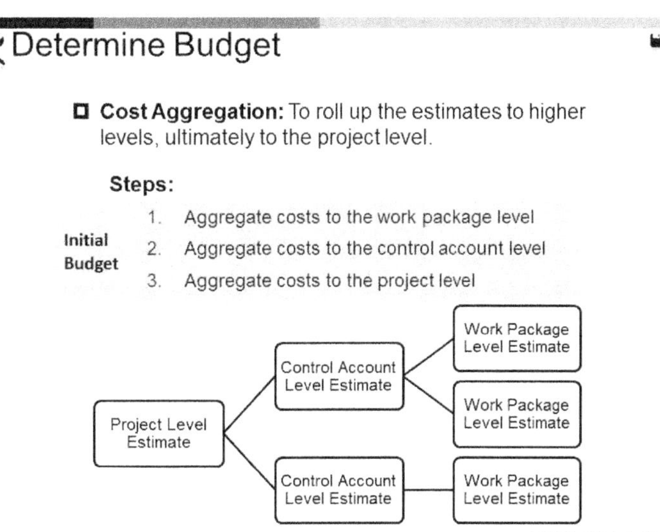

Determine Budget Tools and Techniques

The Determine Budget process has a total of five tools and techniques: *cost aggregation, reserve analysis, expert judgment, historical relationships, and funding limit reconciliation.*

Cost Aggregation

Cost aggregation means to roll up the individual cost estimates to higher levels, ultimately to the project level. The first step is to aggregate the individual activity cost estimates to the work package level, then to the control account level, and then finally, to the project level.

The end result of cost aggregation provides an initial project budget.

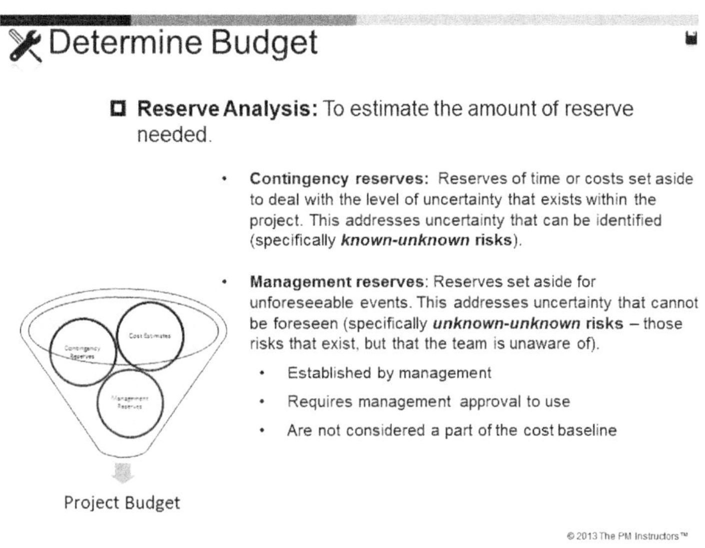

Reserve Analysis

Reserve analysis refers to the total amount of reserve funds needed. There are two types of cost reserves:

- Contingency reserves
- Management reserves

Contingency Reserves

Contingency reserves are reserves of time or costs set aside to deal with the level of uncertainty that exists within the project. This refers to uncertainty that can be identified (to account for known risks). Known risks can be planned for, based on the information acquired to date. Information about known risks can be determined through the risk register input.

Management Reserves

Management reserves, on the other hand, account for unknown-unknown risks – those risks that exist, but we don't know about. They're called management reserves because management sets this reserve level, and it requires management approval to use. The management reserves are not considered to be part of the cost baseline, while contingency reserves are.

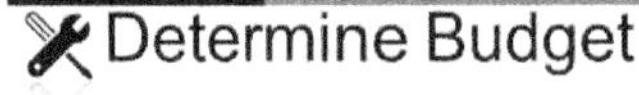
Determine Budget

- **Expert Judgment:** Obtaining feedback from subject matter experts.
- **Historical Relationships:** Involves using the analogous or parametric estimating techniques.
- **Funding Limit Reconciliation:** To level out expenditures.
  - Purpose: to avoid large and inconsistent use of funds
  - Can place imposed date constraints

Helps to get buy-in
© 2013 The PM Instructors™

Expert Judgment

As mentioned previously, any time that estimating is involved – including estimating the overall budget – subject matter experts should be included. This not only improves accuracy, but gets the buy-in of the team.

Historical Relationships

Historical relationships, as a technique, involve reviewing past historical documentation of similar projects to assist in putting together the overall budget. This often utilizes analogous or parametric estimating techniques.

Funding Limit Reconciliation

Funding limit reconciliation is similar to resource leveling – here, the goal is to level out expenditures. This technique looks at the existing expenditure of funds and reconciles them to occur within set limits determined by the customer or the performing organization. As a result, the scheduling of the work may need to be adjusted. The purpose is to avoid large and inconsistent use of funds and even out, or smoothen out, the spending throughout execution of the project work, as is possible. This is done by placing imposed date constraints on some work packages, schedule milestones, or WBS components within the project schedule.

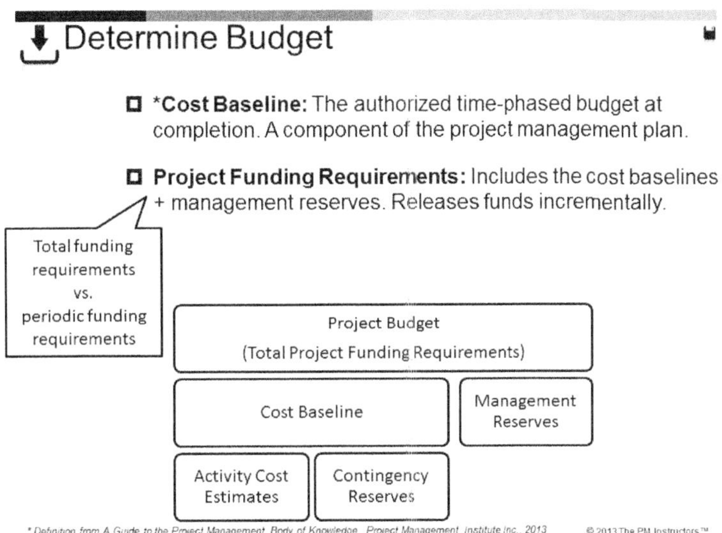
Determine Budget
*Cost Baseline: The authorized time-phased budget at completion. A component of the project management plan.
Project Funding Requirements: Includes the cost baselines + management reserves. Releases funds incrementally.
Total funding requirements vs. periodic funding requirements
Project Budget (Total Project Funding Requirements)
Cost Baseline
Management Reserves
Activity Cost Estimates
Contingency Reserves

Determine Budget Outputs

The Determine Budget process produces three outputs: *cost baseline, project funding requirements, and project documents updates.*

Cost Baseline

The *PMBOK® Guide* describes the cost baseline as the authorized time phased budget at completion. Because it is a baseline, it becomes a part of the project management plan, and will be important to measuring, monitoring, and controlling overall project costs. It is also known as the performance measurement baseline. The cost baseline includes the cost estimates plus the contingency reserves.

Cost Baseline = Activity Cost Estimates + Contingency Reserves

Project Funding Requirements

The project funding requirements come from the cost baseline and are adjusted to reflect early progress or cost overruns. Since funding typically occurs in incremental amounts, versus a continuous steady flow, the funding requirements release funds incrementally throughout the project's lifecycle. Aside from the cost baseline, project funding requirements also include the management reserve amount. This amount is included incrementally throughout the project, or simply when needed. To determine how much of the management reserve was included, you simply subtract the total project funding requirement from the maximum funding authorized. To determine how much of the management reserve was not used at the end of the project, you subtract the total cash flow from the total project funding requirement, and then subtract that by the maximum funding authorized. This number will give you the actual management reserve used, which you can compare with the original estimate.

Total funding requirements refer to the total cost baseline plus the management reserves; periodic funding requirements refer to the portion of the cost baseline and management reserves that are to be released at given points in time (such as quarterly or annually).

Project Funding Requirements = Cost Baseline + Management Reserves

The previously highlighted text shown above reflects how the cost baseline contains activity cost estimates and contingency reserves, while the project funding requirements contains activity cost estimates plus both types of reserves (contingency and management reserves).

Determine Budget

Project Documents Updates	• Updates to the risk register, activity cost estimates, and project schedule

Project Documents Updates

Project documents updated as a result of carrying out this process typically include the risk register, activity cost estimates, and the project schedule.

Control Costs

Purpose: To monitor the status of the project to update the project costs and manage changes to the cost baseline.

Control Costs Process Overview

The Control Costs process is responsible for comparing actual project information, based on current status, to planned costs. The purpose of the process is to monitor status of the project to update the project costs and manage changes to the cost baseline. Using earned value management (EVM), the project management team can calculate status of the project, in terms of how the project is performing according to the schedule and budget, as well as forecasts of how the project will perform.

The Control Costs process is also responsible for influencing the factors that create cost variance within the project, and to control changes to the project budget. Variances can be both positive and negative. In addition to the above, this process is responsible for the following:

- Influencing factors that create changes to the cost baseline
- Managing changes as they occur
- Monitoring cost performance to identify variances from the baseline
- Recording changes to the baseline as they occur
- Informing stakeholders of approved changes

In addition to these items, the process also:

- Ensures that there exists agreement on requested changes
- Monitors cost overruns so that they do not exceed authorized funding
- Ensures that reported cost and resource usage is accurate
- Brings expected cost overruns within acceptable limits

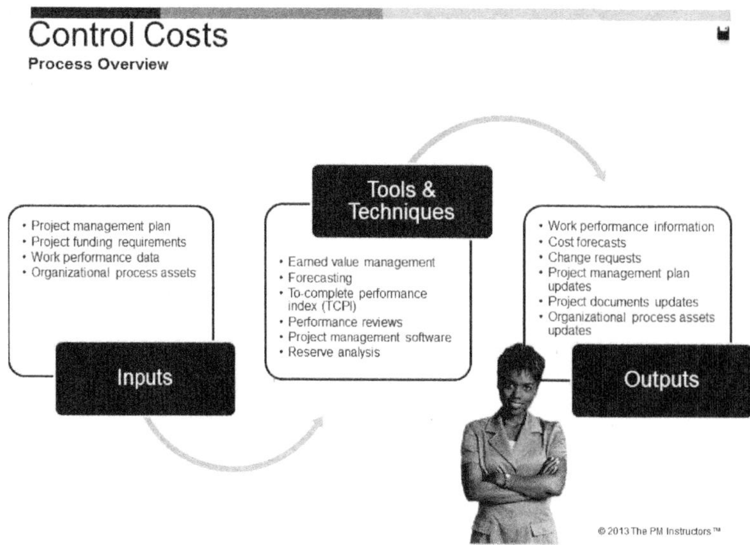
Control Costs
Process Overview
Tools & Techniques
• Project management plan
• Project funding requirements
• Work performance data
• Organizational process assets
• Earned value management
• Forecasting
• To-complete performance index (TCPI)
• Performance reviews
• Project management software
• Reserve analysis
• Work performance information
• Cost forecasts
• Change requests
• Project management plan updates
• Project documents updates
• Organizational process assets updates
Inputs
Outputs
© 2013 The PM Instructors™

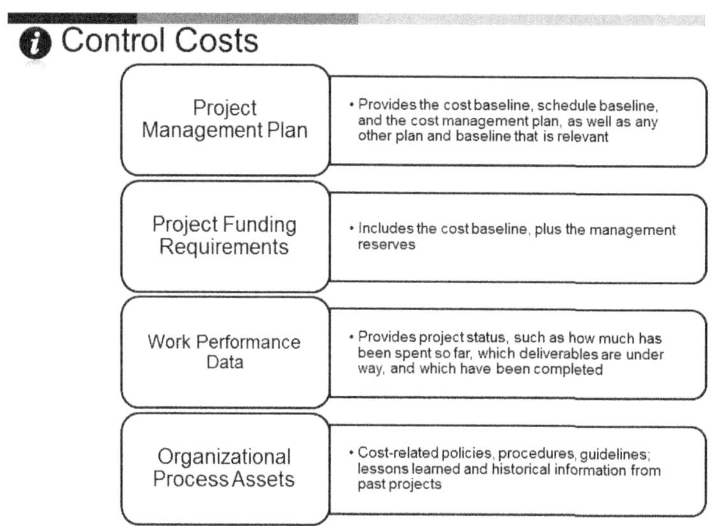
Control Costs
Project Management Plan
• Provides the cost baseline, schedule baseline, and the cost management plan, as well as any other plan and baseline that is relevant
Project Funding Requirements
• Includes the cost baseline, plus the management reserves
Work Performance Data
• Provides project status, such as how much has been spent so far, which deliverables are under way, and which have been completed
Organizational Process Assets
• Cost-related policies, procedures, guidelines; lessons learned and historical information from past projects
© 2013 The PM Instructors™

Control Costs Inputs

The Control Costs process utilizes the following four inputs: *project management plan, project funding requirements, work performance data, and organizational process assets.*

Project Management Plan

The project management plan provides the cost baseline, schedule baseline, and the cost management plan, as well as any other plan and baseline that is relevant.

Project Funding Requirements

Project funding requirements contain not just the cost baseline (which is included in the project management plan input), but also the management reserves. Project funding requirements also contain key information on when funds are disbursed.

Work Performance Data

Work performance data provides current status of the project, such as how much has been spent to date, which deliverables are underway and which have been completed. This can be viewed as the raw data that will be further analyzed through this process to identify and forecast existing or potential variance. This information, along with the planned budget, will be necessary for assessing current and future performance.

Organizational Process Assets

Organizational process assets provide cost-related policies, procedures, and guidelines, as well as cost reporting methods and templates. Lessons learned are also an important component that are found within organizational process assets, which are insightful when carrying out monitoring and controlling activities.

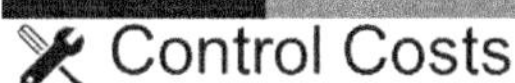

- **Earned Value Management (EVM):** A methodology that is used to assess and measure project performance. There are three key dimensions used as part of EVM: PV, EV, and AC.

Earned Value (EV)	Planned Value (PV)	Actual Cost (AC)
• The measure of work performed expressed in terms of the budget authorized for that work.	• The authorized budget assigned to scheduled work.	• The realized cost incurred for the work performed on an activity during a specific time period (actual funds spent).

- **Budget at Completion (BAC):** Refers to the sum of all budgets established for the work to be performed. The sum of all PVs add up to the BAC.

Control Costs Tools and Techniques

There are six tools and techniques within the Control Costs process, including: earned value management, forecasting, to-complete performance index (TCPI), performance reviews, project management software, and reserve analysis. Earned value management is a key technique used to assess existing and future project performance.

Earned Value Management

Earned value management (EVM) is a methodology that combines scope, schedule, and resource measurements to assess project performance and progress. EVM is the most commonly used method to measuring a project's performance.

Earned Value

Earned value (EV) refers to the measure of work performed expressed in terms of the budget authorized for that work (depending on the level being assessed). To put it simply, it's a snapshot of the value of the work progress, answering the question: "what is the value of work completed?"

EV is often used to represent how much work has been completed for an activity or for the project. How this is measured, however, varies by organization, and is not the recommended use of EV, since EV is meant to represent *value* of work completed.

Planned Value

Planned value is the authorized budget assigned to scheduled work – either an activity or WBS component. This includes the detailed authorized work + the budget for this work. The total PV is referred to as the **performance measurement baseline** (PMB). In addition to planned value, actual cost is also tracked and used in determining project performance.

Actual Cost

Actual cost (AC) refers to the realized cost incurred for the work performed on an activity during a specific time period.

Budget at Completion

Budget at Completion (BAC) refers to the sum of all budgets established for the work to be performed. It is the total planned value of the *project*.

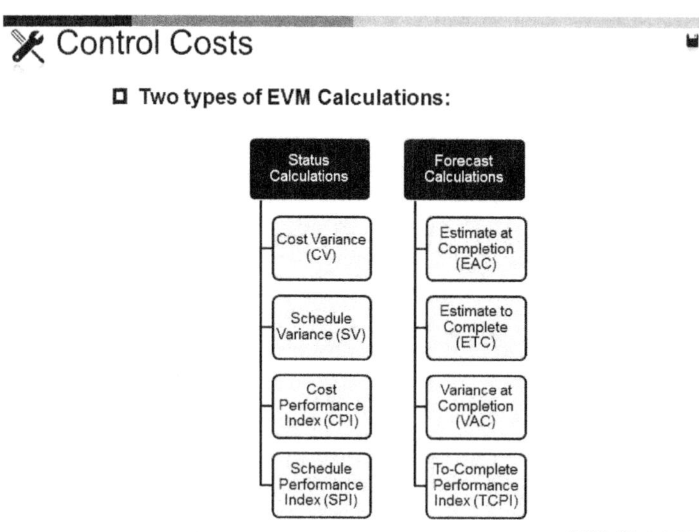

Status versus Forecasts

Earned value management calculations can be divided into two types: status and forecasts.

Status calculations include:

- Cost variance
- Schedule variance
- Cost performance index
- Schedule performance index

Forecast calculations include:

- Estimate at completion
- Estimate to complete
- Variance at completion
- To-complete performance index

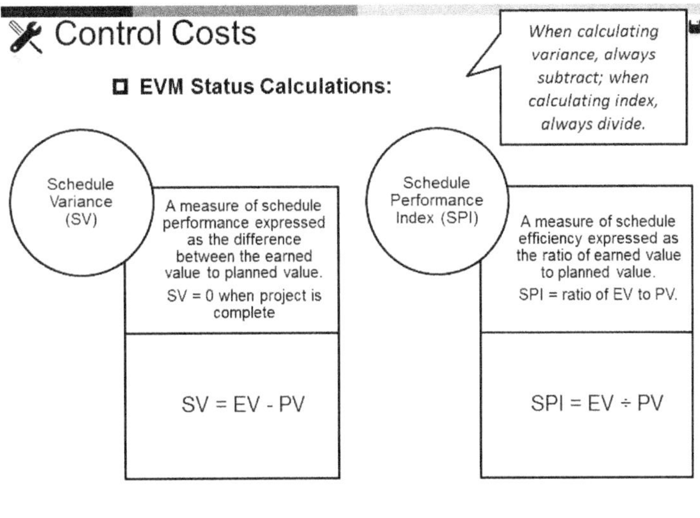

As part of EVM within the Control Schedule and Control Costs processes, schedule variance (SV) and schedule performance index (SPI) are calculated.

Schedule Variance

Schedule variance refers to the measure of schedule performance expressed as the difference between the earned value to planned value. This will therefore reveal whether the project team is ahead or behind schedule. When the project is complete, the SV equals zero. According to the *PMBOK® Guide*, EVM schedule variance is best used "in conjunction with the critical path methodology scheduling and risk management". The formula for calculating SV is EV – PV.

Schedule Performance Index

Schedule Performance Index (SPI) represents the measure of schedule efficiency expressed as the ratio of earned value to planned value. In other words, it is the ratio of EV to PV. The index value identifies the performance efficiency of the team in performing relative to the value accumulation of the schedule. The formula for calculating SPI is EV / PV.

Notice that both SV and SPI formulas use EV and PV. *When calculating variance, always subtract; when calculating index, always divide.*

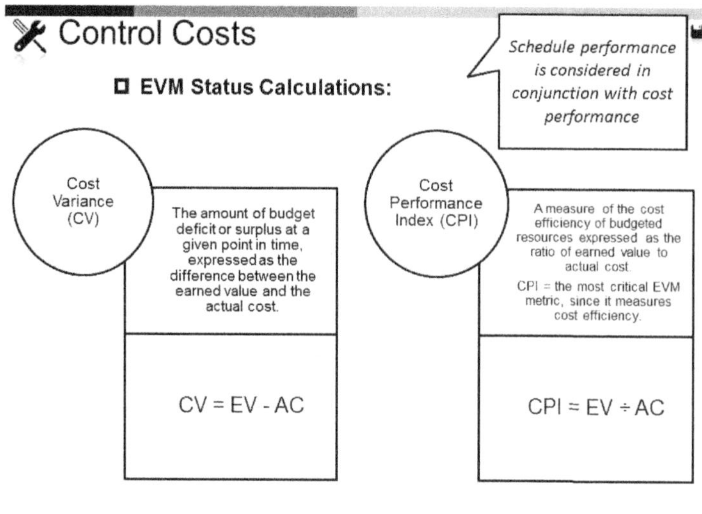

Calculating cost performance is not only tied to the Control Costs process and measuring budget performance. As part of making decisions that relate to the schedule, cost performance will also need to be considered. An example of this is in selecting a schedule compression method: if crashing is considered, are there enough funds to move forward with this technique? There are other, more complex scenarios that combine schedule performance with cost performance that a project manager will use. This is just one example of how EVM is used in various ways and in making various decisions related to the project.

In order to determine cost performance, cost variance and the cost performance index will need to be calculated.

Cost Variance

Cost variance (CV) is the amount of budget deficit or surplus at a given point in time, expressed as the difference between the earned value and the actual cost.

It reflects the relationship of physical performance to the costs spent. To calculate cost variance, simply subtract the actual cost from the earned value (EV – AC).

Cost Performance Index

Cost performance index (CPI) measures the cost efficiency of budgeted resources expressed as the ratio of earned value to actual cost. This is considered to be the most critical EVM metric, since it measures the cost efficiency of the work completed. To calculate CPI, simply divide earned value by actual cost (EV / AC).

EVM Status Interpretations

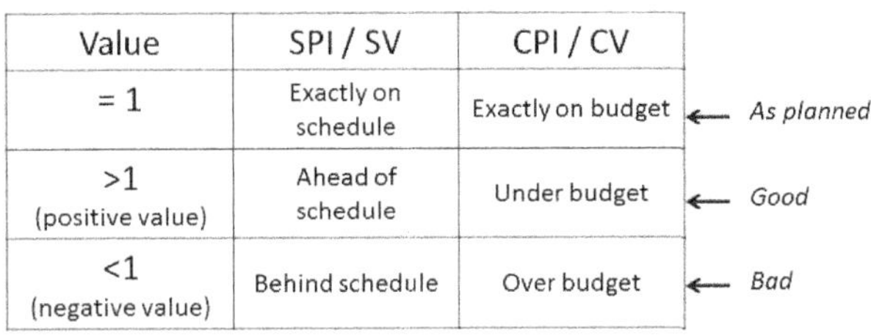

Value	SPI / SV	CPI / CV	
= 1	Exactly on schedule	Exactly on budget	← *As planned*
>1 (positive value)	Ahead of schedule	Under budget	← *Good*
<1 (negative value)	Behind schedule	Over budget	← *Bad*

Assessing the Results: EVM Status Interpretations

Schedule Variance (SV):

- Positive value means that the project team is on or ahead of schedule
- Negative value means that the project team is behind schedule

Cost Variance (CV):

- Positive value means that the project is performing under budget
- Negative value means that the project is performing over budget

Schedule Performance Index (SPI):

SPI = 1 on schedule   SPI >1 ahead of schedule   SPI < 1 behind schedule

Cost Performance Index (CPI):

CPI = 1 on budget   CPI >1 under budget   CPI < 1 over budget

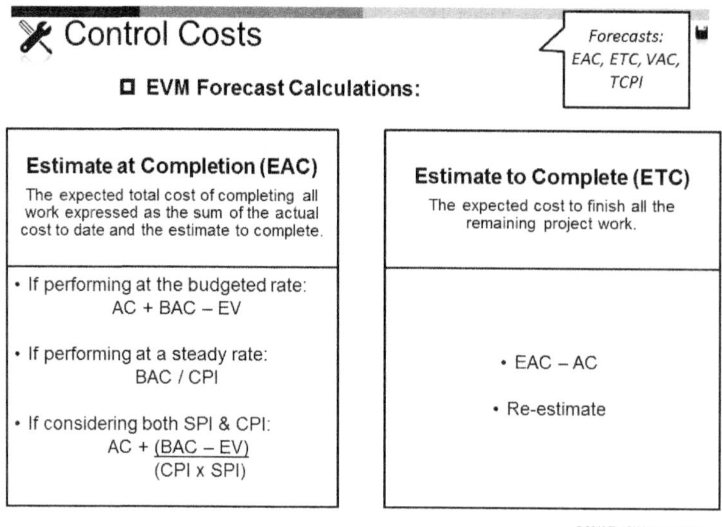

Forecasting

Forecasting performance is an important use of EVM. There are four calculated values:

- Estimate at Completion (EAC)
- Estimate to Complete (ETC)
- Variance at Completion (VAC)
- To-Complete Performance Index (TCPI)

Estimate at Completion (EAC)

EAC refers to the expected total cost of completing all work expressed as the sum of the actual cost to date and the estimate to complete. This may differ from the original BAC if the project is not performing exactly as planned. There are various ways of calculating EAC, depending on whether the project is expected to continue performing at the same rate, or whether unexpected events have occurred.

- If the project is expected to continue performing at a steady rate, meaning at the current CPI, the following formula is used: BAC / CPI. Unless told otherwise within an exam question, assume steady performance.
- If performing at the budgeted rate, use the following formula: AC + BAC – EV. This means that the project team has accepted how the project has performed to date (whether good or bad), and from this point forward, the project will perform as planned.
- If considering current schedule performance *and* cost performance when calculating EAC, use the following formula:

$$AC + \frac{(BAC - EV)}{(CPI \times SPI)}$$

Estimate to Complete (ETC)

ETC is the expected cost to finish all the remaining project work. It answers the question: "how much more do you expect the project to cost from the present point to completion?" Many times, ETC is provided as a bottom-up estimate, but can also be calculated using EAC.

The following two formulas are commonly used to calculate ETC:

- EAC – AC
- Re-estimate (potentially using the bottom-up estimate)

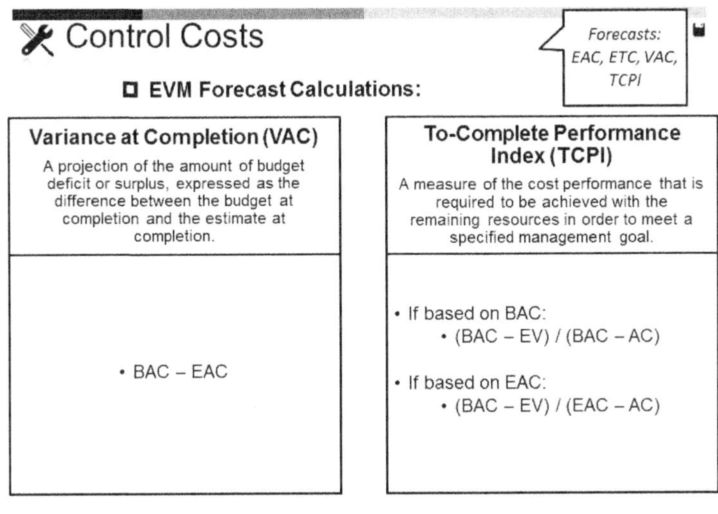

Variance at Completion (VAC)

VAC refers to a projection of the amount of budget deficit or surplus, expressed as the difference between the budget at completion and the estimate at completion. It determines the difference between the BAC and the EAC, to answer the question of how much more or less we anticipate the project to cost, in comparison to the original budget, based on how the project is performing to-date. The formula for calculating VAC is BAC – EAC.

To-Complete Performance Index (TCPI)

TCPI refers to a measure of the cost performance that is required to be achieved with the remaining resources in order to meet a specified management goal, expressed as the ratio of the cost to finish the outstanding work to the remaining budget. It calculates the rate at which the remaining work must be performed, in order to finish at the BAC, or another management goal provided. There are two ways of calculating TCPI:

- If based only on BAC:

$$\frac{BAC - EV}{BAC - AC}$$

- If based on EAC:

$$\frac{BAC - EV}{EAC - AC}$$

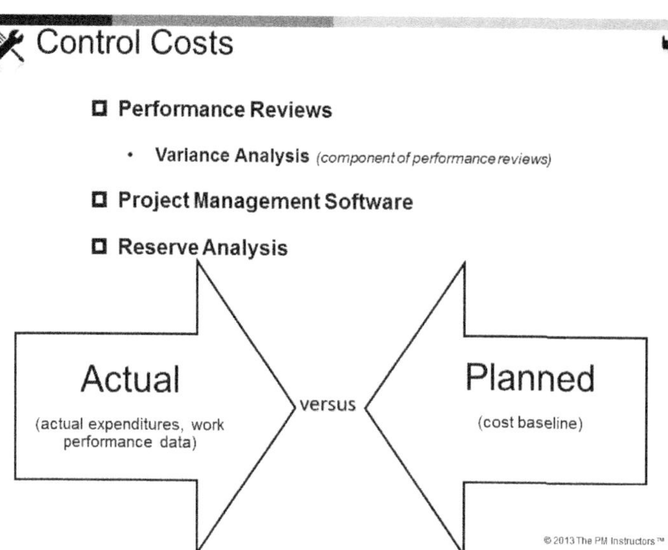

Performance Reviews

Performance reviews involve assessing and measuring performance, as well as reviewing and analyzing it. This includes uncovering variance, surveying trends, and comparing actual performance to the baseline.

Variance Analysis

Variance analysis involves analyzing the variances further to determine the cause and degree of variance, and whether this variance is within the tolerance limits. If not, change requests will need to be submitted. To determine whether variance is within tolerance, the project management team should refer to the cost management plan, where these tolerance limits are documented.

Project Management Software

Project management software may include the use of any software that supports performance analysis and measurement, including EVM software. Although there are various tools available in the marketplace today, this can involve simply using a spreadsheet that calculates performance based on input data.

Reserve Analysis

The reserve analysis technique involves reviewing contingency and management reserves to determine whether a sufficient amount of reserve remains to address the remaining risks. In some cases, reserves remain unused, and can be reduced.

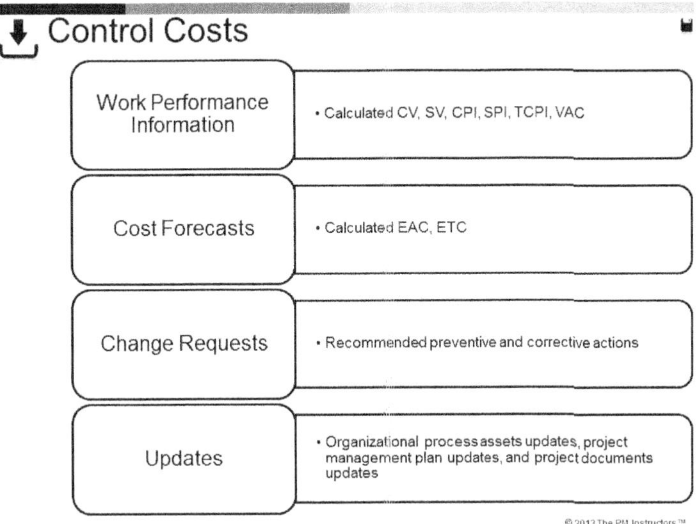
Control Costs
Work Performance Information
• Calculated CV, SV, CPI, SPI, TCPI, VAC
Cost Forecasts
• Calculated EAC, ETC
Change Requests
• Recommended preventive and corrective actions
Updates
• Organizational process assets updates, project management plan updates, and project documents updates
© 2013 The PM Instructors™

Control Costs Outputs

The Control Costs process produces the following six outputs: *work performance information, cost forecasts, change requests, project management plan updates, project documents updates, and organizational process assets updates.*

Work Performance Information

Work performance information refer to the calculated cost variance, schedule variance, cost performance index, schedule performance index, to-complete performance index, and variance at completion values, which were calculated by using the earned value management technique. These values, which are calculated for WBS components, such as work packages and control accounts, are documented as part of this process and then communicated to stakeholders.

Cost Forecasts

Cost forecasts include the calculated estimate at completion and estimate to complete. Like the work performance information, these are calculated as part of this process, documented, and then communicated to stakeholders through the Monitor and Control Project Work process.

Change Requests

If existing cost variance is found to be outside the tolerance limits, change requests will need to be drafted and submitted to the change control board for review. Change requests may be submitted to carry out corrective action, but may also consist of preventive actions if forecasts reflect potential future variance.

Organizational Process Assets Updates

Organizational process assets updates include recording approved corrective actions and whether the actions taken were effective.

Project Management Plan Updates

Common updates to the project management plan include the cost baseline and / or cost management plan.

Project Documents Updates

Common updates to project documents include cost estimates and basis of estimates.

Module Summary

In this module we:

- Defined the purpose of the Project Cost Management Knowledge Area
- Identified the processes of the Project Cost Management Knowledge Area
- Recalled the key outputs of the cost management processes
- Differentiated between the inputs, tools and techniques, and outputs of the cost management processes
- Understood the concept of Earned Value Management (EVM)
- Solved EVM calculations

Chapter Quiz

Exam Practice Questions

1. It has been brought to the attention of the project manager that the defect rate in the widgets that his project is responsible for has increased two fold since the introduction of their laser controlled optical slicer. In order to repair the defects it will cost the company an additional $500,000 and decrease their profit margin by 4%. The project manager decides to look at the cost management plan to get back on course, based on the original approach. Which of the following is not addressed within the cost management plan?
   A. Earned value rules
   B. Money already spent
   C. Defect density
   D. Defined control thresholds

2. Which reserve is included within the cost baseline?
   A. Management reserve
   B. Contingency reserve
   C. Cost budget reserve
   D. Buffer

3. Blazing Broadband Internet Solutions has been developing an innovative software application that will allow them to target advertising to customers based on their favorite channel listings. The application has been in development for 6 years and has already gone over budget by $3 million dollars. The executive stakeholders don't want to cancel the project because of their sunk cost, although the project manager tried to reason with them. Sunk cost refers to:
   A. The money lost when selecting one project for another
   B. Money already spent
   C. Money invested as a result of crashing the schedule
   D. The cost of investing in the project

4. Which of the following is not an input of the Determine Budget process?
   A. Resource calendars
   B. WBS dictionary
   C. Agreements
   D. Project funding requirements

5. A project has an actual cost (AC) of $110 and an estimate at completion (EAC) of $530. What is the estimate to complete (ETC)?
   A. $640
   B. $420
   C. $320
   D. $630

6. During the weekly status meeting, Jim is asked to provide an estimate for his activity. Jim provides the group with an estimate that ranges between –25% to 75%. What type of estimate has Jim provided?
   A. Order of magnitude estimate
   B. Preliminary estimate
   C. Budget estimate
   D. Definite estimate

7. What type of cost is office rent?
   A. Indirect cost
   B. Fixed cost
   C. Direct cost
   D. Sunk cost

8. What is the estimate range of a definitive estimate?
   A. -25% to 75%
   B. -15% to 15%
   C. -10% to 25%
   D. -5% to 10%

9. Imran is the Director of Engineering from the Big Time Software Media Company. He is responding to a request for proposal (RFP) to create a new technology that has never been developed. In order to be as accurate as possible in estimating the project costs and technical feasibility, he enlists the assistance of the company's in-house subject matter experts, such as accountants, project managers and technical architects that have worked on projects involving many of the underlying deliverables that were similar. The goal was to generate an estimate that was high in accuracy. Which type of estimating technique generates a high level of accuracy?
   A. Analogous estimating
   B. Bottom-up estimating
   C. Reserve analysis
   D. Parametric estimating

10. To calculate schedule performance index (SPI), you take the earned value (EV) and:
    A. subtract it by the planned value (PV)
    B. divide it by the planned value (PV)
    C. divide it by the actual cost (AC)
    D. subtract it by the actual cost (AC)

11. If budget at completion (BAC) = 1,325, and cost performance Index (CPI) = 2.03, what is the variance at completion (VAC)?
    A. 652.71
    B. 672.29
    C. 1.325
    D. 2.03

12. You are the project manager for a web design company and have been asked to provide an estimate to create a user-friendly web interface for an online drug store. The problem is that your company only specializes in building user interfaces for military applications. You decide to look through the resumes of all the developers on your staff that have commercial user interface design experience and incorporate their judgment to develop an analogous estimate. What does analogous estimating rely on for information?
    A. Expert judgment
    B. Mathematical models
    C. Work packages
    D. Commercially purchased research

13. Which of the following is a time-phased budget used to measure, monitor and control overall cost performance on the project?
    A. Contingency reserve
    B. Project funding requirement
    C. Cost budget
    D. Cost baseline

14. The project manager for Speedy Dial Aeronautic Parts has been given a budget of 1.3 million dollars to develop a new fire resistant foam that could be used to insulate aircrafts. If the project is successful, it has the potential to save thousands of lives, and generate revenue in excess of 10 billion dollars for the company. However, because he is unable to secure a fixed priced from the preferred vendor he would like to work with to lead up the research, he isn't confident in sharing with the executive team the variance at completion (VAC) information he came up with. What does this calculation reflect?
    A. How much over budget the project will be at completion
    B. How much under budget the project will be at completion
    C. How much over or under budget the project will be at completion
    D. How much the project budget progressed by completion

15. You are the CFO of a global manufacturing company and have been asked to review a project charter from the executive board members to acquire a competitor's office. The project in question could potentially yield a 3% return on the investment in 5 years and an 8% return if completed in 2.5 years, and has been valued at one million dollars. However, in analyzing the numbers carefully, you discover that you'll need to borrow all of the funds from the bank to make the transaction happen and pay a 7.75% over 10 years. You inform the executive board members that you believe that the cost may not be worth following through with the project, and that this may simply need to be considered an opportunity cost. Opportunity cost refers to:
    A. Money lost when selecting one project over another
    B. Money already spent
    C. Money invested as a result of crashing the schedule
    D. Cost of investing in the project

16. What is the SPI of a $2,000 project that has an earned value of $600, a planned value of $550, and an actual cost of $650?
    A. 50
    B. -50
    C. 1.09
    D. 0.92

17. Farmhill Unlimited Inc. produces high-tech products for the poultry industry. A project manager assigned to the newest project has been instructed to use the 20/80 earned value-based earning rule to report activity progress. One of the project's developers informs the scheduler that he is 60% finished with his assigned activity. What percent complete will the scheduler note for this activity?
    A. 100%
    B. 80%
    C. 60%
    D. 20%

18. Sally is the project manager of a government project that involves migrating existing data to an upgraded and more reliable server. This six-month project is currently performing at an SPI of 0.90 and a CPI of 0.75. The project manager recently approached Sally to discuss the possibility of crashing the schedule. What is Sally likely to respond, based on current project performance?
    A. No, crashing is not a viable option, but fast-tracking should be considered
    B. Yes, crashing is a viable option, based on the current project performance
    C. Based on current performance, there is no need to compress the schedule
    D. Based on current performance, the project manager should request additional funds

19. A project with an SPI of 1.20 and a CPI of .80 can be interpreted as:
    A. Ahead of schedule and under budget
    B. Behind schedule and over budget
    C. Ahead of schedule and over budget
    D. Behind schedule and under budget

20. Based on the following values, at what rate will the project team have to perform in order to complete the project at the original budgeted amount of $850? Planned value (PV) = $450, earned value (EV) = $400, actual cost (AC) = $350.
    A. 1.14
    B. 0.90
    C. 1.0
    D. 0.88

Chapter Quiz

Exam Practice Answers

1. Answer: C

   Explanation: There are several things included within the cost management plan, such as the precision level, units of measure, organizational procedures links, defined control thresholds, earned value rules, reporting formats, and process descriptions. The only item included within the list of options not mentioned was defect density, making it the correct choice.

2. Answer: B

   Explanation: Buffer can quickly be eliminated, since it is not a reserve. There are two reserves that were discussed in relation to the cost baseline: management reserve and contingency reserve. Only one is included within the baseline, which is contingency reserve.

3. Answer: B

   Explanation: Sunk cost refers to money already spent / used. As an accounting rule, sunk costs should not be considered when determining whether or not to move forward with the project. Other options refer to opportunity cost, crashing, and direct costs.

4. Answer: D

   Explanation: Resource calendars, WBS dictionary (through the scope baseline), and contracts are all inputs of the Determine Budget process. Project funding requirements is an output of the process, making it the correct answer.

5. Answer: B

   Explanation: The formula for calculating estimate to complete (ETC) is estimate at completion minus actual cost (EAC – AC). After plugging in the numbers, you result in $420.

6. Answer: A

   Explanation: In this scenario, Jim has provided a rough order of magnitude estimate. In order to perform the calculation required by the question, you need to have recalled the range of estimates: -25% to 75%.

7. Answer: A

   Explanation: Office rent is a regular recurring cost that is not necessarily caused as a result of the project, unless the office were rented specifically for carrying out the project activities. Since this is not the typical case, we can safely assume that office rent implies an expense that is overhead for the company and not the project itself. Therefore, the correct choice is indirect cost.

8. Answer: D

   Explanation: Getting this question correct involves knowing the estimate ranges. Rough order of magnitude estimate (-25% to 75%) and definitive estimate (-5% to 10%). The other estimate not mentioned is the actual duration, which is 0%.

9. Answer: B

   Explanation: Of the options provided, bottom-up estimating contains the highest level of accuracy, since it involves subject matter experts decomposing an activity to produce an accurate estimate. Parametric estimating generates the second highest level of accuracy, since it uses mathematical model to calculate cost / schedule estimates through historical data and a numerical factor known of the existing project.

10. Answer: B

Explanation: This question involves knowing the formula for calculating schedule performance index (SPI). The formula for SPI is earned value divided by planned value (SPI = EV / PV).

11. Answer: B

    Explanation: This question involves working through two formulas. Here, we're looking to calculate the variance at completion (VAC), which uses the formula of budget at completion, minus estimate at completion (BAC – EAC). However, we're not given the value of EAC. Since you are provided with the cost performance index (CPI), we can first calculate EAC to get the missing value needed to answer the question correctly. If assuming steady performance, EAC can be calculated by dividing BAC by CPI (BAC / CPI). This gives you a value of 652.71. With the EAC now calculated, you can plug in the needed values into the variance at completion formula to get 672.29.

12. Answer: A

    Explanation: Analogous estimating utilizes expert judgment, which is one of the reasons it is less costly, although less accurate. Expert judgment comes from obtaining estimates from experts who have completed similar activities in the past. These estimates can also be derived from documented information of past, similar projects.

13. Answer: D

    Explanation: The correct answer is the cost baseline, which is the approved time-phased budget. A contingency reserve is estimated costs to be used for known-unknown events. Project funding requirements are taken from the cost baseline, and are adjusted to reflect early progress or cost overruns. Cost budget can refer to the overall budget of the project, although here it doesn't specify. This is not necessarily time phased, however, and would therefore be eliminated.

14. Answer: C

    Explanation: Variance at completion (VAC) reflects the difference between the approved budget and the estimate at completion. This provides a forecast of how much over or under budget the project is anticipated to be, based on performance to date.

15. Answer: A

    Explanation: Opportunity cost refers to money that has been lost as a result of selecting one or more projects over others – it is literally a lost opportunity. The other options refer to other cost related terms.

16. Answer: C

    Explanation: To calculate SPI, divide the earned value by planned value (EV / PV). Plug in the values given ($600 / $550) to result in an SPI of 1.09.

17. Answer: D

    Explanation: The 20/80 rule states that an activity receives a credit of 20% completion from the moment it is started, and receives the remaining 80% credit only after it is fully complete.

18. Answer: A

    Explanation: Based on the CPI and SPI provided within the question, the project is both behind schedule and over budget. Since crashing typically involves adding resources to complete activities faster, it is a costly option that the project can't afford. Another more viable option would be fast-tracking, which looks to perform critical activities in parallel that were originally scheduled to be performed in sequence.

19. Answer: C

    Explanation: Anything over a 1.0 is considered good, and anything under is bad. That means that an SPI of 1.20 is ahead of schedule (performing 120% on schedule) while a CPI of 0.80 is over budget (getting $0.80 of value for every dollar spent).

20. Answer: B

Explanation: The question is asking you to calculate the to-complete performance index (TCPI). Since additional information hasn't been provided, we will assume a TCPI based on the current BAC, which is $850. The formula for calculating TCPI at the current budgeted rate is (BAC – EV) / (BAC – AC). Since these values are provided already, simply plug them into the formula to result in a TCPI of 0.90.

Cost Management Exercises

Earned Value Management Exercise

Instructions: For each of the following scenarios, calculate the following: SV, SPI, CV, CPI, EAC, ETC, VAC, TCPI.

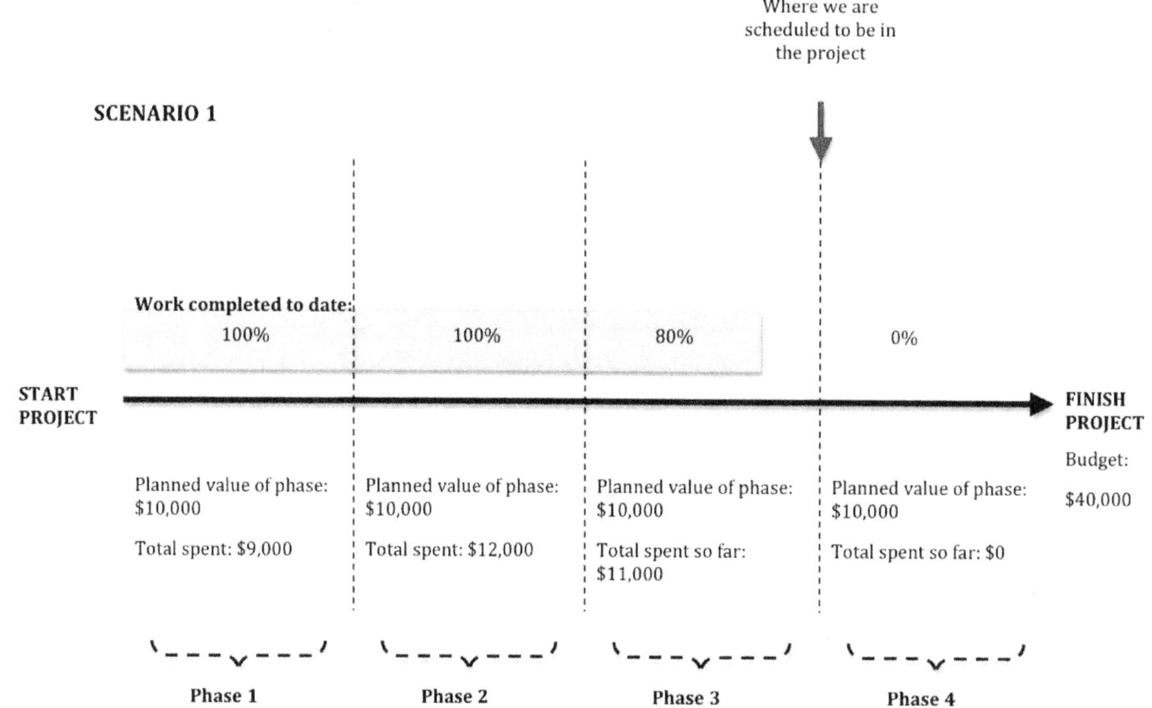

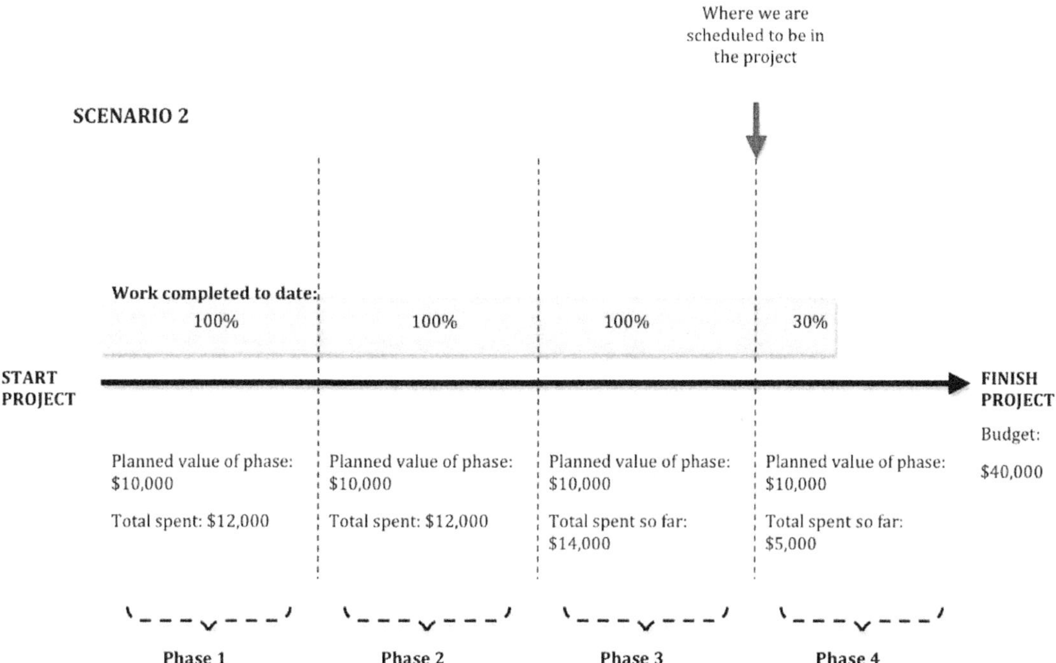
Where we are
scheduled to be in
the project
SCENARIO 2
Work completed to date:
100%
100%
100%
30%
START
PROJECT
FINISH
PROJECT
Budget:
$40,000
Planned value of phase:
$10,000
Total spent: $12,000
Planned value of phase:
$10,000
Total spent: $12,000
Planned value of phase:
$10,000
Total spent so far:
$14,000
Planned value of phase:
$10,000
Total spent so far:
$5,000
Phase 1
Phase 2
Phase 3
Phase 4

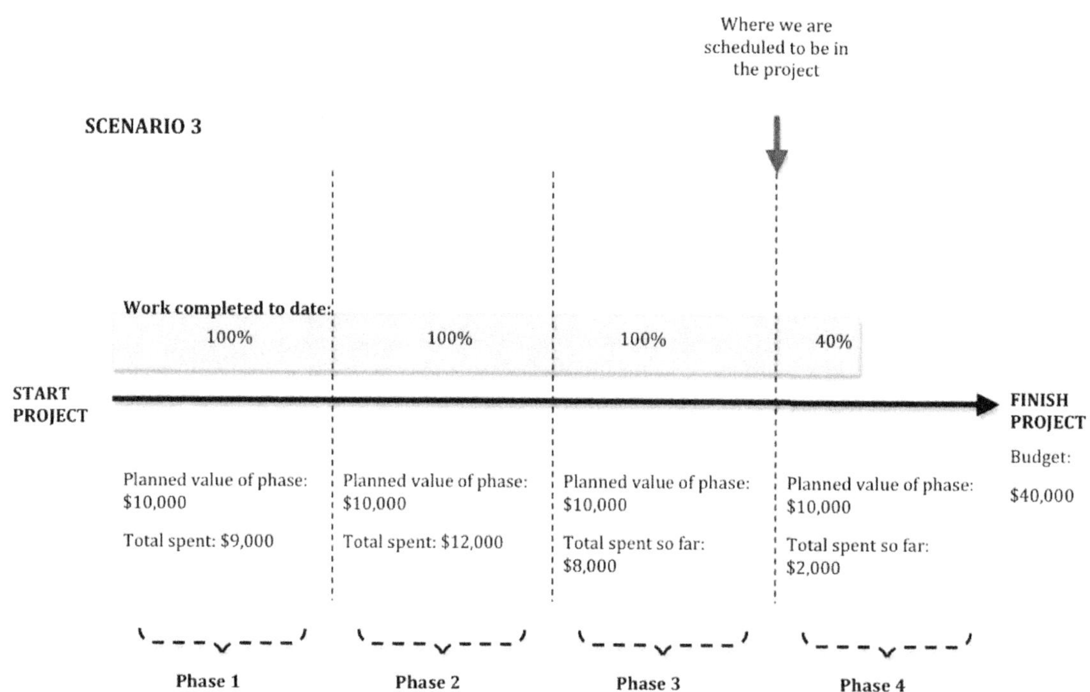
Where we are scheduled to be in the project
SCENARIO 3
Work completed to date:
100%
100%
100%
40%
START PROJECT
FINISH PROJECT
Budget:
$40,000
Planned value of phase: $10,000
Total spent: $9,000
Planned value of phase: $10,000
Total spent: $12,000
Planned value of phase: $10,000
Total spent so far: $8,000
Planned value of phase: $10,000
Total spent so far: $2,000
Phase 1
Phase 2
Phase 3
Phase 4

For each scenario, identify the BAC, EV, PV, and AC, then calculate SV, SPI, CV, CPI, EAC, ETC, TCPI, and VAC. ***How is this project performing?***

Scenario 4

As of the latest report, a project with an overall budget of $50,000 has spent $19,500 to achieve 90% of its $20,000 planned value.

BAC: ______________

EV: ______________

PV: ______________

AC: ______________

SV: ______________

SPI: ______________

CV: ______________

CPI: ______________

EAC: ______________

ETC: ______________

TCPI: ______________

VAC: ______________

Scenario 5

A project that has been divided into four phases has an overall budget of $100,000. Each phase has a planned value of $25,000, and the project is scheduled to have completed up to phase 2. 100% of phase 1 has been completed, and only 60% of phase 2 has been completed. To date, the project has spent $23,000.

BAC: ______________

EV: ______________

PV: ______________

AC: ______________

SV: ______________

SPI: ______________

CV: ______________

CPI: ______________

EAC: ______________

ETC: ______________

TCPI: ______________

VAC: ______________

Scenario 6

A project has a BAC of $40,000, an EV of $32,000, a PV of $30,000, and an AC of $37,000. During the first phase, the project had an unexpected event.

BAC: ______________

EV: ______________

PV: ______________

AC: ______________

SV: ______________

SPI: ______________

CV: ______________

CPI: ______________

EAC: ______________

ETC: ______________

TCPI: ______________

VAC: ______________

Earned Value Management Exercise – Answer Key

<table>
<tr>
<td>

Scenario 1:

- BAC: 40,000
- EV: 28,000
- PV: 30,000
- AC: 32,000

Work Performance Information:

- SV: -2,000
- CV: -4,000
- SPI: 0.933
- CPI: 0.875

Budget Forecasting:

- EAC (steady rate): 45,714.29
- EAC (budgeted rate): 44,000.00
- EAC (with SPI, CPI): 46,699.13
- ETC (at steady rate): 13,714.29
- VAC: -5,714.29
- TCPI (at BAC): 1.50
- TCPI (considering EAC): 0.88

</td>
<td>

Scenario 2:

- BAC: 40,000
- EV: 33,000
- PV: 30,000
- AC: 43,000

Work Performance Information:

- SV: 3,000
- CV: -10,000
- SPI: 1.10
- CPI: 0.767

Budget Forecasting:

- EAC (steady rate): 52,151.24
- EAC (budgeted rate): 50,000
- EAC (with SPI, CPI): 51,296.79
- ETC (at steady rate): 9,151.24
- VAC: -12,151.24
- TCPI (at BAC): -2.33
- TCPI (considering EAC): 0.76

</td>
</tr>
<tr>
<td>

Scenario 3:

- BAC: 40,000
- EV: 34,000
- PV: 30,000
- AC: 31,000

Work Performance Information:

- SV: 4,000
- CV: 3,000
- SPI: 1.133
- CPI: 1.097

Budget Forecasting:

- EAC (steady rate): 36,463.08
- EAC (budgeted rate): 37,000
- EAC (with SPI, CPI): 35,827.42
- ETC (at steady rate): 5,464.08
- VAC: 3,536.92
- TCPI (at BAC): 0.67
- TCPI (considering EAC): 1.10

</td>
<td>

Scenario 4

- BAC: 50,000
- EV: 18,000
- PV: 20,000
- AC: 19,500
- SV: -2,000
- SPI: 0.90
- CV: -1,500
- CPI: 0.923
- EAC: 54,171.18 (steady rate assumed)
- ETC: 34,671.18 (steady rate assumed)
- TCPI: 1.049 (goal of completing at BAC assumed)
- VAC: -4,171.18

</td>
</tr>
</table>

Scenario 5	*Scenario 6*
• BAC: 100,000 • EV: 40,000 • PV: 50,000 • AC: 23,000 • SV: -10,000 • SPI: 0.80 • CV: 17,000 • CPI: 1.739 • EAC: 57,504.31 (steady rate assumed) • ETC: 34,504.31 (stead rate assumed) • TCPI: 0.779 (goal of completing at BAC assumed) • VAC: 42,495.69	• BAC: 40,000 • EV: 32,000 • PV: 30,000 • AC: 37,000 • SV: 2,000 • SPI: 1.067 • CV: -5,000 • CPI: 0.865 • EAC: 45,000 (based on an unexpected event) • ETC: 8,000 (based on an unexpected event, and continuing at the budgeted rate) • TCPI: 2.667 (goal of completing at BAC assumed) • VAC: -5,000

Chapter 8: Project Quality Management

Learning Objectives:

- ☐ Define the purpose of the Project Quality Management Knowledge Area
- ☐ Identify the processes of the Project Quality Management Knowledge Area
- ☐ Recall the key outputs of the quality management processes
- ☐ Differentiate between the inputs, tools and techniques, and outputs of the quality management processes
- ☐ Identify and know when to use quality tools and quality control tools
- ☐ Apply quality tools to simple scenarios to identify issues, root causes, trends, and/or problems

Exam Domain Tasks:

- Develop a quality management plan based on the project scope and requirements, in order to prevent the occurrence of defects and reduce the cost of quality.
- Implement the quality management plan using the appropriate tools and techniques, in order to ensure that work is being performed according to required quality standards.
- Ensure that project deliverables conform to the quality standards established n the quality management plan by using appropriate tools and techniques (e.g. testing, inspection, control charts), in order to satisfy customer requirements.

Project Quality Management
Purpose: To determine quality policies, objectives, and responsibilities so that the project will satisfy the needs for which it was undertaken.
3 Project Management Processes:
Initiating
Planning
• Plan Quality Management
Executing
• Perform Quality Assurance
Monitoring & Controlling
• Control Quality
Closing
© 2013 The PM Instructors™

Project Quality Management Overview

The purpose of the Project Quality Management Knowledge Area is to determine quality policies, objectives, and responsibilities so that the project will satisfy the needs for which it was undertaken. It measures and audits the processes and activities to make sure the results meet the quality requirements, and it is also concerned with the following:

1. Implementing the quality management system through the policy, procedures, and quality management processes;
2. Improving the quality management processes through continuous improvement activities; and
3. Converting project stakeholder's wants, needs, and expectations into quality requirements.

All of this will occur through three quality management processes: Plan Quality Management, Perform Quality Assurance, and Control Quality.

- **Plan Quality Management (Planning Process Group).** Purpose: To identify quality requirements and / or standards for the project and product, and document how the project will demonstrate compliance.
- **Perform Quality Assurance (Executing Process Group).** Purpose: To audit the quality requirements and the results from quality control measurements to ensure appropriate quality standards and operations definitions are used.
- **Control Quality (Monitoring and Controlling Process Group).** Purpose: To monitor and record results of executing the quality activities to assess performance and recommend necessary changes.

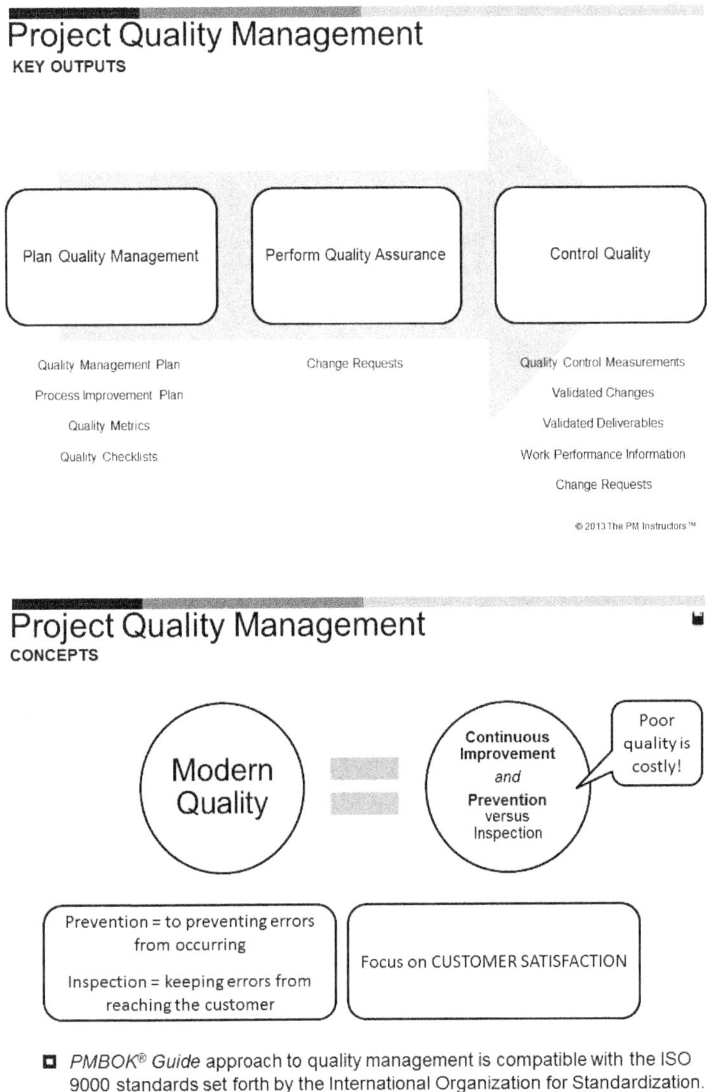
Project Quality Management
KEY OUTPUTS
Plan Quality Management
Perform Quality Assurance
Control Quality
Quality Management Plan
Process Improvement Plan
Quality Metrics
Quality Checklists
Change Requests
Quality Control Measurements
Validated Changes
Validated Deliverables
Work Performance Information
Change Requests
© 2013 The PM Instructors™
Project Quality Management
CONCEPTS
Modern Quality
Continuous Improvement
and
Prevention
versus
Inspection
Poor quality is costly!
Prevention = to preventing errors from occurring
Inspection = keeping errors from reaching the customer
Focus on CUSTOMER SATISFACTION
PMBOK® Guide approach to quality management is compatible with the ISO 9000 standards set forth by the International Organization for Standardization.
© 2013 The PM Instructors™

Quality Management Concepts and Theories

Many quality management theories and concepts used today are based on the modern quality approach. Modern quality is based around the concept of prevention versus inspection, and the idea that teams should seek to reduce variation and produce results that meet requirements. *Prevention* refers to preventing errors from occurring, and *Inspection* refers to keeping errors from reaching the customer. Total Quality management today advocates efforts in prevention. Prevention is considered to involve fewer costs than performing rework, although much of inspection costs can be hidden.

The idea behind prevention of defects is that poor quality is costly and can be detrimental to a project. Here are a few examples of the impact of poor quality:

- Rework, which can be extremely costly
- Poor customer satisfaction
- Schedule delays resulting from rework and resolving defects and issues that arise

In addition to focusing on prevention over inspection, modern quality also focuses on customer satisfaction, continuous improvement, the importance of management responsibility, and cost of quality.

ISO 9000

The *PMBOK® Guide's* basic approach to quality management is compatible with the ISO standards set forth by the International Organization for Standardization. When using this generalized approach, it also becomes compatible with other approaches, such as the Total Quality Management, Six Sigma, Cost of Quality, and others that are both proprietary and non-proprietary approaches to quality.

Project Quality Management

CONCEPTS

- **Quality versus Grade:**
  - **Quality** is defined by the American Society for Quality (ASQ) as **"the degree to which a set of inherent characteristics fulfill requirements"**
  - **Grade** is a category that is assigned to deliverables having the same functional use but different technical characteristics
- **Precision versus Accuracy:**
  - **Precision** refers to a measurement of exactness
  - **Accuracy** refers to an assessment of correctness

Quality versus Grade

Note that there is a difference between quality and grade, and also between precision and accuracy. The American Society for Quality defines quality as *the degree to which a set of inherent characteristics fulfill requirements*. While Grade, on the other hand, is a category that is assigned to products or services having the same functional use but different technical characteristics. For example, it is never acceptable for a result to have low quality, while low grade may be acceptable.

Precision versus Accuracy

Precision refers to the consistency that the value of repeated measurements are clustered and have little scatter –think of it in terms of the definition of how "precise" the measurements are. Accuracy, on the other hand, refers to the level of correctness of a measured value. So although a product may have high precision, it may have low accuracy. It is up to the project management team to determine the appropriate levels of precision and accuracy for a project.

Project Quality Management
CONCEPTS
gold plating
Quality Management Concepts, Theories, Standards
Customer Satisfaction
• Conformance to requirements
• Fitness for use
Prevention over Inspection
Continuous Improvement
• Kaizen
• Total Quality Management
Management Responsibility
Cost of Quality
• Cost of conformance
• Cost of non-conformance
Just in Time

There are several important quality management concepts, theories, and standards that serve as the foundation for the Project Quality Management Knowledge Area, and which are tied to the modern quality movement. Among them are: Customer Satisfaction, Prevention over Inspection, Continuous Improvement, Management Responsibility, Cost of Quality, and Just-in-Time.

Customer Satisfaction

The concept of customer satisfaction highlights two key points: 1) there must be conformance to requirements, in order to ensure that the project results in the output that it set out to create; and 2) the output must be fit for use, meaning that it satisfies the real needs of the customer.

Prevention over Inspection

Prior to the modern quality approach, quality management focused on inspection. Now, the focus is on preventing errors from occurring, which requires that quality be planned and integrated into the project management processes, to avoid the higher cost of mistakes. The idea is that the cost of prevention is lower than the cost of correcting mistakes when found by inspection.

Continuous Improvement / Kaizen

The concept of continuous improvement centers around the idea that small or incremental improvements within a product or processes has the ability to reduce cost and keep consistency of performance. The word Kaizen in Japanese translates to "alter and make better". The purpose is to eliminate waste. This mindset, of making small improvements continuously, a common philosophy in Japan, is a different mindset than the western world where improvements are thought of in terms of big movements or changes. All business functions are subject to these small improvements.

Total Quality Management

Total quality management is a philosophy that encourages a focus on the continuous improvement of quality in the work place, in business practices, and in products or services. The idea is to embed the mindset of quality improvement within the organizational processes – from top management, to all company employees. This is what is behind the word "total" in the title, because it literally encompasses participation of the complete business entity.

Management Responsibility

In order to successfully implement quality management practices effectively, it requires the participation from management. Through this concept, management has the responsibility of providing the resources necessary to implement the appropriate quality approach that is needed by the organization.

Cost of Quality (COQ)

Cost of quality refers to a method of determining the costs incurred to ensure quality. It is defined as the total cost of the conformance work and the nonconformance work that is needed to produce the desired result. *Cost of conformance* includes costs for quality planning, quality control, and quality assurance to comply with requirements. *Cost of nonconformance*, also referred to as *failure costs*, includes costs of rework, processes performed due to non-compliance, cost of warranty work and waste, and loss of reputation.

Just-in-Time

Just in time is an inventory strategy, where the purpose is to reduce inventory costs by not having to store inventory or risk the potentially of non-sale. Therefore, the concept is to have the materials or goods arrive just as they are needed – literally, just in time. A company that is extremely efficient can reduce the storage of inventory to zero. In order for this concept to work, however, a company must be highly efficient, and have a high level of quality, otherwise they will not be able to meet the demands of their customers, or production requirements. This is why it is connected to the concept of quality.

To be efficient, a company relies on signals to tell production processes when the next order is needed. This is called Kanban, which is a Japanese term for these signals. In the United States, this technique was first implemented by Henry Ford. Toyota of Japan later adopted this system, not from Ford, but after visiting Piggly Wiggly (a supermarket chain) that had fully adopted the Just in Time concept and practice.

Gold Plating

Gold plating is a term often tied to quality. It involves giving customers extras that are not included in the approved project scope, meaning that it is a form of scope creep. This can include things like extra features, increasing performance, and adjusting components. This is not recommended, and is not seen as adding value to the project – instead, it is important to follow approved requirements. Project teams sometimes make this error, and even make unapproved adjustments, such as the examples given without customer approval.

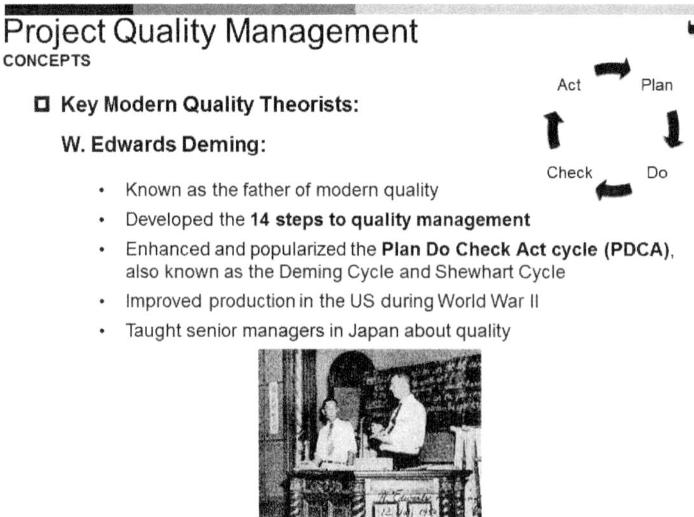

Since the Project Quality Management Knowledge Area is embedded within the concept of modern quality, it is important to become familiar with three modern quality theorists:

W. Edwards Deming

W. Edwards Deming was born in 1900 and was a professor and author. He is known for the following:

- The "14 steps to total quality management"
- An advocate of quality improvement through the Plan-Do-Check-Act Cycle
- Credited with improving overall production in the US during Work War II

- His work in Japan, teaching senior management about quality management

The 14 steps to total quality management come from his book called "Out of the Crisis". It consists of 14 key principles for transforming business effectiveness. Knowing these 14 points is not necessary for the exam. Deming's system of profound knowledge is the basis for applying these 14 points; this system of profound knowledge consists of four parts:

1. Appreciation of a system, which advocates understanding the overall process
2. Knowledge of variation, which refers to the range and causes of variation in quality
3. Theory of knowledge, which are the concepts that explain knowledge and the limits of knowledge
4. Knowledge of psychology, which includes concepts of human nature

Deming also believed that the basis for quality improvement could be achieved through the Plan-Do-Check-Act (PDCA) cycle. The concept of the PDCA cycle stems from the work of Walter Shewhart, an American physicist and statistician whose work on quality control influenced Deming. This cycle is also known as the Deming Cycle, which is a repetitive process meant to determine the next action, and it is based on the Shewhart Cycle, which he modified and popularized.

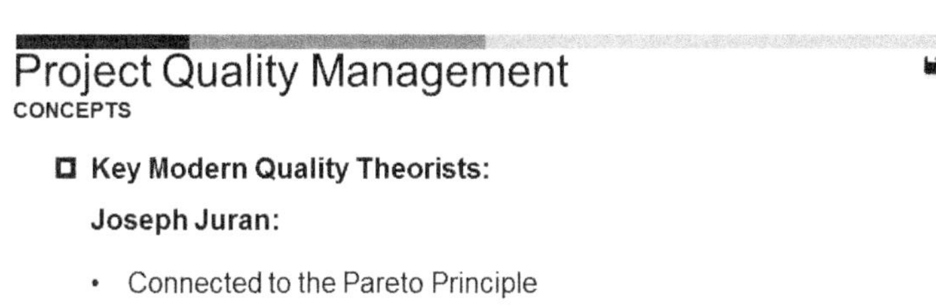
Project Quality Management
CONCEPTS
Key Modern Quality Theorists:
Joseph Juran:
Connected to the Pareto Principle
Believed that the results should be fit for use by the customer
Believed in getting management involved
© 2013 The PM Instructors™

Joseph Juran

Joseph Juran was born in 1904 and was a management consultant who authored several books on the subject of quality. He is connected to:

- the Pareto Principle
- the concept that quality is defined as fitness for use
- an advocate of getting top management involvement

The Pareto principle is also known as the 80/20 Principle or Rule. The principle states that 80% of defects or issues are a result of 20% of the causes. In other words, the majority of the problems are a result of a few causes. This concept will resurface during the Control Quality process. Joseph Juran came up with this principle and named it after Italian economist Vildredo Pareto, who documented the core of this theory in a 1906 economic study of wealth distribution in Italy.

Juran defined quality as fitness for use, with fitness being defined by the customer. This stresses that the end result produced should meet a real need.

Juran also advocated the involvement of top management in regards to quality. He believed that quality training and management should begin at the top and middle management. There was resistance with this concept in the U.S. It wasn't until Japan began to be seen as leaders in quality that this concept became popular. As a result of this, Juran is known for adding the people aspect into quality management (as opposed to being focused purely on statistics).

Project Quality Management

CONCEPTS

- **Key Modern Quality Theorists:**

Phillip Crosby:

- Responsible for the concept of **zero defects**, which states – *get it right the first time*, meaning aim for no rework
- Emphasized the cost of poor quality
- Popularized the idea that quality is "conformance to requirements"

Phillip Crosby

Philip Crosby was born in 1926, and was a businessman and author who contributed to the quality management practices and the management theory. He is connected to 3 things:

1. Zero Defects
2. Cost of Poor Quality
3. The idea that quality is "conformance to requirements"

Zero defects stems from Crosby's "14 Step Quality Improvement Process" (with a focus on step 7). There are four elements to the Zero Defect concept:

1. Quality is conformance to requirements, meaning that if requirements have been met, then quality has been achieved;
2. Defect prevention is preferable to quality inspection and correction. This principle is based on the fact that it is often more costly to go through rework than it is to place efforts and investment into prevention;
3. Zero defects is the quality standard, which means that the goal is literally zero defects, else quality standards overall have not been met and the product or service is not considered to be good. And it also states that if the needs are met but do not reflect the requirements, then the requirements should be altered to reflect this; and
4. The price of nonconformance, which indicates that quality is measured in monetary terms. Crosby believed that every defect represents cost, and these costs should be calculated and brought to the surface for a realistic picture.

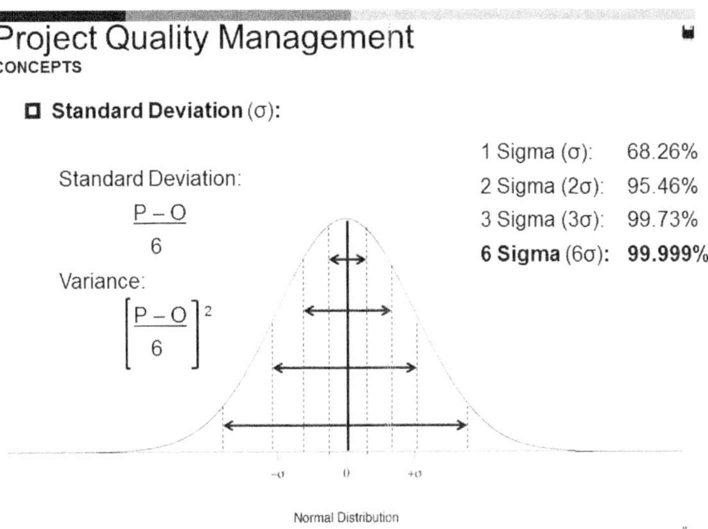

Six Sigma

Six sigma is a business management strategy developed by Motorola, USA in the 1980s. The idea of six sigma is to first identify and then remove the causes of defects within processes, thereby creating a consistency in results and reducing errors.

Sigma (σ) is tied to **standard deviation**, and 1 sigma equals one standard deviation. In order to calculate standard deviation of an estimate, use the following formula:

$$(\text{Pessimistic} - \text{Optimistic}) \div 6$$

Using the same estimates, one can also calculate **variance**. To calculate variance of an estimate, use the following formula:

$$[(\text{Pessimistic} - \text{Optimistic}) \div 6]^2$$

Because sigma is often tied to quality, it has been included here as a concept to know. For the exam, you should also know the following sigma percentages:

- ☐ 1 Sigma = 68.26%
- ☐ 2 Sigma = 95.46%
- ☐ 3 Sigma = 99.73%
- ☐ 6 Sigma = 99.999%

The image shown above is a normal distribution (bell curve) with standard deviation noted (the range of 1, 2, 3, and 6 standard deviations is highlighted). Statistically, 68% of the values plotted will fall within the range of one standard deviation to the left and right of the mean; 95.5% will fall within two standard deviations to the left and right of the mean, and so on. The greater the range considered, the higher the accuracy, but the greater the range of possibilities.

Project Quality Management
CONCEPTS

Example of Standard Deviation (σ):

If the mean of the project's completion date is 30 days, and one standard deviation is equal to 2 days, then the following statements are true:

- There is a 68% likelihood that the project completion date will fall between 28-32 days (or 30 +/- 2 days)
- There is a 95.5% likelihood that the project completion date will fall between 26-34 days (or 30 +/- 4 days)
- There is a 99.73% likelihood that the project completion date will fall between 24-36 days (or 30 +/- 6 days)

Variance and standard deviation are discussed further in Project Risk and Project Cost Management

Example: If the mean of the project's completion date is 30 days, and one standard deviation is equal to 2 days, then the following statements are true:

- There is a 68% likelihood that the project completion date will fall between 28-32 days (or 30 +/- 2 days)
- There is a 95.5% likelihood that the project completion date will fall between 26-34 days (or 30 +/- 4 days)
- There is a 99.73% likelihood that the project completion date will fall between 24-36 days (or 30 +/- 6 days)

Variance and standard deviation will be further discussed within the Project Risk Management Knowledge Area chapter.

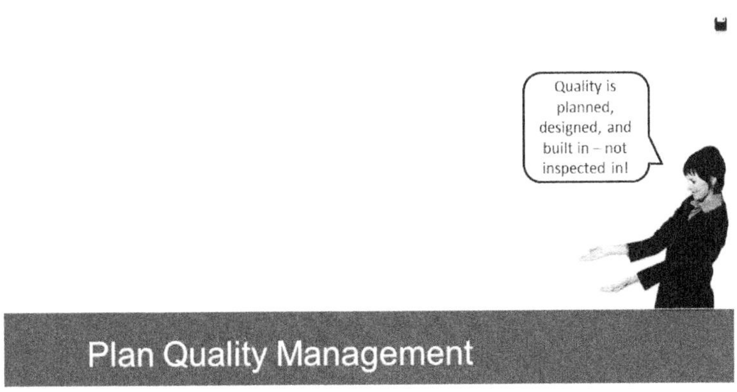
Quality is planned, designed, and built in – not inspected in!
Plan Quality Management
Purpose: To identify quality requirements and/or standards for the project and its deliverables and document how the project will demonstrate compliance with quality requirements.

Plan Quality Management Process Overview

Quality planning plays a key role in the overall planning aspect of a project, and takes place in parallel with other planning processes. This process can impact other planning processes, such as cost and schedule, based on the quality standards that must be incorporated and met within the project. One of the key points of quality management today is that "quality is planned, designed, and built in – not inspected in".

The official purpose of the process is to identify the quality requirements and / or standards for the project and its deliverables and document how the project will demonstrate compliance with quality requirements. This process is also interested in embedding continuous improvement activities into the project.

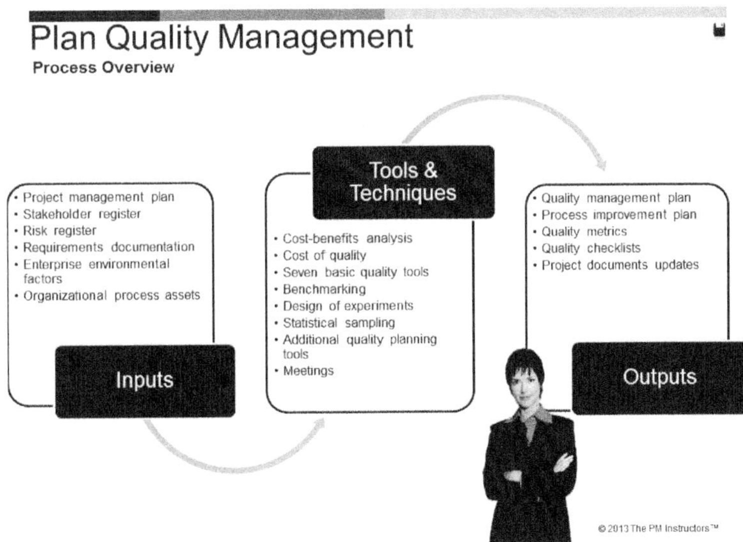
Plan Quality Management
Process Overview
• Project management plan
• Stakeholder register
• Risk register
• Requirements documentation
• Enterprise environmental factors
• Organizational process assets
Inputs
Tools & Techniques
• Cost-benefits analysis
• Cost of quality
• Seven basic quality tools
• Benchmarking
• Design of experiments
• Statistical sampling
• Additional quality planning tools
• Meetings
• Quality management plan
• Process improvement plan
• Quality metrics
• Quality checklists
• Project documents updates
Outputs
© 2013 The PM Instructors™

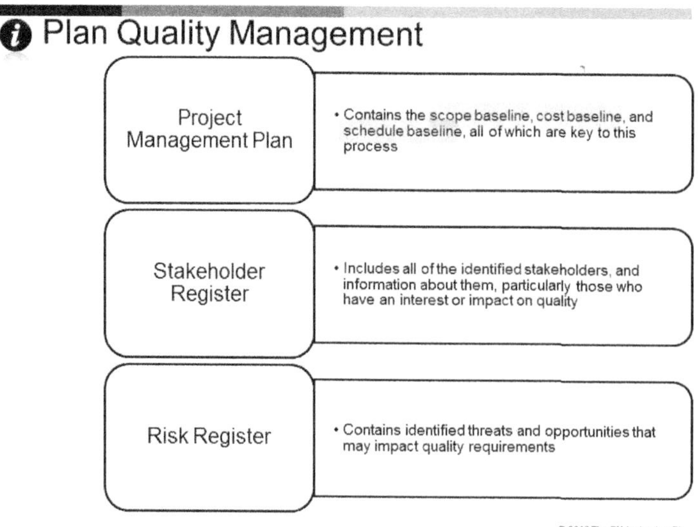

Plan Quality Management Inputs

Plan Quality Management process has a total of six inputs: *project management plan, stakeholder register, risk register, requirements documentation, enterprise environmental factors, and organizational process assets.*

Project Management Plan

The project management plan contains several subsidiary plans and baselines that can be used to create the quality management plan. Of particular importance are the scope baseline, cost baseline, and schedule baseline.

The scope baseline includes the project scope statement, WBS, and WBS dictionary. These documents often provide details of the product, including technical details, and any issues that may impact quality planning.

The cost baseline provides information on when and how much funds are available to measure performance. As part of determining the budget, cost of quality was considered, which would have been included as part of the cost baseline. This means that this process is iterative, since quality activities can be determined as a result of this process.

The schedule baseline represents the approved and signed-off version of the schedule. It documents start and finish dates of performance measurement activities, as well as quality related activities, and when those activities should take place.

Stakeholder Register

The stakeholder register includes all of the identified stakeholders and information about them. The project manager should be particularly interested in those stakeholders who have an interest or impact on quality.

Risk Register

The risk register contains identified threats and opportunities that may impact quality requirements.

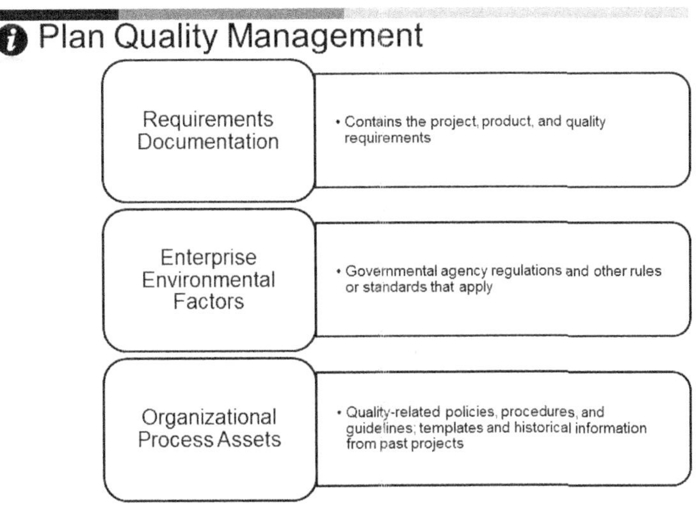

Plan Quality Management
Requirements Documentation
• Contains the project, product, and quality requirements
Enterprise Environmental Factors
• Governmental agency regulations and other rules or standards that apply
Organizational Process Assets
• Quality-related policies, procedures, and guidelines; templates and historical information from past projects
© 2013 The PM Instructors™

Requirements Documentation

The requirements documentation contains all of the requirements gathered for the project to date. It includes project, product, and quality requirements, which will be used by the project team to plan their quality management approach.

Enterprise Environmental Factors

Enterprise environmental factors used as part of this process include governmental agency regulations, rules, standards, and guidelines that are specific to the project.

Organizational Process Assets

Organizational process assets used may include the company's quality policies, procedures, and guidelines, along with the historical databases and lessons learned from previous projects that are similar to the one we are working on.

Quality policy outlines the direction that a company takes in regards to quality and that is endorsed by senior management. If the company has a quality policy, then the project team adopts the policy "as is"; if they do not have a policy, then the project management team develops a quality policy for the project. The project management team has a specific responsibility of notifying the stakeholders of the quality policy used within the project, whether it currently exists or is developed specifically for the project.

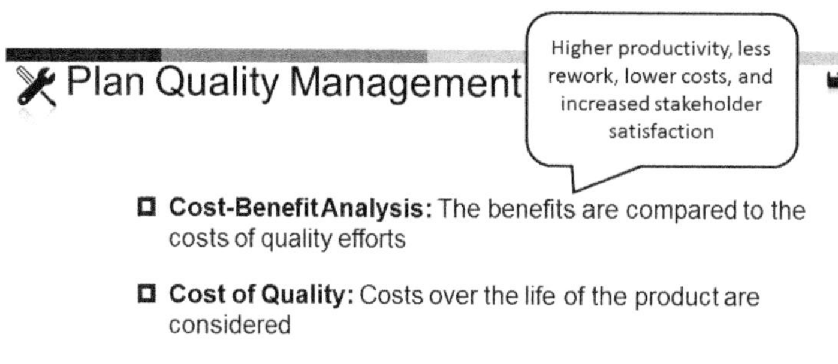
Plan Quality Management
Higher productivity, less rework, lower costs, and increased stakeholder satisfaction
Cost-Benefit Analysis: The benefits are compared to the costs of quality efforts
Cost of Quality: Costs over the life of the product are considered
Conformance refers to money spent during the project to avoid failures
Non-conformance is money spent during and after the project as a result of failures
© 2013 The PM Instructors™

Plan Quality Management Tools and Techniques

Plan Quality Management has a total of eight tools and techniques: *Cost-benefit analysis, cost of quality, seven basic quality tools, benchmarking, design of experiments, statistical sampling, additional quality planning tools, and meetings.*

Cost-Benefit Analysis

Cost benefit analysis is where the benefits are compared to the costs of quality efforts. Cost benefit analysis simply looks at the trade offs between quality planning and cost. The benefits of quality translate into higher productivity, less rework, lower costs, and increased stakeholder satisfaction. The cost of this includes the total cost of quality management activities, such as quality staff, time allotted for quality activities, and any tools necessary to conduct these activities.

Cost of Quality

Costs over the life of the product are considered. This is where costs of conformance versus nonconformance are documented. Conformance refers to money spent during the project to avoid failures, while cost of non-conformance is money spent during and after the project as a result of failures.

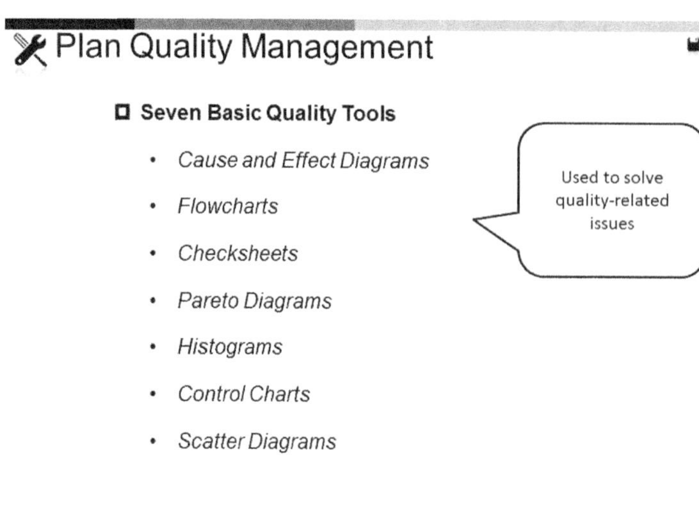
Plan Quality Management
Seven Basic Quality Tools
Cause and Effect Diagrams
Flowcharts
Checksheets
Pareto Diagrams
Histograms
Control Charts
Scatter Diagrams
Used to solve quality-related issues
© 2013 The PM Instructors™

Seven Basic Quality Tools

The seven basic quality tools refer to a series of tools that are commonly used to solve quality-related issues. The seven tools are as follows:

- Cause and Effect Diagrams
- Flowcharts
- Checksheets
- Pareto Diagrams
- Histograms
- Control Charts
- Scatter Diagrams

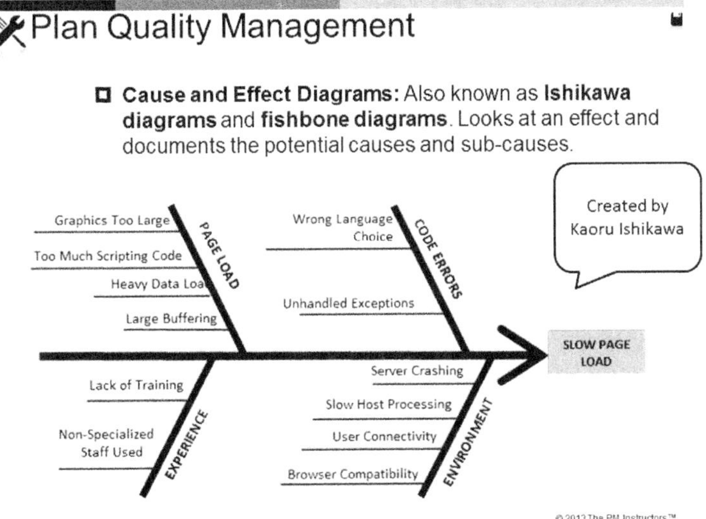

Cause and Effect Diagrams

Cause and effect diagrams, which are also known as Ishikawa diagrams and fishbone diagrams, look at an effect and documents the potential causes and sub-causes. This allows us to illustrate how various factors may be linked to potential problems.

This diagram was created by Kaoru Ishikawa, explaining the second name that it goes by. He is responsible for pioneering quality management processes that were used in shipyards, and he is considered one of the founding fathers of modern management. The diagram is arranged by level of importance and by detail, similar to a tree structure. The point is to end up with the root of the problem, and also to compare various causes of the problem. This explains why it is also known as "cause and effect diagram".

Plan Quality Management

- **Flowcharts:** A tool used in quality that shows the relationships among the steps within a process.

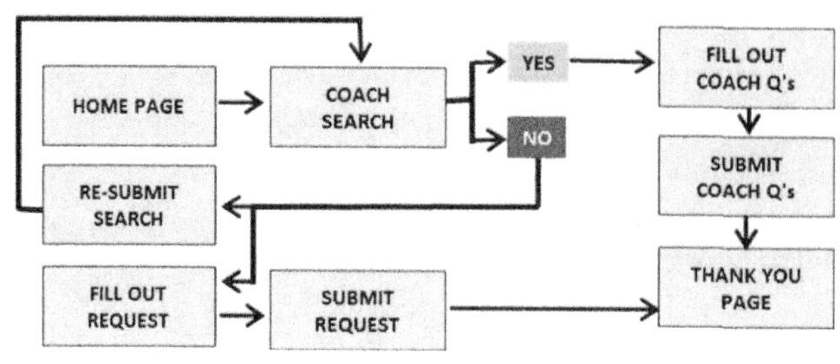

Flowcharts

Flowchart is a tool used in quality that shows the relationships among the steps within a process. Think of a standard flowchart that you've seen in the past, and the various steps that can be taken within it. This is a useful tool to planning out quality activities, including where quality control will measure quality within the process.

Plan Quality Management

- **Checksheets:** A tally sheet that can be used as a checklist when gathering data.

	Frequency			
Part Defect	Week 1	Week 2	Week 3	Week 4
Does not fit	III	I	II	I
Contains chip	I	III	IIII	III
Improper weight	II	I	II	I

Checksheets

A checksheet is a tally sheet that can be used as a checklist when gathering data. These are especially useful when capturing information about quality issues. In the example provided, a checksheet has been used to capture part defects. The tallies reflect frequency of the defect's occurrence by week.

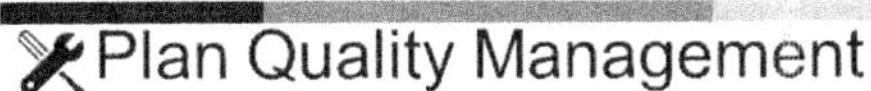

- **Pareto Diagrams:** A type of histogram that is ordered by frequency of occurrence.
  - It shows how many defects have been generated by type or category
  - Based on the 80/20 principle
  - Used when the quality team suspects multiple factors in a process, and as a way of guiding corrective action.

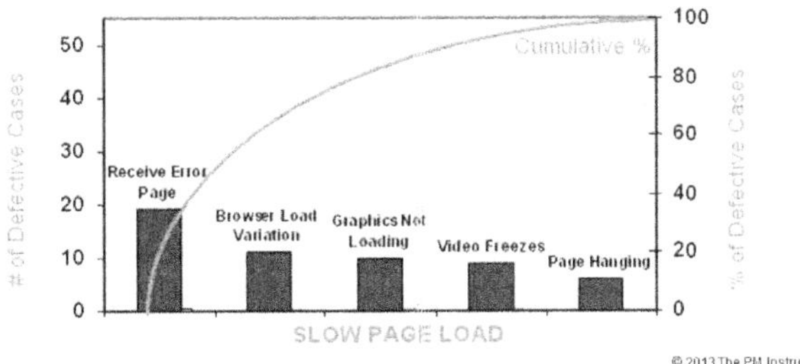

Pareto Diagrams

The Pareto diagram is a type of histogram that is ordered by frequency of occurrence. The Pareto diagram shows how many defects have been generated by type or category. This is done to identify and evaluate nonconformities, and is based on the 80/20 Principle, where 80% of problems are a result of 20% of causes. This tool is used when the quality team suspects multiple factors in a process, and as a way of guiding corrective action.

Plan Quality Management

- **Histograms:** Shows a distribution of variables in a bar chart format.
  - Each column represents an attribute or characteristic of an issue.
  - Histograms show the frequency of distribution for a set of measurements.

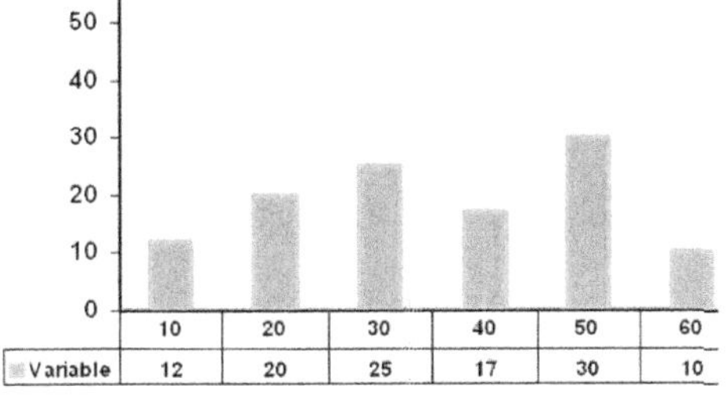

	10	20	30	40	50	60
Variable	12	20	25	17	30	10

Histograms

A histogram shows a distribution of variables in a bar chart format. Each column would represent an attribute or characteristic of an issue. In other words, histograms show the frequency of distribution for a set of measurements. The frequency of each issue is visible through the height of each bar. The quality team can utilize this tool to help identify the cause of issues in a process, since the issue with the highest frequency is readily visible.

Plan Quality Management

Control Charts:

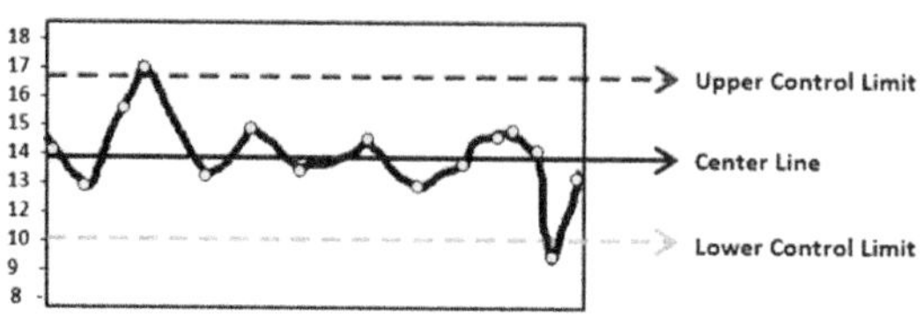

- **Upper Control Limit:** the highest acceptable limit that a process may fall. Typically at 3σ.
- **Center line**, also called median, displays the average point of the plotted data.
- **Lower Control Limit**: the lowest acceptable limit that a process may fall. Typically at 3σ.

Control Charts

Control charts gather data to show when a process experiences an out of control condition. It basically determines whether or not a process is stable or has predictable performance. Shown above is an example of a control chart. With control charts, you can see visually how a process behaves over time, since the interaction of the process variables on a process is mapped out. When looking at a control chart, you're also looking to see whether the processes are within acceptable limits. You do this by plotting out the process result on the control chart and seeing whether it falls within the set limits. A control chart has 3 different designated lines:

- An "Upper Control Limit", which is the highest acceptable limit that a process may fall
- And a center line, also called median, which displays the average of the plotted data
- A "Lower Control Limit", which is the lowest acceptable limit that a process may fall

Plan Quality Management

Control Charts: Gathers data to show when a process experiences an out of control condition. It determines whether or not a process is instable or has predictable performance.

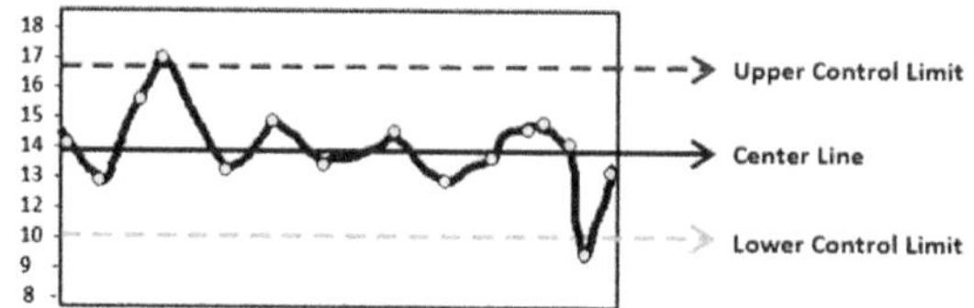

- **Common Cause:** A source of variation that is inherent in the system and predictable.
- **Special Cause / Assignable Cause:** A source of variation that is not inherent in the system, is not predictable, and is intermittent.

Other terms to be familiar with, in connection to control charts, include common cause and special cause / assignable cause.

- Common cause refers to a source of variation within the results plotted that is inherent in the system and predictable.

- Special cause / assignable cause refers to a source of variation within the results plotted that is not inherent in the system, is not predictable, and is intermittent.

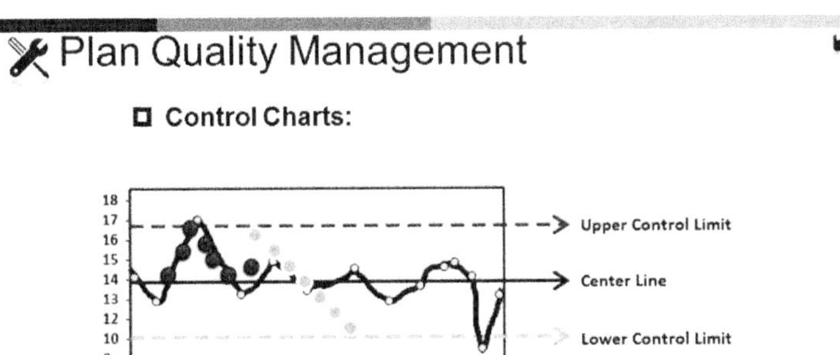

- **Rule of 7:** Applies when 7 or more consecutive processes fall on one side of the mean. This is considered to be an unusual event.
- **Trend of 7:** Applies when 7 or more consecutive processes follow a trend up or down the mean. This is considered to be an unusual event.

When a process is within the limits, it is considered acceptable performance. Some variance within the limits are expected; in fact, when some degree of variation is nonexistent, this may signal that something is amiss. Typically, the rule is that 7 or more processes that fall within the same side of the median are considered an unusual event, which is also called special cause, or assignable cause.

Plan Quality Management

- **Scatter Diagram:** Shows the pattern of relationship between two different variables.
  - Used to analyze the relationship between identified changes within two variables.
  - The closer the variables, the more closely they are related

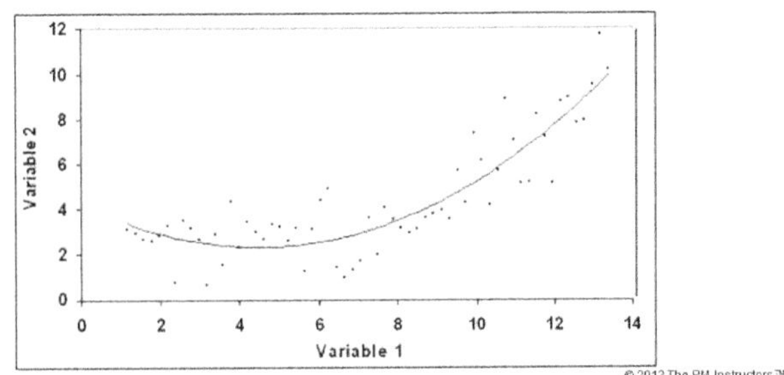

Scatter Diagrams

A scatter diagram shows the pattern of relationship between two different variables. The purpose is to analyze the relationship between identified changes within the two variables. Dependent and independent variables are plotted on a graph, with a diagonal line passing through -- the closer the variables are to each other, the more closely they are related.

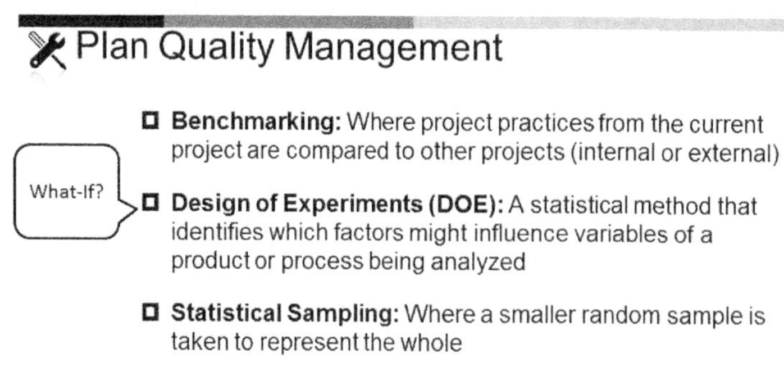

Benchmarking

Benchmarking refers to the comparison of actual or planned project practices to other projects as a way of generating ideas for improvement, and to provide a basis for measuring project performance. The projects used to compare with actual or planned data can be from within the organization or external. The point is to have a relevant basis for comparison.

Design of Experiments

Design of experiments is a statistical method that identifies which factors might influence variables of a product or process being analyzed. It looks at "what if" scenarios to determine the best approach.

Many teams are accustomed to making a single change within a product as an experiment to see whether that change has a positive outcome. This can be a slow process, because there may be many changes to experiment with. The technique of design of experiment, sometimes shown by the acronym DOE, takes a different approach, which is to change all the important factors to see which combination of these factors has a lower or higher impact. As you can imagine, this is a quicker method.

Statistical Sampling

Statistical sampling refers to a smaller random sample taken to represent the whole.

Plan Quality Management

- **Additional Quality Planning Tools:** Includes the use of other quality tools, such as:
  - *Brainstorming*
  - *Force field analysis*
  - *Nominal group technique*
  - *Quality management and control tools*
- **Meetings**

Project team members, sponsor, and others holding quality responsibilities (quality experts)

© 2013 The PM Instructors™

Additional Quality Planning Tools

Additional quality planning tools is a broad reference to other tools and / or techniques that can be put to use towards attaining the appropriate level of quality. The list includes tools such as:

- Brainstorming – used to generate ideas
- Force field analysis – captures the forces for and against change
- Nominal group technique – captures ideas through small groups, who then review them with the larger group
- Quality management and control tools – tools that can be used to link and sequence quality activities identified

Meetings

In many instances, meetings are held to assemble the quality management plan, typically facilitated by the project manager. Attendees include project team members, sponsor, or others who hold quality management responsibilities within the organization.

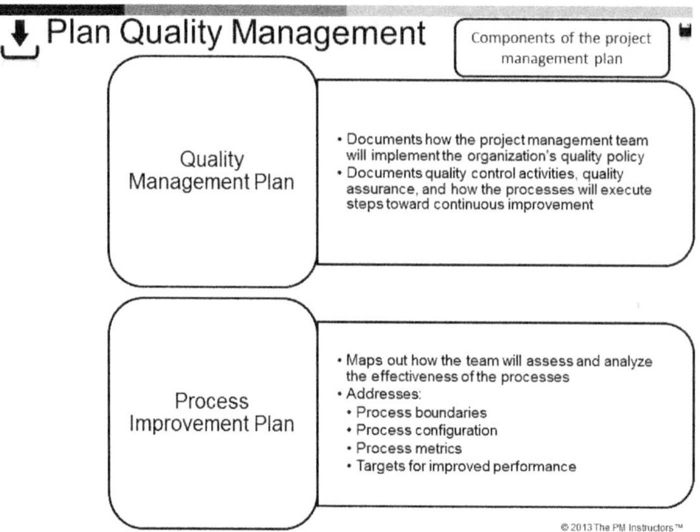

Plan Quality Management Outputs

Plan Quality Management process produces the following five outputs: *quality management plan, process improvement plan, quality metrics, quality checklists, and project documents updates.*

Quality Management Plan

The quality management plan describes how the project team will implement the company's quality policy. The plan addresses quality control, quality assurance, and continuous process improvement. As with all subsidiary plans, it may be formal or informal, broad or detailed, and will detail how to perform an independent peer review.

An independent peer review is conducted from outside of the group working on the material being reviewed, as a way of avoiding bias. The purpose is to ensure that the concepts, designs and tests that were selected for use early on in the project are good or correct. This is useful because it can reduce cost by preventing rework.

Process Improvement Plan

The process improvement plan maps out how the team will assess and analyze the effectiveness of the processes. The idea is to enhance the value of the processes, and increase customer value. This plan will be executed as part of performing quality assurance activities.

The process improvement plan is implemented as part of the Perform Quality Assurance process, and typically addresses the following:

- Process boundaries
- Process configuration
- Process metrics
- Targets for improved performance

Both the quality management plan and process improvement plan are part of the project management plan.

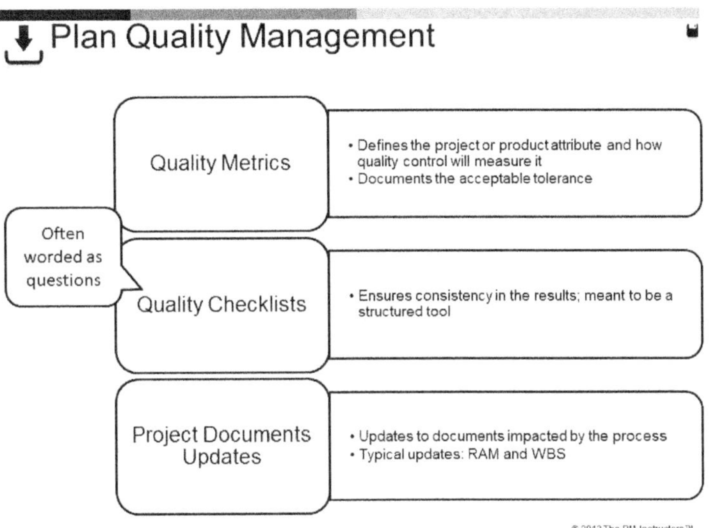

Quality Metrics

Quality metrics describe the measurements, or values, that the project must measure and meet. Basically, quality metrics identify what these measurements are and what results are acceptable. A few examples include: defect density, failure rate, availability, reliability, and test coverage.

Quality metrics define the project or product attribute and how the control quality process will measure it. The acceptable tolerance should be documented as well.

Quality Checklists

Quality checklists exist to make sure that the required quality-related steps are performed. These checklists can be simple or complex, depending on the needs of the project. Here are a few example checklist items:

- Have quality procedures been defined for each project area?
- Are project trends being analyzed and compared to past similar projects?
- Have approved changes to the quality management plan been incorporated?

Notice that they are worded as questions you'd expect on a checklist, or as "to do" items. Think of quality checklists as a quality "to do" list. It ensures consistency in the results, so it is meant to be a structured tool.

Project Documents Updates

Updates to project documents typically involve updating the stakeholder register, the responsibility assignment matrix (RAM), and the WBS.

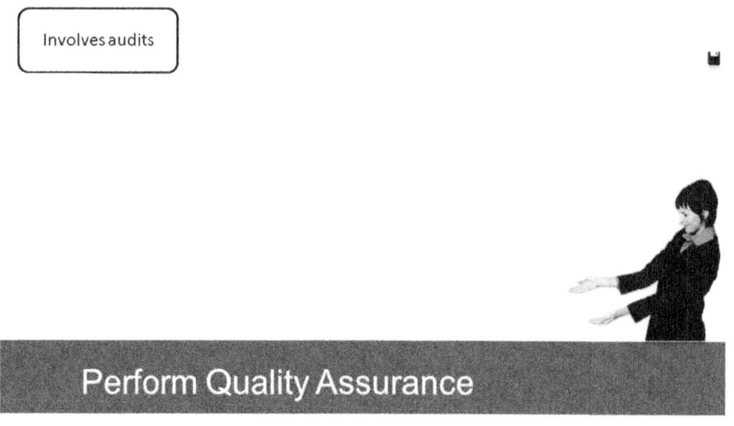

Perform Quality Assurance Process Overview

The purpose of the Perform Quality Assurance process is to audit the quality requirements and the results from quality control measurements to ensure that appropriate quality standards and operational definitions are used. When conducting quality assurance, companies may form a quality department or group to carry out the quality activities. This group can be one put together specifically for the project, or an existing company's quality department. The activities of the group or department include carrying out quality assurance activities and continuous process improvement. The concept behind continuous improvement is to reduce waste and non-value added activities for greater process efficiency and overall effectiveness.

As part of performing quality assurance activities, audits will be carried out – both process audits and audits of quality control results.

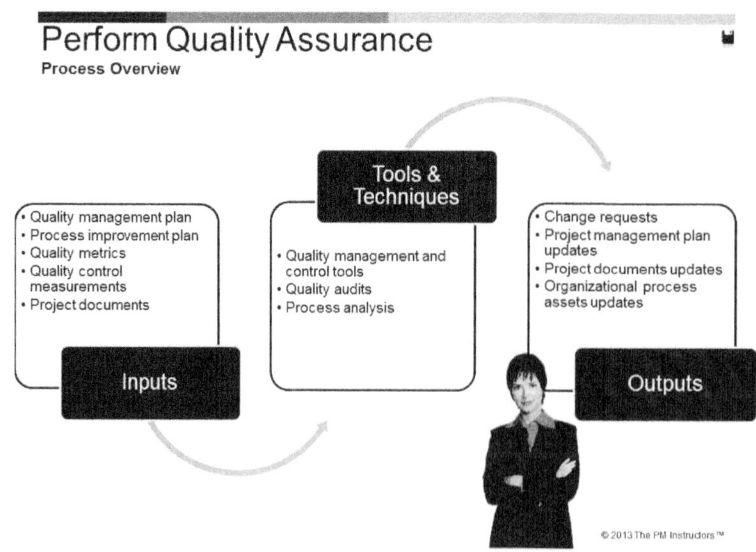

Perform Quality Assurance
Process Overview
Tools & Techniques
• Quality management plan
• Process improvement plan
• Quality metrics
• Quality control measurements
• Project documents
Inputs
• Quality management and control tools
• Quality audits
• Process analysis
• Change requests
• Project management plan updates
• Project documents updates
• Organizational process assets updates
Outputs
© 2013 The PM Instructors ™

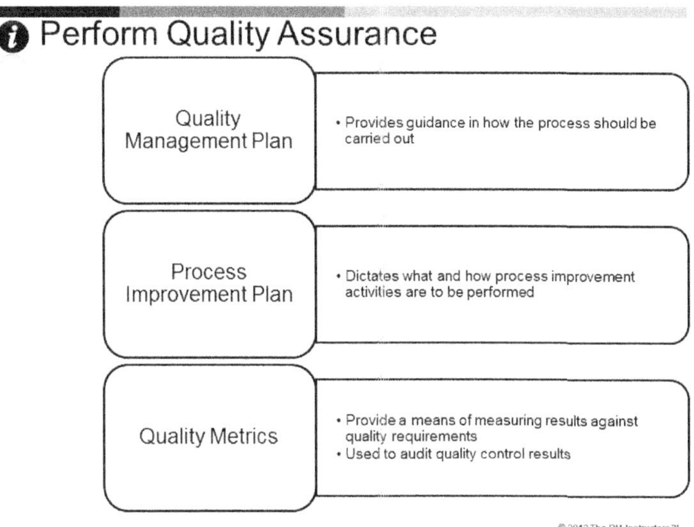

Perform Quality Assurance Inputs

The Perform Quality Assurance process utilizes the following five input: *quality management plan, process improvement plan, quality metrics, quality control measurements, and project documents.*

Quality Management Plan

The quality management plan will provide the project and / or quality team with guidance in carrying out this process. It describes how quality assurance will be performed.

Process Improvement Plan

The process improvement plan dictates what and how process improvement activities are to be performed. It is through this process that the plan is executed.

Quality Metrics

Quality Metrics provide important measurements that provide insight into the performance of the project. These limits have identified values of what results are acceptable, so knowing the results of these identified quality metrics within project executing activities is important to ensuring that quality control activities (which are audited as part of this process) were performed correctly.

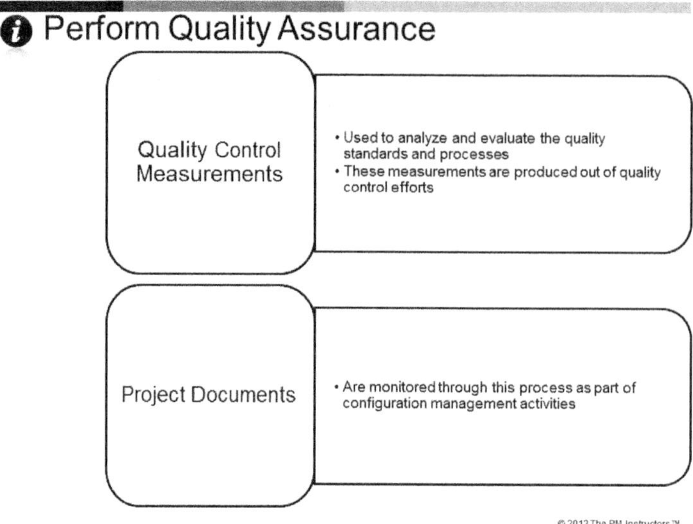

Quality Control Measurements

Quality control measurements are needed to analyze and evaluate the quality standards and processes. They are an output of the Control Quality process, and are reviewed as part of quality auditing activities.

Project Documents

Project documents are monitored as part of performing quality assurance activities, as part of performing configuration management. Project documents may influence quality assurance work.

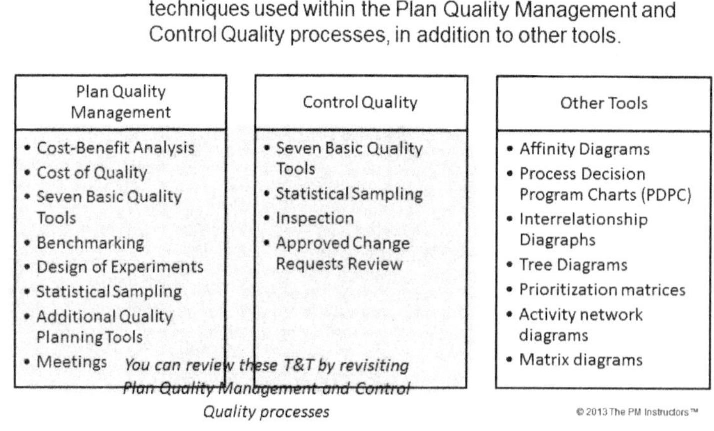

Perform Quality Assurance Tools and Techniques

There are three tools and techniques that are used within the Perform Quality Assurance process: *quality management and control tools, quality audits, and process analysis.*

Quality Management and Control Tools

Plan Quality Management and Control Quality tools and techniques may all be used as part of this process. In addition to these tools and techniques, the following are also used: affinity diagrams, process decision program charts (PDPC), interrelationship diagraphs, tree diagrams, prioritization matrices, activity network diagrams, and matrix diagrams.

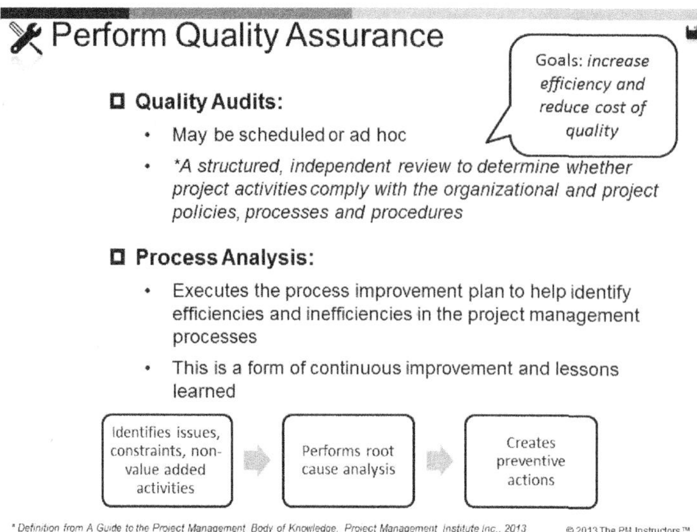

Quality Audits

Quality audits are typically performed by a quality assurance department. These audits may be scheduled or ad hoc. The *PMBOK® Guide* defines quality audits as a "structured, independent review to determine whether project activities comply with the organizational and project policies, processes and procedures."

This tool has two primary goals: to increase efficiency and to reduce the cost of quality. Doing the latter will also increase the chances of product or service acceptance. To meet these goals, quality audits look to identify inefficient and ineffective policies, processes, and procedures. By identifying these deficiencies, they can be corrected, and this is what increases efficiency and saves money by reducing the cost of quality.

Process Analysis

Process analysis involves executing the process improvement plan to help identify efficiencies and inefficiencies in the project management processes. This is a form of continuous improvement and gathering of lessons learned.

Process analysis also looks at the issues discovered, constraints and non-value added activities experienced. It then carries out root cause analysis, which is a technique that analyzes issues and determines the causes that led to it, then creates preventive actions. In simpler terms, process analysis takes what you've learned from carrying out recent activities, and applies those lessons learned to the next round of similar activities – it continues to improve the processes for greater efficiency and as a way of preventing issues that occurred previously .

Perform Quality Assurance

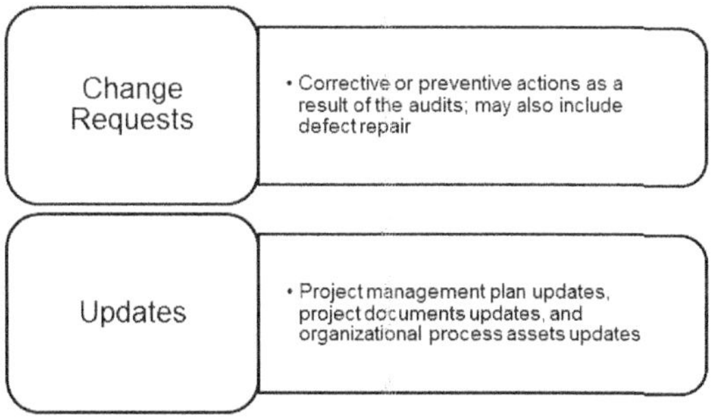

Change Requests	• Corrective or preventive actions as a result of the audits; may also include defect repair
Updates	• Project management plan updates, project documents updates, and organizational process assets updates

Perform Quality Assurance Outputs

The Perform Quality Assurance process produces four outputs: *change requests, project management plan updates, project documents updates, and organizational process assets updates.*

Change Requests

Change request are an important output of this process, and may entail corrective or preventive actions as a result of the audits or defect repair performed.

Project Management Plan Updates

Updates to the project management plan typically include the quality management plan, schedule management plan, scope management plan and / or cost management plan.

Project Documents Updates

Project documents that are updated often include quality audit reports, training plans, and process documentation.

Organizational Process Assets Updates

Updates to the organizational process assets as a result of performing this process typically include updates to the organization's quality standards.

Control Quality
Purpose: To monitor and record results of executing the quality activities to assess performance and recommend necessary changes.

Control Quality Process Overview

The purpose of the Control Quality process is to monitor and record results of executing the quality activities to assess performance and recommend necessary changes. The following should also be noted:

- Part of quality control includes action taken to eliminate causes of poor project performance.
- Quality control is often carried out by a quality control department, if one exists within the company, or a quality control team put together for the project. This team should have a working knowledge of statistical quality control, such as sampling and probability. They will need this to evaluate the outputs of the process.

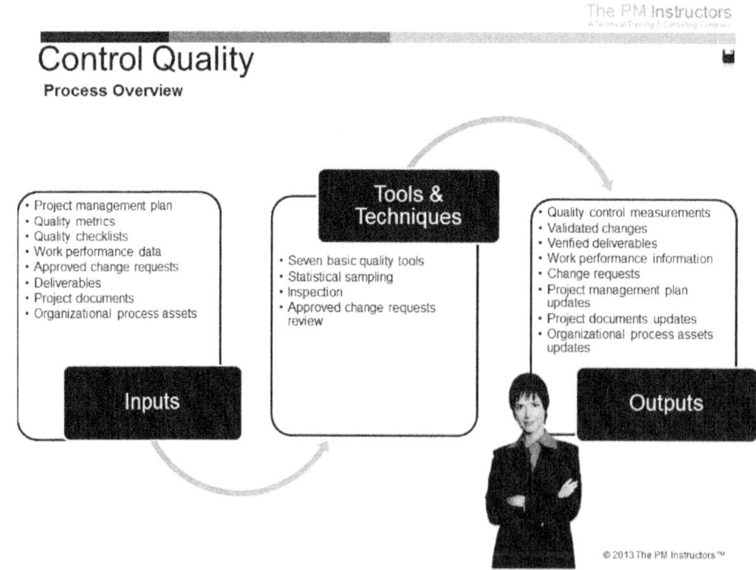
The PM Instructors
Control Quality
Process Overview
• Project management plan
• Quality metrics
• Quality checklists
• Work performance data
• Approved change requests
• Deliverables
• Project documents
• Organizational process assets
Inputs
Tools & Techniques
• Seven basic quality tools
• Statistical sampling
• Inspection
• Approved change requests review
• Quality control measurements
• Validated changes
• Verified deliverables
• Work performance information
• Change requests
• Project management plan updates
• Project documents updates
• Organizational process assets updates
Outputs
© 2013 The PM Instructors™

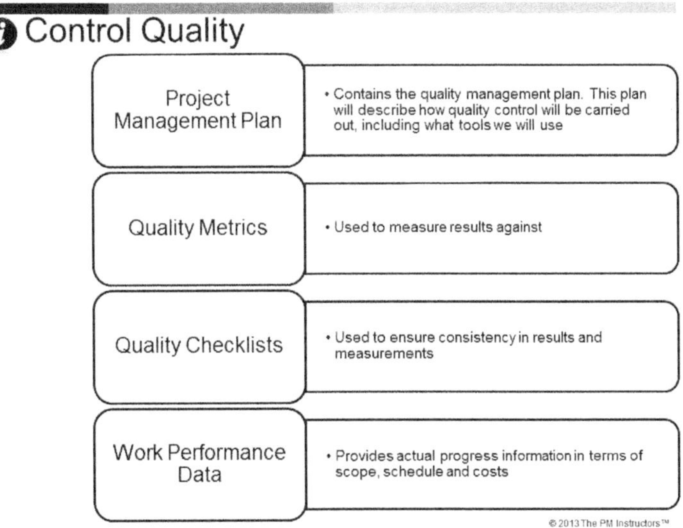

Control Quality Inputs

The Control Quality process contains a total of eight inputs: *project management plan, quality metrics, quality checklists, work performance data, approved change requests, deliverables, project documents, and organizational process assets.*

Project Management Plan

The project management plan contains the quality management plan. This plan will describe how quality control will be carried out, including what tools the team should use.

Quality Metrics

Quality metrics describe how the quality control process should measure the results. It provides what to measure within the project and the values that the results should fall within.

Quality Checklists

Quality checklists is a checklist of quality related activities that should be performed. Quality checklists are typically used to ensure consistency in results and measurements. In some industries, quality checklists are a requirement.

Work Performance Data

Work performance data provides actual progress information in terms of scope, schedule and costs, which will be used to measure progress against and to understand where the project is currently at in the present.

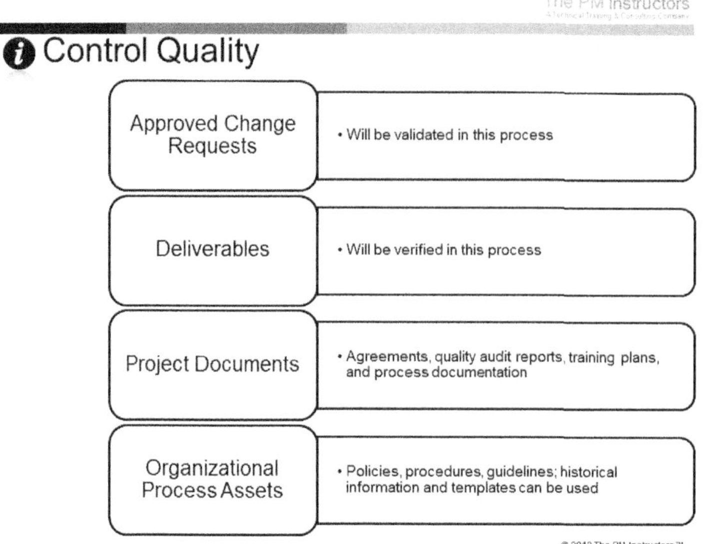
The PM Instructors
Control Quality
Approved Change Requests
• Will be validated in this process
Deliverables
• Will be verified in this process
Project Documents
• Agreements, quality audit reports, training plans, and process documentation
Organizational Process Assets
• Policies, procedures, guidelines; historical information and templates can be used
© 2013 The PM Instructors™

Approved Change Requests

We'll also be validating two things in this process: Approved change requests and Deliverables, so we'll also need these items.

Deliverables

Deliverables refer to the list of project deliverables generated, which we'll need as a point of reference to measure the completion and status of these deliverables and to determine whether they comply with the quality standards. If the deliverables pass inspection, they will be considered "verified".

Project Documents

Project documents that are typically used for quality control purposes include agreements, quality audit reports, training plans, and process documentation.

Organizational Process Assets

Organizational process assets used as part of quality control activities include quality standards and policies, standard work guidelines, and issues and defect reporting procedures of the organization.

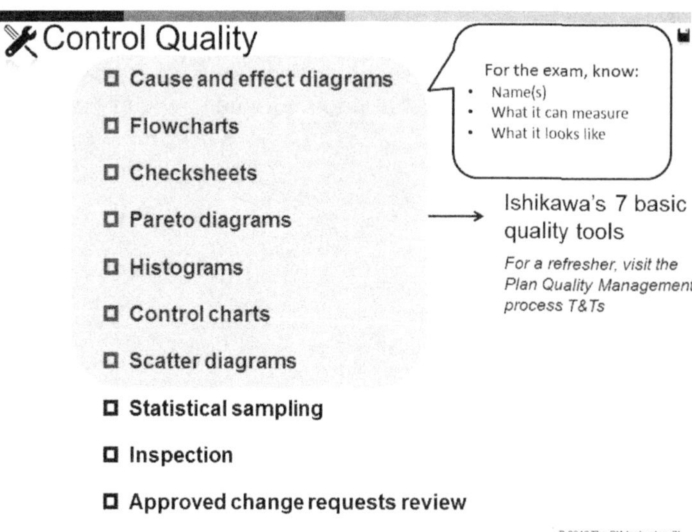
Control Quality
Cause and effect diagrams
Flowcharts
Checksheets
Pareto diagrams
Histograms
Control charts
Scatter diagrams
Statistical sampling
Inspection
Approved change requests review
For the exam, know:
• Name(s)
• What it can measure
• What it looks like
Ishikawa's 7 basic quality tools
For a refresher, visit the Plan Quality Management process T&Ts
© 2013 The PM Instructors™

Control Quality Tools and Techniques

The Control Quality process utilizes the following four tools and techniques: *seven basic quality tools, statistical sampling, inspection, and approved change requests review.*

Many of the tools and techniques included within the list for the Control Quality process are either charts, graphs, or some other visual form of analysis, where we can convert a measurement into an actual result that can be followed through with an action. For the exam, you'll need to know *when* to use *what type* of graph or chart. For each, you should be familiar with the following: their name, the name that they also go by if applicable, what it can measure, and what it looks like.

The first seven on the list included within the associated image are known as the "7 basic quality tools"

For a description or refresher of the seven basic quality tools and statistical sampling, refer to the Plan Quality Management process.

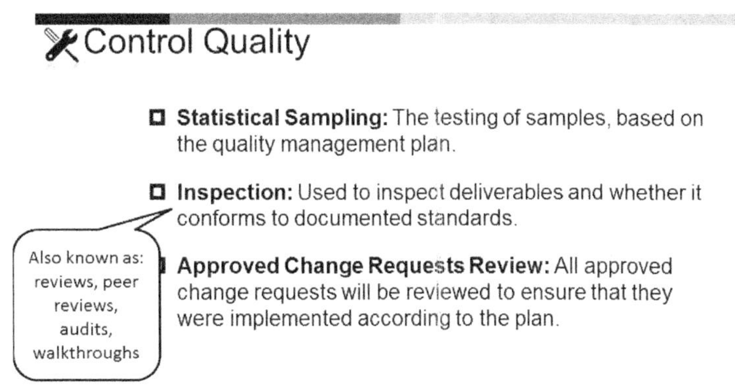

Statistical Sampling

Statistical sampling refers to the testing of samples, as specified within the quality management plan.

Inspection

Inspection is the examination of a work product, such as through measurements, to determine whether it conforms to standards. This is also known as reviews, peer reviews, audits, and walkthroughs. Inspections can also be used to validate defect repairs.

Approved Change Requests Review

Approved change requests review is where all approved change requests will be reviewed to ensure that they were implemented according to the plan.

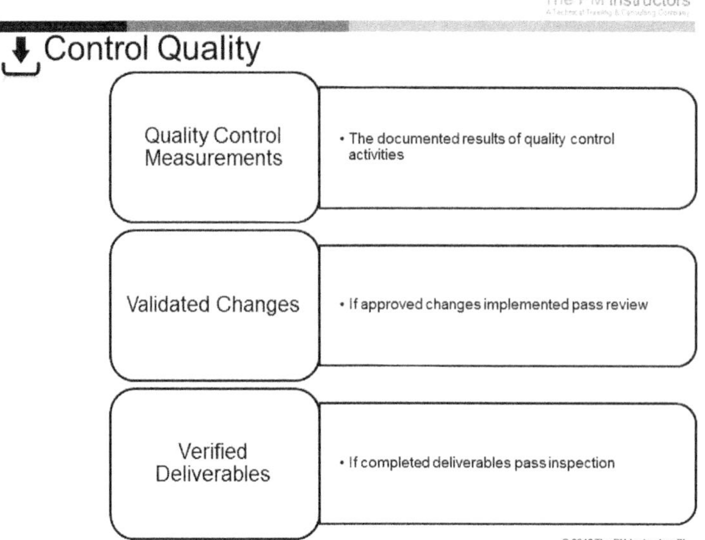

Control Quality Outputs

The Control Quality process has a total of eight outputs: *quality control measurements, validated changes, verified deliverables, work performance information, change requests, project management plan updates, project documents updates, and organizational process assets updates.*

Quality Control Measurements

Quality control measurements are the measurements that result out of the quality control activities. These measurements will be submitted into the quality assurance process as an input for auditing purposes. The purpose of this action is to reevaluate and analyze the quality standards and processes of the company while performing the quality assurance activities.

Validated Changes

Validated changes refer to those implemented changes that were inspected as a way of ensuring that they were implemented correctly, and that they yielded the desired results.

Verified Deliverables

Verified deliverables are a result of the execution of quality control processes. This means that the correctness of a deliverable has been verified.

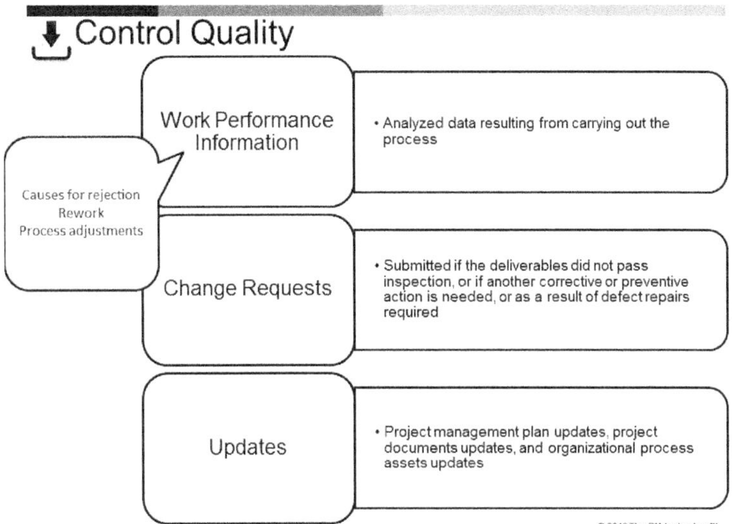
Control Quality
Work Performance Information
• Analyzed data resulting from carrying out the process
Causes for rejection
Rework
Process adjustments
Change Requests
• Submitted if the deliverables did not pass inspection, or if another corrective or preventive action is needed, or as a result of defect repairs required
Updates
• Project management plan updates, project documents updates, and organizational process assets updates
© 2013 The PM Instructors™

Work Performance Information

Work performance information consists of the analyzed data and information resulting from carrying out this process. Examples provided by the *PMBOK® Guide* include causes for rejections, rework, or process adjustments.

Change Requests

If the changes or the deliverables did not pass inspection, a change request will need to be submitted for corrective action, preventive action, or defect repair.

Project Management Plan Updates

Project management plan updates reflect changes made to the quality management plan and the process improvement plan that result out of carrying out the quality control process.

Project Documents Updates

Updates to the project documents typically involve updating the quality standards or process documentation.

Organizational Process Assets Updates

Organizational process assets updates includes completed checklists, which become a part of the project's records, and lessons learned documentation that includes causes of variances, the reason behind the corrective action taken, and any other lessons learned that should be archived as part of the historical database.

Module Summary

In this module we:

- Defined the purpose of the Project Quality Management Knowledge Area
- Identified the processes of the Project Quality Management Knowledge Area
- Recalled the key outputs of the quality management processes
- Differentiated between the inputs, tools and techniques, and outputs of the quality management processes
- Identified and know when to use quality tools and quality control tools
- Applied quality tools to simple scenarios to identify issues, root causes, trends, and/or problems

Chapter Quiz

Exam Practice Questions

1. The project manager needed to convince the executive team that adding more developers to the project, in order to reach the project deadline, would provide little benefit. In fact, because of the time required to ramp up the new team members, it would likely cause further delay to the project. To visually explain this to the executives, the project manager used an Ishikawa diagram, which is also known as:
   A. Influence diagram
   B. Process flow diagram
   C. Kaizen diagram
   D. Cause and effect diagram

2. A project manager reviewing a control chart noticed that three of the processes were climbing up towards the upper control limit. What should the project manager do?
   A. Investigate what is causing the processes to move in this direction
   B. Nothing, since the processes are within the control limits
   C. Do everything possible to prevent the future processes from following the trend
   D. Follow up with the quality department to see what they are doing about it, since this shows potential risks

3. Speedy Dial Aeronautic Parts manufactures widgets for a large government funded space exploration program. In order for them to remain in compliance to maintain good standing with their buyer, all of their parts must be delivered within 3 Sigma of the specifications. What is the accuracy level of 3 Sigma (3 σ)?
   A. 99.985%
   B. 99.73%
   C. 95.46%
   D. 68.27%

4. Susan and David are both project managers for Blazing Broadband Internet Solutions, but they work in different divisions of the company, each having led numerous successful projects for the organization. Another division of their company is planning to release a new software package, but it has been plagued with many obstacles and unique problems. The CEO has asked his two top performing project managers to collaborate in order to find a solution to these unique issues they have been experiencing. Susan and David decided to look at other projects for ideas. Comparing actual or planned project practices to other projects as a way of generating ideas for improvement refers to:
   A. Cost-benefit analysis
   B. Design of experiments
   C. Cost of quality
   D. Benchmarking

5. Which of the following are not tools and techniques of the Control Quality process?
   A. Quality control measurements
   B. Pareto diagram
   C. Inspection
   D. Control charts

6. ZipFast Auto Parts recently started working with a new vendor to provide them with windshield wipers that will be distributed in the retails stores. Since switching to the new vendor, customers of ZipFast Auto Parts have begun receiving complaints that the new windshield wipers are leaving scratches on their windshield and affecting their ability to drive. The project manager informs the new vendor of the problem, who adamantly insists that his windshield wipers cannot be the cause because his quality control measures require that every product that leaves his assembly line get approved, documented and inspected by 3 quality control managers who use a variety of basic quality tools. Which of the following are not considered to be a basic tool of quality?
   A. Inspection
   B. Histogram
   C. Pareto diagram
   D. Cause and effect diagram

7. Inspection is also known as:
   A. Walkthroughs
   B. Re-planning
   C. Product analysis
   D. Expert judgment

8. Which quality theorist believed that quality is conformance to requirements, and that we should strive for zero defects within results?
   A. Philip Crosby
   B. Joseph Juran
   C. W. Edwards Deming
   D. Kaizen

9. Which of the following quality theories reduces inventory costs by having materials or goods arrive right when they are needed?
   A. Gold Plating
   B. Kaizen Theory
   C. Total Quality Management
   D. Just in Time

10. The Project Quality Management Knowledge Area contains the following processes:
   A. Plan Quality Management, Report Performance, Control Quality
   B. Plan Quality Management, Validate Quality, Control Quality
   C. Plan Quality Management, Report Performance, Control Quality
   D. Plan Quality Management, Perform Quality Assurance, Control Quality

11. In looking at the latest control charts, the project manager notices that more than half a dozen processes fall on the same side of the median, raising a red flag. What BEST describes the reason for the project manager's concern?
   A. Assignable cause
   B. Special cause
   C. Processes out of control
   D. Rule of seven

12. John is the lead team member of the group assigned to execute the project's quality activities. John references a document that asks whether his team has performed a series of quality procedures. Based on this information, what document is John likely utilizing?
   A. Process improvement plan
   B. Quality metrics
   C. Quality management plan
   D. Quality checklist

13. Based on the following control chart, what is the lower control limit?

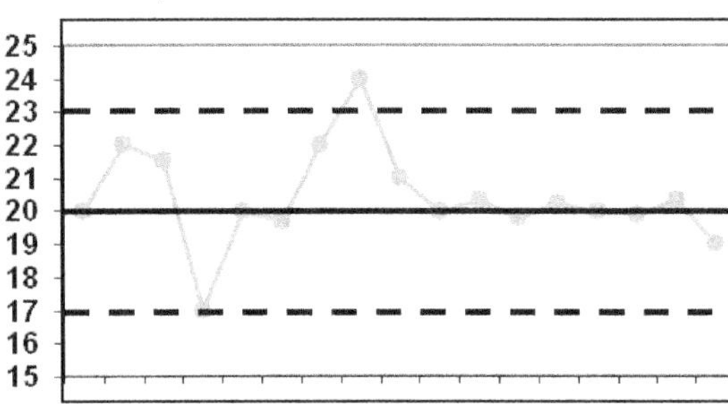

A. 15
B. 17
C. 23
D. 25

14. How is the design of experiments approach different from the standard process of determining which factors should be changed?
    A. It changes all the important factors to see which combination has a higher impact
    B. It changes one important factor at a time to see which factor has a higher impact
    C. Changes two important factors at a time to see which dual combination has a higher impact
    D. Both approaches are the same

15. Henry's Meat Emporium encourages all its employees to focus on contributing toward improving the company's practices and products. This is an example of what philosophy?
    A. Total Quality Management
    B. Kaizen Theory
    C. Just in Time
    D. Zero Defects

16. Joseph Juran is widely known for the following:
    A. Zero Defects
    B. Fit for Use
    C. 14 Steps to Total Quality Management
    D. Plan-Do-Check-Act Cycle

17. A global healthcare provider has recently begun experiencing a high employee attrition rate. The CEO has asked the HR department and managers to compile a report that shows the overall history of the employee satisfaction within the company and compare it to the current satisfaction rate of employees. Upon reading the report he comes across a diagram that reveals an alarming trend. The trend shows the highest level of dissatisfaction and turn-over rate as having taken place immediately following the periods where the work week spiked up to 57 hours prior to the release of new project. Which of the following diagrams shows the various factors that may be connected to potential problems or effects, used by the CEO in this scenario?
    A. Histogram
    B. Pareto chart
    C. Ishikawa diagram
    D. Flowchart diagram

18. Cost of quality is an investment made towards preventing all but which of the following?
    A. Non-conformance to requirements
    B. Appraising products for "conformance" made to requirements
    C. Rework
    D. Customer satisfaction

19. You are the project manager for a widget company and have just been informed by your fabrication foreman that your customer's order of 5,000 rust resistant screws are completed, but there is one problem. The screws are within the specifications and requirements defined by the customer, however, he noticed that the width of the screws are 1 nanometer less than the company's quality policy. A rework of the order will cause a slip in the schedule by 7 days and take their profit margin down to .001%. When implementing the company's quality policy, what does the project management team utilize as a guide?
    A. Quality baseline
    B. Quality management plan
    C. Process improvement plan
    D. Quality checklist

20. In response to the information you received from your foreman about the 5,000 rust resistant screws not meeting the company quality standards, you try to figure out what cased this error to occur. Your first question to the foreman is "who is responsible for the inspection and prevention". What is the difference between inspection and prevention, in regards to quality management?
    A. Inspection focuses on the cause of errors found, while prevention focuses on resolving the errors
    B. Prevention focuses on the cause of errors found, while inspection focuses on resolving the errors
    C. Inspection keeps errors from reaching the customer, while prevention prevents errors from occurring
    D. Prevention keeps errors from reaching the customer, while inspection prevents errors from occurring

Chapter Quiz

Exam Practice Answers

1. Answer: D

   Explanation: Ishikawa diagrams are also known as cause and effect diagrams and fishbone diagrams. These diagrams show how an effect (or defect) relates to potential causes and sub-causes.

2. Answer: B

   Explanation: All three processes fall within the upper and lower control limits. This variation is acceptable and is known as common causes. If a process falls outside of these limits, or if it follows the rule of seven or trend of seven, then the project manager should immediately investigate, since it means that the process has fallen out of control or may be influenced by an external factor.

3. Answer: B

   Explanation: 6 sigma is considered to be the highest level of quality, which is 99.999%; 3 sigma is the next level down, which is 99.73%; 2 sigma is 95.46%, and 1 sigma is 68.2%.

4. Answer: D

   Explanation: Cost benefit analysis looks at the trade-offs between quality planning and cost, so this option can be eliminated. Design of experiments is a statistical method that tries to identify factors that may influence variables of a product that's being developed, also not the correct choice. Cost of quality simply refers to the investment of the quality activities, again one that we can cross off. And finally, we are left with benchmarking, which compares the actual or planned project practices to other projects as a way of generating ideas for improvement and to provide a basis for measuring project performance, making it the correct answer.

5. Answer: A

   Explanation: All of the options provided relate to the Control Quality process. However, one of them is an output, and that is "quality control measurements". Pareto diagram, inspection, and control charts, are all tools and techniques of the process.

6. Answer: A

   Explanation: There are seven items that make up the basic tools of quality, which are used as part of the Control Quality process: cause and effect diagram, control charts, flowcharts, histograms, Pareto diagram, checksheets, and scatter diagram. Notice that all options except "inspection" were mentioned. Therefore, inspection, which is also a tool and technique of the Control Quality process, is the correct answer.

7. Answer: A

   Explanation: There were four additional names provided for inspection, and they include: reviews, product reviews, audits, and walkthroughs. This makes walkthroughs the correct answer.

8. Answer: A

   Explanation: The correct theorist tied to the idea that quality is conformance to requirement, is Philip Crosby. He also believed in zero defects and the idea behind the cost of poor quality.

9. Answer: D

   Explanation: This describes the Just in Time theory, which involves receiving goods or materials just before they are needed. The idea behind this theory is to reduce the cost of inventory. But to implement this, a company must be very efficient with a high focus in quality; otherwise, coordinating and knowing when the goods must arrive will not work.

10. Answer: D

    Explanation: The Project Quality Management Knowledge Area consists of three processes: Plan Quality Management, Perform Quality Assurance, and Control Quality.

11. Answer: D

    Explanation: The question describes the rule of seven, where if 7 or more processes fall on the same side of the median, it indicates that an external factor may be influencing the results. This raises a red flag. This also means that a process may be out of control, so there are multiple viable options included. In this case, rule of seven is the most relevant and direct answer, making it the best choice.

12. Answer: D

    Explanation: Notice that the document is providing John with a reference, displayed in the format of a question, and checking to ensure that the team has performed a series of procedures. This sounds like a quality checklist. Additional notes: the process improvement plan provides the steps for determining waste and non-value added activities; quality metrics focuses on what measurements are acceptable, and the quality management plan is the guide for implementing the quality policy and approach.

13. Answer: B

    Explanation: The upper and lower control limits are identified as dotted lines directly above / under the median (center) line, typically placed at a 3 Sigma level from the median. This would point to line 17 as the lower control limit.

14. Answer: A

    Explanation: Design of experiments takes all the important factors and attempts different combinations of changes to see which has a lower or higher impact. This provides a quicker way of reaching the desired result. The standard approach, on the other hand, makes a single change at a time.

15. Answer: A

    Explanation: Total Quality Management embeds the mindset of participating in improvement within all employees. Kaizen theory is the focus on continuous improvement; Just in Time is when inventory and goods are obtained just before they are needed; and Zero Defects focuses on achieving zero defects as part of meeting quality requirements.

16. Answer: B

    Explanation: Juran is widely known for the concept that the project's end result should be fit for use by the customer.

17. Answer: C

    Explanation: The correct answer is Ishikawa diagrams, also known as cause and effect diagrams and fishbone diagrams.

18. Answer: D

    Explanation: It is almost counter intuitive to have the word *except* and customer *satisfaction* together, but the question asks for what is quality NOT attempting to prevent.

19. Answer: B

    Explanation: Each Knowledge Area after Project Integration Management produces a subsidiary plan, which becomes part of the project management plan. Part of what these subsidiary plans do is guide the implementation and execution of the processes from within their respective Knowledge Areas. They outline how to go through the related processes ("how to" plans). The question here asks for what is utilized as a guide in carrying out quality related activities, based on the quality policies. This would point to the quality management plan.

20. Answer: C

    Explanation: We have two statements here with the two terms reversed. Prevention and Inspection are both looking to eliminate issues, defects, or problems. Prevention focuses on preventing something, while inspection's primary focus is on fixing something that already contains a defect, prior to reaching the customer.

Chapter 9: Project Human Resource Management

Learning Objectives:

- ☐ Define the purpose of the Project Human Resource Management Knowledge Area
- ☐ Identify the processes of the Project Human Resource Management Knowledge Area
- ☐ Recall the key outputs of the human resource management processes
- ☐ Differentiate between the inputs, tools and techniques, and outputs of the human resource management processes
- ☐ Interpret an organization chart and position descriptions for a project team
- ☐ Identify the specific differences between operational and project team management
- ☐ Identify and describe the five general techniques for managing conflict

Exam Domain Tasks:

- Develop a human resource management plan by defining the roles and responsibilities of the project team members in order to create an effective project organization structure and provide guidance regarding how resources will be utilized and managed.
- Obtain and manage project resources including outsourced deliverables by following the procurement plan, in order to ensure successful project execution.
- Maximize team performance through leading, mentoring, training, and motivating team members.

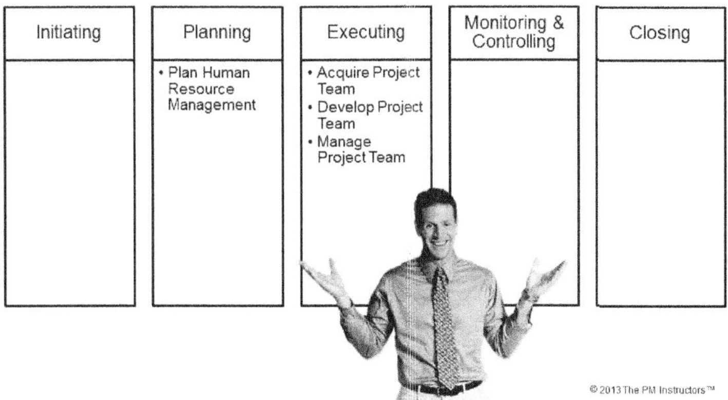
Project Human Resource Management
Purpose: To organize, manage, and lead the project team.
4 Project Management Processes:
Initiating
Planning
Executing
Monitoring & Controlling
Closing
• Plan Human Resource Management
• Acquire Project Team
• Develop Project Team
• Manage Project Team
© 2013 The PM Instructors™

Project Human Resource Management Overview

The purpose of the Project Human Resource Management Knowledge Area is to organize, manage, and lead the project team. Here is where the project management team identifies the roles and responsibilities of the team, how staffing will be managed, and project assignments are issued. In short, this Knowledge Area is concerned with all aspects of people management in relation to the project. And just like the goal of improving processes and overall organizational efficiency, we are also interested in enhancing the skills and efficiency of the team. The increase in skill and competency of the project staff will translate into better project performance, resulting in a win-win.

It is important to understand the difference between the project management team and the project team, and also the responsibilities of the project manager.

Project Human Resource Management

CONCEPT

Project Manager	Project Management Team	Project Team
• Responsible for managing and leading the project team. This includes the following responsibilities: • Influencing the project team • Maintaining accountability over professional and ethical behavior of the team	• A subset of the project team that is responsible for project management and leadership activities, including: • Performing or supporting the implementation of the project management processes • Working with the sponsor	• A set of individuals who support the project manager in performing the work of the project to achieve its objectives • Serve as SMEs • Perform project activities

© 2013 The PM Instructors™

Project Manager

In the context of managing and leading, the project manager has two main responsibilities as part of this Knowledge Area:

- Influencing the project team; and

- Maintaining accountability over professional and ethical behavior

Depending on the organizational structure that the project team works within, the project manager may need to collaborate and work closely with operational leadership, in order to effectively lead and manage the project team. Operational management involves managing and running the day-to-day operations of the business. In many instances, project team members have operational responsibilities that they are accountable for completing. The project manager and functional manager must be aware of, and help balance, this set of responsibilities from the project responsibilities of the team.

Project Management Team

The project management team is a subset of the project team. They are responsible for performing project management and leadership activities, including activities related to the five Process Groups. In some organizations, this team is referred to as the core team, leadership team, or leads of the project.

An aim of the project management team is to develop the project team and to involve the team as early on as possible in the planning efforts and also in decision-making efforts when the opportunity exists. Individuals that are involved in this way have a greater commitment to the project, and also, their expertise will be a valuable addition.

Project Team

The project team refers to a set of individuals who support the project manager in performing the work of the project to achieve its objectives. They often serve as subject matter experts (SMEs) and perform the activities / work of the project.

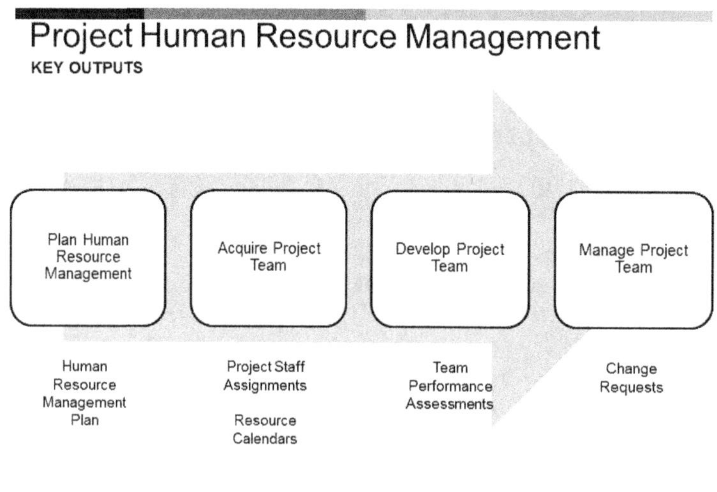

The Project Human Resource Management Knowledge Area has a total of four processes:

- **Plan Human Resource Management (Planning Process Group).** Purpose: To identify and document the project roles, responsibilities, required skills, reporting relationships and to create a staffing management plan.
- **Acquire Project Team (Executing Process Group).** Purpose: To confirm human resource availability and obtain the team necessary to complete the project activities.
- **Develop Project Team (Executing Process Group).** Purpose: To improve the competencies, team member interaction, and the overall team environment to enhance project performance.
- **Manage Project Team (Executing Process Group).** Purpose: To track team member performance, provide feedback, resolve issues, and manage changes to optimize project performance.

Plan Human Resource Management
Purpose: To identify and document project roles, responsibilities, required skills, reporting relationships, and to create a staffing management plan.

Plan Human Resource Management Process Overview

The purpose of the Plan Human Resource Management process is to identify and document the project roles, responsibilities and reporting relationships, and to create the staffing management plan. The staffing management plan will be critical in obtaining, managing, and releasing the resources that make up the project team.

Understanding this process helps to see the overall picture and how several processes are tied and work together, since there are several interdependencies between the people resources and the ability to carry out the work of the project.

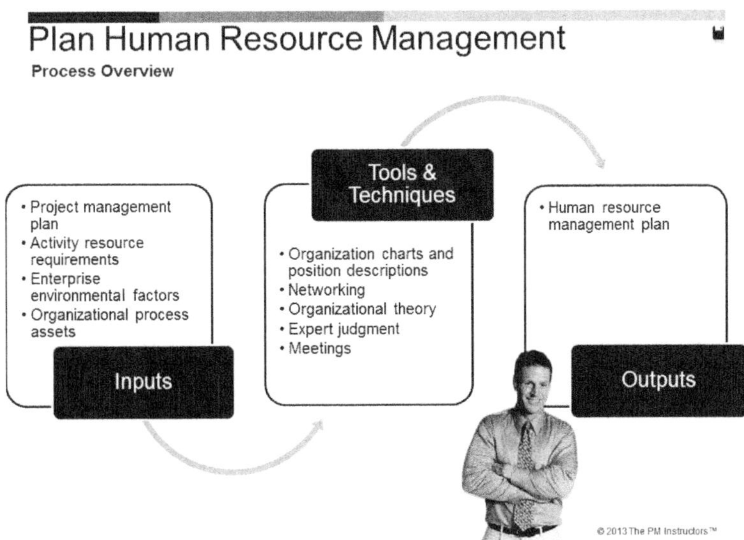
Plan Human Resource Management
Process Overview
• Project management plan
• Activity resource requirements
• Enterprise environmental factors
• Organizational process assets
Inputs
Tools & Techniques
• Organization charts and position descriptions
• Networking
• Organizational theory
• Expert judgment
• Meetings
• Human resource management plan
Outputs
© 2013 The PM Instructors™

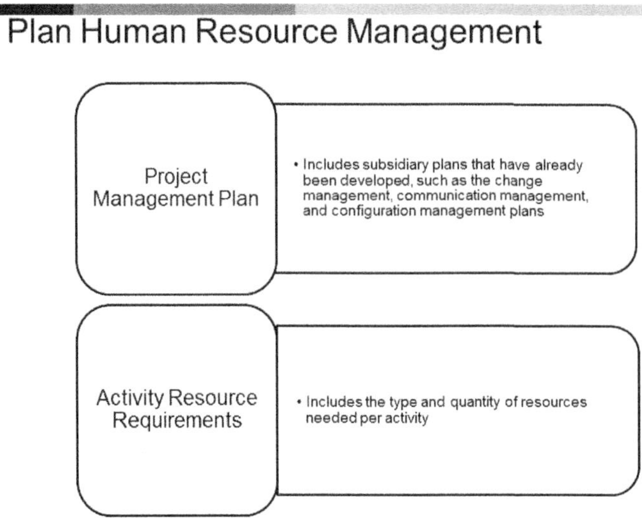
Plan Human Resource Management
Project Management Plan
• Includes subsidiary plans that have already been developed, such as the change management, communication management, and configuration management plans
Activity Resource Requirements
• Includes the type and quantity of resources needed per activity
© 2013 The PM Instructors™

Plan Human Resource Management Inputs

The Plan Human Resource Management process has a total of four inputs: *project management plan, activity resource requirements, enterprise environmental factors, and organizational process assets.*

Project Management Plan

The project management plan is often referenced when developing subsidiary plans, such as the human resource management plan. Typical subsidiary plans used include the change management, communication management, and configuration management plans.

Activity Resource Requirements

Activity resource requirements includes the type and quantity of resources needed per activity. Remember that this was generated in the Project Time Management Knowledge Area, out of the process called Estimate Activity Resources. Activity resource requirements include the basis of estimates for each resource, any assumptions made, the resource availability, and the quantity of resources needed.

Plan Human Resource Management

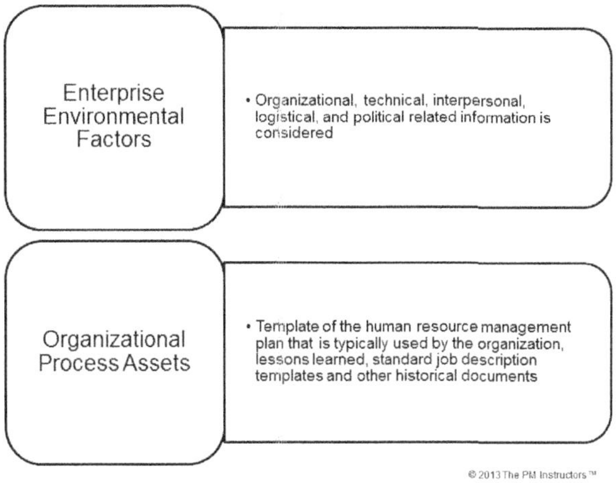

Enterprise Environmental Factors	• Organizational, technical, interpersonal, logistical, and political related information is considered
Organizational Process Assets	• Template of the human resource management plan that is typically used by the organization, lessons learned, standard job description templates and other historical documents

Enterprise Environmental Factors

There are several items from within the enterprise environmental factors that may be used as part of this process, and which reveal how the organization functions. This is key for this process, because the roles and responsibilities will be developed with the organization's current structure and processes in mind. Here are the items to consider and that will be utilized:

- **Organizational.** This identifies the departments that will be involved in the project, and how they currently interact with one another. In order to develop realistic and workable roles and responsibilities it's important to understand current working arrangements .
- **Technical.** The project team must consider the disciplines and specialties that are needed to carry out the project activities. Just saying that three programmers are required is not sufficient. What type of programming language do they need to know? And at what skill level?
- **Interpersonal,** which looks at the formal and informal relationships that exist among specific individuals that are being considered for the roles. For these individuals being considered, what is their current job description, working relationships, cultural or language differences that will impact the job, and even existing trust levels?
- **Logistical.** These logistics refer to the distance separating team members, such as time zones, countries, and even buildings.
- **Politics** are also taken into consideration. This looks at the goals and agenda of potential project stakeholders. What is their current level of power and alliances?

Organizational Process Assets

Organizational process assets provide a template of the human resource management plan that is typically used by the organization, as well as lessons learned, standard job description templates and other historical documents that could be of help here to make the creation of the plan more efficient.

Plan Human Resource Management

- **Organization Charts and Position Descriptions:** There are three formats used: hierarchical, matrix, and text descriptions.

Hierarchical	Matrix	Text Format
• A standard company org chart provides information on the reporting structure of the various roles, as well as the roles that exist	• Example: a responsibility assignment matrix (RAM) • RACI chart (type of RAM) • responsible • accountable • consult • inform	• Standard job description for each role • Each role should outline the capabilities and skill level required of each role, and their designated authority level

Plan Human Resource Management Tools and Techniques

There are a total of five tools and techniques used within the Plan Human Resource Management process: *organization charts and position descriptions, networking, organizational theory, expert judgment, and meetings.*

Organization Charts and Position Descriptions

Because the human resource management plan will include roles and descriptions as part of it, as well as a project org chart, the organization charts and position descriptions tool and technique becomes an important item that contributes toward generating them. There are three formats to this tool and technique: hierarchical, matrix, and text descriptions of the roles and responsibilities.

Hierarchical

Hierarchical refers to the organization charts (org charts). A standard company org chart provides information on the reporting structure of the various roles, as well as the roles that exist. Since the project manager will be putting together a project org chart inside of this plan, this tool and technique is important.

Matrix

Matrix refers to the use of responsibility assignment matrix (RAM). A common type of RAM is the RACI chart – RACI stands for responsible, accountable, consult, and inform. A RACI chart can indicate who has what type of responsibility for the activities.

Text Format

Text format refers to a standard job description for each role. Each role should outline the capabilities and skill level required of each role, and their designated authority level. Think of a standard job description that you've seen in the past. This will be generated as part of the human resource management plan.

Plan Human Resource Management

- **Networking:** Networking within the organization and outside of it to obtain the information needed to put together the plan, as well as establish relationships within the company and within the industry.

  Proactive correspondence
  Luncheons
  Informal conversations
  Trade conferences
  Industry Association meetings
  Committee gatherings
  Virtual meetings

- **Organizational Theory:** This theory states that the behaviors and actions of individuals will be influenced by the type of organizational structure and its culture that they work within.

Networking

Networking refers to networking within the organization and outside of it to obtain the information needed to put together the human resource management plan, as well as establish relationships within the company and within the industry. Networking can involve interacting with people either within your industry or organization in an informal way in order to understand political and interpersonal factors impacting staffing management. Here is a list of examples that relate to human resource networking:

- Proactive correspondence
- Luncheons
- Informal conversations
- Trade conferences
- Industry Association meetings
- Committee gatherings or virtual meetings

Organizational Theory

Organizational theory states that the behaviors and actions of individuals will be influenced by the type of organizational structure and its culture that they work within. For example, if you work within a functional organization, which tends to be much more structured, formal, and conservative, the decisions that you make will reflect this.

Plan Human Resource Management

- **Expert Judgment:** Necessary to assess and determine role requirements, and to assess staff related risks, training, and security needs.
- **Meetings:** Held to assemble the plan and apply the tools and techniques of the process.

Expert Judgment

Expert judgment is used to develop the plan as a way of assessing and determining the role requirements and reporting relationships. Expert judgment is also needed to assess staff related risks, training, and security needs.

Meetings

Meetings are often held by the project management team to assemble the human resource management plan, and to apply the tools and techniques of the process.

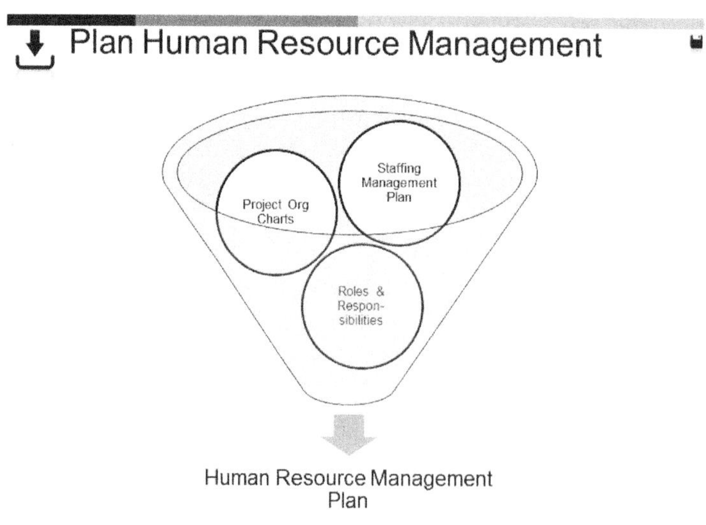

Plan Human Resource Management Outputs

The Plan Human Resource Management process has a single output: *the human resource management plan.*

Human Resource Management Plan

The human resource management plan contains three components: roles and responsibilities, project org charts, and staffing management plan. The human resource management plan itself is a part of the project management plan.

Roles and Responsibilities

When generating and documenting roles and responsibilities, it should include the role, level of authority, responsibility, and competency.

- A role is the label that describes the work that a person is accountable for. An example of this is senior programmer, architect, programming analyst, and so forth. But to a company, or even to a project, the role of a senior programmer can mean different things. And for this reason, having good clarity on what the role encompasses is important.
- The level of authority indicates whether the individual holding this role has the ability to assign resources, make decisions, and sign approvals. Clarifying this is very beneficial and helps to prevent confusion, mix-ups, and conflict within a project.
- Responsibility refers to the work that an individual within this role is required to perform.
- Competency is the skill and capacity that's required to complete the project activities. The required competencies should be clearly laid out to address any training needs if necessary, and to make sure the right people are placed in the role.

Project Org Charts

Project org charts are a graphic display of project team members and their reporting relationships. This org chart focuses on the project, versus the organization.

Staffing Management Plan

The staffing management plan contains all of the details of how the project team will be acquired, managed, and then released. It also contains training and safety needs of the team, and compliance. This also includes how resources will be acquired externally. Additional detail of the staffing management plan can be found on the next page.

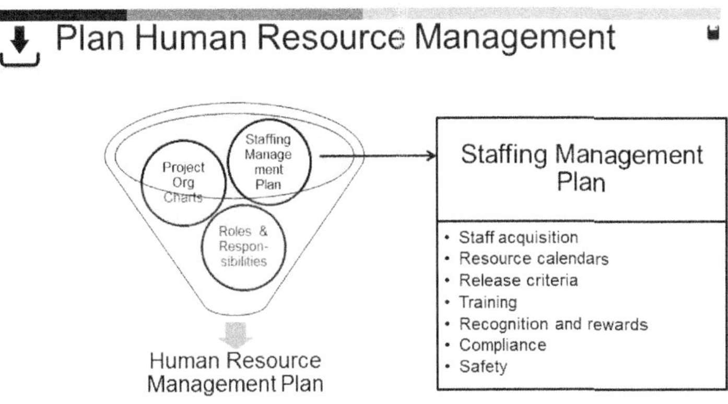

In the previous page, a high level review of the staffing management plan contents were provided. The following is a more descriptive breakdown of the staffing management plan contents:

- **Staff acquisition,** which specifies whether resources will come from contracted sources or internal to the company, whether they will work in a centralized location, the costs associated with the various levels of expertise, and the assistance that will be provided in obtaining the resources by the company's human resource department.

- **Resource calendars / timetable**, which shows when human resources and acquisition activities will occur by time frames. Resource histograms are often used as a tool in charting a timetable. It illustrates the number of hours that an individual, department or entire project team will be needed by week or by month. Project management software typically includes this and makes creating the timetable simple and quick.
- **Release criteria** determine the method and timing of releasing project team members in a way that benefits the project and the individuals. Planning this well helps to keep morale high, costs down, and transitions over to other projects smooth.
- **Training** needs are also included. This is especially important if senior resources are needed, but cannot be obtained due to availability or costs.
- **Recognition and rewards**, which should be based on activities and performance. These rewards will be awarded during the develop project team process within this knowledge area. Planning recognition and rewards helps to promote desired behavior.
- **Compliance** covers the adherence of government regulations, union contracts, and other applicable human resource related policies.
- **Safety**, which include policies and procedures that are established to protect team members from hazards and other risks. This is either included here, in the staffing management plan, or can be addressed as a part of the risk register.

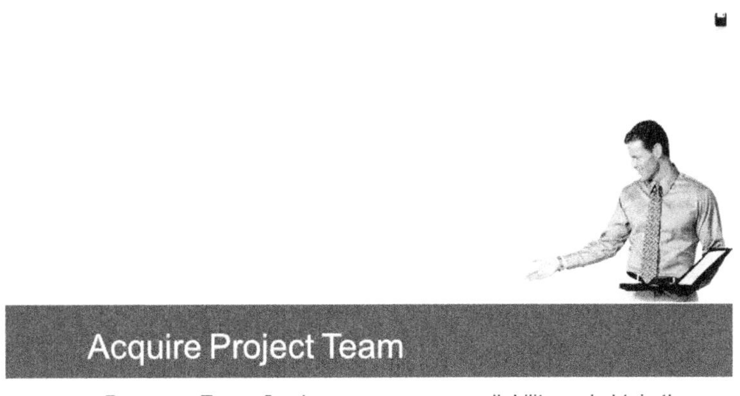

Acquire Project Team
Purpose: To confirm human resource availability and obtain the team necessary to complete project activities.

Acquire Project Team Process Overview

The Acquire Project Team process is responsible for obtaining the human resources needed to complete the project. Depending on the type of organizational structure that the project is functioning within will depend on whether or not the project management team has control over which team members are selected, and whether or not they will be contracted.

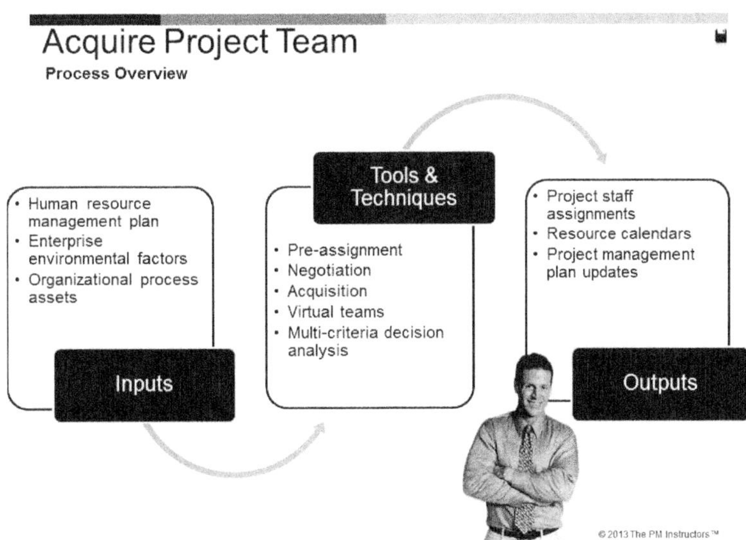

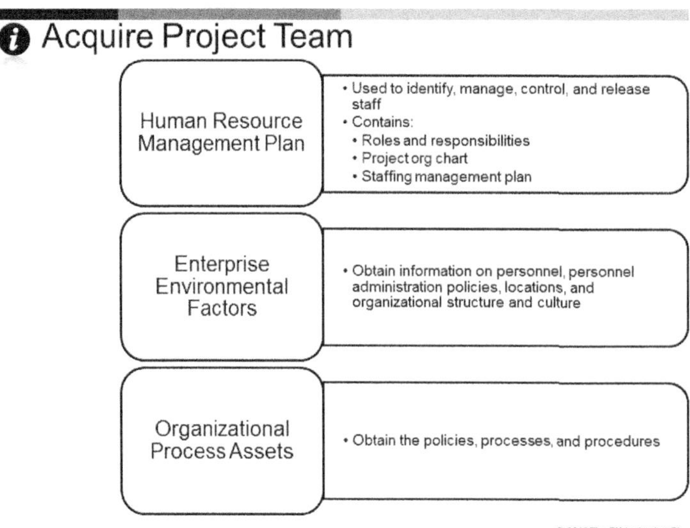
Acquire Project Team
Human Resource Management Plan
• Used to identify, manage, control, and release staff
• Contains:
• Roles and responsibilities
• Project org chart
• Staffing management plan
Enterprise Environmental Factors
• Obtain information on personnel, personnel administration policies, locations, and organizational structure and culture
Organizational Process Assets
• Obtain the policies, processes, and procedures
© 2013 The PM Instructors™

Acquire Project Team Inputs

The Acquire Project Team process has a total of three inputs: *human resource management plan, enterprise environmental factors, and organizational process assets.*

Human Resource Management Plan

The human resource management plan contains several key items that are necessary to making assignments, such as roles and descriptions, the project org chart, and the staffing management plan.

Enterprise Environmental Factors

Enterprise environmental factors contain all personnel related information, including availability of company resources, their competence or skill level, personnel related policies, company locations and facilities, and the company's organizational structure and culture.

Organizational Process Assets

The organizational process assets contain the company's policies, procedures, and processes.

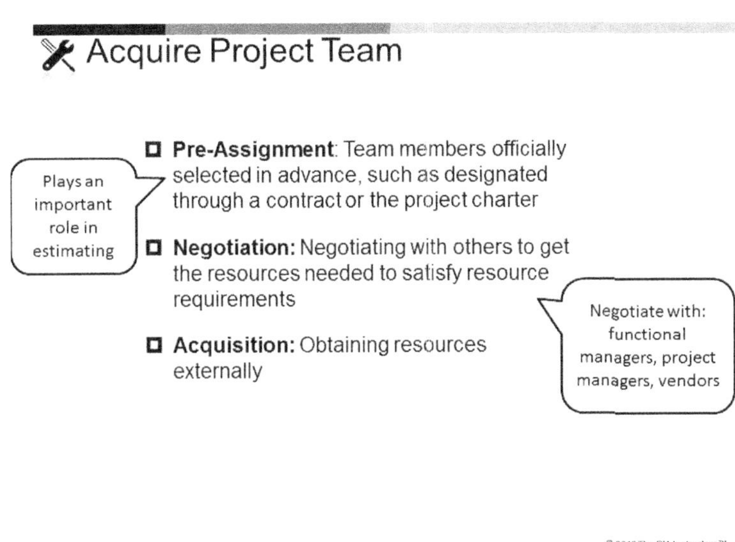

Acquire Project Team Tools and Techniques

There are a total of five tools and techniques within the Acquire Project Team process: *pre-assignment, negotiation, acquisition, virtual teams, and multi-criteria decision analysis.*

Pre-Assignment

In certain cases, individuals will be promised as part of a contract to a customer, or they will be assigned as early as the project charter. This is typically the case when a specific expertise is required, or the demand for a specific resource's skill set is high, in which case they may be assigned early to guarantee availability. Pre-assignments play an important role in estimating the activity resource requirements.

Examples of pre-assignments include a resource noted in an agreement or within the project charter.

Negotiation

In many cases, project managers must negotiate with others to get the resources needed for the project and to satisfy the resource requirements. This negotiation may take place with functional managers, it may be with other project managers, and it may occur externally with vendors.

Acquisition

Acquisition is needed when necessary resources are not available within the organization, and the project management team must look externally for the resources. The staffing management plan provides the guidance as to how to go about this.

Acquire Project Team

- **Virtual Teams:** Staff who have minimal face-to-face time (located outside of office)

Specialized skills more accessible
Provides cost savings

- **Multi-Criteria Decision Analysis:** A tool that rates potential project team members based on criteria defined by the project management team

Availability
Cost
Experience
Ability
Knowledge
Skills
Attitude
International Factors

Virtual Teams

The use of virtual teams has greatly broadened the ability for project management teams to acquire resources, especially those that require very specialized skills. If a particular specialty is not available within the project's facility, it may be available within another location from within the organization, and that resource can participate as a virtual team member. Virtual teams can provide a project with savings from reducing the need for constant travel.

Multi-Criteria Decision Analysis

Multi-criteria decision analysis refers to a tool that incorporates project team member selection criteria. Team members are rated based on criteria that are defined by the project management team. Examples of criteria provided within the *PMBOK® Guide* includes team member availability, cost, experience, ability, knowledge, skills, attitude and international factors.

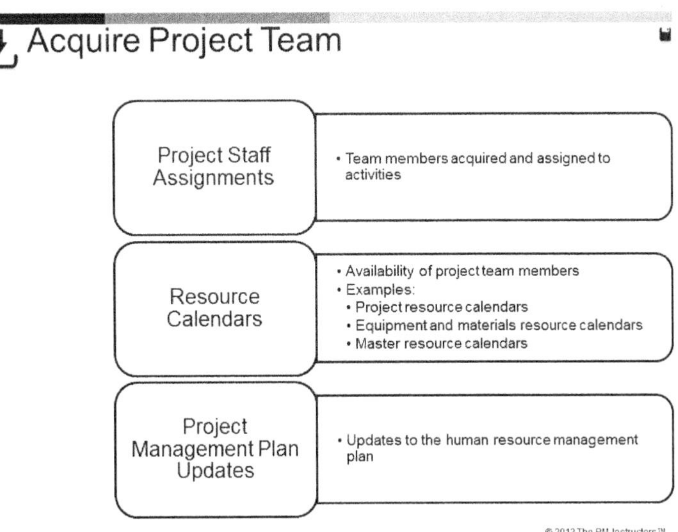

Acquire Project Team Outputs

The Acquire Project Team process has a total of three outputs: *project staff assignments, resource calendars,* and *project management plan updates.*

Project Staff Assignments

Official assignments of individual team members to the roles and responsibilities described within the human resource management plan are made as a result of the Acquire Project Team process. The project management team documents these assignments through a team directory, memos to current team members already working within the project, and inserts the names of the assigned resources within several areas of the project management plan.

Resource Calendars

Several types of resource calendars may exist, such as resource calendars specific to a project (such as project calendars), resource calendars specific to equipment and materials, and a master resource calendar for the organization. Once staffing assignments are made, the appropriate calendars must be updated to reflect the availability of the affected resources.

Project Management Plan Updates

The *PMBOK® Guide* specifies that the most likely updates made as a result of carrying out this process include the human resource management plan. Within this plan, changes may be made to the project's RAM or RACI chart, as well as to the project organizational chart.

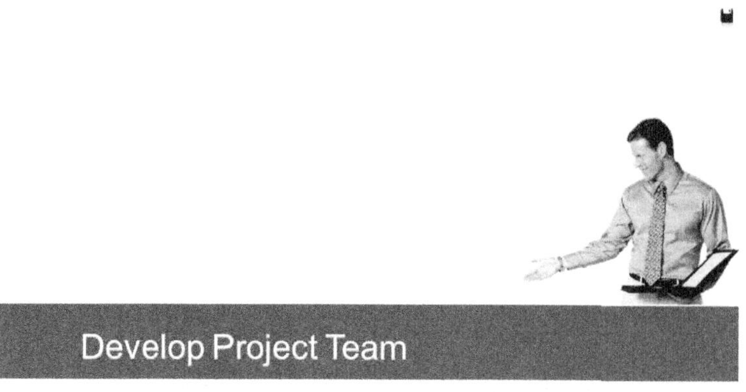
Develop Project Team
Purpose: To improve the competencies, team member interaction, and the overall team environment to enhance project performance.

Develop Project Team Process Overview

The purpose of the Develop Project Team process is to improve the competencies, team member interaction, and the overall team environment to enhance project performance. This is where team building and the focus on enhancing the team's skill set takes place. The process has the following objectives:

- Increase the ability of team members to complete project activities by improving the skill of team members
- Raise productivity through greater teamwork by increasing the level of trust and cohesiveness among team members

When the project team functions effectively, team members are more likely to assist one another and work together versus as isolated project groups.

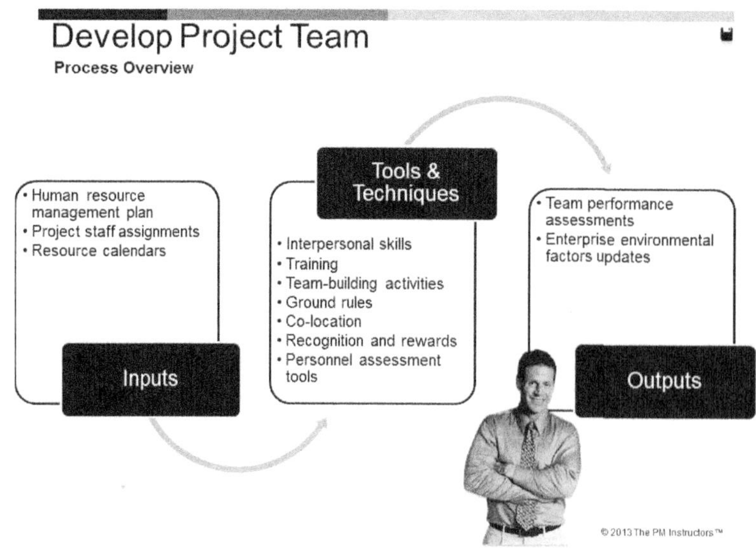
Develop Project Team
Process Overview
• Human resource management plan
• Project staff assignments
• Resource calendars
Inputs
Tools & Techniques
• Interpersonal skills
• Training
• Team-building activities
• Ground rules
• Co-location
• Recognition and rewards
• Personnel assessment tools
• Team performance assessments
• Enterprise environmental factors updates
Outputs
© 2013 The PM Instructors™

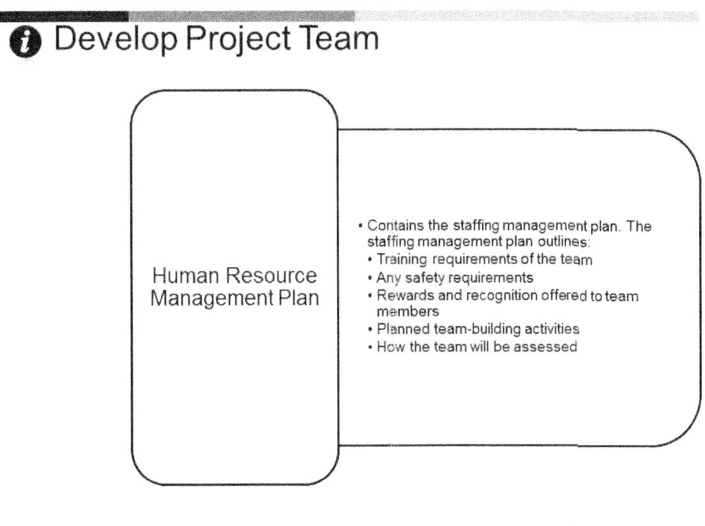

Develop Project Team Inputs

The Develop Project Team process has three inputs: *human resource management plan, project staff assignments, and resource calendars.*

Human Resource Management Plan

The human resource management plan contains the staffing management plan. The staffing management plan outlines the training requirements of the team, any safety requirements, and also what rewards and recognition we will offer team members. It also outlines team-building activities that have been planned in advance. Another important item addressed by the staffing management plan is how the team will be assessed.

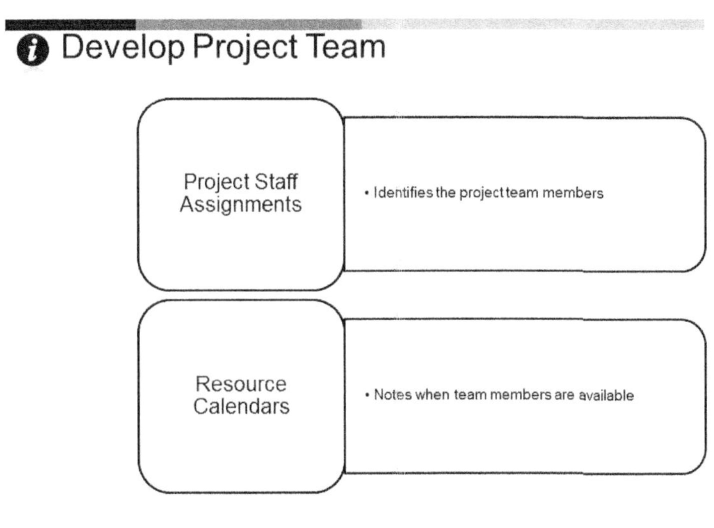

Project Staff Assignments

Project staff assignments simply identify who is assigned to which project activities. In order to develop the project team members, it's only logical that you would need to have access to who they are.

Resource Calendars

Resource calendars indicate when team members are available. This is important to consider when planning team-building activities and other motivational or team-related events.

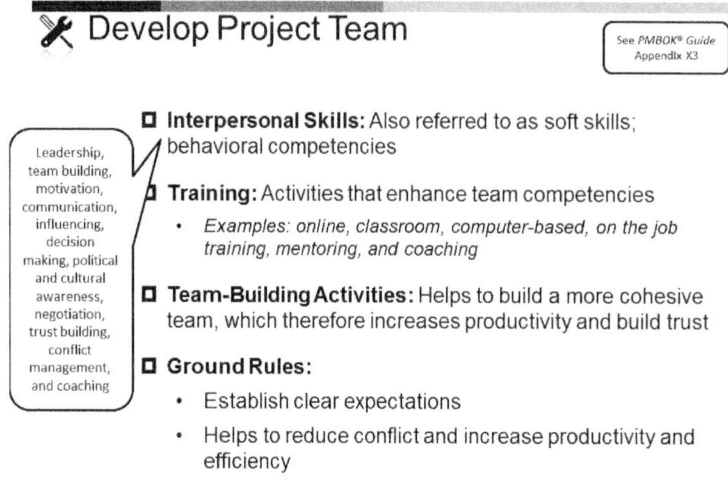

Develop Project Team
See PMBOK® Guide Appendix X3
Leadership, team building, motivation, communication, influencing, decision making, political and cultural awareness, negotiation, trust building, conflict management, and coaching
Interpersonal Skills: Also referred to as soft skills; behavioral competencies
Training: Activities that enhance team competencies
Examples: online, classroom, computer-based, on the job training, mentoring, and coaching
Team-Building Activities: Helps to build a more cohesive team, which therefore increases productivity and build trust
Ground Rules:
Establish clear expectations
Helps to reduce conflict and increase productivity and efficiency
© 2013 The PM Instructors™

Develop Project Team Tools and Techniques

The Develop Project Team process has seven tools and techniques: *interpersonal skills, training, team-building activities, ground rules, colocation, recognition and rewards, and personnel assessment tools.*

Interpersonal Skills

Interpersonal skills are commonly called "soft skills". It is thought that the project management team can decrease issues and increase cooperation by understanding how project team members are feeling, knowing what their concerns are, and being able to follow up on existing issues. The *PMBOK® Guide* notes the following skills as being valuable to managing a project team: empathy, influence, creativity, and group facilitation.

Training

Training refers to all the activities that are meant to enhance the competencies of the team. Whether informal or formal, training can be provided in various formats and venues. Here are a few examples: online, classroom, computer-based, on the job training, and even mentoring and coaching, whether internal to the group or provided externally.

Mentoring and coaching can be both planned and unplanned. Even providing guidance through a simple conversation can be considered coaching.

Team-Building Activities

The idea behind team building activities is to grow interpersonal relationships among the team, both professionally and personally, with the goal of enhancing the team's cohesiveness and ability to work together. It also helps to build trust and establish good working relationships. This can be very important for those team members that work virtually or simply from remote locations, such as different company offices.

Ground Rules

Ground rules is something that should be discussed and communicated early on in the project. Ground rules establish clear expectations regarding what is and isn't considered to be acceptable behavior within the project team. This helps to provide clarity on acceptable behavior, and decreases misunderstandings while increasing productivity. It is the responsibility of all team members to ensure that ground rules are enforced. Ground rules tend to reduce conflict and increase productivity and efficiency, particularly when it comes to instances of team interaction, such as meetings.

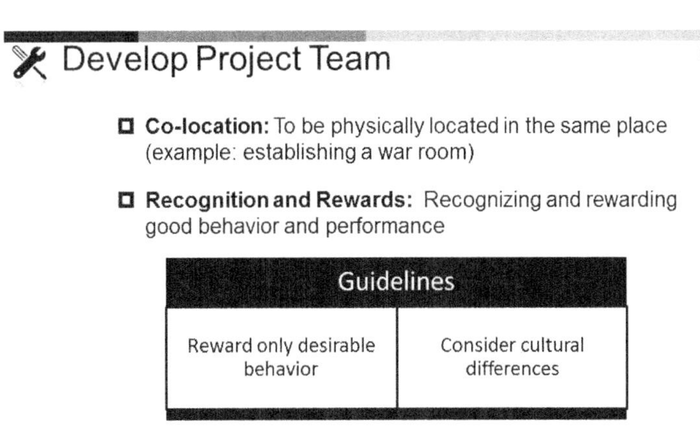

Co-Location

Co-location refers to placing most or all of the active project team members in the same physical location, as a way of enhancing their ability to perform as a team. This can be a temporary arrangement or last through the entire project. When co-location takes place, team members often work within what's called a "war room", which is simply a meeting room with project information posted throughout. While co-location is a great way to enhance communication and a sense of community, it can be difficult to do with virtual and remote teams.

When and if this is needed depends on the situation; usually as crunch time nears, it can become necessary to have the team together in one place where the sole focus is the project.

Recognition and Rewards

Recognition and rewards are meant to recognize and reward good behavior and performance. Awards are decided on during the next process: manage project team. Here are a few guidelines for recognizing and rewards team member behavior:

- Only desirable behavior should be rewarded
- Cultural differences should be considered

Personnel Assessment Tools

Personnel assessment tools provide insight into team member strengths and weaknesses. Examples of types of tools used provided by the *PMBOK® Guide* include attitudinal surveys, specific assessments, structured interviews, ability tests, and focus groups.

Develop Project Team

THEORIES OF MOTIVATION

- Maslow's Hierarchy of Needs
- McGregor's Theory of X and Y
- Herzberg's Motivation / Hygiene Theory
- Achievement Theory
- Expectancy Theory

CONCEPTS

- Power / Authority Types
- Tuckman's Stages of Team Development

Motivational Theories and Concepts

As part of the exam, you will need to know several motivational theories and other concepts, including: *Maslow's Hierarchy of Needs, McGregor's Theory of X and Y, Herzberg's Motivation Theory, Achievement Theory, Expectancy Theory, Power Types, and Tuckman's Stages of Team Development.*

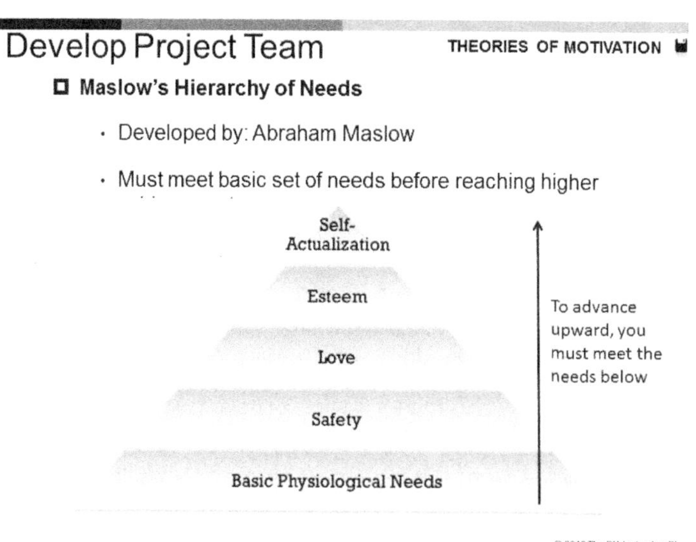

Maslow's Hierarchy of Needs

Maslow's hierarchy of needs was developed by **Abraham Maslow**, a psychologist. The theory states that people must first meet a basic set of needs before reaching for higher achievement. Maslow developed a pyramid shaped set of needs, with the basic needs shown at the bottom, and the desire for higher achievement at the top.

1. First (bottom of the pyramid) are the basic Physiological needs. This includes things like food, shelter, water, breathing, and sleeping.
2. Next is Safety, which includes the security of health, property, employment, and resources.
3. The third is Love / Belonging, which includes things like friendship, family, and sexual intimacy.

4. Next is Esteem, which includes self-esteem, confidence, respect, and achievement.
5. And the top is Self-Actualization, which includes morality, problem solving, acceptance of facts, creativity, and lack of prejudice.

In order to advance up the pyramid, the set of needs below it must be met. For example, someone will not strive for esteem if safety is not met. Therefore, to reach self-actualization, all the other needs must be met. Also, it should be noted that an individual may go up and down the pyramid throughout their lives.

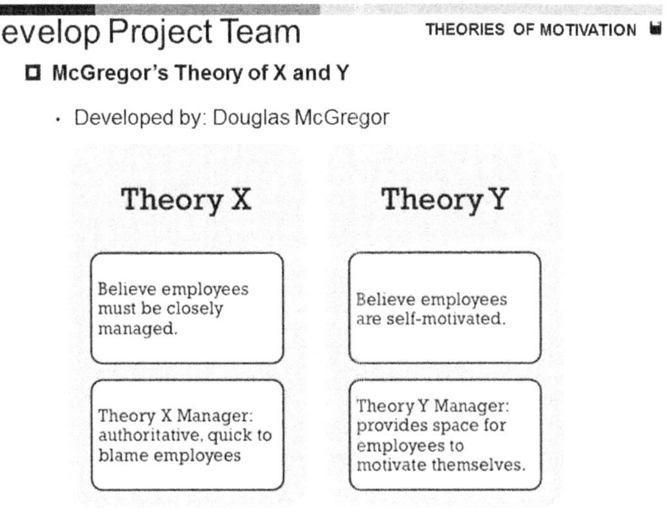

McGregor's Theory of X and Y

McGregor's Theory of X and Y was developed in the 1960s by **Douglas McGregor**. The theory revolves around two different types of attitudes toward work: Theory X and Theory Y.

Theory X

In Theory X, management functions with the belief that employees are inherently lazy and that they avoid work whenever possible. As a result, they must be closely managed and supervised with a tight level of control, and preferably within a hierarchical structure. In order to motivate employees, you'd therefore need a very big incentive plan.

Theory X Manager Profile: authoritative, believes that interests of employees revolve around money, and is quick to blame employees in any situation.

Theory Y

In Theory Y, management functions with the belief that employees may be ambitious, self-motivated, are empowered, and anxious to take on greater responsibility. As a result, they must be given freedom to utilize their abilities without having their creativity restricted by many rules.

Theory Y Manager Profile: removes barriers that restrict employees, allow the space for employees to motivate themselves through good performance.

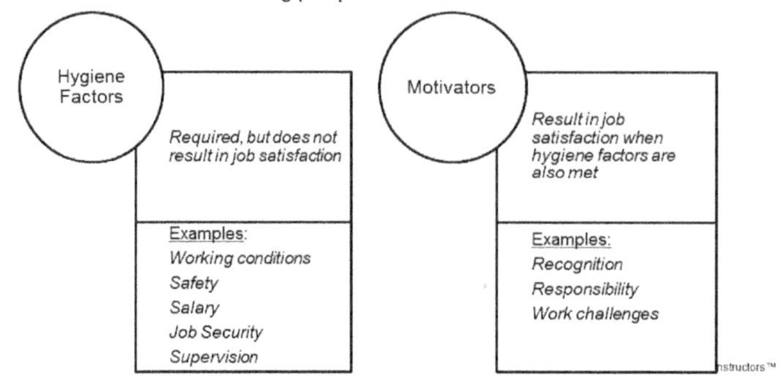

Herzerg's Motivation / Hygiene Theory

Herzberg's Theory of Motivation was developed by **Frederick Herzberg**, a psychologist who believed that there are multiple job motivating factors and hygiene factors that affect people's attitude at work. It is also often referred to as **Herzberg's Motivator-Hygiene theory.**

Hygiene factors are those that if absent, would result in job dissatisfaction, but if present, does not necessarily translate to job satisfaction. Employees expect these types of things to be present in their job and work environment. These include things like:

- Working conditions
- Safety
- Salary
- Job Security
- Supervision

Motivators are factors that could bring about job satisfaction, if hygiene factors have been met, include things like:

- Recognition
- Responsibility
- Work challenges

Note: These two sets of factors are independent of each other.

Develop Project Team

THEORIES OF MOTIVATION

Achievement Theory:

- Developed by David McClelland
- Believed that people were motivated by their need for achievement, power, and affiliation

Achievement	Power	Affiliation

Achievement Theory

The next theory is the Achievement Theory, developed by **David McClelland**. McClelland believed that people were motivated by their need for achievement, power, and affiliation

The need for achievement, power and affiliation can be found to varying degrees among various types of individuals. This is why the three motivational needs of this theory are often displayed as "n", representing the degree:

> Achievement motivation (n-ach): Where an individual needs to feel challenged, continue to advance within their job, and seeks achievements.
>
> Power / authority (n-pow): Where an individual needs to feel that they are impactful, influential, and effective.
>
> Affiliation (n-affil): Where an individual needs to interact with others, be liked and feel popular.

According to McClelland, most team members will display a combination of the characteristics described above, and may exhibit a stronger bias toward one of the motivational needs.

Develop Project Team

THEORIES OF MOTIVATION

Expectancy Theory

- Developed by Victor Vroom
- States that employees will place more effort into better performance if it leads to rewards valued by them

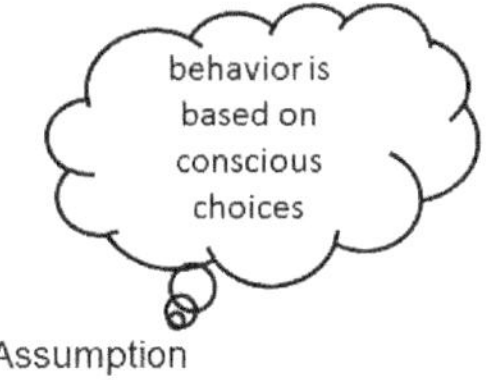
behavior is
based on
conscious
choices
Assumption

Expectancy Theory

The Expectancy Theory was created by **Victor Vroom**, and deals with motivation and management. The theory states that employees who believe that putting in more effort will lead to better performance, that this better performance will lead to rewards, and that the reward is valued by them individually, will continue to be productive.

The underlying assumption of this theory is that behavior stems from conscious choices. Individual factors that play a role in an individual's performance include things like skills, experience, ability, knowledge, and personality.

Note: The rewards must be specifically aligned with the personal factors and goals of that individual in order for them to be motivated.

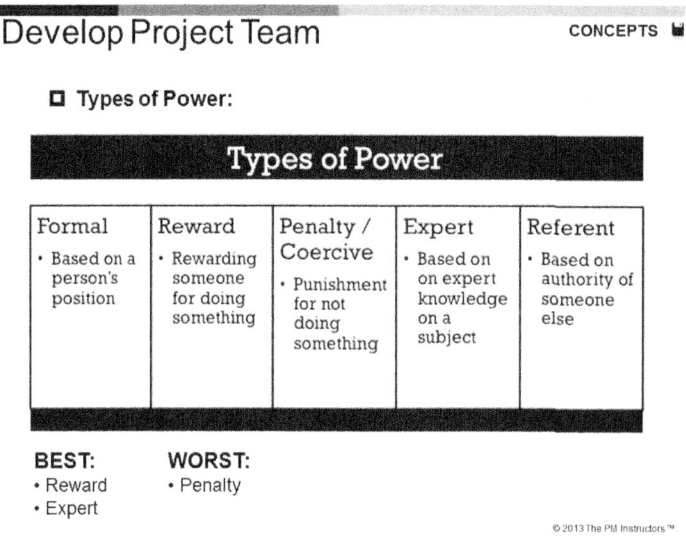

Power / Authority Types

When addressing conflict, a project manager may utilize various methods to influence stakeholders or other individuals connected to the project. These methods are types of power used to reach a desired result. For instance, a project manager may utilize power to get a contingency response plan approved. There are 5 types of power / authority:

- Formal, which is based on a person's position
- Reward, which is based on rewarding someone for doing something
- Penalty, also known as Coercive power, is punishment for not doing something
- Expert, where an individual is an expert on a subject, and their knowledge gives them a heightened status and authority
- Referent, which is based on the authority of someone else within a higher position who has formal power

The best types of power are reward and expert. The worst type of power is obtained through penalty, which should be used as a last resort. Expert is earned power, whereas formal, reward and penalty can be obtained simply through position.

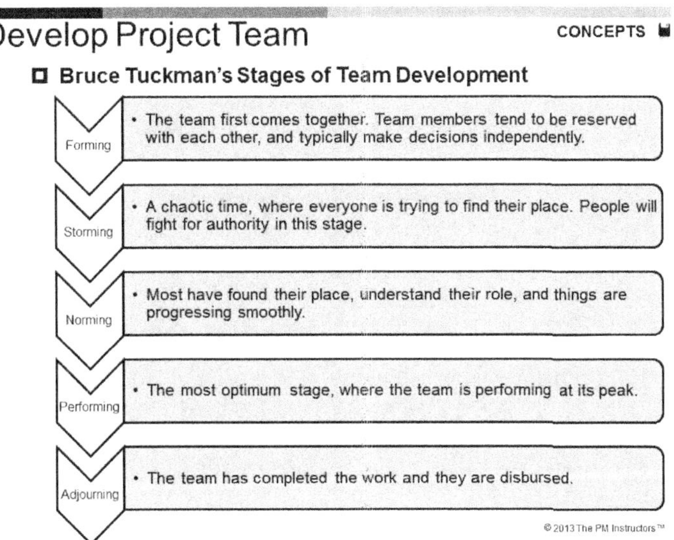

Tuckman's Stages of Team Development

Bruce Tuckman's five stages of team development reflect how the project team as a whole progresses through the following stages together:

- Forming, where the team first comes together. During this stage, the team is usually somewhat shy and reserved with each other, and typically make decisions independently.
- Storming is a chaotic time amongst the team, where everyone is trying to find their place. People will fight for authority in this stage.
- Norming is a stage where the team members have found their place, understand their role, and things are progressing smoothly.
- Performing is the most optimum stage, where the team is performing at its peak, as one group. Conflicts tend to be far less here, and again, productivity and efficiency is at its highest.
- Adjourning is the final stage, where the team has completed the work and they are released.

When a new team member is added, this takes the group back to stage 1, although they may progress through the stages quicker than the initial forming of the team.

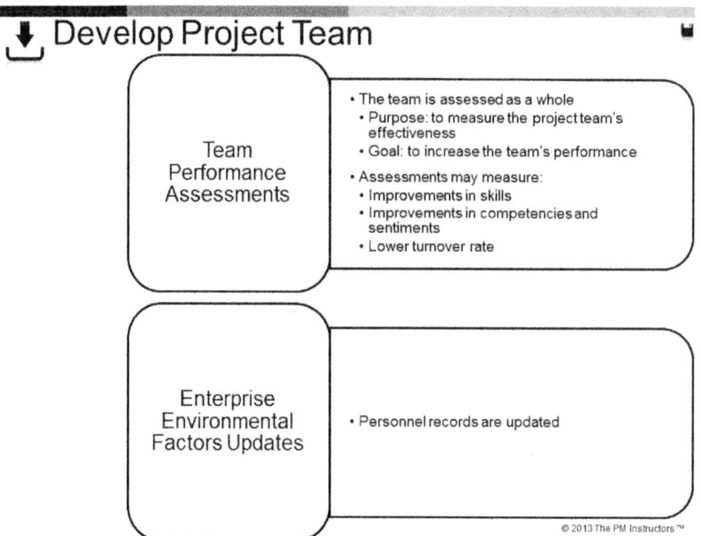

Develop Project Team Outputs

There are two outputs of the Develop Project Team process: *team performance assessments,* and *enterprise environmental factors updates.*

Team Performance Assessment

Team performance assessments can be both informal or formal, and is generated by the project management team. This is where the team is assessed as a whole. The purpose is to measure the project team's effectiveness, and the goal is to increase the team's performance, which will in turn increase the chances of meeting the project objectives. The effectiveness of team performance assessments can be determined based on the following factors:

- Improvements in team member skills
- Improvements in competencies and sentiments that would result in the team performing better as a group
- Lower staff turnover rate

Enterprise Environmental Factors Updates

Enterprise environmental factor updates involve updating personnel records with completed training and skill assessments, and any other personnel administration necessary.

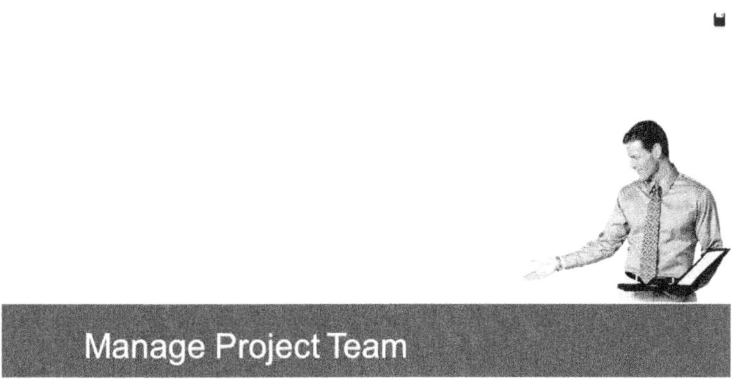
Manage Project Team
Purpose: To track team member performance, provide feedback, resolve issues, and manage changes to optimize project performance.

Manage Project Team Process Overview

The purpose of the Manage Project Team process is to track team member performance, provide feedback, resolve issues, and manage changes to optimize project performance.

While in the previous process our interest was in the team as a whole, here, we're looking at team members individually.

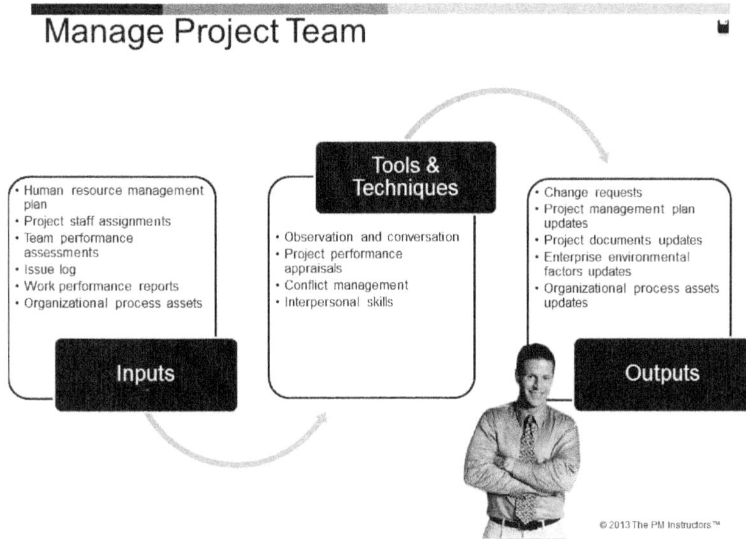
Manage Project Team
• Human resource management plan
• Project staff assignments
• Team performance assessments
• Issue log
• Work performance reports
• Organizational process assets
Inputs
Tools & Techniques
• Observation and conversation
• Project performance appraisals
• Conflict management
• Interpersonal skills
• Change requests
• Project management plan updates
• Project documents updates
• Enterprise environmental factors updates
• Organizational process assets updates
Outputs
© 2013 The PM Instructors™

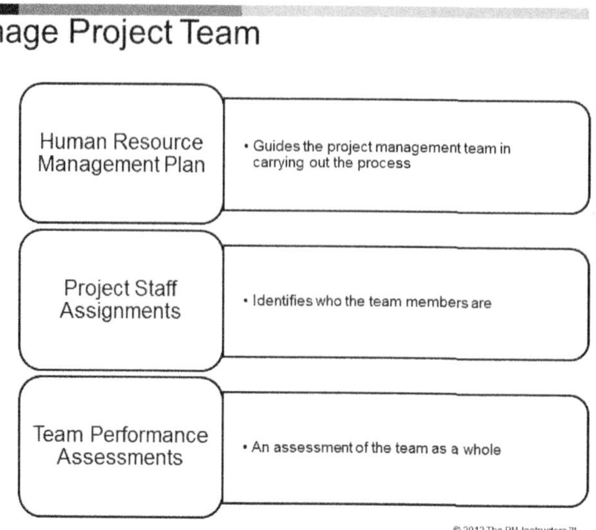

Manage Project Team Inputs

The Manage Project Team process has six inputs: *human resource management plan, project staff assignments, team performance assessments, issue log, work performance reports, and organizational process assets.*

Human Resource Management Plan

The human resource management plan guides the project management team in carrying out the process. This includes how the project team should be managed, controlled, and released.

Project Staff Assignments

Project staff assignments provide the project management team with the list of team members that will be evaluated during the course of the process.

Team Performance Assessments

Team performance assessments are team evaluations that are generated as a result of the Develop Project Team process. This assesses the team's performance as a group.

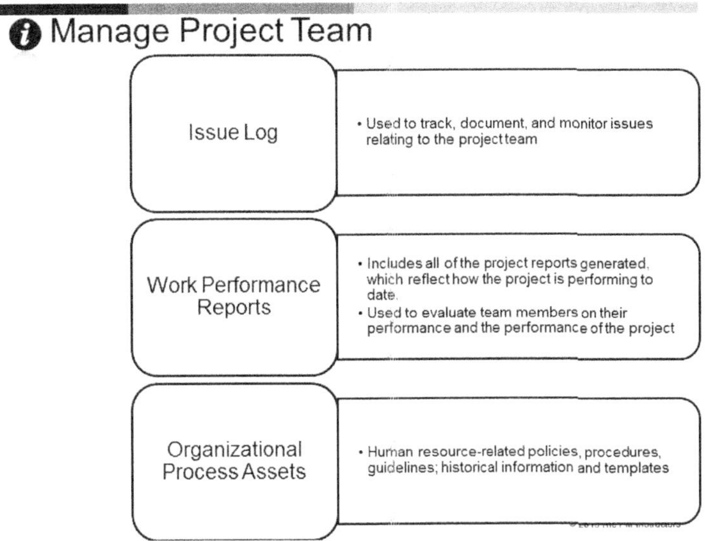

Issue Log

The issue log is used to track, document, and monitor issues relating to the project team, as they arise. Issues logged should always contain an owner, who is accountable for ensuring that the issue is addressed effectively.

Work Performance Reports

Work performance reports include all of the reports generated out of the project, which reflect how the project is performing to date. These reports are a result of the Monitor and Control Project Work process, a process that belongs to the Project Integration Management Knowledge Area. This will become important information to evaluating the team members on their performance, and the performance of the project.

Organizational Process Assets

In regards to organizational process assets, the project management team utilizes the organization's policies, procedures, and systems for rewarding employees throughout the project. Although the staffing management plan incorporates recognition and rewards, it's important to align with the guidelines set by the company.

Manage Project Team

Observation and Conversation:

- Used to find out how the team members are feeling, whether any conflicts exist
- A type of temperature check of our resources

Project Performance Appraisals:

- Team members receive evaluations through this process from their managers
- May use 360 degree feedback

Objectives:
- Re-clarification of roles and responsibilities
- Structured time to ensure team members receive positive feedback
- Discovery of unknown or unresolved issues
- Development of individual training plans
- Establishment of specific goals for future time periods

Manage Project Team Tools and Techniques

The Manage Project Team process has a total of four tools and techniques: *observation and conversation, project performance appraisals, conflict management, and interpersonal skills.*

Observation and Conversation

The project manager can use observation and conversation as a way of finding out how the team members are feeling, and whether any conflicts exist. It is a type of temperature check of our resources. Talking with your team members is important, and although it seems like a common sense item that should go without mention, it is easily forgotten in the daily management of the project, yet it's extremely important. Observing and speaking with team members is used as a way of staying in touch with the work and also the attitudes of project team members. This is done by the project management team, who monitors the project's progress, accomplishments, and interpersonal issues.

Project Performance Appraisals

Project Performance Appraisals can be given in formal or informal formats, and focus on the performance of individual project team members. Feedback is given by those who manage the project team member's work directly, and 360 degree feedback can also be utilized as a way of providing them with more thorough feedback. 360 degree feedback refers to feedback that is received from all levels of interaction with the team member receiving the feedback, such as the manager, colleagues, and direct reports if applicable. Keep in mind that the organizational type can play an important factor here, particularly when a dual reporting relationship exists. The *PMBOK® Guide* lists the following objectives of project performance appraisals:

- Re-clarification of roles and responsibilities
- Structured time to ensure team members receive positive feedback
- Discovery of unknown or unresolved issues
- Development of individual training plans
- Establishment of specific goals for future time periods

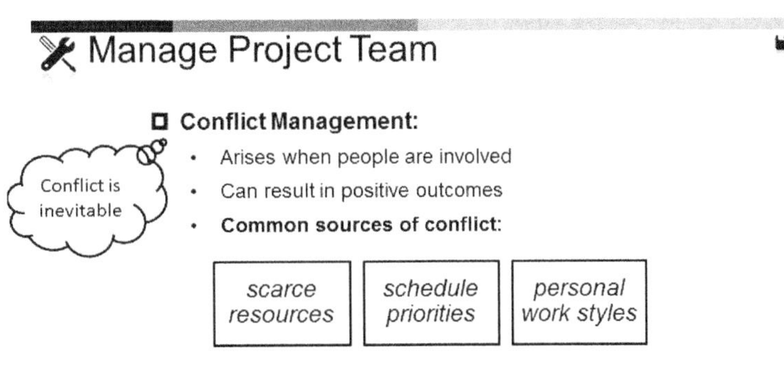

Conflict Management

Whenever people are involved, conflicts will arise. It used to be that conflict was viewed as a negative thing; but the mindset now is that conflict is actually a positive thing. It can challenge us to look at our processes and approach and change for the better. Common sources of conflict tend to be scarce resources, schedule priorities, and personal work styles.

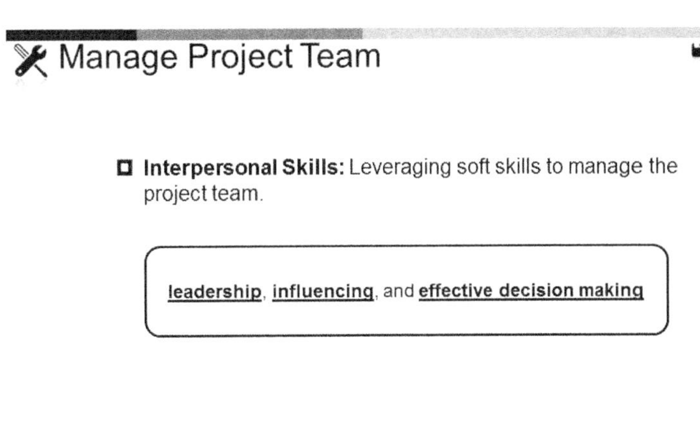

Interpersonal Skills

Interpersonal skills, which are soft skills, are critical to the proper management of the project team. The *PMBOK® Guide* calls out specific examples of interpersonal skills that a project manager can leverage, including:

- Leadership
- Influencing
- Effective decision making

Conflict within a project is inevitable, making the ability to manage conflict a critical skill for the project manager to master. According to the *PMBOK® Guide*, conflict often comes about as a result of scarce resources, scheduling priorities, and varying personal work styles.

While it is not possible to fully avoid conflict, the project manager can establish ground rules for the team, along with group norms, to reduce the amount of conflict. Establishing and following solid project management practices can also aid in reducing conflict.

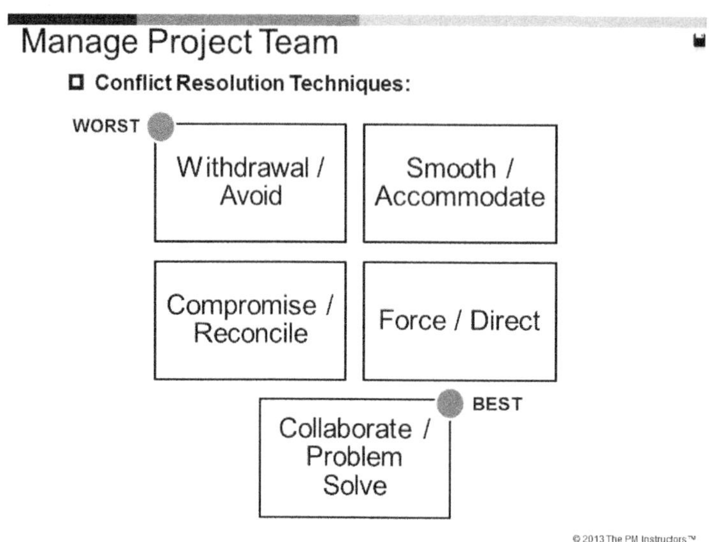

Conflict Resolution Techniques

The *PMBOK® Guide* highlights the following conflict resolution techniques that you should know for the exam:

- **Withdrawal, also known as avoiding**, where there is no solution made, and the problem is ignored in hopes that it goes away.
- **Smoothing, also known as accommodating,** where emphasis is on agreement - getting to an agreement so that everyone can move on, even if it's not the best solution.
- **Compromising, also known as reconciling,** which is a lose-lose, where both parties give up something
- **Forcing, also known as directing**, which is a win-lose, where one party gets what they want and the other doesn't.
- **Collaborative, also known as problem solving**, where a solution is reached by consensus. This is considered to be a win-win where you look to solve the heart of the problem to the best interest of all parties.

Collaborative is the best type of conflict resolution technique, while withdrawal is the worst.

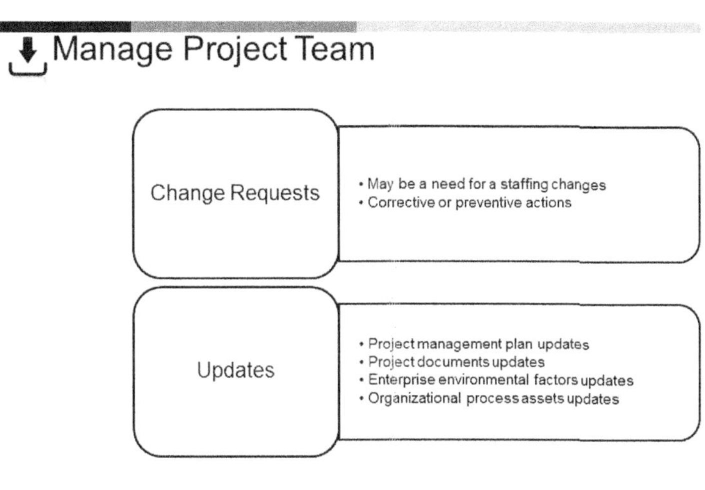
Manage Project Team
Change Requests
• May be a need for a staffing changes
• Corrective or preventive actions
Updates
• Project management plan updates
• Project documents updates
• Enterprise environmental factors updates
• Organizational process assets updates
© 2013 The PM Instructors™

Manage Project Team Outputs

Manage Project Team has a total of five outputs: *change requests, project management plan updates, project documents updates, enterprise environmental factors updates,* and *organizational process assets updates.*

Change Requests

In this process, requested changes tend to deal with staffing changes. The need of staffing changes can come about due to budgetary reasons, scheduling reasons, or other issues that can disrupt the project plan. As with all requested changes, they are submitted into the integrated change control process for review and approval before implementation.

Change requests may also deal with corrective actions. Corrective actions are meant to bring project performance back in line with the project management plan. In relation to human resource management, this may include staffing changes, training, or disciplinary actions.

Project Management Plan Updates

Project management plan updates typically include updates made to the human resource management plan – specifically, the staffing management plan.

Project Documents Updates

Project documents typically updated as a result of carrying out this process include the issue log, roles description, and project staff assignments.

Enterprise Environmental Factors Updates

Enterprise environmental factors updates typically include updates to personnel records.

Organizational Process Assets Updates

Updates made to the organizational process assets include archiving project documents and lessons learned documentation. Examples include:

- Project org charts, position descriptions and staffing management plan. These can later be used as templates for other similar projects
- Ground rules, conflict management techniques, recognition events
- Procedures for virtual teams, co-location, negotiation, training and team building
- Specific team member special skills or competencies that emerged
- Project issue log

Module Summary

In this module we:

- Defined the purpose of the Project Human Resource Management Knowledge Area
- Identified the processes of the Project Human Resource Management Knowledge Area
- Recalled the key outputs of the human resource management processes
- Differentiated between the inputs, tools and techniques, and outputs of the human resource management processes
- Interpreted an organization chart and position descriptions for a project team
- Identified the specific differences between operational and project team management
- Identified and describe the five general techniques for managing conflict

Chapter Quiz

Exam Practice Questions

1. A project manager liked to hold meetings on a weekly basis with his team members. These meetings resembled brainstorming sessions, where ideas were generated regarding existing risks and project issues. The project manager never struck down any idea, and instead, attempted to foster an environment where creativity and sharing of ideas was encouraged. What type of leadership style does this project manager use?
   A. Facilitating
   B. Directing
   C. Consultative
   D. Co-Managing

2. During a status meeting, two project team members began a heated argument that quickly escalated. The project manager had her hands full in keeping the room under control. What are the team members most likely arguing about?
   A. Resources
   B. Schedule
   C. Cost
   D. Priorities

3. Who developed the Expectancy Theory?
   A. Douglas McGregor
   B. Victor Vroom
   C. Frederick Herzberg
   D. Abraham Maslow

4. Eric has over 18 years of hands-on software development experience and has recently decided to move into the field of project management. As a developer, he has been accustomed to working on his own, isolated from the business and customers. In order to be effective in his new role, the director advised that Eric be more empathetic toward others and seek creative ways to influence them. These are all forms of:
   A. Communication skills
   B. Management skills
   C. Leadership skills
   D. Interpersonal skills

5. 5551212 is the latest mobile phone provider, expanding to a new region that is estimated to add three million users. The risk manager of the expansion project has just been hired as part of the project to assist in risk planning activities. Immediately, the risk manager arranged a planning meeting with the risk management team and began issuing assignments to each team member. What leadership style is the risk manager using?
   A. Directing
   B. Facilitating
   C. Autocratic
   D. Supporting

6. Which of the following statements is inaccurate?
   A. Working conditions are considered a hygiene factor.
   B. Hygiene factors must be present for motivators to result in job satisfaction.
   C. Theory of X and Y deals with hygiene factors and motivators.
   D. Work challenges is a type of motivator.

7. During project execution, the project team was experiencing several tense moments, as activities were underway and holes within the plans were emerging. The project manager was most recently called in to deal with two project team members that had become involved in a heated argument over resources. The project manager was determined to deal with this and result in a win-win situation. What type of conflict resolution technique is the project manager most likely to use?
   A. Withdrawal
   B. Compromising
   C. Smoothing
   D. Confronting

8. Purse Centric is a clothing retail company with eleven stores throughout Europe. The company is planning to expand to North America, beginning with two stores opening concurrently. The project manager heading the opening of the western region store has dealt with several conflicts within the project over the past three weeks. In the recent project meeting, two stakeholders were nearly at each other's throats. What would be the most likely reason for the conflict between the two stakeholders?
   A. Different priorities
   B. Resources
   C. Schedule
   D. Personality

9. Joy is the technical lead of the testing department at Bing Bonk software. After bringing an issue to the attention of the CEO of the company, the CEO has instructed Joy to tell the project manager to increase the duration of the testing phase by 2 weeks as a means of guaranteeing their upcoming release has no defects. Which of the following types of power is based on the authority of someone else?
   A. Expert
   B. Referent
   C. Formal
   D. Coercive

10. While developing risk responses, a project manager came across a stumbling block with one of the project stakeholders. The stakeholder insisted that a contingency reserve was not necessary for this project. Based on previous experience working in projects with similar types of risks, the project manager felt that to not allocate a risk contingency reserve would be a mistake. What type of power would be BEST for the project manager to use?
    A. Penalty
    B. Formal
    C. Referent
    D. Expert

11. Which of the following items is not present within Maslow's Hierarchy of Needs?
    A. Hygiene
    B. Physiological Needs
    C. Self-Actualization
    D. Love

12. Which of the following motivational theories states that hygiene factors are a requirement in the workplace, but do not alone result in job satisfaction?
    A. Utility Theory
    B. Maslow's Hierarchy of Needs
    C. Herzberg's Theory of Motivation
    D. Theory of X and Y

13. Which of the following theorists is responsible for developing the Theory of X and Y?
    A. Frederick Herzberg
    B. Abraham Maslow
    C. Victor Vroom
    D. Douglas McGregor

14. Which of the following is displayed in table format?
    A. Responsibility assignment matrix
    B. Resource breakdown structure
    C. Text oriented description
    D. Risk register

15. As the project manager, you've noticed that several project team members appear tense and withdrawn. It's unclear whether this is stemming from the recent issues that have emerged from within the project. How can you best discover what the attitudes of the project team members are toward the project?
    A. Use observation and conversation
    B. Perform a project performance appraisal
    C. Institute ground rules
    D. Perform conflict management

16. Sue, the project manager of a pet facility build out project, plans on attending an upcoming *Pets for the Environment* expo to mingle with other pet facilities and see the latest gadgets and technology used by the industry. This is an example of:
    A. Pre-assignment
    B. Research
    C. Vacation
    D. Networking

17. Under project team roles and responsibilities, which of the following clarifies whether a role has the ability to assign resources, make decisions, and sign approvals?
    A. Role
    B. Authority
    C. Responsibility
    D. Competency

18. Chuck, the department manager heading one of the key work packages of the project, notices that one of the activities has fallen behind by two days. He chalks this up to the fact that he has been on vacation over the past week and a bad company incentive program. Based on McGregor's theory, what type of manager is Chuck?
    A. Theory X manager
    B. Theory Y manager
    C. Formal manager
    D. Referent manager

19. Kishore is located in Las Vegas and works remotely from his home. Bryan is also remote and works from home as well. Their project manager is co-located with 4 of the other team members, and the stakeholders reside on the same campus as the project manager and team, but are located in a different building. Every morning at 9:00am the four co-located team members meet in the project manager's office, and Kishore and Bryan call in using a phone bridge to take part in the same morning meeting. All team members connect to discuss a shared goal: successfully completing the project. A group of individuals with a shared goal, who fulfill their roles with little or no time meeting face to face BEST describes:
    A. Co-location
    B. Stakeholders
    C. Virtual teams
    D. Project team

20. Blazing Broadband Internet Solutions is in the process of piloting a technical support group that would work onsite exclusively for the benefit of one of their larger customers. In order for the new venture to be successful, the project would require spinning up a staffing management plan that aligns with the objectives of both the project and the needs of the customers. The staffing management plan should contain all of the following except for which one?
    A. Roles and responsibilities
    B. Recognition and rewards
    C. Compliance
    D. Safety

Chapter Quiz

Exam Practice Answers

1. Answer: C

   Explanation: Consultative is a form of leadership style, where the leader encourages ideas of others.

2. Answer: B

   Explanation: "Schedule" is considered to be one of the top reasons for conflict. This can include how the schedule is approached, when tasks or resources should be scheduled and utilized, and determining schedule status.

3. Answer: B

   Explanation: The Expectancy theory was developed by Victor Vroom, and deals with motivation and management. The theory states that employees who believe that putting in more effort will lead to better performance will increase their performance if the reward is valued by them.

4. Answer: D

   Explanation: These are interpersonal skills, also referred to as "soft" skills. Interpersonal skills itself is part of general management skills. It is thought that the project / risk manager can decrease issues and increase cooperation by understanding how project team members are feeling, knowing what their concerns are, and being able to follow up on existing issues.

5. Answer: A

   Explanation: Directing involves the manager telling others what to do. By general consensus, the directing technique is best used in the beginning of a project when team members are not familiar with their assignments yet. As the team becomes more familiar with the work, the manager is better off using styles such as coaching, supporting and facilitating.

6. Answer: C

   Explanation: The Theory of X and Y do not relate to Hygiene Factors or Motivators. The latter are part of Herzberg's Theory of Motivation.

7. Answer: D

   Explanation: Confronting, also known as problem solving, is the best conflict resolution technique. Because it seeks to resolve the problem, it is considered a win-win situation.

8. Answer: C

   Explanation: Schedule is the most common reason for conflict. Schedule is followed by: varying priorities, resources, technical beliefs, administrative procedures, cost and personality.

9. Answer: B

   Explanation: Referent power is based on the authority of someone else within a higher position who has formal power.

10. Answer: D

    Explanation: The best type of power overall is either expert or reward. Since reward is not an option, this leaves only expert to consider. On the other end of the spectrum, penalty is the worst type of power to use, and one that should be used as a last resort.

11. Answer: A

Explanation: Hygiene is a factor in Herzberg's Theory of Motivation. Maslow's Hierarchy includes the following set of needs, from bottom to top of the pyramid: basic physiological needs, safety, love/belonging, esteem and self-actualization.

12. Answer: C

    Explanation: The Theory of Motivation states that Hygiene factors are those that if absent, would result in job dissatisfaction, but if present, do not necessarily translate to job satisfaction; Motivators can bring about job satisfaction, if hygiene factors have been met.

13. Answer: D

    Explanation: Douglas McGregor developed this theory in the 1960s. The theory revolves around two different types of attitudes towards work: Theory X and Theory Y. Herzberg is responsible for the Theory of Motivation; Abraham Maslow is responsible for Maslow's Hierarchy of Needs, and Victor Vroom is responsible for the Expectancy Theory.

14. Answer: A

    Explanation: The responsibility assignment matrix (RAM) is a matrix-based chart displayed in the format of a table.

15. Answer: A

    Explanation: The correct choice is observation and conversation. This is a technique that allows the project manager to observe the attitudes of team members towards the project, and better gauge what is going on. The project manager also gets direct feedback from team members.

16. Answer: D

    Explanation: In this question, you're taken to the Plan Human Resource Management process. What Sue is doing is adding value to the project. Networking is a form of informal interaction with others as a way of understanding political and interpersonal factors that impact the project, and developing industry relationships and partnerships (if done within the company, it would be building of relationships and partnerships internally).

17. Answer: B

    Explanation: Within the options provided, authority is the correct answer. This defines and describes what level of authority an individual has.

18. Answer: A

    Explanation: The question specifically asks what type of manager Chuck is, as opposed to what type of power he uses to manage. Formal and Referent are types of power. Douglas McGregor's Theory is known as the Theory X and Y, and describes two types of management styles and approaches. In Theory X, management functions with the belief that employees are inherently lazy and will avoid work whenever possible, while in Theory Y, management functions with the belief that employees may be ambitious, self-motivated, empowered and anxious to take on greater responsibility. Chuck fits in with the Theory X group, since he believes that the activity is delayed because he was on vacation, and because the team members are motivated by money.

19. Answer: C

    Explanation: This statement describes virtual teams. Virtual teams may consist of individuals located around the globe, or perhaps the same city but that interact primarily through technology, such as video conference, online, chat, telephone, etc. The point is that there is minimal to no face to time. As a side note, co-location is the exact opposite, where team members are physically located in the same place.

20. Answer: A

    Explanation: The staffing management plan describes when and how human resource requirements will be met. It addresses staff acquisition, timetable of when the team will be acquired, resource release criteria, training needs, recognition & rewards, compliance, and safety. It does not, however, define the roles and responsibilities. The staffing management plan is a component of the human resource management plan, which itself is a subsidiary plan of the project management plan.

Chapter 10: Project Communications Management

Learning Objectives:

- ☐ Define the purpose of the Project Communications Management Knowledge Area
- ☐ Identify the processes of the Project Communications Management Knowledge Area
- ☐ Recall the key outputs of the communications management processes
- ☐ Differentiate between the inputs, tools and techniques, and outputs of the communications management processes
- ☐ Identify and describe the communications skills necessary for project management
- ☐ Outline the components contained in a communications management plan

Exam Domain Tasks:

- Develop a communication plan based on the project organization structure and external stakeholder requirements, in order to manage the flow of project information.
- Communicate project status to stakeholders for their feedback, in order to ensure the project aligns with business needs.

Project Communications Management
Purpose: To ensure timely and appropriate planning, collection, creation, distribution, storage, retrieval, management, control, monitoring, and the ultimate disposition of project information.
3 Project Management Processes:
Initiating
Planning
• Plan Communications Management
Executing
• Manage Communications
Monitoring & Controlling
• Control Communications
Closing
© 2013 The PM Instructors™

Project Communications Management Overview

The Project Communications Management Knowledge Area focuses on connecting people and information in order to result in successful communications within the project. The purpose of this Knowledge Area is to ensure timely and appropriate planning, collection, creation, distribution, storage, retrieval, management, control, monitoring, and the ultimate disposition of project information. It is also concerned with managing the overall project communications. In a sense, you can think of communication as being a part of everything within the project – it is intertwined with the majority of the other processes.

Project communication is an important part of project management, particularly in understanding the expectations and needs of the project's stakeholders. This includes both internal and external stakeholders of the project. The majority of these communication activities are addressed in this Knowledge Area. According to PMI, a good project manager spends 90% of their time communicating, which is a good indicator of how important this area is to a project manager.

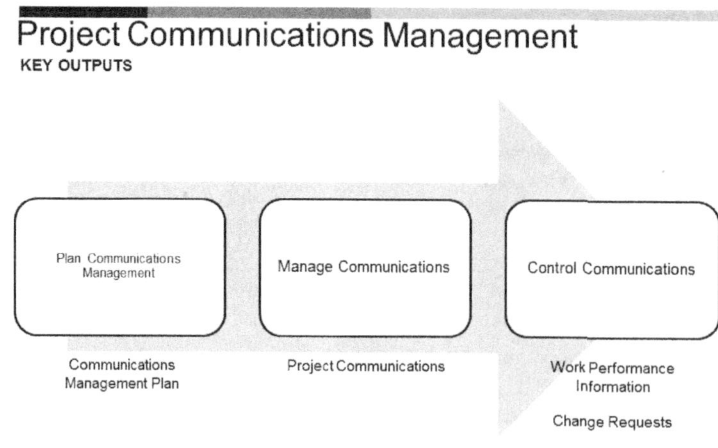

The Project Communications Management Knowledge Area is responsible for connecting people and information to result in successful communications within the project. There are three processes:

- **Plan Communications Management (Planning Process Group).** Purpose: To develop an appropriate approach and plan for project communications based on stakeholder's information needs and requirements, and available organizational assets.
- **Manage Communications (Executing Process Group).** Purpose: To create, collect, distribute, store, retrieve and ultimately dispose of project information in accordance with the communications management plan.
- **Control Communications (Monitoring and Controlling Process Group).** Purpose: To monitor and control communications throughout the entire project life cycle to ensure the information needs of the project stakeholders are met.

Plan Communications Management
Purpose: To develop an appropriate approach and plan for project communications based on stakeholder's information needs and requirements, and available organizational assets.

Plan Communications Management Process Overview

Plan Communications Management is the first process of the Project Communications Management Knowledge Area. This process is concerned with determining the project stakeholder information needs and defining a communication approach. Along with other key aspects of a project, this includes the communication requirements relating to the project schedule. The official purpose of the process is to develop an appropriate approach and plan for project communications based on stakeholder's information needs and requirements, and available organizational assets.

The communications management plan, which is the primary result of this process, is critical to successfully managing stakeholders and communicating with them. For this reason, planning out how communication will be managed is generally done during the early stages of the project.

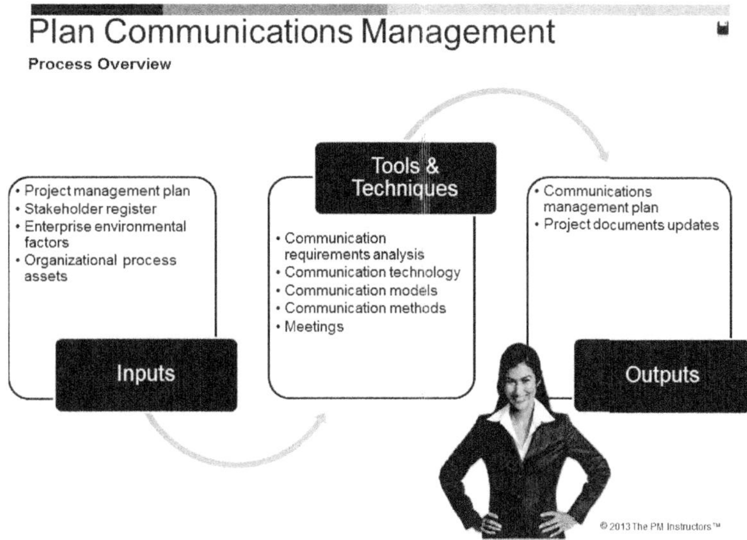
Plan Communications Management
Process Overview
• Project management plan
• Stakeholder register
• Enterprise environmental factors
• Organizational process assets
Inputs
Tools & Techniques
• Communication requirements analysis
• Communication technology
• Communication models
• Communication methods
• Meetings
• Communications management plan
• Project documents updates
Outputs
© 2013 The PM Instructors™

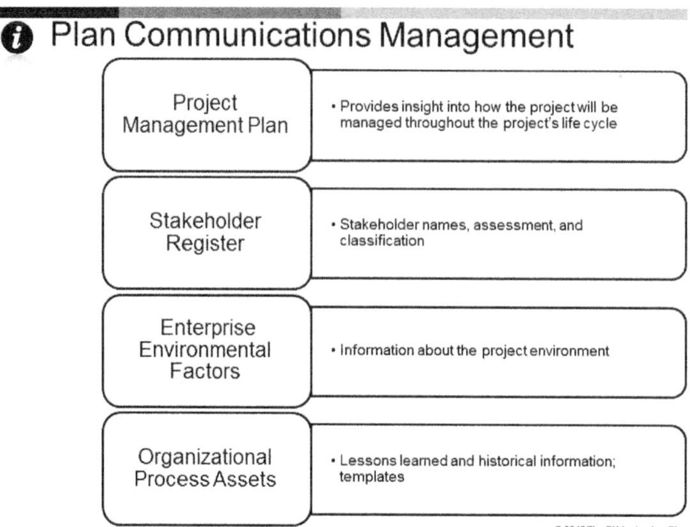

Plan Communications Management Inputs

The Plan Communications Management process utilizes the following four inputs: *project management plan, stakeholder register, enterprise environmental factors, and organizational process assets.*

Project Management Plan

The project management plan provides insight into how the project will be managed throughout the project's life cycle. The stakeholder management plan is typically one of the subsidiary plans that are created and used as a reference point for creating the communications management plan.

Stakeholder Register

The stakeholder register is generated out of the first stakeholder management related process: Identify Stakeholders. This register contains all of the details about stakeholders that have been identified. Establishing a communications management plan should be based around the communication needs of the stakeholders outlined within this register.

Enterprise Environmental Factors

All of the existing enterprise environmental factors are considered.

Organizational Process Assets

Organizational process assets provide lessons learned and historical information from previous projects; these items can provide the results and decisions made from previous communication issues. In addition to this, templates are an important asset used in this process.

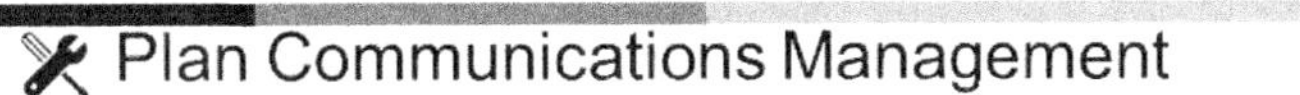

Plan Communications Management

- **Communication Requirements Analysis:**
  - Determines the communication needs of stakeholders
  - Combines the type and format of the information needed
  - Ensures information communicated is valuable

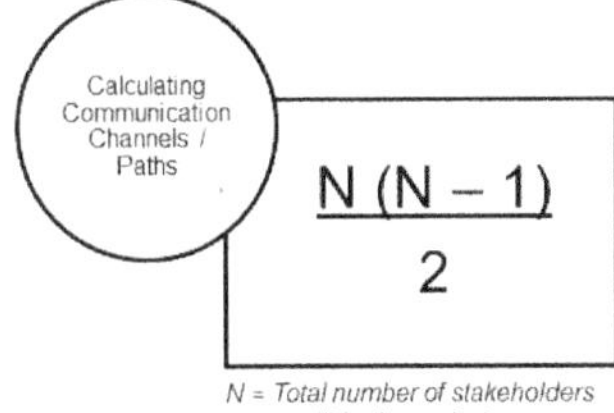

Calculating Communication Channels / Paths
N (N – 1)
2
N = Total number of stakeholders within the project

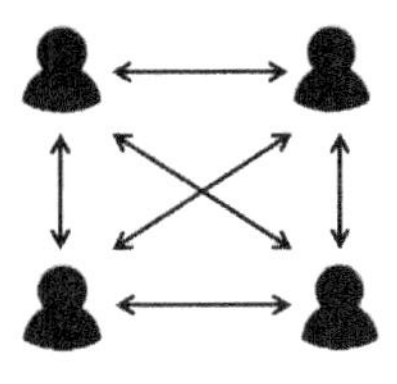

Plan Communications Management Tools and Techniques

The Plan Communications Management process utilizes the following five tools and techniques: *communication requirements analysis, communication technology, communication models, communication methods, and meetings.*

Communication Requirements Analysis

Communication requirements analysis involves combining the type and format of the information needed within an analysis of the value of that information. The aim and result of this analysis is a summary and compilation of the information needs of the project stakeholders. Here, the focus is on communicating information that contributes to the success of the project, and also communicating information that, if not communicated, would lead to the failure of the project. The reason for this is to make sure that the information being communicated is valuable and with purpose in order to prevent communication overload.

According to the *PMBOK® Guide*, the following information is needed to determine project communications requirements:

- Organization charts; project and stakeholder responsibility relationships
- Project disciplines, specialties and departments
- Project logistics
- Internal and external information needs
- Stakeholder information and communication requirements

As part of the explanation above, the project manager should consider the total number of communication channels, or paths, that exist. Calculating communication channels requires a simple formula:

$$\frac{n(n-1)}{2}$$

"n" represents the total number of stakeholders (or individuals) associated with the project

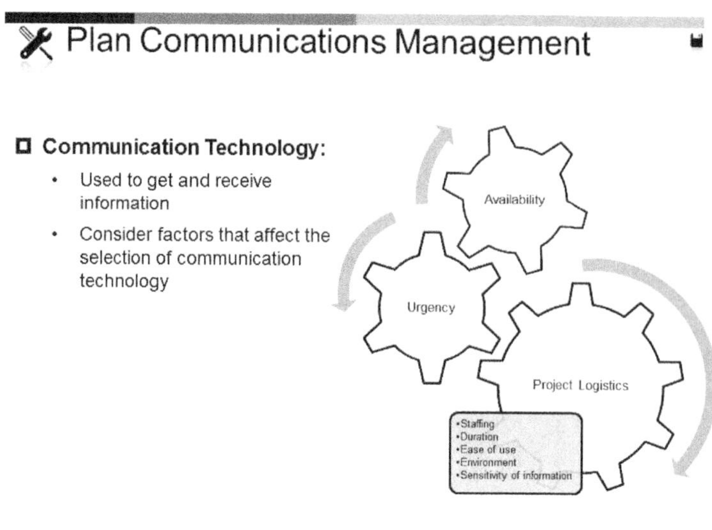

Communication Technology

Communications technology is used to get and receive information to stakeholders. The *PMBOK® Guide* outlines the following as technology factors that can influence the project:

- Availability of the technology used
- Urgency of the information needed
- Project logistics, such as:
  - Staffing
  - Duration
  - Ease of use
  - Project environment
  - Sensitivity and confidentiality of the information

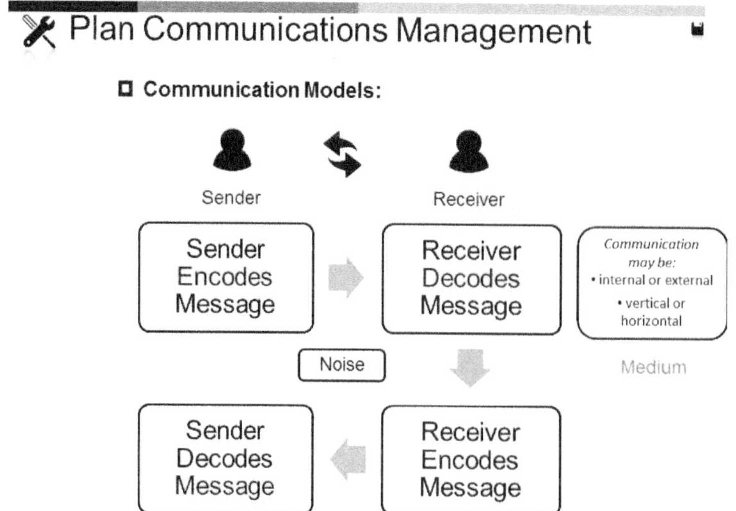

Communication Models

The basic model of communication reflects an exchange between the Sender of the information and the Receiver of that information. The concept behind the basic model of communication is communicating effectively. The cycle is presented in the figure shown above. Throughout the communication steps, the message must pass through noise, which poses a challenge to the individual receiving it.

Defining the Terms and Responsibilities

- **Sender:** responsible for confirming that the information has been understood correctly and making sure the information is clear and complete.
- **Receiver:** responsible for making sure that the information is understood correctly and received in its entirety.
- **Encode:** to pass on thoughts or ideas in a way that can be understood by others.
- **Decode:** to receive the message and translate it back into meaningful thoughts.
- **Message:** information that is being encoded and then decoded between the sender and receiver.
- **Medium**: the method that is used to convey the message.
- **Noise:** anything that may interfere with getting or receiving the message, such as background noise, technology, distance, language and cultural factors, and so forth.

Communication can be internal within the project, or external to the project. Communication may also occur vertically, as in up or down the chain of command, or horizontally with peers.

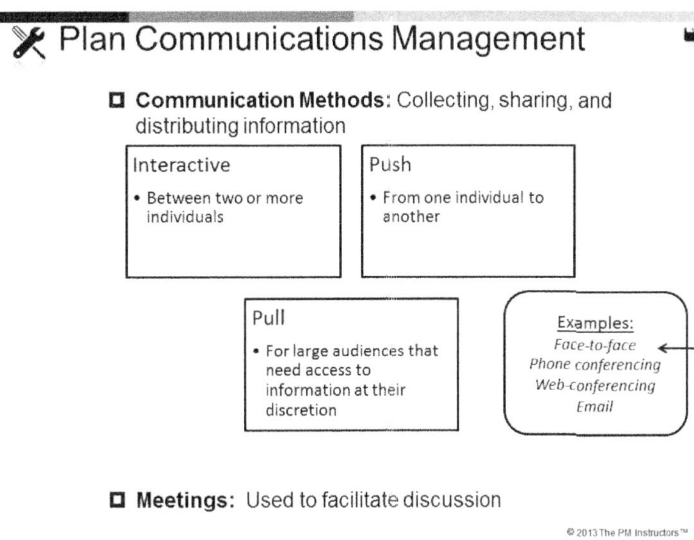

Communication Methods

Communication methods refer to the communications methods identified within the communications management plan for each stakeholder. Examples of communication methods, as outlined by the *PMBOK® Guide*, include:

- **Interactive:** between 2 or more individuals. Examples: meetings, conference calls, phone calls, etc.
- **Push:** from one individual to another. Examples: letters, email, fax, voicemails, memos, etc.
- **Pull:** for large audiences that need to access information at their discretion. Examples: online learning, intranet, knowledge hub, etc.

Communication methods involve collecting, sharing, and distributing information. Distribution methods include the mediums used to get stakeholders the information that they need. The distribution method used is tied into the communication type appropriate for the given scenario.

Other examples of communication methods include:

- Face-to-face meetings
- Phone conferencing
- Web-conferencing
- Email

Out of these methods, the preferred and best type is face-to-face meetings, which is a form of interactive communication. Face-to-face meetings are also the preferred method used when dealing with stakeholders or complex situations.

Meetings

Meetings are used to facilitate a discussion amongst stakeholders to determine how communication for the project should be managed, and identification of their communication needs.

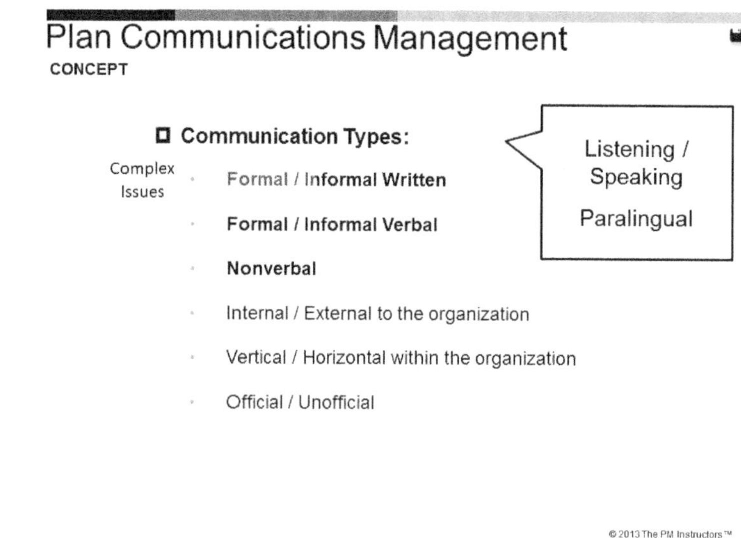

Communication Types

There are 5 primary types of communication:

- **Formal Written**, such as reports and written requests
- **Informal Written**, such as emails
- **Formal Verbal**, such as through presentations
- **Informal Verbal**, such as through meetings or standard conversation
- **Nonverbal** communication, such as paying attention to another's physical mannerisms

In addition to the above, it should also be noted that communication can be internal within the project, or external to the project. It may also occur vertically or horizontally within the organization, and that it may be considered official or unofficial communication.

The type of communication used depends on the scenario. For instance, when dealing with complex issues, a formal and documented approach is best, making formal written the preferred type in this instance.

The act of listening and speaking also plays a role in effective communication, as is demonstrated within the basic model of communication. Using the right pitch and tone when **speaking**, and using the right nonverbal mannerisms while **listening** are part of communication. Listening also involves picking up the pitch and tone of the speaker, which is what is meant by paralingual.

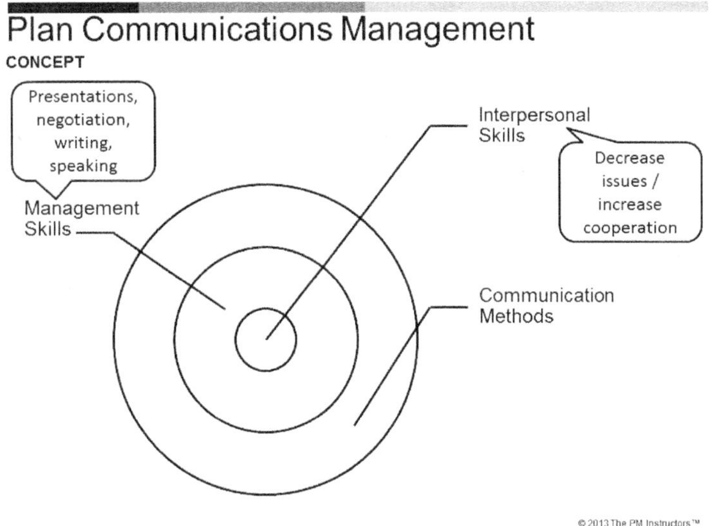

Concept

Interpersonal and management skills play an important role in communicating effectively, and they are at the core of using communication methods.

Interpersonal Skills

Interpersonal skills are commonly called "soft skills". It is thought that the project manager can decrease issues and increase cooperation by understanding how stakeholders are feeling, knowing what their concerns are, and being able to follow up on existing issues. These skills are important to effectively managing a project and controlling the schedule. Interpersonal skills are a tool and technique of the Develop Project Team process from within the Project Human Resource Management Knowledge Area. Utilizing soft skills allows the project manager to build trust with stakeholders, resolve conflict, overcome resistance to change, and practice active listening.

Management Skills

Management and interpersonal skills are both useful when dealing with people. Examples of management skills include: utilizing presentation skills, negotiating, writing skills, and public speaking.

By leveraging interpersonal and management skills, along with leveraging the various communication methods available, the project manager can more effectively carry out several communication activities. Examples of communication activities include the following:

- Listening
- Questioning & probing
- Educating
- Fact-finding
- Setting and managing expectations
- Persuading
- Motivating
- Coaching
- Negotiating
- Resolving conflict
- Summarizing & identifying next steps

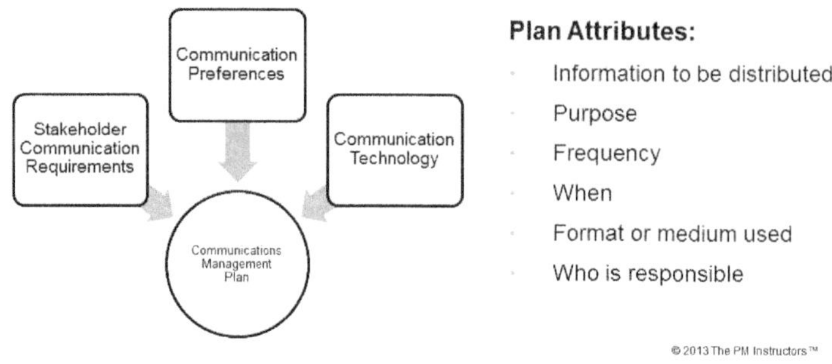
Plan Communications Management
Communications Management Plan:
Identifies, analyzes, and documents the needs and expectations of stakeholders
Subsidiary plan of the project management plan
Communication Preferences
Stakeholder Communication Requirements
Communication Technology
Communications Management Plan
Plan Attributes:
Information to be distributed
Purpose
Frequency
When
Format or medium used
Who is responsible
© 2013 The PM Instructors™

Plan Communications Management Outputs

The Plan Communications Management process produces two outputs: *communications management plan and project documents updates.*

Communications Management Plan

The communications management plan identifies, analyzes and documents the needs and expectations of the stakeholders, which in turn allows the project manager insight into the stakeholders' goals and objectives. Understanding stakeholder priorities is important to managing projects, and the communications management plan clues the project manager into these priorities and communication needs. It is developed by carefully evaluating the stakeholder communication requirements and preferences, and considers the communication technology needed and available.

At a minimum, the plan should address the following attributes when considering the various types of information that is to be communicated to stakeholders:

- What information needs to be distributed
- The purpose of the information
- The frequency in which it is to be distributed
- The format or medium used to distribute it
- And who is responsible for distributing it

Like all subsidiary plans, the communications management plan is a part of the project management plan.

Plan Communications Management

- **Communication Management Plan** Sample Contents:
  - Stakeholder communication requirements
  - Information to be communicated
  - Communication guidelines
  - Frequency
  - Escalation Process
  - Responsibility
  - Recipients
  - Communication methods used
  - Communication constraints
  - Communication flow chart
  - Glossary of terms
  - Method for updating and refining

According to the *PMBOK® Guide*, the communications management plan typically includes the following:

- The communication requirements of the project stakeholders
- The information that will be communicated, including the format, content, and how detailed it should be
- Guidelines for holding team meetings, status meetings, conference calls, etc.
- How often the information is updated and communicated
- The escalation process for resolving issues that cannot be resolved among those directly involved
- Who is responsible, or what groups are responsible for communicating the information
- Who the recipient or recipients are that the information is being distributed to
- The methods and technologies that will be used to provide the information, such as email, memos, meetings, summit, etc.
- Any communication constraints that exist
- A communication flow chart
- Glossary of communications-related terms used
- The methods for updating and revising the communications management plan. This is a standard item within subsidiary plans, and is utilized as the project progresses and changes are made

Plan Communications Management
Project Documents Updates
• Documents updated may include: project schedule, stakeholder register, and other documents impacted by the process
© 2013 The PM Instructors™

Project Document Updates

Project documents updated as a result of carrying out this process include the project schedule, stakeholder register, and other documents impacted by the process.

Manage Communications

Purpose: To create, collect, distribute, store, retrieve and ultimately dispose of project information in accordance with the communications management plan.

Manage Communications Process Overview

The purpose of the Manage Communications process is to create, collect, distribute, store, retrieve and ultimately dispose of project information in accordance with the communications management plan. The process itself is very important, since it addresses balancing and managing the expectations of stakeholders, in regards to communication.

According to the *PMBOK® Guide*, techniques and considerations used for effectively managing communication includes:

- Basic model of communication, also referred to as sender-receiver models
- Choice of media
- Writing style
- Meeting management techniques
- Presentation techniques
- Facilitation techniques
- Listening techniques

As previously mentioned, it is important for a project manager to have strong interpersonal and management skills, in order to effectively manage communications.

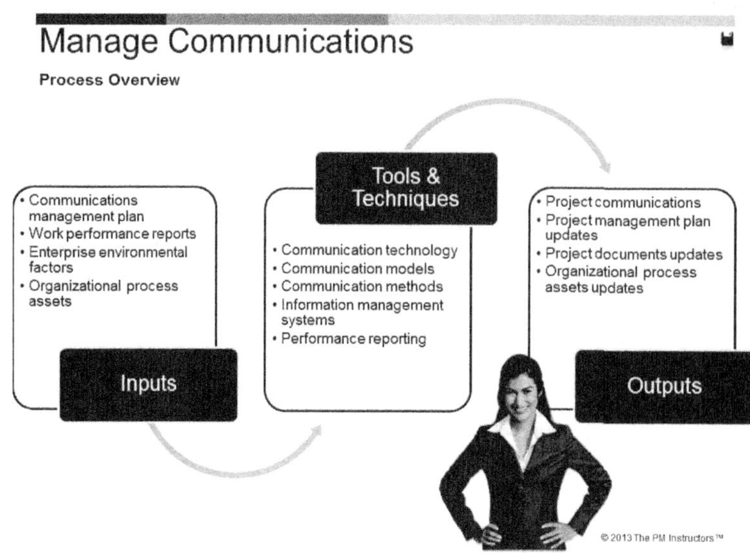
Manage Communications
Process Overview
Tools & Techniques
• Communications management plan
• Work performance reports
• Enterprise environmental factors
• Organizational process assets
Inputs
• Communication technology
• Communication models
• Communication methods
• Information management systems
• Performance reporting
• Project communications
• Project management plan updates
• Project documents updates
• Organizational process assets updates
Outputs
© 2013 The PM Instructors™

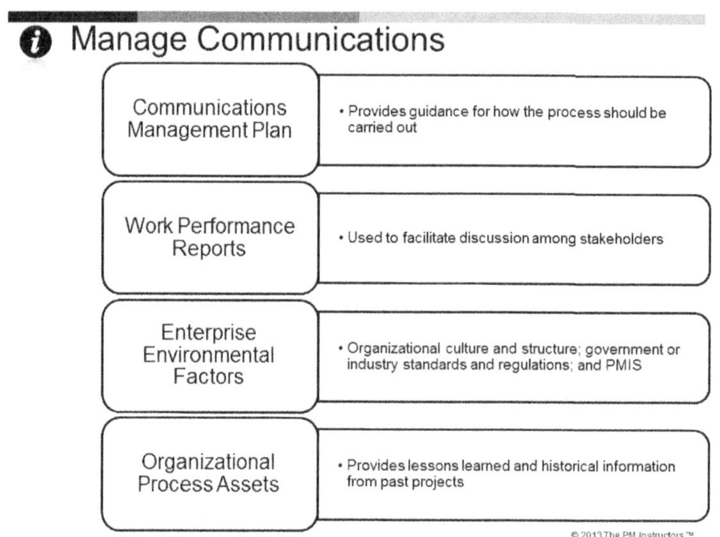
Manage Communications
Communications Management Plan
• Provides guidance for how the process should be carried out
Work Performance Reports
• Used to facilitate discussion among stakeholders
Enterprise Environmental Factors
• Organizational culture and structure; government or industry standards and regulations; and PMIS
Organizational Process Assets
• Provides lessons learned and historical information from past projects
© 2013 The PM Instructors™

Manage Communications Inputs

The Manage Communications process contains four inputs: *communications management plan, work performance reports, enterprise environmental factors,* and *organizational process assets.*

Communications Management Plan

The communications management plan outlines how this process is to be carried out, the goals and objectives of the stakeholders, as well as the communication requirements of the stakeholders.

Work Performance Reports

Work performance reports, which contain information about the progress of the project, are used to facilitate discussions among stakeholders.

Enterprise Environmental Factors

According to the *PMBOK® Guide*, enterprise environmental factors typically used to manage stakeholders includes the organizational culture and structure, government or industry standards and regulations, as well as the PMIS.

Organizational Process Assets

Organizational process assets that influence this process include communication, issue, and change control procedures, as well as historical information from previous projects. This historical information can provide insight as to how stakeholders have behaved in the past.

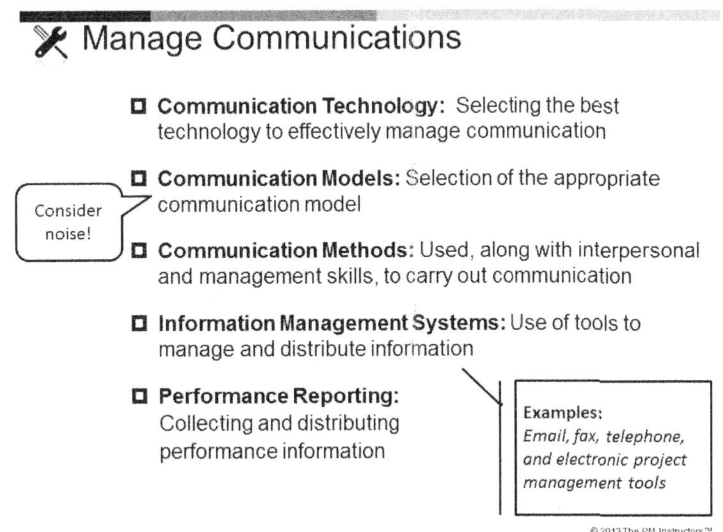

Manage Communications Tools and Techniques

The Manage Communications process contains five tools and techniques: *communication technology, communication models, communication methods, information management systems,* and *performance reporting.*

Communication Technology

Communication technology involves selecting the best technology for the project that can be used to effectively manage communication. This should be in line with what is described within the communications management plan.

Communication Models

Just as with communication technology, the appropriate communication model used should be based on the needs of the project and situation. The level of noise that exists should also be taken into account, to ensure that communication is managed appropriately.

Communication Methods

Communication in general is important throughout all of project management, and it is through these skills that the project manager can properly communicate with stakeholders. Communication methods, along with interpersonal and management skills, are utilized while interacting with and managing stakeholders.

Information Management Systems

Information management systems refer to the use of several tools to manage and distribute information. Examples provided by the *PMBOK® Guide* include hard copy documents, electronic communication such as email, fax, and telephone, and electronic project management tools, such as software, virtual meeting programs, and web portals.

Performance Reporting

Performance reporting refers to collecting and distributing performance information, including assembling status reports and other reports distributed by the project manager. These reports may include performance analysis, current status reports, an update on risks and issues, and summary of changes.

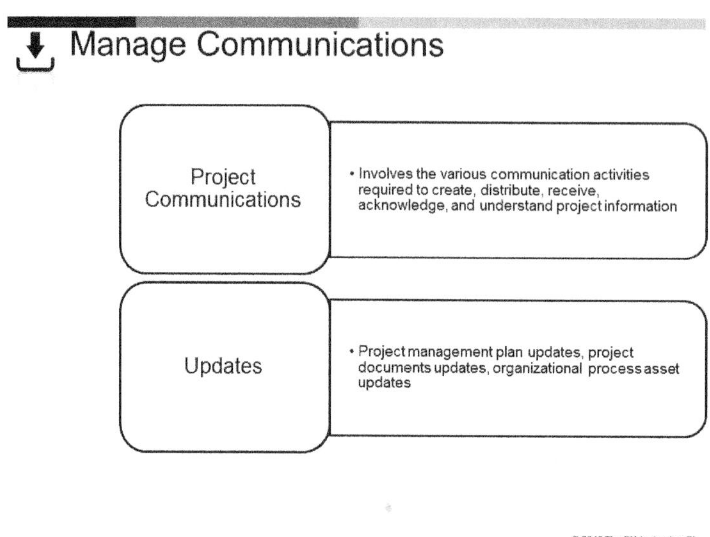
Manage Communications
Project Communications
• Involves the various communication activities required to create, distribute, receive, acknowledge, and understand project information
Updates
• Project management plan updates, project documents updates, organizational process asset updates
© 2013 The PM Instructors™

Manage Communications Outputs

The Manage Communications process has four outputs: *project communications, project management plan updates, project documents updates,* and *organizational process assets updates.*

Project Communications

Project communications refers to various communication activities that involve creating, distributing, receiving, acknowledging, and understanding project information. Examples of project communications include performance reports, status on deliverables, schedule progress, and costs incurred.

Project Management Plan Updates

Updates to the project management plan typically include the communications management plan.

Project Documents Updates

Updates to the project documents typically include the schedule, project funding requirements, stakeholder register, and issue log.

Organizational Process Asset Updates

Organizational process assets often updated as a result of carrying out this process include causes of issues, corrective action taken as a result, and whether the actions were effective. Lessons learned are also documented.

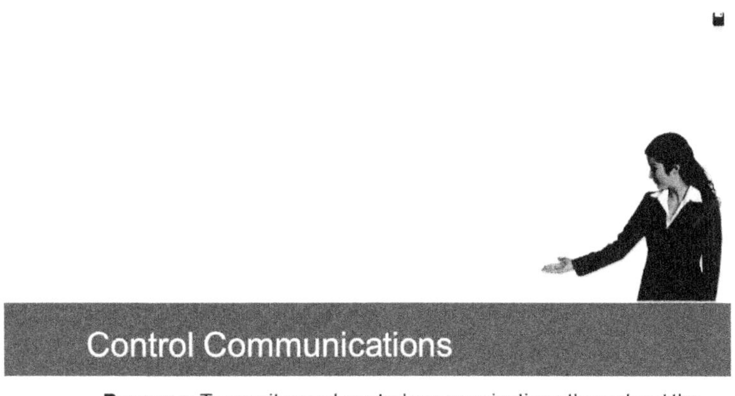
Control Communications
Purpose: To monitor and control communications throughout the entire project life cycle to ensure the information needs of the project stakeholders are met.

Control Communications Process Overview

Control Communications is the third and final process of the Project Communications Management Knowledge Area. This process is part of the Monitoring and Controlling Process Group and is responsible for ensuring that the project maintains an optimal level of information flow of communication among stakeholders.

The official purpose of the process is to monitor and control communications throughout the entire project life cycle to ensure the information needs of the project stakeholders are met.

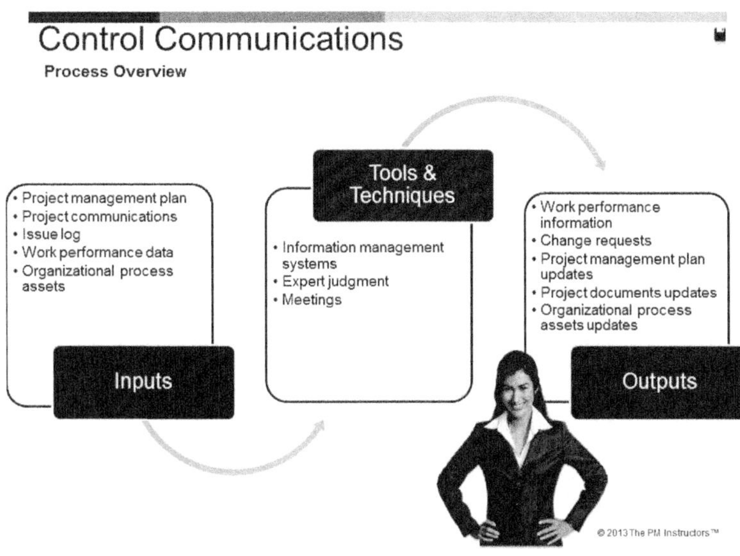
Control Communications
Process Overview
Tools & Techniques
• Project management plan
• Project communications
• Issue log
• Work performance data
• Organizational process assets
• Information management systems
• Expert judgment
• Meetings
• Work performance information
• Change requests
• Project management plan updates
• Project documents updates
• Organizational process assets updates
Inputs
Outputs
© 2013 The PM Instructors™

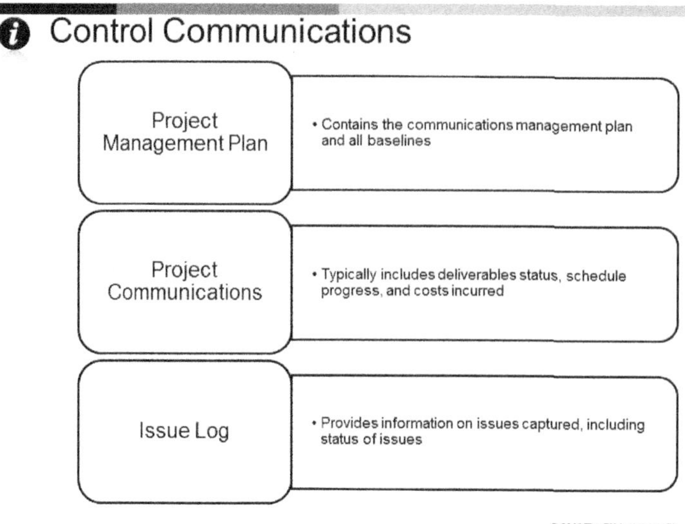
Control Communications
Project Management Plan
• Contains the communications management plan and all baselines
Project Communications
• Typically includes deliverables status, schedule progress, and costs incurred
Issue Log
• Provides information on issues captured, including status of issues
© 2013 The PM Instructors™

Control Communications Inputs

The Control Communications process has a total of five inputs: *project management plan, project communications, issue log, work performance data,* and *organizational process assets.*

Project Management Plan

The communications management plan is the primary document used from within the project management plan, although the scope, schedule, and cost baselines are all typically referenced. These documents are important to measuring and communicating actual performance against plan.

Project Communications

Project communications typically used by this process include deliverables status, schedule progress, and costs incurred.

Issue Log

The issue log contains all of the issues identified and captured, and information about them, including status, response, and ownership. The issue log provides key information needed for monitoring and controlling the communications of the project.

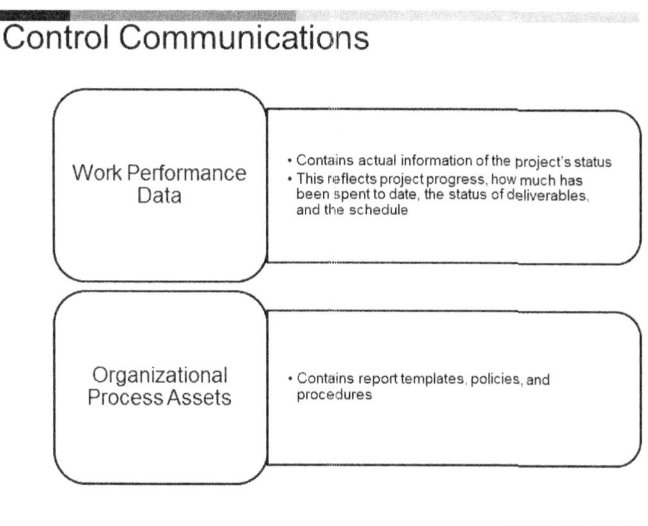

Work Performance Data

As part of measuring progress, the project manager will need actual information of the project's status, which is why work performance data is used. This reflects project progress, and includes how much has been spent to date, the status of deliverables, and the schedule.

Organizational Process Assets

Organizational process assets used as part of this process include report templates, policies, and procedures.

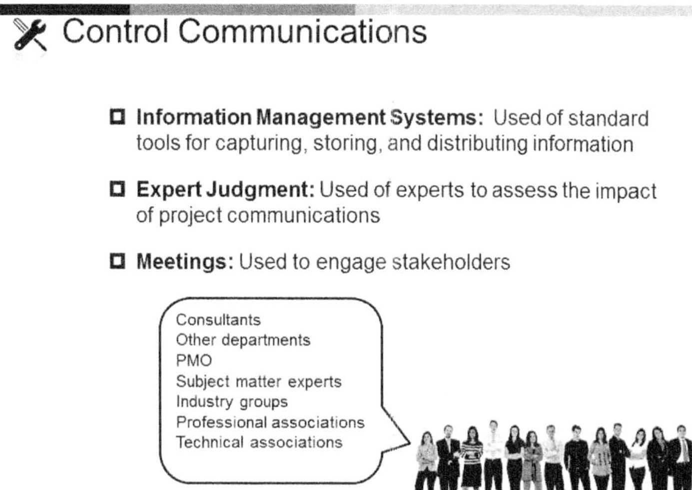

Control Communications Tools and Techniques

The Control Communications process contains three tools and techniques used: *information management systems, expert judgment,* and *meetings.*

Information Management Systems

Information management systems, which also appeared as a tool and technique of the Manage Communications process, refers to the usage of standard tools for capturing, storing, and distributing information to stakeholders. An example of this would be using SharePoint as a central repository for storing and sharing project documents.

Expert Judgment

When monitoring and controlling communications, expert judgment is often used. This involves using experts to assess the impact of project communications, or to take needed actions for getting the project back on track. Examples of expert judgment, in the context of this process, includes:

- Consultants
- Other departments within the organization
- PMO
- Subject matter experts
- Industry groups
- Professional and technical associations

Meetings

Meetings are used to engage stakeholders and have a direct dialogue about how the project is progressing. These meetings may occur as face-to-face engagements or through virtual meetings.

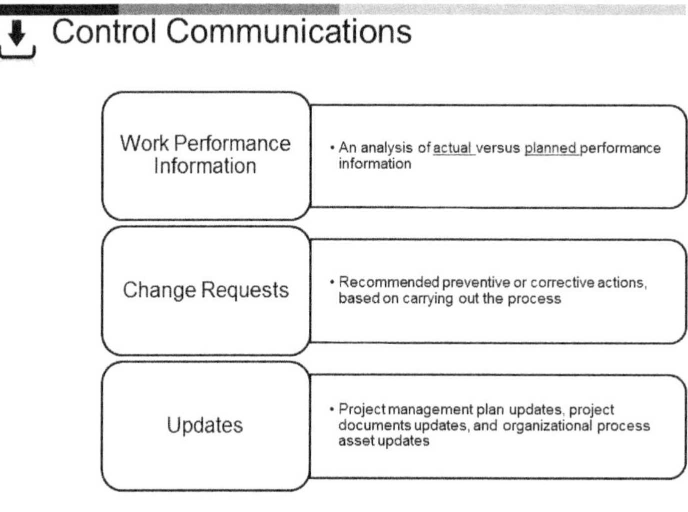
Control Communications
Work Performance Information
• An analysis of actual versus planned performance information
Change Requests
• Recommended preventive or corrective actions, based on carrying out the process
Updates
• Project management plan updates, project documents updates, and organizational process asset updates
© 2013 The PM Instructors™

Control Communications Outputs

Control Communications contains five outputs: *work performance information, change requests, project management plan updates, project documents updates,* and *organizational process assets updates.*

Work Performance Information

As with the majority of processes that fall in this process group, Control Communications compares actual project progress with planned progress, as a way of uncovering any variances that may exist. Any deviations from the project management plan are evaluated and corrective or preventive actions are submitted through formal change requests. This analysis of progress is generated as work performance information.

Actual Performance

Actual performance is evaluated through the use of work performance data, which includes the raw data of the project, and details the progress. For example, this can include activities started, in progress, and completed.

Planned Performance

Planned performance is obtained through the project management plan, which itself contains the project's baselines. The performance measurement baseline refers to an approved plan for the project work and integrates scope, schedule, and cost parameters, and may also include technical and quality parameters as well.

Change Requests

Change requests may include recommended corrective actions or preventive actions as a result of carrying out an analysis of project performance.

Project Management Plan Updates

Updates to the project management plan that result out of this process typically include the communications management plan, stakeholder management plan, and human resource management plan.

Project Documents Updates

Project documents typically updated as a result of this process include forecasts, performance reports, and the issue log.

Organizational Process Assets Updates

Updates to the organizational process assets typically include lessons learned, causes of issues and corrective action taken to resolve the issues; archiving documents for use by future projects.

Module Summary

In this module we:

- Defined the purpose of the Project Communications Management Knowledge Area
- Identified the processes of the Project Communications Management Knowledge Area
- Recalled the key outputs of the communications management processes
- Differentiated between the inputs, tools and techniques, and outputs of the communications management processes
- Identified and describe the communications skills necessary for project management
- Outlined the components contained in a communications management plan

Chapter Quiz

Exam Practice Questions

1. A project manager has just received news that symptoms were discovered signaling that a high rated risk is about to occur. This risk had the potential of bringing failure to the entire project. Due to the level of impact this risk would have on the project, all stakeholders needed to be informed. What should the project manager do?
   A. Hold a meeting with all of the stakeholders
   B. Call each stakeholder individually
   C. Meet with each stakeholder one-on-one
   D. Send an email to all stakeholders with the news

2. A project manager currently working on a pharmaceutical project was in the process of developing risk responses. A project team member approached her with a question regarding risk reporting formats. There seemed to be confusion on how one of the risk reports scheduled for delivery during this process was to be delivered to the group of stakeholders. Where would the project manager look to clarify the confusion?
   A. Risk register
   B. Communications management plan
   C. Risk management plan
   D. Risk register

3. A project team member called the project manager to notify him that there seemed to be confusion about the resources needed to complete her activity. The project manager, who was running late for a meeting, told the team member not to worry about it and ended the conversation by telling her to have a good day, and that they would touch base in the coming weeks. The project team member was left wondering whether or not the project manager understood the severity of the situation, since without the resources, her activity could not proceed and the deadline would be missed. In this scenario, what was the communication role of the project manager?
   A. Sender
   B. Encoder
   C. Receiver
   D. Decoder

4. A project team member called the project manager to notify him that there seemed to be confusion about the resources needed to complete her activity. The project manager, who was running late for a meeting, told the team member not to worry about it and ended the conversation by telling her to have a good day, and that they would touch base in the coming weeks. The project team member was left wondering whether or not the project manager understood the severity of the situation, since without the resources, her activity could not proceed and the deadline would be missed. What did the project team member fail to do during the conversation?
   A. Ask the project manager whether it was a good time to talk.
   B. Confirm that the project manager understood the message correctly.
   C. Schedule a follow up conversation.
   D. Increase the pitch of her voice so that the project manager understood the severity of the situation.

5. The project manager of a pharmaceutical company sent an email to one of his project team members apologizing for ending their recent conversation abruptly. What type of communication did the project manager use?
   A. Formal Written
   B. Informal Written
   C. Written
   D. Informal Electronic

6. During the project kick-off meeting, the project manager decided that an information portal will be created as a means to communicate with team members in different time zones. The communications management plan, where this information was documented, is an output of which of the following processes?
   A. Communications Process
   B. Manage Communications
   C. Plan Communications Management
   D. Control Communications

7. Purse Centric is a clothing retail company with eleven stores throughout Europe. The company is planning to expand to North America, beginning with two stores opening concurrently. The project manager heading the opening of the west region store has just discovered a critical risk that may affect the location of the store. What type of communication should the project manager use to document the potential risk?
   A. Formal written
   B. Informal written
   C. Informal verbal
   D. Formal verbal

8. Purse Centric is a clothing retail company with eleven stores throughout Europe. The company is planning to expand to North America, beginning with two stores opening concurrently. The project manager heading the opening of the west region store has just discovered a critical risk that may affect the location of the store and needs to communicate the risk to stakeholders. What method of communication should the project manager use to communicate the risk with stakeholders?
   A. Individual phone calls
   B. Phone conference
   C. One-on-one meetings
   D. Face-to-face meeting

9. A large RV rental company is launching a consignment program for private owners who are looking to rent out their vehicles. The project manager of the project has just determined that there are 22 stakeholders total within the project. How many communication paths are there within the project?
   A. 484
   B. 242
   C. 231
   D. 462

10. Which of the following items is not addressed within the communications management plan?
    A. Frequency of communication
    B. Risk reporting formats
    C. Glossary of communication terms
    D. Method for updating and refining the plan

11. The project manager needs to keep stakeholders informed about the status of a high risk project that has been delayed several times this year. In order to provide them with comprehensive updates of the project on a regular basis, she will need to include several pieces of information within the report. Which of the following is not an input utilized in generating the communications management plan?
    A. Enterprise environmental factors
    B. Performance reports
    C. Stakeholder register
    D. Organizational process assets

12. Gaby is the project manager of a multi-million dollar project that will roll out a major upgrade to the network of her organization's data center. Gaby is in the process of collecting and distributing information about the project's progress to the project team. What process is she carrying out?
    A. Plan Communications Management
    B. Manage Communications
    C. Distribute Information
    D. Control Communications

13. A project manager of Cyber Channels Inc. was in the process of planning how communications would be handled throughout the project. Since there were a high number of stakeholders involved in the project, the project manager held a planning meeting with the project management team to define and document the stakeholder communications requirements. Which of the following tools and techniques can the project management team utilize to define and document the stakeholder communications requirements?
    A. Communications skills
    B. Communications technology
    C. Communications requirements analysis
    D. Communications methods

14. Gaby is the project manager of a multi-million dollar project that will roll out a major upgrade to the network of her organization's data center. As standard within her organization, Gaby has created an internal SharePoint site to store project documentation, and to serve as the central repository for all project communications. This site contains various workflows for managing communications that exist among the project's stakeholders. The SharePoint site can BEST be described as:
    A. A record management system
    B. A distribution tool
    C. A communication method
    D. An information management system

15. A project manager of Cyber Channels Inc. was in the process of planning how communications would be handled throughout the project. While identifying stakeholders, the project manager determined that there were a total of 16 stakeholders. How many communication paths exist within this project?
    A. 120
    B. 128
    C. 240
    D. 256

16. Which of the following processes is responsible for ensuring that there is an optimal information flow among all project stakeholders?
    A. Plan Communications Management
    B. Manage Communications
    C. Distribute Information
    D. Control Communications

17. A good project manager spends 90% of their time doing the following:
    A. Communicating
    B. Planning
    C. Directing
    D. Organizing

18. Which of the following is not an example of general management skills?
    A. Creativity
    B. Smoothing
    C. Influence
    D. Empathy

19. You have just discovered that one of the deliverables will be delayed by one day. Your project staff has assured you that it will be completed. However, stakeholder updates are scheduled to go out today, and the delay of the deliverable will likely cause some anxiety amongst the group. What should you do?
    A. Don't mention the delay since the project team has assured you it will be completed
    B. Include the delay in your update report
    C. Mention that the deliverable has been completed. After all, it is guaranteed to complete by tomorrow
    D. Send the update one day late to reflect the completion of the deliverable

20. Richard, the current director of marketing, approaches Amy who is managing the project that Richard is indirectly involved in at a marketing level. Knowing that the project began a month prior, Richard inquires as to when the next meeting will be held so that he can make sure that he receives the necessary information requested from the customer's marketing manager. Amy appears confused, since project staff assignments were already underway and planning had occurred a week after the roll out. What step did Amy omit to carefully address?
    A. Networking with key managers
    B. Performing observation and conversation
    C. Analyzing communication requirements
    D. Co-locating the team

Chapter Quiz

Exam Practice Answers

1. Answer: A

   Explanation: When dealing with an issue, it is always preferred that the project manager communicate with stakeholders directly. While face-to-face is the preferred method, it is not necessary that the project manager meet with each stakeholder individually.

2. Answer: B

   Explanation: The risk management plan contains information on risk-related reporting formats, while the communications management plan contains information regarding distribution frequency, medium, and tool used to distribute reports.

3. Answer: C

   Explanation: The sender, who initiated the communication, is the project team member; the receiver of the information is the project manager.

4. Answer: B

   Explanation: As the sender of the information, the project team member is responsible for confirming that the project manager understood the information, and that the information is complete and clear. On the other end, the project manager also failed to meet the responsibilities of a receiver, which is to make sure that they understood the information correctly and that it was received in its entirety.

5. Answer: B

   Explanation: Formal and informal written are communication types. Emails are an informal way of communicating, and are also written. Therefore, informal written is the correct answer.

6. Answer: C

   Explanation: The communications management plan is generated out of the first process within the Project Communications Management Knowledge Area, which is Plan Communications Management. Manage Communications and Control Communications are also processes within the Project Communications Management Knowledge Area, whereas Communications Process is not a formal process.

7. Answer: A

   Explanation: Notice that the question asks for the type of communication used to "document" the risk. Risks should always be documented formally.

8. Answer: D

   Explanation: When communicating with stakeholders, it is best to meet face-to-face. It is not necessary, however, to meet with each stakeholder individually (unless the situation itself warrants it).

9. Answer: C

   Explanation: In order to calculate the communication paths, you would need to know the following formula: n (n – 1) / 2, where "n" represents the total number of stakeholders. When you plug in the total number of stakeholders, you result in the following calculation: 22 (22 – 1) / 2. Solve the problem and you end up with 231 communication paths.

10. Answer: B

Explanation: Risk reporting formats are addressed within the risk management plan. All the remaining items are included within the communications management plan.

11. Answer: B

    Explanation: Performance reports are not necessary in creating the communications management plan. Aside from enterprise environmental factors, stakeholder register, project management plan, and organizational process assets are also used as inputs.

12. Answer: B

    Explanation: Gaby is in the process of carrying out the Manage Communications process. The purpose of this process is to create, collect, distribute, store, retrieve, and ultimately dispose of project information in accordance with the communications management plan.

13. Answer: C

    Explanation: Communication requirements analysis is a tool and technique of the Plan Communications Management process, which is used to define and document stakeholder communication requirements, and to determine who will communicate with who, and what will be communicated.

14. Answer: D

    Explanation: An information management system is defined as facilities processes, and procedures used to collect, store, and distribute information between producers and consumers of information in physical or electronic format. In the context of the Project Communications Management processes, information management systems refer to the usage of tools to manage communication, including project management tools, software, and products.

15. Answer: A

    Explanation: In order to answer this question correctly, you would need to know the formula for calculating communication channels. The formula is n (n – 1) / 2, where "n" represents the total number of stakeholders. Plug in 16 into the formula and you get the following calculation: 16 (16 – 1) / 2. Therefore, there are a total of 120 communication paths within the project.

16. Answer: D

    Explanation: The Control Communications process is responsible for ensuring that the information needs of the project stakeholders are met, including ensuring that there is an optimal information flow among all project stakeholders, at any moment in time.

17. Answer: A

    Explanation: While all options appear valid, it has been documented that a good project manager spends 90% of their time communicating. When reviewing the project management processes, notice that most require that the project manager perform some type of communication.

18. Answer: B

    Explanation: General management skills often encompass soft skills. All options included are examples of soft skills except for smoothing, which is a conflict resolution technique that focuses on getting agreement by all parties involved.

19. Answer: B

    Explanation: The answer is to include the delay within your update report. It is important to always be truthful when communicating or sending information about the project.

20. Answer: C

    Explanation: Co-location means to bring the project team together physically in the same location, and wouldn't have helped the situation. Here, Amy missed Richard when addressing the communication requirements of the stakeholders. It is clear that Richard hasn't been involved to date, meaning that Amy did not carefully analyze the communication requirements, which occurs as part of the Plan Communications Management process. Going through this would have summarized the information needs of the project stakeholders.

Chapter 11: Project Risk Management

Learning Objectives:

- ☐ Define the purpose of the Project Risk Management Knowledge Area
- ☐ Identify the processes of the Project Risk Management Knowledge Area
- ☐ Recall the key outputs of the risk management processes
- ☐ Differentiate between the inputs, tools and techniques, and outputs of the risk management processes
- ☐ Perform simple qualitative risk calculations

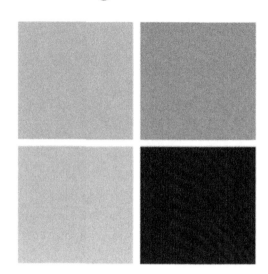

Exam Domain Tasks:

- Plan risk management by developing a risk management plan, and identifying, analyzing, and prioritizing project risks in the risk register and defining risk response strategies, in order to manage uncertainty throughout the project life cycle.
- Implement approved actions and follow the risk management plan and risk register, in order to minimize the impact of negative risk events on the project.
- Update the risk register and risk response plan by identifying any new risks, assessing old risks, and determining and implementing appropriate response strategies, in order to manage the impact of risks on the project.

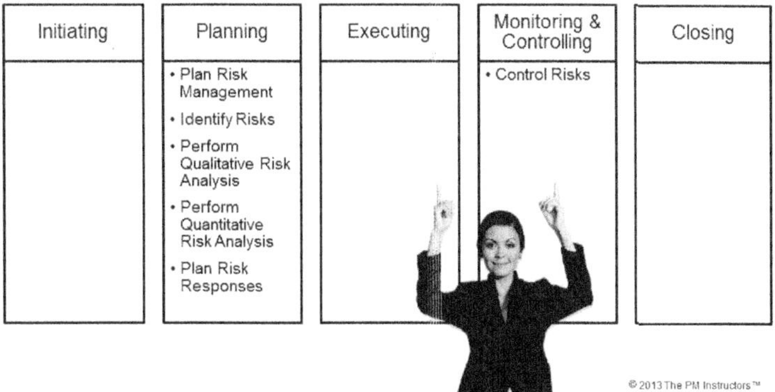
Project Risk Management
Purpose: To conduct risk management planning, identification, analysis, response planning, and controlling risk on a project.
6 Project Risk Management Processes:
Initiating
Planning
Executing
Monitoring & Controlling
Closing
• Plan Risk Management
• Identify Risks
• Perform Qualitative Risk Analysis
• Perform Quantitative Risk Analysis
• Plan Risk Responses
• Control Risks
© 2013 The PM Instructors™

Project Risk Management Overview

The purpose of the Project Risk Management Knowledge Area is to conduct risk management planning, identification, analysis, response planning, and controlling risk on a project.

This Knowledge Area is concerned with increasing the probability and impact of positive events, and decreasing the probability and impact of negative events. Risk is something that should be monitored and addressed during the entire lifecycle of the project.

The definition of risk, as defined by the *PMBOK® Guide*, is *an uncertain event or condition that, if it occurs, has a positive or negative effect on one or more project objective*s. By objective, we are referring to time, cost, scope, and quality. It should also be noted that risk and issue are two separate things. A risk is something that may or may not occur in the future, while an issue is something that is occurring in the present or is certain to occur in the future. So if not addressed, a negative risk can convert into an issue.

Many project managers and team members don't realize that there are risks considered to be positive, since we're so accustomed to thinking of risks with a negative undertone. Positive risks are simply opportunities, while negative risks are threats.

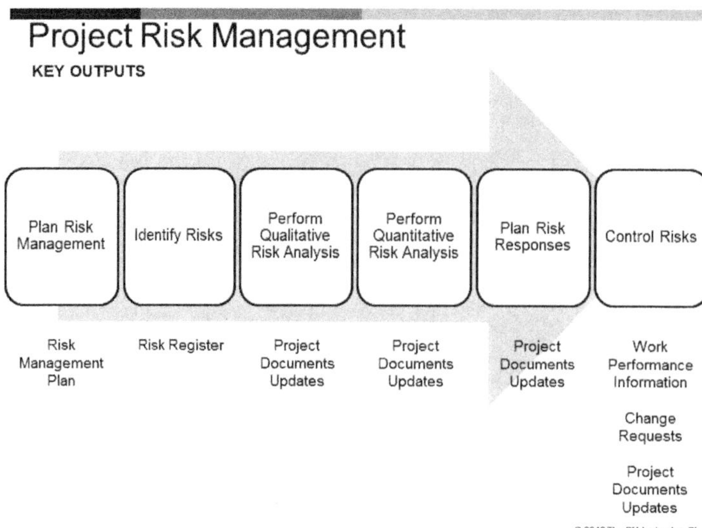

The Project Risk Management Knowledge Area consists of six processes:

- **Plan Risk Management (Planning Process Group).** Purpose: To define how to conduct risk management activities for a project.
- **Identify Risks (Planning Process Group).** Purpose: To determine which risks may affect the project and document their characteristics.
- **Perform Qualitative Risk Analysis (Planning Process Group).** Purpose: To prioritize risks for further analysis or action by assessing and combining their probability of occurrence and impact.
- **Perform Quantitative Risk Analysis (Planning Process Group).** Purpose: To numerically analyze the effect of identified risks on overall project objectives.
- **Plan Risk Responses (Planning Process Group).** Purpose: To develop options and actions to enhance opportunities and to reduce threats to project objectives.
- **Control Risks (Monitoring and Controlling Process Group).** Purpose: To implement risk response plans, track identified risks, monitor residual risks, identify new risks, and evaluate risk process effectiveness throughout the project.

Plan Risk Management
Purpose: To define how to conduct risk management activities for a project.

Plan Risk Management Process Overview

The purpose of the Plan Risk Management process is to define how to conduct risk management activities for a project, and it is responsible for creating the risk management plan. The risk management plan is the heart of carrying out risk management activities of the project and will guide the project/risk management teams in carrying out risk activities. The purpose of the risk management plan is to define how risks will be managed, monitored, and controlled throughout the project.

After its creation, the risk management plan becomes an input to the remaining risk management processes.

It is important to note that the risk management plan is generated during the early stages of project planning. Risk management itself begins as early as the start of the project.

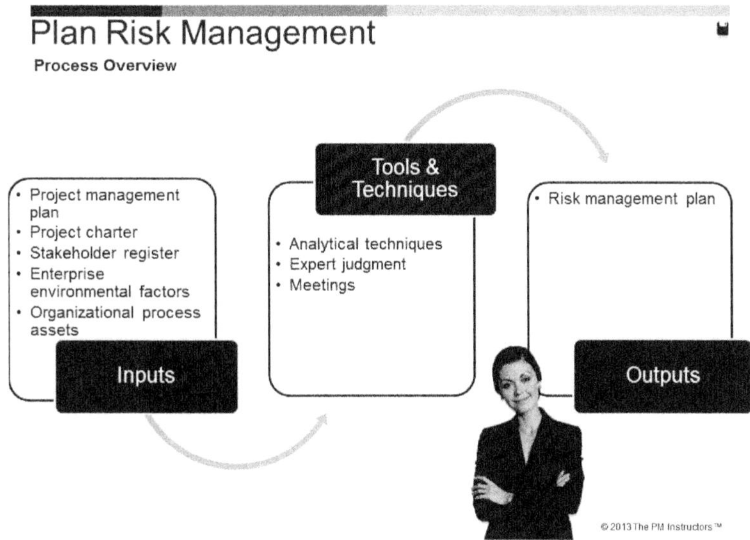
Plan Risk Management
Process Overview
• Project management plan
• Project charter
• Stakeholder register
• Enterprise environmental factors
• Organizational process assets
Inputs
Tools & Techniques
• Analytical techniques
• Expert judgment
• Meetings
• Risk management plan
Outputs
© 2013 The PM Instructors™

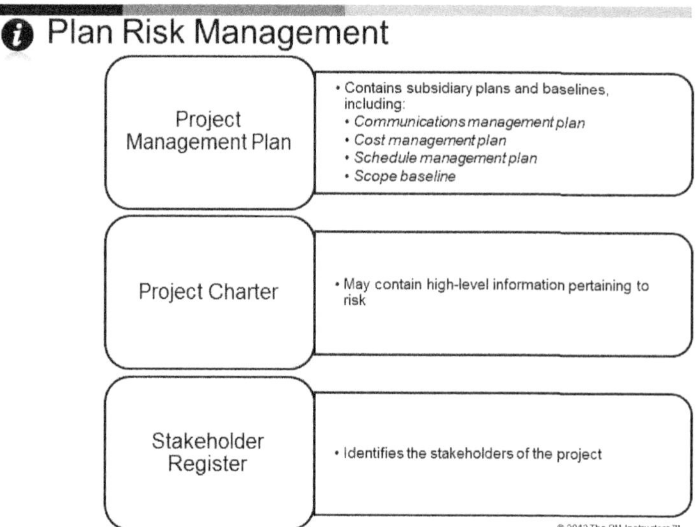
Plan Risk Management
Project Management Plan
• Contains subsidiary plans and baselines, including:
• Communications management plan
• Cost management plan
• Schedule management plan
• Scope baseline
Project Charter
• May contain high-level information pertaining to risk
Stakeholder Register
• Identifies the stakeholders of the project
© 2013 The PM Instructors™

Plan Risk Management Inputs

The Plan Risk Management process contains five inputs: *project management plan, project charter, stakeholder register, enterprise environmental factors* and *organizational process assets.*

Project Management Plan

The project management plan provides the various subsidiary plans and baselines needed to develop the risk management plan. Of particular interest are the communication, cost and schedule management plans, as well as the scope baseline.

Communications Management Plan

The communications management plan defines the interactions that will take place and who is responsible for sharing information and when.

Cost Management Plan

The cost management plan provides the information needed for the risk budget, contingencies and also management reserves.

Schedule Management Plan

The schedule management plan is necessary to assess and report schedule contingencies.

Scope Baseline

The project scope statement, which is a part of the scope baseline, provides the project deliverables and what it is that the project has set out to accomplish. This is used as a guideline to determine how to conduct risk management efforts, and how risk will be measured. The constraints, assumptions, acceptance criteria are all detailed in the project scope statement. The scope baseline also provides an indication of whether the project is setting out to produce something new that the team has not undertaken before, which may call for a higher level of rigor in risk management planning.

Project Charter

The project charter contains high-level information captured at the inception of the project. Of critical importance is any risk management related items documented within the charter, including identified risks.

Stakeholder Register

The stakeholder register contains the list of identified stakeholders, which is important when considering who should participate in the development of the risk management plan.

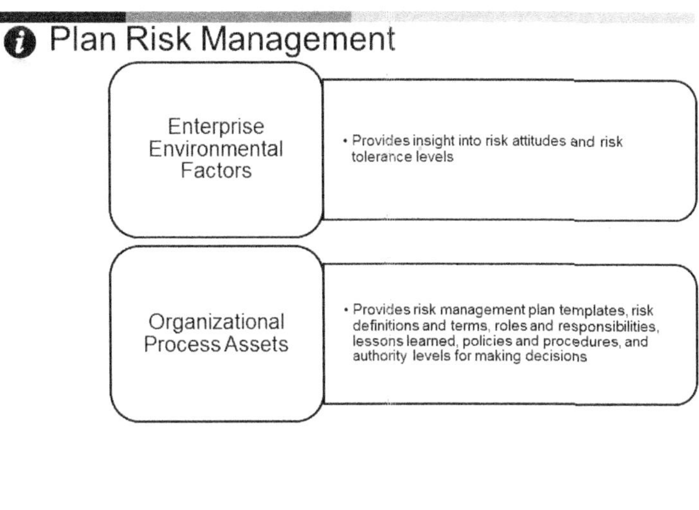

Enterprise Environmental Factors

Enterprise environmental factors provide an understanding of risk attitudes and risk tolerances of the organization. This is very important for planning the risk approach and strategy. Risk tolerance levels are commonly revealed through the organization's policies and actions.

Organizational Process Assets

Organizational process assets provide several key pieces of information that may impact the risk management plan, including: risk templates (such as risk management plan templates, risk categories, risk statements, and risk registers), definitions and terms relating to risk, defined roles and responsibilities, policies and procedures, and authority levels for making decisions, and lessons learned.

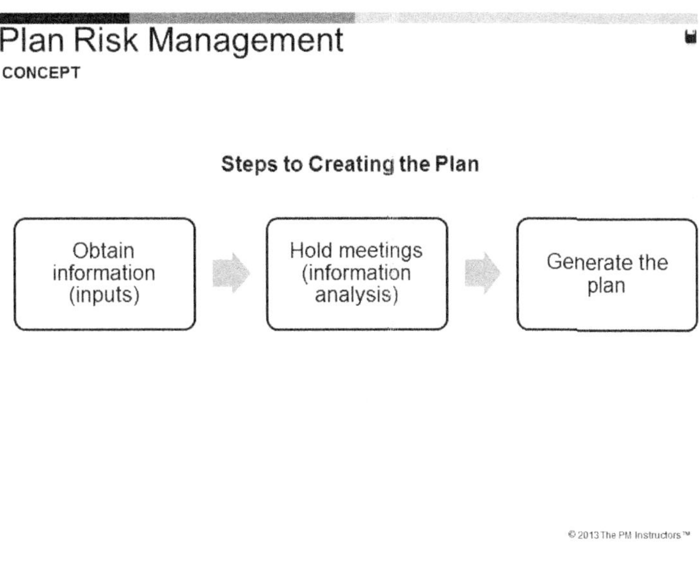

The creation of the risk management plan follows a smooth and clear flow when charted in the following three steps:

1. First, information is obtained using the inputs previously outlined;
2. Planning meetings are held to analyze the existing information available and to develop the risk management plan;
3. Based on the results of these meetings, the risk management plan is generated.

These inputs, along with the tools and techniques that will be covered next, provide the project and risk manager with the necessary information to develop the risk management plan.

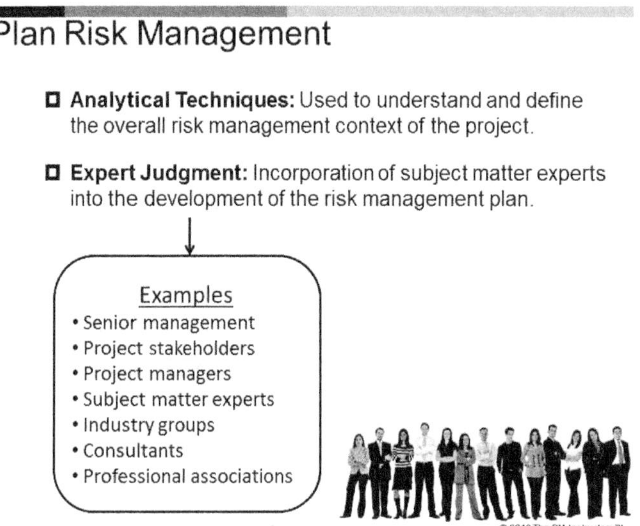

Plan Risk Management Tools and Techniques

The Plan Risk Management process contains three tools and techniques: *analytical techniques, expert judgment,* and *meetings.*

Analytical Techniques

Analytical techniques, in the context of developing the risk management plan, are used to define the overall risk management context of the project. This refers to deciphering the risk attitude of the stakeholders and organization, which provides insight into the level of risk management activities that should be performed on the project.

Expert Judgment

In development the risk management plan, the project manager should consider various perspectives and expertise, to determine the appropriate level of rigor needed. Oftentimes, the risk management plan is developed through a series of meetings with the project management team and experts that can assist in facilitating the development of the plan.

Examples of expert judgment provided by the *PMBOK® Guide* include: senior management, project stakeholders other project managers, subject matter experts, industry groups and consultants, and professional and technical associations.

Plan Risk Management

- **Meetings:**

Who

- Project manager, project team members, other stakeholders, etc.

What

- Develop risk activities and estimate costs
- Assign risk responsibilities
- Identify risk categories
- Define levels of probability and impact
- Create / modify probability and impact matrix
- Create / modify risk templates

When

- Early on within the project

Meetings

Planning meetings are held in conjunction with the other two tools and techniques of this process. The results of these meetings will be summarized and documented within the risk management plan.

Meeting Attendees

Meeting attendees tend to include anyone that has a voice regarding risk management. A typical list of participants includes: the project manager, selected project team members and other stakeholders, as well as anyone involved in risk planning and risk execution activities.

Meeting Agenda

The meeting agenda is included under the "What" heading in the slide above. The agenda should include all items that are covered within the risk management plan.

Plan Risk Management Outputs

The Plan Risk Management process contains a single output: *risk management plan.*

Risk Management Plan

The risk management plan contains the following items within it:

- **Methodology** describes the approach used to carry out risk management. This should cover the methods, tools, and sources of the data.
- **Roles and responsibilities** identifies who is responsible for the risk activities outlined in the risk management plan; this could be a single individual or a group of team members, and it also clarifies what they will be responsible for doing, similar to a job description.
- **Budgeting** provides the amount of funds that are set aside for risk activities. The risk management plan details the estimated amount that will be spent on risk management activities, assigns resources, and outlines the protocol for using the contingency reserve. This information becomes a part of the cost baseline.
- **Timing** outlines when and how often the risk management processes are carried out. It also details the protocols for using schedule contingency reserves, and inclusion of the risk management activities into the project schedule.
- **Risk categories** used are identified and documented to ensure consistency and to systematically classify risks. This may include a risk category list or the risk breakdown structure (RBS).
- **Definitions of risk probability and impact** literally define risk probability and impact using a scale or rating system. This scale or rating system is defined in the risk management plan so that negative and positive risks can be easily and consistently rated.
- **Probability and impact matrix** is used to prioritize risks and to determine which risks require a response. The probability and impact matrix serves as a look-up table and combines the probability and impact rating so that a risk can be assigned an overall rating.
- **Stakeholder risk tolerances** describes the level of risk acceptable to the project stakeholders.
- **Reporting formats** describes how the risk register will be formatted and updated. It also notes how the results of the various risk management processes will be captured, analyzed and communicated.
- **Tracking** describes how the risk management team will go about documenting the various risk activities that are performed throughout the risk management processes.

The risk management plan becomes a component of the project management plan.

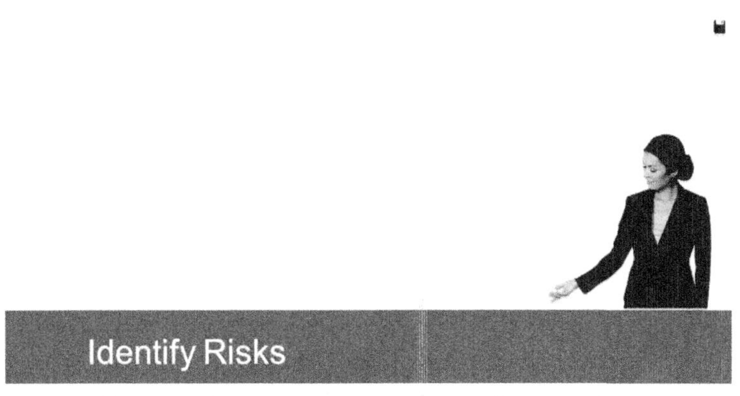

Identify Risks
Purpose: To determine which risks may affect the project and document their characteristics.

Identify Risks Process Overview

The Identify Risks process is an important part of risk management, and is where the risk register is created. This is where risks are first identified and documented. Identify Risks is an iterative process, meaning that it is repeated multiple times throughout the life of the project, since new risks are discovered as the project moves forward.

Typically, the completion of this process leads right into qualitative risk analysis. However, an experienced project or risk manager may move right into the process of quantitative risk analysis.

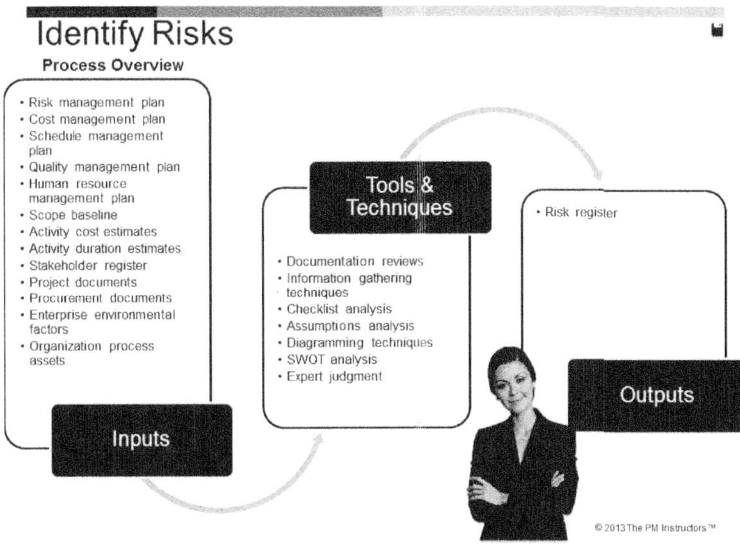

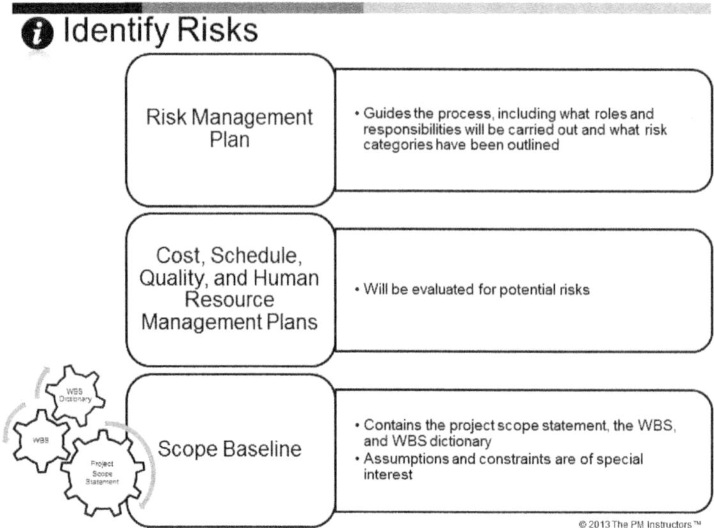

Identify Risks
Risk Management Plan
• Guides the process, including what roles and responsibilities will be carried out and what risk categories have been outlined
Cost, Schedule, Quality, and Human Resource Management Plans
• Will be evaluated for potential risks
Scope Baseline
• Contains the project scope statement, the WBS, and WBS dictionary
• Assumptions and constraints are of special interest
© 2013 The PM Instructors™

Identify Risks Inputs

The Identify Risks process has a total of thirteen inputs: *risk management plan, cost management plan, schedule management plan, quality management plan, human resource management plan, scope baseline, activity cost estimates, activity duration estimates, stakeholder register, project documents, procurement documents, enterprise environmental factors,* and *organizational process assets.*

Risk Management Plan

The risk management plan defines how the processes will be carried out and how risks are to be measured. The following items are utilized from within the plan:

- The assignment of roles and responsibilities
- What budget and schedule provisions have been made for risk management activities
- The categories of risk or RBS (if one was included)

Cost Management Plan

It is important to know the approach of the cost management plan, which may either increase or decrease potential risk. If, for example, the project is working on a very tight budget with little room for change or surprises, risks relating to cost overruns or insufficient funds will be greater. If reserves or provisions for risk have already been set aside, the level or risk of the items may decrease.

Schedule Management Plan

It is important to be familiar with a project's schedule management plan to know whether the schedule allows room for any surprises, or whether there is a greater risk of missing deadlines as a result of some activities.

Quality Management Plan

The quality management plan provides insight into risk identification. How quality is managed can either alleviate or increase risk. For example, if a project has a very refined and detailed plan for carrying out quality activities, the project's level of risk will decrease. However, if a project does not have the systems and methods in place to identify quality inefficiencies, or statistically measuring the accuracy of variances and so forth, the level of risk increases, since the chances of catching deficiencies within the product or service being created are not as probable.

Human Resource Management Plan

As with the other plans included as inputs, the human resource management plan is an important artifact to review as part of risk identification activities. Without a good plan in place for managing resources, risks can be introduced into the project.

Scope Baseline

The scope baseline consists of three documents: project scope statement, WBS, and WBS dictionary. Assumptions and constraints of the project are especially important to this process, which are obtained through the project scope statement. There is always uncertainty where assumptions are present.

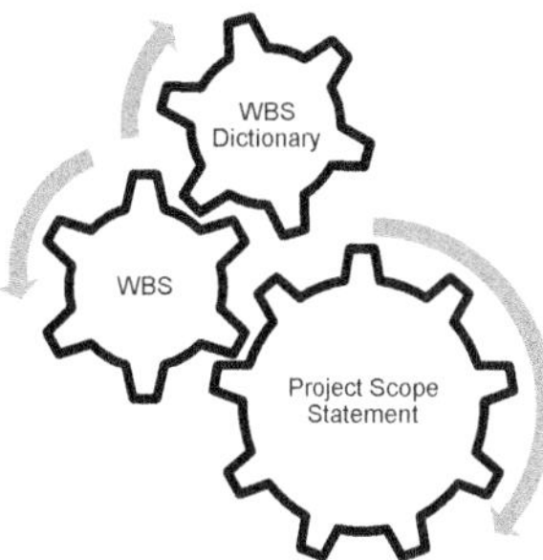

Constraints can also pose several risks, since options are limited.

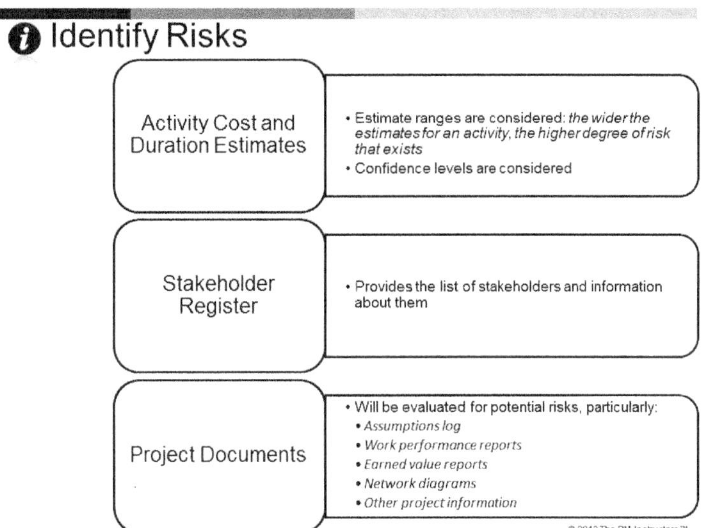

Activity Cost Estimates

Activity cost estimates provide a quantitative assessment of what activities will cost, represented as a range.

Activity Duration Estimates

Activity duration estimates provide an assessment of the estimated duration of activities, also represented as a range.

Stakeholder Register

The stakeholder register provides a list of project stakeholders. This list is important, since it provides an indication of who must be included in risk identification activities.

Project Documents

Project documents utilized for risk identification purposes typically include:

- Assumptions log

- Work performance reports
- Earned value reports
- Network diagrams
- Other project information

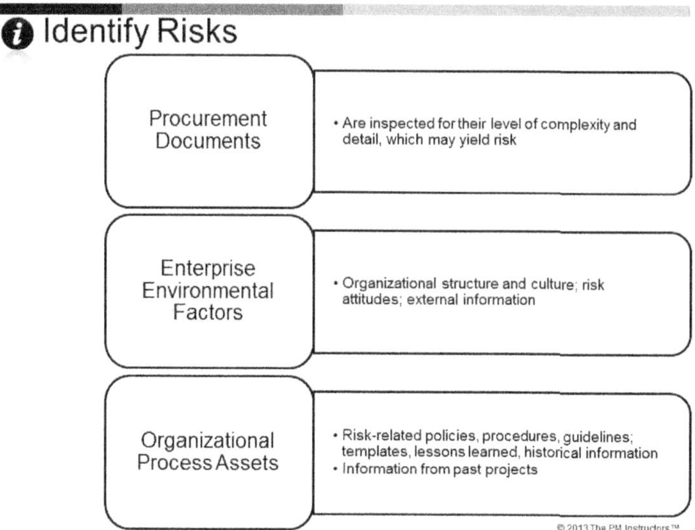
Identify Risks
Procurement Documents
• Are inspected for their level of complexity and detail, which may yield risk
Enterprise Environmental Factors
• Organizational structure and culture; risk attitudes; external information
Organizational Process Assets
• Risk-related policies, procedures, guidelines; templates, lessons learned, historical information
• Information from past projects
© 2013 The PM Instructors™

Procurement Documents

Procurement documents are inspected for their level of complexity and level of detail included. This inspection can yield new risks, as a result of these documents.

Enterprise Environmental Factors:

Enterprise environmental factors utilized can include published information, such as commercial databases, and public and industry studies. These policies and the information provided can reveal risks.

Organizational Process Assets

Organizational process assets provide information and experience from past projects, such as:

- Existing project files, including actual data from previous projects, particularly those projects that were similar to the one currently being managed. Studying what the risks were in previous projects and also what the actual outcome and responses to those risks were at the end of the project provides major insight into the risks within the current project
- Any project process controls that the company already has in place
- Risk templates
- Lessons learned

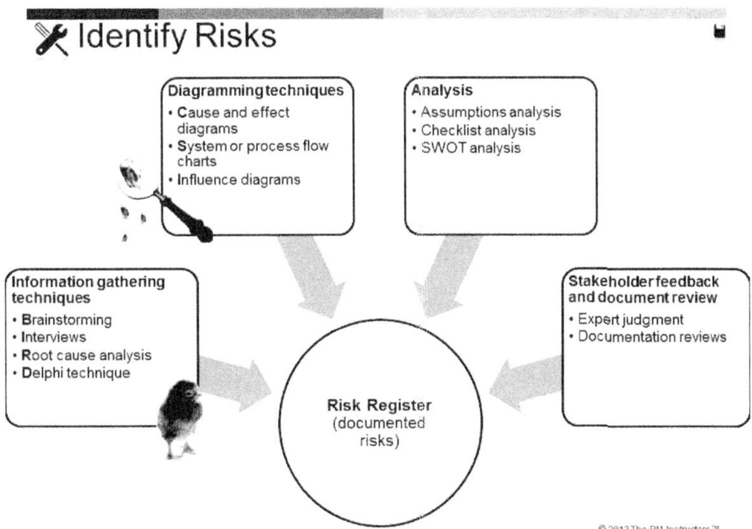

Identify Risks Tools and Techniques

The Identify Risks process contains seven tools and techniques: *documentation reviews, information gathering techniques, checklist analysis, assumptions analysis, diagramming techniques, SWOT analysis,* and *expert judgment.*

Two of the tools and techniques used by this process contain multiple techniques within them (information gathering techniques and diagramming techniques). These tools and techniques take the inputs of the process, and convert the information into information that can be used to identify risks.

Participants of risk identification include a wide array of individuals. The following is an example of who typically participates in this process:

- Project manager
- Project team
- Risk management team (if applicable)
- The customers
- Stakeholders
- End users
- Subject matter experts who are not a part of the project team
- Risk management experts
- Other project managers

To help remember the list of tools and techniques, along with the sub-list items, they can be grouped as indicated within the image shown above (note acronyms for the two sub-lists).

Documentation Reviews: Reviews project plans, documents, and other information to determine:

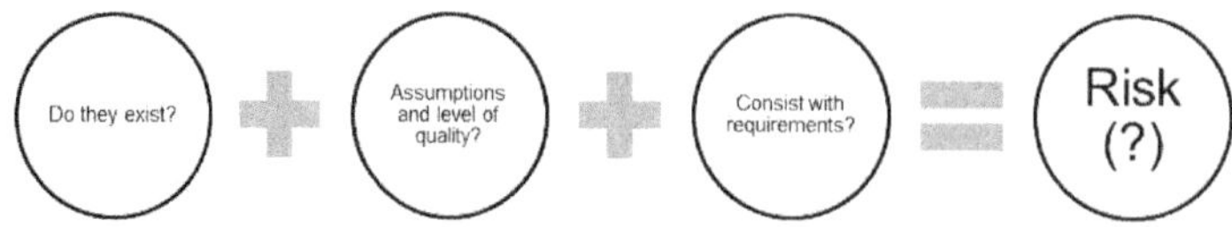

Checklist Analysis: Creation of risk checklists. May utilize:

- Historical information from previous projects
- RBS

Documentation Reviews

Documentation reviews look at the project plans and documents, and perform a structured review to determine the following:

- Do the plans exist, and if so, are they consistent with the project requirements?
- What are the assumptions made within the plans and documents?
- Do the plans and documents cover everything that they should?

The answers to these types of questions can be indicators of risk. For example, plans not consistent with the project requirements reveal risks.

Most projects fail due to lack of planning; therefore, it is viable to say that projects fail for lack of risk management, since risk management identifies where lack of planning exists and flags it for investigation and for a response.

Checklist Analysis

Checklist analysis involves the creation of risk checklists, which can be simple, short lists, or lengthy comprehensive lists. These checklists help to make sure that all items within the project have been considered for risks. Checklists can be created using:

- Historical information from previous projects, such as actual checklists previously used, or information and knowledge that can assist in the creation of new (or refined) checklists.
- The risk breakdown structure (RBS) is a good source for checklist analysis. In this case, the lowest level of the RBS can be used as a checklist.

Identify Risks

Information Gathering Techniques:

Brainstorming	Interviewing	Root Cause Analysis	Delphi Technique
• Group session that gets together to generate ideas and develop a comprehensive list of project risks. • Large group setting • Nominal group technique • Use RBS	• Primary source of risk identification data gathering • Includes SMEs, stakeholders, experienced project participants	• Steps to root cause identification include: • 1) Identify issue or potential issue; • 2) Determine underlying causes; • 3) Develop preventive actions	• Experts participate *anonymously* by completing a questionnaire on important risks; facilitator collects and summarizes responses, then redistributes. • This reduces bias in the data

Information Gathering Techniques

Information gathering techniques contains a group of techniques under one umbrella. When placed in a specific order (brainstorming, interviewing, root cause analysis, Delphi technique), it creates the following acronym: B.I.R.D.

Brainstorming

Brainstorming involves a large group getting together to develop a comprehensive list of project risks. The purpose is to get several relevant individuals together to generate ideas about risk. Typically, brainstorming sessions are led by a facilitator, and participants include the project team and a multidisciplinary set of experts not part of the project team.

There are two general methods of holding brainstorming sessions:

1. A large group setting where all of the participants come together at the same time in a free-flowing environment.
2. Using the nominal group technique. This is where many small sessions are held at different times, and the results are then reviewed and discussed in a larger meeting.

Risk categories and risk breakdown structures can provide a good framework for identifying risks within brainstorming sessions. Remember that the RBS shows the risk categories used and breaks them down into subcategories. As risks are identified, they are categorized by type.

Interviewing

Interviewing typically includes interviews with subject matter experts, stakeholders, and experienced project participants who assist in identifying risks. Interviews are one of the primary sources of risk identification data gathering.

Root Cause Analysis

Root cause analysis involves identifying causes, determining what the underlying cause or causes are that are creating it, and then developing preventive action to resolve it. This technique attempts to get to the real problem by asking "why": *why does this risk exist?*

Delphi Technique

The Delphi technique has a unique way of utilizing expert ideas and feedback. One of the most important characteristics about this method to know is that experts participate anonymously. A facilitator sends the group of participating experts a questionnaire to obtain their ideas on project risks. The responses are collected and then summarized by the facilitator and then redistributed to the experts for further feedback. This process occurs multiple times until consensus is reached, which may occur within just a few rounds.

Another important characteristic to know about the Delphi technique is that it helps reduce bias in the data and it also prevents one or more experts from having influence over the opinion or feedback of the others – this is why it is conducted anonymously. Experts that participate are specifically risk experts.

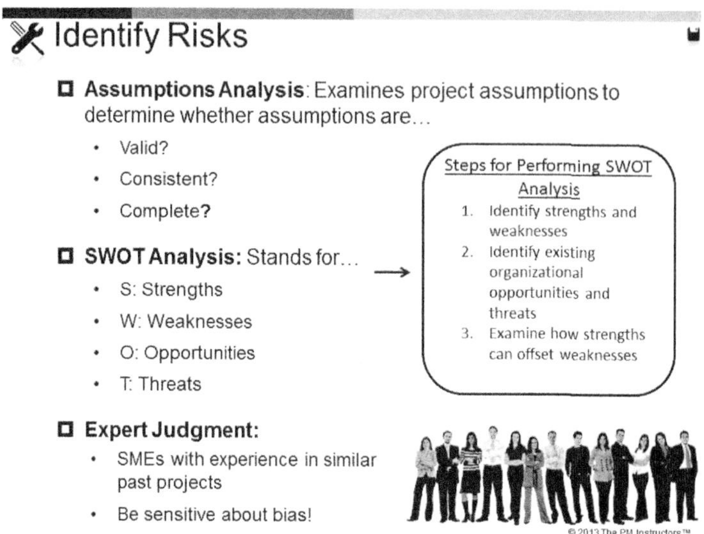

Assumptions Analysis

Assumptions analysis involves examining the project assumptions. This technique looks at whether the assumptions are valid. Risks can be identified by determining whether the assumptions are inaccurate, inconsistent, or incomplete. Assumptions can be obtained from the project scope statement, which is an input of the process.

SWOT Analysis

SWOT stands for strengths, weaknesses, opportunities, and threats. Steps to conducting SWOT analysis are as follow:

1. Identify strengths and weaknesses
2. Identify existing opportunities and threats resulting from organization's strengths and weaknesses
3. Examine how strengths can offset weaknesses

Expert Judgment

Expert judgment is used throughout the process in various ways. This may entail risk experts, project team members, or others that have experience in similar past projects. The project manager should be sensitive to experts' bias as risks are identified and evaluated.

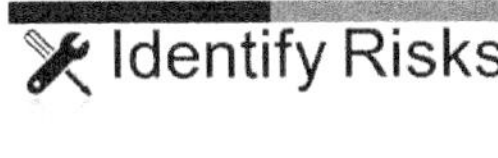

Identify Risks

- **Diagramming Techniques:**
  - **C**ause and Effect Diagrams
  - **S**ystem or Process Flowcharts
  - **I**nfluence Diagrams

Diagramming Techniques

Diagramming techniques used within risk identification activities typically include the following:

- Cause and effect diagrams
- System or process flow charts
- Influence diagrams

Identify Risks

Diagramming Techniques

- **Cause and Effect Diagrams:** Useful in identifying the potential causes of risks
  - Show how various factors may be connected to potential problems or effects

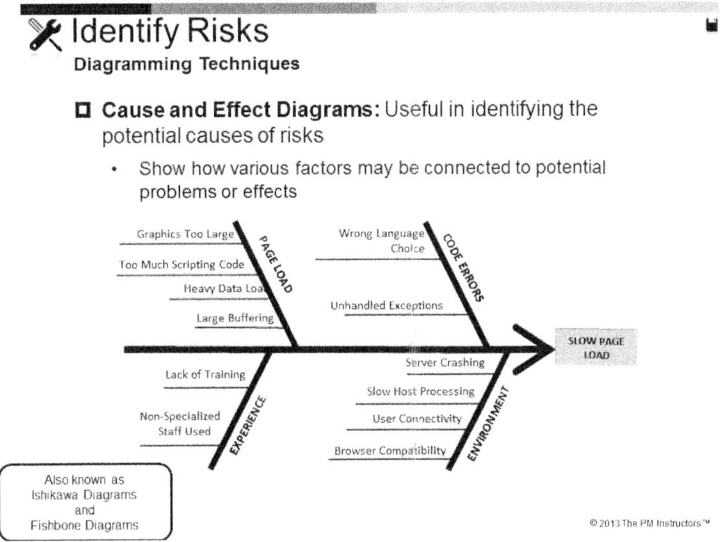

Cause and Effect Diagrams

Cause and effect diagrams are useful in identifying the potential causes of risks. If you can identify the causes, then you can identify additional risks, as well as develop a better and more efficient response. Cause and effect diagrams take a different approach to determining the causes than root cause analysis. Cause and effect diagrams are a technique used in quality management.

They are also known as Ishikawa Diagrams and Fishbone Diagrams. Any one of these three names may appear on the exam.

Cause and effect diagrams show how various factors may be connected to potential problems or effects. In other words, it helps to determine all the possible causes, or reasons, for a single effect.

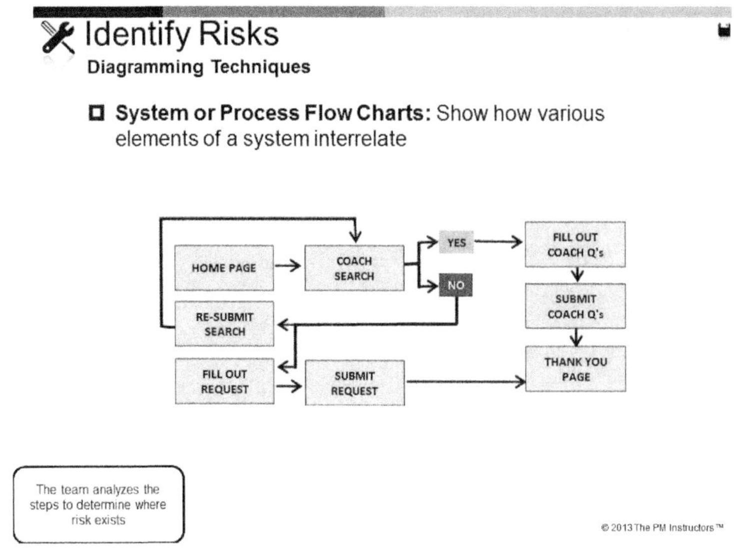

System or Process Flowcharts

The purpose of flow charts is to show how the various elements of a system interrelate, thereby showing how a problem occurs. In other words, these diagrams help determine the cause of an issue, and how you arrive at that cause within a system.

A flowchart shows the process in a graphical format from beginning to end, including the activities, decision points, the order of processing, and how the system elements interrelate. The risk management team takes a flowchart and analyzes the steps to determine where risks may occur, and based on this, the root cause of the risk. This information is extremely useful for determining potential responses. Risk identification also includes documenting potential responses to risk that become evident by utilizing these tools and techniques.

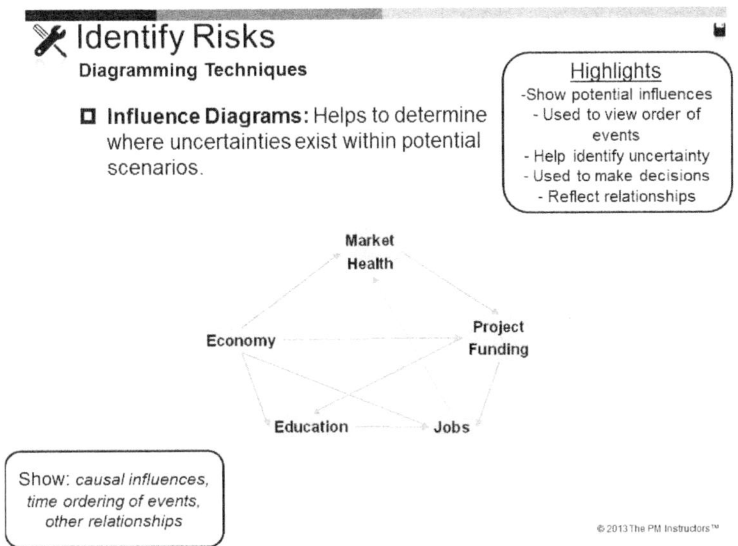

Influence Diagrams

Influence diagrams show the following:

- Causal influences
- Time ordering of events
- Other relationships among variables and outcomes

Within existing project decisions, the project or risk management team can determine where uncertainties exist within potential scenarios. Influence diagrams are a great way of looking at situations and determining how a destination can be arrived at, similar to a decision tree.

Influence diagrams reflect uncertainty within potential paths. As the risk management team moves through the diagram, they can see the elements that influence one another. Within influence diagrams, decisions and uncertainties can be visually distinguished from one another to better highlight the various factors within the diagram more clearly.

Highlights about influence diagrams:

- They are diagrams that show potential influences that elements or situations can have on others
- They can be used to view the order of potential events
- They help to spot uncertainty, and therefore potential risk
- They are used to make decisions
- They reflect relationships among the variables and the outcomes

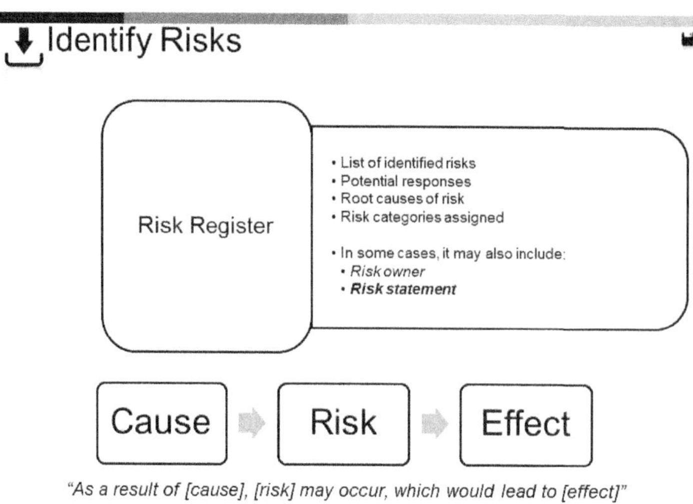

Identify Risks
Risk Register
• List of identified risks
• Potential responses
• Root causes of risk
• Risk categories assigned
• In some cases, it may also include:
• Risk owner
• Risk statement
Cause
Risk
Effect
"As a result of [cause], [risk] may occur, which would lead to [effect]"
© 2013 The PM Instructors™

Identify Risks Outputs

The Identify Risks process contains one output: *risk register.*

Risk Register

As a result of carrying out the Identify Risks process, the risk register is created as the single output. When it is first created, the risk register typically contains the following within it:

- List of all the identified risks.
- Potential responses. The potential responses, if identified, will be used within the Plan Risk Responses process. It isn't until that process that responses become official.
- Root causes of risk, for those risks where they were identified.
- Risk categories assigned, if identified.

It is also possible that a risk owner be assigned at this point as well, although this is not a requirement. In addition to this, the risk management team may document a risk statement within the risk register. The following is an example of a **risk statement**:

"As a result of [cause], [risk] may occur, which would lead to [effect]"

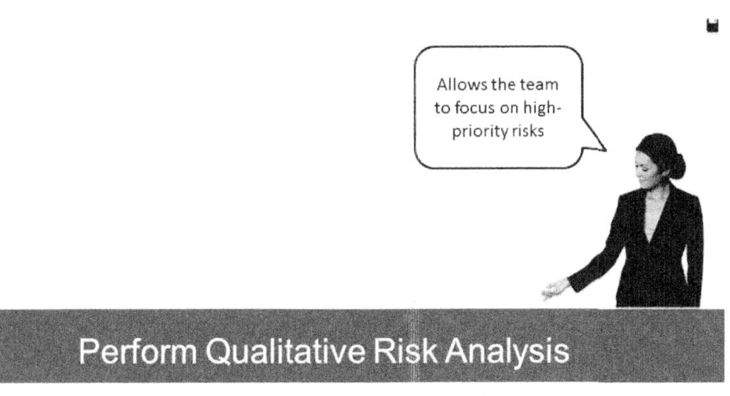
Allows the team to focus on high-priority risks
Perform Qualitative Risk Analysis
Purpose: To prioritize risks for further analysis or action by assessing and combining their probability of occurrence and impact.

Perform Qualitative Risk Analysis Process Overview

Perform Qualitative Risk Analysis is the third process within the Project Risk Management Knowledge Area. The purpose of the process is to prioritize risks for further analysis or action by assessing and combining their probability of occurrence and impact. This is the first step in analyzing the identified project risks and determining which risks require further analysis and action. Qualitative risk analysis allows the risk management team to focus on high-priority risks by assessing which risks have a higher probability of occurring and a higher impact to the project objectives, should the risk occur.

There are several updates made to the risk register as a result of this process, with the largest being the list of prioritized risks.

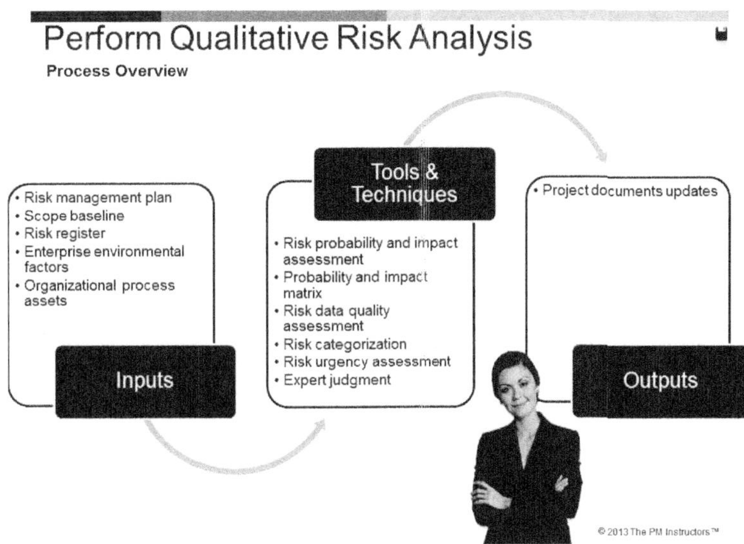
Perform Qualitative Risk Analysis
Process Overview
• Risk management plan
• Scope baseline
• Risk register
• Enterprise environmental factors
• Organizational process assets
Inputs
Tools & Techniques
• Risk probability and impact assessment
• Probability and impact matrix
• Risk data quality assessment
• Risk categorization
• Risk urgency assessment
• Expert judgment
• Project documents updates
Outputs
© 2013 The PM Instructors™

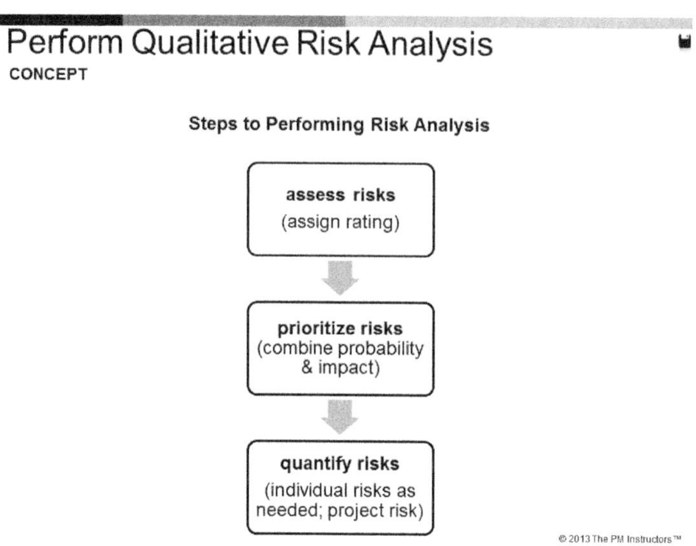

Steps to Performing Risk Analysis

When performing risk analysis, there are several steps involved.

1. First, risks must be assessed. This is done by assigning a probability rating and an impact rating, based on the documented definitions included within the risk management plan.
2. Next, the probability and impact rating should be combined into an overall score. This is commonly done using a probability and impact matrix.
3. And the third step involves quantifying risks. Overall project risks can be derived by using several quantitative risk analysis tools, such as Monte Carlo Technique and Sensitivity Analysis.

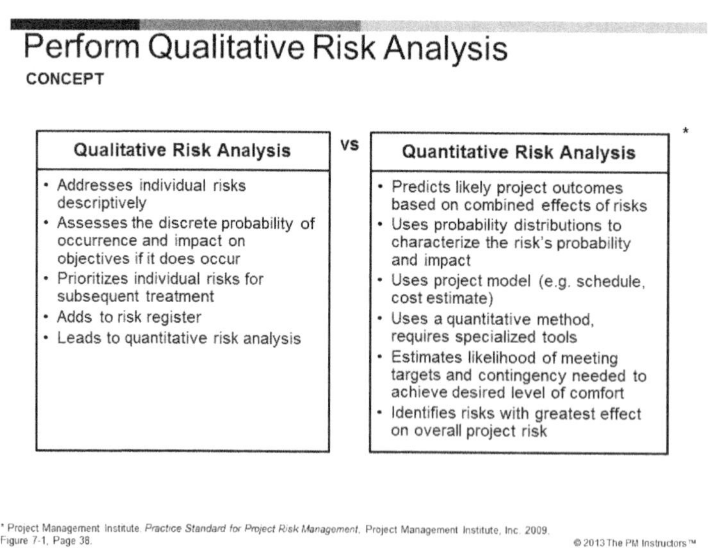

Qualitative vs. Quantitative Risk Analysis

Qualitative and quantitative risk analysis both offer valuable information. It is recommended that risks be evaluated on a qualitative level first, and then quantitative as needed. Qualitative risk analysis is considered to be a quick and cost effective form of risk analysis, whereas quantitative risk analysis requires additional expertise and tools. Another key difference between qualitative and quantitative risk analysis is that qualitative risk analysis focuses more on individual risks, and quantitative risk analysis focuses more on project risk.

The table on the screen reflects the differences highlighted within the Practice Standard for Project Risk Management. Take a moment to pause the course, and read the two tables, and consider the differences. It is not necessary for you to memorize the contents of this table, but to understand the differences.

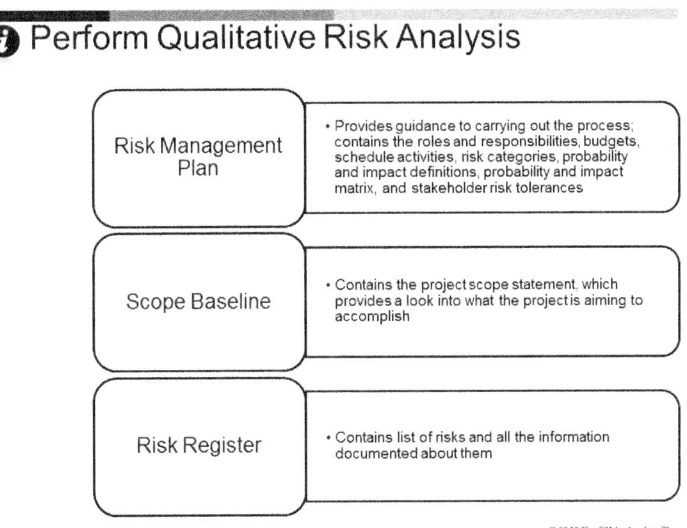
Perform Qualitative Risk Analysis
Risk Management Plan
• Provides guidance to carrying out the process; contains the roles and responsibilities, budgets, schedule activities, risk categories, probability and impact definitions, probability and impact matrix, and stakeholder risk tolerances
Scope Baseline
• Contains the project scope statement, which provides a look into what the project is aiming to accomplish
Risk Register
• Contains list of risks and all the information documented about them
© 2013 The PM Instructors™

Perform Qualitative Risk Analysis Inputs

The Perform Qualitative Risk Analysis process consists of five inputs: *risk management plan, scope baseline, risk register, enterprise environmental factors,* and *organizational process assets.*

Risk Management Plan

The risk management plan is essential to carrying out the risk management processes. Elements of the risk management plan utilized within this process include:

- Roles and responsibilities
- Budgets
- Schedule activities
- Risk categories
- Definition of probability and impact
- Probability and impact matrix
- Revised stakeholders' risk tolerances

Those elements mentioned above that were not defined or refined in the risk management plan are developed during qualitative risk analysis.

Scope Baseline

The scope baseline contains the project scope statement, which provides insight as to whether the project is aiming at accomplishing something new, as opposed to a similar project performed in the past. A project that aims at creating a product or service that is state-of-the-art (such as new technology) is likely to have larger risks; a project that has been conducted similarly in the past is likely to have risks that are better understood.

Risk Register

The risk register provides the list of identified risks that were documented during the Identify Risks process.

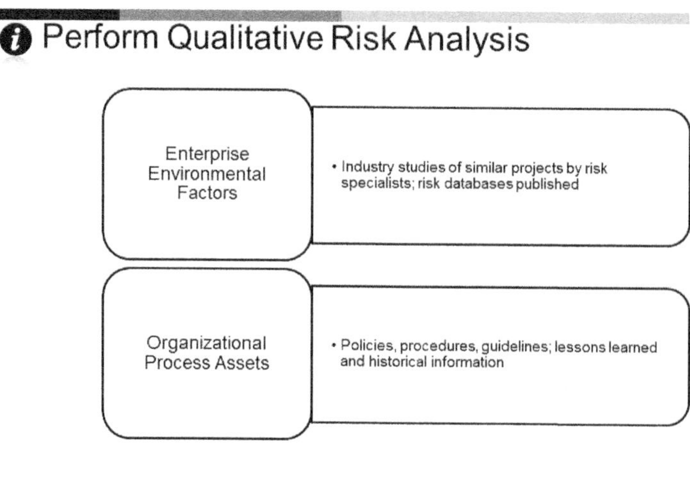
Perform Qualitative Risk Analysis
Enterprise Environmental Factors
• Industry studies of similar projects by risk specialists; risk databases published
Organizational Process Assets
• Policies, procedures, guidelines; lessons learned and historical information
© 2013 The PM Instructors™

Enterprise Environmental Factors

The enterprise environmental factors used as part of this process typically include the industry studies of similar projects by risk specialists, and risk databases that are published by industry or proprietary sources.

Organizational Process Assets

Organizational process assets provide information from the lessons learned knowledge base, as well as information and data from past projects. Similar risks may have already been analyzed from past projects, and knowing the outcome of these risks and how the risk management team responded is extremely valuable.

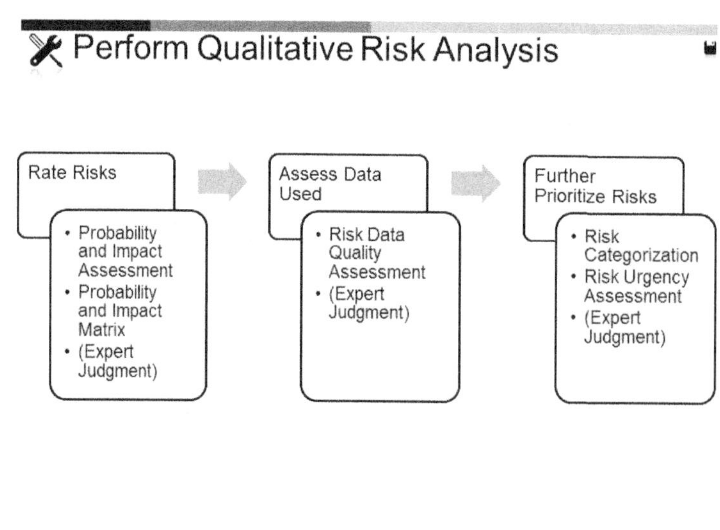
Perform Qualitative Risk Analysis
Rate Risks
• Probability and Impact Assessment
• Probability and Impact Matrix
• (Expert Judgment)
Assess Data Used
• Risk Data Quality Assessment
• (Expert Judgment)
Further Prioritize Risks
• Risk Categorization
• Risk Urgency Assessment
• (Expert Judgment)
© 2013 The PM Instructors™

Perform Qualitative Risk Analysis Tools and Techniques

The Perform Qualitative Risk Analysis process utilizes six tools and techniques: *risk probability and impact assessment, probability and impact matrix, risk data quality assessment, risk categorization, risk urgency assessment,* and *expert judgment.*

The image shown above breaks the tools and technique into categories, which are further organized as steps.

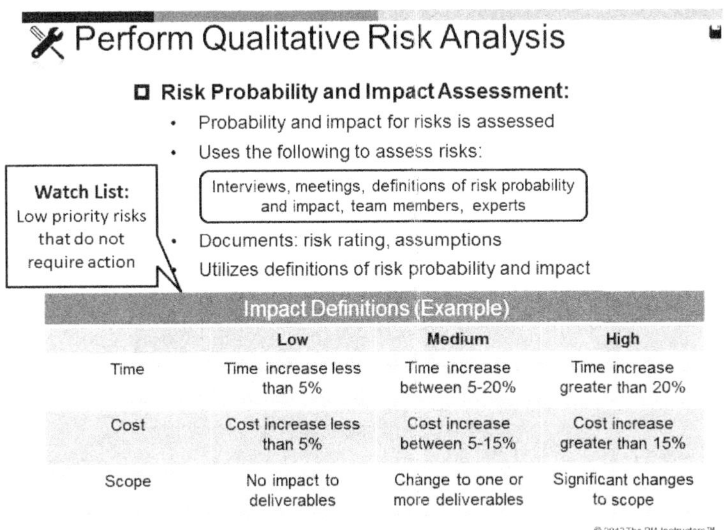
Perform Qualitative Risk Analysis
Risk Probability and Impact Assessment:
Probability and impact for risks is assessed
Uses the following to assess risks:
Interviews, meetings, definitions of risk probability and impact, team members, experts
Documents: risk rating, assumptions
Utilizes definitions of risk probability and impact
Watch List:
Low priority risks that do not require action
Impact Definitions (Example)
© 2013 The PM Instructors™

	Low	Medium	High
Time	Time increase less than 5%	Time increase between 5-20%	Time increase greater than 20%
Cost	Cost increase less than 5%	Cost increase between 5-15%	Cost increase greater than 15%
Scope	No impact to deliverables	Change to one or more deliverables	Significant changes to scope

Risk Probability and Impact Assessment

The image shown above provides a basic example of an impact definitions table. This information provides guidelines that will be used for rating risk, which will help in ranking and prioritizing risks during the Perform Qualitative Risk Analysis process. There are various ways of documenting risk probability and impact. Some companies choose a high-medium-low approach, while others use a numeric scale. In the example provided, risks are defined as low, medium, or high.

Probability and impact for each positive and negative risk is assessed with the purpose of identifying the likelihood that each specific risk will occur and the potential effects on project objectives (such as time, cost, scope or quality).

To assess the probability and impact of each risk, the risk management team utilizes the following:

- Interviews or meetings (led by a facilitator)
- Definitions of risk probability and impact developed and documented within the risk management plan
- Participation from project team members
- Participation from experts outside of the project

The probability and impact ratings of risks resulting from interviews and/or meetings are documented. These results typically entail the following:

- Risk rating (probability and impact)
- Assumptions justifying the levels assigned

A **watch list** of low priority risks will watch list include those risks that have low ratings of probability and impact and therefore do not require action. These risks are put aside within the risk register, so that the team may monitor them for any changes.

Perform Qualitative Risk Analysis

Risk Probability and Impact Matrix:

- Included in the risk management plan
- Used to prioritize risks based on the risk assessment
- Look up table
- Combination of probability and impact yields a risk score

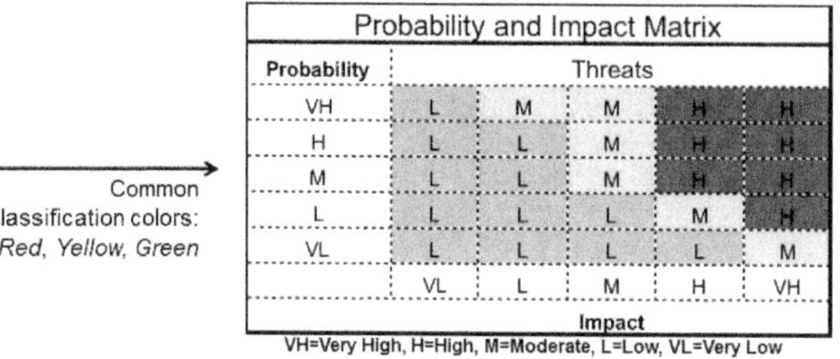
Common classification colors:
Red, Yellow, Green

Probability and Impact Matrix

Probability	Threats				
VH	L	M	M	H	H
H	L	L	M	H	H
M	L	L	M	H	H
L	L	L	L	M	H
VL	L	L	L	L	M
	VL	L	M	H	VH
	Impact				

VH=Very High, H=High, M=Moderate, L=Low, VL=Very Low

Risk Probability and Impact Matrix

The image shown above is an example of a probability and impact matrix, which combines the impact rating and probability rating to generate an overall risk rating. This combined risk rating will then allow the team to better prioritize the risks.

The risk probability and impact matrix is developed and documented as part of the risk management plan. If this step was omitted, and a risk probability and impact matrix does not exist, then it is developed as part of the Perform Qualitative Risk Analysis process. The matrix leads to a risk rating of low, moderate, or high priority, or a numeric value, depending on the practices or preferences of the organization.

The risk probability and impact matrix serves as a look up table using the risk ratings. This leads to a risk score previously mentioned (low, moderate, high; or numeric value). Within the matrix, a further color-coded classification exists. Common colors used are:

- Red condition: high risk
- Yellow condition: moderate risk
- Green condition: low risk

The risk rating guidelines of the organization are commonly included within the organizational process assets, and then tailored during the creation of the risk management plan, as previously mentioned.

Note: An organization may rate risks individually or separately by project objective. Positive and negative risks may utilize a different matrix.

Risk Data Quality Assessment

Part of accurately assessing risk is to measure the confidence and accuracy of the data used in risk management and risk analysis. Risk data quality assessment holds a similar purpose as assumptions analysis covered within the Identify Risks process. Risk data quality assessment checks to make sure that the data is accurate and unbiased. Specifically, it evaluates the data for the following:

- Accuracy
- Reliability
- Integrity
- Quality

Information and data used in risk analysis that is found to be lacking in the items mentioned above results in analysis that is useless to risk management. When this occurs, new or better data will need to be collected.

Risk Categorization

Risk categorization involves grouping risks by source or area of the project affected by the risks. This can be achieved by using the risk breakdown structure and the work breakdown structure. The purpose of this technique is to uncover the areas of the project that are impacted the most by risk. This type of information is valuable in developing more effective risk responses.

Perform Qualitative Risk Analysis

- **Risk Urgency Assessment:** Determines the level of urgency in addressing risks

"near term" risks

- Examine:
  - Time to execute a risk response
  - Symptoms and warning signs
  - Risk rating

- **Expert Judgment:** Required to assess risks
  - Experts have experience with previous similar projects or tasks, and evaluate risks during workshops or interviews
  - Consider:
    - Bias
    - Experience
    - Feedback and input

Risk Urgency Assessment

Prioritizing risks is important to risk response, since effort is better spent on those risks that have a higher impact and probability of occurring. The theory behind risk urgency assessment is similar to the saying, "the squeaky wheel gets the grease". Identifying those risks that have a higher urgency allows the risk management team to focus on those risks first. These risks are referred to as risks that require a "near-term" response.

The following should be examined to determine where risks require a near-term response:

- Time to execute a risk response
- Symptoms and warning signs
- Risk rating

Expert Judgment

Expert judgment plays an important role in the Perform Qualitative Risk Analysis process. Experts typically assess risks during workshops or interviews that are facilitated by a risk expert. Notes to keep in mind:

- Bias of experts should be considered
- Experts should have experience with similar projects or activities
- Expert feedback and input is required in assessing risks

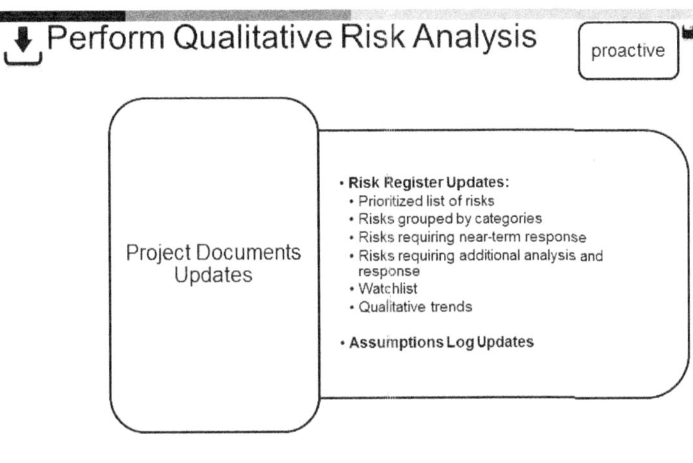
Perform Qualitative Risk Analysis
proactive
Project Documents Updates
• Risk Register Updates:
• Prioritized list of risks
• Risks grouped by categories
• Risks requiring near-term response
• Risks requiring additional analysis and response
• Watchlist
• Qualitative trends
• Assumptions Log Updates
© 2013 The PM Instructors™

Perform Qualitative Risk Analysis Outputs

The Perform Qualitative Risk Analysis process has a single output: *project documents updates*.

Project Documents Updates

The project documents updated primarily consist of the risk register, but also include the assumptions log. The risk register is updated with the results of carrying out the Perform Qualitative Risk Analysis process. The results typically include the following elements:

- Prioritized list of risks, or relative ranking of risks, including a description of how the risks were assessed. This can include one large list or a list by project objective. This is used to classify risks by their significance, allowing the risk manager to focus on high priority risks
- Risks grouped by category, revealing the root causes of risk. This allows for a more effective risk response plan
- Near-term response risks
- Risks requiring additional response and analysis
- Watch list
- Qualitative risk analysis trends. Risk management is a very proactive practice within project management. The documenting of trends within risk analysis is a part of this proactive measure. Noting trends within the results of qualitative risk analysis is documented as part of risk register updates. This involves noting those trends that emerge as the process is repeated. Qualitative risk analysis trends help to understand whether risk response or further analysis of a risk is required.

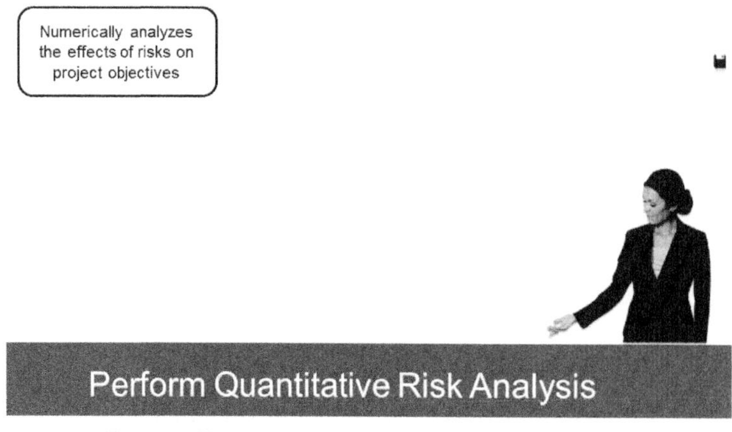
Numerically analyzes the effects of risks on project objectives
Perform Quantitative Risk Analysis
Purpose: To numerically analyze the effect of identified risks on overall project objectives.

Perform Quantitative Risk Analysis Process Overview

The purpose of the Perform Quantitative Risk Analysis is to numerically analyze the effect of identified risks on overall project objectives. This process assigns a numerical rating to risks prioritized by the Qualitative Risk Analysis process. This allows the risk management team to numerically analyze the effects that identified risks have on project objectives. The process then becomes an aid to making decisions using a quantitative approach.

Carrying out the Perform Quantitative Risk Analysis process results in several updates to the risk register, with a prioritized list of quantified risks among them.

Quantified risk analysis is typically carried out after qualitative risk analysis. An experienced risk manager may conduct quantitative risk analysis directly after identifying risks. The Quantified Risk Analysis process is not always necessary to conduct risk response planning, and is dependent on the project needs, time and budget.

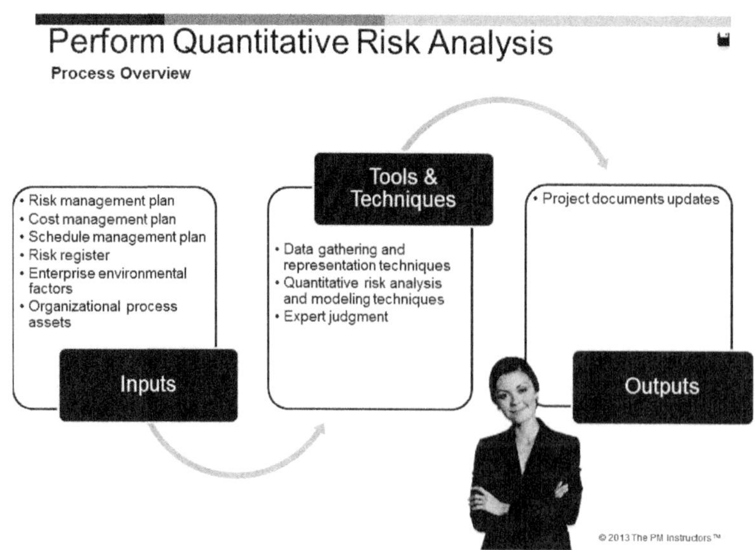
Perform Quantitative Risk Analysis
Process Overview
• Risk management plan
• Cost management plan
• Schedule management plan
• Risk register
• Enterprise environmental factors
• Organizational process assets
Inputs
Tools & Techniques
• Data gathering and representation techniques
• Quantitative risk analysis and modeling techniques
• Expert judgment
• Project documents updates
Outputs
© 2013 The PM Instructors™

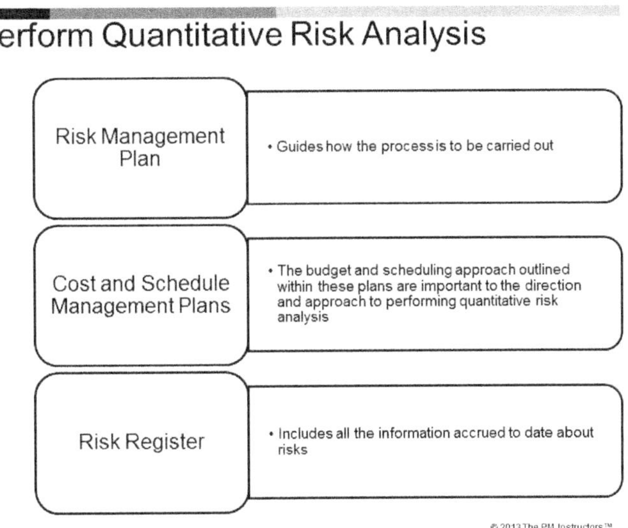

Perform Quantitative Risk Analysis
Risk Management Plan
• Guides how the process is to be carried out
Cost and Schedule Management Plans
• The budget and scheduling approach outlined within these plans are important to the direction and approach to performing quantitative risk analysis
Risk Register
• Includes all the information accrued to date about risks
© 2013 The PM Instructors™

Perform Quantitative Risk Analysis Inputs

The Perform Quantitative Risk Analysis process has a total of six inputs: *risk management plan, cost management plan, schedule management plan, risk register, enterprise environmental factors,* and *organizational process assets.*

Risk Management Plan

The risk management plan contains the roles and responsibilities, budgets, schedule, risk categories, RBS, and revised stakeholders' risk tolerances, all used by this process.

Cost Management Plan

The cost management plan provides the necessary information to establish the criteria for controlling the project costs.

Schedule Management Plan

The schedule management plan provides the information necessary to develop and control the project schedule.

Risk Register

The risk register contains the list of identified and prioritized risks, and risks grouped by categories.

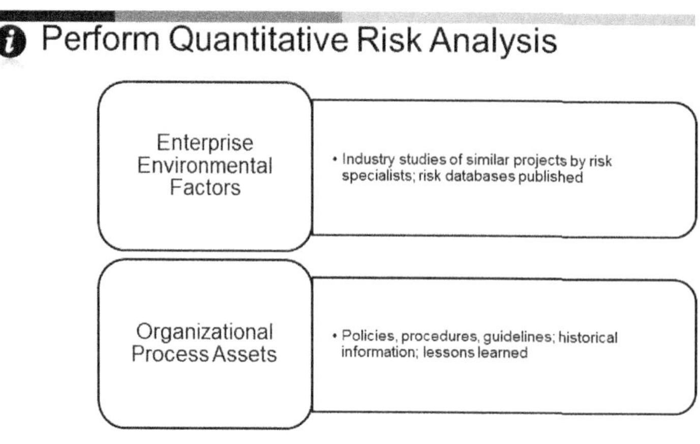
Perform Quantitative Risk Analysis
Enterprise Environmental Factors
• Industry studies of similar projects by risk specialists; risk databases published
Organizational Process Assets
• Policies, procedures, guidelines; historical information; lessons learned
© 2013 The PM Instructors™

Enterprise Environmental Factors

Enterprise environmental factors used as part of performing quantitative risk analysis are similar to those used in performing qualitative risk analysis:

- Industry studies of similar projects by risk specialists
- Risk databases published by industry or proprietary sources

Organizational Process Assets

Organizational process assets are also used, which contain risk databases, information from previous similar projects, and studies conducted of similar projects by internal risk specialists.

Perform Quantitative Risk Analysis

- **Data gathering and representation techniques:**
  - Interviewing
  - Probability distributions
- **Quantitative risk analysis and modeling techniques:**
  - Sensitivity analysis
  - Expected monetary value analysis
  - Modeling and simulation
- **Expert judgment**
  - Validates the tools and techniques used in this process

Perform Quantitative Risk Analysis Tools and Techniques

The Perform Quantitative Risk Analysis process contains three tools and techniques: *data gathering and representation techniques, quantitative risk analysis and modeling techniques,* and *expert judgment.* Aside from expert judgment, these techniques have been grouped into two primary techniques:

Data gathering and representation techniques, containing:

- Interviewing
- Probability distributions

Quantitative risk analysis and modeling techniques, containing:

- Sensitivity analysis
- Expected monetary value analysis (includes Decision Tree analysis)
- Modeling and simulation (utilizes the Monte Carlo technique)

Expert judgment validates the tools and techniques used in this process. It is also necessary for identifying potential cost and schedule impacts.

The image below groups the sub-list items to better clarify the steps involved in quantifying risks:

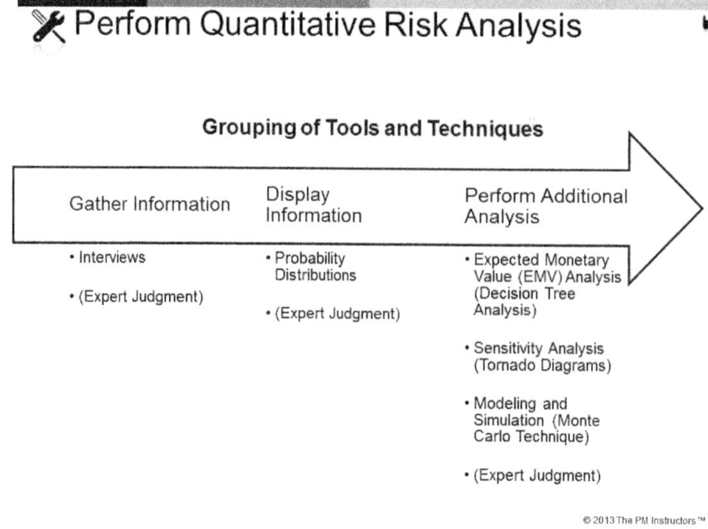
Perform Quantitative Risk Analysis
Grouping of Tools and Techniques
Gather Information
Display Information
Perform Additional Analysis
• Interviews
• (Expert Judgment)
• Probability Distributions
• (Expert Judgment)
• Expected Monetary Value (EMV) Analysis (Decision Tree Analysis)
• Sensitivity Analysis (Tornado Diagrams)
• Modeling and Simulation (Monte Carlo Technique)
• (Expert Judgment)
© 2013 The PM Instructors™

Perform Quantitative Risk Analysis
Data Gathering and Representation Techniques

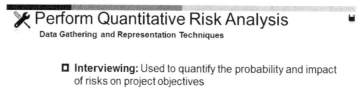

- **Interviewing:** Used to quantify the probability and impact of risks on project objectives
  - Gathers 3-Point Estimates: *Pessimistic (P) estimate, Most Likely (ML) estimate, Optimistic (O) estimate*
  - Utilizes the following formulas:

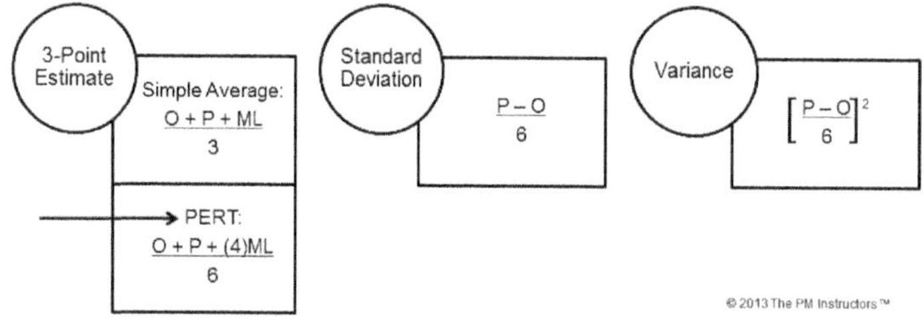
3-Point Estimate
Simple Average: O + P + ML / 3
PERT: O + P + (4)ML / 6
Standard Deviation
P – O / 6
Variance
[P – O / 6]²
© 2013 The PM Instructors™

Interviewing

Interviewing is used to quantify the probability and impact that risks have on the project objectives, and is based on the type of probability distributions used to reflect the expert's uncertainty. The information gathered during risk interviews consist of optimistic estimates, most likely estimates, and pessimistic estimates for scenarios, which are needed to calculate a 3-point estimate and also the mean and standard deviation. The three-point estimates can also be used to calculate a weighted average using the program evaluation and review technique (PERT). PERT assigns a higher weight to the most likely estimate, thereby resulting in a more accurate estimate.

The formula for calculating PERT is shown above, as is the formula for calculating the standard deviation. Variance may also be calculated by squaring standard deviation.

The basis for the risk ranges gathered during risk interviews is documented to provide the credibility of the analysis.

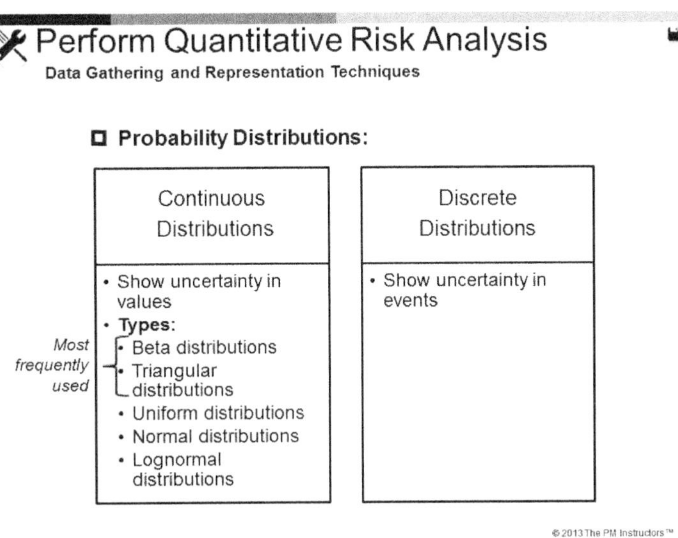

Probability Distributions

For the exam, you'll need to be familiar with two types of probability distributions: continuous and discrete distributions. Continuous distributions show uncertainty in values, while discrete distributions show uncertainty in events. Types of continuous distributions you should be familiar with include beta, triangular, uniform, normal, and lognormal.

According to the *PMBOK® Guide*, Beta distributions, along with triangular, are considered to be the most frequently used in quantitative risk analysis.

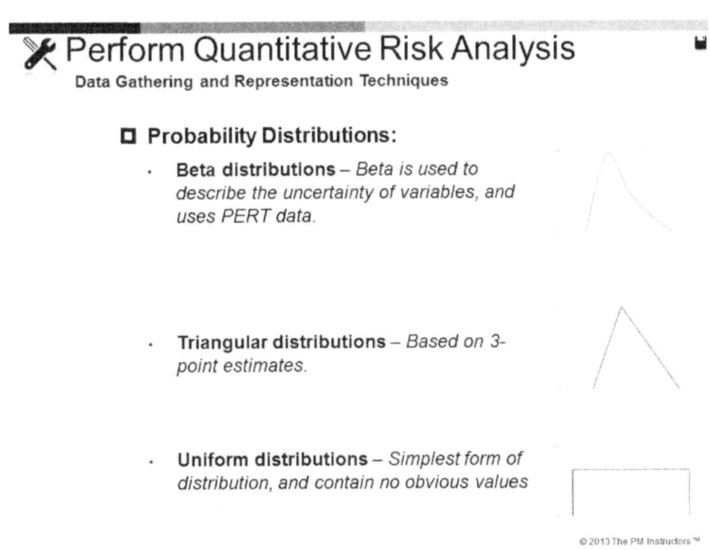

Beta Distributions (continuous distribution)

According to the *PMBOK® Guide*, Beta distributions, along with triangular, are considered to be the most frequently used in quantitative risk analysis. Beta is used to describe the uncertainty of variables, and uses PERT data. These probability distributions range from 0 to 1 and can take on several types of shapes.

Triangular Distributions (continuous distribution)

Triangular distributions are based on the three-point estimates and form the shape of a triangle. This is a commonly used distribution type in quantitative risk analysis.

Uniform Distributions (continuous distribution)

Uniform distributions are considered to be the simplest form of distribution. All values are of the same length and equally probable. In order to use this distribution type, it is necessary to know the upper and lower bounds of the range of possible values.

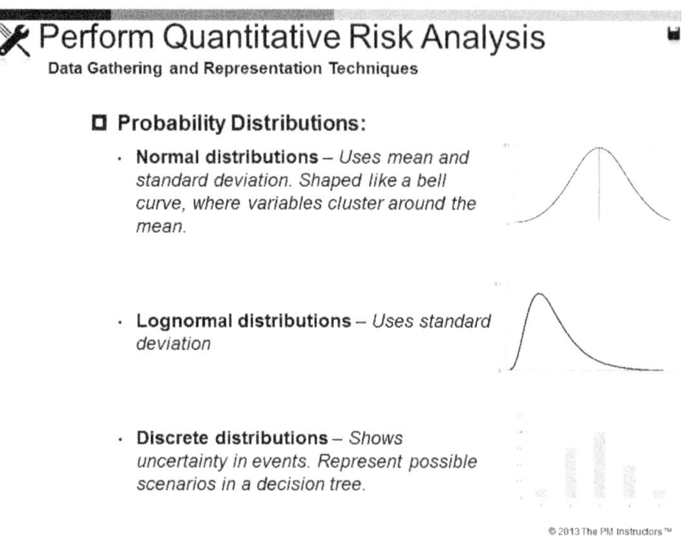

Normal Distributions (continuous distribution)

Normal distributions use mean and standard deviations to quantify risk. This distribution type is shaped like a bell curve and is typically used for variables that cluster around the mean. This is perhaps the most widely recognized distribution.

Lognormal Distributions (continuous distribution)

Lognormal distributions use any random value, which plot as a normal distribution. This distribution type also uses mean and standard deviations to quantify risk, and results are positively skewed, giving it the shape shown below.

Discrete Distributions (discrete distribution)

Discrete distributions, which are based on a whole number, are used to show uncertainty in events where the probability of occurrence can be calculated. Within quantitative risk analysis, discrete distributions are typically used to represent possible scenarios in a decision tree.

Additional Review Notes

- Continuous probability distributions show uncertainty in values
- Discrete distributions show uncertainty in events

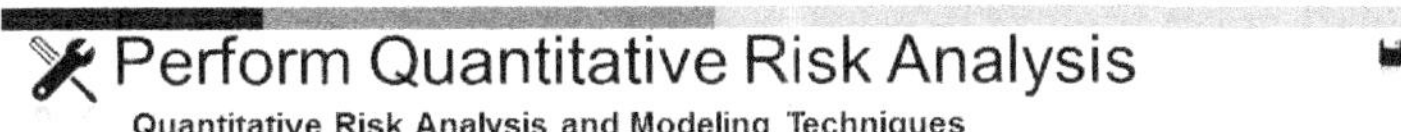
Perform Quantitative Risk Analysis
Quantitative Risk Analysis and Modeling Techniques

Sensitivity analysis:

- Determines which risks have the most potential impact on the project objectives
- What-if scenarios
- Displays results using the **tornado diagram**

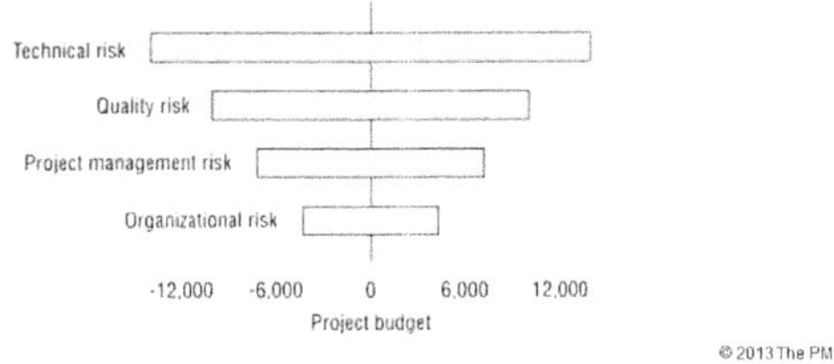
Technical risk
Quality risk
Project management risk
Organizational risk
-12,000
-6,000
0
6,000
12,000
Project budget

Sensitivity Analysis

Sensitivity analysis determines which risks have the highest impact on the project objectives. It uses a series of "what if" scenarios to examine the uncertainty of project elements. This technique looks at the effects that a project element has on a project objective when all other uncertain elements are held at their baseline values.

A **tornado diagram** is a common way of displaying sensitivity analysis. This type of diagram compares the importance of variables that have a high degree of uncertainty to more stable variables.

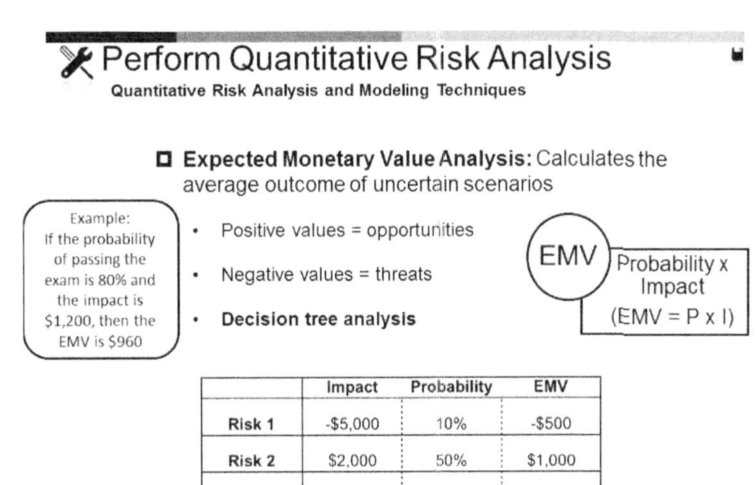
Perform Quantitative Risk Analysis
Quantitative Risk Analysis and Modeling Techniques
Expected Monetary Value Analysis: Calculates the average outcome of uncertain scenarios
Example: If the probability of passing the exam is 80% and the impact is $1,200, then the EMV is $960
Positive values = opportunities
Negative values = threats
Decision tree analysis
EMV
Probability x Impact
(EMV = P x I)
© 2013 The PM Instructors™

	Impact	Probability	EMV
Risk 1	-$5,000	10%	-$500
Risk 2	$2,000	50%	$1,000
Risk 3	-$2,000	65%	-$1,300
		Total EMV:	**-$800**

Expected Monetary Value Analysis

Expected Monetary Value (EMV) analysis calculates the average outcome of future scenarios that may or may not occur. The EMV formula is very straightforward: multiply probability and impact. Positive values represent opportunities, while negative values represent a threat.

Example: if the probability of passing the exam is 80% and the impact is $1,200, the EMV is $960.

An additional example is shown in the table above. Note that the EMV of the three risks calculated is added together to calculate an overall EMV, and that the impact of positive risks are shown as a gain, and the impact of negative risks are shown as a loss:

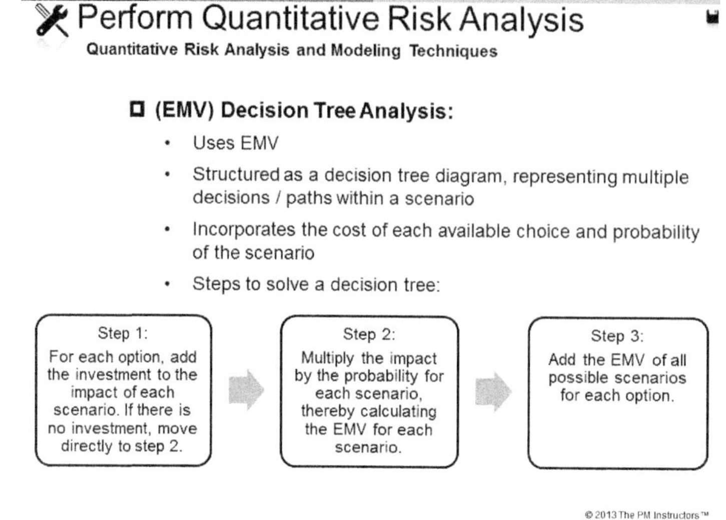
Perform Quantitative Risk Analysis
Quantitative Risk Analysis and Modeling Techniques
(EMV) Decision Tree Analysis:
Uses EMV
Structured as a decision tree diagram, representing multiple decisions / paths within a scenario
Incorporates the cost of each available choice and probability of the scenario
Steps to solve a decision tree:
Step 1: For each option, add the investment to the impact of each scenario. If there is no investment, move directly to step 2.
Step 2: Multiply the impact by the probability for each scenario, thereby calculating the EMV for each scenario.
Step 3: Add the EMV of all possible scenarios for each option.
© 2013 The PM Instructors™

Decision Tree Analysis

Decision tree analysis uses EMV to make decisions under uncertain circumstances. It is structured as a decision tree diagram that represents multiple decisions (or paths) within a scenario that is being considered. Each path contains the impact and the probability if that scenario were to occur.

The EMV is calculated for each of the decisions using EMV, allowing for a comparison of the potential paths. This, therefore, allows cost and the benefits of the paths to play a role in making decisions. Use the steps noted below to work through a decision tree:

- Step 1: For each option, add the investment to the impact of each scenario (note that an investment is outgoing cash flow). If there is no investment, move directly to step 2
- Step 2: Multiply the impact by the probability for each scenario, thereby calculating the EMV for each scenario
- Step 3: Add the EMV of all possible scenarios for each option to get an overall EMV

Perform Quantitative Risk Analysis

Quantitative Risk Analysis and Modeling Techniques

(EMV) Decision Tree Analysis:

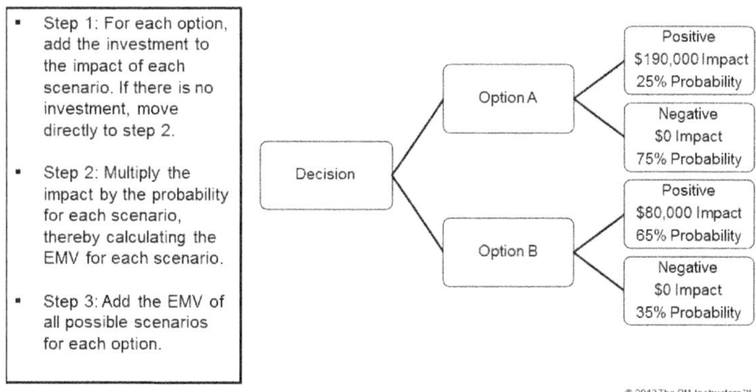

Step 1: For each option, add the investment to the impact of each scenario. If there is no investment, move directly to step 2.
Step 2: Multiply the impact by the probability for each scenario, thereby calculating the EMV for each scenario.
Step 3: Add the EMV of all possible scenarios for each option.
Decision
Option A
Option B
Positive
$190,000 Impact
25% Probability
Negative
$0 Impact
75% Probability
Positive
$80,000 Impact
65% Probability
Negative
$0 Impact
35% Probability
© 2013 The PM Instructors™

EXAMPLE 1: In the example shown above, multiply $190,000 impact by 25% probability to result in an EMV of $47,500 for the first scenario of Option A. Next, multiply $0 impact by 75% probability to result in an EMV of $0 for scenario 2 of Option A. From here, add them together to get an overall EMV of $47,500 for Option A.

Next, multiply $80,000 impact by 65% probability to result in an EMV of $52,000 for the first scenario of Option B. Next, multiply $0 impact by 35% probability to result in an EMV of $0 scenario 2 of Option B. From here, add them together to get an overall EMV of $52,000 for Option B.

Based on the EMV, the best option would be Option B.

Perform Quantitative Risk Analysis
Quantitative Risk Analysis and Modeling Techniques

(EMV) Decision Tree Analysis:

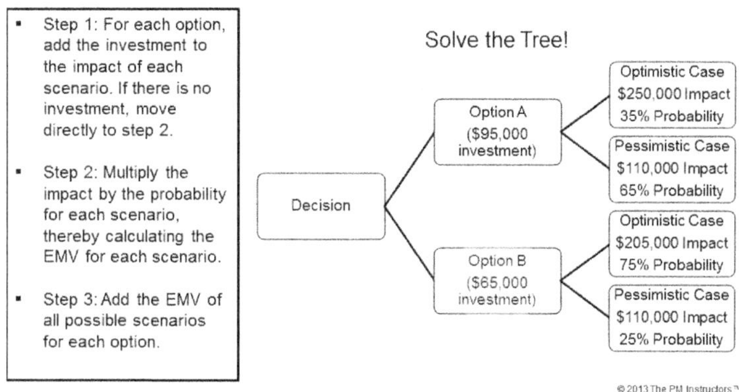

Step 1: For each option, add the investment to the impact of each scenario. If there is no investment, move directly to step 2.
Step 2: Multiply the impact by the probability for each scenario, thereby calculating the EMV for each scenario.
Step 3: Add the EMV of all possible scenarios for each option.
Solve the Tree!
Decision
Option A
($95,000 investment)
Option B
($65,000 investment)
Optimistic Case
$250,000 Impact
35% Probability
Pessimistic Case
$110,000 Impact
65% Probability
Optimistic Case
$205,000 Impact
75% Probability
Pessimistic Case
$110,000 Impact
25% Probability
© 2013 The PM Instructors™

EXAMPLE 2: In the example shown above, you must first account for the investment of each option. Calculating Option A:

1. For the first scenario, add the -$95,000 investment to the $250,000 impact to get $155,000. Multiply the revised impact by 35% probability, which comes to $54,250.
2. Repeat step 1 for scenario 2: add the -$95,000 investment to the $110,000 impact to get $15,000. Multiply the revised impact by 65% probability, which comes to $9,750.

3. Add the EMV of the two options together to get an overall EMV of $64,000 for Option A.

Calculating Option B:

1. For the first scenario, add the -$65,000 investment to the $205,000 impact to get $140,000. Multiply the revised impact by 75% probability, which comes to $105,000.
2. Repeat step 1 for scenario 2: add the -$65,000 investment to the $110,000 impact to get $45,000. Multiply the revised impact by 25% probability, which comes to $11,250.
3. Add the EMV of the two options together to get an overall EMV of $116,250 for Option B.

Based on the calculations, Option B is the best choice.

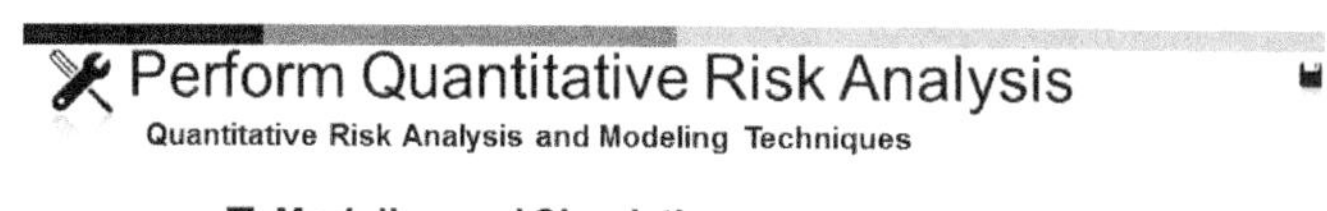

Modeling and Simulation:

- Translates uncertainties into potential impact on project objectives
- Uncertainties are specified at a detailed level of the project

Probability	Date Complete
100%	1-Jun
95%	30-May
90%	28-May
85%	26-May
80%	24-May
75%	22-May
70%	20-May
65%	18-May
60%	16-May
55%	14-May
50%	12-May
45%	10-May
40%	8-May
35%	6-May

- Typically performed using the Monte Carlo technique
- Computes the project model many times
- Completed using a software program
- Randomizes values from a probability distribution function
- Results in the calculation of a probability distribution – S-shaped curve that widens as probability increases

Modeling and Simulation

Modeling and simulation is a technique that translates uncertainties provided at a detailed level of the project into the potential impacts that they could have on project objectives. This technique allows for the risk management team to track how the results were derived. Examples of how modeling and simulation can be used include:

- Calculates probable cost and value of the project, and probable time to complete the project
- Determines which activities may likely be on the critical path
- Performs cost-benefit analysis when deciding on a response

The Monte Carlo technique is a common modeling and simulation technique used. This type of technique normally requires a software program to perform the analysis, since it generates a large number of scenarios. It looks at possible cost and schedule outcomes by randomizing values from a probability distribution function, and is therefore typically used for cost or schedule risks. Results are

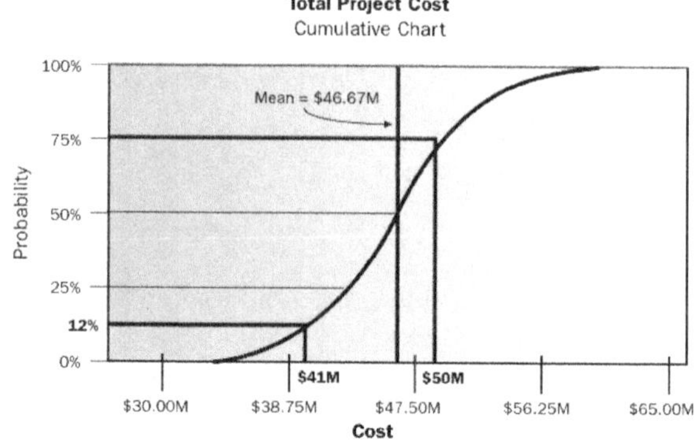

commonly displayed using a cumulative chart or distribution (S-curve). Example of an S-curve chart:[7]

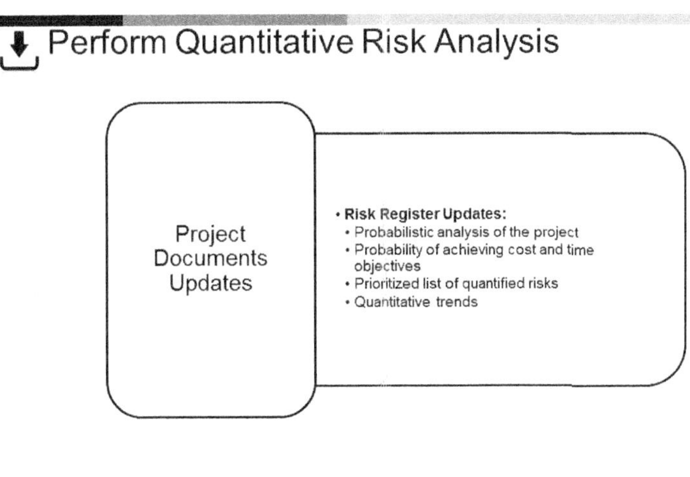
Perform Quantitative Risk Analysis
Project Documents Updates
• Risk Register Updates:
• Probabilistic analysis of the project
• Probability of achieving cost and time objectives
• Prioritized list of quantified risks
• Quantitative trends
© 2013 The PM Instructors™

Perform Quantitative Risk Analysis Outputs

Perform Quantitative Risk Analysis process has a single output: *project documents updates.*

Project Documents Updates

The outputs, or results, of the Perform Quantitative Risk Analysis process emerge as updates to the project documents, which primarily consist of updates to the risk register. This includes the following additions:

- The probabilistic analysis of the project. This includes estimates of potential schedule and cost outcomes. This is normally displayed as a cumulative distribution, which, when used with stakeholder risk tolerances, allows the quantification of cost and time contingency reserves. These reserves help the risk management team in determining whether the project has a risk of going over budget or schedule.
- Probability of achieving cost and time objectives. Quantitative risk analysis results help determine the probability of achieving the project objectives under present circumstances.
- Prioritized list of quantified risks. These are the risks that pose the greatest threat or opportunity, and therefore the ones that require the largest contingency reserves.
- Trends in quantitative risk analysis results. Documenting trends resulting from quantitative risk analysis holds the same purpose as documenting qualitative risk analysis trends. These trends emerge as the process is repeated, which results in information that may affect risk response.

[7] Project Management Institute, *A Guide to the Project Management Body of Knowledge*, (*PMBOK® Guide*) – Fourth Edition, Project Management Institute, Inc. 2013, Figure 11-16, Page 300. Material from this publication has been reproduced with the permission of PMI.

Plan Risk Responses
Purpose: To develop options and actions to enhance opportunities and to reduce threats to project objectives.

Plan Risk Responses Process Overview

The purpose of the Plan Risk Responses process is to develop options and actions to enhance opportunities and to reduce threats to project objectives. It involves developing responses to the identified risks in order to increase the probability and impact of potential opportunities, and decrease the probability and impact of potential threats. This process develops options for risks and determines what actions to follow if certain risk events occur.

Within this process, several potential approaches will be discussed, and planned responses will need to consider the significance of the cost and time required to execute a response. An owner is assigned to each risk.

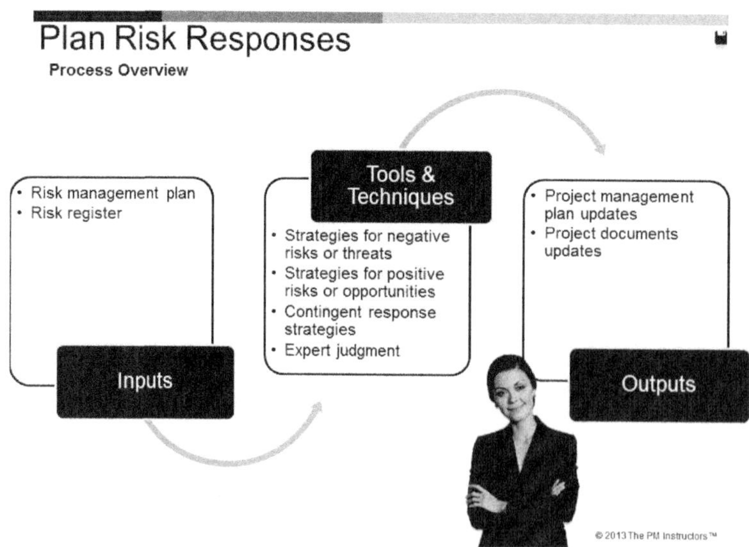
Plan Risk Responses
Process Overview
Inputs
• Risk management plan
• Risk register
Tools & Techniques
• Strategies for negative risks or threats
• Strategies for positive risks or opportunities
• Contingent response strategies
• Expert judgment
Outputs
• Project management plan updates
• Project documents updates
© 2013 The PM Instructors™

Plan Risk Responses

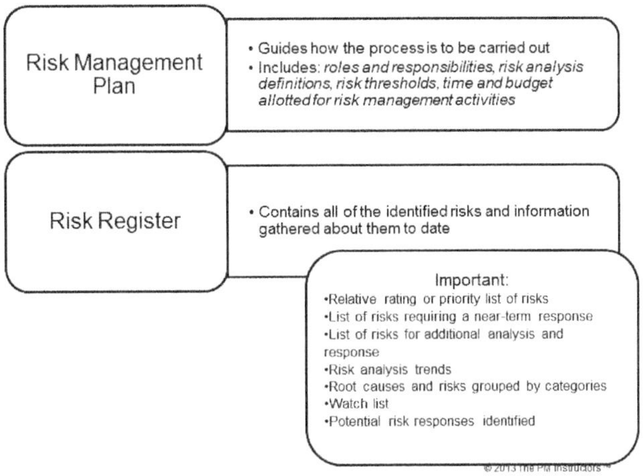

Risk Management Plan

- Guides how the process is to be carried out
- Includes: *roles and responsibilities, risk analysis definitions, risk thresholds, time and budget allotted for risk management activities*

Risk Register

- Contains all of the identified risks and information gathered about them to date

Important:
- Relative rating or priority list of risks
- List of risks requiring a near-term response
- List of risks for additional analysis and response
- Risk analysis trends
- Root causes and risks grouped by categories
- Watch list
- Potential risk responses identified

Plan Risk Responses Inputs

The Plan Risk Responses process has two inputs: *risk management plan* and *risk register.* Information from within the risk management plan and risk register is utilized in developing a risk response plan and contingency response plan.

Risk Management Plan

The risk management plan includes the following, which are utilized by this process:

- Roles and responsibilities
- Risk analysis definitions
- Risk thresholds for low, moderate and high risks
- Time and budget allotted for risk management activities

Risk Register

The risk register includes all the information covered to date that has been documented about the identified risks. The following are particularly important to carrying out this process:

- Relative rating or priority list of project risks
- List of risks requiring a near-term response
- List of risks for additional analysis and response
- Qualitative and quantitative risk analysis trends
- Root causes and risks grouped by categories
- Watch list
- Potential risk responses identified

Plan Risk Responses

- Strategies for Negative Risks or Threats
- Strategies for Positive Risks or Opportunities
- Contingent Response Strategies
- Expert Judgment

Plan Risk Responses Tools and Techniques

The Plan Risk Responses process has four tools and techniques: *strategies for negative risks or threats, strategies for positive risks or opportunities, contingent response strategies,* and *expert judgment.*

In developing risk responses, there are several strategies to consider for negative risks and positive risks. In addition to this, a contingent response strategy will be developed as part of this process. Understanding the two types of reserves is also important in connection to this process. The two types of reserves are: contingency reserves and management reserves.

Plan Risk Responses

Strategies for Negative Risks or Threats

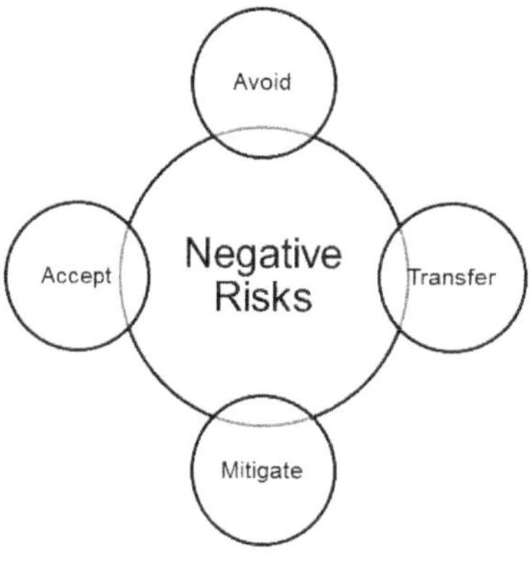

Plan Risk Responses

Strategies for Negative Risks or Threats

Avoid	Transfer	Mitigate	Accept
• To alter the project in some way to remove the possibility of the risk from occurring • *Examples:* • *Changing the project management plan* • *Clarifying requirements*	• To shift the impact of the risk to a third party • *Examples:* • *Purchasing insurance, bonds, warranties, or guaranties* • *A form of payment made to a 3rd party*	• To reduce the probability and / or impact of a risk, bringing it down to a level that is acceptable to the organization • *Examples:* • *Tests* • *Reducing complexity* • *Conservative approach* • Less costly • Used when eliminating risk is not feasible	• To accept the risk • Two types of Acceptance: • **Passive Acceptance:** To do nothing about the risk • **Active Acceptance:** To add contingency reserve to prepare for the risk

Strategies for Negative Risks or Threats

Avoid

Avoiding risks includes altering the project in some way to remove the possibility of the risk from occurring (altering the probability to 0%). An example of this is changing the project management plan to eliminate the threat, isolating project objectives from the risk's impact, or relaxing the objective affected by the risk. In cases of risk that have been identified early on in the project, simply clarifying the requirements or increasing the information or expertise used can eliminate the threat.

Transfer

Transfer means to shift the impact of the risk to a third party. This involves transferring the responsibility of the risk in question to a third party that takes ownership and management of that risk. An example of this is purchasing insurance, bonds, warranties, or guaranties. Transferring the liability of risk is normally a way of dealing with financial risk exposure. Transfer normally requires some form of payment made to the third party taking on the risk.

Mitigate

Mitigate means to reduce the probability and / or impact of a risk, bringing it down to a level that is acceptable to the organization and stakeholders (within their risk tolerance thresholds). An example of this is conducting more tests, reducing the complexity of processes, taking a more conservative approach, such as using stable vendors, and so forth. While this does not eliminate risk, it reduces the chances and the effects if the risk were to occur. Mitigating risk is also considered to be less costly than dealing with the issue if the risk were to materialize. Mitigation is used when eliminating the risk is not feasible.

Accept

Accept is a type of risk response that is used for both negative and positive risks. There are two forms of acceptance: passive and active.

- **Passive acceptance** means to do nothing about the risk;
- **Active acceptance** normally means to add a contingency reserve, such as time, funds, or resources to prepare for the risk.

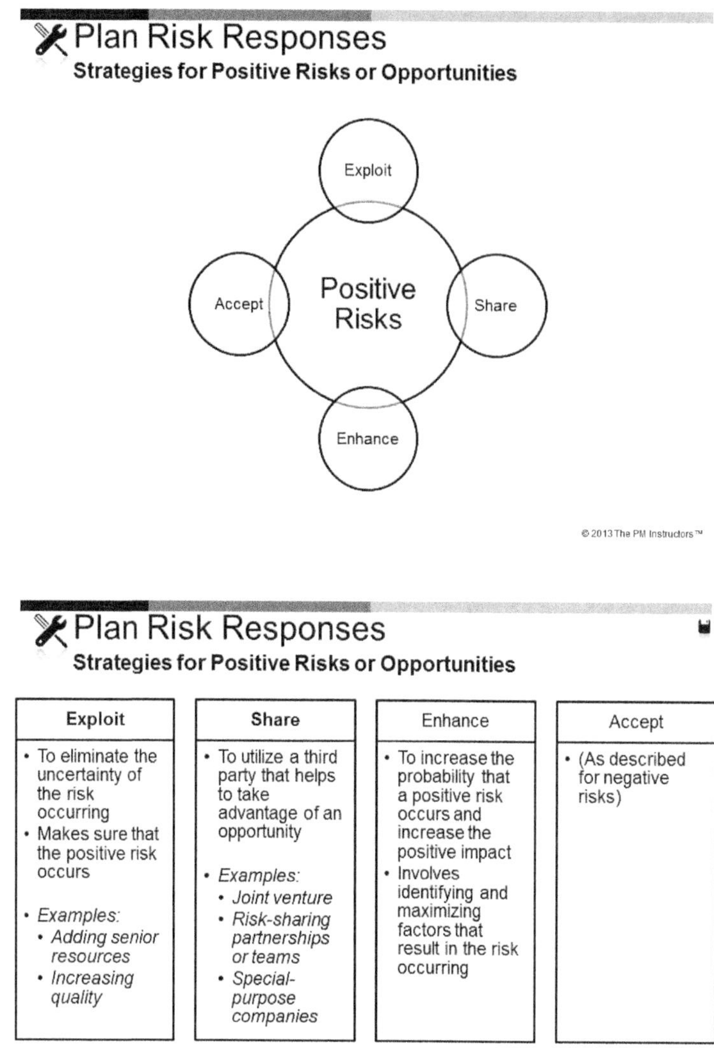

Strategies for Positive Risks or Opportunities

Exploit

Exploit is a strategy used when the organization is interested in making sure that the positive risk occurs (altering the probability to 100%). This is the opposite of the "avoid" strategy used for negative risks. Exploit looks to eliminate the uncertainty of the risk occurring. An example of exploiting a risk includes adding senior resources to make sure that certain tasks are completed quickly, or increasing the quality.

Share

Sharing is a strategy that involves utilizing a third party that can help make sure that the organization can take advantage of an opportunity. Ownership is given to the third party who can best make it happen. An example is forming a joint venture, risk-sharing partnerships or teams, or special-purpose companies. The idea is to seize opportunities. This literally involves sharing the benefits of a risk.

Enhance

The enhance strategy looks to increase the probability that a positive risk occurs and increasing the positive impact of the risk. Enhancing involves identifying and maximizing the factors that result in the risk occurring. This strategy is similar to mitigating negative risks, although instead of decreasing the impact and probability, it looks to increase the impact and probability.

Accept

Acceptance strategy is the same as described for negative risks.

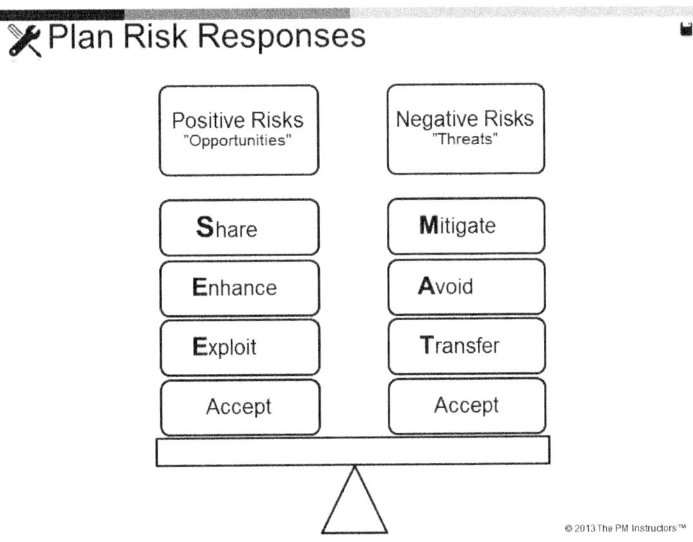

The image above can be used as an aid in remembering the strategies for positive risks and negative risks. The acronyms of the three unique strategies, combined with the strategy shared by both, forms the saying: "**SEE MAT Accept**".

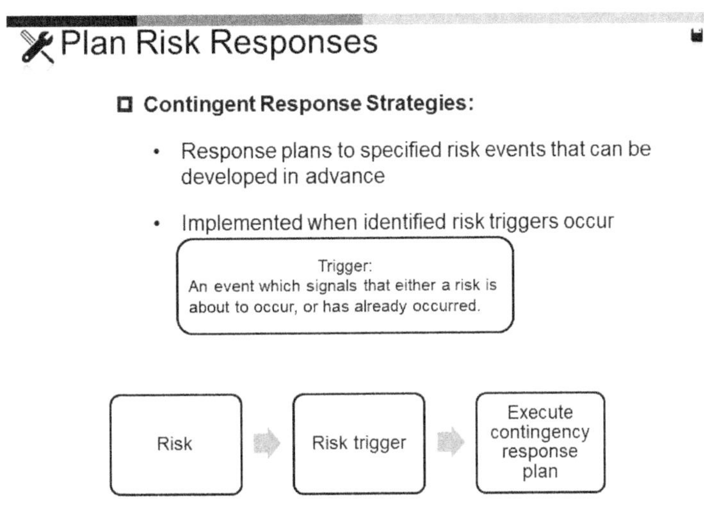

Contingent Response Strategies

The contingent response strategy is created for certain risks where a response plan can be developed in advance and that are connected to a trigger. This contingency plan is executed when predefined risk triggers (symptoms or warning signs) occur. A trigger is an event which signals that either a risk is about to occur, or has already occurred.

An example of a risk trigger may be missing a schedule milestone. This may be a warning sign of a particular risk, thereby triggering the execution of a contingency response plan.

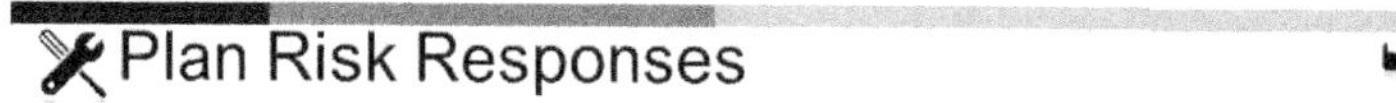

Contingent Response Strategies:

- Contingency reserves: To account for known risk
- Management reserves: To account for unknown-unknown risk

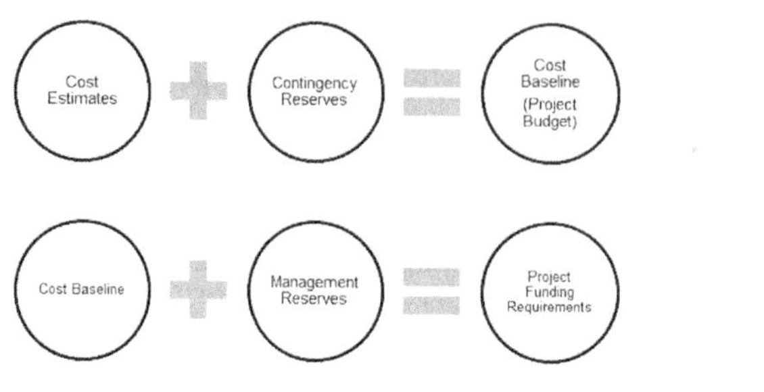

According to the *PMBOK® Guide,* there are two types of reserves: **contingency reserves** and **management reserves**. Contingency reserves are used to account for known risks (or identifiable uncertainty that leads to risk). These reserves are included as part of the project budget and schedule.

Management reserves, on the other hand, are used to account for unknown-unknown risks and are not considered to be part of the project budget. Management determines how much management reserve will be set aside, and management must approve its use. Project funding requirements is used to describe the cost baseline *plus* the management reserves.

Plan Risk Responses

Fallback Plans:

- A secondary plan, for use if the initial plan is ineffective ("Plan B")

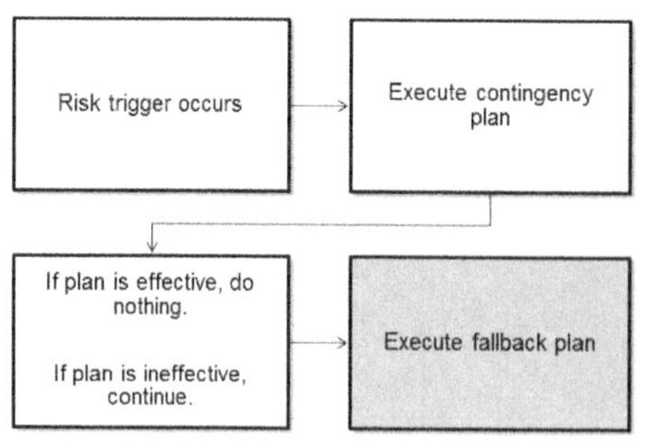

When a contingency response plan is executed, but is not effective, a fallback plan may also be planned in advance for use. **Fallback plans** are planned responses to risk, used when the other planned responses prove to be ineffective. They are considered secondary plans, which is why they are often referred to as plan B. The image above highlights the use of fallback plans. In this scenario, only fallback plans are considered to be a secondary plan (the contingency plan in this example is the first or initial plan).

Plan Risk Responses

Key Definitions:

- *Residual risks: A risk that remains after risk responses have been implemented.
- *Secondary risks: A risk that arises as a direct result of implementing a risk response.

* Definition from *A Guide to the Project Management Body of Knowledge*, *Project Management Institute Inc.*, 2013

Residual risks: *A risk that remains after risk responses have been implemented.*

Secondary risks: *A risk that arises as a direct result of implementing a risk response.*

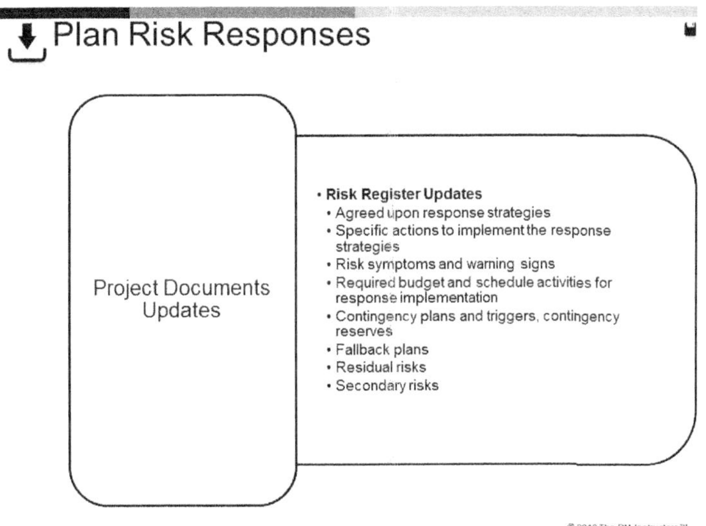

Plan Risk Responses Outputs

The Plan Risk Responses process has two outputs: *project management plan updates and project documents updates.*

Project Documents Updates

Risk register is the primary document updated within the list of project documents. This includes the following additions to the register:

- Agreed upon risk response strategies for those risks requiring a response
- Risk owners and assigned responsibilities
- Risk symptoms and warning signs which signal that a risk is about to occur
- The required budget and schedule activities for implementing risk responses
- Contingency plans and triggers

- Time and cost contingency reserves, which are meant to meet the risk tolerance levels of stakeholders
- Fallback plans, which are used when the other planned responses prove ineffective

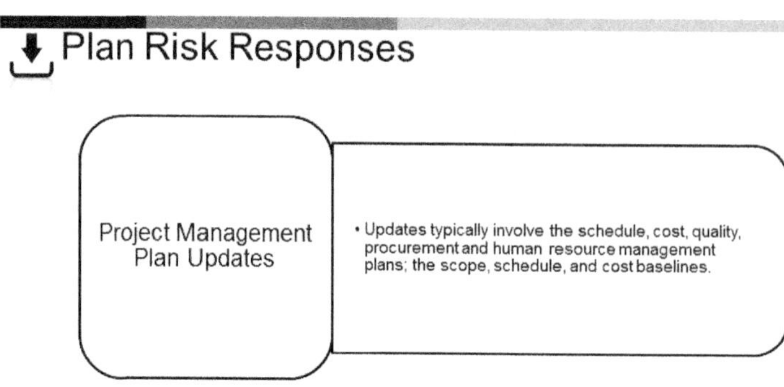
Plan Risk Responses
Project Management Plan Updates
• Updates typically involve the schedule, cost, quality, procurement and human resource management plans; the scope, schedule, and cost baselines.
© 2013 The PM Instructors™

Project Management Plan Updates

Project management plan updates resulting out of carrying out this process typically include the schedule management plan, cost management plan, quality management plan, procurement management plan, human resource management plan, scope baseline, schedule baseline, and cost baseline.

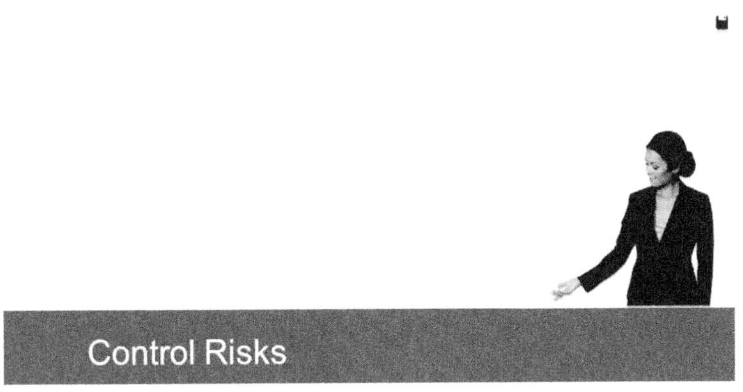
Control Risks
Purpose: To implement risk response plans, track identified risks, monitor residual risks, identify new risks, and evaluate risk process effectiveness throughout the project.

Control Risks Process Overview

The purpose of the Control Risks process is to implement risk response plans, track identified risks, monitor residual risks, identify new risks, and evaluate risk process effectiveness throughout the project. It is the only risk-related process within the Project Risk Management Knowledge Area that is not a part of the Planning Process Group. This process belongs to the Monitoring and Controlling Process Group, as the name of the process implies. This process is responsible for the following:

- Tracking identified risks
- Monitoring the residual risks
- Identifying new risks
- Executing risk response plans
- Evaluating the effectiveness of risk response plans
- Evaluating the effectiveness of the risk management processes

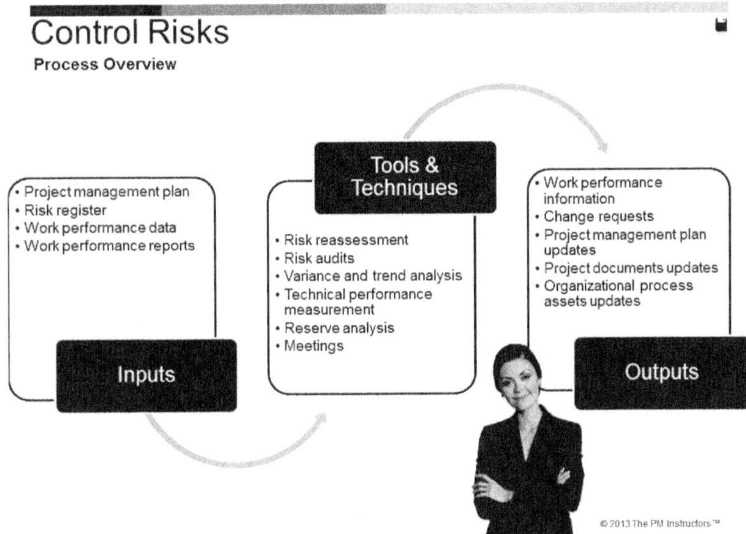
Control Risks
Process Overview
• Project management plan
• Risk register
• Work performance data
• Work performance reports
Inputs
Tools & Techniques
• Risk reassessment
• Risk audits
• Variance and trend analysis
• Technical performance measurement
• Reserve analysis
• Meetings
• Work performance information
• Change requests
• Project management plan updates
• Project documents updates
• Organizational process assets updates
Outputs
© 2013 The PM Instructors™

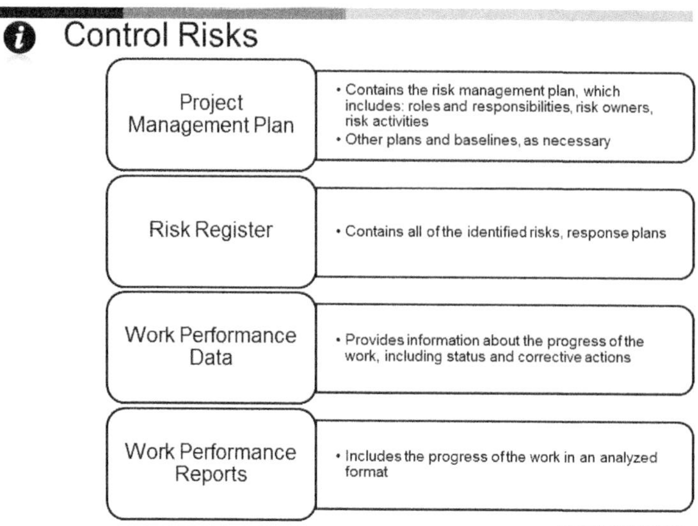
Control Risks
Project Management Plan
• Contains the risk management plan, which includes: roles and responsibilities, risk owners, risk activities
• Other plans and baselines, as necessary
Risk Register
• Contains all of the identified risks, response plans
Work Performance Data
• Provides information about the progress of the work, including status and corrective actions
Work Performance Reports
• Includes the progress of the work in an analyzed format
© 2013 The PM Instructors™

Control Risks Inputs

The Control Risks process has four inputs: *project management plan, risk register, work performance data,* and *work performance reports.*

Project Management Plan

Project management plan includes the risk management plan, which itself provides the following: risk-related roles and responsibilities, risk owners, time allocated for risk activities, and any other resources dedicated to risk monitoring and control. The project management plan also provides access to other plans as needed, as well as baselines.

Risk Register

The risk register includes all the information added to the risk register to date, particularly:

- Agreed-upon risk responses (which are executed as needed during this process)
- Implementation actions
- Symptoms and warning signs indicating that risk is about to occur
- Residual and secondary risks
- Risks on the watch list
- Time and cost reserves

Work Performance Data

Work performance data is an output of the Direct and Manage Project Work process, within Project Integration Management Knowledge Area. Work performance data includes information on the following:

- Status of project deliverables
- Corrective actions

Work Performance Reports

Work performance reports are an output of the Monitor and Control Project Work process, which is part of the Project Integration Management Knowledge Area. Work performance reports provide information on the project's work performance.

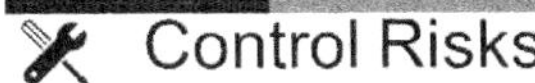

Control Risks

Risk Reassessment:

- Reassessment of existing risks and identification of new risks.
- Reviews the watch list
- Often an agenda item of project status meetings

Risk Audits:

- Examines the effectiveness of risk responses and risk management processes

Variance and Trend Analysis:

- Examines trends using performance data using work performance reports, work performance data
- Forecasts potential cost/schedule deviations

Control Risks Tools and Techniques

Control Risks has six tools and techniques: *risk reassessment, risk audits, variance and trend analysis, technical performance measurement, reserve analysis,* and *meetings.*

Risk Reassessment

Risk reassessment involves reassessing existing risks and also identifying new risks using the risk management processes. As part of risk-reassessment, risks that are on the watch list should be carefully monitored and revisited often for changes in status. Conducting risk reassessment is scheduled regularly, and is typically added as an agenda item to project status meetings.

Risk Audits

Risk audits are an important part of process improvement. Risk audits are not only concerned with measuring the effectiveness of risk responses, but also the effectiveness of the risk management processes. Through risk audits, the risk policies and practices can be better refined.

Variance and Trend Analysis

Variance trend analysis examines trends using performance data. Performance data can be obtained through the following inputs:

- Work performance reports
- Work performance data

The purpose is to forecast any potential cost and/or schedule deviations of the project at completion, which may indicate potential risks. Actual performance is measured against baseline information, using earned value analysis, to determine whether any variances do exist.

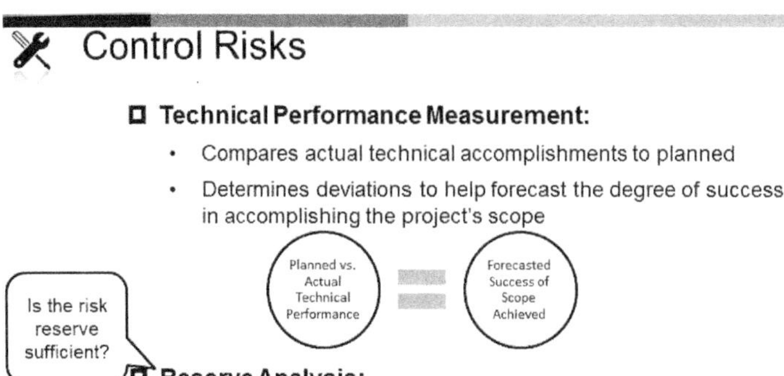

Technical Performance Measurement

Technical performance measurement compares actual technical performance accomplishments to forecasted technical performance milestones. The purpose is to uncover any deviations that may exist, such as differing functionalities. This information allows the risk management team to forecast the degree of success in achieving the scope of the project.

Reserve Analysis

As the project progresses, and contingency reserves are utilized, it becomes important to stay on top of whether the remaining reserves are sufficient to cover the remaining risks. This describes the purpose of reserve analysis. Reserve analysis compares the remaining contingency reserves to the remaining risks and determines whether the funds are sufficient, or whether changes are necessary.

Meetings

Status meetings are used as a tool for discussing risk. Risk reassessment is one example of an agenda item that should be addressed within project status meetings as needed. It can be difficult to gather the project team and other necessary individuals to meet and discuss important risk items; status meetings allow the risk management team to efficiently utilize the time of the project team members and stakeholders, and ensure that risk agenda items are covered.

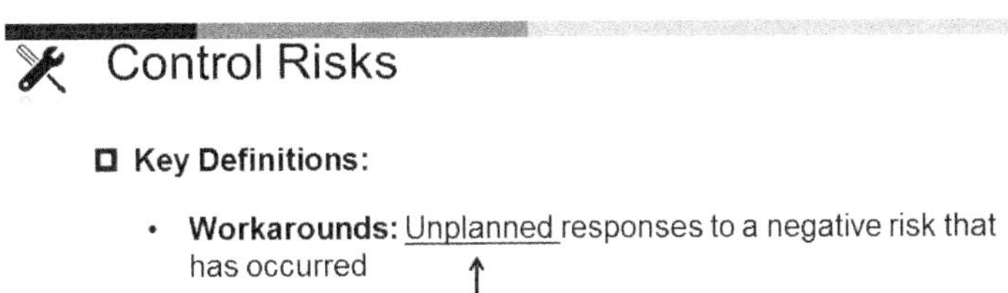

Control Risks
Key Definitions:
Workarounds: Unplanned responses to a negative risk that has occurred
© 2013 The PM Instructors™

Workarounds are unplanned responses to a negative risk that has occurred. It is realistic to expect some risks to go undetected, and then suddenly materialize. Workarounds are the risk management team's response to these types of risks.

Important note: Workarounds differ from other risk responses because they are **unplanned**. In comparison, contingency plans and fallback plans are **planned** responses.

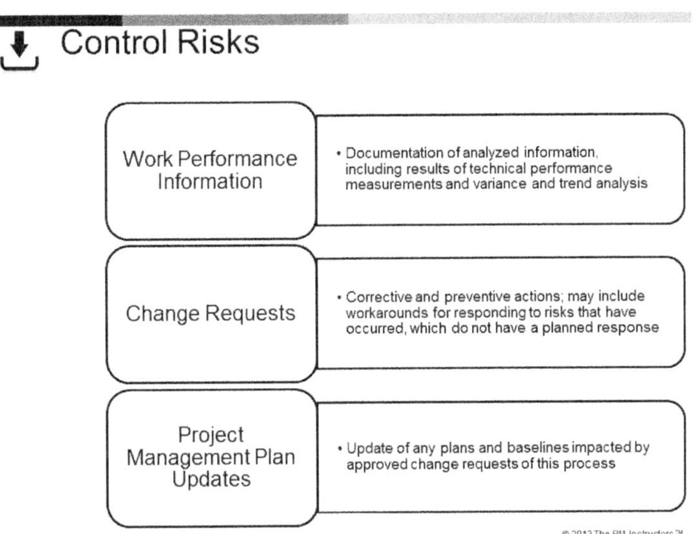

Control Risks
Work Performance Information
• Documentation of analyzed information, including results of technical performance measurements and variance and trend analysis
Change Requests
• Corrective and preventive actions; may include workarounds for responding to risks that have occurred, which do not have a planned response
Project Management Plan Updates
• Update of any plans and baselines impacted by approved change requests of this process
© 2013 The PM Instructors™

Control Risks Outputs

The Control Risks process contains five outputs: *work performance information, change requests, project management plan updates, project documents updates,* and *organizational process assets updates.*

Work Performance Information

Work performance information typically includes results of performing the technical performance measurements and variance and trend analysis techniques. It is a documentation of the analyzed information of this process.

Change Requests

Processes that fall in the Monitoring and Controlling Process Group often yield change requests as an output. As the project and risk management teams are monitoring risks, a change request may be needed, based on identified variances, or opportunities to implement preventive measures to prevent variance. Change requests may also involve implementing workarounds for unknown-unknown risks that have occurred.

Project Management Plan Updates

Any of the subsidiary plans and baselines impacted by this process may be updated, based on change requests that have been approved.

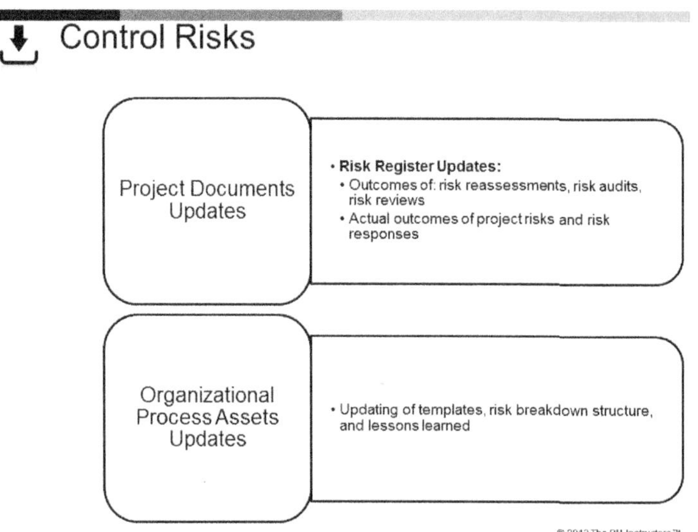

Project Documents Updates

Among the project documents updates are updates to the risk register. These updates typically include:

- Outcomes of risk reassessments, risk audits, and risk reviews. If the outcomes included any updates affecting other elements within the risk register (such as response plans, priority, and so forth), these items are then updated as well.
- Actual outcomes of project risks and risk responses. Actual outcomes provide extremely valuable information to future projects that will utilize this and other risk registers during the risk management planning processes. The actual outcomes are the final updates made to the risk register, and become an input into the Close Project or Phase process and a part of project closure documents.

Organizational Process Assets Updates

Organizational process assets updated as a result of this process typically include archival of templates, risk breakdown structure, and lessons learned.

Module Summary

In this module we:

- Defined the purpose of the Project Risk Management Knowledge Area
- Identified the processes of the Project Risk Management Knowledge Area
- Recalled the key outputs of the risk management processes
- Differentiated between the inputs, tools and techniques, and outputs of the risk management processes
- Performed simple qualitative risk calculations

Chapter Quiz

Exam Practice Questions

1. Meetings is a tool and technique of which process?
    A. Perform Qualitative Risk Analysis
    B. Perform Quantitative Risk Analysis
    C. Plan Risk Management
    D. Plan Risk Responses

2. During the creation of the risk management plan, you decide to start by analyzing the risk tolerance levels of the organization and of stakeholders. What information are you most likely to utilize?
    A. Project management plan
    B. Risk management plan
    C. Organizational process assets
    D. Enterprise environmental factors

3. A risk manager had just been hired to take over risk management responsibilities for a company producing a new pharmaceutical drug for diabetics. During the first cycle of risk identification, it was determined that the project had a high level of risk, and an expert was needed. The risk manager's first order of business is to look over the risk management plan. Which of the following is not likely to be addressed within the plan?
    A. Stakeholder risk tolerances
    B. Budget for risk activities
    C. Definitions of risk probability and impact
    D. Risk owners

4. Thomas is a project manager at ACME Media Productions. Technical support has informed him that there is a risk that the release of their new dual sided DVDs may cause consumers to believe that they've only received half of the movie they purchased. Since the probability was very low, the team decided that this risk should be placed on the watch list. Which of the following BEST describes a watch list?
    A. Contains a list of low priority risks
    B. Contains a list of high priority risks
    C. Contains a list of risk for further analysis
    D. Contains risks with high impact

5. You are a project manager for Strong Tech Solutions, a company that markets products using the latest in technology. You have just finished performing a risk urgency assessment. What process are you currently in?
    A. Identify Risks
    B. Perform Qualitative Risk Analysis
    C. Perform Quantitative Risk Analysis
    D. Plan Risk Responses

6. What is the expected monetary value of a project with an impact of $42,000 and a probability of 85%?
    A. $77,700
    B. $35,700
    C. $6,300
    D. Insufficient information

7. You are a project manager for Strong Tech Solutions, a company that markets products using the latest in technology. You've just discovered a risk that could have negative consequences on the project. To date, the risk management team has been unable to mitigate the risk or eliminate it. What response strategy should be taken to deal with this risk?
    A. Avoid
    B. Share
    C. Mitigate
    D. Accept

8. Which of the following BEST describes secondary risks?
    A. Risks that emerge as a direct result of implementing a risk response
    B. Risks that are expected to remain after risk responses have been executed
    C. Risks that are identified during the monitoring and controlling stage of the project
    D. Low priority risks that should not receive too much effort, but should be monitored

9. To date, 13 of the 42 identified risks have occurred; 5 of those risks were considered to have held a high-risk rating. At this point, it is unclear whether there are enough funds remaining to deal with the other 29 risks that remain. What should the project manager do?
    A. Perform quantitative risk analysis on the remaining 29 risks
    B. Perform reserve analysis as soon as possible
    C. Hold a status meeting to inform stakeholders of the concern
    D. Perform technical performance measurement

10. The senior solution architect and the project manager are in an emotionally charged disagreement about the vulnerability of a new feature being added to their software package. To determine the potential impact of the vulnerability and its level of severity, they agree to place their concerns on the board and numerically assign a level of risk to each of their concerns. After going through this exercise, they rate the risks, prioritize them, and move on to perform a more thorough numerical analysis. Which of the following risk management processes numerically analyzes the effects of identified risks on the project objectives?
    A. Identify Risks
    B. Perform Qualitative Risk Analysis
    C. Perform Quantitative Risk Analysis
    D. Plan Risk Responses

11. Which of the following statements is inaccurate?
    A. Risk management is a proactive approach to project management.
    B. Risk management should begin with a thorough and realistic review of the project.
    C. Risk management begins early on in the project, when information is minimal.
    D. Risk management begins early on in the project, as soon as the project scope is defined.

12. While conducting risk management planning, the project manager led the meeting participants, which included project team members and stakeholders, in a collaborative effort to break down the risk categories into subcategories. The end result was displayed as a hierarchical structure, containing the risk categories and subcategories. The project manager and meeting participants are utilizing which of the following?
    A. Work breakdown structure
    B. Risk category structure
    C. Risk breakdown structure
    D. Resource breakdown structure

13. A project manager leading a multi-phased construction project is beginning the risk management process. Because of the project's complexity, and the amount of money invested within the project, the project sponsor stressed the critical nature of managing risks. The project manager took this advice seriously and brought together a risk management team. Along with the risk management team, the project manager worked on the development of the risk management plan. All of the following are likely to be covered within the risk management plan except for which of the following?
    A. When and how often to conduct risk management activities.
    B. When and how often to communicate with stakeholders throughout the project.
    C. The amount of funds set aside for risk management activities.
    D. The approach used to carry out risk management.

14. 5551212 is the latest mobile phone provider, expanding to a new region that is estimated to add three million users. The risk manager of the expansion project has just been hired as part of the project to assist in risk planning activities. The project manager, who has been with the organization for five years, offers his services to the risk manager whenever it is needed. She decides to take him up on his offer by asking whether or not the organization has the documented definitions of the risk ratings. What is the risk manager looking for?
    A. Risk categories
    B. Probability and impact matrix
    C. Definitions of risk probability and impact
    D. Reporting formats

15. Which of the following diagramming techniques is not used within the Identify Risks process?
    A. Herzberg Diagram
    B. Ishikawa Diagram
    C. Fishbone Diagram
    D. Influence Diagram

16. A project manager of Cyber Channels Inc. is in the process of identifying project risks. While reviewing how the elements of a particular system interrelate, she discovers two risks relating to the cause of another risk that were both initially overlooked. Which of the following techniques is the project manager using?
    A. Influence diagram
    B. Flow chart
    C. Cause and effect diagram
    D. Control chart

17. A project manager of a retail chain of hardware stores is in the process of conducting risk identification activities. Along with the risk management team, the project manager examined the existing project plans to determine whether they were consistent with the project requirements. What technique is the project manager currently using?
    A. Process flow chart
    B. Checklist analysis
    C. Brainstorming
    D. Documentation reviews

18. A project manager currently working on a mid-level pharmaceutical project is performing risk management activities. The project manager is now assessing the probability and impact of each risk. Which of the following is the project manager least likely to use?
    A. Facilitated interviews
    B. Project team members
    C. Probability and impact definitions
    D. Watch list

19. Two stakeholders approached the project manager about the integrity of the data used for risk management. They both felt that the risks identified weren't in alignment with what they'd seen in previous past projects. The project manager informed them that the accuracy of the data had already been analyzed, and therefore, the integrity of the information and data used had been validated. The project manager then spent 20 minutes with the stakeholders going through the results of the data's validation. What technique did the project manager most likely use to check the integrity of the data used for risk management?
    A. Risk data quality assessment
    B. Assumptions analysis
    C. Checklist analysis
    D. Data validation analysis

20. A project manager of Cyber Channels Inc. is in the process of prioritizing risks. A project team member expressed concerns with one of the risks, informing the project manager that if not responded to quickly, it may have dire consequences for the project. What should the project manager do first?
    A. Develop a response to the risk in question
    B. Perform risk urgency assessment
    C. Assure the team member that the risk will be addressed
    D. Create a risk probability and impact matrix to prioritize the risk

Chapter Quiz

Exam Practice Answers

1. Answer: C

   Explanation: Meetings is a tool and technique used by the first process within the Project Risk Management Knowledge Area: Plan Risk Management. Through meetings, the contents of the risk management plan are developed.

2. Answer: D

   Explanation: Enterprise environmental factors encompass internal and external factors that impact or influence the project. This includes risk tolerance levels of the project stakeholders, and of the organization as a whole.

3. Answer: D

   Explanation: The risk management plan reflects how risk management activities will be carried out. It does not contain actual risks that have been identified, which are documented within the risk register. As a result, risk owners cannot be documented within this plan. The appropriate place to document risk owners would be within the risk register.

4. Answer: A

   Explanation: A watch list is a list of low priority risks, which will not be responded to. Instead, they will be continuously monitored for a change in status. The watch list is first generated out of the Perform Qualitative Risk Analysis process, where risks are prioritized.

5. Answer: B

   Explanation: The Perform Qualitative Risk Analysis process is responsible for prioritizing the list of identified risks. Assessing the level of urgency of risks is done to properly prioritize them.

6. Answer: B

   Explanation: To calculate expected monetary value (EMV), simply multiple impact by probability (I x P). The result is $35,700.

7. Answer: D

   Explanation: There are four potential responses to negative risks: avoid, transfer, mitigate, or accept. The question notes that mitigation and avoidance have been attempted without success. This leaves accept as the best possible alternative.

8. Answer: A

   Explanation: A secondary risk refers to a new risk that emerges as a direct result of implementing a risk response.

9. Answer: B

   Explanation: In this scenario, the project manager is unsure if the remaining risk reserve is sufficient to cover the remaining active risks. In response, the project manager should perform reserve analysis to clarify whether or not there is enough reserve remaining.

10. Answer: C

    Explanation: Perform Quantitative Risk Analysis is responsible for numerically analyzing the prioritized list of risks.

11. Answer: D

Explanation: Risk management begins as soon as the project begins, even when minimal information is available. It is not necessary to wait until the project scope has been defined, which occurs during the planning phase of the project (as opposed to the Initiating phase).

12. Answer: C

    Explanation: The risk breakdown structure (RBS) displays risks by their categories, and then breaks them down further by subcategories.

13. Answer: B

    Explanation: While the risk management plan covers the details of risk-related reports and formats, it does not cover all of the communication requirements of project stakeholders. This is addressed within the communications management plan.

14. Answer: C

    Explanation: The risk manager is referring to definitions of risk probability and impact, which literally defines risk probability and impact using a scale or rating system. Organizations maintaining organizational process assets archive this information from previous, past projects. Previous or existing definitions of probability and impact are refined and tailored according to the current project.

15. Answer: A

    Explanation: Herzberg is the name of a management theorist, and is not related to a diagramming technique, making it the correct answer. Ishikawa and fishbone diagram are other names used to identify cause and effect diagrams, which is a diagramming technique used to identify risks.

16. Answer: B

    Explanation: System or process flow charts show how the various elements of a system interrelate, which can reveal how a problem occurs. This is done by analyzing the steps of a system, and is very useful in identifying potential responses to risks.

17. Answer: D

    Explanation: Documentation reviews involve examining the project plans and documents to ensure that they are consistent with project requirements, that they include everything necessary within the plans, and also evaluate the assumptions made. This technique allows the project manager to determine whether the documents are thorough enough, and whether any risks exists as a result of planning.

18. Answer: D

    Explanation: Watch lists, which contain low-priority risks, are developed during the Perform Qualitative Risk Analysis process, which is the process that the project is currently in (Perform Qualitative Risk Analysis is where the impact and probability of risks are assessed). Therefore, watch lists cannot be used by the project manager to assess the risks.

19. Answer: A

    Explanation: Risk data quality assessment measures the confidence and accuracy of the data used for risk management purposes. Overall, this technique evaluates the accuracy, reliability, integrity, and quality of the data and information.

20. Answer: B

    Explanation: Risk urgency assessment determines the level of urgency in addressing risk. This should be performed for all prioritized risks so that effort is spent on those risks that have a higher impact and probability of occurring. The result is the identification of near-term risks, which are those risks that require a near-term response.

Chapter 12: Project Procurement Management

Learning Objectives:

- ☐ Define the purpose of the Project Procurement Management Knowledge Area
- ☐ Identify the processes of the Project Procurement Management Knowledge Area
- ☐ Recall the key outputs of the procurement management processes
- ☐ Differentiate between the inputs, tools and techniques, and outputs of the procurement management processes
- ☐ Identify various types of fixed-price, cost-reimbursable and Time and Material contractual agreements

Exam Domain Tasks:

- Develop a procurement plan based on the project scope and schedule, in order to ensure that the required project resources will be available.

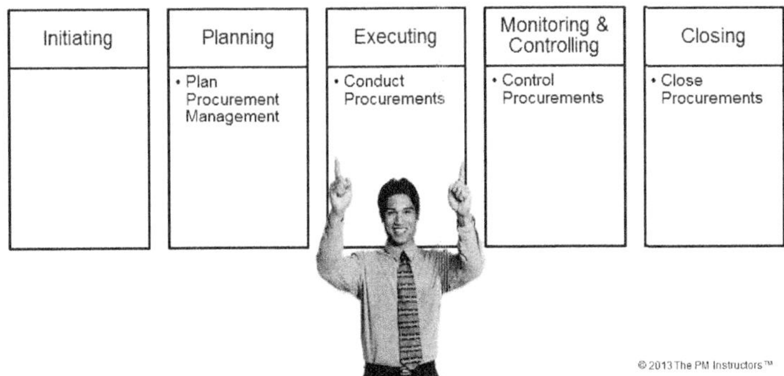
Project Procurement Management
Purpose: "To purchase or acquire products, services, or results needed from outside the project team."
4 Project Management Processes:
Initiating
Planning
• Plan Procurement Management
Executing
• Conduct Procurements
Monitoring & Controlling
• Control Procurements
Closing
• Close Procurements
© 2013 The PM Instructors™

Project Procurement Management Overview

The purpose of the Project Procurement Management Knowledge Area is to purchase or acquire the products, services, or results needed from outside the project team. It is concerned with the following things:

- Contract management and change control, which includes the administration of contracts or purchase orders that are issued by authorized team members
- Administration of contracts issued from outside the organization, and the administration of contractual obligations of the project team defined within the contract

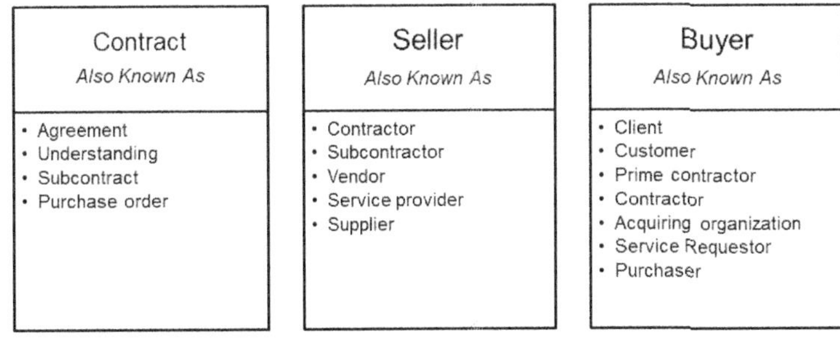
Project Procurement Management
CONCEPT
*Contract: A mutually binding agreement that obligates the seller to provide the specified product or service or result and obligates the buyer to pay for it.
Contract
Also Known As
• Agreement
• Understanding
• Subcontract
• Purchase order
Seller
Also Known As
• Contractor
• Subcontractor
• Vendor
• Service provider
• Supplier
Buyer
Also Known As
• Client
• Customer
• Prime contractor
• Contractor
• Acquiring organization
• Service Requestor
• Purchaser
* Definition from A Guide to the Project Management Body of Knowledge, Project Management Institute Inc., 2013
© 2013 The PM Instructors™

The *PMBOK® Guide* defines contacts as *a mutually binding agreement that obligates the seller to provide the specified product or service or result and obligates the buyer to pay for it.* The terms contract, seller, and buyer can be referred to by several different names, such as the following:

- Contract: agreement, understanding, subcontract, or purchase order
- Seller: contractor, subcontractor, vendor, service provider, or supplier

- Buyer: client, customer, prime contractor, contractor, acquiring organization, service requestor, or purchaser

There are three categories of procurement:

1. Major complexity procurements, also known as high risk procurements, such as a product that is being developed or created specifically for the project;
2. Minor complexity procurements, also known as low risk procurements, such as a product that already exists but is costly;
3. Routine purchases, which are commercial off the shelf purchases

Within the project's procurement activities, project managers may manage the life cycle of the procurement process, and the purchasing activities. This includes determining which products or services will need to occur outside of the organization. The project team helps to tailor the contract to the needs of the project. Keep in mind that procurement management is different for various organizations. In some instances, procurements are solely managed by a vendor management or procurement management team, and not the project manager.

The Project Procurement Management Knowledge Area is written from the perspective of the buyer.

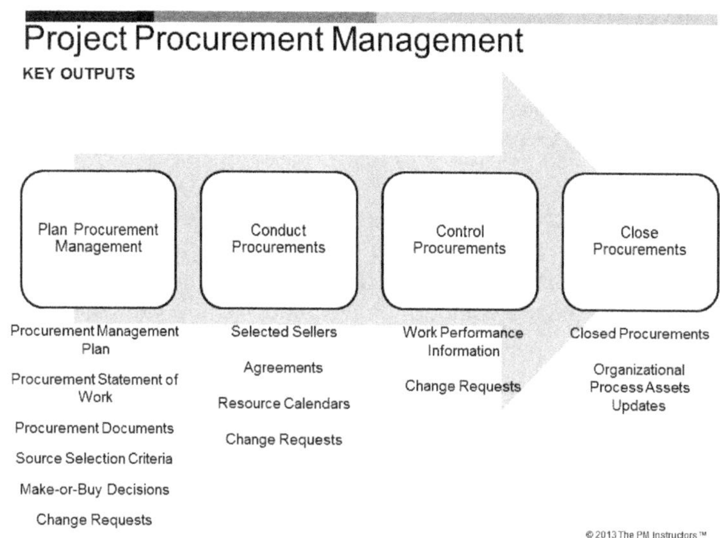

The Project Procurement Management Knowledge Area consists of four processes:

- **Plan Procurement Management (Planning Process Group).** Purpose: To document project procurement decisions, specify approach, and identify potential sellers.
- **Conduct Procurements (Executing Process Group).** Purpose: To obtain seller responses, select a seller, and award a contract.
- **Control Procurements (Monitoring and Controlling Process Group).** Purpose: To manage procurement relationships, monitor contract performance, and make changes and corrections as appropriate.
- **Close Procurements (Closing Process Group).** Purpose: To complete each project procurement.

Purpose: To document project procurement decisions, specify the approach, and identify potential sellers.

Plan Procurement Management Process Overview

Plan Procurement Management is an important process, because it is where all of the planning efforts in relation to procurements will take place. The purpose of the process is to document project procurement decisions, specify the approach, and identify potential sellers. The project management team looks at the project work and determines what can be done internally, by the project team, and what needs to be contracted out or purchased. A few additional notes on the process include the following:

- This process considers whether part or all of the project work should be completed internally or externally, how, what, how much, and when
- This process, along with the other procurement related processes, are completed for each item within the project that is purchased or acquired
- This process considers potential sellers
- The project schedule has a significant influence over this process, and vice versa
- Risks are reviewed and considered when deciding on a make-or-buy decision

There are several important decisions and documents that take place and are created as part of this process, including the creation of the procurement management plan, and decisions on what contract types to use for procurement activities.

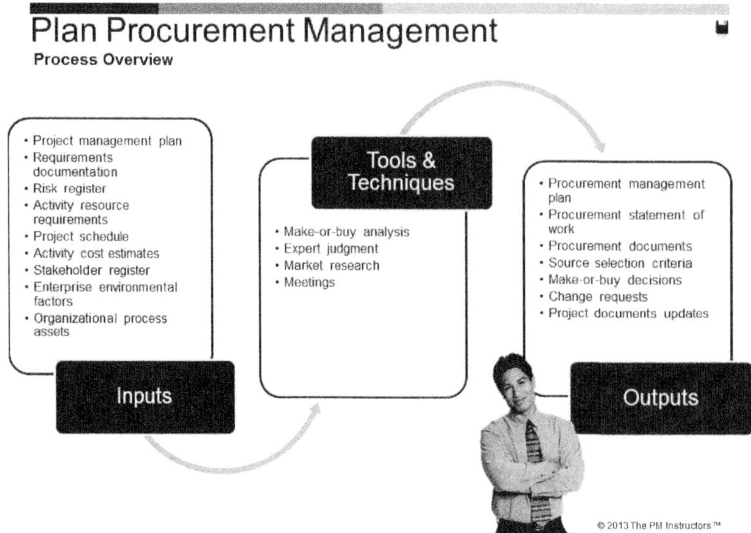

Plan Procurement Management
Process Overview
• Project management plan
• Requirements documentation
• Risk register
• Activity resource requirements
• Project schedule
• Activity cost estimates
• Stakeholder register
• Enterprise environmental factors
• Organizational process assets
Inputs
Tools & Techniques
• Make-or-buy analysis
• Expert judgment
• Market research
• Meetings
• Procurement management plan
• Procurement statement of work
• Procurement documents
• Source selection criteria
• Make-or-buy decisions
• Change requests
• Project documents updates
Outputs
© 2013 The PM Instructors™

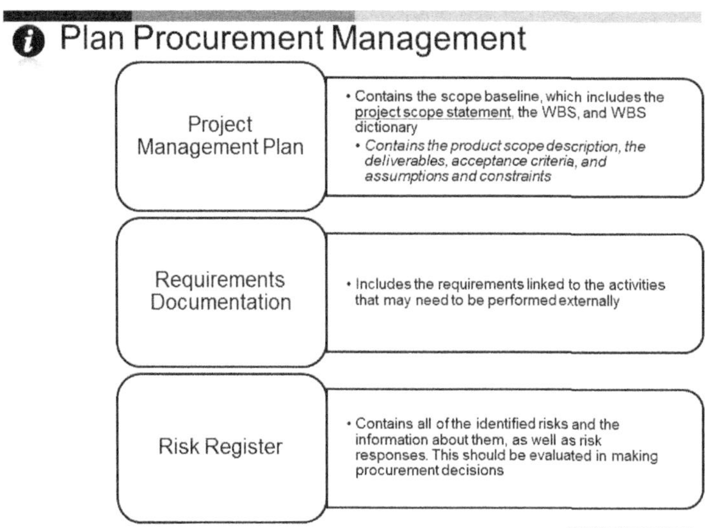

Plan Procurement Management
Project Management Plan
• Contains the scope baseline, which includes the project scope statement, the WBS, and WBS dictionary
• Contains the product scope description, the deliverables, acceptance criteria, and assumptions and constraints
Requirements Documentation
• Includes the requirements linked to the activities that may need to be performed externally
Risk Register
• Contains all of the identified risks and the information about them, as well as risk responses. This should be evaluated in making procurement decisions
© 2013 The PM Instructors™

Plan Procurement Management Inputs

The Plan Procurement Management process has nine inputs: *project management plan, requirements documentation, risk register, activity resource requirements, project schedule, activity cost estimates, stakeholder register, enterprise environmental factors,* and *organizational process assets.*

Project Management Plan

The project management plan contains the subsidiary plans and baselines. Of particular interest to this process is the scope baseline. The scope baseline itself includes the project scope statement, the WBS, and WBS dictionary. This provides the project management team with the product scope description, the deliverables, acceptance criteria, and importantly, assumptions and constraints. Under constraints, the team will need to evaluate whether it is acceptable to procure an activity.

Requirements Documentation

Requirements documentation provides constraints and assumption of the individual requirements, which have been prioritized as part of this document. Of special interest will be those requirements that are being considered as part of the procurement, including those with contractual or legal ramifications.

Risk Register

The risk register contains all of the identified risks and the information about them, including the risk responses documented. As a result of opting for the transfer or share risk strategies, risk-related contract decisions may exist. These become an important input into this process, since this is where they will be carried out. This should be evaluated in making procurement decisions.

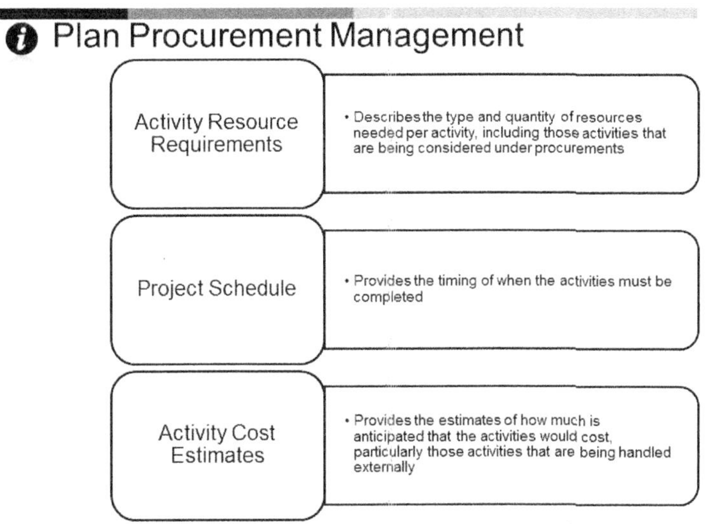

Activity Resource Requirements

Activity resource requirements describe the type and quantity of resources needed per activity. Of special interest will be those activities that are being considered as part of the procurement.

Project Schedule

The project schedule provides the timing of when the activities must be completed. It is important to ensure that enough time has been allocated toward selecting a seller.

Activity Cost Estimates

The activity cost estimates provide estimates of how much the project management team anticipates that the activities will cost. Again, we're interested in those activities that are being considered as part of the procurement, and which will be performed by an external seller.

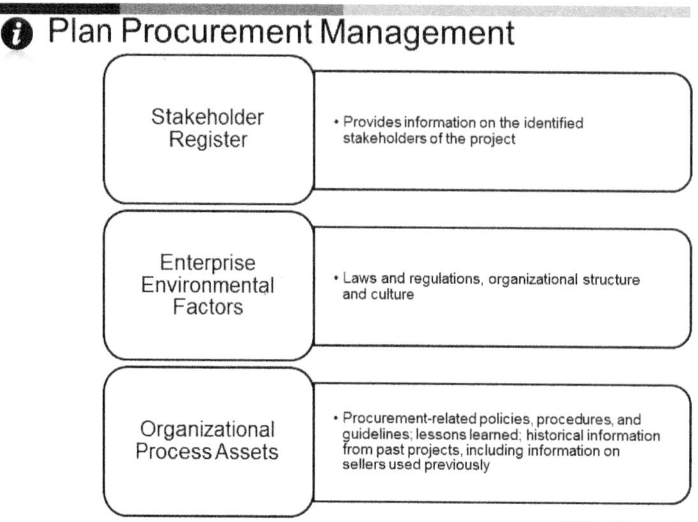

Plan Procurement Management
Stakeholder Register
• Provides information on the identified stakeholders of the project
Enterprise Environmental Factors
• Laws and regulations, organizational structure and culture
Organizational Process Assets
• Procurement-related policies, procedures, and guidelines; lessons learned; historical information from past projects, including information on sellers used previously
© 2013 The PM Instructors™

Stakeholder Register

The stakeholder register provides a list of identified stakeholders of the project, thereby providing information on who should be involved in the procurement process. This includes reviewing the interest of participants in the project.

Enterprise Environmental Factors

Within the enterprise environmental factors, the purchasing or contracting team considers what products, services and results are available in the marketplace, along with all the details associated with purchasing or acquiring the item or services. The conditions of the marketplace are also taken into consideration. If the company does not have a purchasing or contracting team or group, then the responsibility falls on the project team.

Organizational Process Assets

Under organizational process assets, the project management team utilizes the policies, procedures, guidelines, and management systems that pertain to procurement. It's important to understand how the company currently conducts procurement activities, which will aid the project team in compiling a good procurement management plan. Every company approaches things differently, especially when purchasing or acquiring products or services externally. Understanding what existing limitations are, procedures, approval processes, whether there are pre-qualified sellers, etc, will result in a realistic plan of action.

Plan Procurement Management

- **Make-or-Buy Analysis:** Used to determine whether a product or service can be produced internally by the project team, or must be procured externally

Considerations include:

Budget constraints	Rent versus buy	Direct and indirect cost analysis	Long term organizational needs

- **Expert Judgment:** Expertise used to assess process inputs and outputs. May involve legal and technical expertise

Plan Procurement Management Tools and Techniques

The Plan Procurement Management process contains four tools and techniques: *make-or-buy analysis, expert judgment, market research,* and *meetings.*

Make-or-Buy Analysis

Make-or-buy analysis is a technique used to determine whether a product or service can be produced internally by the project team, or whether it must be procured externally. When making these determinations, budget constraints are factored into the decision. If the option to buy is chosen, then a decision of whether to purchase or rent is selected, and analysis of the direct and indirect costs are made, such as what the out-of-pocket costs are, as well as the indirect cost of managing the purchasing process. In regards to the purchase or rent option, the project team should consider whether the company as a whole has a long term need for the goods, materials, or equipment – if this is the case, then a portion of the item's cost should be applied to the project, as opposed to the full cost.

Expert Judgment

Expert judgment is used to assess the process's inputs and outputs, to modify evaluation criteria for proposals and offers. Aside from this type of expertise and judgment used, it could also involve legal expertise, such as from a lawyer, business expertise, and technical expertise.

Plan Procurement Management

- **Market Research:** Use of industry research and research / review of vendor capabilities
- **Meetings:** Held with potential bidders to obtain information needed to form a procurement strategy

win-win!

Market Research

The use of research that is published or provided by the industry, such as through conferences, trade shows, product and showcasing. This may also involve researching and reviewing vendor capabilities.

Meetings

Meetings are held with potential bidders in order to provide information and answer questions. The purpose of the meetings is to obtain information needed to form the appropriate procurement strategy. This becomes a win-win situation for the buyer and potential sellers.

Plan Procurement Management

- **Contract Types:**
  - The type of contract used is determined and documented within the procurement management plan.
  - There are three primary types of contracts:

Fixed Price | Cost Reimbursable | Time and Materials

Contract Types

Contract types involves determining the type of contract that will be used, and documenting it within the procurement management plan. There are three primary types of contracts:

- Fixed price
- Cost reimbursable
- Time and materials

Plan Procurement Management

FFP = Most commonly used

Fixed Price
(also known as lump sum)

Summary	Greatest Risk	Sub-Types
• The seller provides an estimate for the work, negotiates with the buyer, and commits to doing the work at that price.	• Seller	• Firm Fixed Price (FFP) • Fixed Price Incentive Fee (FPIF) • Fixed Price with Economic Price Adjustments (FP-EPA)

Fixed Price

Fixed price, also known as lump sum, is where the seller provides an estimate for the work, negotiates with the buyer, and commits to doing the work at that price. The seller has the greatest risk, because if the estimate is not good, they may end up with little to no profit.

There are various types of fixed price contracts, such as firm fixed price, fixed price incentive fee, and fixed price with economic price adjustments.

Firm Fixed Price: The seller sets a price for good or services up front that is not subject to change, unless approved scope changes are made to the agreement. This is the most commonly used type of agreement.

Fixed Price Incentive Fee: Provides financial incentives to the seller upon achieving specific metrics documented within the agreement, on top of a fixed price for the goods or services procured.

Fixed Price with Economic Price Adjustment: Provides special provisions for adjustments needed to address inflation changes or cost changes for specific commodities. This is typically used for contracts that span multiple years.

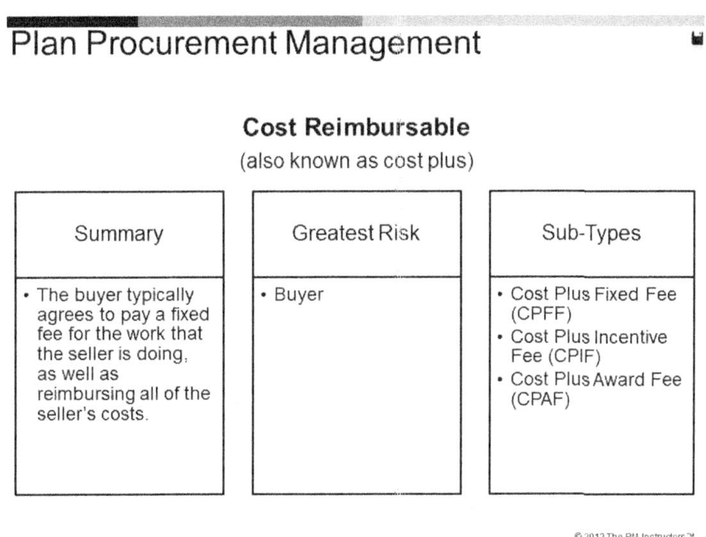
Plan Procurement Management
Cost Reimbursable
(also known as cost plus)
Summary
Greatest Risk
Sub-Types
• The buyer typically agrees to pay a fixed fee for the work that the seller is doing, as well as reimbursing all of the seller's costs.
• Buyer
• Cost Plus Fixed Fee (CPFF)
• Cost Plus Incentive Fee (CPIF)
• Cost Plus Award Fee (CPAF)
© 2013 The PM Instructors™

Cost-Reimbursable

Cost-reimbursable, also known as cost plus, is where the buyer typically agrees to pay a fixed fee for the work that the seller is doing, as well as reimbursing all of the seller's costs. The buyer is the one with the highest risk, since they may have little control over the seller's spending. There are different types of cost plus contracts, such as cost plus fixed fee, cost plus incentive fee, and cost plus award fee.

Cost-Plus-Award-Fee or Cost-Plus-Percentage of Cost: In both cases, the seller is reimbursed for approved costs, and also receives a fee of an agreed-upon percentage of the costs. This is an extremely risky type of contract for a buyer. In the latter sub-contract type, the buyer pays the seller's costs and on top of that, an additional percentage of those costs as a fee.

Cost-Plus-Fixed-Fee: The seller is reimbursed for costs for performing the work and receives a fixed fee payment that is calculated based on the percentage of the estimated project costs. This additional fixed fee is agreed upon at the start of the work and does not change. This is the most common type of cost-reimbursable contract out of the three.

Cost-Plus-Incentive-Fee: In this type, the seller is reimbursed for costs for performing the project work and receives a predetermined fee, and an incentive bonus for achieving certain performance targets.

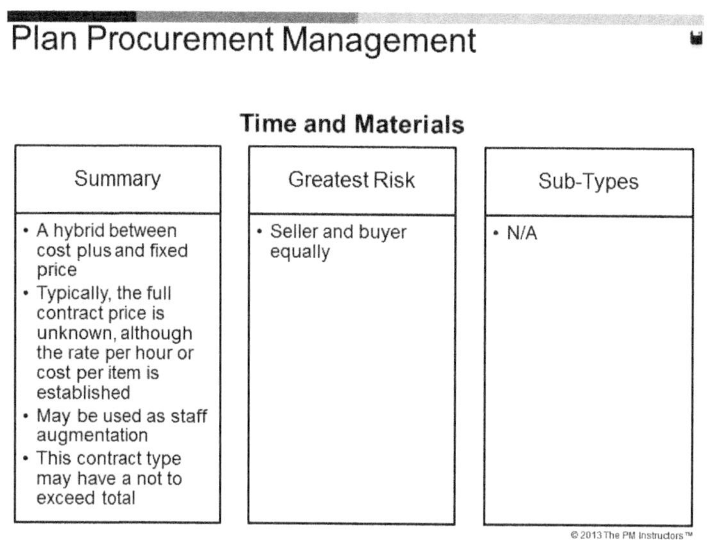
Plan Procurement Management
Time and Materials
Summary
• A hybrid between cost plus and fixed price
• Typically, the full contract price is unknown, although the rate per hour or cost per item is established
• May be used as staff augmentation
• This contract type may have a not to exceed total
Greatest Risk
• Seller and buyer equally
Sub-Types
• N/A
© 2013 The PM Instructors™

Time and Materials

Time and materials is a hybrid between cost plus and fixed price. Typically, the full contract price is unknown, although the rate per hour or cost per item is established. Hiring a contract resource, for instance, is an example of a time and materials contract, where the hourly rate of the resource is known, but the total hours of the full contract is not. As this statement describes, it can be used for staff augmentation purposes. This contract type may have a not to exceed total set by the customer.

The risk of this contract is shared equally between the buyer and the seller.

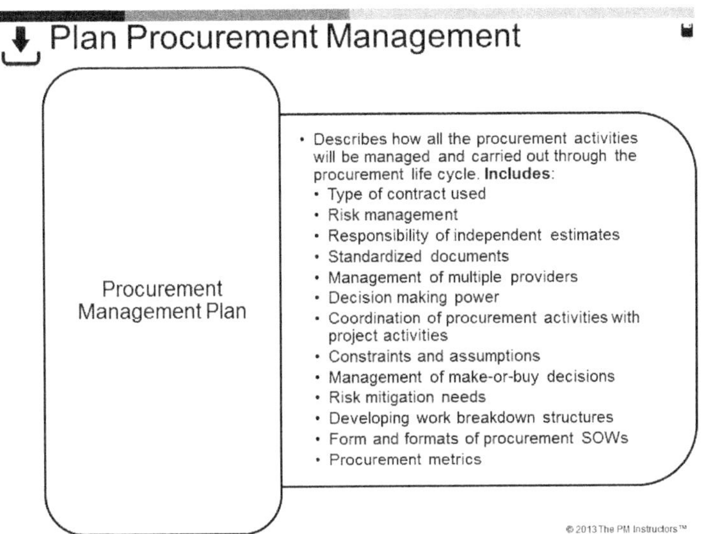

Plan Procurement Management
Procurement Management Plan
• Describes how all the procurement activities will be managed and carried out through the procurement life cycle. Includes:
• Type of contract used
• Risk management
• Responsibility of independent estimates
• Standardized documents
• Management of multiple providers
• Decision making power
• Coordination of procurement activities with project activities
• Constraints and assumptions
• Management of make-or-buy decisions
• Risk mitigation needs
• Developing work breakdown structures
• Form and formats of procurement SOWs
• Procurement metrics
© 2013 The PM Instructors™

Plan Procurement Management Outputs

Plan Procurement Management has seven outputs: *procurement management plan, procurement statement of work, procurement documents, source selection criteria, make-or-buy decisions, change requests,* and *project documents updates.*

Procurement Management Plan

The procurement management plan describes how the procurement related processes will be managed and carried out, from the initiation of the procurement contract to the closing of the contract. According to the *PMBOK® Guide*, it may include the following:

- The type of contract(s) to be used
- Risk management considerations
- Who is responsible for preparing independent estimates;
- Standardized procurement documents
- Management of multiple providers
- The decision making power of the procurement, contracting, or purchasing department
- Coordinating procurement alongside other project components; Identifying pre-qualified sellers
- Constraints and assumptions that could impact purchasing and acquisition activities and decisions; The management of lead times to purchase or acquire items and managing that with the project schedule
- Managing make-or-buy decisions and linking them to the activity resource estimating and schedule development processes
- Identifying performance bonds and insurance contracts to mitigate project risk as needed
- Establishing direction for the seller on developing the contract work breakdown structure
- Establishing the form and format of the procurement statement of work
- Procurement metrics to be used in managing contracts and evaluating sellers

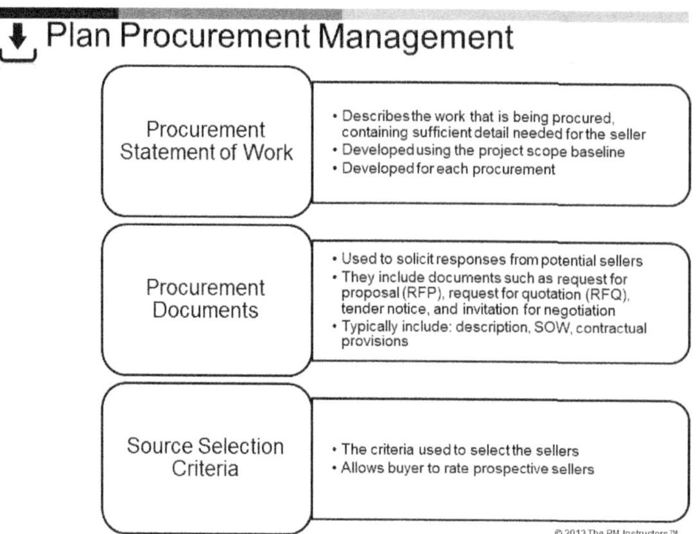

Procurement Statement of Work

The procurement statement of work defines the portion of the scope that is being purchased or acquired, and describes the product, service, or result that is to be supplied by the seller. It includes just enough detail so that prospective sellers can determine whether they can provide the product or service. It may include various requirements and specifications, such as the quantity, quality, performance data, time frame of work, and location. This statement of work is developed using the project scope statement, WBS, and the WBS dictionary. A statement of work is developed for each purchase or acquisition, unless it involves multiple products or services that can be grouped as one.

Procurement Documents

Procurement documents are documents used to solicit responses from potential sellers. They include documents such as request for proposal, request for quotation, tender notice, and invitation for negotiation. Procurement documents should provide prospective sellers with sufficient information that will allow them to determine whether they can provide their services and meet the objectives. It should also detail information needed so that buyers receive a complete and accurate response from the prospective sellers.

When a decision is based on price, the terms bid, tender, or quote are typically used; when it is based on technical skill or approach, it is called a proposal – *keep in mind that this can vary*. The initial request for prospective sellers to respond include: invitation for bid, request for proposal, request for quotation, tender notice, invitation for negotiation, and contractor initial response.

Procurement documents typically include:

- Description of the form for the prospective seller response
- The procurement statement of work
- Contractual provisions, if any (such as non-disclosure agreements)

Source Selection Criteria

Source selection criteria refer to the criteria used to select the vendors or sellers. This will be important to the next process. The criteria allows the buyer to rate and evaluate all the prospective sellers. The criteria used can be objective or subjective, and is sometimes included within the procurement documents. The following are additional examples of source selection criteria:

- Understanding of need
- Overall or life-cycle cost
- Technical capability

- The prospective seller's management approach
- Financial capacity – this is especially important if a large quantity of an item is involved or aggressive schedule targets. Can the prospective seller meet the needs?
- Production capacity and interest
- Business size and type of the prospective seller
- References
- Intellectual property rights

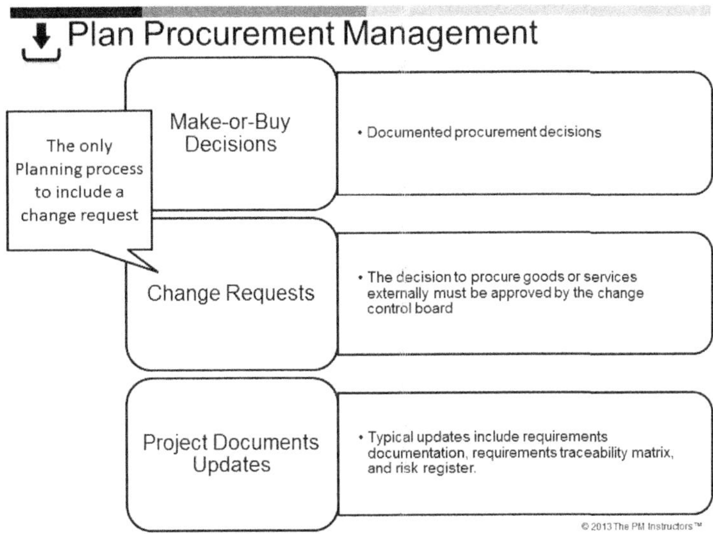
Plan Procurement Management
The only Planning process to include a change request
Make-or-Buy Decisions
• Documented procurement decisions
Change Requests
• The decision to procure goods or services externally must be approved by the change control board
Project Documents Updates
• Typical updates include requirements documentation, requirements traceability matrix, and risk register.
© 2013 The PM Instructors™

Make-or-Buy Decisions

Make-or-buy decisions are the documented decisions of what products, services or results will be acquired and purchased, or developed internally by the project team.

Change Requests

Plan Procurement Management is the only process that falls within the Planning Process Group to have change requests as an output. This is because during planning efforts, it is not necessary to submit change requests – these are submitted when attempting to make changes to a baseline or to carry out a corrective or preventive action. In this case procuring resources, goods, services, or anything else that is external to the organization often calls for an approval.

Project Documents Updates

As a result of carrying out this process, several project documents will require updates. Typical documents updated include the requirements documentation, requirements traceability matrix, and risk register.

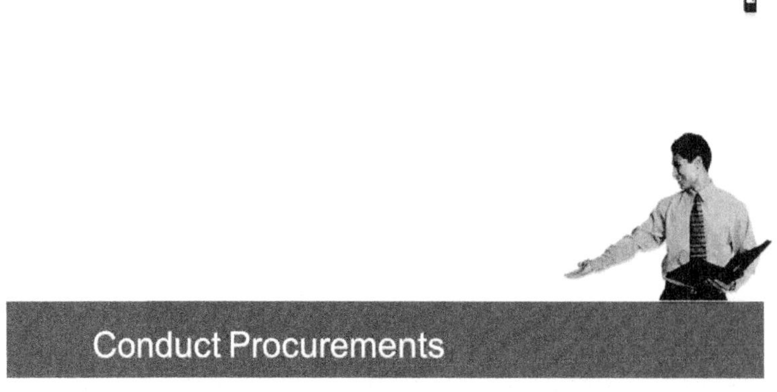
Conduct Procurements
Purpose: To obtain seller responses, select a seller, and award a contract.

Conduct Procurements Process Overview

The purpose of the Conduct Procurements process is to obtain seller responses, select a seller, and award a contract.

Depending on what is being procured, carrying out this process may vary. For instance, if a seller is chosen from a pre-qualified list, or if a partner agreement already exists, then selecting a seller may be a quick and easy process. In other cases, gathering a good number of proposals may require effort on the part of the buyer, as well as evaluating and ranking the incoming proposals.

In the end, the buyer will award a contract, resulting in a seller.

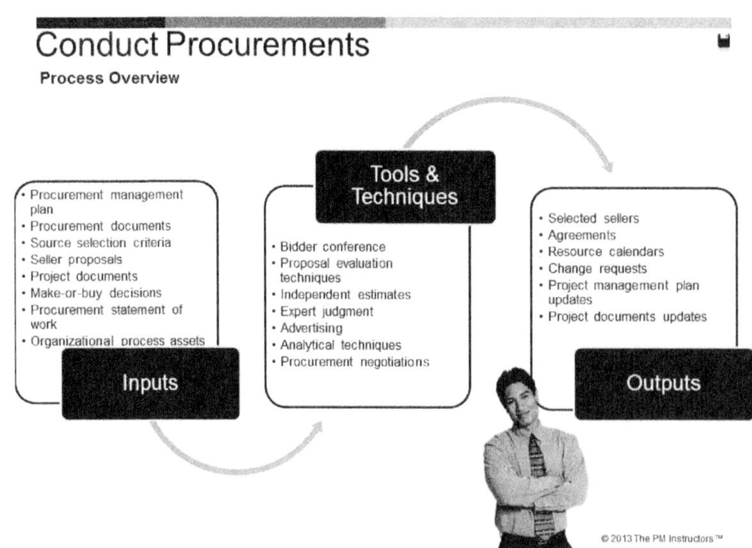
Conduct Procurements
Process Overview
Inputs
• Procurement management plan
• Procurement documents
• Source selection criteria
• Seller proposals
• Project documents
• Make-or-buy decisions
• Procurement statement of work
• Organizational process assets
Tools & Techniques
• Bidder conference
• Proposal evaluation techniques
• Independent estimates
• Expert judgment
• Advertising
• Analytical techniques
• Procurement negotiations
Outputs
• Selected sellers
• Agreements
• Resource calendars
• Change requests
• Project management plan updates
• Project documents updates
© 2013 The PM Instructors™

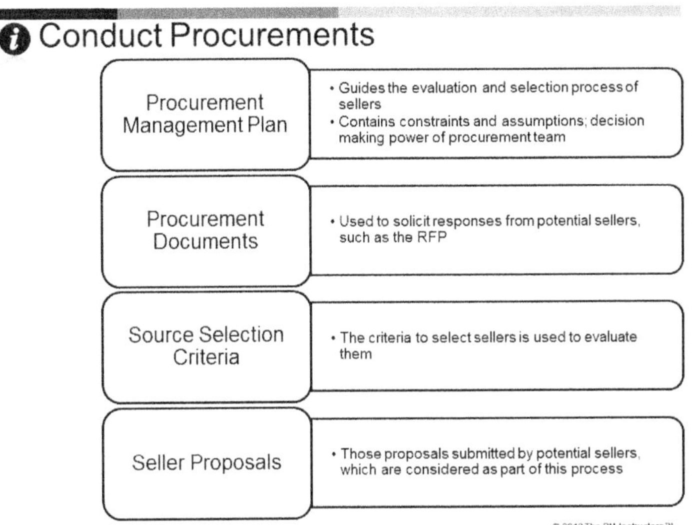

Conduct Procurements Inputs

The Conduct Procurements process has eight inputs: *procurement management plan, procurement documents, source selection criteria, seller proposals, project documents, make-or-buy decisions, procurement statement of work,* and *organizational process assets.*

Procurement Management Plan

The procurement management plan contains several key items used to guide the team in carrying out this process. For example, it contains constraints and assumptions impacting procurement, management of multiple providers, and the decision making power of the procurement team. The primary significance of the procurement management plan is that it guides the project manager in carrying out the seller evaluation and selection process.

Procurement Documents

Procurement documents are used to solicit responses from potential sellers, such as an RFP. This will be needed to ensure that proposals submitted by potential sellers are complete. It should also contain the selection process published to potential sellers.

Source Selection Criteria

Source selection criteria was developed and generated as an output of the previous process. This will be used to screen incoming proposals.

Seller Proposals

As potential sellers submit proposals, they will enter the process here, through this input. This is the group of proposals that will be evaluated. These are the responses submitted by the potential sellers to the procurement documents. The project or procurement team will evaluate the potential sellers based on the proposals, which provide the basic set of information from the potential sellers that will be used by the buyer to make a decision.

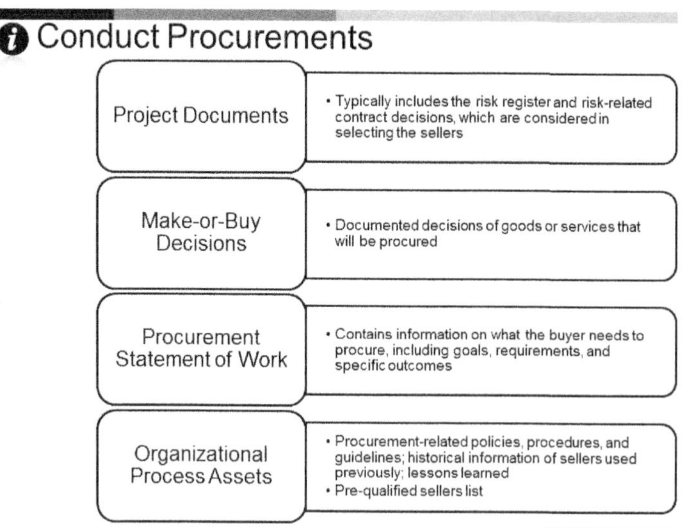

Conduct Procurements
Project Documents
• Typically includes the risk register and risk-related contract decisions, which are considered in selecting the sellers
Make-or-Buy Decisions
• Documented decisions of goods or services that will be procured
Procurement Statement of Work
• Contains information on what the buyer needs to procure, including goals, requirements, and specific outcomes
Organizational Process Assets
• Procurement-related policies, procedures, and guidelines; historical information of sellers used previously; lessons learned
• Pre-qualified sellers list
© 2013 The PM Instructors™

Project Documents

Project documents typically include the risk register and risk-related contract decisions, which are considered when selecting a seller.

Make-or-Buy Decisions

Make-or-buy decisions that were made in the previous process will be needed for documentation purposes.

Procurement Statement of Work

The procurement statement of work provides prospective sellers with information on what the buyer needs to procure. This can include goals, requirements, and specific outcomes of the goods or services needed, which will allow the prospective sellers to determine whether they will submit a proposal.

Organizational Process Assets

In this process, organizational process assets are used to access procurement policies, guidelines, and procedures, particularly those that pertain to the evaluation of seller proposals. Organizational process assets also contain lessons learned and past historical information. This information can be very useful if a previous potential seller was used.

If a pre-qualified seller list exists, then it will be needed in this process. These are the sellers that have already gone through a screening process previously, and have been authorized to provide the organization with their services.

Conduct Procurements

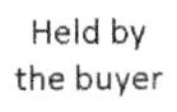

Bidder Conference: Provides a venue for all potential sellers to come together and have their questions answered in an open and fair platform

- The buyer has the responsibility of making sure that all potential sellers receive the same opportunity (no preferential treatment) and receive answers to questions asked

- **Proposal Evaluation Techniques:** Includes those techniques used to review the proposals against the selection criteria, such as a weighted scoring model, or checklist

Conduct Procurements Tools and Techniques

The Conduct Procurements process has a total of seven tools and techniques: *bidder conferences, proposal evaluation techniques, independent estimates, expert judgment, advertising, analytical techniques,* and *procurement negotiations.*

Bidder Conference

Bidder conferences are held by the buyer and provide a venue for all potential sellers to come together and have their questions answered in an open and fair platform. The buyer has the responsibility of making sure that all potential sellers receive the same opportunity (no preferential treatment) and receive answers to questions asked.

Proposal Evaluation Techniques

Proposal evaluation techniques are used to review the proposals against the selection criteria. A weighted scoring model may be used, a basic checklist, screening systems, etc.

Conduct Procurements

- **Independent Estimates:** Estimates obtained by the buyer through a non-biased third party, or an internally prepared estimate. This is used to compare against the incoming bids.
- **Expert Judgment:** Used to evaluate proposals. May include:
  - Contract administrator
  - Those with negotiation expertise
  - Multi-discipline review team
- **Advertising:**
  - Buyer may be required to advertise the work
  - Buyer may opt to advertise in order to widen the potential resource pool

Independent Estimates

The buyer may opt for obtaining independent estimates from a non-biased third party, or prepare its own independent estimates to compare against the incoming bids. These estimates provide a way of checking the quotes submitted by the prospective sellers. This is also known as a "should-cost" estimate. Sometimes, large differences between the independent estimate and the quotes can signal that the procurement statement of work was not clear.

Expert Judgment

Expert judgment is used to evaluate the proposals submitted by prospective sellers. It may involve a contract administrator and others with expertise to negotiate and authorize a contract. Expert judgment may also consist of a multi-discipline review team with expertise in the areas covered within the procurement documents and contract.

Advertising

In some cases, the buyer may be required to advertise the work (this is common in the government sector), while in other cases, the buyer may opt to advertise in order to widen the potential resource pool.

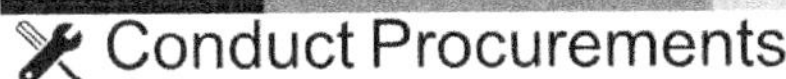

Conduct Procurements

- **Analytical Techniques:** An analysis carried out to determine whether vendor has the capability of providing the goods or services needed. Examples:

Past Performance	Evaluating Risk	Ability to Meet Schedule / Cost Constraints

- **Procurement Negotiations:** Where the contract is negotiated, including contract terms.

Sample Terms Negotiated:
Responsibilities and authorities
Applicable terms and law
Technical and business management approaches
Proprietary rights
Technical solution
Overall schedule
Contract financing, payments, and price

Analytical Techniques

Analytical techniques can be used to further assess whether a vendor has the capability to provide the goods or services needed by the buyer. This may involve analyzing past performance, evaluating risk, the ability to meet schedule and cost constraints, etc.

Procurement Negotiations

Procurement negotiations is where the contract between the buyer and seller is negotiated. This involves working out the contract terms. Here are some of the items included within contract negotiations:

- Responsibilities and authorities
- Applicable terms and law
- Technical and business management approaches
- Proprietary rights
- Technical solution
- Overall schedule
- Contract financing, payments, and price

The result of contract negotiation is the awarded contract. While the project management team may be included within the negotiations, the project manager may not be the lead negotiator.

Conduct Procurements

Selected Sellers	Agreements
• Those that were ranked highest or most competitive • Have negotiated a draft contract	• Official contract awarded to selected seller • May be complex or simple • Legally binding

Conduct Procurements Outputs

The Conduct Procurements process has six outputs: *selected sellers, agreements, resource calendars, change requests, project management plan updates,* and *project documents updates.*

Selected Sellers

The selected sellers are those that have been determined as the highest ranked or most competitive based vendors on the proposal and bid evaluation, and that have also been able to negotiate a draft contract.

Agreements

Agreements refer to the official contract awarded to the selected seller. The contract can be a complex document, or simply a purchase order for off-the-shelf items. In all cases, it is considered to be a legally binding agreement that obligates the seller to provide the specified product or services, and obligates the buyer to pay the seller. There are several potential components within the contract, and how complex it is depends on the procurement item. Here are examples of these:

- Section headings
- Statement of work
- Schedule
- Period of performance
- Roles and responsibilities
- Pricing and payment
- Inflation adjustments
- Acceptance criteria
- Warranty
- Product support
- Limitation of liability
- Fees
- Retainers
- Penalties
- Incentives
- Insurance
- Performance bonds
- Subcontractor approval
- Change request handling

- Termination and disputes resolution

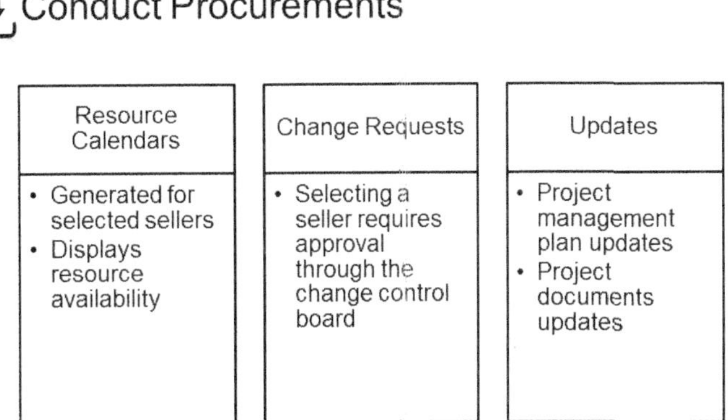
Conduct Procurements
Resource Calendars
• Generated for selected sellers
• Displays resource availability
Change Requests
• Selecting a seller requires approval through the change control board
Updates
• Project management plan updates
• Project documents updates
© 2013 The PM Instructors™

Resource Calendars

Once a seller is selected, resource calendars will be generated for the resources procured (if applicable). This displays the availability of those resources.

Change Requests

Selecting a seller may require several changes, and these must go through the change control board through the Perform Integrated Change Control process.

Project Management Plan Updates

Project management plan updates typically involve updates to one of three baselines (scope, schedule, cost) and the procurement management plan.

Project Documents Updates

Project documents updates typically involve updates to the requirements documentation, requirements traceability matrix, and the risk register.

Purpose: To manage procurement relationships, monitor contract performance, and make changes and corrections as appropriate.

Control Procurements Process Overview

The purpose of the Control Procurements process is to manage procurement relationships, monitor contract performance, and make changes and corrections as appropriate. Both the buyer and seller are tasked with ensuring that contract terms are followed.

How contracts are managed varies from organization to organization. In some instances, a contract administrator is responsible for management of the contract.

The following applies to this process:

- Both the buyer and seller have an interest in making sure that the other meets their contractual obligations
- It's important that the project management team be aware and understands the legal implications of the contract. For this reason, contract administration may occur separate from the project group
- The outputs of this process are integrated into the overall project
- This process is also concerned with monitoring the payments made to the seller, and that the contract requirements for compensation are met
- The seller's performance is monitored, reviewed, and documented in this process. The documentation of the seller's performance is important for future relationships. A performance evaluation is carried out by the buyer at regular intervals
- Early termination of the contracted work is also managed through this process, in accordance to the contract
- This process is also concerned with managing changes to the contract, with the terms of managing changes usually addressed within the contract itself

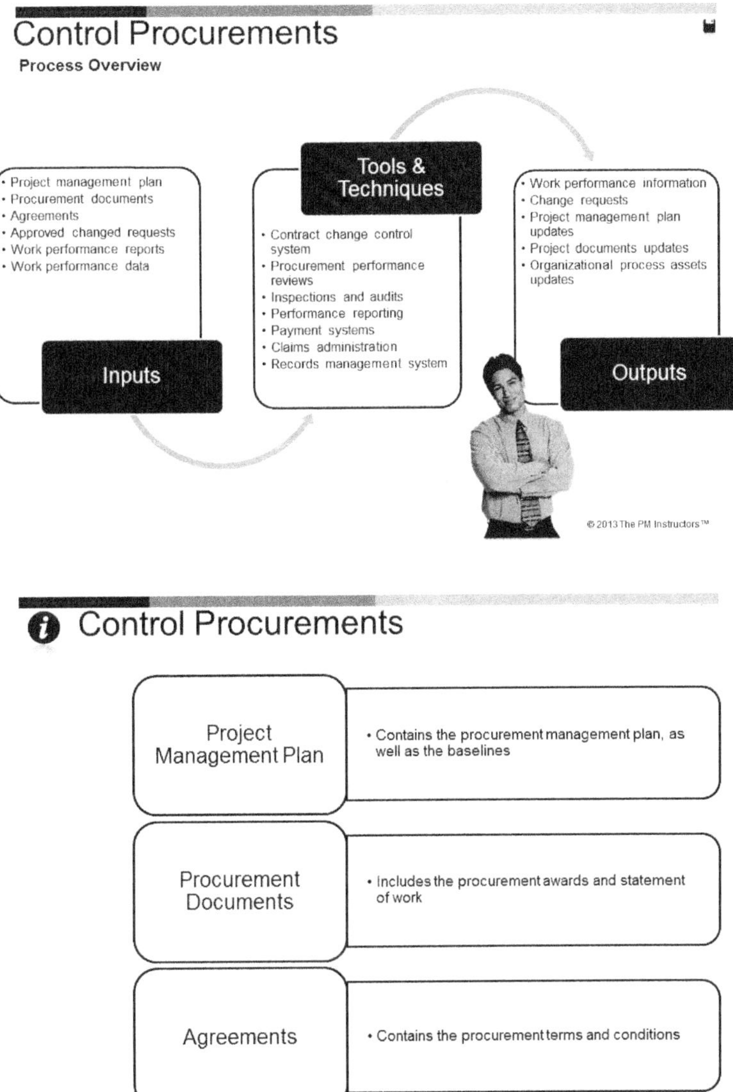
Control Procurements
Process Overview
Tools & Techniques
• Project management plan
• Procurement documents
• Agreements
• Approved changed requests
• Work performance reports
• Work performance data
Inputs
• Contract change control system
• Procurement performance reviews
• Inspections and audits
• Performance reporting
• Payment systems
• Claims administration
• Records management system
• Work performance information
• Change requests
• Project management plan updates
• Project documents updates
• Organizational process assets updates
Outputs
© 2013 The PM Instructors™
Control Procurements
Project Management Plan
• Contains the procurement management plan, as well as the baselines
Procurement Documents
• Includes the procurement awards and statement of work
Agreements
• Contains the procurement terms and conditions
© 2013 The PM Instructors™

Control Procurements Inputs

The Control Procurements process has a total of six inputs: *project management plan, procurement documents, agreements, approved change requests, work performance reports,* and *work performance data.*

Project Management Plan

The project management plan contains the procurement management plan as well as the baselines. The procurement management plan guides the project management team in carrying out the process, while the baselines are relevant to measuring how the seller is progressing.

Procurement Documents

Procurement documents include the procurement awards and statement of work.

Agreements

Agreements refers to the contract that will be administered and carried out within this process. The contract dictates the terms and conditions of the relationship between the buyer and the seller.

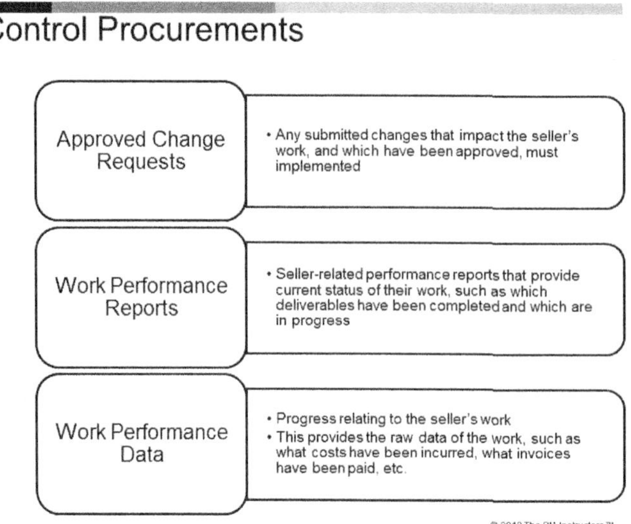

Approved Change Requests

Any submitted changes that impact the seller's work, and which have been approved, must come through this process as an input for implementation. This may even include approved changes made to the contract. All approved changes come through the Perform Integrated Change Control process.

Work Performance Reports

Work performance reports refer to seller-related reports. This provides current status of the seller's work, such as which deliverables have been completed, and which are in progress.

Work Performance Data

Work performance data refers to information about the seller's progress. This provides the raw data of their work, such as what costs have been incurred, what invoices have been paid, etc.

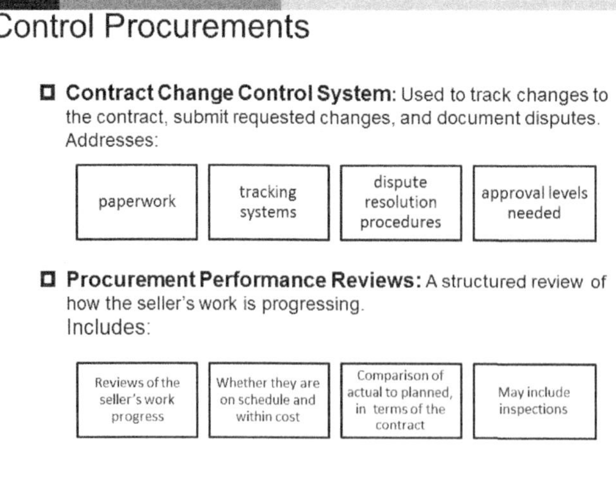

Control Procurements Tools and Techniques

The Control Procurements process contains the following tools and techniques: *contract change control system, procurement performance reviews, inspections and audits, performance reporting, payment systems, claims administration, and records management system.*

Contract Change Control System

The contract change control system is used to track changes to the contract, submit requested changes, and document disputes. This system simply outlines the procedures to follow in the event that the contract needs to be modified. It covers: the paperwork, tracking systems, dispute resolution procedures, and approval levels needed to authorize the changes. This system is integrated and works with the integrated change control system used to manage project changes.

Procurement Performance Reviews

Procurement performance reviews are structured reviews meant to identify successes and failures of the seller's work within the project, monitor the progress in respect to the contract statement of work, and for the buyer to determine whether non-compliance exists and the seller's ability to perform the work. It includes reviews of the seller's work progress in terms of delivering on the scope and quality of the project, whether they are on schedule, within cost, in comparison to the terms of the contract. The reviews may include inspections completed by the buyer, and documentation prepared by the seller.

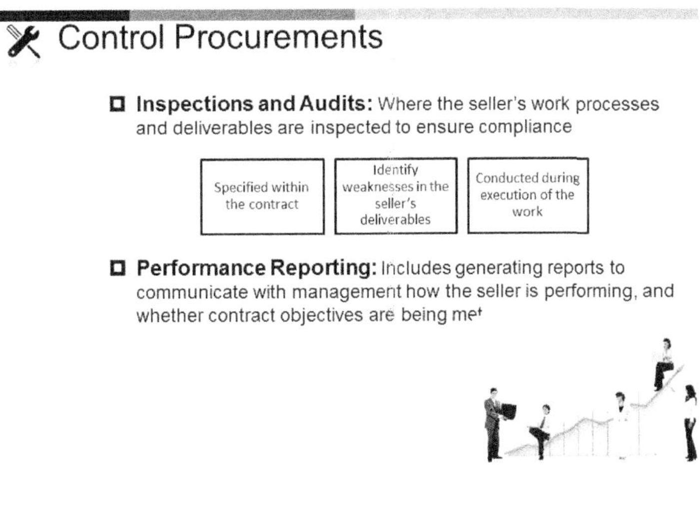

Inspections and Audits

Inspections and audits is where the seller's work processes and deliverables are inspected to ensure compliance. If you have a cost-reimbursable contract type, the audits become very important to ensure that the seller is controlling costs.

These are usually specified within the contract, and therefore required by the buyer. The purpose behind inspections and audits is to identify weaknesses in the seller's work processes or deliverables. These are conducted during the execution of the project work, and supported by the seller.

Performance Reporting

Performance reporting generates reports to communicate with management how the seller is performing, and whether contract objectives are being met.

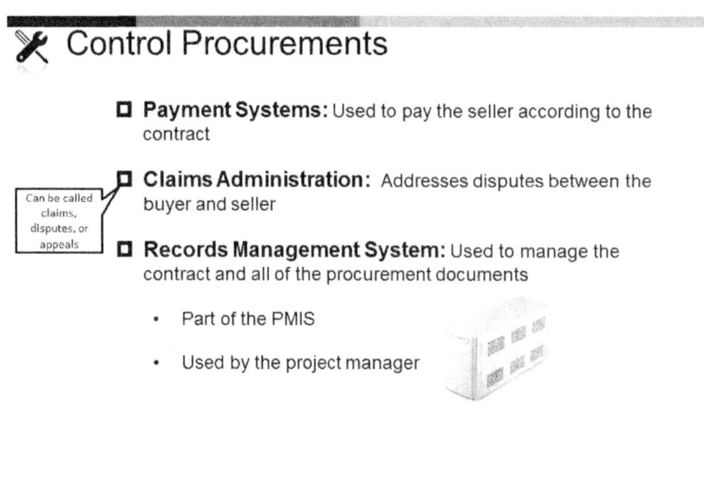
Control Procurements
Payment Systems: Used to pay the seller according to the contract
Claims Administration: Addresses disputes between the buyer and seller
Can be called claims, disputes, or appeals
Records Management System: Used to manage the contract and all of the procurement documents
Part of the PMIS
Used by the project manager
© 2013 The PM Instructors™

Payment Systems

Payment systems refer to payments made to the seller by the buyer, handled by the buyer's accounts payable system. If the project is large enough, then it may include its own payment system. Both of these scenarios should involve reviews and approvals by the project management team as appropriate and according to the terms of the contract.

Claims Administration

Claims administration deals with disputes between the seller and buyer, when a resolution cannot be reached, or regarding a change to the contract. These issues tend to be called claims, disputes, or appeals. Claims are documented, processed, monitored and managed through the contract's life cycle and following the terms specified within the contract. When a claim cannot be resolved, they are handled as specified within the contract, typically noted as dispute resolution procedures, and may involve litigation or arbitration.

Records Management System

The records management system is used to manage the contract and all of the procurement documents. It is a part of the project management information system, and is considered to be a set of processes, related control functions, and automation tools. The project manager uses the records management system to manage contract documentation and records. This system is very helpful in tracking contract documents and correspondence, and then archiving them.

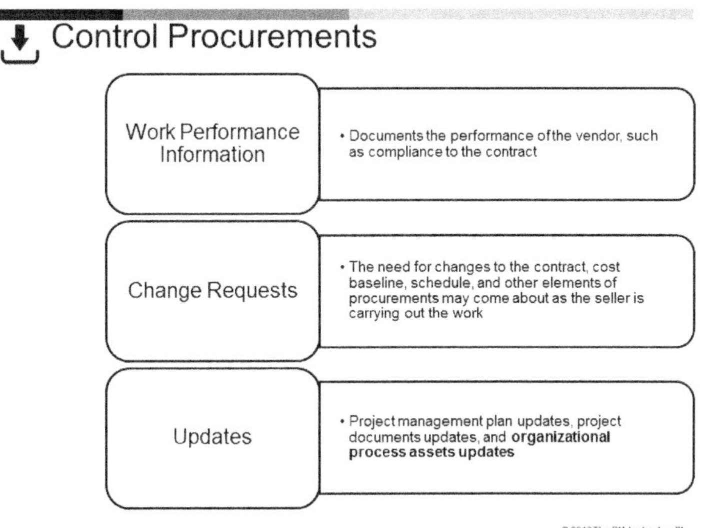
Control Procurements
Work Performance Information
• Documents the performance of the vendor, such as compliance to the contract
Change Requests
• The need for changes to the contract, cost baseline, schedule, and other elements of procurements may come about as the seller is carrying out the work
Updates
• Project management plan updates, project documents updates, and organizational process assets updates
© 2013 The PM Instructors™

Control Procurements Outputs

The Control Procurements process produces five outputs: *work performance information, change requests, project management plan updates, project documents updates, and organizational process assets updates.*

Work Performance Information

Work performance information refers to the performance of the vendor, including compliance to the contract. This information allows the project manager to better forecast and make effective decisions, as well as manage risks.

Change Requests

Change requests is an important output, since changes to the contract, cost baseline, schedule, and other elements of procurements may come about as the seller is carrying out the work. If requested changes are approved by the change control board, they will come in as an input to be implemented through this process.

Project Management Plan Updates

Project management plan updates typically involve updates to the procurement management plan, reflecting any approved change requests that impact procurement management.

Project Documents Updates

Project documents typically updated as a result of carrying out this process include: procurement documentation, including the contract, schedules, unapproved contract changes, and other information pertaining to information that makes up procurement documents.

Organizational Process Assets Updates

Updates to organizational process assets may include:

1. Correspondence regarding contract terms and conditions, warnings of unsatisfactory performance, requests for contract changes or clarifications, and buyer audits and inspections. This record of correspondence is maintained by both parties and includes both written and oral communication;
2. Payment schedules and requests. The project may utilize the buyer's accounts payable system or, if big enough, the project would have it's own payable system. If it uses the external accounts payable system, then it would include updates of payment schedules and requests. Otherwise, it would only include payments;

3. Seller performance evaluation documentation, which is prepared by the buyer. The buyer documents the seller's performance, rating them on how well they are performing the project work, and whether they should be considered for future work. These documents can also be used if early termination of the seller's contract is needed.

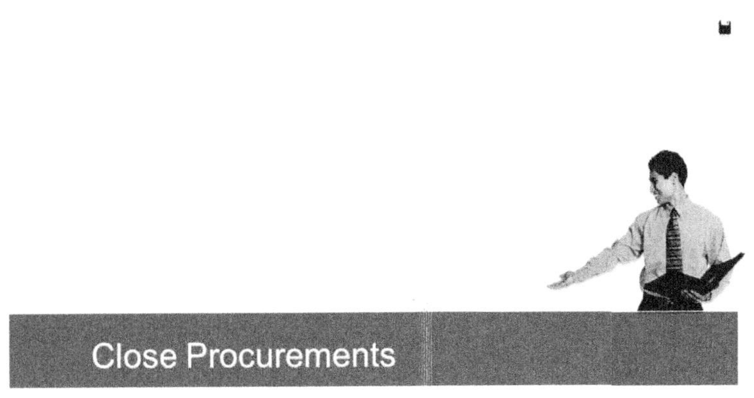

Close Procurements
Purpose: To complete each project procurement.

Close Procurements Process Overview

The purpose of the Close Procurements process is to complete and settle each contract, including resolution of open items and closing each contract applicable to the project.

The following should be considered when carrying out this process:

- This process works with the Close Project or Phase process, supporting this process by verifying that all work and deliverables are acceptable
- This process involves administrative activities
- Each procurement contract related to the project is addressed within this process, and if a project exists that is multi-phased, then the process closes that portion of the contract relating to the phase
- This process may involve early termination of a contract when applicable

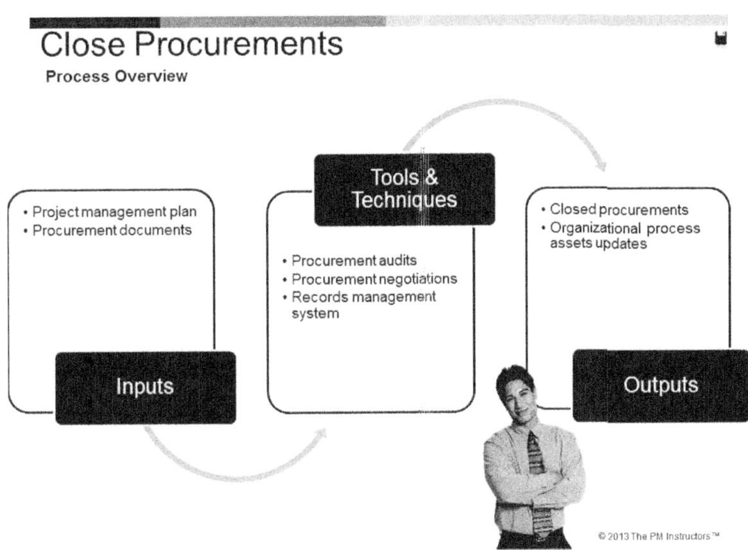

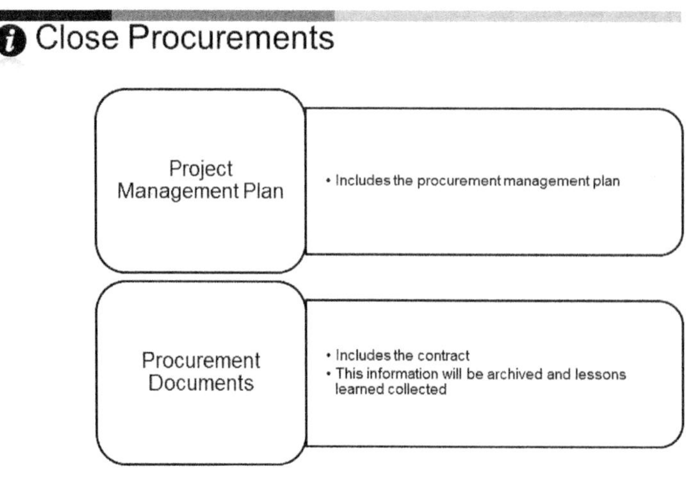
Close Procurements
Project Management Plan
• Includes the procurement management plan
Procurement Documents
• Includes the contract
• This information will be archived and lessons learned collected
© 2013 The PM Instructors™

Close Procurements Inputs

The Close Procurements process has two inputs: *project management plan* and *procurement documents.*

Project Management Plan

Project management plan contains the procurement management plan. This sub-plan provides the details of the procedures involved in closing out the contract.

Procurement Documents

Procurement documents includes the contract, along with other seller-specific information. The contract will be essential to confirming that all requirements have been met by the seller; it also outlines closing procedures agreed to between the buyer and seller. This information will also be archived and lessons learned will be collected.

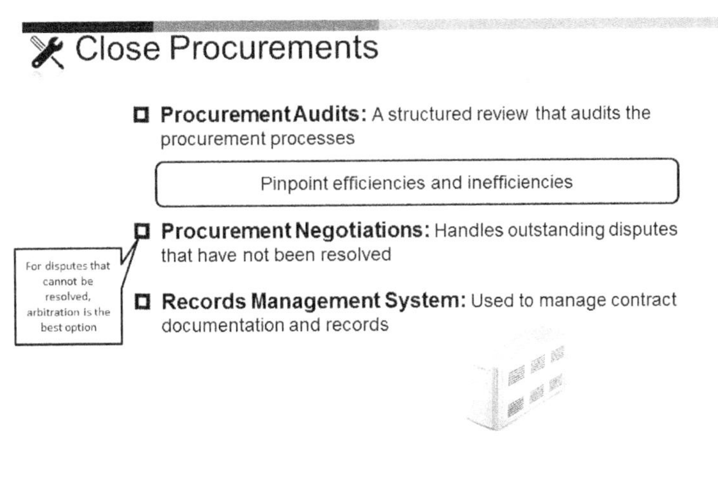

Close Procurements Tools and Techniques

The Close Procurements process has three tools and techniques: *procurement audits, procurement negotiations,* and *records management system.*

Procurement Audits

Procurement audits are structured reviews that audit the procurement management processes. The idea is to pinpoint what the efficiencies and inefficiencies were within the processes, which will be documented as part of the lessons learned. This information is important for future procurements, whether for the current project or future projects.

Procurement Negotiations

Procurement negotiations refer to outstanding disputes that have been negotiated. If the dispute cannot be resolved, then arbitration is an option; according to the *PMBOK® Guide*, litigation in the courts is the least desirable option, but is an option nevertheless.

Records Management System

The records management system is part of the project management information system, and is used by the project manager, and/or procurement management team, to manage contract documentation and records.

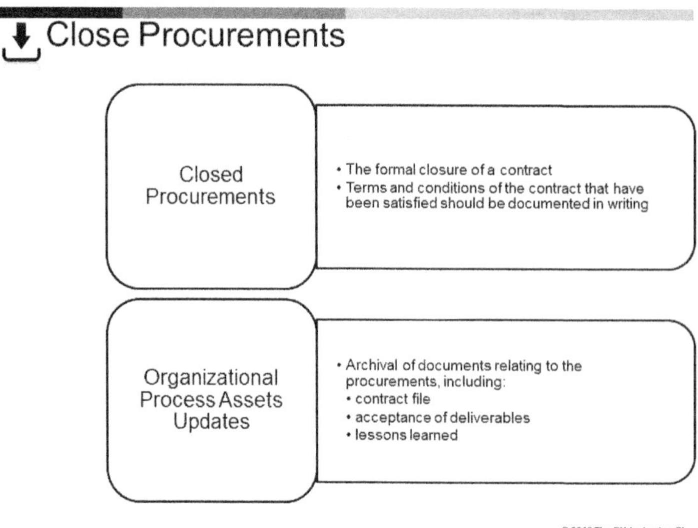

Close Procurements Outputs

The Closed Procurements process has two outputs: *closed procurements* and *organizational process assets updates*.

Closed Procurements

Closed procurements refer to the formal closure of a contract. It is important that a formal written notice is provided to the seller that the contract has been completed, and that this be provided by the buyer through an authorized contract administrator. The requirements for formal closure of the contract are included within the contract terms and the procurement management plan.

Organizational Process Assets Updates

All of the documents relating to the procurements will be archived, including the archiving of the documented deliverable acceptance, and lessons learned will be collected once again at the end of the procurement cycle.

Updates to the organizational process assets include three archived items:

1. Contract file, which includes a complete set of contract documentation that includes the closed contract
2. Deliverable acceptance, which is the formal written notice of accepted or rejected deliverables
3. Lessons learned documentation, including recommendations that would be helpful for future procurement planning and implementation

Module Summary

In this module we:

- Defined the purpose of the Project Procurement Management Knowledge Area
- Identified the processes of the Project Procurement Management Knowledge Area
- Recalled the key outputs of the procurement management processes
- Differentiated between the inputs, tools and techniques, and outputs of the procurement management processes
- Identified various types of fixed-price, cost-reimbursable and time and material contractual agreements

Chapter Quiz

Exam Practice Questions

1. Eight weeks ago, Jody provided the last set of deliverables to her customer and received 75% of the payment for her services, and will be sending out an invoice for the remaining 25% at the end of the week. She has already completed the process of disbanding her team and assigning them to new projects, since their current project is now closed. However, today, the customer called to inform her that they've just had a chance to examine the deliverables that were provided and have come to the conclusion that the product doesn't meet their needs. In order to remain in compliance with the terms of the contract, she needs to reassemble the original team to rework the deliverables and officially bring the project to a close. A project is considered complete when:
   A. The lessons learned have been archived
   B. Project team has been released
   C. All payments for the project have been received
   D. Formal documented acceptance has been received by the customer

2. You are coordinating a contract between your company and Mac Burger, who sells commercial deep fryers for $155 each. This purchase will replace existing deep fryers in 450 of your fast food stores, but will continue to replace the deep fryers of additional stores out of the 800 locations over the next six months. What is the BEST contract type for this purchase?
   A. Fixed price
   B. Cost-reimbursable
   C. Time and material
   D. Cost-plus-fixed-fee

3. One of the vendors of the project you are managing offers you two tickets to a local jazz concert event as a thank you for working with them. What should you do?
   A. Decline the tickets, since you don't like jazz, but thank them for their thoughtfulness
   B. Accept the tickets, but give them to the project sponsor, since they are the ones funding the project and therefore should receive them instead
   C. Accept the tickets and hold a drawing amongst the project team since everyone collectively worked with the vendor
   D. Decline the tickets, since it is considered unethical to accept gifts from vendors

4. Which of the following processes documents the products, services, and results needed to be procured externally?
   A. Plan Procurement Management
   B. Plan Contracts
   C. Conduct Procurements
   D. Control Procurements

5. Which of the following identifies successes and failures that should be brought to light and considered within the preparation or administration of other procurement contracts within the project?
   A. Weighting System
   B. Records Management System
   C. Procurement Audits
   D. Buyer-Conducted Performance Reviews

6. The City of Los Angeles is seeking a vendor to construct a new bridge between their offices on 1st Street and 2nd Street. In order to generate as many bids as possible, while ensuring that all vendors have an equal opportunity to bid on the project, they decide to hold a bidder conference. Bidder conferences can BEST be described as:
   A. Meetings held by the seller for the buyer to prepare the bid or proposal
   B. Meetings held by the seller to provide the buyer with an oral presentation after submitting the proposal
   C. Meetings held by the buyer with a group of prospective sellers that takes place before the preparation of the bid or proposal
   D. Meetings held by the buyer with a group of prospective sellers that takes place after the preparation of the bid or proposal

7. Jet Red airlines is in need of a vendor to provide them with a new GPS tracking system that would enable customers to see flights in route by logging onto JetRedAirlines.com. Tanya is the project manager responsible for creating the request for proposal (RFP) to locate the right vendor. In addition to finding a vendor that can deliver the service at the lowest cost, the executive team has informed her that the contract should ensure that Jet Red has the least amount of exposure to risk on the contract. Which contract type poses a higher risk to the buyer?
   A. Fixed price
   B. Cost-reimbursable
   C. Time and material
   D. Cost-plus-fixed-fee

8. Which of the following are tools and techniques is not utilized by the Control Procurements process?
   A. Procurement performance reviews
   B. Records management system
   C. Payment system
   D. Make-or-buy analysis

9. As part of the general requirements for responding to RFPs posted by the Jet Red Airlines company, the procurement team always informs sellers of the following two requirements that must be met in order for a response to be considered: 1) Provide a supplemental description of any projects worked on that were similar to the one listed in the RFP, and 2) return the response to the procurement office no later than 12pm from the deadline date noted on the RFP. Which of the following establishes a minimum set of performance requirements for one or more of the seller evaluation criteria, as stated above?
   A. Weighting systems
   B. Screening systems
   C. Seller rating systems
   D. Proposal evaluation techniques

10. Which of the following is not included as part of procurement documents?
   A. Agreement
   B. Approved change requests
   C. Work performance data
   D. Seller proposals

11. You have just stated that the deadline for sellers to submit their RFPs is 45 days from the official release date, and your Administrator has arrived to assist you with writing up the RFP announcement that will be sent out and posted for potential sellers. Next, you begin creating the source selection criteria. What project management process are you in?
    A. Plan Procurement Management
    B. Conduct Procurements
    C. Control Procurements
    D. Develop Project Management Plan

12. The accounts receivable department of ZipFast Auto Parts has just sent Richard an email informing him that the buyer of the project has sent them the final payment. Since Richard works for ZipFast Auto Parts, the accounting department has asked him to provide them with an email stating the project has been closed so that they can officially close out related POs. Before this can be done, what must the buyer provide to ZipFast Auto Parts to officially close out the contract?
    A. Formal written notice of completion
    B. Final payment receipt
    C. Lessons learned documentation
    D. Contract file

13. Which of the following is not an output of the Conduct Procurements process?
    A. Source selection criteria
    B. Selected sellers
    C. Agreement
    D. Change requests

14. Which of the following processes is responsible for monitoring the work of sellers?
    A. Plan Procurement Management
    B. Conduct Procurements
    C. Control Procurements
    D. Close Procurements

15. Prime Pictures Company is looking to procure the development of an interactive website. After issuing a request for proposal (RFP), they are finding themselves with a small number of incoming proposals from potential sellers. What can the company do to increase the number of proposals under consideration?
    A. Advertise
    B. Get an independent estimate
    C. Use the internet
    D. Nothing

16. You have just finalized an agreement between your company and Mac Burger, who sells commercial deep fryers for $155 each. What process have you just completed?
    A. Plan Procurement Management
    B. Conduct Procurements
    C. Control Procurements
    D. Close Procurements

17. You have just finalized an agreement between your company and Mac Burger, who sells commercial deep fryers for $155 each, and the work is currently in progress. What process will most likely be carried out next?
    A. Plan Procurement Management
    B. Conduct Procurements
    C. Control Procurements
    D. Close Procurements

18. Prime Pictures Company is procuring the development of an interactive website. After issuing a request for proposal (RFP), several proposals were submitted by prospective sellers. One of the selection criteria that the company is using is that only pre-qualified sellers will be considered. Which input provides this information?
    A. Organizational process assets
    B. Procurement management plan
    C. Seller proposals
    D. Enterprise environmental factors

19. Prime Pictures Company is procuring the development of an interactive website. The vendor selected has asked for a one week extension to complete a major deliverable that is contractually due in two weeks. They notified the Prime Pictures Company project manager that the delay was due to a key team member winning the lottery, and resigning the next day. What should the project manager do?
    A. Agree to give them the additional week
    B. Decline, since this is a major deliverable
    C. Nothing
    D. Submit a change request

20. Which of the following is responsible for performing a structured review of the procurement processes?
    A. Procurement negotiation
    B. Procurement audit
    C. Expert judgment
    D. Performance reporting

Chapter Quiz

Exam Practice Answers

1. Answer: D

   Explanation: A project is not officially considered closed until the customer or buyer signs off on it. This is a mistake many companies make, which leaves the door open for further requests or conflict as to whether or not the project was really closed or not. Sign-off addresses it directly and also obtains agreement from the customer that the deliverables and scope have indeed been met.

2. Answer: C

   Explanation: One thing you will notice in this example is that the price is fixed, ruling out cost-reimbursable and cost-plus-fixed-fee as potential options. Another important detail is that the total number of products purchased is left open, fixed price as well, since the total cost of the purchase has not been determined. The correct answer is time and material, which is a combination of fixed price and cost plus.

3. Answer: D

   Explanation: Accepting any gifts or favors from vendors, even if it appears innocent, is not acceptable for the exam, since we do not know what the defined policies are around doing so (unless the question specifies what the policies or guidelines are). Although it may have been a very genuine gift or offer, it is your responsibility to decline it. Declining the gift simply because you don't like it, is also not a good choice. The correct answer involves respectfully declining the gift.

4. Answer: A

   Explanation: The question describes the purpose of the Plan Procurement Management process, which puts together the procurement management plan, analyzes what work must be taken care of outside of the project team, and compiles selection criteria for evaluating seller proposals.

5. Answer: C

   Explanation: Procurement audits focus on the procurement processes, with the intent of making them more efficient and effective. Other items included within the options are specific to the project. Procurement audits are something similar to what exists within the quality processes, which are also audited for future improvement.

6. Answer: C

   Explanation: Bidder conferences are held by the buyer with the purpose of making sure that all prospective sellers have a clear and common understanding of the buyer's procurement request.

7. Answer: D

   Explanation: Cost-reimbursable contracts (also known as cost plus) are a higher risk to the buyer. This is because the buyer reimburses the seller for the seller's actual costs, plus an additional fixed amount, meaning that the total cost of the contract to the buyer is unknown. Depending on the type of cost-reimbursable contract will determine whether or not this additional fee is constrained.

8. Answer: D

   Explanation: The Control Procurements process has several tools and techniques, including: contract change control system, procurement performance reviews, inspections and audits, performance reporting, payment systems, claims administration, and records management system. The only one not mentioned is make-or-buy analysis. This is a technique used in the Plan Procurement

Management process, where a decision is first made to determine whether the project team must procure a service, product, or goods externally.

9. Answer: B

   Explanation: Screening systems require that potential sellers first pass pre-set requirements / criteria set by the seller (such as fully completing an RFP, or submitting a response on time). This is the correct answer. Weighting systems is a method that quantifies the qualitative data for a unbiased review of the potential sellers, ruling it out as an option. Seller rating systems rate prospective sellers by using the seller's past performance, quality ratings, delivery performance, and contractual compliance, and therefore does not appear to be a match. And lastly, proposal evaluation techniques is where the buyer evaluates the potential sellers through objective and subjective criteria that has been assigned a predefined weight.

10. Answer: D

    Explanation: The correct answer is seller proposals, since by this stage, sellers have already been selected and a contract signed. Procurement documents includes all seller-specific documentation, including the agreement, and is used during the Close Procurements process to determine whether the seller met all contract terms and conditions.

11. Answer: A

    Explanation: Source selection criteria is an output of the Plan Procurement Management process. It will be used by the Conduct Procurements process to evaluate seller proposals.

12. Answer: A

    Explanation: Final payment does not constitute the closure of the contract; instead, the buyer must provide the seller with formal written notice that the seller has completed the contract. Remember that the contract is a legal document, and the closure of it must be official and documented. Final payment alone does not necessarily indicate that the deliverables have been met.

13. Answer: A

    Explanation: Source selection criteria is an input, not an output, of the Conduct Procurements process.

14. Answer: C

    Explanation: The Control Procurements process is responsible for managing procurement relationships, monitoring contract performance, and making changes and corrections as needed.

15. Answer: A

    Explanation: Advertising can be used by buyers as a means of attempting to increase or widen the potential pool of prospective sellers. Although the internet may be a means of advertising, the option does not clearly state what it is to be used for.

16. Answer: B

    Explanation: Since an agreement has already been finalized with Mac Burger, you know that you have just completed the Conduct Procurements process. This process is responsible for obtaining seller responses, selecting a seller, and awarding a contract.

17. Answer: C

    Explanation: Since an agreement has already been finalized with Mac Burger, you know that the Plan Procurement Management and Conduct Procurement Management processes have already been carried out. The next process to be carried

18. Answer: A

Explanation: Organizational process assets contain the organization's policies, procedures, guidelines, historical information, and lessons learned. It also contains other assets belonging to the organization, such as pre-qualified sellers list.

19. Answer: D

    Explanation: The project manager should submit a change request, since this is a request to extend the due date of a deliverable. Any changes to the agreement must first go through the change control board.

20. Answer: B

    Explanation: Procurement audits are responsible for performing a structured review of the procurement management processes to identify successes and failures. This is a tool and technique of the Close Procurements process.

Chapter 13: Project Stakeholder Management

Learning Objectives:

- ☐ Define the purpose of the Project Stakeholder Management Knowledge Area
- ☐ Identify the processes of the Project Stakeholder Management Knowledge Area
- ☐ Recall the key outputs of the stakeholder management processes
- ☐ Differentiate between the inputs, tools and techniques, and outputs of the stakeholder management processes
- ☐ Describe the four classification models used for stakeholder analysis

Exam Domain Tasks:

- Perform key stakeholder analysis using brainstorming, interviewing, and other data-gathering techniques, in order to ensure expectation alignment and gain support for the project.

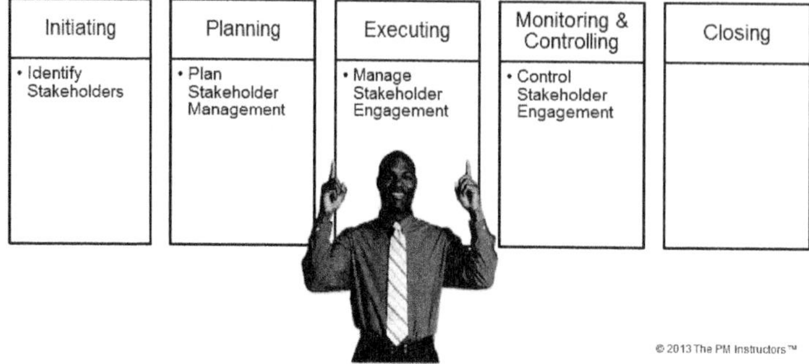
Project Stakeholder Management
Purpose: "To identify the people, groups, or organizations that could impact or be impacted by the project, to analyze stakeholder expectations and their impact on the project, and to develop appropriate management strategies for effectively engaging stakeholders in project decisions and execution."
4 Project Management Processes:
Initiating
• Identify Stakeholders
Planning
• Plan Stakeholder Management
Executing
• Manage Stakeholder Engagement
Monitoring & Controlling
• Control Stakeholder Engagement
Closing
© 2013 The PM Instructors™

Project Stakeholder Management Overview

The purpose of the Project Stakeholder Management Knowledge Area is to identify the people, groups, or organizations that could impact or be impacted by the project, to analyze stakeholder expectations and their impact on the project, and to develop appropriate management strategies for effectively engaging stakeholders in project decisions and execution. It focuses on engaging with stakeholders in order to understand their needs and expectations, as well as to address issues and manage conflict regularly. But we can't do this until we identify them, which is the first step that takes place in this Knowledge Area. It's also concerned with fostering the right level of stakeholder engagement in project activities and in making project decisions.

Failure to identify and engage stakeholders can result in costly rework, unnecessary issues or conflict, as well as potential failure of the project itself. The project manager is responsible for managing the activities described through the stakeholder management processes, to ensure that the project delivers its expected outcomes.

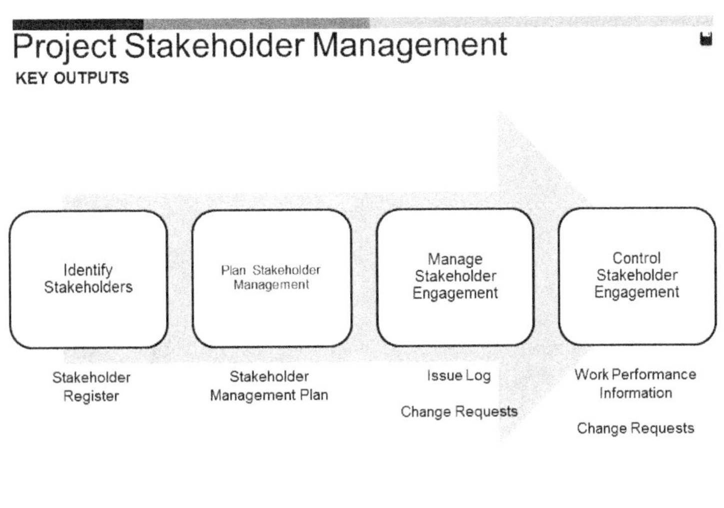

The Project Stakeholder Management Knowledge Area consists of four project management processes:

- **Identify Stakeholders (Initiating Process Group).** Purpose: To identify the people, groups, or organizations that could impact or be impacted by a decision, activity, or outcome of the project; and analyze and document relevant information regarding their interests, involvement, interdependencies, influence, and potential impact on project success.
- **Plan Stakeholder Management (Planning Process Group).** Purpose: To develop appropriate management strategies to effectively engage stakeholders throughout the project life cycle, based on the analysis of their needs, interests, and potential impact on project success.
- **Manage Stakeholder Engagement (Executing Process Group).** Purpose: To communicate and work with stakeholders to meet their needs/expectations, address issues as they occur, and foster appropriate stakeholder engagement in project activities throughout the project life cycle.
- **Control Stakeholder Engagement (Monitoring and Controlling Process Group).** Purpose: To monitor overall project stakeholder relationships and adjust strategies and plans for engaging stakeholders.

Carried out early and iterated many times within the project life cycle
Identify Stakeholders
Purpose: To identify the people, groups, or organizations that could impact or be impacted by a decision, activity, or outcome of the project; and analyze and document relevant information regarding their interests, involvement, interdependencies, influence, and potential impact on project success.

Identify Stakeholders Process Overview

The purpose of the Identify Stakeholders process is to identify the people, groups, or organizations that could impact or be impacted by a decision, activity, or outcome of the project; and analyze and document relevant information regarding their interests, involvement, interdependencies, influence, and potential impact on project success. Remember that this process occurs within the Initiating Process Group, so the first time that it is carried out, it is very early within the life cycle of the project. Since stakeholders tend to change throughout the project, particularly for long projects, this process should be carried out regularly.

The Identify Stakeholders process results in the creation of the stakeholder register.

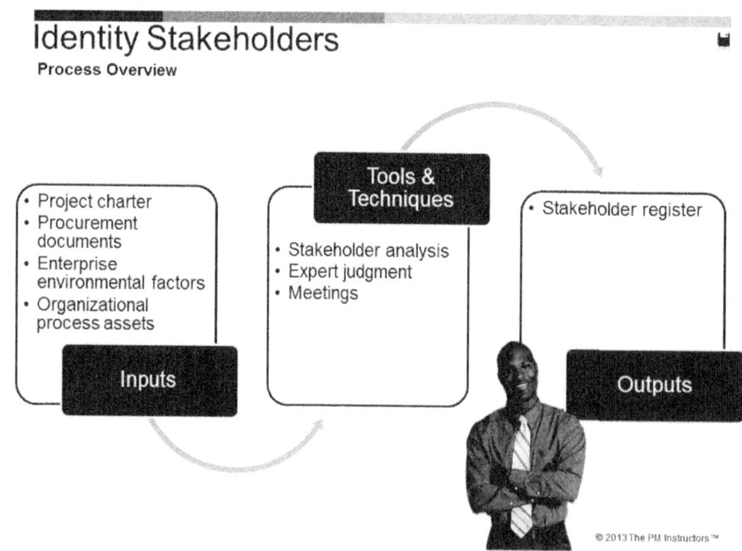
Identity Stakeholders
Process Overview
• Project charter
• Procurement documents
• Enterprise environmental factors
• Organizational process assets
Inputs
Tools & Techniques
• Stakeholder analysis
• Expert judgment
• Meetings
• Stakeholder register
Outputs
© 2013 The PM Instructors™

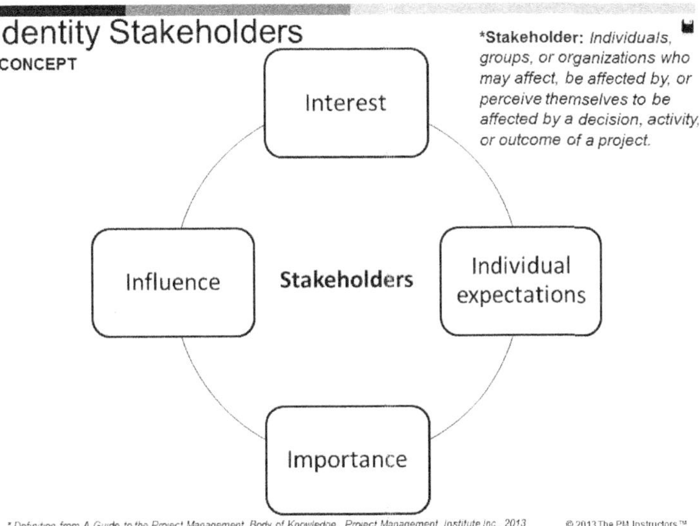
Identity Stakeholders
CONCEPT
Interest
*Stakeholder: Individuals, groups, or organizations who may affect, be affected by, or perceive themselves to be affected by a decision, activity, or outcome of a project.
Influence
Stakeholders
Individual expectations
Importance
* Definition from A Guide to the Project Management Body of Knowledge, Project Management Institute Inc., 2013
© 2013 The PM Instructors™

A stakeholder[8] is defined as individuals, groups, or organizations who may affect, be affected by, or perceive themselves to be affected by a decision, activity, or outcome of a project. The project manager, along with the project management team, will need to ascertain the following of the individual stakeholders:

1. Level of interest
2. Individual expectations
3. Level of importance
4. Level of influence

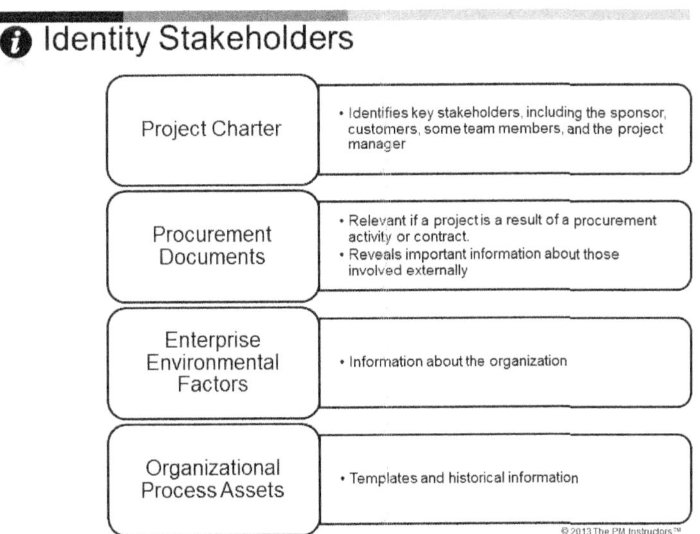
Identity Stakeholders
Project Charter
• Identifies key stakeholders, including the sponsor, customers, some team members, and the project manager
Procurement Documents
• Relevant if a project is a result of a procurement activity or contract.
• Reveals important information about those involved externally
Enterprise Environmental Factors
• Information about the organization
Organizational Process Assets
• Templates and historical information
© 2013 The PM Instructors™

Identify Stakeholders Inputs

The Identify Stakeholders process contains four inputs: *project charter, procurement documents, enterprise environmental factors,* and *organizational process assets.*

---

[8] * *Definition from A Guide to the Project Management Body of Knowledge, Project Management Institute Inc., 2013*

Project Charter

During the early stages of the project, the project charter is one of few documents that exists. The project charter usually identifies several key stakeholders, including the sponsor, customers, some team members and departments participating in the project, and in some cases, the project manager.

Procurement Documents

Procurement documents are applicable as an input when a project is a result of a procurement activity or contract. If this is the case, then procurement documents will reveal important information about those involved in a contract, as well as suppliers.

Enterprise Environmental Factors

Enterprise environmental factors can provide important information about the stakeholders, particularly when performing stakeholder analysis.

Organizational Process Assets

Organizational process assets contain the organization's policies, procedures, and guidelines. It also contains lessons learned, historical information from past projects, as well as templates that can be used toward carrying out this process.

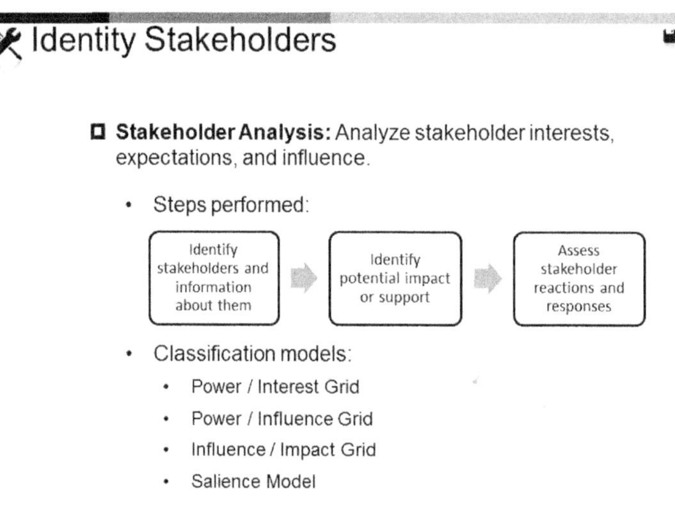

Identify Stakeholders Tools and Techniques

The Identify Stakeholders process utilizes the following three tools and techniques: *stakeholder analysis, expert judgment, and meetings.*

Stakeholder Analysis

Stakeholder analysis is a tool and technique of the Identify Stakeholders process and is used to create the stakeholder register. This technique further analyzes the influences and interests of stakeholders using a qualitative and quantitative approach. Specifically, it helps to identify stakeholder interests, expectations, and influence.

Stakeholder analysis includes a three-step process:

1. Identify stakeholders and information about stakeholders
2. Identify the potential impact or support of each stakeholder
3. Assess stakeholder reactions and responses given various scenarios

There are various classification models that can be leveraged to performing stakeholder analysis. According to the *PMBOK® Guide*, there are four that are of particular importance, and which you should also know for the exam:

- **Power / Interest Grid:** Groups stakeholders according to their level of authority (power) and their level of concern (interest)
- **Power / Influence Grid:** Groups stakeholders according to their level of authority (power) and active involvement (influence)
- **Influence / Impact Grid:** Groups stakeholders according to their active involvement (influence) and ability to effect changes to the project (impact)
- **Salience Model:** Describes classes of stakeholders according to their power, urgency, and legitimacy.

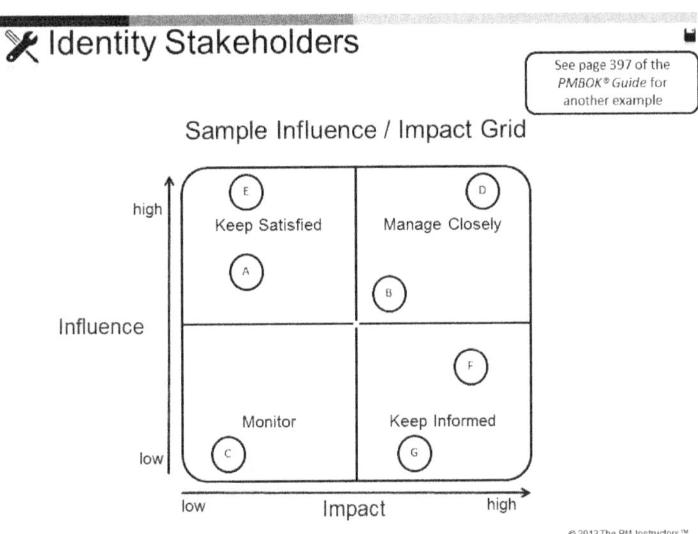

The image shown above depicts an Influence / Impact Grid for a project. An example of a Power / Interest Grid can be found within the *PMBOK® Guide*, page 397.

Identity Stakeholders

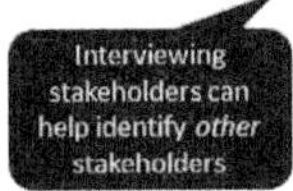

- **Expert Judgment:** Used to identify and assess stakeholders. Examples of expert judgment leveraged:
  - Senior management
  - Other units within the organization
  - Identified stakeholders
  - Other project managers
  - Subject matter experts
  - Industry groups and consultants
  - Other professional and technical associations and organizations
- **Meetings**: Held to engage stakeholders and further assess their level interest, influence, expectations, and importance

Expert Judgment

Throughout this process, expert judgment will be used and needed. This can include the identified stakeholders and more, as appropriate. In many instances, the project manager will be able to easily identify key (important) stakeholders, but additional stakeholders will be identified through interviews and discussion with others, including those already identified.

According to the *PMBOK® Guide*, experts often include:

- Senior management
- Other units within the organization
- Identified stakeholders
- Other project managers
- Subject matter experts
- Industry groups and consultants
- Other professional and technical associations and organizations

Meetings

Meetings are often held to engage stakeholders, including for identification and assessment purposes. Through these meetings, stakeholders may discuss their interests, level of knowledge, and other information that is relevant to assessing their level of interest, influence, expectations, and importance.

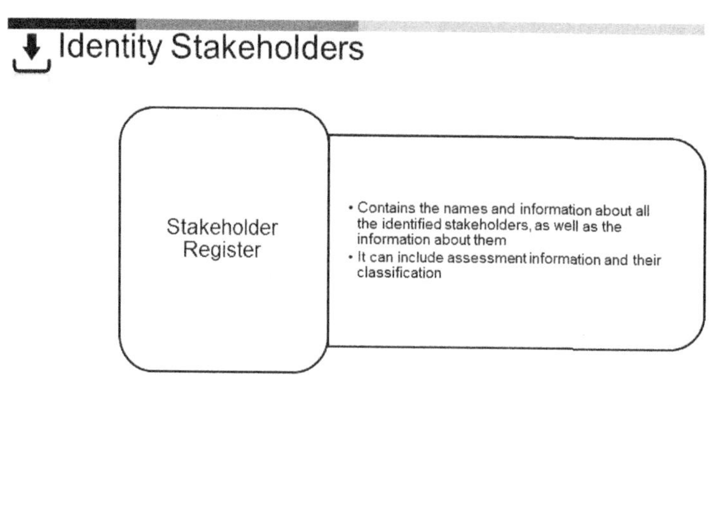
Identity Stakeholders
Stakeholder Register
• Contains the names and information about all the identified stakeholders, as well as the information about them
• It can include assessment information and their classification
© 2013 The PM Instructors™

Identify Stakeholders Outputs

The Identify Stakeholders process has a single output: *stakeholder register.*

Stakeholder Register

The stakeholder register typically contains the following information about each identified stakeholder:

- Identification information, such as name, position, location, contact information, and project role
- Assessment information, such as expectations, major requirements, individual project interests, and potential influence in the project
- Stakeholder classification, such as whether they are internal or external, and a supporter, neutral, or resistor of the project

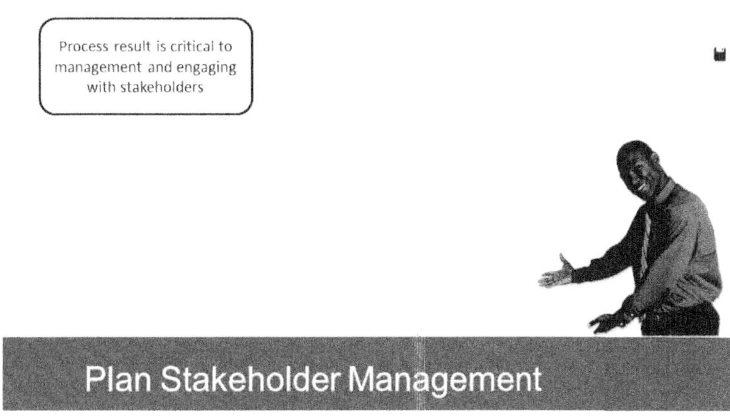
Process result is critical to management and engaging with stakeholders
Plan Stakeholder Management
Purpose: To develop appropriate management strategies to effectively engage stakeholders throughout the project life cycle, based on the analysis of their needs, interests, and potential impact on project success.

Plan Stakeholder Management Process Overview

Plan Stakeholder Management is the second process of the Project Stakeholder Management Knowledge Area – Identify Stakeholders being the first. The purpose of the process is to develop appropriate management strategies to effectively engage stakeholders throughout the project life cycle, based on the analysis of their needs, interests, and potential impact on project success.

The stakeholder management plan, which is the primary result of this process, is critical to successfully managing stakeholders and engaging with them. Within the plan, the project manager will document the approach to effectively engage with stakeholders and how their expectations will be managed.

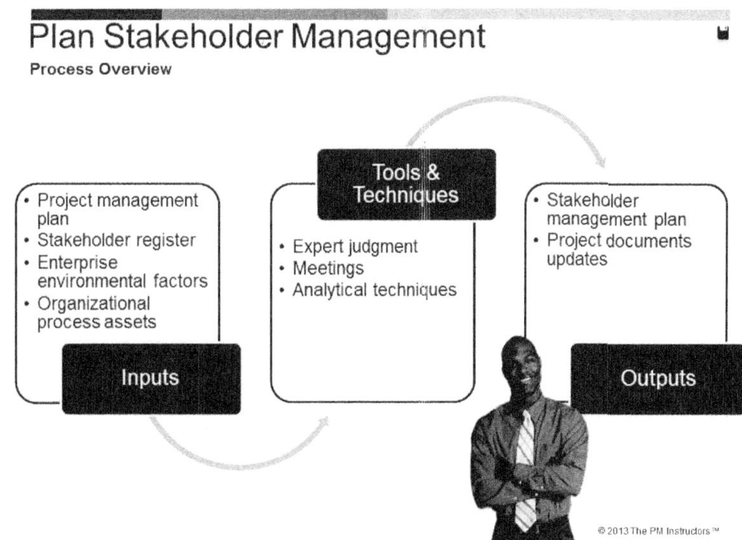
Plan Stakeholder Management
Process Overview
• Project management plan
• Stakeholder register
• Enterprise environmental factors
• Organizational process assets
Inputs
Tools & Techniques
• Expert judgment
• Meetings
• Analytical techniques
• Stakeholder management plan
• Project documents updates
Outputs
© 2013 The PM Instructors™

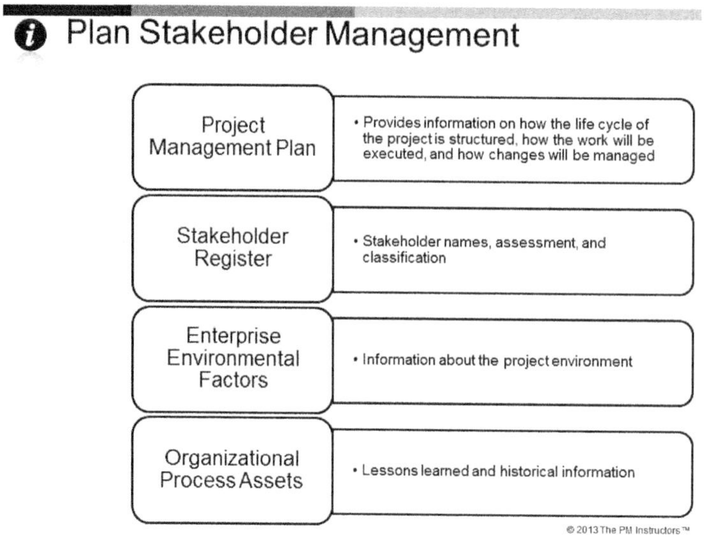

Plan Stakeholder Management

Project Management Plan	• Provides information on how the life cycle of the project is structured, how the work will be executed, and how changes will be managed
Stakeholder Register	• Stakeholder names, assessment, and classification
Enterprise Environmental Factors	• Information about the project environment
Organizational Process Assets	• Lessons learned and historical information

Plan Stakeholder Management Inputs

The Plan Stakeholder Management process has a total of four inputs: *project management plan, stakeholder register, enterprise environmental factors,* and *organizational process assets.*

Project Management Plan

The project management plan contains subsidiary plans and baselines. Since the stakeholder management plan is typically created early on within the life cycle of the project, the typical components referenced include the descriptions of how the project will be structured, in terms of the life cycle, how the work will be executed, and how changes will be managed.

Stakeholder Register

The stakeholder register contains all of the details about stakeholders identified. Establishing a stakeholder management plan should be based around the needs of the stakeholders outlined within this register. Of particular importance will be stakeholder names, assessment, and classification information.

Enterprise Environmental Factors

All of the existing enterprise environmental factors are considered that impact the project environment.

Organizational Process Assets

Organizational process assets provide lessons learned and historical information from previous projects; these items can provide the results and decisions made from previous stakeholder management and communication issues.

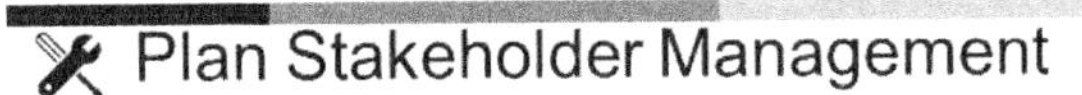

Plan Stakeholder Management

- **Expert Judgment:** Used to determine the level of engagement needed from stakeholders
- **Meetings:** Used gather feedback and information from stakeholders
- **Analytical Techniques:** Used to capture the level of stakeholder engagement throughout the project life cycle.

Engagement categories:

Plan Stakeholder Management Tools and Techniques

The Plan Stakeholder Management process has three tools and techniques: *expert judgment, meetings,* and *analytical techniques.*

Expert Judgment

Expert judgment is used to determine the level of engagement needed for the various stakeholders of the project, based on the analysis captured within the stakeholder register, along with lessons learned of past projects.

The project manager may interview experts, send surveys to obtain additional information, or hold focus groups to get feedback from a larger group of individuals.

Meetings

Meetings are held in combination with expert judgment and analytical techniques, two other tools and techniques of the process. Meetings are a way of gathering feedback and information from stakeholders, and can be used as workshops to assemble the stakeholder management plan.

Analytical Techniques

Analytical techniques can be used within this process as a way of capturing the level of stakeholder engagement throughout the life cycle of the project. The approach chosen should be documented within the stakeholder management plan, for ongoing assessment of engagement.

According to the *PMBOK® Guide*, engagement levels of stakeholders can be classified using the following categories:

- **Unaware:** *unaware of project and potential impacts*
- **Resistant:** *Aware of project and potential impacts and resistant to change*
- **Neutral:** *aware of project yet neither supportive or resistant*
- **Supportive:** *aware of project and potential impacts and supportive to change*
- **Leading:** *aware of project and potential impacts and actively engaged in ensuring the project is a success*

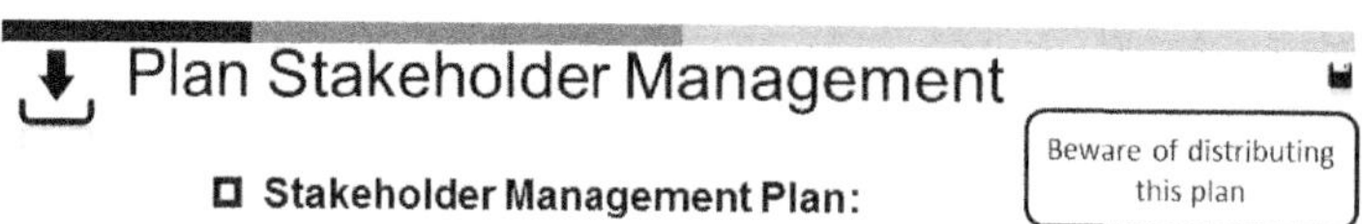

Plan Stakeholder Management
Beware of distributing this plan

Stakeholder Management Plan:

- Identifies the strategies needed to effectively engage stakeholders
- Component of the project management plan

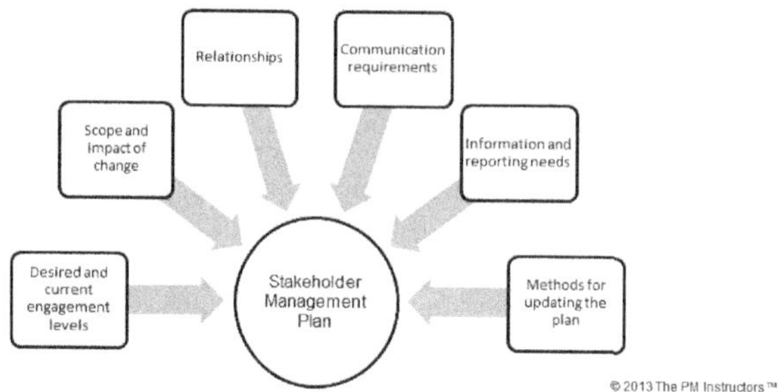

Plan Stakeholder Management Outputs

The Plan Stakeholder Management process has two outputs: *stakeholder management plan* and *project documents updates.*

Stakeholder Management Plan

The stakeholder management plan identifies and documents the strategy necessary to effectively engage stakeholders, which in turn allows the project manager insight into the stakeholders' goals and objectives. Understanding stakeholder priorities is important to managing projects, and the stakeholder management plan provides the project manager with insight into these priorities and needs of the stakeholders.

According to the *PMBOK® Guide*, the stakeholder management plan typically includes the following:

- Desired and current engagement levels of key stakeholders
- Scope and impact of change to stakeholders
- Relationships among stakeholders
- Communication requirements of stakeholders
- Information and reporting needs of stakeholders
- Methods for updating the plan

The project manager should take special care to ensure that the contents of this plan are distributed to only the appropriate individuals, as a result of its sensitive content.

Plan Stakeholder Management

Project Documents Updates
• Typical updates resulting from the process include:
• project schedule
• stakeholder register
© 2013 The PM Instructors™

Project Document Updates

Project documents updated as a result of carrying out this process include the project schedule, and stakeholder register.

The project manager should address stakeholder expectations and influence them

Manage Stakeholder Engagement

Purpose: To communicate and work with stakeholders to meet their needs/expectations, address issues as they occur, and foster appropriate stakeholder engagement in project activities throughout the project life cycle.

Manage Stakeholders Expectations Process Overview

The purpose of the Manage Stakeholder Engagement process is to communicate and work with stakeholders to meet their needs/expectations, address issues as they occur, and foster appropriate stakeholder engagement in project activities throughout the project life cycle.

The process itself is very important, since it addresses balancing and managing the expectations of stakeholders. The project manager must address their expectations and influence them, as well as resolve issues as they come up. It's important for the project manager to actively manage their expectations in order to increase the chances of successful project completion. The idea is to address problems before they grow into major issues. Remember that PMI promotes *proactive* behavior.

In addition to the statements above, note that this process is responsible for keeping the stakeholders updated about issues and changes.

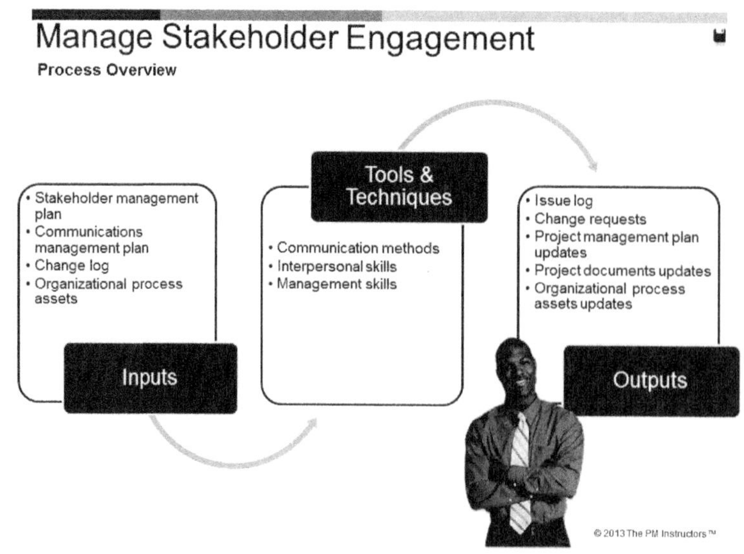
Manage Stakeholder Engagement
Process Overview
Stakeholder management plan
Communications management plan
Change log
Organizational process assets
Inputs
Tools & Techniques
Communication methods
Interpersonal skills
Management skills
Issue log
Change requests
Project management plan updates
Project documents updates
Organizational process assets updates
Outputs
© 2013 The PM Instructors ™

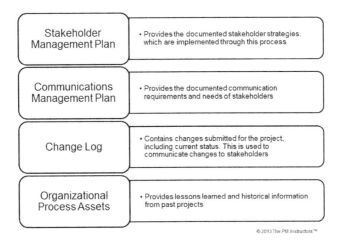

Manage Stakeholder Engagement

Stakeholder Management Plan	• Provides the documented stakeholder strategies, which are implemented through this process
Communications Management Plan	• Provides the documented communication requirements and needs of stakeholders
Change Log	• Contains changes submitted for the project, including current status. This is used to communicate changes to stakeholders
Organizational Process Assets	• Provides lessons learned and historical information from past projects

Manage Stakeholder Engagement Inputs

The Manage Stakeholder Engagement process has four inputs: *stakeholder management plan, communications management plan, change log,* and *organizational process assets.*

Stakeholder Management Plan

The stakeholder management plan contains the strategies identified and documented for managing stakeholder expectations and engagement. This process is where this document is primarily used and executed.

Communications Management Plan

The communications management plan documents what the communication requirements of the stakeholders are, including what information must be communicated and distributed, who the recipients of the information are, and the escalation process.

Change Log

Like issues, changes should also be communicated regularly with stakeholders. The change log contains the list of change requests and decisions, as well as the impact of changes.

Organizational Process Assets

Organizational process assets that influence this process include communication, issue, and change control procedures, as well as historical information from previous projects. This historical information can provide insight as to how stakeholders have behaved in the past.

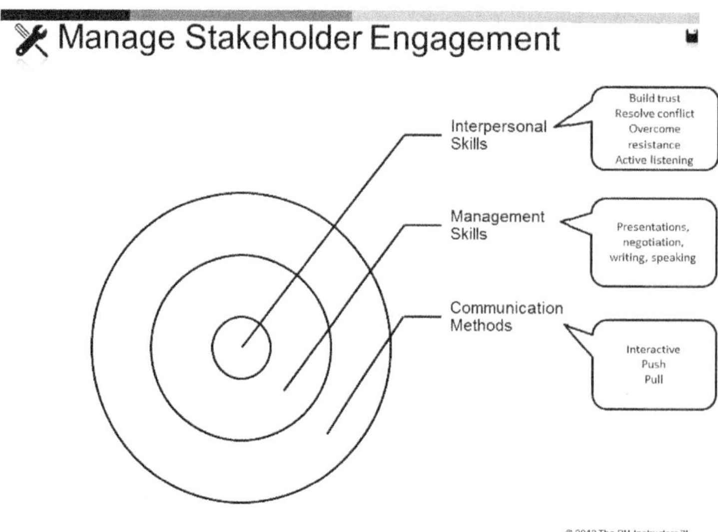

Manage Stakeholder Engagement Tools and Techniques

The Manage Stakeholder Engagement process has three tools and techniques: *communication methods, interpersonal skills,* and *management skills.*

Communication Methods

Communication in general is important throughout all of project management, and it is through these skills that the project manager can properly communicate with stakeholders. Communication methods are also utilized while interacting with and managing stakeholders.

Communication methods also consist of the interactive, pull, and push methods described within the Project Communications Management Knowledge Area chapter. Based on the plan and situation, the project manager will need to determine which method is the most appropriate.

Interpersonal Skills

Interpersonal skills are commonly called "soft skills". It is thought that the project manager can decrease issues and increase cooperation by understanding how stakeholders are feeling, knowing what their concerns are, and being able to follow up on existing issues. These skills are important to effectively managing a project and controlling the schedule. Interpersonal skills is a tool and technique of the Develop Project Team process from within the Project Human Resource Management Knowledge Area, and also this process. Utilizing soft skills allows the project manager to build trust with stakeholders, resolve conflict, overcome resistance to change, and practice active listening.

Management Skills

Management and interpersonal skills are both useful when dealing with people. Examples of management skills include: utilizing presentation skills, negotiating, writing skills, and public speaking. The project manager will need to use these skills to influence stakeholders and to facilitate positive and productive engagement among the group.

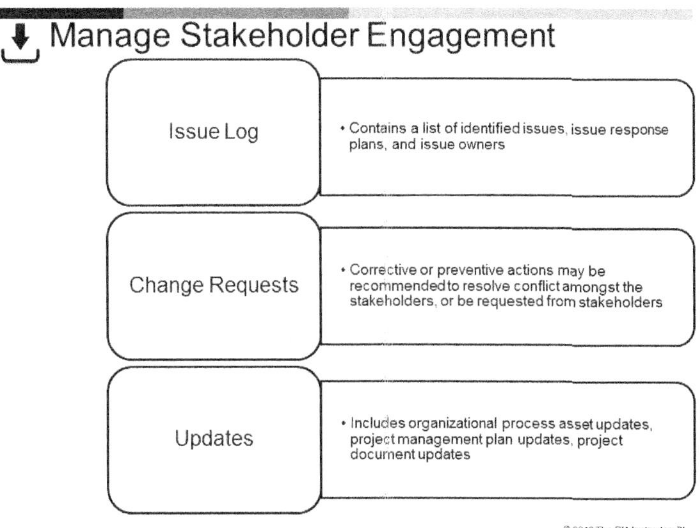
Manage Stakeholder Engagement
Issue Log
• Contains a list of identified issues, issue response plans, and issue owners
Change Requests
• Corrective or preventive actions may be recommendedto resolve conflict amongst the stakeholders, or be requested from stakeholders
Updates
• Includes organizational process asset updates, project management plan updates, project document updates
© 2013 The PM Instructors™

Manage Stakeholder Engagement Outputs

The Manage Stakeholder Engagement process has five outputs: *issue log, change requests, project management plan updates, project documents updates,* and *organizational process assets updates.*

Issue Log

The issue log contains the list of identified issues, issue response plans, and issue owners. Issue logs should also contain the urgency level of the issues, as well as their impact. This will be important to ensuring that issues are communicated appropriately with the stakeholders.

Change Requests

Conflict may arise amongst the stakeholders, and it may call for corrective action to be taken. But change requests also come about as a result of requested changes to the product or project by the stakeholders, so it can also include corrective and preventive actions that have nothing to do with conflict.

Project Management Plan Updates

Updates to the project management plan typically include the communications management plan and stakeholder management plan.

Project Documents Updates

Updates to the project documents typically include the stakeholder register and issue log.

Organizational Process Asset Updates

Organizational process assets often updated as a result of carrying out this process include causes of issues, corrective action taken as a result, and whether the actions were effective. Lessons learned are also documented.

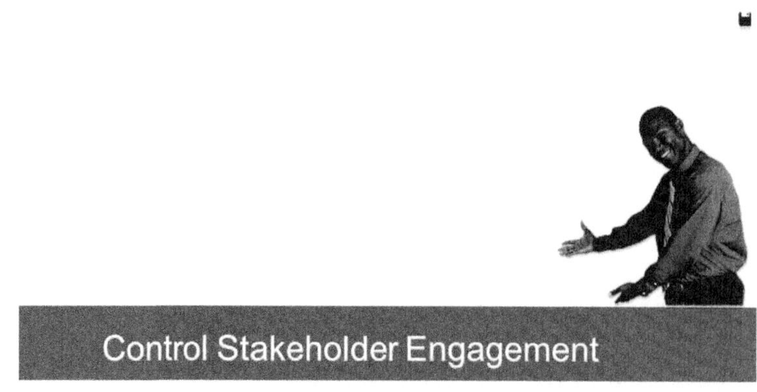
Control Stakeholder Engagement
Purpose: To monitor overall project stakeholder relationships and adjust strategies and plans for engaging stakeholders.

Control Stakeholder Engagement Process Overview

Control Stakeholder Engagement is the final process of the Project Stakeholder Management Knowledge Area. This process is part of the Monitoring and Controlling Process Group and is responsible for controlling stakeholder engagement.

The official purpose of the process is to monitor overall project stakeholder relationships and adjust strategies and plans for engaging stakeholders.

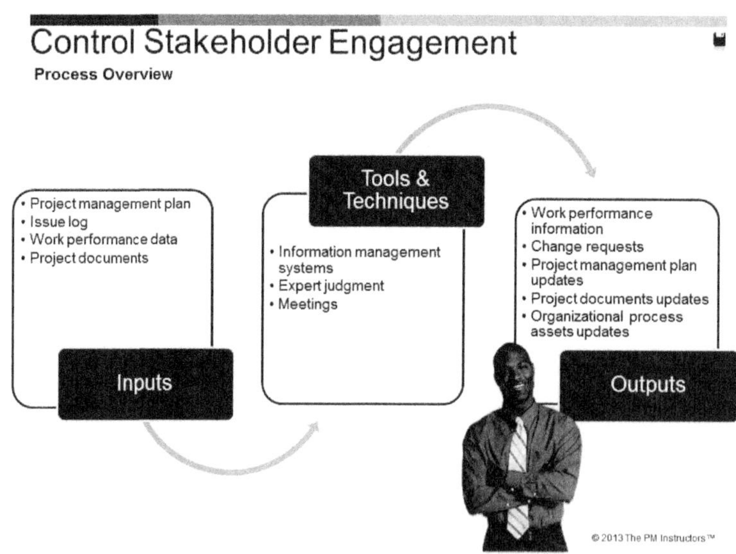
Control Stakeholder Engagement
Process Overview
• Project management plan
• Issue log
• Work performance data
• Project documents
Inputs
Tools & Techniques
• Information management systems
• Expert judgment
• Meetings
• Work performance information
• Change requests
• Project management plan updates
• Project documents updates
• Organizational process assets updates
Outputs
© 2013 The PM Instructors™

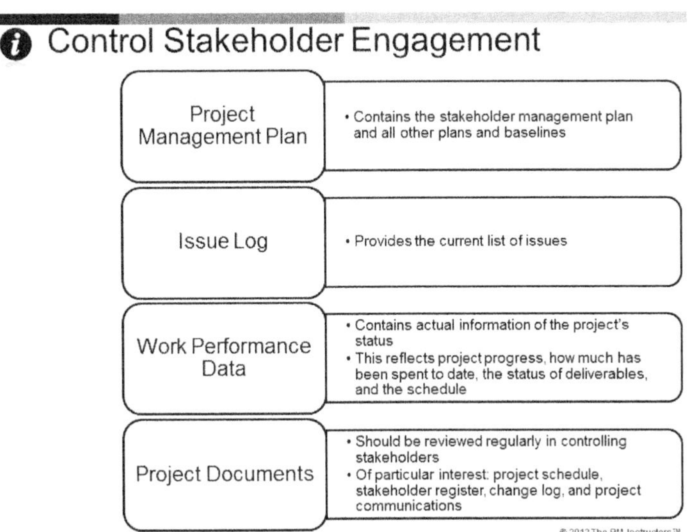

Control Stakeholder Engagement Inputs

The Control Stakeholder Engagement process has four inputs: *project management plan, issue log, work performance data,* and *project documents.*

Project Management Plan

The stakeholder management plan is the primary document used from within the project management plan, although the communications management plan, scope, schedule, and cost management plans and baselines are all typically referenced.

Issue Log

The issue log is continuously updated as new issues arise or as existing issues are resolved. As part of controlling stakeholder engagement, issues will need to be continuously reviewed.

Work Performance Data

As part of measuring progress, the project manager will need actual information of the project's status, which is why work performance data is used. This reflects project progress, and includes how much has been spent to date, the status of deliverables, and the schedule.

Project Documents

Project documents will need to be reviewed regularly, as the information contained within them may influence stakeholder engagement. Of particular interest will be the project schedule, stakeholder register, change log, and project communications.

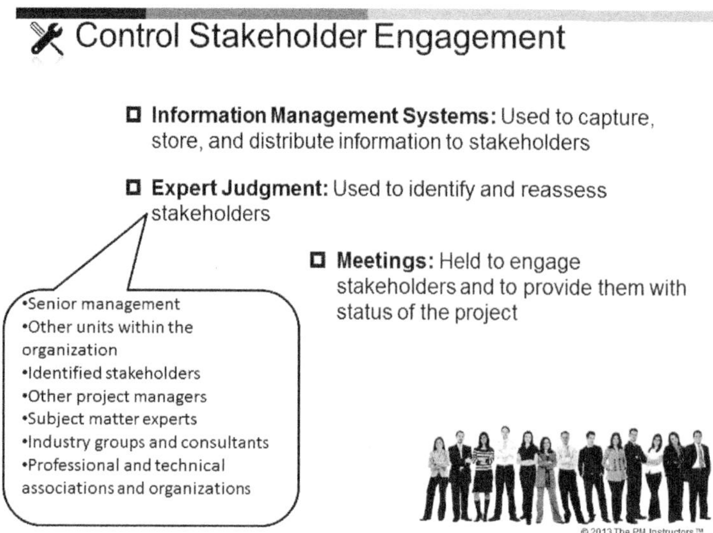

Control Stakeholder Engagement Tools and Techniques

The Control Stakeholder Engagement process contains three tools and techniques: *information management systems, expert judgment,* and *meetings.*

Information Management Systems

The information management system is a tool used by the project manager to capture, store, and distribute information to stakeholders.

Expert Judgment

Expert judgment is used in this process to reassess stakeholders. Experts may include:

- Senior management
- Other units within the organization
- Identified stakeholders
- Other project managers
- Subject matter experts
- Industry groups and consultants
- Other professional and technical associations and organizations

Meetings

Status review meetings are often held and facilitated by the project manager to engage stakeholders and to provide and obtain status of the project's progress. This can also be an interactive means of communicating changes and issues to stakeholders.

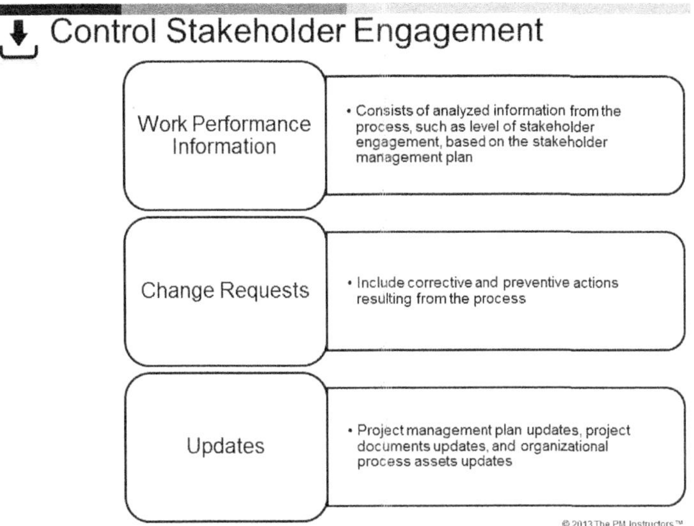
Control Stakeholder Engagement
Work Performance Information
• Consists of analyzed information from the process, such as level of stakeholder engagement, based on the stakeholder management plan
Change Requests
• Include corrective and preventive actions resulting from the process
Updates
• Project management plan updates, project documents updates, and organizational process assets updates
© 2013 The PM Instructors™

Control Stakeholder Engagement Outputs

The Control Stakeholder Engagement process has five outputs: *work performance information, change requests, project management plan updates, project documents updates,* and *organizational process assets updates.*

Work Performance Information

Work performance information includes the analyzed information of the process. This may include a measure of stakeholders' engagement, according to the stakeholder management plan.

Change Requests

Change requests may include recommended corrective actions or preventive actions as a result of carrying out this process.

Project Management Plan Updates

As a result of carrying out this process, several updates may be made to the components of the project management plan, particularly, the various subsidiary plans.

Project Documents Updates

Project documents typically updated as a result of carrying out this process include the stakeholder register and issue log.

Organizational Process Assets Updates

Updates to the organizational process assets typically include lessons learned, causes of issues and corrective action taken to resolve the issues; archiving documents for use by future projects.

Module Summary

In this module we:

- Defined the purpose of the Project Stakeholder Management Knowledge Area
- Identified the processes of the Project Stakeholder Management Knowledge Area
- Recalled the key outputs of the stakeholder management processes
- Differentiated between the inputs, tools and techniques, and outputs of the stakeholder management processes
- Described the four classification models used for stakeholder analysis

Chapter Quiz

Exam Practice Questions

1. During the beta release of a new software application, the project manager was informed that many of the features in the software did not meet the expectations of the stakeholders, and as result, they are displeased with the amount of time and money that was wasted on this effort. As part of their lessons learned, the project manager realized that there was very little time dedicated toward stakeholder analysis. Stakeholder analysis is a tool and technique that analyzes the influences and interests of stakeholders, and is utilized by which of the following processes?
    A. Identify Stakeholders
    B. Communications Planning
    C. Plan Risk Management
    D. Information Distribution

2. You are currently assigned to work on a project involving the release of a new pharmaceutical drug. The vice president (VP) of strategic partnerships, who to date has not been a part of the project, asked to see the work performance data. This raises a red flag for the following reason:
    A. The VP of strategic partnerships is not a part of the project, and should therefore not have access to the report.
    B. The VP may have heard of existing performance issues and is investigating.
    C. All stakeholders of the project have not been identified to date.
    D. There are no red flags raised for this project, and the project manager has nothing to worry about.

3. A small project team is in the process of performing a feasibility study on the potential build out of an offshore data center. Several team members have expressed excitement about the project, since early indications from the study show that this may be a cost effective solution that can save the organization millions of dollars in annual expenses. The Operations team, however, has expressed strong concerns about the impact to the team's morale if this project were to proceed forward. Where would the project manager document the various strategies for engaging with stakeholders, based on their needs and reactions to the project?
    A. Stakeholder register
    B. Stakeholder management plan
    C. Stakeholder management strategy
    D. Project management plan

4. Which of the following processes does not belong to the Project Stakeholder Management Knowledge Area?
    A. Plan Stakeholder Management
    B. Identify Stakeholders
    C. Manage Stakeholder Engagement
    D. Manage Project Team

5. Tony is the CEO of a new startup company called Power Cloud Stock Trading Online. In his excitement to make the company public, he has launched a project that will potentially increase the revenue of the business by 496%. Grant, who is the project manager of this project, performs an analysis of the stakeholders identified to date, using an influence / impact grid. He assesses Tony as having a high level of influence and a high level of impact. What type of strategy is Grant likely to choose in managing Tony's expectations throughout the project?
   A. Monitor
   B. Keep informed
   C. Manage closely
   D. Keep satisfied

6. A stakeholder register has just been issued. What comes next?
   A. An issue log will be created
   B. A stakeholder management plan will be created
   C. Stakeholder analysis will be performed
   D. Project team will be acquired

7. Martha has just been told that she will be assigned as the project manager for the new office expansion project. After the project charter is created and approved, she begins the process of performing stakeholder analysis. She decides to group stakeholders by their level of authority and level of concern. What type of classification model has she chosen to use?
   A. Power / Influence Grid
   B. Power / Interest Grid
   C. Influence / Impact Grid
   D. Salience Model

8. In order to determine how the project is progressing, the project manager evaluates the overall project stakeholder relationships and their level of engagement. What process is the project manager performing?
   A. Manage Stakeholder Engagement
   B. Control Stakeholder Engagement
   C. Direct and Manage Project Work
   D. Monitor and Control Project Work

9. In what process is the issue log created?
   A. Manage Stakeholder Engagement
   B. Control Stakeholder Engagement
   C. Direct and Manage Project Work
   D. Monitor and Control Project Work

10. Susan and David are both project managers for Blazing Broadband Internet Solutions, but they work in different divisions of the company, each having led numerous successful projects for the organization. They have been teamed together in order to find innovative solutions to problems on a new project, including ways of harmonizing the group of stakeholders toward accomplishing the project objectives. What skill set will Susan and David need to use to facilitate consensus toward project objectives, influence stakeholders to support the project, and negotiate agreements?
    A. Conflict management techniques
    B. Communication methods
    C. General management skills
    D. Interpersonal skills

11. Ronald Pierce is a high-end furniture store chain. The company is in the process of developing a new renaissance style edition for release in six months. The project manager leading the development of the new edition is evaluating the engagement level of stakeholders needs using the approach documented in the stakeholder management plan. He identifies some stakeholders as unaware, resistant, neutral, supportive, and leading. What tool and technique is the project manager performing to evaluate stakeholder engagement?
    A. Stakeholder analysis
    B. Analytical techniques
    C. Management skills
    D. Expert judgment

12. Which of the following is not a tool and technique of the Control Stakeholder Engagement process?
    A. Stakeholder analysis
    B. Information management systems
    C. Expert judgment
    D. Meetings

13. Which of the following does a project manager use to build trust with stakeholders and overcome resistance to change?
    A. Conflict management techniques
    B. Communication methods
    C. General management skills
    D. Interpersonal skills

14. Alfred is holding a status meeting with several members of the project team to generate engagement amongst the team, and to exchange information on progress of various planned activities. At the conclusion of the meeting, Alfred distributes meeting minutes to attendees, and archives the documentation to the project's central repository. What is this central repository used to capture, store, and distribute information to stakeholders called?
    A. Project management software
    B. SharePoint site
    C. Record management system
    D. Information management system

15. Big Food Co. is wholesale distributer of food products available to the public. They have recently decided to take on a modernization program that would bring their legacy systems into the current standards of web-based applications. The project, now in its sixth month of execution, has experienced several communication hurdles, with stakeholders who have varying agendas and expectations. In one particular scenario, the project manager is working to resolve a new issue that has been identified. The sponsor of the project has expressed concerns around the project's progress, and requested that a specific course of action be taken. What should the project manager do next?
    A. Implement the course of action
    B. Submit a change request
    C. Schedule a team meeting to discuss the sponsor's reaction
    D. Deny the request, since the project is in execution

16. In order to determine how the project is progressing, the project manager evaluates the overall project stakeholder relationships and their level of engagement. As part of these activities, she also considers work performance data collected so far. The results of this evaluation and analysis will be documented as:
    A. Work performance information
    B. Work performance reports
    C. Work performance data
    D. Change requests

17. In order to determine how the project is progressing, the project manager evaluates the overall project stakeholder relationships and their level of engagement. As part of these activities, she generates corrective and preventive actions to bring the project back in line with the plan. The corrective and preventive actions will be documented as:
    A. Work performance information
    B. Work performance reports
    C. Work performance data
    D. Change requests

18. Susan and David are both project managers for Blazing Broadband Internet Solutions, but they work in different divisions of the company, each having led numerous successful projects for the organization. They have been teamed together in order to find innovative solutions to problems on a new project. As a starting point, they determine that stakeholders have not been properly identified or analyzed. They decide to classify stakeholders based on their power, urgency, and legitimacy. What type of classification model have they chosen to use?
    A. Power / Influence Grid
    B. Power / Interest Grid
    C. Influence / Impact Grid
    D. Salience Model

19. Which of the following BEST describes how the change log is used within the Manage Stakeholder Engagement process?
    A. It is used as an input to the process, to document and communicate changes to stakeholders
    B. It is used as a tool as part of the process, to document and communicate changes to stakeholders
    C. It is generated as an output of the process, to document and communicate changes to stakeholders
    D. It is not used by this process

20. Which of the following is not an output of the Manage Stakeholder Engagement process?
    A. Issue log
    B. Change log
    C. Project management plan updates
    D. Project documents updates

Chapter Quiz

Exam Practice Answers

1. Answer: A

   Explanation: According to the *PMBOK® Guide, 5th edition,* stakeholder analysis occurs as part of the Identify Stakeholders process. Here, the influences, interests, needs, wants, and expectations of stakeholders are identified and documented.

2. Answer: C

   Explanation: Based on the question, the VP is clearly a stakeholder of the project, which means that they were not previously identified. If all stakeholders have not been identified, this means that all expectations, needs, and requirements have not been fully documented and resolved, which can create major issues within the project.

3. Answer: B

   Explanation: The stakeholder management plan, which is created out of the Plan Stakeholder Management process, identifies the strategies needed to effectively engage stakeholders. The plan is based on the stakeholder analysis completed as part of creating the stakeholder register. While the project management plan is also technically correct, it is not the best answer as a more specific option was available.

4. Answer: D

   Explanation: The Project Stakeholder Management Knowledge Area has four processes: Identify Stakeholders, Plan Stakeholder Management, Manage Stakeholder Engagement, and Control Stakeholder Engagement. Manage Project Team is a process of the Project Human Resource Management Knowledge Area.

5. Answer: C

   Explanation: An influence / impact grid can be split into four quadrants, where stakeholders will be plotted against, according to their level of influence and impact. Stakeholders with low influence / low impact are likely to be monitored; stakeholders with high influence / low impact will likely be kept satisfied; stakeholders with low influence / high impact are likely to be kept informed; and stakeholders with high influence / high impact are likely to be managed closely. Tony falls in the latter of the options stated.

6. Answer: B

   Explanation: After the stakeholder register has been created through the Identify Stakeholders process, the Plan Stakeholder Management process will need to be performed, which will produce the stakeholder management plan.

7. Answer: B

   Explanation: The power / interest grid groups stakeholders based on their level of authority, a reference to *power*, and by level of concern, a reference to *interest*.

8. Answer: B

   Explanation: The Control Stakeholder Engagement process is responsible for monitoring the overall project stakeholder relationships and adjusting strategies and plans for engaging stakeholders.

9. Answer: A

   Explanation: The Manage Stakeholder Engagement process is concerned with communicating and working with stakeholders to meet their needs / expectations, address issues as they occur, and fostering appropriate stakeholder engagement in project activities throughout the project life cycle. This process produces the following outputs: issue log, change requests, project management plan updates, project documents updates, and organizational process assets updates.

10. Answer: C

    Explanation: The project manager applies general management skills to coordinate and harmonize the group of stakeholders toward accomplishing the project objectives. General management skills is a technique of the Manage Stakeholder Engagement process.

11. Answer: B

    Explanation: Analytical techniques can be used to evaluate the current engagement level of stakeholders. One approach involves classifying the levels of stakeholder engagement as follows: unaware, resistant, neutral, supportive, or leading. Throughout the project, a project manager can use this approach to note the desired level of engagement of individual stakeholders, versus their current engagement. Analytical techniques is a tool and technique of the Plan Stakeholder Management process.

12. Answer: A

    Explanation: The Control Stakeholder Engagement process uses the following tools and techniques: information management systems, expert judgment, and meetings.

13. Answer: D

    Explanation: Interpersonal skills is used by the project manager to build trust, resolve conflict, actively listen to stakeholders, and overcome resistance to change. It is a technique used by the Manage Stakeholder Engagement, Develop Project Team, and Manage Project Team processes.

14. Answer: C

    Explanation: Alfred is using an information management system, which captures, stores, and distributes information to stakeholders of the project.

15. Answer: B

    Explanation: Although the concerns and course of action requested comes from the sponsor, the project manager should submit the requested corrective action as a change request. Addressing issues is an activity of the Control Stakeholder Engagement process, where change requests is an output.

16. Answer: A

    Explanation: The project manager is carrying out the Control Stakeholder Engagement process, and will document the results of her evaluation and analysis as work performance information, an output of this process.

17. Answer: D

    Explanation: Corrective and preventive actions are submitted as change requests, typically to bring the project back in line with the project management plan. These actions must always be processed through the formal change control process before implementation.

18. Answer: D

    Explanation: The salience model is a stakeholder classification model used to carry out stakeholder analysis within the Identify Stakeholders process. It classifies stakeholders based on their power, urgency, and legitimacy.

19. Answer: A

    Explanation: Change log is an input to the Manage Stakeholder Management process. It documents changes that occur throughout the project; these changes are communicated to stakeholders as part of this process.

20. Answer: B

    Explanation: The Manage Stakeholder Engagement process has the following outputs: issue log, change requests, project management plan updates, project documents updates, and organizational process assets updates.

Full Length Practice Exam

Exam Questions

1. The project manager of an accounting software upgrade project was approached by the Vice President of Marketing regarding the schedule milestone update report. The VP was concerned because the report was not being sent out weekly as scheduled. The project manager understood that this report was scheduled for bi-weekly distribution. Where would the project manager go to clarify the report distribution frequency?
   A. The project team member responsible for distributing the report
   B. The communications management plan
   C. The risk management plan
   D. The project management plan

2. All of the following statements are true except for which of the following?
   A. Risk management is a proactive practice within project management.
   B. Risks are prioritized during qualitative risk analysis.
   C. Watch lists contain near-term risks that must be monitored carefully.
   D. Risk symptoms are considered when evaluating if a risk is a near-term risk.

3. You are the project manager for Kitchens Plus Inc. The latest project involves the development of an automatic dicer with unique industry features. Currently, you are analyzing schedule performance. Based on the information provided by the scheduling team, the current schedule performance index (SPI) is at 1.10, while the cost performance index (CPI) is at 0.80. What might be a good strategy for balancing out performance between the schedule and budget?
   A. Crash the schedule by adding additional resources to critical activities
   B. Fast-track the longest activities that fall on the critical path
   C. Level out resource usage to further spread out cost over time
   D. Nothing, since the project is performing as planned

4. There are 10 stakeholders within your project. As the project manager, you must therefore manage 45 communication channels. Two additional stakeholders have been added. How many MORE channels of communication must you manage?
   A. 47
   B. 45
   C. 21
   D. 66

5. If the duration of activity B were changed to 6, what would be the impact to the following network diagram?

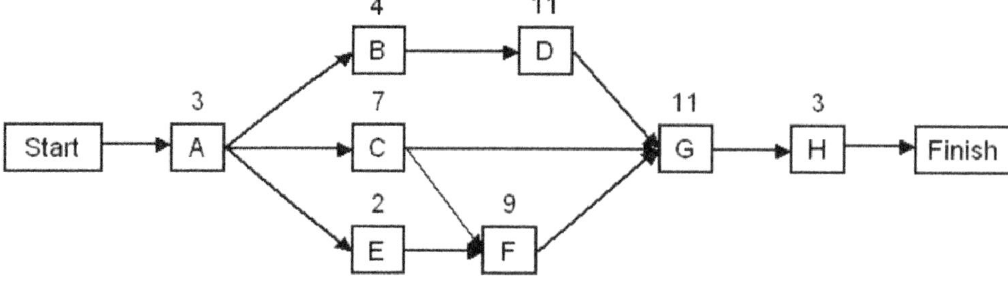

   A. The critical path changes
   B. Activity B's network path becomes the near-critical path
   C. There will be two critical paths
   D. There is no impact to the project

6. The project manager had received two complaints that three project team members were arguing over the interpretation of schedule analysis results conducted the previous day. The project manager had waited to see if they would work it out amongst themselves, but another two complaints were made that the situation was affecting the work of others. What should the project manager do?
   A. Give the disputing team members more time to work it out amongst themselves
   B. Issue corrective action to the team members negatively affecting the work of others
   C. Look at the results of the analysis and make a decision
   D. Collaborate to resolve the dispute

7. Around 2:37 pm, Bruce Bethor, the project manager for the Happy Holiday Cruise Ships, Inc. walks around the office to interact with each member of his team. The majority of his team members enjoy this type of informal interaction because it gives them an opportunity to bring up issues they may have forgetten to mention during the morning meetings or those issues that were recently uncovered during the day. Which of the following techniques does Bruce use to stay in touch with the work and attitudes of his project team members?
   A. 360-degree feedback
   B. Observation and conversation
   C. Issue log
   D. Team-building activities

8. Which type of estimating technique can have a high level of accuracy?
   A. Analogous estimating
   B. Bottom-up estimating
   C. Reserve analysis
   D. Parametric estimating

9. Janet is a project manager for the consulting division of The Java Architects. She has just been informed that the proposal she provided for a prospective client last week has gained approval from the company's governance board, and a project charter has been approved. What process is most likely to be carried out next?
   A. Develop Project Management Plan
   B. Define Scope
   C. Identify Stakeholders
   D. Develop Project Charter

10. The project management team is coordinating the decision between making or buying a product. Making the product would require an initial investment of $35,000 and has a probability of 15% failure and impact of $15,000. Buying the product would require an initial investment of $25,000 but has a probability of 35% failure and $10,000 impact. What is the expected monetary value of making the product?
   A. $37,250
   B. $20,250
   C. $5,250
   D. $2,250

11. The following processes make up the Project Human Resource Management Knowledge Area:
   A. Plan Human Resource Management, Acquire Project Team, Develop Project Team, Manage Project Team
   B. Plan Human Resource Management, Acquire Project Team, Manage Project Team
   C. Plan Human Resource Management, Acquire Project Team, Develop Project Team
   D. Plan Human Resource Management, Acquire Project Team, Develop Project Team, Manage Stakeholder Engagement

12. Activity A has a probability of 10% and an impact of $4,000. What is the expected monetary value of Activity A?
   A. $4,000
   B. $4,400
   C. $400
   D. $3,600

13. The project manager of a multi-phased gaming project made a phone call to one of her virtual project team members abroad regarding an upcoming schedule activity that the team member was responsible for. The project manager notified the team member that due to an unplanned risk, a prototype would be built into the schedule, and it was important that her activity be completed according to the plan. The project manager noticed that the team member did not say much during the call, and she hoped that the team member understood. What did the project manager fail to do?
    A. Requested that the team member respond with a status report
    B. Have been more attuned to existing noise on the call
    C. Request that the team member write down the request and confirm status through the use of a written medium
    D. Request that the team member repeat the message back to ensure it was understood

14. Which of the following techniques can provide the probability of a project completing on any given date?
    A. Critical chain method
    B. Critical path method
    C. Precedence diagramming method
    D. What-if scenario analysis

15. A risk manager of a software company is performing quantitative risk analysis. While numerically analyzing risks, she decided to utilize external subject matter experts. What can the risk manager gain through this technique?
    A. Assess the likelihood that all risks have been identified
    B. Gain unbiased feedback on the evaluated risks
    C. Better evaluate the results of modeling and simulation techniques
    D. Validate the data and techniques used within the process

16. Which of the following are not inputs of the Acquire Project Team process?
    A. Roles and responsibilities
    B. Project organization charts
    C. Staffing management plan
    D. Resource availability

17. Which of the following is not a characteristic of earned value management?
    A. It is used as a means of controlling the schedule
    B. It looks to measure performance variance the baseline values
    C. It is used in determining what activities may fall on the critical path
    D. It is used to forecast project performance

18. Immediately after a morning planning meeting, the project manager and the development lead held an impromptu discussion about the schedule for a project they are working on. During their discussion they uncover that each thought a set of deliverables was going to be completed at different points in the schedule. In light of this new revelation, they agree to update the schedule and share the information with the rest of the team. What is the BEST type of communication to use when dealing with complex issues, such as this one?
    A. Informal written
    B. Formal written
    C. Informal verbal
    D. Formal verbal

19. Frank has just performed forecasting analysis and presented the findings to the project's stakeholders. What Process Group is the project currently in?
    A. Planning
    B. Executing
    C. Monitoring and Controlling
    D. Closing

20. Which of the following techniques uses a weighted average?
    A. Reserve analysis
    B. What-if scenario analysis
    C. Parametric estimating
    D. PERT analysis

21. As the project manager, you are in the middle of creating vendor evaluation criteria. What process are you in?
    A. Develop Project Management Plan
    B. Plan Procurement Management
    C. Conduct Procurements
    D. Control Procurements

22. Which of the following processes documents the products, services, and results requirements of work being procured, and results in seller proposals received?
    A. Develop Project Management Plan
    B. Plan Procurement Management
    C. Conduct Procurements
    D. Control Procurements

23. A key stakeholder approached the project manager for a list of significant events in the project that can be used to benchmark the project's progress. What document will the project manager provide the key stakeholder with?
    A. Schedule management plan
    B. Schedule baseline
    C. Project schedule
    D. Milestone list

24. You are the project manager for a pharmaceutical company. The latest project involves a new drug that will be released in six months. The project for the release is going well and closely mirrors the release of a drug that took place the previous year. With accurate historical information and quantifiable parameters in hand, what is the BEST type of cost estimating technique to use during the Determine Budget process?
    A. Cost aggregation
    B. Analogous estimating
    C. Earned value
    D. Parametric estimating

25. A project manager using probability distributions to display data is most likely to use which of the following:
    A. Uniform distributions
    B. Normal distributions
    C. Beta distributions
    D. Lognormal distributions

26. Richard, the project manager, has a difficult time with Rob, who is the department manager of Information Systems, when it comes to dealing with risk. Rob does everything possible to avoid risk, even if it means negatively impacting the project. What type of risk attitude does Rob have?
    A. Risk averse
    B. Risk tolerant
    C. Risk neutral
    D. Risk seeking

27. A project has an earned value (EV) of 95 and an actual cost (AC) of 112. What is the cost performance index (CPI)?
    A. .848
    B. –17
    C. 1.18
    D. .984

28. All of the following statements are true except for which one?
    A. Precedence Diagramming Method (PDM) uses dummy activities
    B. Precedence Diagramming Method (PDM) displays activities on the node
    C. Arrow Diagramming Method (ADM) uses only one type of logical relationship
    D. Both Precedence Diagramming Method (PDM) and Arrow Diagramming Method (ADM) use the finish-to-start dependency

29. Ricardo was late to the Monday morning project meeting and had to dial into the phone bridge in order to join the meeting. Unfortunately, he was 20 minutes late and the majority of the topics that were of interest to him had already been discussed. He sent an email to the meeting chairperson and asked if the notes for the meeting would be distributed by email or placed on the team wiki site because he was unable to attend the full meeting. Meetings, email, web publishing and telephone, when used for sharing information, are all examples of:
    A. Communication tools
    B. Lessons learned
    C. Information gathering and retrieval systems
    D. Information management systems

30. While defining the activities needed to perform the work of the project, the project manager needs to review the deliverables, constraints and assumptions of the project. Where will the project manager find this information?
    A. Organizational process assets
    B. Enterprise environmental factors
    C. Scope baseline
    D. Work breakdown structure

31. Which process handles the distribution of information?
    A. Plan Communications Management
    B. Control Communications
    C. Manage Communications
    D. Communicate Information

32. With the first major milestone around the corner, the project manager has decided to move all the active project team members to a war room. This is an example of:
    A. a virtual team
    B. ground rules
    C. co-location
    D. team building

33. Two project team members have been involved in a dispute that has escalated to the point of involving the project manager. What is the most likely source of the dispute?
    A. Scarce resources
    B. Technology used
    C. Budget
    D. Schedule priorities

34. Which of the following is not an input of the Develop Project Team process?
    A. Resource calendars
    B. Project staff assignments
    C. Staffing management plan
    D. Recognition and rewards

35. You are the project manager for Kitchens Plus Inc. The latest project involves the development of an automatic dicer with unique industry features, and has a project budget of $95,000. Based on the latest data, the project has a planned value of $70,200, an earned value of $59,000, and an actual cost of $65,500. How is the project currently performing according to the schedule and budget?
A. The project is ahead of schedule and under budget
B. The project is ahead of schedule and over budget
C. The project is behind schedule and under budget
D. The project is behind schedule and over budget

36. Al is a lead testing manager and Veronica is a development manager, both working for Power Cloud Stock Trading Online. They are requesting a meeting with the project manager because every milestone that has been set for the project seems to experience a conflict. The top three reasons for conflict are:
A. Technical beliefs, resources, scheduling priorities
B. Personality, scheduling priorities, cost priorities
C. Personality, varying priorities, resources
D. Scheduling priorities, scarce resources, personal work styles

37. What is the expected monetary value of a risk with an impact of $1,500 and probability of 65%?
A. $2,475
B. $750
C. $525
D. $975

38. Jane, who is the project manager, has a question about the Research activity's progress and is interested in knowing why it appears to have fallen behind. According to the RACI chart provided, who is to perform the work of this activity?

Activity	Todd	Alfred	Anne	Henry
Define	A	R	C	I
Research	I	R	A	I
Compile	A	I	R	I

A. Todd
B. Alfred
C. Anne
D. Henry

39. Hal has been assigned as part of the research team on a project that involves working with the latest lab software. You've noticed Hal working longer hours than the rest of the research team. When approaching him about this, he shares that he hasn't quite grasped how to utilize the new program, and has been wrestling with it for some time. As the project manager, what should you do?
A. Provide a sounding board for Hal so that he can channel the frustration within a controlled conversation
B. Look into providing training for Hal and others in the research team that may be in need of it as well
C. Replace Hal, since he is clearly not qualified for the role
D. Commend Hal on his hard work and dedication in staying longer hours to learn the program

40. Frank has just submitted a report outlining the forecasted future performance of the project to management. What stage is the project currently in?
A. Planning
B. Executing
C. Monitoring and Controlling
D. Closing

41. The 100% rule signifies that:
    A. 100% of the deliverables be included within the work breakdown structure
    B. 100% of the scope baseline represent the project scope statement
    C. 100% of activities be included within the activity list
    D. 100% of the scope be represented within the work breakdown structure

42. Ron meets with Bob, the assigned project manager, to ask when the other project team members will be assigned to the project he is scheduled for. Since team assignments have not been issued as of yet, how does Ron know he will be assigned to the project?
    A. Bob is a friend of Ron's, and mentioned the assignment early on
    B. Ron must have heard about the assignment in passing
    C. Ron was pre-assigned and listed in the project charter
    D. Ron must have looked in Bob's files and should be reported

43. Ronald Pierce is a high-end furniture store chain. The company is in the process of developing a new renaissance style edition for release in six months. The project manager leading the development of the new edition is in the process of estimating the durations of the project activities. He uses information from the previous edition's project as the primary basis of his estimates. What estimating technique is the project manager using?
    A. Analogous estimating
    B. Parametric estimating
    C. Bottom-up estimating
    D. PERT estimating

44. During quantitative risk analysis, a project manager held a planning meeting with key stakeholders to share the results of the latest analysis conducted. What-if scenarios were performed on several important risks, and then displayed using a tornado diagram. This is an example of:
    A. Expected monetary value analysis
    B. Decision tree analysis
    C. Sensitivity analysis
    D. Data validation analysis

45. During the execution phase of a bio-tech project, a new issue has surfaced. What is one of the first things that the project manager should do?
    A. Contact the stakeholders to report the issue
    B. Note the issue within an issues log
    C. Notify the team of the issue in the next status meeting
    D. Attempt to resolve the issue immediately

46. You will be participating in a weekly project team status meeting, along with ten other team members. The meeting will take place by conference call, with only two of the participants located in the same office. What is this an example of?
    A. Negotiation
    B. Virtual team
    C. Co-location
    D. Project staff assignments

47. Every Friday the development teams at Blazing Broadband Internet Solutions are treated to a free massage and a catered lunch. The CEO authorized this extra activity as a means of retaining top performers at the company and to give the human resource department extra leverage in attracting new employees as an added benefit. Benefits provided to employees who are doing a great job is known as:
    A. Fringe benefits
    B. Perquisites
    C. Halo effect
    D. Performance bonus

48. During the most recent team meeting, Nick left dissatisfied after not having had an opportunity to express his concerns over the schedule. When broaching the subject, he was cut off repeatedly by John, who felt that the focus of the meeting should center around the recent server crash. What went wrong?
 A. Nick did not have the correct priorities, since the server crash was the most pressing issue at hand.
 B. The project manager had not set clear ground rules.
 C. John should be disciplined for repeatedly cutting Nick off, which was not a display of team cohesiveness.
 D. Nick should have been advised to submit his concern through documentation.

49. Based on the following network diagram, what is the critical path?

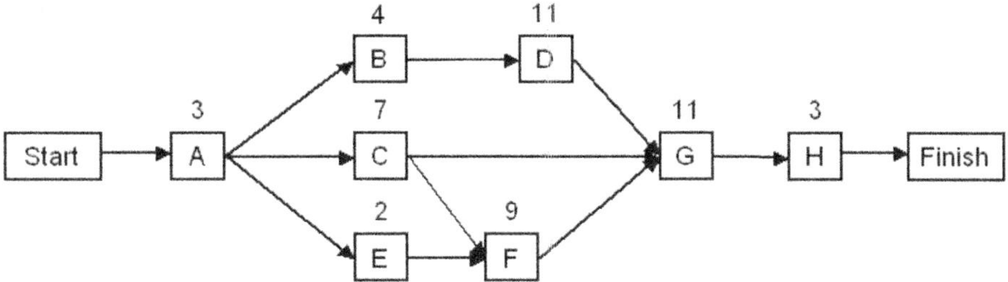

 A. A-E-F-G-H
 B. A-C-F-G-H
 C. A-B-D-G-H
 D. A-C-G-H

50. A project team member called the project manager to notify him that there seemed to be confusion about the resources needed to complete her activity. The project manager, who was running late for a meeting, told the team member not to worry about it and ended the conversation by telling her to have a good day, and that they would touch base in the coming weeks. The project team member was left wondering whether or not the project manager understood the severity of the situation, since without the resources, her activity could not proceed and the deadline would be missed. In this scenario, what was the communication role of the project manager?
 A. Sender
 B. Encoder
 C. Receiver
 D. Decoder

51. Bob has been assigned as the project manager for a new supplement that his company, who is in the fitness and wellness industry, will be releasing in the next quarter. To prepare for the project, Bob has decided to attend an upcoming fitness expo, which will be attended by many colleagues in the industry. This is an example of:
 A. Spying on the competition
 B. Research
 C. A leisure activity
 D. Networking

52. A project manager is currently working on a pharmaceutical project. The activities that will produce the deliverables of Phase 1 are currently being planned out in detail. All other work will be planned out at higher levels until additional product details are known through testing results. This strategy is known as:
 A. Rolling wave planning
 B. Progressive elaboration
 C. Scope creep
 D. Initiating

53. A project manager is working through potential options using a decision tree. Scenario A has a failure impact of -$5,000 with a probability of 25%, and no impact if successful; and scenario B has a failure impact of -$3,500 with a probability of 65%, and no impact if successful. Which scenario should the project manager choose?
    A. Scenario A
    B. Scenario B
    C. Neither scenario
    D. Insufficient information provided

54. What quality theorist believed that the quality standard should be zero defects?
    A. Edward Shewhart
    B. W. Edwards Deming
    C. Philip Crosby
    D. Joseph Juran

55. There are 24 stakeholders within a project. How many communication channels exist?
    A. 276
    B. 288
    C. 552
    D. 24

56. Sally, a member of the project management team, walks into a room where two project team members are seen arguing over the schedule. One team member feels that an additional resource is needed in order to meet an upcoming deadline, while another feels that the risk is not as high and that the schedule should be left alone. Sally takes a moment to review the schedule, and instructs the team members to leave it. What type of resolution technique did Sally use?
    A. Collaborating
    B. Smoothing
    C. Withdrawing
    D. Forcing

57. If activity A has a duration of 10 days, and activity B has a duration of 7 days with a 2 day lag, what is the overall duration of both activities combined, given a start-to-start relationship with an assumption that both activities will begin as soon as possible?
    A. 9
    B. 10
    C. 17
    D. 7

58. Joseph Juran is known for the following:
    A. Zero Defects
    B. Fitness for Use
    C. 14 Steps to Total Quality Management
    D. Plan-Do-Check-Act Cycle

59. Frank's team is working on a gaming software product for a long-term customer. It was unanimously thought by Frank's team that the product needed the addition of a scoreboard on the screen as an enhancement. With the intention of increasing the quality of the product, a scoreboard was added. What has Frank's team done?
    A. Prevented rework
    B. Quality enhancement
    C. Performed gold plating
    D. Followed concept of "fitness for use"

60. What is the highest level a person can reach, according to Maslow's Theory?
   A. Belonging
   B. Self-Actualization
   C. Safety
   D. Esteem

61. Jon, a senior research technician, has been with the company for one year and is considered to be the top performer of his group. Because of his exceptional performance, the company has decided to promote him to the role of project manager of his department. This is an example of:
   A. Fringe benefits
   B. Perquisites
   C. Halo effect
   D. Performance bonus

62. The duration of a milestone is:
   A. the duration equal to half the length of the project
   B. the duration equal to the length of the project
   C. zero
   D. typically one

63. Who developed the 14 Steps to Quality Management?
   A. Edward Shewhart
   B. W. Edwards Deming
   C. Philip Crosby
   D. Joseph Juran

64. As part of controlling the schedule, cost, and scope, variance analysis and performance reviews will be used. These technique compare actual data to planned in order to:
   A. perform a forward pass and backward pass
   B. determine whether corrective action is needed
   C. generate revised schedule completion dates
   D. satisfy the project sponsor

65. What type of contract poses the greatest risk to the buyer?
   A. Fixed price
   B. Lump sum
   C. Cost plus
   D. Time and materials

66. Purse Centric is a clothing retail company with eleven stores throughout Europe. The company is planning to expand to North America, beginning with two stores opening concurrently. The project manager heading the opening of the western region store has been working diligently with the project management team to document all the potential risks. Based on information from previous expansions, the project manager was able to include potential responses for a third of the identified risks. What risk management process is the project currently in?
   A. Plan Risk Management
   B. Identify Risks
   C. Plan Risk Responses
   D. Control Risks

67. Which of the following BEST describes virtual teams?
   A. Team members located outside of the primary physical office where the project takes place
   B. Co-locating team members in order to increase the efficiency of the project overall
   C. Team members located within another branch of the organization
   D. Specialized resources that access meetings via web or other technology tools

68. A project manager leading a multi-phase construction project is beginning to perform the risk management processes. Because of the project's complexity, and the amount of money invested in the project, the project sponsor stressed the critical nature of managing risks. The project manager took this advice seriously and brought together a risk management team. Alongside the risk management team, the project manager worked on the development of the risk management plan. Which of the following is not likely to be covered within the risk management plan?
    A. When and how often to conduct risk management activities
    B. When and how often to communicate with stakeholders throughout the project
    C. The amount of funds set aside for risk management activities
    D. The approach used to carry out risk management

69. Which of the following BEST describes a RACI chart?
    A. A chart arranged by company departments, units, or teams
    B. A chart that displays categories by types of resources
    C. A chart that appears similar to a job description
    D. A type of RAM that stands for Responsible, Accountable, Consult and Inform

70. During a status meeting, the project sponsor made a rare appearance to address questions on project funding, and asked for an update on the project's overall progress. At one point, the sponsor asked the project manager for a copy of the schedule baseline to see what work has already been accomplished. What is wrong with the sponsor's request?
    A. The sponsor should not be asking for project specific information, particularly in regards to the schedule
    B. What they are really looking for is the project management plan with all of the baselines
    C. The schedule baseline provides the original schedule, plus the approved changes, but not the current schedule
    D. Nothing. It was a valid request

71. The project manager of an accounting firm has team members located across the globe for his latest high-tech project. The project will make use of cutting edge technology that is not widely used yet. In this scenario, what is the key benefit to having a virtual team?
    A. It widens the potential resource pool
    B. It reduces the cost of travel
    C. It allows for multiple cultures to collaborate
    D. The work continues around the clock

72. After Bruce, the project manager for the Happy Holiday Cruise Ships, Inc., makes his rounds through the office he usually compiles the notes he's collected from talking to his team into a quick performance report and shares it on their team wiki site. Performance reports are an example of what type of communication?
    A. Informal written
    B. Formal written
    C. Informal verbal
    D. Formal verbal

73. A project is considered to be complete when:
    A. The lessons learned have been archived
    B. Project team has been released
    C. All payments for the project have been received
    D. Formal documented acceptance has been received by the customer

74. The project charter has just been approved. What comes next?
    A. Develop the project management plan
    B. Develop the project scope statement
    C. Develop the project scope statement
    D. Perform stakeholder analysis

75. The following is included within the cost baseline:
  A. Management reserve
  B. Contingency reserve
  C. Cost aggregation
  D. Cash flow

76. In order to prevent the problem from happening again, the project manager has instructed the quality team to focus on the top 20% of causes that resulted in the identified defect. This is an example of:
  A. Specification limits
  B. 80 / 20 rule
  C. Assignable cause
  D. Trend analysis

77. Which of the following statements is inaccurate?
  A. Gathering three-point estimates helps generate a more accurate estimate of activity resources needed
  B. Bottom-up estimating is a time-consuming technique that generates confident resource estimates
  C. Resource breakdown structures are generated as part of the Estimate Activity Resources process
  D. Project management software helps increase the level of accuracy, organization, and data accessibility

78. Which of the following are displayed as a table format chart?
  A. Responsibility assignment matrix
  B. Resource breakdown structure
  C. Text oriented description
  D. Risk register

79. Cloud Divine is a start-up company that provides SaaS using Cloud computing. The first major project launched by the company experienced a few issues, including a large number of changes to the project deliverables, nearly resulting in a failed project. What is the most likely cause for the lack of change control?
  A. The project manager is not PMI certified
  B. A poorly written scope
  C. Informal change control procedures
  D. The lack of a configuration management system

80. Which of the following statements is inaccurate?
  A. The risk register is a part of the project documents
  B. The risk register is first created during the Identify Risks process
  C. The contents of the risk register are updated during project planning
  D. After its creation, the risk register becomes an input and output of the remaining risk management processes

81. While acquiring the project team, the project manager discovers that a key resource has just resigned from the company. This was the only resource available with the necessary skill set to perform the activity requiring the given expertise. Since hiring and getting a new resource up to speed would take up to three months, the project sponsor authorized the procurement of a specialized contractor. Where will the project management team look to determine how resources are to be acquired externally?
  A. Requirements management plan
  B. Project management plan
  C. Human resource management plan
  D. Schedule management plan

82. A project manager of Cyber Channels Inc. is in the process of identifying project risks. While reviewing how the elements of a particular system interrelate, she discovers two risks relating to the cause of another risk that were both initially overlooked. Which of the following techniques is the project manager using?
  A. Influence diagram
  B. Flow chart
  C. Cause and effect diagram
  D. Control chart

83. Which of the following is not contained within the staffing management plan?
   A. Roles and responsibilities
   B. Recognition and rewards
   C. Compliance
   D. Safety

84. Eric is a project manager that has teams located in two buildings on their corporate campus. As part of being a good project manager he knows that in order to keep the team functioning well, he has to spend time with them equally. Which of the following is used to stay in touch with the work and attitudes of project team members?
   A. 360 Degree feedback
   B. Observation and conversation
   C. Issue log
   D. Team-building activities

85. Molly is the lead project manager for Cube Systems Plus. A project that she is managing is utilizing three different vendors to perform various components of work. Molly's customer has just requested that the delivery date be pushed up by one month. To determine whether this is possible, she sits down with the account managers of the three vendor companies to discuss availability. Where will Molly and the account managers look to view resource availability?
   A. Resource management plan
   B. Seller Gantt charts
   C. Contract
   D. Resource calendars

86. Al is a lead testing manager and Veronica is a development manager, both working for Power Cloud Stock Trading Online in the same team. They are requesting a meeting with the project manager because every milestone that has been set for the project seems to have a conflict, resulting from conflict between two specific team members. Who is responsible for resolving conflict between the two project team members?
   A. The project manager
   B. The project sponsor
   C. The two project team members
   D. The functional manager

87. Which of the following statements is inaccurate?
   A. The scheduling tool is used along with the project management software to perform schedule network analysis
   B. Crashing the schedule is a costly schedule compression technique applied to critical activities only
   C. A negative cost variance (CV) indicates that the project is performing under budget
   D. Monte Carlo technique is a commonly used form of what-if scenario analysis

88. Which communication type will the project manager use to update the schedule management plan?
   A. Informal written
   B. Formal written
   C. Informal verbal
   D. Formal verbal

89. An RV rental company is launching a consignment program for private owners to participate in, who are looking to rent out their vehicles. The project manager of the project has just begun carrying out risk management activities. Since the project manager is experienced in managing risk, she immediately moved into the Identify Risks process. Based on this information, which of the following is most likely to occur?
   A. The project manager is likely to carry out risk management activities effectively, given her level of experience
   B. The project manager is unlikely to carry out risk management activities effectively, regardless of her level of experience
   C. The project manager is likely to generate a useful risk register
   D. The project manager is likely to identify more risks, based on her experience

90. Which of the following is not addressed within the communications management plan?
   A. Roles and responsibilities
   B. Information to be distributed
   C. Communication responsibility
   D. Glossary of communication terms

91. Which contract type poses a higher risk on the buyer?
   A. Fixed price
   B. Cost-reimbursable
   C. Time and material
   D. Cost-plus-fixed-fee

92. Which of the following BEST describes activity duration estimates:
   A. A duration estimate of the critical activities within the project that are required to complete the deliverables
   B. Quantitative assessments of the likely number of work periods required to complete an activity
   C. Quantitative assessments of the likely number of work periods, leads, and lags required to complete an activity
   D. A specific estimate of the likely number of work periods required to complete an activity

93. Which of the following is not an official component that makes up the human resource management plan?
   A. Roles and responsibilities
   B. RACI chart
   C. Project organizational charts
   D. Staffing management plan

94. Ronald Pierce is a high-end furniture store chain. The company is in the process of developing a new renaissance style edition for release in six months. The project manager leading the development of the new edition is currently developing risk responses, alongside the risk management team. In response to one of the threats, insurance was purchased to cover any potential losses, should the risk emerge. What type of response did the team utilize?
   A. Mitigate
   B. Avoid
   C. Transfer
   D. Exploit

95. Schedule variance (SV) can BEST be described as:
   A. Measure of progress achieved versus progress planned
   B. A measure of the value of work completed versus actual cost
   C. The measurement of schedule performance versus the baseline schedule
   D. The difference between the overall project budget and the revised estimate

96. A project team member called the project manager to notify him that there seemed to be confusion about the resources needed to complete her activity. The project manager, who was running late for a meeting, told the team member not to worry about it and ended the conversation by telling her to have a good day, and that they would touch base in the coming weeks. The project team member was left wondering whether or not the project manager understood the severity of the situation, since without the resources, her activity could not proceed and the deadline would be missed. What did the project team member fail to do during the conversation?
   A. Ask the project manager whether it was a good time to talk
   B. Confirm that the project manager understood the message correctly
   C. Schedule a follow up conversation
   D. Increase the pitch of her voice so that the project manager understood the severity of the situation

97. During risk analysis, a project manager of a construction project uses historical data and the required labor hours to calculate the cost estimate of a schedule activity. What type of cost estimate did the project manager use?
A. Parametric estimating
B. Bottom-up estimating
C. Analogous estimating
D. Reserve analysis estimating

98. A project manager is working on a residential housing project. Currently, the project manager is estimating the duration of laying down interior carpeting per home. Based on past similar projects, a carpenter is able to install 10 square feet of carpeting per hour, and each home will require 2,000 square feet of carpeting. Given the variables used to estimate this activity, what type of estimating technique is the project manager using?
A. Analogous estimating
B. Bottom-up estimating
C. Parametric estimating
D. PERT

99. Based on the following information, what is the duration of the critical path?

Activity	Prede-cessor	Duration
A	Start	2
B	A	5
C	A	6
D	B	9

Activity	Prede-cessor	Duration
E	B,C	3
F	D,E	4

A. 16
B. 20
C. 15
D. 21

100. A project manager of a retail chain of hardware stores is in the process of conducting risk identification activities. Along with the risk management team, the project manager examined the existing project plans to determine whether they were consistent with the project requirements. What technique is the project manager currently using?
A. Process flow chart
B. Checklist analysis
C. Brainstorming
D. Documentation reviews

101. Variance at completion tells you:
A. How much over the project will be at completion
B. How much under the project will be at completion
C. How much over or under the project will be at completion
D. How much the project progressed by completion

102. You are a project manager working as a consultant for a company that is in start-up mode. One of your responsibilities for this week is to create an organizational chart. Which of the following is not a format you are likely to use to display an organizational chart?
A. Hierarchical type
B. Matrix-based
C. Run chart
D. Text-oriented

103. Robert is a project manager and Sergio is a business analyst working on a project. As part of their project planning strategy they have scheduled a daily team meeting. Robert and Sergio tend to have more direct conflicts with one another during the discussions that take place as part of these meetings than other attendees. Which of the following is not likely to be a source of conflict between the two?

A. Personal work styles
B. Personality clashes
C. Scheduling priorities
D. Scarce resources

104. A the end of each quarter, the PMO of the Big Bang Software Development Company performs a review that focuses on measuring the project team's effectiveness. This type of activity can BEST be described as:

A. Co-location
B. Team building activities
C. Team performance assessments
D. Project performance appraisals

105. The lowest level of the work breakdown structure (WBS) is the:

A. work package
B. activity list
C. planning package
D. control account

106. You are the project manager of a software organization leading a project to develop a new reservation system. A new scheduling risk has been identified and determined to be critical to the project. As a result, you need to meet with project stakeholders to discuss the situation. What is the BEST method in dealing with stakeholders?

A. Call each stakeholder individually to get feedback
B. Schedule one-on-one meetings with all of the stakeholders
C. Schedule a phone conference with all of the stakeholders
D. Schedule an in-person meeting with all of the stakeholders

107. Which of the following is not an example of utilizing transfer as a risk response?

A. Prototypes
B. Bonds
C. Warranties
D. Guaranties

108. The project management team spent several days negotiating with a functional manager and another project manager to utilize the senior developer of the company as part of their project. This was the final resource needed to meet the resource requirements of the project. What process has the project management team just completed?

A. Acquire Project Team
B. Estimate Activity Resources
C. Estimate Activity Durations
D. Plan Human Resource Management

109. Al and Veronica have agreed to put an end to the bickering about the project by settling their personal differences on the Go Kart track. In fact, they have made it a team building activity by giving their team members half of a day off so that they could join in the race. Team building activities accomplish the following:

A. Clarify what is considered to be acceptable behavior
B. Provide isolated team members with a better social life
C. Encourage individuality
D. Build trust

110. Susan is the Director of Engineering for a software consulting company. She needs to hire 7 people for a project that will be starting over the next month, and has just filled out the roles and responsibilities of the positions and provided them to the human resources department. Which of the following is not considered in the development of roles and responsibilities?
   A. Technical
   B. Political
   C. Interpersonal
   D. Background

111. 360 degree feedback is an example of:
   A. Team performance assessment
   B. Observation and conversation
   C. Project performance appraisal
   D. Conflict management

112. Changes to the baseline must first be approved, and change control is an important responsibility of the project manager. Which project management process is concerned with reviewing submitted changes and taking the requests through the proper change control procedures?
   A. Develop Project Management Plan
   B. Perform Integrated Change Control
   C. Control Schedule
   D. Direct and Manage Project Work

113. First Strike Engineering Co. has won a contract to produce 1,000,000 night-time vision goggles for the military. However, part of the requirement is that they must ensure the product accuracy is within 6 Sigma. This prevents a problem for First Strike Engineering Co. because they are not accustomed to delivering products within a 6 Sigma level of accuracy, and as a result, the cost of quality to achieve that level of accuracy will decrease their profit margin by 67%. Cost of quality, which is a factor in this scenario, can BEST be defined as:
   A. The prevention of rework
   B. The cost of conformance to requirements
   C. The investment made toward customer service
   D. Providing customers with extras

114. Molly is the lead project manager for Cube Systems Plus. A project that she is managing is utilizing three different vendors to perform various components of work. At the present time, Molly is monitoring the performance of the sellers and managing changes to the contract, involving the company's contract administrator and change control board when necessary. What process describes the work that Molly is currently performing?
   A. Conduct Procurements
   B. Control Procurements
   C. Manage Procurements
   D. Close Procurements

115. If the duration of activity D were compressed to 6 days within the following network diagram, what would be the impact to the schedule?

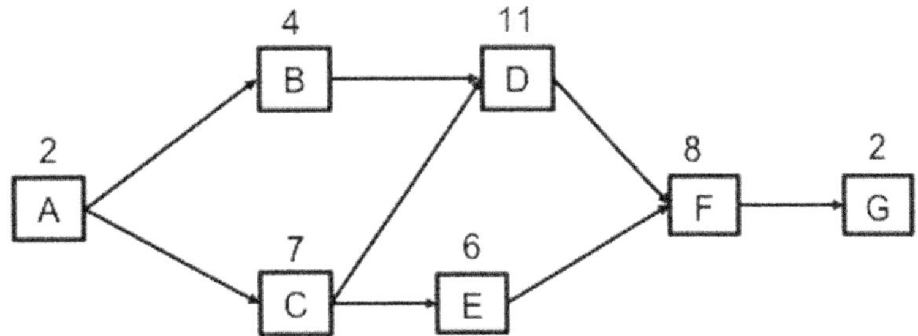

A. Activity D will have a float of 1
B. There will be one critical path
C. The risk increases
D. There is no impact

116. Which of the following statements BEST describes mitigation of a risk?
A. To transfer a risk to a third party
B. To remove the possibility of a risk occurring
C. To increase the probability and / or impact of a risk
D. To reduce the probability and / or impact of a risk

117. The scheduler has just received earned value reports indicating that the project is performing at a cost performance index (CPI) of .95 and a schedule performance index (SPI) of 1.3. What do these performance indicators tell the scheduler?
A. The project is under budget and behind schedule
B. The project is over budget and behind schedule
C. The project is under budget and ahead of schedule
D. The project is over budget and ahead of schedule

118. Astral Bank is known for providing its customers with superior online services through its use of cutting edge technology. The latest project includes the ability for customers to electronically sign for loans. Currently, the project is in its third week of executing the project work, and the project manager noticed that a key resource has been over-allocated. What technique is the project manager likely to use to resolve this issue?
A. Resource leveling
B. Monte Carlo technique
C. An adjustment of leads and lags
D. Critical chain method

119. Which of the following tools and techniques is used to generate the communications management plan?
A. Calculation of communication paths
B. Communication skills
C. Communication requirements analysis
D. Communication methods

120. Two stakeholders approached the project manager about the integrity of the data used for risk management. They both felt that the risks identified weren't in alignment with what they'd seen in previous past projects. The project manager informed them that the accuracy of the data had already been analyzed, and therefore, the integrity of the information and data used had been validated. The project manager then spent 20 minutes with the stakeholders going through the results of the data's validation. What technique did the project manager most likely use to check the integrity of the data used for risk management?
A. Risk data quality assessment
B. Assumptions analysis
C. Checklist analysis
D. Data validation analysis

121. Templates are beneficial to the project manager in which way?
   A. It allows more time available to spend with the project team
   B. It lessens the repercussions of procrastination
   C. It removes the need of using the project team to create the list of activities
   D. It allows for greater efficiency and consistency of results

122. The human resources associate at the Uptime Software Development Corporation is finding it difficult to attract new recruits due to the competitive nature of finding software developers. In response, she has suggested to her manager that the company increase the standard benefits package. Standard benefits provided to all employees is known as:
   A. Fringe benefits
   B. Perquisites
   C. Halo effect
   D. Performance bonus

123. Tim works for a project management consulting firm that has just assisted a client implement a new process improvement plan. The executives of the company are pleased with the outcome of the project but are unsure how they will be able to maintain this new level of productivity. In response, Tim suggested that they use Kaizen events based around The Kaizen Theory. The Kaizen Theory is also known as:
   A. Kanban
   B. Continuous Improvement
   C. Prevention
   D. Zero Defects

124. A project manager of a construction company uncovered a risk that, if it were to occur, could shorten the length of the project by 2 months. This would mean a savings of $75,000 for the company. All of the stakeholders agreed that anything within reason should be done to make sure that this risk happens. What risk response strategy is the project manager most likely to use?
   A. Exploit
   B. Share
   C. Enhance
   D. Accept

125. Which of the following BEST describes procurement audits?
   A. Structured reviews that audit the project manager's adherence to company procurement policies
   B. Structured reviews that audit the seller's deliverables
   C. Structured reviews that audit the procurement management processes
   D. Structured reviews that audit the procurement closing procedures

126. A project manager of a retail chain of hardware stores is in the process of generating the project schedule. After issuing the project assignments, a team member approaches the project manager to say that he has a two week planned vacation right in the middle of a critical activity. What did the project manager fail to do?
   A. Call the team member in advance to see if their vacation can be re-scheduled
   B. Check the resource requirements for the affected activities
   C. Cancel the team member's scheduled vacation in advance
   D. Check the resource calendars for team member schedule conflicts

127. A software architect provides the scheduler with the following duration estimates for his assigned activity: that it can be completed as soon as 13 days, as late as 45 days, and most likely at 20 days. Based on this information, what can the scheduler determine about the activity?
   A. The activity contains schedule risk
   B. The software architect is padding the estimate
   C. The scheduler is using PERT
   D. This is a junior software architect

128. Igor is a software developer for a large IT consulting company. Mary, the team lead, has just informed him that the project manager has compressed the schedule by 2 weeks, and as a result, she is requiring the team to work weekends to accommodate the release. Which of the following is a type of power that is based on the authority of someone else, such as the type that Mary is using in this example?
   A. Formal
   B. Reward
   C. Referent
   D. Expert

129. Which of the following is not a component of the scope baseline?
   A. Project scope statement
   B. Deliverables
   C. WBS
   D. WBS Dictionary

130. A project manager of Cyber Channels Inc. is in the process of prioritizing risks. A project team member expressed concerns with one of the risks, informing the project manager that if not responded to quickly, it may have dire consequences for the project. What should the project manager do first?
   A. Develop a response to the risk in question
   B. Perform risk urgency assessment
   C. Assure the team member that the risk will be addressed
   D. Create a risk probability and impact matrix to prioritize the risk

131. Which of the following risk response strategies utilizes warranties and bonds?
   A. Transfer
   B. Mitigate
   C. Avoid
   D. Accept

132. The risk management team has exhausted all potential scenarios of dealing with a particular risk. The possibility of eliminating the risk had been found to be impossible, and the possibility of reducing the risk was also minimal. In the end, the risk management team, with the approval of the project stakeholders, decided to do nothing about the risk. What strategy did the risk management team take in dealing with the risk?
   A. Active acceptance
   B. Passive acceptance
   C. Mitigate
   D. Avoid

133. An uncertain event or condition that, if it occurs, has a positive or negative effect on a project's objectives is known as:
   A. Workaround
   B. Issue
   C. Risk
   D. Trigger

134. Which of the following BEST describes procurement documents?
   A. Documents used to identify the sellers that have already gone through a screening process
   B. Responses submitted by the potential sellers to the procurement documents
   C. Documents used to solicit responses from potential sellers
   D. Documents used to review the seller proposals against the selection criteria

135. The Big Mouth grocery food chain is planning to modernize their IT department by developing a new bar coding system that will allow them to keep their shelves stocked more efficiently by using the Just In Time Strategy. However, during the project chartering phase the project manager explained to them that in order to execute the Just in Time strategy, a company must have a high level of:
A. Quality
B. Resources
C. Experience
D. Financing

136. A project manager was holding a one-on-one meeting with the scheduler located across the globe. The meeting was difficult to manage, due to sporadic static. The static can BEST be described as:
A. Noise
B. Medium
C. Obstacle
D. Interference

137. Which of the following risk responses are unplanned?
A. Workarounds
B. Fallback plans
C. Contingency plans
D. Response plans

138. You are the project manager for Kitchens Plus Inc. The latest project involves the development of an automatic dicer with unique industry features, and has a project budget of $95,000. Based on the latest data, the project has a planned value of $70,200, an earned value of $59,000, and an actual cost of $65,500. In order to finish according to the original budget, at what rate must the project perform at moving forward?
A. 1.22
B. 0.90
C. 0.84
D. 1.00

139. You are the project manager for Kitchens Plus Inc. The latest project involves the development of an automatic dicer with unique industry features. Currently, you are analyzing schedule performance. Based on the information provided by the scheduling team, the current schedule performance index (SPI) is at 1.10, while the cost performance index (CPI) is at 0.80. What might be a good strategy for balancing out performance between the schedule and budget?
A. Crash the schedule by adding additional resources to critical activities
B. Fast-track the longest activities that fall on the critical path
C. Level out resource usage to further spread out cost over time
D. Nothing, since the project is performing as planned

140. Which of the following describes a resource that has been committed to a project as part of a contract or within the project charter?
A. Committed
B. Pre-assignment
C. Negotiated
D. Asset

141. A project manager of Cyber Channels Inc. is in the process of assigning resources to her current project. At the end of the day, she received an angry call from the director of engineering, who was upset that his senior systems administrator was assigned to the project without his consent. At this stage, what should the project manager do to keep this resource?
A. Negotiate with the director for the resource
B. Agree by phone but keep the resource
C. Get the project sponsor involved
D. Call the CEO, who is a personal friend

142. A project manager looking to increase the probability that a positive event will occur, and increase the impact will use which of the following response strategies?
 A. Enhance
 B. Mitigate
 C. Exploit
 D. Share

143. The project manager has facilitated the creation of the WBS, broken down the work packages into the activity list, generated the list of milestones, and inspected the project scope statement for existing constraints. What should the project manager do NEXT?
 A. Create and document the activity attributes
 B. Place the activities in proper sequence
 C. Define the activities
 D. Estimate the duration of the activities

144. The project manager of a pharmaceutical company sent an email to one of his project team members apologizing for ending their recent conversation abruptly. What type of communication did the project manager use?
 A. Formal written
 B. Informal written
 C. Written
 D. Informal electronic

145. Alfred has just been assigned as the project manager for the Realtor Dual Co project, which has just kicked off its second phase. As part of getting up to speed on the project, Alfred investigates the procurement activities that will be required to carry out this phase of the project. He discovers that a key deliverable has been flagged as requiring external resources, and begins working immediately to procure those resources. Where can Alfred look to review the company's existing procurement policies, procedures, and guidelines?
 A. Enterprise environmental factors
 B. Organizational process assets
 C. Procurement documents
 D. Procurement documentation

146. Which of the following statements is inaccurate?
 A. Resource calendars provide information on non-working days of resources
 B. Published estimating data can be used to estimate resource types and quantities
 C. Bottom-up estimating is a quick and cost efficient estimating technique
 D. The scheduler should consider various options in carrying out an activity

147. How many network paths exist within the following diagram?

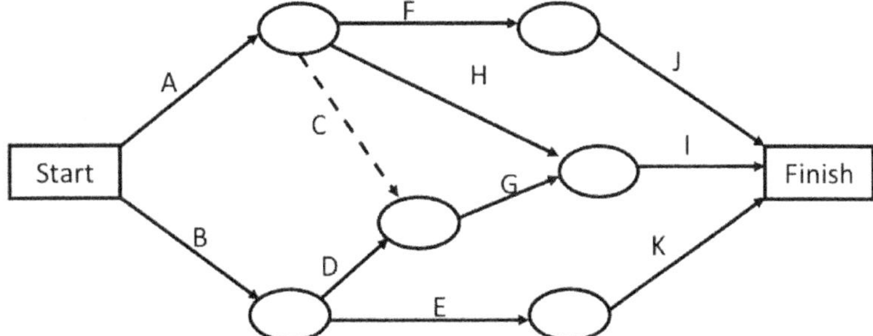

 A. 5
 B. 4
 C. 6
 D. 3

148. What assumption is made in the Expectancy theory?
   A. Behavior is based on conscious choices
   B. Behavior is based on unconscious choices
   C. Behavior is based on cognitive bias
   D. The two sets of factors operate independently from each other

149. Which of the following is not a type of leadership style?
   A. Directing
   B. Supporting
   C. Forcing
   D. Facilitating

150. A project manager was working through potential options using a decision tree. Scenario A has a failure impact of -$5,000 with a probability of 25% and no impact if successful, and scenario B has a failure impact of -$3,500 with a probability of 65% and no impact if successful. Which scenario should the project manager choose?
   A. Scenario A
   B. Scenario B
   C. Neither scenario
   D. Insufficient information provided

151. Thomas is the project manager for a software consulting company. The project he is working on has encountered numerous overruns due to regulatory compliance obstacles. A new bill passed by the government may even make it impossible for the deliverable to be distributed. He suggests to the CEO that it may be in the company's best interest to end the project and write off costs they have incurred thus far. What type of cost refers to money already spent?
   A. Sunk cost
   B. Opportunity cost
   C. Direct costs
   D. Fixed costs

152. Janet is the project manager for First Strike Engineering, a company that specializes in providing military devices for jet fighters. Her departmental projects usually require that all deliverables be within an accuracy of 6 Sigma. Today, she received her first contract stating that the accuracy of the deliverable can be within 1 Sigma. What is the level of accuracy of 1 Sigma?
   A. 68.27%
   B. 95.46%
   C. 99.73%
   D. 99.99%

153. Which of the following is considered to be the BEST type of power that a project manager can use?
   A. Formal
   B. Reward
   C. Referent
   D. Penalty

154. Which of the following is triggered when pre-defined risk warning signs occur?
   A. Active acceptance
   B. Passive acceptance
   C. Contingency response
   D. Fallback plan

155. If Earned Value (EV) = 145, Planned Value (PV) = 162, Cumulative Cost Performance Index (CPI) = 1.3, Budget at Completion (BAC) = 200, and Estimate to Complete (ETC) = 55, what is Variance at Completion (VAC)? Assume future performance will be the same as past performance.
A. 46
B. 8
C. 145
D. 190

156. A stakeholder approaches the project manager of a project to express concerns about the schedule. Based on calculations from the earned value team, the project has a CPI of 2.1 and an SPI of 0.8. The project manager is already aware that the two longest critical activities cannot be altered to occur in parallel. Based on the reported performance, what will the project manager most likely do?
A. Perform a what-if scenario analysis
B. Perform resource leveling
C. Fast-track the schedule
D. Crash the schedule

157. Which of following statements is inaccurate?
A. The human resource management plan is a component of the project management plan
B. Team member assignments occur during the final weeks of the planning phase
C. Activity resource requirements are used as an input in the development of the human resource management plan
D. The staffing management plan is a component of the human resource management plan

158. Empathy, influence and creativity are all forms of:
A. Communication skills
B. Management skills
C. Leadership skills
D. Interpersonal skills

159. Alfred has just been assigned as the project manager for the Realtor Dual Co project, which has just kicked off its second phase. To date, the procurement management plan and procurement statement of work have been written, and a seller has been awarded a contract for work that is to be carried out by external resources. What procurement-related process will Alfred carry out next?
A. Plan Procurement Management
B. Conduct Procurements
C. Control Procurements
D. Close Procurements

160. While creating the list of activities for the latest project, a project manager decided to work incrementally by only generating detailed activities within a four-week window, and planning the remaining activities at a high level. This is an example of:
A. Rolling wave planning
B. Progressive elaboration
C. Decomposition
D. Scope creep

161. A project manager has just received news that the initial planned response for a particular risk proved ineffective. The stakeholders had given the project manager authority to make decisions regarding risk responses. What should the project manager do next?
A. Implement the planned response
B. Accept the outcome
C. Implement a contingency plan
D. Implement a fallback plan

162. Further decomposing an activity to more accurately calculate estimates is an example of which estimating technique?
A. Analogous estimating
B. PERT analysis
C. Parametric estimating
D. Bottom-up estimating

163. After conducting a lessons learned session at the end of each project phase, the project manager is responsible for collecting feedback from the team and creating a process improvement plan. The process improvement plan contains all of the following except for which one?
A. Process boundaries
B. Process configuration
C. Failure rate
D. Targets for improved performance

164. Jason is the project manager for the Jingles Toy Company. His department has received their first order from a new client. Since this is the first run of a new product, he has suggested they add an additional week to the schedule to perform statistical sampling before shipping to the customer. The primary benefit of statistical sampling is:
A. Reduces the cost of quality control
B. Increases the cost of quality control
C. Identifies causes of errors
D. Prevents errors

165. Your project is progressing nicely. One of the key deliverables for your project was contracted out to a vendor, but your organization is performing all the remaining work of the project. The completion of this deliverable marks the end of the design phase of the project. Two project phases remain. Which of the following Closing processes should be performed, if any?
A. Close Project or Phase and Close Procurements
B. Close Project or Phase only
C. Close Procurements only
D. None

166. Ronald Pierce is a high-end furniture store chain. The company is in the process of developing a new renaissance style edition for release in six months. The project manager leading the development of the new edition is currently developing risk responses, alongside the risk management team. In response to one of the threats, insurance was purchased to cover any potential losses, should the risk emerge. What type of response did the team utilize?
A. Mitigate
B. Avoid
C. Transfer
D. Exploit

167. A project management team is in the process of acquiring the necessary resources to complete the project activities, as specified within the human resource management plan. After considering those resources that had been promised as part of the customer contract, they discover that a key resource was not included within the initial agreement, and was already committed to two other projects. In order to work through the best scenario, what technique can the team use?
A. Virtual Teams
B. Pre-Assignment
C. Acquisition
D. Negotiation

168. The project team has had to re-architect a product that did not meet project standards. This has resulted in a one-week schedule delay, in addition to the cost of rework. This is an example of:
 A. Poorly trained resources
 B. Lack of specifications
 C. Poor quality
 D. Poorly structured scope

169. Company Amex is a respectable organization within the travel industry. The organization will be launching a new product to make booking reservations quicker and more efficient for customers using a website containing the latest in user interface technology. As part of developing the list of activities necessary to carry out the work of the project, the project manager obtained a copy of the work breakdown structure (WBS). What will the project manager do with this document?
 A. Perform rolling wave planning
 B. Decompose the deliverables into work packages
 C. Decompose the work packages into activities
 D. Progressively elaborate the components

170. A benefit of bottom-up estimating is:
 A. it produces a good level of accuracy
 B. it is cost efficient
 C. it is a quick method
 D. it does not require expert judgment

171. Identifying new risks occurs in which of the following processes?
 A. Identify Risks
 B. Identify Risks and Control Risks
 C. Control Risks
 D. Identify Risks and Plan Risk Responses

172. What is the difference between a contingency reserve and management reserve?
 A. Contingency Reserves are estimated costs used for known events, while management reserves are used for known-unknown events
 B. Contingency reserves are actual costs used for known-unknown events, while management reserves are used for unknown-unknown events
 C. Contingency reserves come from unused project funds, while management reserves come from a second wave of project funding
 D. Contingency reserves are estimated costs used for known-unknown events, while management reserves are used for unknown-unknown events

173. In order to expedite the scheduling process, a project manager alters an existing schedule management plan from a previous project for use on the current project. In this case, the schedule management plan represents:
 A. a lazy project manager
 B. a best practice
 C. an enterprise environmental factor
 D. an organizational process asset

174. If earned value (EV) = 205, and planned value (PV) = 210, what does it tell us about the schedule?
 A. Nothing, since there is insufficient information provided to calculate schedule progress
 B. That the schedule is 3.4% behind schedule
 C. That the schedule is 97.6% ahead of schedule
 D. That the schedule should be adjusted

175. A project manager received feedback from team members that a certain team member was not up to speed on the project's technology, and it was impacting the progress of the work. The project manager then realized his error, since the team member was brought on board after the initial project training had occurred. Where can the project manager look to view the training needs and training plans for the team?
A. Project schedule
B. Schedule management plan
C. Project management plan
D. Staffing management plan

176. A quantitative assessment of the likely resource cost necessary to complete the schedule activity refers to:
A. Variance management
B. Project performance reviews
C. Cost management plan
D. Activity cost estimates

177. Benchmarking refers to:
A. determining where the project team should be through a status meeting
B. the investment made towards preventing non-conformance to requirements
C. comparing actual or planned project practices to other projects as a way of generating ideas for improvement
D. identifying the factors that may influence variables of a product or process being developed

178. In which Process Group is the work outlined within the project management plan carried out?
A. Executing
B. Monitoring and Controlling
C. Initiating
D. Planning

179. Which of the following is risk management not concerned with?
A. Identifying and analyzing project risks
B. Preventing risks from occurring
C. Risk response planning
D. Continuous process improvement

180. Which of the following is not addressed in the procurement management plan?
A. The type of contract(s) to be used
B. The portion of the scope that is being purchased or acquired
C. The form and format of the procurement statement of work
D. Constraints and assumptions that could impact purchasing and acquisition activities and decisions

181. A project manager of a construction company uncovered several new risks after the project work was executed. After conducting analysis, the project manager became concerned that there would not be enough funds to cover these additional risks, should they occur. What should the project manager do?
A. Request additional funds
B. Reassess risks
C. Perform risk audits
D. Perform reserve analysis

182. Alfred is holding a brainstorming meeting with select members of the project team to help generate different approaches and ideas for executing the project work. This is an example of:
A. Lateral thinking
B. Expert judgment
C. Product analysis
D. Alternatives analysis

183. Which of the following statements is inaccurate?
   A. Gathering three-point estimates helps generate a more accurate estimate of activity resources needed
   B. Bottom-up estimating is a time-consuming technique that generates confident resource estimates
   C. Resource breakdown structures are generated as part of the Estimate Activity Resources process
   D. Project management software helps increase the level of accuracy, organization, and data accessibility

184. Which of the following represents a level at which cost estimates will not be aggregated to?
   A. Work package
   B. Control account
   C. Network path
   D. Overall project

185. As a proactive approach to dealing with a recent issue, the project team has been asked to determine all the possible causes of the issue. Which of the following tools would be the BEST choice for the project team to use?
   A. Histogram
   B. Scatter diagram
   C. Cause and effect diagram
   D. Control chart

186. Upon returning from lunch, you discover that a quality audit will be taking place. Some of the team members are upset, since there is an approaching deadline, and have therefore requested that the audit be moved to the following day. As the project manager, what should you do?
   A. Request that the audit be rescheduled
   B. Allow the audit to take place
   C. Express your dissatisfaction along with the team, and allow the audit only if your own manager requires it
   D. Allow the audit to take place, but do not offer assistance, since you and your team are too busy

187. The stakeholder approaches the project manager to report that the schedule must be adjusted to finish one week earlier than originally planned. What would be the preferred approach for the project manager to take in order to make this happen?
   A. Crash the schedule
   B. Fast-track the schedule
   C. Add duration buffers
   D. Level out resources

188. You are the project manager for Kitchens Plus Inc. The latest project involves the development of an automatic dicer with unique industry features, and has a project budget of $95,000. Based on the latest data date, the project has a planned value of $70,200, an earned value of $59,000, and an actual cost of $65,500. How much more is the project expected to cost, based on current performance?
   A. $24,800
   B. $29,500
   C. $39,938
   D. $36,000

189. Quality metrics can BEST be described as:
   A. Identifies what to measure within the project, and what measurements are considered acceptable
   B. A tool to ensure that quality related steps are performed
   C. Ensures that the concepts, designs and tests selected at the beginning of the project are correct
   D. Detailed steps for determining waste and non-value added activities within the processes

190. Which of the following is not considered to be a cost of quality?
   A. Quality staff
   B. Time spent on quality activities
   C. Rework
   D. Quality tools

191. The company's quality research team has been assigned to review the project materials. This team is not part of the group that developed the material. This is an example of what type of review?
   A. Design of experiments
   B. Independent peer review
   C. Quality audits
   D. Defect repair review

192. Which of the following risk responses are unplanned?
   A. Workarounds
   B. Fallback plans
   C. Contingency plans
   D. Response plans

193. A senior project manager is working on a project that will allow two servers across the globe to communicate with one another using web-based technology. Part of the project includes working with technology that is outdated, resulting in the need for a vendor with specific expertise. Because the vendor was in high demand, they included a requirement within the awarded contract that the parts provided by the buyer must be available before the start of the vendor's work. This is an example of which type of dependency?
   A. External
   B. Discretionary
   C. Mandatory
   D. Preferential

194. Which of the following BEST describes rolling wave planning?
   A. To plan out near term work in detail and future work at higher levels of the work breakdown structure
   B. To pick up where the work packages leave off
   C. To begin with a broadly defined scope and add additional detail incrementally
   D. To make unplanned additions to the scope of the project as the work progresses

195. What is the difference between inspection and prevention, in regards to quality?
   A. Inspection focuses on the cause of errors found, while prevention focuses on resolving the errors
   B. Prevention focuses on the cause of errors found, while inspection focuses on resolving the errors
   C. Inspection keeps errors from reaching the customer, while prevention prevents errors from occurring
   D. Prevention keeps errors from reaching the customer, while inspection prevents errors from occurring

196. Martha has just been told that she will be assigned as the project manager for the new office expansion project that will begin during the next quarter. Martha's assignment was identified within the project charter. During which Process Group did her assignment occur?
   A. Initiating
   B. Planning
   C. Monitoring and Controlling
   D. Executing

197. The project manager has just generated probabilities of project completion dates, prior to finalizing the schedule. Which process is the project currently in?
   A. Define Activities
   B. Sequence Activities
   C. Develop Schedule
   D. Estimate Costs

198. You are the project manager of a project heading the development of a government simulation program. The risk management team has just disbanded from a meeting on the project, reporting the outcome of risk activities and adding these outcomes to the risk register. What process is the project currently going through?
   A. Plan Risk Responses
   B. Control Risks
   C. Plan Risk Management
   D. Identify Risks

199. Impact of risk is highest during which phase of the project?
   A. Initiating
   B. Planning
   C. Executing
   D. Closing

200. Based on the following diagram, what is the total float of activity B?

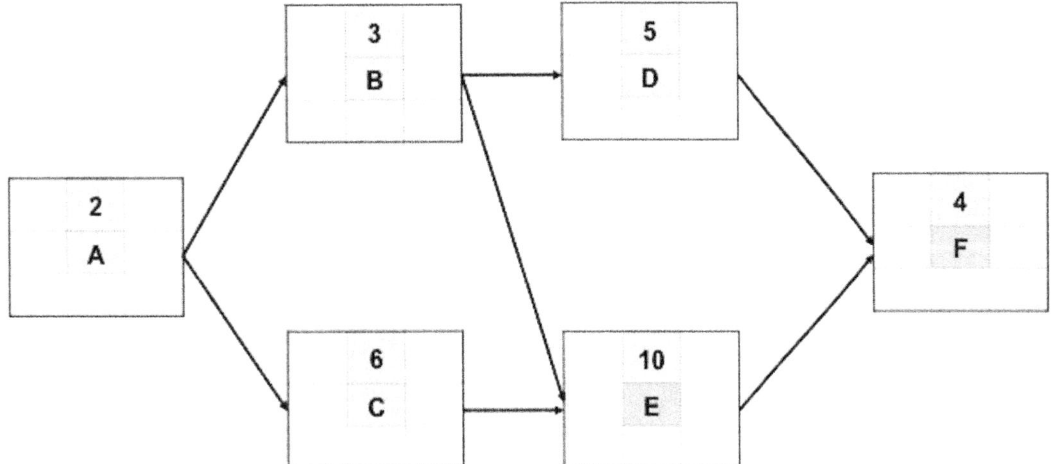

   A. 3
   B. 2
   C. 5
   D. 0

Full Length Practice Exam

Exam Answers

1. Answer: B
Explanation: The communications management plan offers the who, what, where, why, and when of communications and reporting. This plan should contain the detailed information of when the report in question is scheduled for distribution.

2. Answer: C
Explanation: Watch lists contain the opposite type of risks than described in the scenario. The risks on the watch list are low-priority risks that are determined to contain a minimal amount of threat, but that should be monitored regularly for a change of status as the project moves forward. Keep in mind that the risk management team should spend time on the risks that have the highest probability and impact; therefore, placing high effort on low-priority risks is not efficient.

3. Answer: C
Explanation: Based on the performance indexes provided, the project is 10% ahead of schedule, but over budget. Leveling out resource usage is a strategy used to spread out costs over time. This helps in reducing sudden spikes in spending, although it may lead to lengthening the schedule.

4. Answer: C
Explanation: The addition of two stakeholders brought the total number of communication channels to 66. Remember that you must apply the formula for calculating communication channels, which is:
$$N (N-1) \div 2$$
The question, however, asks how many *more* communication channels you will need to manage, meaning that you must now subtract the new number of channels by the original number of channels to get the answer (66 – 45). The answer is 21.

5. Answer: A
Explanation: Prior to the duration change of activity B, activity B's network path had a duration of 32. The original critical path has a duration of 33. If activity B's duration is increased to 6, then its path becomes the critical path, with a duration of 34.

6. Answer: D
Explanation: The project manager should allow team members to resolve their own conflict. However, when the issue escalates and requires the involvement of the project manager, the best method is to collaborate (or problem solve) to resolve the issue. This is a recommended conflict resolution technique because it leads to a win-win situation.

7. Answer: B
Explanation: Observation and conversation is a technique from the Manage Project Team process, and describes a way for the project manager to monitor the team's progress, accomplishments, and interpersonal issues, and is therefore the correct answer. 360-degree feedback is a type of project performance appraisal, where feedback is received from all levels of interaction with a team member. This provides information about a team member, but not from the team member themselves. Issue log tracks issues so is not relevant here, and team-building activities seems like a good choice, except that the purpose is to grow relationships among the team, with a focus on establishing cohesiveness, not of assessing work attitudes.

8. Answer: D
Explanation: Parametric estimating uses mathematical models to calculate cost estimates through historical data, resulting in a fairly accurate estimate.

9. Answer: C
Explanation: The project charter is generated out of the Initiating Process Group, through the Develop Project Charter process. Since this process has already been carried out, it is not the correct choice. The only other process belonging to the Initiating Process Group is Identify Stakeholders, where the stakeholder register is created, along with the stakeholder management strategy. Identify Stakeholders is the correct answer.

10. Answer: A

Explanation: Getting this question correct involves knowing how to calculate the expected monetary value, as well as understanding decision tree analysis. The correct answer is $37,250. Based on the question, our focus is on the *make* scenario. To calculate the expected monetary value, take the impact of $15,000 and multiply it by the probability of 15%, then add the initial investment of $35,000.

11. Answer: A
Explanation: There are a total of four processes within the Project Human Resource Management Knowledge Area. Manage Stakeholder Engagement is part of the Project Stakeholder Management Knowledge Area. The correct answer is: Plan Human Resource Management, Acquire Project Team, Develop Project Team, Manage Project Team.

12. Answer: C
Explanation: The formula for calculating expected monetary value is probability x impact. Therefore, multiply $4,000 by 10% to get $400.

13. Answer: D
Explanation: As the sender of the message, the project manager is responsible for confirming that the message was understood correctly and that the information was clear and complete. In this scenario, the project manager made the assumption that the message was understood.

14. Answer: D
Explanation: What–if scenario analysis is typically performed using the Monte Carlo technique, which simulates hundreds of scenarios by using existing project data and considering uncertainty. This is used as part of modeling techniques performed through the Develop Schedule and Control Schedule processes, as well as the Perform Quantitative Risk Analysis process.

15. Answer: D
Explanation: The risk manager is utilizing the expert judgment technique. This involves subject matter experts that are internal or external to the project, who validate the data and techniques used to conduct the process.

16. Answer: D
Explanation: The answer to this question is resource availability. This is an output of the process (through resource calendars) along with project staff assignments and updates to the project management plan.

17. Answer: C
Explanation: The correct choice (and inaccurate statement) is a characteristic of what-if scenario analysis and not of EVM.

18. Answer: B
Explanation: All of the options listed are types of communication. When dealing with complex issues, it is best to use a written format that is formal. Formal written is also the best choice when working with other cultures, communicating through long distances, updating a plan, or dealing with legal matters.

19. Answer: C
Explanation: Forecasting methods is part of the analytical technique used in the Monitor and Control Project Work process, which produces work performance reports, and is carried out as part of Monitoring and Controlling activities.

20. Answer: D
Explanation: PERT stands for program evaluation and review technique, and uses a weighted average of the following three estimates: optimistic, pessimistic, and most likely. PERT analysis is used as part of the three-point estimates tool and technique, within the Estimate Activity Durations and Estimate Costs processes.

21. Answer: B
Explanation: Source selection criteria, which is a type of vendor evaluation criteria, is an output of the Plan Procurement Management process.

22. Answer: B
Explanation: The question describes the purpose of the Plan Procurement Management process. This process carries out all of the planning-related activities relating to procurements.

23. Answer: D

Explanation: This refers to a milestone list, which contains all of the project's milestones. It also notes whether or not a milestone is optional or mandatory. A milestone is a significant point or event in the project, and as the project progresses and the work is under way, the milestone list can be used as a benchmark to measure progress against.

24. Answer: D
Explanation: The key pieces of information within the question reveal that you have accurate historical information and quantifiable parameters. Both items that are needed to utilize the parametric estimating technique.

25. Answer: C
Explanation: All of the options are types of probability distributions. The most commonly used probability distributions are beta distributions and triangular distributions. Since beta is the only one of the two included as an option, it is the best choice.

26. Answer: A
Explanation: All of the options included are actual risk attitudes. The names of the risk attitudes are fairly descriptive, making them easy to understand at face value. Even if you don't know anything about risk attitudes, risk averse stands out as a good choice, which is correct.

27. Answer: A
Explanation: To answer this question, you would need to know the formula for calculating CPI, which is: EV ÷ AC. Simply plug in the numbers, then work out the problem to get the answer, which is .848. As a side note, this CPI indicates that the project is not performing well, in terms of the budget.

28. Answer: A
Explanation: Only the Arrow Diagramming Method (ADM) uses dummy activities, which are not real activities, but instead are meant to show that a relationship between two activities exists. All of the other statements are accurate.

29. Answer: D
Explanation: The question provides examples of information management systems, which is a tool and technique of the Manage Communications process. Information management systems are tools used to facilitate communication.

30. Answer: C
Explanation: The scope baseline contains the project scope statement, the WBS, and the WBS dictionary. Constraints and assumptions are documented within the project scope statement. The deliverables can be found within the project scope statement, and also within the WBS.

31. Answer: C
Explanation: Manage Communications, a process that belongs to the Project Communications Management Knowledge Area, is responsible for creating, collecting, distributing, storing, retrieving and ultimately disposing of project information in accordance with the communications management plan. It is part of the Executing Process Group.

32. Answer: C
Explanation: Co-location refers to team members working out of the same location physically. This is relevant to the question, and creating a war room is a method of co-location. Co-location is a tool and technique used in the Develop Project Team process.

33. Answer: A
Explanation: The question is asking for the most common source of conflict. The correct answer is scarce resources. The other common sources of conflict include scheduling priorities and personal work styles.

34. Answer: D
Explanation: Inputs of the Develop Project Team process include project staff assignments, human resource management plan, and resource calendars. In this instance, all four options can be considered technically accurate as being part of the process' inputs. Both resource calendars and project staff assignments are direct inputs, while the other two are indirect inputs. Indirect meaning that they are used through the inclusion of the human resource management plan. However, of the two, recognition and rewards is the best answer.

35. Answer: D
Explanation: In order to answer this question, you will need to calculate the cumulative SPI and CPI. All values needed to do this have been provided within the question. The formula for calculating SPI, which will tell us how the project is performing according to the schedule, is EV ÷ PV. Plug in the values provided to result in the following: ($59,000 / $70,200) = 0.84. Anything under 1.0 means that the project is behind schedule. Now, calculate CPI by using the following formula: EV ÷ AC. Plug in the values provided to result in the following: ($59,000 / $64,500) = 0.91. A CPI under 1.0 means that the project is over budget. Therefore, the project is behind schedule and over budget.

36. Answer: D
Explanation: The top three sources of conflict include scarce resources, scheduling priorities, and personal work styles.

37. Answer: D
Explanation: To calculate the expected monetary value, simply multiply the impact by the probability. In this case, multiply $1,500 by 65% to get $975.

38. Answer: B
Explanation: RACI stands for: responsible, accountable, consult, and inform. The chart identifies Alfred as being responsible for the Research activity, making him the correct answer. Responsible indicates who will be performing the work.

39. Answer: B
Explanation: The project manager is responsible for providing project team members with the appropriate level of training needed to perform the work.

40. Answer: C
Explanation: Work performance reports are generated as an output of the Monitor and Control Project Work process, which occurs during the Monitoring and Controlling Process Group. Forecasts are also generated out of the Control Schedule and Control Costs process, with the results of those efforts fed into the Monitor and Control Project Work process, where the end reports that will be distributed to the team are put together.

41. Answer: D
Explanation: According to the *PMBOK® Guide*, the 100% rule refers to the work breakdown structure including all of the work of the project. The WBS therefore represents all of the product and project work, which can best be described as the scope of the project.

42. Answer: C
Explanation: The question is referring to pre-assignments, which can be negotiated within the contract, included in the project charter, or it can be a result of a project that revolves around a staff member's expertise. Pre-assignments is used as a tool and technique of the Acquire Project Team process.

43. Answer: A
Explanation: Analogous estimating involves the use of historical information from past similar projects as the basis for determining the activity duration estimates. This is what the project manager has done within the question by using the estimates from the past edition's project.

44. Answer: C
Explanation: Sensitivity analysis is a tool and technique that determines which risks have the most potential impact on the project, and utilizes tornado diagrams. This type of diagram compares the importance of variables that have a high degree of uncertainty, to the more stable variables. Sensitivity analysis is used as part of the Perform Quantitative Risk Analysis process.

45. Answer: B
Explanation: The best choice is to note the issue within the issue log. The reason for this is that an owner can then be assigned to the issue, and a target resolution date set. This allows for more structured and documented resolution. The issues log is also something that will be archived later on within the project files.

46. Answer: B
Explanation: Negotiation and staff assignments don't pertain to where a team member is located. That leaves virtual team and co-location. Virtual team includes project team members who are located at different locations, often never even meeting face to face. This can include working from home offices, from a remote location in

general, and different company sites. Co-location is when project team members are brought to work together at the same physical location. Based on these descriptions, virtual team is the correct choice.

47. Answer: B
Explanation: Perquisites is another type of benefits offered, and is often called "perks", making it the correct answer.

48. Answer: B
Explanation: In team meetings, this is something that happens regularly, and is something that can be avoided. The option that should immediately stick out is setting ground rules. Although it seems common sense not to cut someone off, directly outlining what acceptable behavior is could have taken care of this issue from the start. Even though John felt that Nick's issue was not an immediate priority, all issues should be allowed to be brought to the table, or through the outlined procedures.

49. Answer: B
Explanation: The critical path contains the longest path within a network diagram. To calculate which path is the longest within the diagram presented by the question, first count the total number of paths and add the duration of all activities that fall on each path. There are a total of four paths. The longest path, which is A-C-F-G-H, has a duration of 33.

50. Answer: C
Explanation: The sender, who initiated the communication, is the project team member; the receiver of the information is the project manager.

51. Answer: D
Explanation: Attending an expo does not translate to spying on the competition, and is an example of networking. On a smaller scale, examples of networking include informal conversations, committee gatherings, luncheons, and so on. In this scenario, Bob is being proactive through his actions.

52. Answer: A
Explanation: Rolling wave planning is where work in the near term is planned out in detail, while work in the future is planned out at higher levels of the WBS. While this is a form of progressive elaboration, rolling wave planning is a more specific choice. Progressive elaboration and rolling wave planning are different from scope creep in that they are planned and controlled.

53. Answer: A
Explanation: To solve a decision tree, calculate the expected monetary value of each scenario. Expected monetary value can be calculated by multiplying the impact by the probability. Scenario A has a potential implication of -$1,250, and scenario B has a potential implication of -$2,275. Therefore, scenario A is the best choice.

54. Answer: C
Explanation: Philip Crosby believed that quality is achieved when zero defects are present, and if a defect is present and considered acceptable, then the requirements should be altered to reflect this fact.

55. Answer: A
Explanation: This question involves applying the communication channels formula, which is:

$$N (N-1) \div 2$$

Plugging 24 in place of the N results in 276.

56. Answer: D
Explanation: Notice that Sally took in the facts and made a choice on the spot, without listening to the two-team members or attempting to discuss the choices. This type of conflict resolution technique is known as forcing, where one person makes a decision without taking into account others' feedback. Forcing is also known as Directing.

57. Answer: B
Explanation: In a start-to-start relationship, the successor activity (activity B) must wait for its predecessor (activity A) to start before it can start. Since both activities are beginning as soon as possible, we can assume that activity B will begin immediately after activity A starts. However, there is a lag of 2 days, meaning that activity B must wait two days to start after activity A has started. That means that from the moment that A starts, activity B will not be completed until 9 days have passed (just add the duration of the activity, plus the two day

lag). Since the activities overlap in this scenario, then the duration that has passed for both of these two activities to finish will have been ten days total.

58. Answer: B
Explanation: Joseph Juran is connected to the concept that the results produced should be fit for use by the customer.

59. Answer: C
Explanation: Gold plating is when additional functionality is added that is outside of the project scope. Sometimes, this is done with good intention, but is not considered acceptable actions, no matter what the intent is. If the addition was not a part of the project requirements, quality is not considered as having been met.

60. Answer: B
Explanation: To answer this correctly, you'd need to recall Maslow's pyramid and the five steps within the pyramid. The question asks for the highest level, which according to the pyramid, is self-actualization.

61. Answer: C
Explanation: Halo effect is when a person's strong trait(s) is perceived as an indication of another trait. In this example, it is though that because Jon is good at his job, he must therefore be a good project manager. But the job of a research technician has different required skills than the job of a project manager. The most common example given is that an attractive person, such as a celebrity, must be intelligent, which is why they are often used in advertising.

62. Answer: C
Explanation: A milestone has a duration of zero; it is a significant *point or event* in the project, such as the completion of a deliverable.

63. Answer: B
Explanation: The theorist responsible for the 14 Steps to Quality Management is W. Edwards Deming.

64. Answer: B
Explanation: Processes that fall within the Monitoring and Controlling Process Group are often designed to compare actual versus planned data as a way of identifying existing or potential variance. From there, the project management team can determine whether any corrective action is needed in order to keep the project in line with the overall project management plan.

65. Answer: C
Explanation: Cost-reimbursable, also known as cost plus, is where the buyer typically agrees to pay a fixed fee for the work that the seller is doing, as well as reimbursing all of the seller's costs. The buyer is the one with the highest risk, since they may have little control over the seller's spending. There are different types of cost plus contracts, such as cost plus fixed fee, cost plus incentive fee, and cost plus award fee.

66. Answer: B
Explanation: Potential responses that are available during risk identification are noted within the risk register early on in the risk management process. Potential responses can be determined during the Identify Risks process while risks are being identified. These potential responses are then utilized within the Plan Risk Responses process.

67. Answer: A
Explanation: Virtual teams are team members located outside of the physical office where the project is primarily taking place.

68. Answer: B
Explanation: While the risk management plan covers the details of risk-related reports and formats, it does not cover all of the communication requirements of project stakeholders. This is addressed within the communications management plan.

69. Answer: D
Explanation: A RACI is a type of responsibility assignment matrix (RAM), and it stands for responsible, accountable, consult, and inform.

70. Answer: C

Explanation: What the project sponsor is looking for is an updated project schedule that reflects where the project is currently at in terms of work accomplished. The schedule baseline contains the planned information, not actual work progress. Instead, the schedule baseline is typically compared to the current project schedule to determine what variances exist.

71. Answer: A
Explanation: While several actual benefits to virtual teams are included within the various options, this particular project requires a specialized skill set. Since virtual teams widen the resource pool available, with team members potentially located across the globe, it allows for this unique resource need to be met. Without the use of virtual teams, the project may not have been possible, or it may have been very costly due to relocating team members or frequent travel.

72. Answer: B
Explanation: Reports are considered formal written, since they are an official report of the project, and they are delivered in written format.

73. Answer: D
Explanation: The project is not officially considered to be complete until the customer or buyer signs off on it. This is a mistake many companies make, which leaves the door open for further requests, or conflict as to whether or not the project was really closed or not. This addresses it directly, and also obtains agreement from the customer that the deliverables and scope have indeed been met.

74. Answer: D
Explanation: The project charter is generated during the Initiating Process Group. Before we can move on to the planning stages of the project, there is one additional item generated within this Process Group, and that is the stakeholder register. This is created as a result of performing stakeholder analysis.

75. Answer: B
Explanation: The correct answer is contingency reserve, which are funds set aside for responding to risk that remain after carrying out the risk response plan. Management reserves are funds that have been set aside to cover unforeseen risks. Cost aggregation deals with aggregating cost estimates, so was a clear elimination, and cash flow refers to needed, or used funds.

76. Answer: B
Explanation: Specification limits and assignable cause are related to control charts, and are therefore not the correct answers; trend analysis relates to run chart, also not the answer. That leaves the 80 / 20 rule, also known as Pareto's Law or Pareto Principle, which states that 80% of problems result from 20% of causes. This is exactly what the project manager in this scenario is looking for.

77. Answer: A
Explanation: While it's true that gathering three-point estimates helps to generate estimates with higher accuracy, this is a technique that we use to generate duration estimates, not resource estimates. All other statements are accurate.

78. Answer: A
Explanation: The answer to this question is responsibility assignment matrix, which is a matrixed-based chart displayed in the format of a table.

79. Answer: B
Explanation: While all options may have contributed to the project issues, a poorly written scope can quickly result in project failure, no matter how good the change control procedures or systems are. A lack of formal project management may have contributed as well, but being certified does not guarantee that this type of scenario will not occur. The scope baseline is often used for change control purposes and in making project decisions. This is why a poorly written scope will result in a large number of project changes, and oftentimes, scope creep.

80. Answer: C
Explanation: The contents of the risk register continue to be updated after the project moves out of the planning phase. This is reflected within the updates made as a result of the Control Risks process, which is part of the Monitoring and Controlling Process Group. If the risk register were only updated during the planning phase of the project, it could not contain actual outcomes of risks and the outcomes of risk response plans.

81. Answer: B
Explanation: The project management plan contains the procurement management plan, which will serve as a guide to carrying out procurement-related activities.

82. Answer: B
Explanation: System or process flow charts show how the various elements of a system interrelate, which can reveal how a problem occurs. This is done by analyzing the steps of a system, and is very useful in identifying potential responses to risks.

83. Answer: A
Explanation: The staffing management plan describes when and how human resource requirements will be met. It addresses things like staff acquisition, timetable of when the team will be acquired, release criteria, training needs, recognition and rewards, compliance, and safety. It doesn't, however, define the roles and responsibilities, which is a separate output of the human resource management planning process.

84. Answer: B
Explanation: 360 degree feedback is a type of project performance appraisal, where feedback is received from all levels of interaction with a team member. This provides information about a team member, but not from a team member. Next, observation and conversation is a technique from the manage project team process. It's a way for the project manager to monitor the team's progress, accomplishments, and interpersonal issues and is therefore the correct answer. Issue log simply tracks issues so is not relevant here, and team-building activities seems like a good choice, except that the purpose is to grow relationships among the team so the focus is on establishing this cohesiveness and of working together, not of assessing work attitudes.

85. Answer: D
Explanation: Once a seller is selected, resource calendars will be generated for the resources procured. This displays the availability of those resources.

86. Answer: C
Explanation: It's often thought that the project manager or functional manager are the ones responsible for resolving this type of conflict. But in actuality, these individuals should be brought in only to provide assistance, or to address the conflict in a formal manner. The best option is that the project team members resolve the conflict on their own, directly.

87. Answer: C
Explanation: Negative variance, whether cost or schedule, is an indication of poor performance. In the case of cost, it indicates that the project is *over* budget, not under (where actual cost is greater than the value earned). All other statements are true.

88. Answer: B
Explanation: Updating a project plan, or any other type of formal plan or document, is considered to be a formal written type of communication.

89. Answer: B
Explanation: The risk manager has omitted the initial process of risk management, which involves creating the risk management plan. The risk management plan is an essential part of carrying out the other risk management processes, since it outlines how risks will be identified, analyzed, monitored, and so forth. Therefore, the project manager in this scenario has a low likelihood of developing a risk register that will be useful to carrying out risk management. For exam purposes, the risk management plan is a requirement.

90. Answer: A
Explanation: Roles and responsibilities is the correct answer. This is something addressed within the human resource management plan, and the one that doesn't pertain to communication or information distribution. The other three are included within the communications management plan.

91. Answer: B
Explanation: Cost-reimbursable contracts are a higher risk to the buyer. This is because the buyer reimburses the seller for the seller's actual cost, plus an additional amount, and depending on the type of cost-reimbursable contract will determine whether or not this additional fee is capped. For this reason, this contract is typically used when the buyer can describe the work, but not how to go about the work.

92. Answer: B

Explanation: This correct option provides the best and closest description of activity duration estimates as provided by the *PMBOK® Guide*. This, therefore, makes it the *best* option to choose from the four. Activity duration estimates do not include lags, and the estimates are not required to be specific – they may be specific, presented in a range, or as a percentage of probability.

93. Answer: B
Explanation: The human resource management plan consists of roles and responsibilities, project organizational charts, and the staffing management plan. The responsibility assignment matrix (RAM) is used to define the roles and responsibilities of the project team and falls under the "roles and responsibilities" component of the human resource management plan. RACI is a common type of RAM used.

94. Answer: C
Explanation: The transfer strategy involves the transfer of a risk to a third party. In this case, the third party takes on the responsibility of managing and taking responsibility for the risk. Insurance is one example of risk transference.

95. Answer: C
Explanation: Schedule variance is an indication of schedule performance, which is calculated by subtracting the planned value from earned value. The result provides a measurement of the schedule's performance, as opposed to the baseline schedule. All other options are definitions relating to other EVM terms.

96. Answer: B
Explanation: As the sender of the information, the project team member is responsible for confirming that the project manager understood the information, and that the information is complete and clear. On the other end, the project manager also failed to meet the responsibilities of a receiver, which are to make sure that they understood the information correctly and that it was received in its entirety. Remember to choose the BEST answer from a PMI perspective.

97. Answer: A
Explanation: Quantitative risk analysis can utilize cost estimating techniques to determine whether there are existing risks of cost or schedule overruns. Parametric estimating is a technique that provides a high level of accuracy and it uses a statistical relationship between historical data and other variables (such as labor hours used in this example).

98. Answer: C
Explanation: Parametric estimating involves using a combination of past historical data from similar projects, along with other variables from the current project.

99. Answer: B
Explanation: First, draw out the network diagram based on the activity relationships indicated within the chart. Next, add the total activity durations of each network path. There are a total of three paths. The critical path is the longest path through the network diagram, which is 20 days.

100. Answer: D
Explanation: Documentation reviews involve examining the project plans and documents to ensure that they are consistent with project requirements, that they include everything necessary within the plans, and also evaluate the assumptions made. This technique allows the project manager to determine whether the documents are thorough enough, and whether any risks exists as a result of planning.

101. Answer: C
Explanation: The correct answer is "how much over or under the project will be at completion". Variance compares actual progress of the project to planned progress, in order to identify whether there is any variance between the two.

102. Answer: C
Explanation: A run chart is a quality tool, and therefore not a format you would use to display an organizational chart.

103. Answer: B
Explanation: Personal work styles, scheduling priorities, and scarce resources are the top three reasons for conflict. The correct answer is therefore personality clashes.

104. Answer: C
Explanation: A team performance assessment has a goal of increasing the team's performance while project performance appraisals refers to feedback given directly to project team members. Team performance assessments are an output of the Develop Project Team process.

105. Answer: A
Explanation: The lowest level of the WBS is the work package level. The next step from there would be to decompose the work packages into the activity lists, which is done through the second time management-related process: Define Activities. The activity list, however, is not considered to be part of the WBS itself. Planning packages and control accounts are placed within the WBS, but are not the lowest levels.

106. Answer: D
Explanation: A face-to-face meeting is the preferred method for dealing with stakeholders. There is nothing within the question to indicate that a one-on-one meeting with stakeholders is required, which makes "an in-person meeting" the BEST and most efficient choice.

107. Answer: A
Explanation: Bonds, warranties, and guaranties are all examples of the transfer risk response strategy. The most common type of transfer is purchasing insurance. All of these methods involve transferring the risk to a third party. Prototype is used as a way of refining requirements early on within the life cycle of the project, and could therefore be viewed as a mitigation strategy.

108. Answer: A
Explanation: Negotiations and project staff assignments take place within the Acquire Project Team process, the second process within the Project Human Resource Management Knowledge Area.

109. Answer: D
Explanation: Team building activities build trust among the project team, allowing them to work in a more efficient and cohesive manner.

110. Answer: D
Explanation: In this question, you simply have to recognize the factors. Background may have stood out from the rest of the group, since it doesn't necessarily apply to a factor dealing with the organization's current structure or processes. The factors include organizational, technical, interpersonal, logistical, and political.

111. Answer: C
Explanation: Conflict management is not a form of feedback, is it is incorrect; 360 degree feedback is a formal type of feedback, as opposed to observation and conversation. 360 degree feedback is a type of appraisal, whereas team performance assessment focuses on the team's performance.

112. Answer: B
Explanation: All change requests are submitted into the Perform Integrated Change Control process. This process is part of Project Integration Management Knowledge Area, and is responsible for reviewing changes through a change control board, which then makes a decision. If a change request is approved, it is then executed through the Direct and Manage Project Work process (which is also responsible for executing the overall project management plan).

113. Answer: B
Explanation: The answer is cost of conformance to requirements. While quality works towards preventing rework and providing better customer satisfaction, these are results of conforming to the project requirements.

114. Answer: B
Explanation: The purpose of the Control Procurements process is to manage the contract with the seller and monitor contract performance and changes. Both the buyer and seller are tasked with ensuring that contract terms are followed.

115. Answer: C
Explanation: Since the question provides only the activity durations and sequencing, you must first calculate the impact to the critical path. Activity D currently falls on the critical path, and lies on two network paths. When the duration of activity D changes to 6 days, it results in 2 critical paths – both with a duration of 25 days. Multiple

critical paths increase the amount of risk within the project, since there are a large number of activities with zero flexibility.

116. Answer: D
Explanation: Mitigation reduces the probability and / or the impact of a risk. Other options describe the transfer, avoid, and enhance strategies.

117. Answer: D
Explanation: A CPI of less than 1 is bad, meaning that the project is over budget; a CPI of 1 or greater is good, meaning that the project is on or ahead of schedule.

118. Answer: A
Explanation: Resource leveling involves leveling out resource usage to resolve over-allocation of resources, and / or to level out the peaks and valleys of resource usage over time.

119. Answer: C
Explanation: The communications management plan is generated out of the Plan Communications Management process. The primary tool and technique used that analyzes the communications requirements and preferences of stakeholders is the communications requirements analysis technique.

120. Answer: A
Explanation: Risk data quality assessment measures the confidence and accuracy of the data used for risk management purposes. Overall, this technique evaluates the accuracy, reliability, integrity, and quality of the data and information.

121. Answer: D
Explanation: Templates are stored within the organizational process assets. When using templates from previous similar projects, the project manager can create a consistency of results, such as by using portions of activity lists or network diagrams, thereby making more efficient use of their time. It also allows for improved results.

122. Answer: A
Explanation: The correct choice is fringe benefits, which are those benefits provided to all employees.

123. Answer: B
Explanation: The correct answer is continuous improvement. The word Kaizen means to alter and make better in Japanese.

124. Answer: A
Explanation: Exploit is a strategy used when the organization is interested in making sure that the risk occurs, as well as increasing the impact of the positive risks. Exploit is the exact opposite of avoid, which seeks to eliminate the possibility of the risk from *not* occurring.

125. Answer: C
Explanation: Procurement audits are structured reviews that audit the procurement management processes, and are used as part of the Close Procurements process. The idea is to pinpoint what the efficiencies and inefficiencies were within the procurement management processes, which will be documented as part of the lessons learned. This information is important for future procurements, whether for the current project or future projects.

126. Answer: D
Explanation: It's clear that the project manager did not check the resource calendars when creating the schedule. Resource calendars contain working and nonworking days of resources. This includes holidays, vacations, as well as when resources are idle.

127. Answer: A
Explanation: When the duration estimates contain a wide range between the optimistic and pessimistic estimates, it is an indicator of uncertainty. Uncertainty typically leads to risk.

128. Answer: C
Explanation: There are 5 types of power that a project manager can utilize. These include: formal, reward, penalty, expert, and referent. The question asks for the one that is based on the authority of someone else. This would be referent power. As a quick review on the other types of power, formal is power that stems from one's

position, reward where you reward someone for doing something; and expert is power that comes from knowledge and expertise.

129. Answer: B
Explanation: The scope baseline consists of three things: the project scope statement, the WBS, and the WBS dictionary. Technically, deliverables are also a large part of the scope baseline, since they are documented within the project scope statement and are decomposed as part of the WBS. However, always choose the BEST answer.

130. Answer: B
Explanation: Risk urgency assessment determines the level of urgency in addressing risk. This should be performed for all prioritized risks so that effort is spent on those risks that have a higher impact and probability of occurring. The result is the identification of near-term risks, which are those risks that require a near-term response.

131. Answer: A
Explanation: The transfer risk response strategy uses warranties, bonds, and purchasing of insurance to transfer the risk to a third party, usually requiring some form of payment to the third party.

132. Answer: B
Explanation: Passive acceptance is when nothing is done about the risk; active acceptance, on the other hand, is where a contingency reserve of time, funds, or resources are set aside to deal with the risk if it materializes. Mitigate and avoid are two types of negative risk responses that involve some sort of action taken.

133. Answer: C
Explanation: This is the definition of risk as defined by the *PMBOK® Guide*. A workaround is put into action for an unidentified negative risk that has occurred; an issue can be described as a negative risk or event that is occurring in the present; while a trigger, or risk trigger, is an event that signifies a risk is about to materialize.

134. Answer: C
Explanation: Procurement documents are used to solicit responses from potential sellers, such as an RFP. This will be needed to ensure that proposals submitted by potential sellers are complete. It should also contain the selection process published to potential sellers, and will also eventually include the agreement and work performance information and results of the seller.

135. Answer: A
Explanation: With the Just in Time strategy, inventory costs are brought in just as they are needed. But in order to implement this type of strategy, a company must be highly efficient and have a high focus on quality, else the strategy won't work, and the goods will either arrive too early or too late.

136. Answer: A
Explanation: Noise is defined as anything that may interfere with getting or receiving the message (such as static). Only noise and medium were official terms provided within the four options, according to the basic model of communication.

137. Answer: A
Explanation: Workarounds differ from contingency and fallback plans because they are unplanned responses to a negative risk that has occurred.

138. Answer: A
Explanation: The question is asking that you calculate the to-complete performance index (TCPI) based on the budget at completion (BAC). The formula for calculating this is (BAC – EV) ÷ (BAC – AC). Plug in the values to result in the following: ($95,000 - $59,000) ÷ ($95,000 - $65,500). Work out the calculations to result in a TCPI of 1.22, meaning that the project must achieve a greater value for every dollar spent in order to finish at the original BAC.

139. Answer: C
Explanation: Based on the performance indexes provided, the project is 10% ahead of schedule, but over budget. Leveling out resource usage is a strategy used to spread out costs over time. This helps in reducing sudden spikes in spending, although it may lead to lengthening the schedule.

140. Answer: B

Explanation: Pre-assignments occur when individuals have been promised as part of a contract to a customer, or they have been assigned as early as the project charter. In either case, the resource has *officially* been committed to the project.

141. Answer: A
Explanation: Negotiation is a common technique used by project managers to acquire resources for a project. Ideally, the project manager would have first approached the director of engineering for approval, but at this stage, the best option was to attempt to negotiate with the resource's manager. The project sponsor should not get involved in cases like this unless it is detrimental to the project.

142. Answer: A
Explanation: Enhance is the exact opposite of mitigate. Enhance is used in handling positive risks when the organization wishes to increase the probability and/or impact of the risk; to mitigate a risk means to *decrease* the probability and/or impact of the risk from occurring.

143. Answer: B
Explanation: Now that the project manager has generated the list of activities, it's time to place them in proper sequence. Inspecting the project scope statement for any constraints or product characteristics that may impact sequencing is one of the first steps in getting this done.

144. Answer: B
Explanation: Only "formal written" and "informal written" are communication types. Emails are an informal way of communicating and are also written, which makes "informal written" the best choice.

145. Answer: C
Explanation: Under organizational process assets, the project management team utilizes the policies, procedures, guidelines, and management systems that pertain to procurement. It's important to understand how the company currently conducts procurement activities, which will aid the project team in compiling a good procurement management plan.

146. Answer: C
Explanation: Bottom-up estimating may be an estimating technique that provides a more accurate result, but it is not quick and low-cost. This estimating technique involves further decomposing an activity until it can be confidently estimated. These smaller components are then rolled up to the original activity level to determine an overall estimate of resources. This can be time-consuming, and therefore costly.

147. Answer: A
Explanation: There are five possible paths within the sample network diagram: Start-A-F-J, Start-A-H-I, Start-C-G-I, Start-B-D-G-I, and Start-B-E-K.

148. Answer: A
Explanation: The Expectancy theory states that employees who believe that more effort will lead to better performance, which will then lead to rewards that they personally value, will continue to be productive. This is a conscious choice, else if they don't value the rewards, their incentive to be productive is lost.

149. Answer: C
Explanation: The correct answer is forcing, which is a type of conflict resolution technique, not a leadership style. There are 7 primary leadership styles: directing, facilitating, coaching, supporting, autocratic, consultative, and consensus.

150. Answer: A
Explanation: To solve a decision tree, calculate the expected monetary value of each scenario. Expected monetary value can be calculated by multiplying the impact by the probability. Scenario A has a potential implication of -$1,250, and scenario B has a potential implication of -$2,275. Therefore, scenario A is the best choice.

151. Answer: A
Explanation: Money already spent refers to sunk costs. Opportunity cost refers to money lost when selecting one project over another, equaling the value of the project that was passed up; direct dosts are costs that are directly attributed to the work on the project; and fixed costs are costs that remain the same throughout the project, such as rentals.

152. Answer: A
Explanation: In order to get this question correct, you need to remember the different levels of accuracy for Sigma. 1 Sigma is 68.27%.

153. Answer: B
Explanation: There are two types of power that are considered to be the preferred type that a manager use. This includes reward and expert, which would make "reward" the correct choice. As a side note, penalty is considered to be the least preferred.

154. Answer: C
Explanation: A contingent response strategy is created for certain risks where a response plan can be developed in advance, and dependent on a trigger occurring. This contingency plan is executed when predefined risk triggers (symptoms or warning signs) occur.

155. Answer: A
Explanation: First, you need to know EAC. The EAC formula for this question is: (BAC ÷ CPI). Plugging in the numbers, the equation is as follows: (200 ÷ 1.3). The EAC is therefore 153.85. Next, to calculate VAC, subtract BAC and EAC (200 – 153.85), which is 46.15. When rounded to the nearest whole number, the answer is 46.

156. Answer: D
Explanation: Based on the SPI, the schedule must be compressed, and the CPI indicates that funds exist to add additional resources to critical activities where possible. This is referred to as "crashing" the schedule. While fast-tracking is another schedule compression technique, the question indicates that this technique was already attempted.

157. Answer: B
Explanation: Team members are assigned during the executing phase of a project, unless a pre-assignment has taken place. This occurs as an official output of the Acquire Project Team process, which is a process of the project human resource management knowledge area. All other statements are true.

158. Answer: D
Explanation: These are interpersonal skills, also referred to as "soft" skills. Interpersonal skills itself is part of general management skills. It is thought that the project manager can decrease issues and increase cooperation by understanding how project team members are feeling, knowing what their concerns are, and being able to follow up on existing issues.

159. Answer: C
Explanation: The purpose of the Control Procurements process is to manage the contract with the seller and monitor contract performance and changes. Both the buyer and seller are tasked with ensuring that contract terms are followed.

160. Answer: A
Explanation: Rolling wave planning is a form of progressive elaboration. It's where the work done in the near term is planned out in great detail, while future work is planned at higher levels of the WBS, typically decomposed to the milestone level. Although rolling wave planning is a form of progressive elaboration, rolling wave planning is a more specific choice, which makes it the best answer.

161. Answer: D
Explanation: Fallback plans are planned responses that are executed when the initial planned response proves ineffective.

162. Answer: D
Explanation: Bottom-up estimating is a tool and technique of the Estimate Activity Resources and Estimate Costs processes. It involves further decomposing an activity until it can be more accurately estimated. Then these smaller components are aggregated to the original activity level to determine the activity's estimates. While this estimate is high on the accuracy scale, it is also time consuming and costly.

163. Answer: C
Explanation: There are four primary items that the process improvement plan contains, and that is process boundaries, process configuration, process metrics, and targets for improved performance. Therefore, "failure rate" is the option that should be selected as the answer.

164. Answer: C
Explanation: Prevention and Inspection are both looking to eliminate issues, defects, or problems, which rules out one of the statements that mention focusing on the cause. It makes sense to think of prevention as preventing something, which points to "identifying causes of errors" as the correct answer.

165. Answer: A
Explanation: Both Close Project or Phase and Close Procurements should be performed. The contract is complete, which requires the Close Procurements process. Close Project or Phase is performed as the project phases are completed.

166. Answer: C
Explanation: Transfer involves the transfer of a risk to a third party. In this case, the third party takes on the responsibility of managing and taking responsibility for the risk. Insurance is one example of risk transference.

167. Answer: D
Explanation: At this point, pre-assignments is a technique already used, and the issue is that a key resource was not pre-assigned and is now unavailable. The best option would be to negotiate with the project managers of the other two projects, along with the resource's functional manager, to open up availability for participation in the project in question. Acquisition may be a potential option, but not until negotiation has been attempted.

168. Answer: C
Explanation: The correct answer is poor quality. Remember that quality also looks to remove waste and non-value added processes. It looks to improve processes and make sure that project requirements are being met.

169. Answer: C
Explanation: The lowest level of the WBS is the work package. In order to create the list of activities, the project manager will further decompose the work packages into activities with the help of experts who are familiar with the work to be performed. At this stage, the deliverables have already been decomposed down to the work package level to create the WBS, so this step is not necessary, and we are not provided with sufficient information to determine whether the project manager will use rolling wave planning.

170. Answer: A
Explanation: Bottom-up estimating involves decomposing an activity into smaller components for estimating purposes, and the estimates are then aggregated up to the original activity level. This is typically used when the type and quantity of resources needed cannot be confidently estimated. While results in a fairly high accuracy level, it is time consuming and therefore costly to perform.

171. Answer: B
Explanation: The identification of new risks can also occur while monitoring risks, particularly those risks that emerge as a result of risk response plans, or that are detected as the project work is executed and underway.

172. Answer: D
Explanation: Contingency reserve is included in the cost baseline, and is used to account for known unknown events. While management reserves are set aside for those events that are unforeseen, making them unknown-unknown events.

173. Answer: D
Explanation: Organizational process assets contain historical information from past archived projects, lessons learned, templates, policies, procedures, and other valuable information. In this case, the project manager is using a previous schedule management plan as a template, and tailoring it for use by the current project. This is recommended practice and prevents having to re-invent the wheel for every project. Instead, the effort is placed on increasing the efficiency and refining existing practices and templates.

174. Answer: B
Explanation: Here we have a formula question, inquiring about the schedule. This would be a clue as to what we are calculating, which is either the schedule variance or the schedule performance index. No matter which formula you chose, you would have come to the same conclusion: that the project is slightly behind schedule.

175. Answer: D
Explanation: The staffing management plan is a component of the human resource management plan. It outlines the training needs, safety needs, and compliance of the project. As an extra note, it also contains details of how the project team will be acquired, managed, and released.

176. Answer: D
Explanation: The cost management plan can be ruled out, since this is not a type of assessment; neither is variance management. The correct choice is activity cost estimates.

177. Answer: C
Explanation: Benchmarking takes the current project and compares it to other projects, using the previous projects as the point of comparison.

178. Answer: A
Explanation: In the Executing Process Group, the work outlined in the project management plan is executed and carried out. This is where the actual work gets done, just as the name itself implies, and where the team works to satisfy the project specifications.

179. Answer: B
Explanation: Preventing risks from occurring is an inaccurate statement since risks can also represent an opportunity that the project team may decide to enhance or exploit.

180. Answer: B
Explanation: The procurement statement of work defines the portion of the scope that is being purchased or acquired, and describes the product, service, or result that is to be supplied by the seller. All other options are addressed within the procurement management plan.

181. Answer: D
Explanation: At this point, the project manager does not know whether there are enough funds remaining within the contingency reserve. To obtain this information, reserve analysis would need to be performed. This technique compares the remaining risks to the remaining amount of contingency reserve, to determine whether the contingency reserve is sufficient to cover the existing risks.

182. Answer: D
Explanation: Brainstorming is a part of alternatives generation, which is a tool and technique of the Define Scope process. Lateral thinking is also a type of alternatives generation.

183. Answer: A
Explanation: While it's true that gathering three-point estimates helps to generate estimates with higher accuracy, this is a technique that we use to generate duration estimates, not resource estimates. All other estimates are accurate.

184. Answer: C
Explanation: The question refers to cost aggregation, which is a technique of the Determine Budget process. Cost estimates are aggregated to the work package level, control account, and also the overall project.

185. Answer: C
Explanation: The question is asking for the project team to get to all the possible causes. There are a few potential answers, but based on the question and options provided, cause and effect diagram is the best choice. This is the diagram that resembles a fishbone, and shows how various factors can be connected to potential problems.

186. Answer: B
Explanation: The correct response is to allow the audit to take place. Audits are not always planned, and the purpose is to increase efficiency and reduce the cost of quality. Discovering existing inefficiencies will highly benefit the team. Audits are a win-win, even if sometimes it feels like an inconvenience, the big picture must remain at the forefront.

187. Answer: B
Explanation: The project manager has told the scheduler that the schedule must be compressed by one week. That means that we will use one of two schedule compression techniques: crashing or fast tracking, both of which are options. When possible, select the lowest cost option first, which would be fast-tracking.

188. Answer: C
Explanation: The question asks that you calculate the estimate to complete (ETC), which determines how much more the project is expected to cost, from the current data date to project completion. If the project is expected to

continue performing at the current rate, the formula for ETC is as follows: ETC = EAC – AC. Before we can plug in the numbers, we would need to calculate EAC (EAC = BAC ÷ CPI) and CPI (CPI = EV ÷ AC):

CPI = 59,000 ÷ 65,500 CPI = 0.901
EAC (at steady rate) = 95,000 ÷ 0.901 EAC = 105,438.40
ETC = 105,438.40 – 65,500 ETC = 39,938.40

189. Answer: D
Explanation: Quality metrics determine what to measure and what the acceptable measurements are. They are first created out of the Plan Quality Management process.

190. Answer: C
Explanation: Cost of quality is any related costs that result out of carrying out quality activities. This is considered to be an investment of time, money, and resources, which technically all boils down to an investment in money. The correct choice is rework.

191. Answer: B
Explanation: Independent peer review is the correct answer. This type of review ensures that the concepts, the designs and tests that are utilized at the beginning of the project, were good choices.

192. Answer: A
Explanation: Workarounds differ from contingency and fallback plans because they are unplanned responses to a negative risk that has occurred.

193. Answer: C
Explanation: Notice that the constraint impacts the sequence of events of the project, since the project manager must work around the deadline of providing the necessary parts before the vendor can begin, based on a contractual requirement. Dependencies that result out of a physical or contractual requirement are known as mandatory dependencies, or hard logic.

194. Answer: A
Explanation: Rolling wave planning is a form of progressive elaboration, and plans out the near term work in detail and future work at higher levels of the WBS.

195. Answer: C
Explanation: The correct answer is that inspection keeps errors from reaching the customer, while prevention prevents errors from occurring.

196. Answer: A
Explanation: There are only two processes within the Initiating Process Group: Develop Project Charter and Identify Stakeholders.

197. Answer: C
Explanation: The project manager is using the Monte-Carlo technique, a common simulation program that is part of the what-if scenario analysis tool and technique. This technique is part of the Develop Schedule process and can generate the potential outcomes of the project – including the probability of completing the project on any given day.

198. Answer: B
Explanation: The risk register is created through the second risk related process, Identify Risks, and is updated as a result of carrying out the remaining risk management processes. Only the Control Risks process, the final process of the Project Risk Management Knowledge Area, generates updates on outcomes of risk activities and risks overall, making it the correct choice.

199. Answer: D
Explanation: During the initiating phase of the project, very few resources and funds have been utilized for the project. For this reason, the level of impact of risk is at its lowest. As funds are expended and resources are utilized, the level of impact that a risk may have continues to increase on an upward hill.

200. Answer: A

Explanation: To calculate total float, subtract either LS and ES, or LF and EF. To do this, you would first need to perform a forward pass and a backward pass to determine what the ES, EF, LS, and LF values are. Activity B should result in an early start of 2, a late start of 5, an early finish of 5, and a late finish of 8. Plug in the values into either of the two formulas mentioned previously to result in a total float of 3.

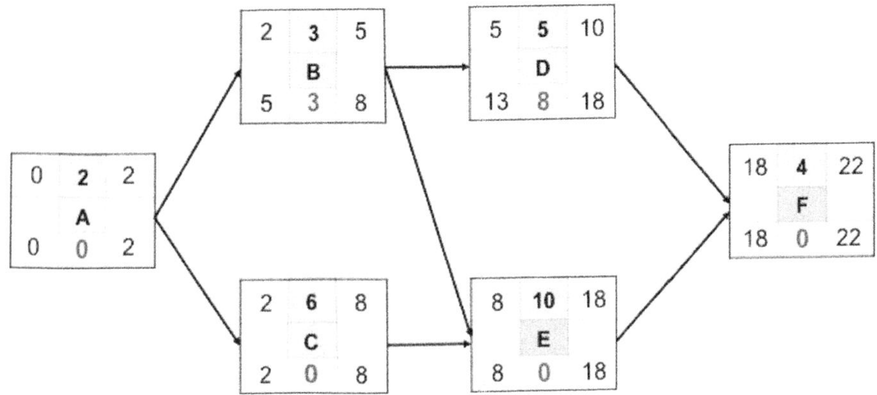

Supplemental Material

Formula Summary

Communication Channels:

$$\frac{N(N-1)}{2}$$

Program Evaluation and Review Technique (PERT)

$$\frac{O + P + 4(ML)}{6}$$

Standard Deviation:

$$\frac{P - O}{6}$$

Variance:

$$\left(\frac{P - O}{6}\right)^2$$

Expected Monetary Value (EMV)

Probability x Impact

Earned Value Management – Status Formula Summary

EVM Value	Formula	Note
Schedule Performance Index (SPI)	EV / PV	>1 = good, ahead of schedule 1 = on schedule <1 = bad, behind schedule
Schedule Variance (SV)	EV – PV	Positive variance = good Negative variance = bad
Cost Performance Index (CPI)	EV / AC	>1 = good, under budget 1 = on budget <1 = bad, over budget
Cost Variance (CV)	EV – AC	Positive variance = good Negative variance = bad

Earned Value Management – Forecast Formula Summary

Estimate at Completion (EAC)		EAC determines what the project is expected to cost overall, based on current performance.
	$\frac{BAC}{CPI}$	Use this formula when expecting the work to continue at a steady rate. This is your default formula.
	AC + BAC – EV	Use this formula when an unexpected event occurs. It looks at work performed at the budgeted rate.
	$AC + \frac{BAC - EV}{CPI \times SPI}$	Use this formula if taking into account both the CPI and the SPI.
Estimate to Complete (ETC)	EAC – AC	ETC looks at how much *more* the project is expected to cost. Use this formula if work is proceeding to plan.
	Reestimate	Reestimate the remaining work from the bottom up if work is not proceeding to plan.
To Complete Performance Index (TCPI)		TCPI determines the performance that must be achieved on the remaining work in order to finish within budget (example: if you are over budget, how much better must you perform from this point forward to end within budget?)
	$\frac{BAC - EV}{BAC - AC}$	This formula is based on BAC, and is your (default) formula.
	$\frac{BAC - EV}{EAC - AC}$	This formula is based on EAC or a new goal, use this formula.
Variance at Completion (VAC)	BAC – EAC	VAC determines how much over or under budget the project is expected to finish at.

Risk Register Update Cycle

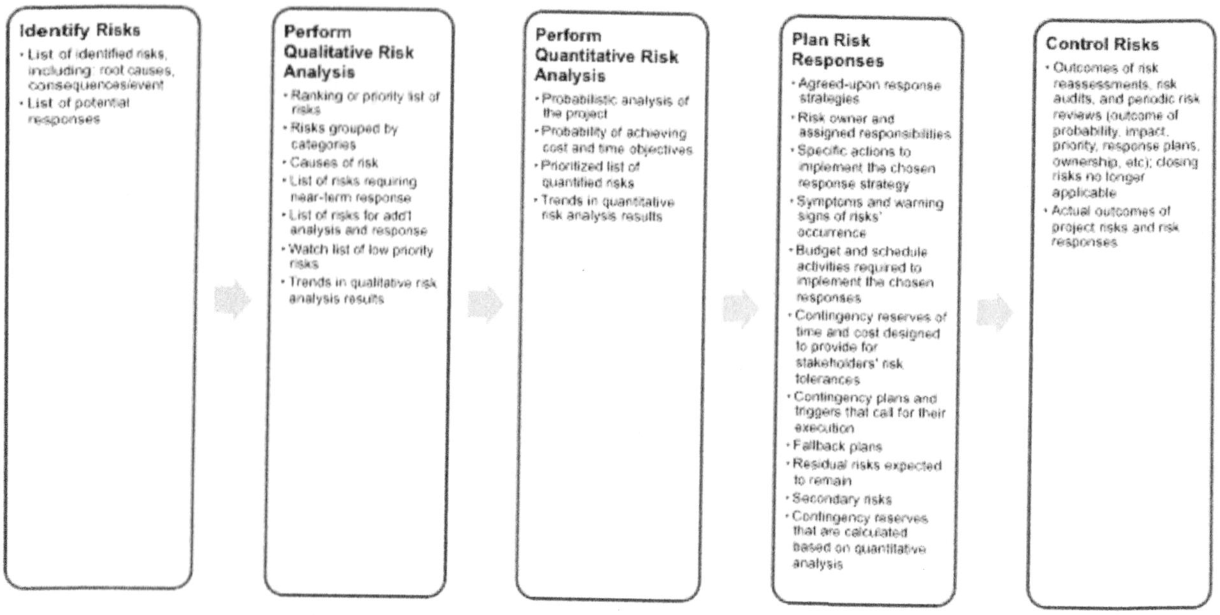

Identify Risks

- List of identified risks, including: root causes, consequences/event
- List of potential responses

Perform Qualitative Risk Analysis

- Ranking or priority list of risks
- Risks grouped by categories
- Causes of risk
- List of risks requiring near-term response
- List of risks for add'l analysis and response
- Watch list of low priority risks
- Trends in qualitative risk analysis results

Perform Quantitative Risk Analysis

- Probabilistic analysis of the project
- Probability of achieving cost and time objectives
- Prioritized list of quantified risks
- Trends in quantitative risk analysis results

Plan Risk Responses

- Agreed-upon response strategies
- Risk owner and assigned responsibilities
- Specific actions to implement the chosen response strategy
- Symptoms and warning signs of risks' occurrence
- Budget and schedule activities required to implement the chosen responses
- Contingency reserves of time and cost designed to provide for stakeholders' risk tolerances
- Contingency plans and triggers that call for their execution
- Fallback plans
- Residual risks expected to remain
- Secondary risks
- Contingency reserves that are calculated based on quantitative analysis

Control Risks

- Outcomes of risk reassessments, risk audits, and periodic risk reviews (outcome of probability, impact, priority, response plans, ownership, etc); closing risks no longer applicable
- Actual outcomes of project risks and risk responses

Calculating Forward Pass and Backward Pass

Steps to Calculating Forward Pass

1. Begin with the first activity within a network diagram and work forward within the diagram, meaning from left to right.
2. Add a zero as the early start of the first activity. This means that we are not working with calendar days, but instead with durations
3. Add the duration of the first activity to the ES of zero to calculate the EF.
4. To calculate the ES of the successor activity, simply carry over the EF (the ES of an activity is the EF of its predecessor).
5. Continue calculating the ES and EF of each activity within the network diagram. In the instance where an activity has more than one predecessor, carry over the highest EF number.

Steps to Calculating Backward Pass

1. Begin with the last activity within a network diagram and work backward within the diagram, meaning from right to left.
2. The LF of the final activity will be the activity's EF (this activity will automatically fall on the critical path, and therefore represents the duration of the project).
3. Subtract the duration of the last activity from its LF to calculate the LS.
4. To calculate the LF of the predecessor activity, simply carry over the LS (the LF of an activity is the LS of its successor).
5. Continue calculating the LS and LF of each activity within the network diagram. In the instance where an activity has more than one successor, carry over the lowest LS number.

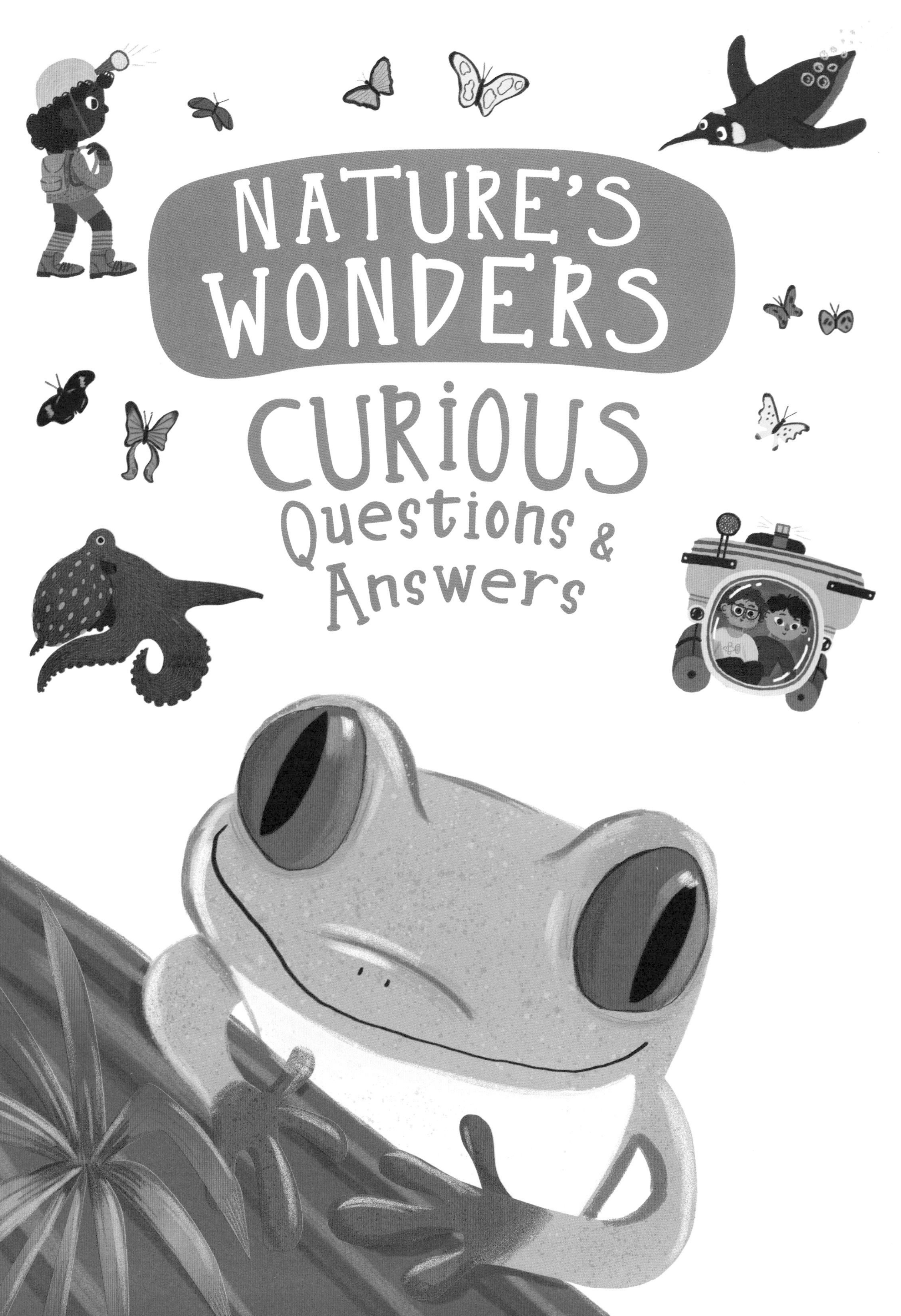
NATURE'S WONDERS
CURIOUS
Questions &
Answers

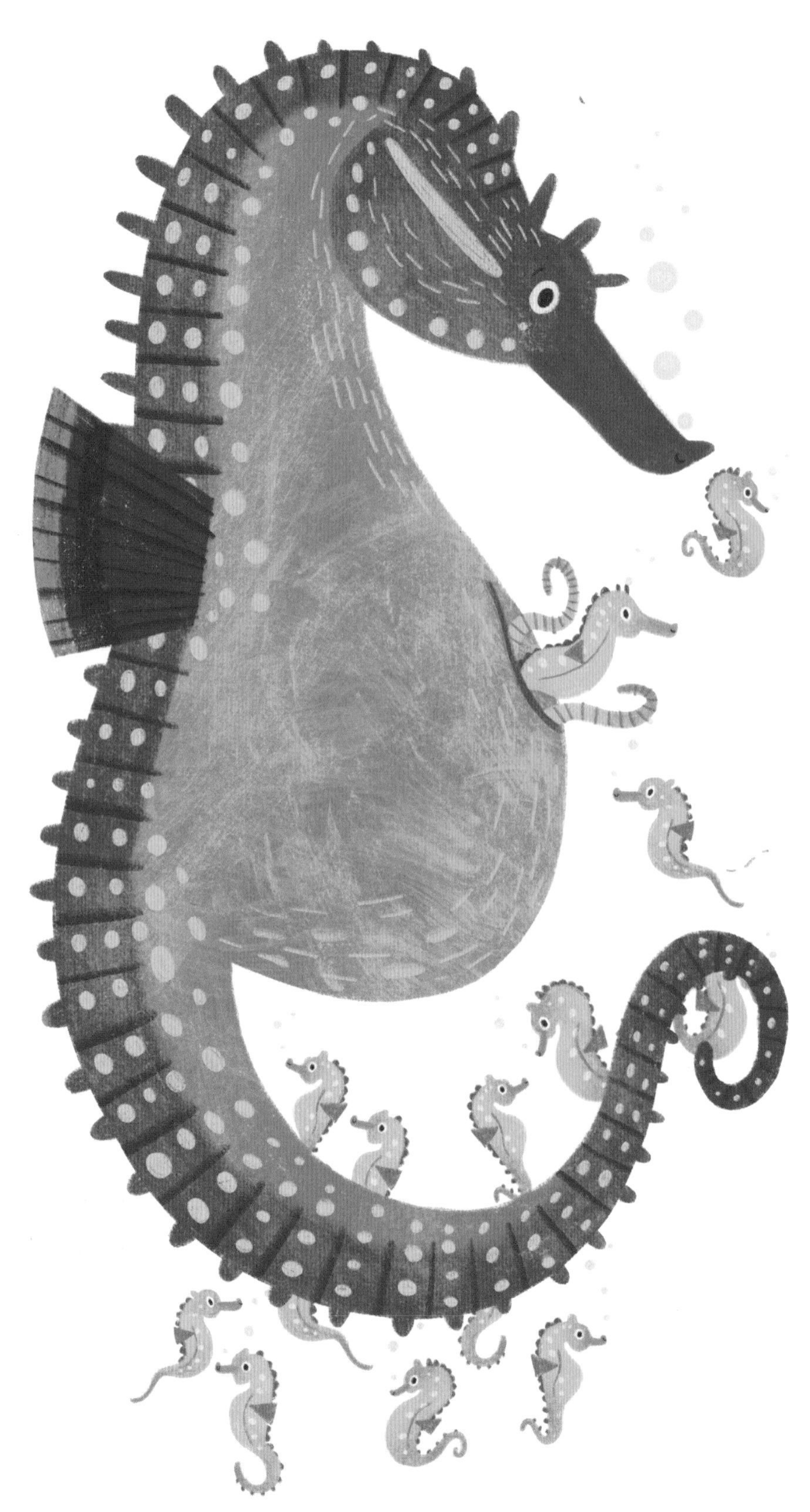

NATURE'S WONDERS

CURIOUS Questions & Answers

Words by Sue Nicholson, Anne Rooney and Philip Steele

Illustrations by Veronika Kotyk, Jean Claude, Ana Gomez and Mike Moran

Miles Kelly

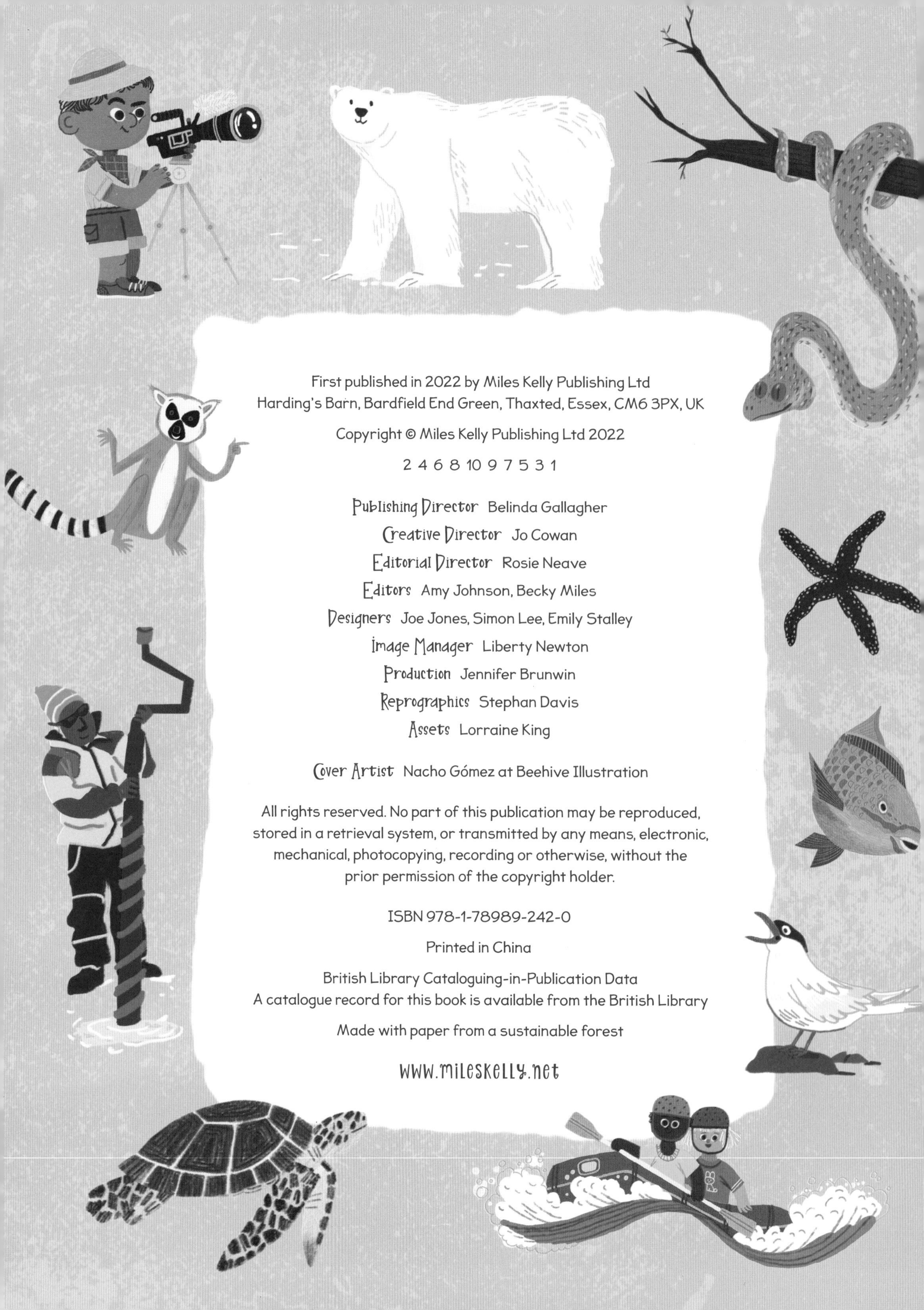

First published in 2022 by Miles Kelly Publishing Ltd
Harding's Barn, Bardfield End Green, Thaxted, Essex, CM6 3PX, UK

2 4 6 8 10 9 7 5 3 1

Publishing Director Belinda Gallagher
Creative Director Jo Cowan
Editorial Director Rosie Neave
Editors Amy Johnson, Becky Miles
Designers Joe Jones, Simon Lee, Emily Stalley
Image Manager Liberty Newton
Production Jennifer Brunwin
Reprographics Stephan Davis
Assets Lorraine King

Cover Artist Nacho Gómez at Beehive Illustration

ISBN 978-1-78989-242-0

Printed in China

British Library Cataloguing-in-Publication Data
A catalogue record for this book is available from the British Library

Made with paper from a sustainable forest

www.mileskelly.net

CONTENTS

Would you rather explore a desert or a rainforest?
Where would you go on an adventure?
What activity do you do for fun?

Have you ever seen a waterfall?
Where do you live on planet Earth?
NATURE'S WONDERS
If you could be any animal for a day, which would you choose?
Are you an explosive volcano or as cool as an iceberg?

Where can I see nature's wonders?

Everywhere! Planet Earth is bursting with amazing life and weird and wonderful places. Many of Earth's wonders are also important to the health of the planet.

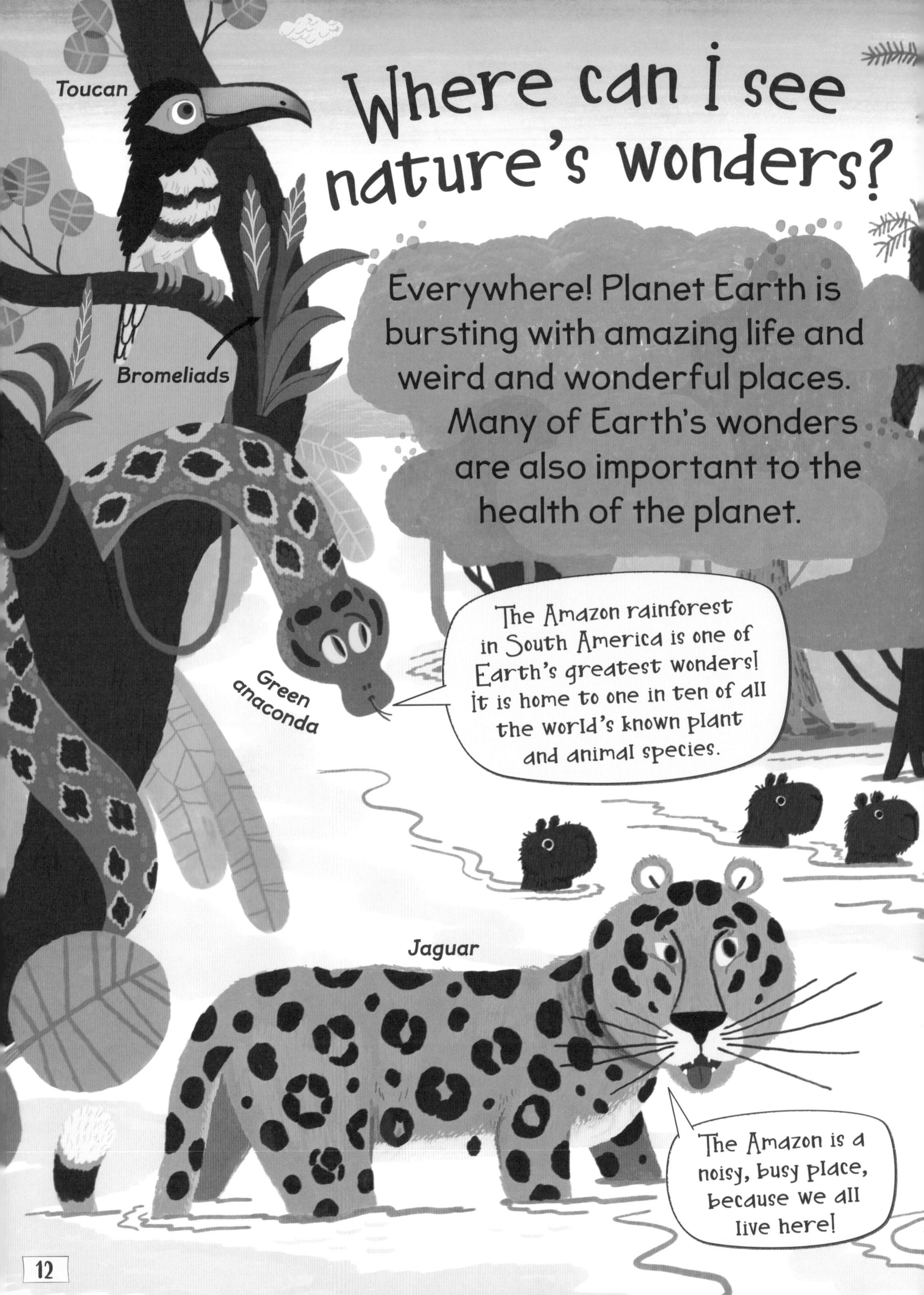

Toucan
Bromeliads
Green anaconda
The Amazon rainforest in South America is one of Earth's greatest wonders! It is home to one in ten of all the world's known plant and animal species.
Jaguar
The Amazon is a noisy, busy place, because we all live here!

Why are forests called 'green lungs'?

Forests are so important because trees soak up carbon dioxide, one of the gases that are over-heating our planet. They also give out oxygen, the gas we breathe.

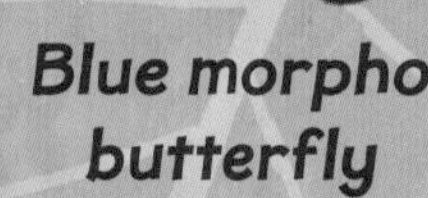

Blue morpho butterfly

Orchid

Over 1000 rivers and streams join the mighty Amazon river as it flows across South America.

Heron

Capybaras

How many trees are in the Amazon?

There may be around 390 billion! It is the world's biggest tropical rainforest.

Caiman

Yellow-spotted river turtles

What is 'the Smoke that Thunders'?

Mosi-oa-Tunya is the local name for the Victoria Falls on the Zambezi river in southern Africa. During the wet season, huge amounts of water thunder over a 108-metre drop, causing a mist of spray to rise high into the air.

Half-collared kingfisher

Victoria Falls are not the tallest or widest, but they're the greatest curtain of falling water in the world.

African paradise flycatcher

In November and December, the dry season, there's barely any water at all!

Why is Uluru so special?

Uluru is a massive sandstone rock at the heart of Australia. It is a sacred place for the region's Anangu people, central to their creation myths and stories of their ancestors.

Kangaroo
A hill or small mountain that stands alone is called an inselberg – island mountain. Most of Uluru is actually underground!
I'm Irish giant Finn MacCool! In an old legend, I made the Causeway as a bridge to fight a Scottish giant.

Who made the Giant's Causeway?

No one! In many parts of the world a volcanic rock called basalt forms six-sided columns. It's hard to believe that these coastal rocks in Northern Ireland were not shaped by humans.

Why do volcanoes blow their tops?

The plates of rock that form Earth's crust are always shifting and shoving against each other. Beneath them is a layer of gooey molten rock (magma). Mighty forces inside Earth build up until the magma bursts out.

An eruption blasts rock, ash and gases high into the air.

Crash!
Whoosh!
Side vent
Crater
Vent
Eruptions can cause flows of scorching liquid rock called lava
Extreme heat and pressure force the magma upwards

What are

Where can monkeys enjoy a hot tub?
In the north of Japan, winters are cold and snowy.
We keep warm in pools and springs heated by hot rocks underground.
Japanese macaques
Magma builds up deep below Earth's surface
underground pockets of water boil until a scalding jet of water and steam spurts high into the air.

Did you know?

The trunk of an **African elephant** has over 40,000 muscles!

A **leatherback sea turtle** can grow to over 2 metres long – more than the average height of a man.

Mount Everest is the highest peak above sea level, at 8849 metres. But Hawaiian volcano **Mauna Kea** is the highest from its base on the ocean floor to its peak, at 10,210 metres.

The **oceans** cover over 70 percent of the Earth's surface – we really are a blue planet.

Mount Everest

Everyone thinks I'm the tallest!

But I am really!

Mauna Kea

The **river Nile** is 6650 kilometres lon

Honey bees perform dances when they return to the hive, waggling their bodies. This tells the other bees where to find flowers with the best nectar.
carries rainfall all the way from tropical Africa through the deserts of Sudan and Egypt to the Mediterranean Sea.
We live in Africa's longest river!
CLICK!
CLICK!
Whales communicate underwater with songs and clicks, over thousands of kilometres.
Animals often know that a **volcano** is going to erupt before humans do.
We wriggle down the mountainside to escape the blast.

Who puts on great displays?

Whether swooping, scuttling or splashing, these animals create incredible sights.

Red crabs on Kirimati (Christmas Island) live on the forest floor, but they return to the sea each year to breed. About 45 million of them head for the beach at the same time! It's a crab traffic jam.

Flying fish get their name because they are super gliders. They have fins like wings, and if they are chased by hungry swordfish or tuna they can escape by gliding above the waves.

At dusk in winter up to 100,000 **starlings** may gather in a flock called a murmuration. They swirl and swoop in tight formation, making amazing shapes. Their aim is to confuse predators.
CRABS CROSS HERE
Excuse me!
There is safety in numbers for us!
Our long, narrow bodies help us swim fast enough to jump out of the water.
We can glide for up to 200 metres before splashing back down and leaping again.

Why do lakes turn blood red?

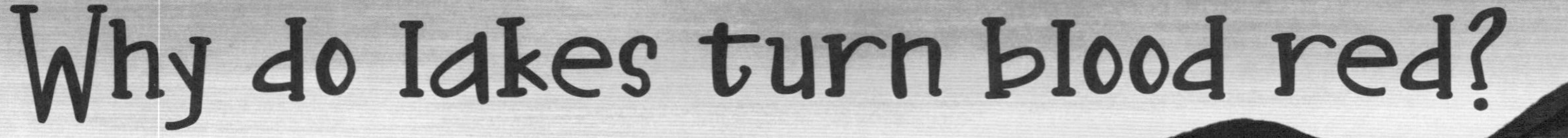

We feed off little shrimps and insects in the lake. Their red colouring turns our feathers pink.

This is Laguna Colorada in Bolivia. Salt lakes in many parts of the world turn red because they take their colour from tiny organisms called algae in the water. Red algae can put up with high levels of salt. Creatures living in the lakes also turn red.

Where are there colourful acid pools?

Dallol in Ethiopia is a volcanic landscape that looks like an alien world! The strange colours are caused by salt reacting with volcanic minerals.

Heated by magma below the surface, Dallol has geysers, salt mounds and highly acidic hot springs.

Where does the sky glow green?

In the far north or south, around the Poles, you might see the night sky shimmer with coloured light. This is an aurora.
Auroras are caused when particles of energy from the Sun disturb the magnetic forces surrounding the Earth.

What is the Great Blue Hole?

In the Caribbean Sea, off the coast of Belize, there is a big sinkhole in the ocean. This was once a cave, formed during the Ice Age when sea levels were low. Later, sea levels rose and the cave was drowned.

The Great Blue Hole is such a dark blue because it's very deep

Around it there is an atoll, a ring of coral reefs

Would you rather?

Film **anacondas** in the Amazon rainforest...
...or a fierce **tiger** in India?
Explore a giant **cave**...
Stalactites hang down from the cave ceiling and stalagmites point up from the ground.
...or dive to a **coral reef**?
Study **mountain gorillas** in Rwanda...
...or watch **whales** in the Pacific?

Explore the Alps in a **balloon**...
...or the bottom of the ocean in a **submersible**?
Raft through the **Grand Canyon**...
... or trek across the vast **Gobi desert** in Mongolia?
Plant new trees as a **forester** or study rocks as a **geologist**?
Find an ancient **fossil** or discover a new species of **bird**?

Where do the wildebeest go?

As many as 1.5 million wildebeest thunder across the plains of Kenya and Tanzania each rainy season, in search of fresh grazing. This journey is called a migration.

The wildebeest are also joined by herds of zebra and gazelle.
As the seasons change, some animals make amazing migrations to find the best places to feed and breed.

Which insects are great travellers?

Each year about 500,000 monarch butterflies fly from Canada and the USA to spend the winter in southwest Mexico, a journey of 4800 kilometres. One super generation of butterflies makes this migration, but it takes three new generations to complete the return journey.

Which birds go global?

Arctic terns are little seabirds that make incredible journeys. They can fly up to 40,000 kilometres in a year, from the Arctic to the Antarctic and back again.

We experience more daylight than any other animal on Earth!
We make the most of two summer seasons – the northern and the southern.
SPLASH!
This is a risky journey – an attack by hungry lions or an ambush by crocodiles at a river crossing can cause a stampede.

How do trees talk?

Trees and other plants can send chemical 'messages' to each other. They use an amazing underground network of thread-like fungi that connect their roots. This is known as the wood wide web.

Douglas fir tree saplings
We're all connected. We send each other nutrients, information, and even warnings of danger.
Help! We're small so we're not getting enough sunlight. All plants need energy from sunlight to make sugar for food.
Roots
Messages from the fir trees
Nutrients from the birch tree
Harmful chemicals from the walnut tree

The fungi spread out through the soil and join with the tips of the tree roots, forming the wood wide web.

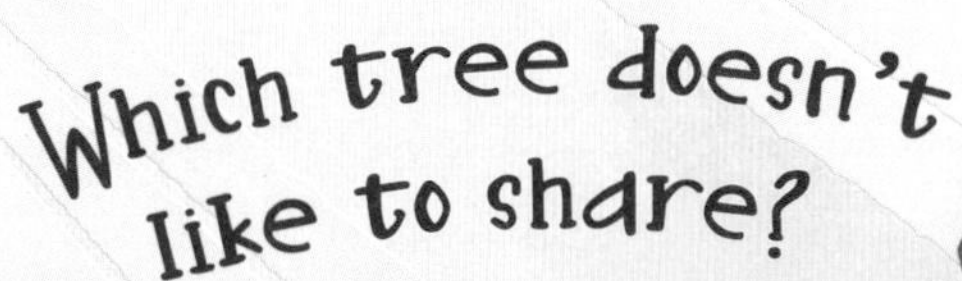

Which tree doesn't like to share?

I don't! I release a nasty chemical into the network to stop nearby plants growing. This means I get more water and sunlight for myself!
Those saplings need food – I can use the network to give them extra sugars that will help them survive and grow.
Black walnut tree
Paper birch tree
Fungi

The trees and fungi are useful to each other. The fungi pass on nutrients from the soil and in return, get sugars from the trees.

How many?

40 million

The number of krill (tiny shrimp-like creatures) that can be swallowed by a blue whale in just one day.

125

The length in centimetres of the longest tail feathers, belonging to the ribbon-tailed astrapia of Papua New Guinea.

22.4

The height in metres of a giant wave surfed at Praia del Norte, Portugal, in 2020.

15,000

The number of seeds that can be spread by one dandelion plant!

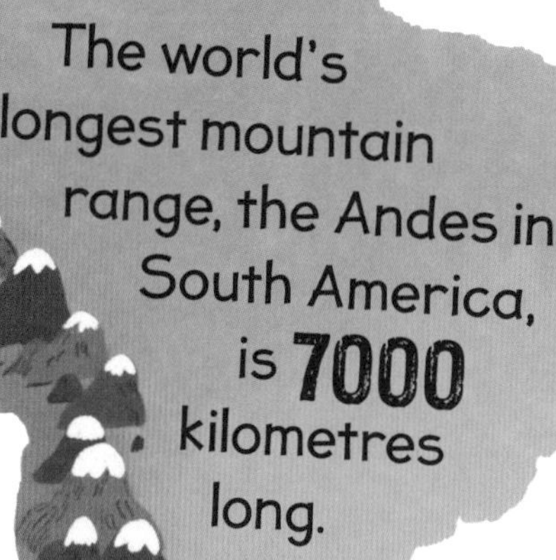

The world's longest mountain range, the Andes in South America, is **7000** kilometres long.

Welcome to the bat cave!

20 million

The number of bats that live in Bracken Cave in Texas, USA.

I'm a Mariana snailfish, I've been found at 8000 metres. It's amazing I can live at these crushing depths!

A bolt of lightning can be as hot as **30,000°** Celsius. That's five times the temperature at the Sun's surface!

The Mariana trench in the Pacific is the deepest part of the ocean, reaching **11,034** metres below the surface.

Ball's Pyramid in Australia is the world's tallest sea stack. It reaches **562** metres above the Pacific Ocean.

An avalanche, a massive flow of snow and ice, reaches **130** kilometres an hour in just **5** seconds as it roars down a mountainside.

How are icebergs made?

Icebergs are large chunks of ice that break off from a glacier or an ice shelf. The creation of an iceberg is an amazing sight!

The end of a glacier is called the snout.

A glacier is a deep freshwater river of ice. It moves slowly, gouging out rock. It heads to the sea, where it forms a cliff of ice.

The warmer, salty sea water makes huge chunks of the ice break away. This is called calving.

The iceberg floats into open sea. About two-thirds of it is under the water.

A pointed iceberg like this one is called a pinnacle.

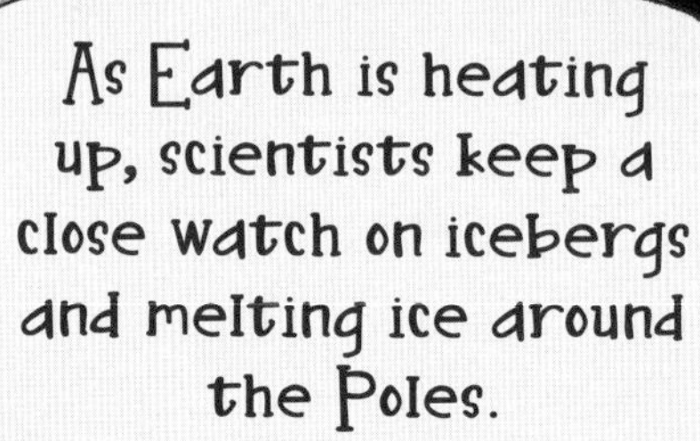

As Earth is heating up, scientists keep a close watch on icebergs and melting ice around the Poles.

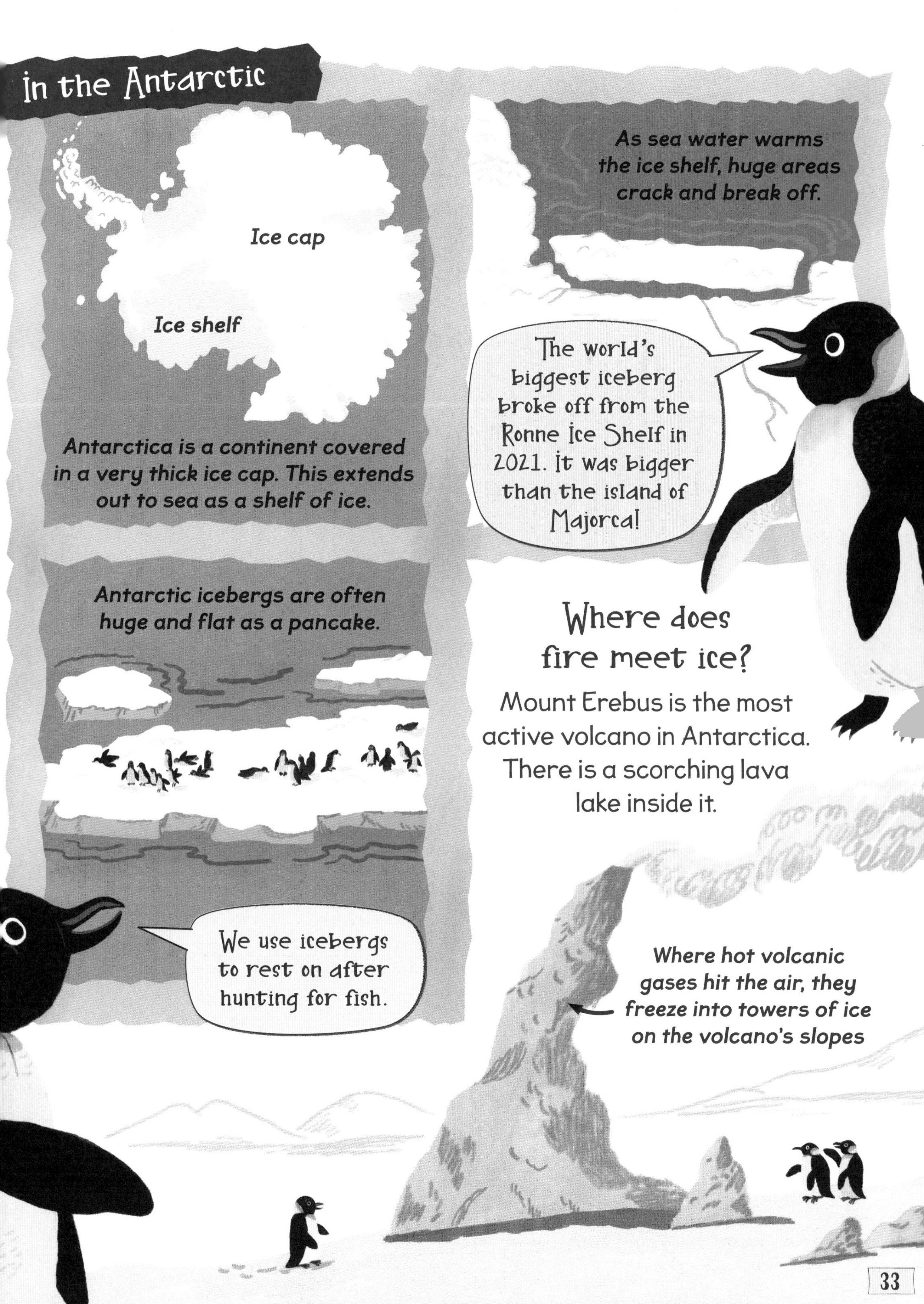
In the Antarctic
Ice cap
Ice shelf
Antarctica is a continent covered in a very thick ice cap. This extends out to sea as a shelf of ice.
As sea water warms the ice shelf, huge areas crack and break off.
The world's biggest iceberg broke off from the Ronne Ice Shelf in 2021. It was bigger than the island of Majorca!
Antarctic icebergs are often huge and flat as a pancake.
We use icebergs to rest on after hunting for fish.
Where does fire meet ice?
Mount Erebus is the most active volcano in Antarctica. There is a scorching lava lake inside it.
Where hot volcanic gases hit the air, they freeze into towers of ice on the volcano's slopes

How does water slice through rock?

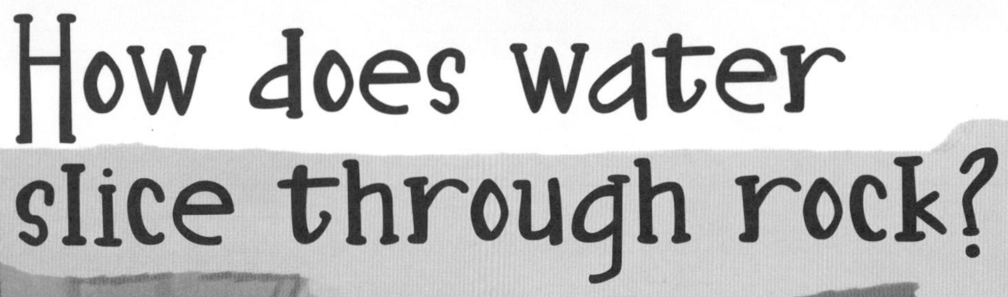

Earth's surface is shaped and carved by the forces of nature. Wind, rain, rivers, ocean waves, ice, heat and dust storms all erode (wear down) rocks over time.

The Grand Canyon in Arizona, USA, was formed around six million years ago by the Colorado river gradually eroding the rock.

The stripes in the rock show us layers of Earth's crust. The oldest layers at the bottom are 1.8 billion years old!

Ringtail

The canyon is 446 kilometres long, 1.6 kilometres deep and up to 29 kilometres wide.

I glide overhead in search of dead animals to eat. Yum!

The river is still wearing away the rock, gradually making the canyon wider and deeper.

Short-horned lizard

Where do rocks make weird shapes?

In Shilin, China, there is a forest of limestone pillars that look like tree trunks. They were eroded by wind and rain over 270 million years.

Water in caves dissolves minerals as it soaks through the rock. The minerals form spiky stalactites and stalagmites.

Arches National Park in Utah, USA, has over 2000 sandstone arches, formed by rocks shifting and being worn down.

Who lights up the ocean?

Many ocean creatures, from the surface to the darkest depths, can make glowing light through a chemical reaction in their bodies.

Plankton

At the surface, luminous plankton (tiny plants and creatures) sparkle as waves break, or when ripples lap the shore.

Hawaiian bobtail squid

I have luminous bacteria living in me! The glow they make helps me blend in with light from the surface above, so predators below don't catch me!

Lanternfish

I signal with my lights like a headlight to help me attract mates.

Bamboo coral

There are lots of deep-ocean animals that use light to find and catch prey and attract mates in the darkness.

Dragonfish

Only dragonfish can see and give out red light. The organ below my eye is like a searchlight, helping me spot prey.

Anglerfish

I have a long 'fishing rod' on my head with a light on the end. This lures my prey, which I quickly gobble up.

This deep-sea coral glows blue when it is disturbed.

A compendium of questions

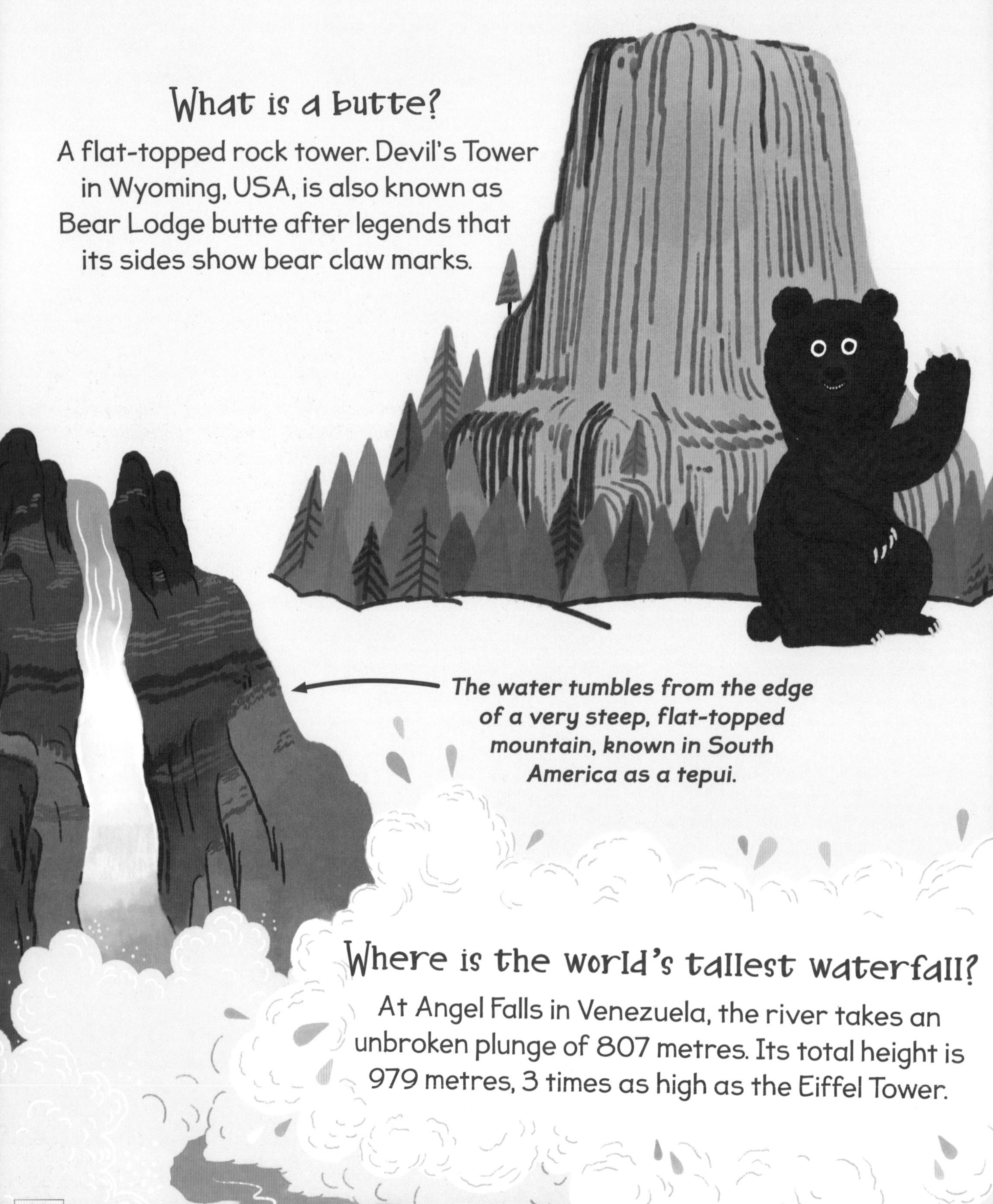

What is a butte?

A flat-topped rock tower. Devil's Tower in Wyoming, USA, is also known as Bear Lodge butte after legends that its sides show bear claw marks.

The water tumbles from the edge of a very steep, flat-topped mountain, known in South America as a tepui.

Where is the world's tallest waterfall?

At Angel Falls in Venezuela, the river takes an unbroken plunge of 807 metres. Its total height is 979 metres, 3 times as high as the Eiffel Tower.

The new trees trap moisture in the soil and stop it blowing away.

Where are people building green walls?

In Africa and China people are planting large areas of land with trees. They aim to stop the deserts spreading as the world becomes hotter.

Find out what you can do to help save the planet – turn to page 133 for some ideas!

Do trees bleed?

No, but the Dragon's blood tree, found on Socotra island in Yemen, has bright red sap, so it looks like it's bleeding!

I'm not really bleeding – I'm fine!

Dragon's blood trees can live to be thousands of years old!

Can pebbles burst into flower?

The Lithops plants of Namibia and South Africa look exactly like stone pebbles. Animals barely notice them, until...

... they bloom into beautiful flowers!

Whoosh!

The Chocolate Hills consist of over 1200 cone-shaped mounds.

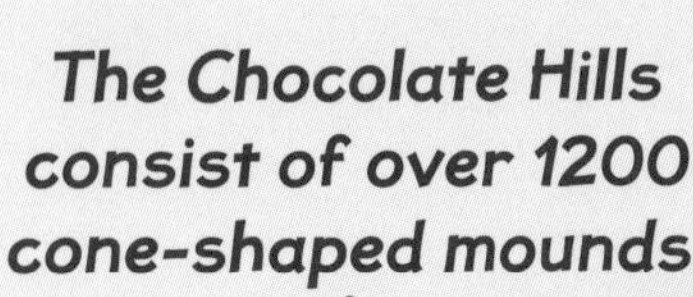

Are there hills made of chocolate?

Sadly, no! The Chocolate Hills in the Philippines get their name because the grass turns from green to chocolatey-brown in the dry season.

CRASH!

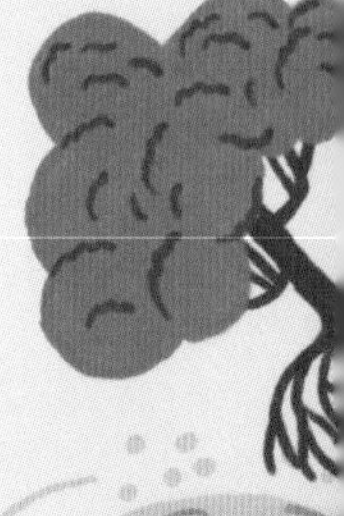

Where is the desert always moving?

In vast areas of sand dunes called ergs, fierce winds whip up the sand into constantly shifting piles and banks.

We herd camels in the Sahara Desert. The ergs are very difficult to cross!

What is Tornado Alley?

It's a danger zone in the USA, where fearsome tornadoes are common. It stretches from Texas through the Great Plains to Nebraska.

What is the Great Barrier Reef made of?

Coral polyps, tiny animals which live inside a hard chalky structure. Over millions of years they can grow to create incredible reefs.

If you could chat to a seal or a sea turtle, which would you choose?
What would you like to be when you grow up?
What's your favourite coral reef creature?

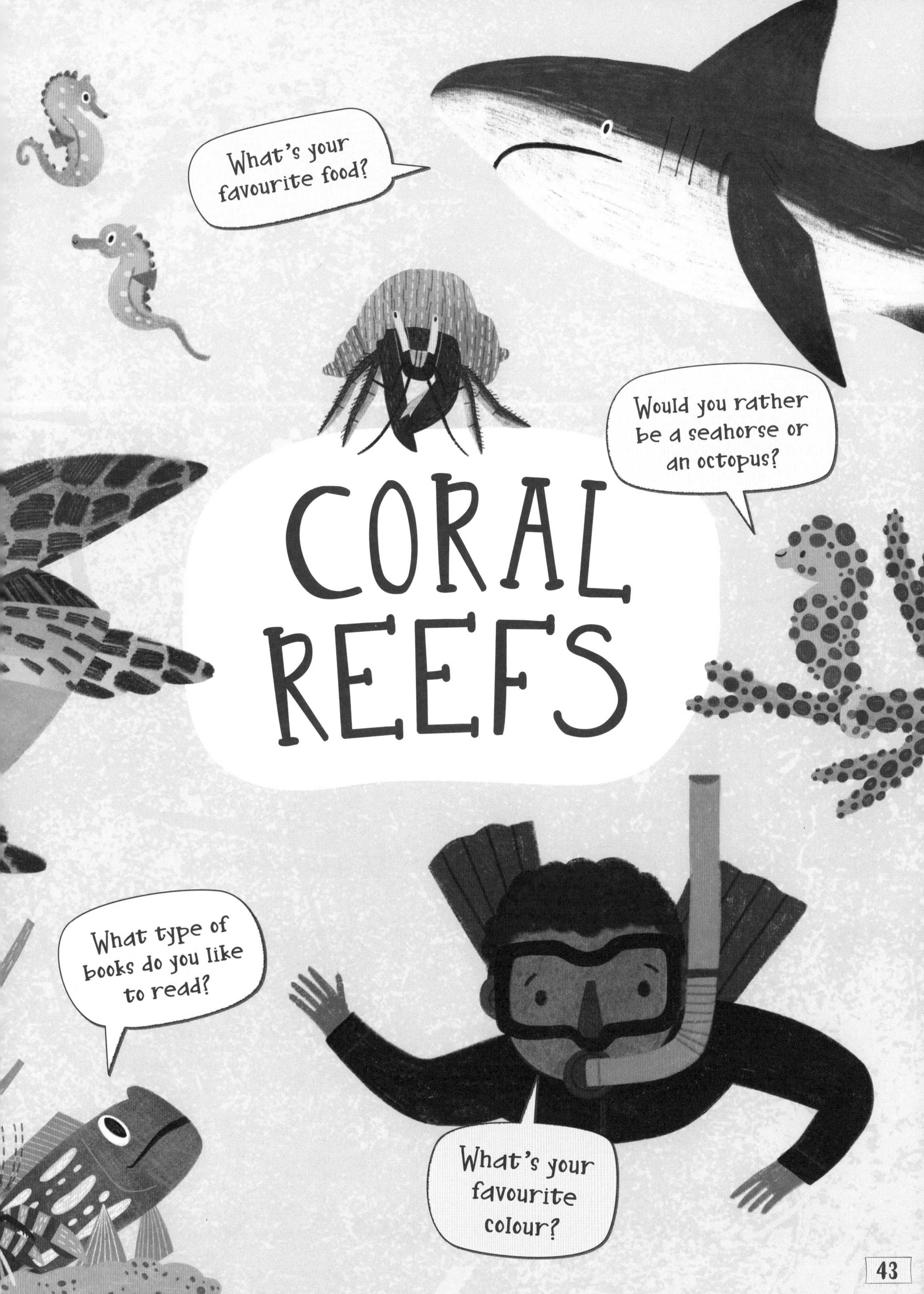
What's your favourite food?
Would you rather be a seahorse or an octopus?
CORAL REEFS
What type of books do you like to read?
What's your favourite colour?

What is a coral reef?

Reefs have been called the 'rainforests of the sea'. They're colourful and crowded underwater habitats teeming with sea creatures all swimming, darting and creeping over living rock called coral.

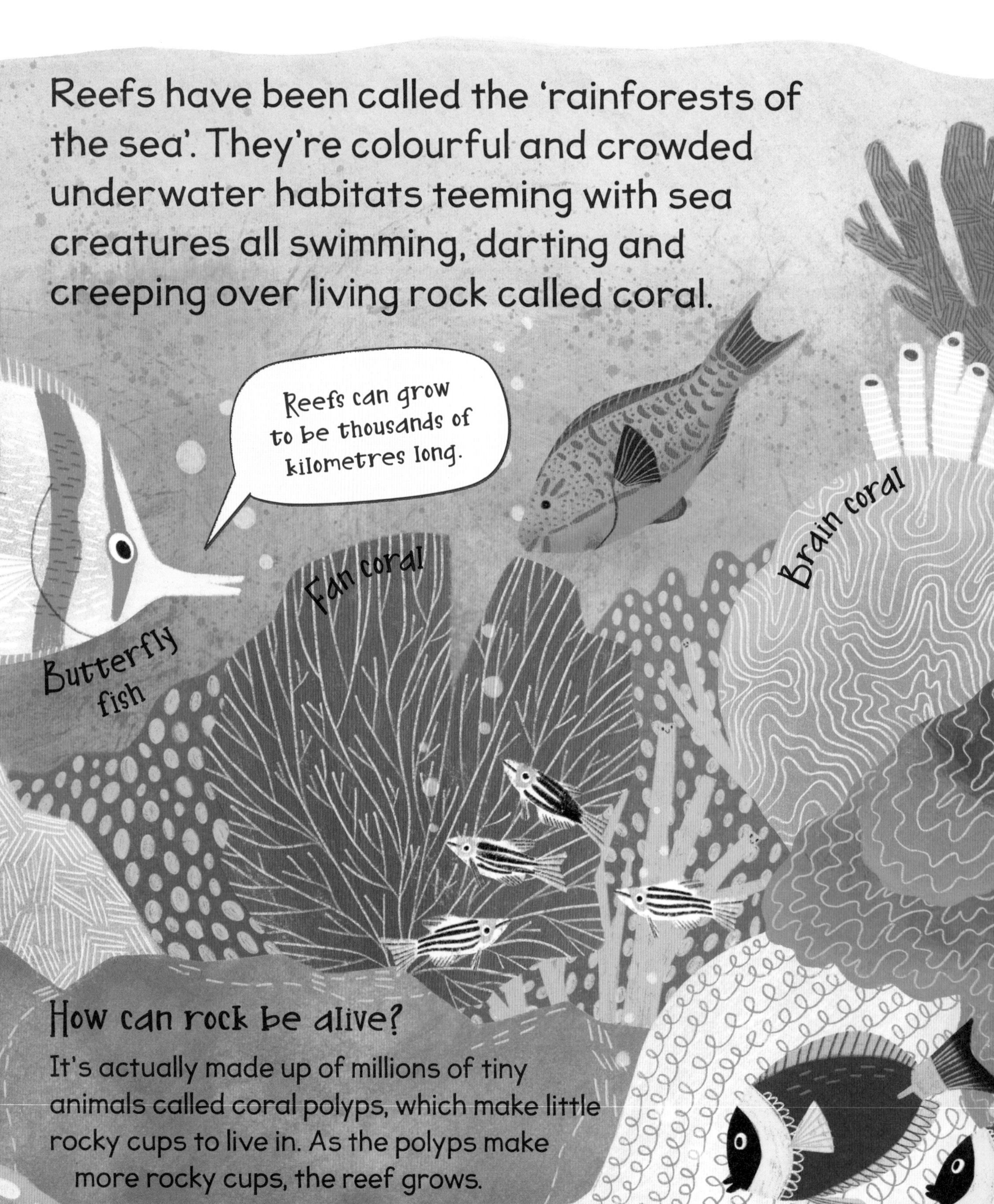

Reefs can grow to be thousands of kilometres long.
Fan coral
Brain coral
Butterfly fish

How can rock be alive?

It's actually made up of millions of tiny animals called coral polyps, which make little rocky cups to live in. As the polyps make more rocky cups, the reef grows.

Is it a good home?

A coral reef provides lots of places for plants to attach themselves as well as nooks and crannies where creatures can live.

Reefs are at risk of disappearing due to climate change. They need our help!
Elkhorn coral

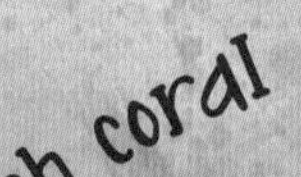

ivory bush coral

Why are reefs so special?

They are home to billions of animals and plants, many of which can live nowhere else. Coral reefs have been around for at least 230 million years.

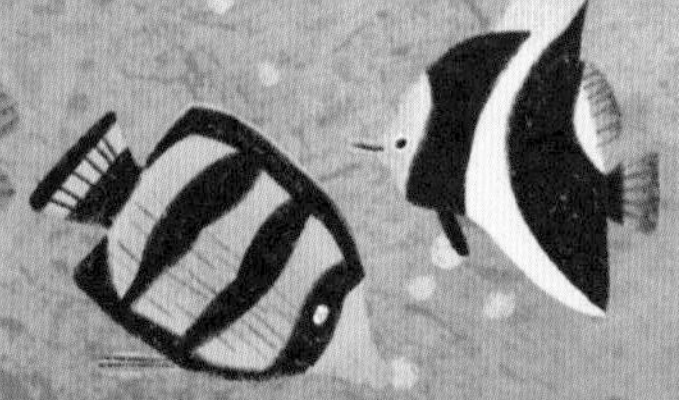

Does all coral look the same?

No, there are lots of different shapes and styles. Coral can make structures like tree branches or antlers, a lettuce or a brain.
Star coral
Lettuce coral

How busy is a reef?

Very busy indeed! Although reefs cover just one percent of the seabed, about a quarter of ALL sea life lives there. Most reef animals live only in water, but a few breathe the air and sometimes go on land.

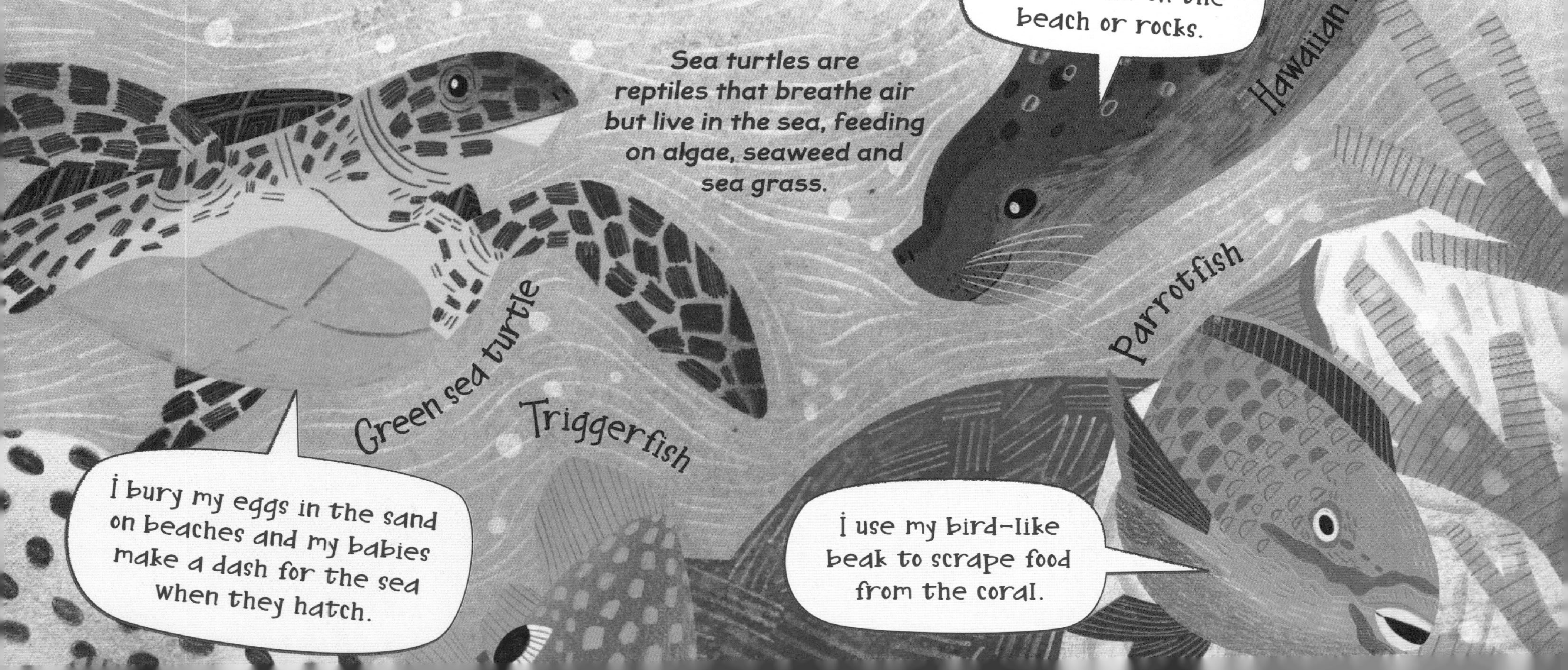

Hawaiian monk seal

I search the reef for food to eat, but also lie on the beach or rocks.

Sea turtles are reptiles that breathe air but live in the sea, feeding on algae, seaweed and sea grass.

Green sea turtle

Triggerfish

Parrotfish

I bury my eggs in the sand on beaches and my babies make a dash for the sea when they hatch.

I use my bird-like beak to scrape food from the coral.

Some corals don't live in hard rocky cups. They are called soft corals.
My name in Hawaii is humuhumunukunukuapua'a!
Butterfly fish
i'm a trumpetfish. i suck up small fish with my tube-like mouth.
Yum!
Blue starfish
Starfish crawl over the rocks and seabed hunting small, slow-moving animals.
Anemones like me wrap our arms around prey – then throw our stomach out of our body to digest it!
We hermit crabs find a shell left by another animal and move in.
Anemones are soft, squishy animals. Stuck to a rock, they wave their tentacles and wait for a meal to come along.

Did you know?

Goby fish and blind **pistol shrimps** are best friends. The shrimp digs a burrow where they both live and the goby keeps a lookout for predators.

Baby seahorses grow in a pouch on their dad's tummy until they're old enough to fend for themselves. Then the dad gives birth to up to 2000 kids!

Two **giant clams** weigh as much as a **polar bear**.

Collector urchins eat tiny algae. They can be used to help a reef in danger of being taken over by algae.

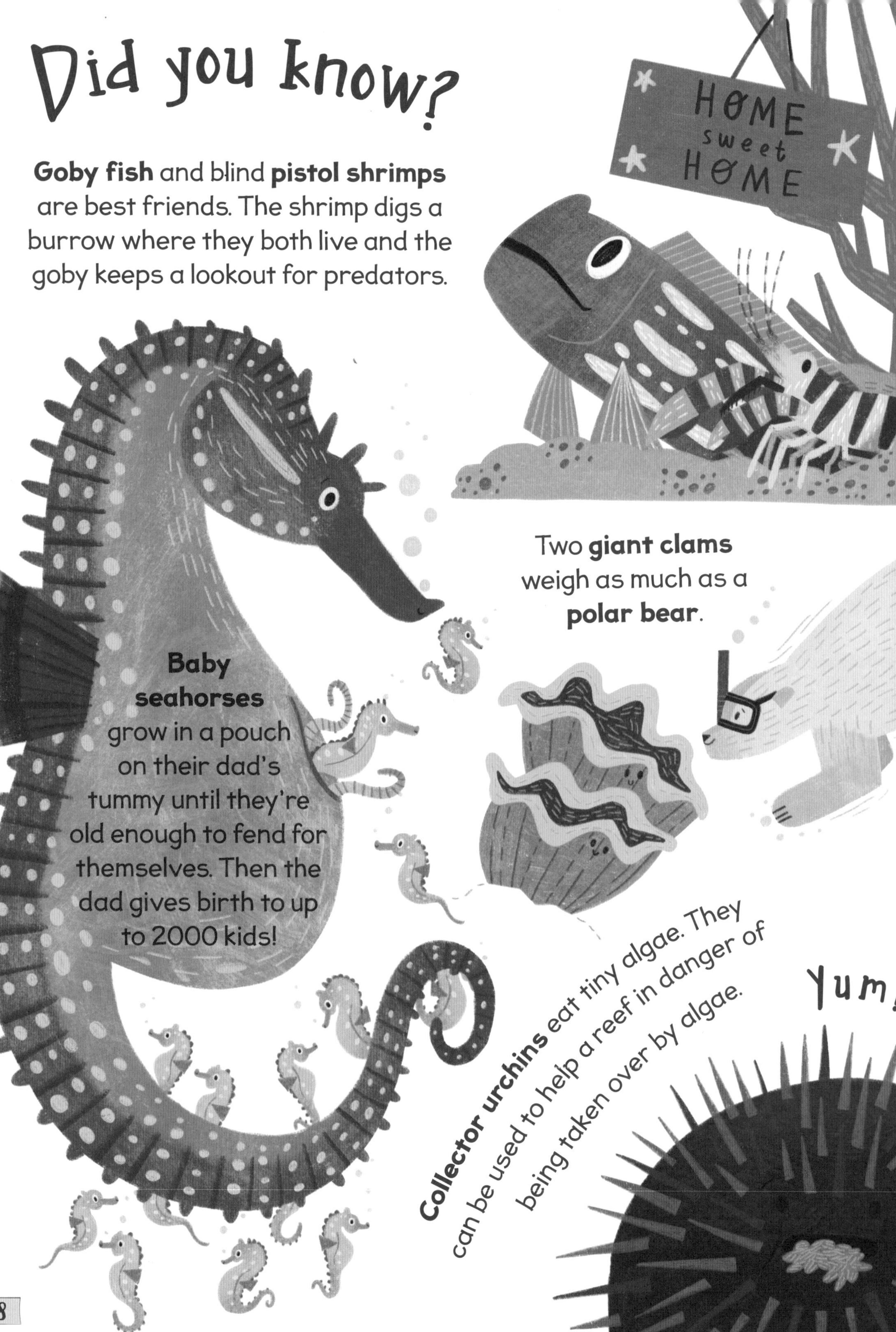

Many reef creatures, such as coral and sponges, are **fixed to one spot**. Their offspring are carried by the water and grow where they settle.

I wish I lived over there.

Corals grow best in crystal-clear water. **Sponges** and **corals** help keep seawater clean by eating the tiny bits and pieces that make it cloudy.

Mmmm, blobby bits of dead stuff – my favourite!

I used to be under the sea, you know.

Fish can be lured to a new, growing reef if scientists play the sounds recorded in a healthy reef on **loudspeakers**.

Some entire **mountain ranges** are made from old coral reefs and parts of the seabed that were under the sea millions of years ago. They still have fossils of reef animals!

Are there reefs near me?

Possibly, if you live somewhere warm by the sea. Coastal reefs love warm, shallow water, but there are also colder, deep-water reefs we know less about.

Microbialites
Scientists look at our reef to study what life in underground lakes on Mars might be like!
We love clean, clear water!
ATLANTIC OCEAN
PACIFIC OCEAN
SOUTHERN OCEAN
Key
warm-water reefs
cold-water reefs

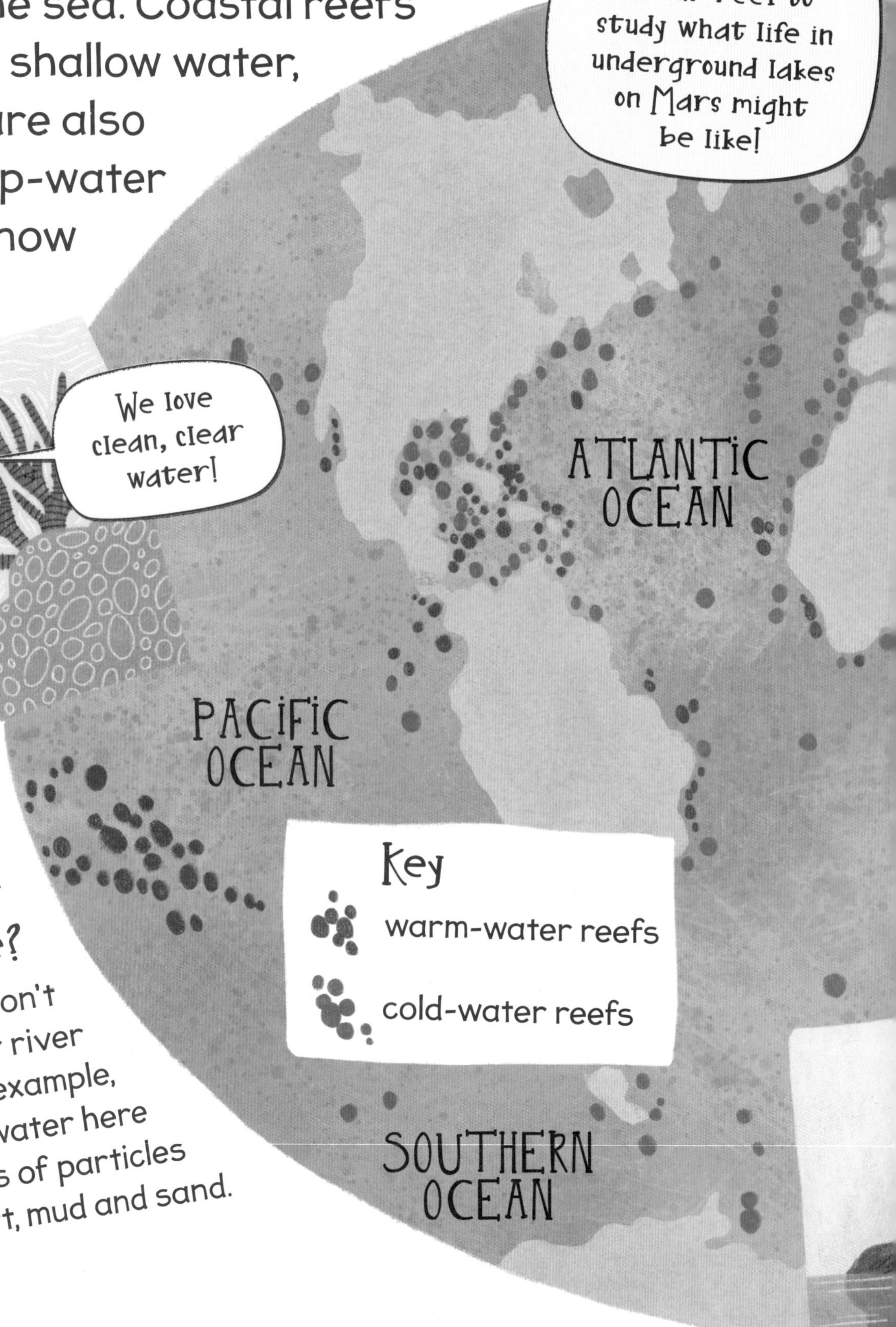

Are coral polyps fussy about their home?

Yes. They don't grow near river mouths, for example, because the water here carries lots of particles of dirt, mud and sand.

Are reefs all in the sea?

Most are, but a few freshwater lakes have rocky reef-like structures called microbialites. One in Canada shows scientists what very early life on Earth might have been like.

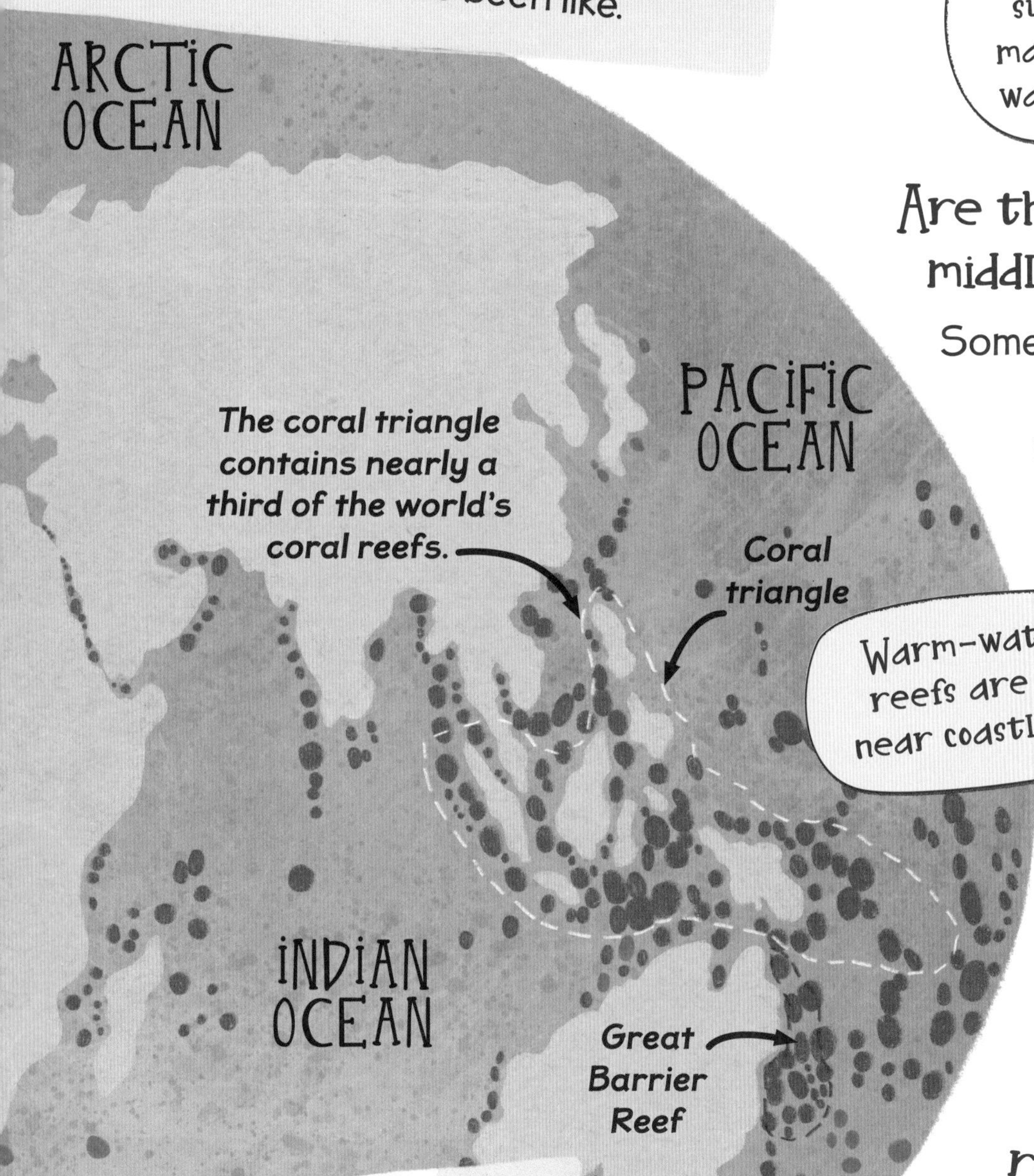

Cold water corals

We don't rely on sunlight to help us make food, unlike our warm-water cousins.

ARCTIC OCEAN

PACIFIC OCEAN

INDIAN OCEAN

The coral triangle contains nearly a third of the world's coral reefs.

Coral triangle

Great Barrier Reef

Are there any in the middle of the ocean?

Some cold-water reefs are on mid-ocean ridges (mountains beneath the sea).

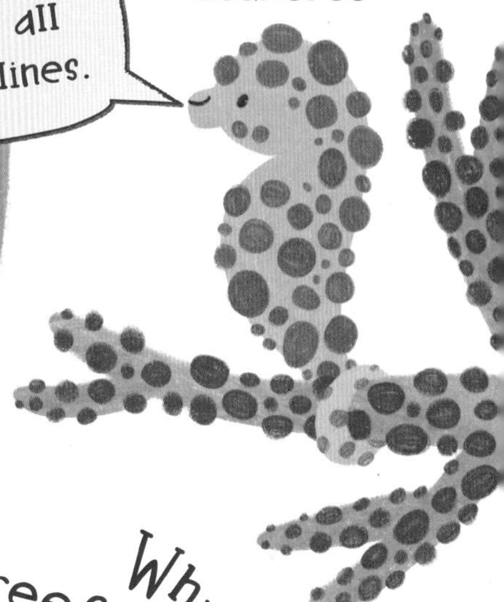

Pygmy seahorse

Warm-water reefs are all near coastlines.

Why do reefs love the Pacific Ocean?

Reefs often form where there are volcanic islands, and the Pacific Ocean has more than its fair share of volcanoes!

Is a reef really alive?

Each reef is not a single living thing – it is a huge collection of living coral polyps. These tiny animals are like a little bag of jelly with tentacles.

Coral polyp

We're related to jellyfish and anemones.

Although we're mostly soft and squishy creatures, special 'glass sponges' have a hard skeleton that can form a reef.

Sponges

Reefs are classed as the largest living structures on Earth.

Can you have a reef without coral?

Yes, sometimes. The very earliest reefs were made by sponges and a small number exist today.

How does coral get food?

Tiny algae (a plant-like organism) living inside the coral polyp use energy from sunlight and chemicals from the water to make food for the coral.

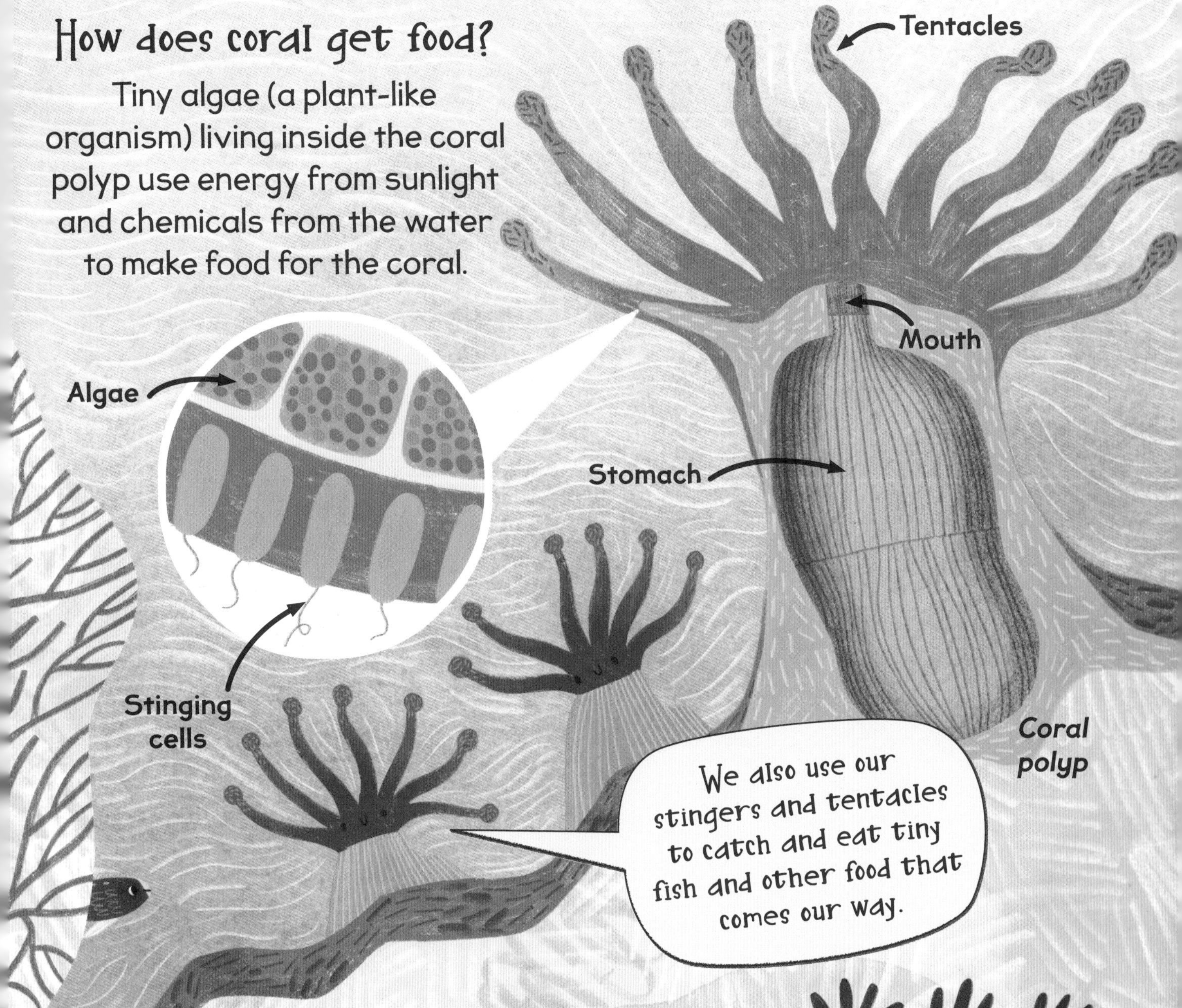

Tentacles

Mouth

Algae

Stomach

Stinging cells

Coral polyp

We also use our stingers and tentacles to catch and eat tiny fish and other food that comes our way.

How do squashy polyps make a hard reef?

They take chemicals from seawater to make rocky limestone cups around themselves. New polyps build on top of old empty ones.

My hard, rocky cup protects me.

Over thousands of years, this grows into a huge reef.

How many?

6000
The depth in metres below the ocean's surface of the deepest cold-water reef.

2 million
The number of eggs laid by a female lionfish each year.

High six!

6
The number of tentacles belonging to each stony coral polyp.

3 The length in metres of the longest sea snakes.

1 million
tiny algae live inside just one square centimetre of coral.

It's a bit crowded in here!

Whale sharks have more than **3000** tiny teeth that help them strain the tiny plankton they eat from the seawater.

I'm a tasselled wobbegong shark and have got to be one of the weirdest!
134 different shark and ray species live around the Great Barrier Reef.
A green sea turtle can travel 2600 kilometres between its reef feeding ground and its nesting site on a beach.
5000 stinging cells are found in each tentacle of the highly poisonous box jellyfish.
60 The number of sea snake species that live around coral reefs.
Like snakes that live on land, some of us are poisonous.

Here the water is shallow, calm and usually warm.

Spiny lobster

Back reef

Reef crest

Coral polyps that live on the reef crest have to survive strong winds and waves.

Do reefs have different neighbourhoods?

Yes, and different types of organisms live in each one. The part closest to the shore is called the back reef. The part closest to the surface is the reef crest. And the side that faces the open sea – where most of the corals grow – is the fore reef.

How many types of coral reef are there?

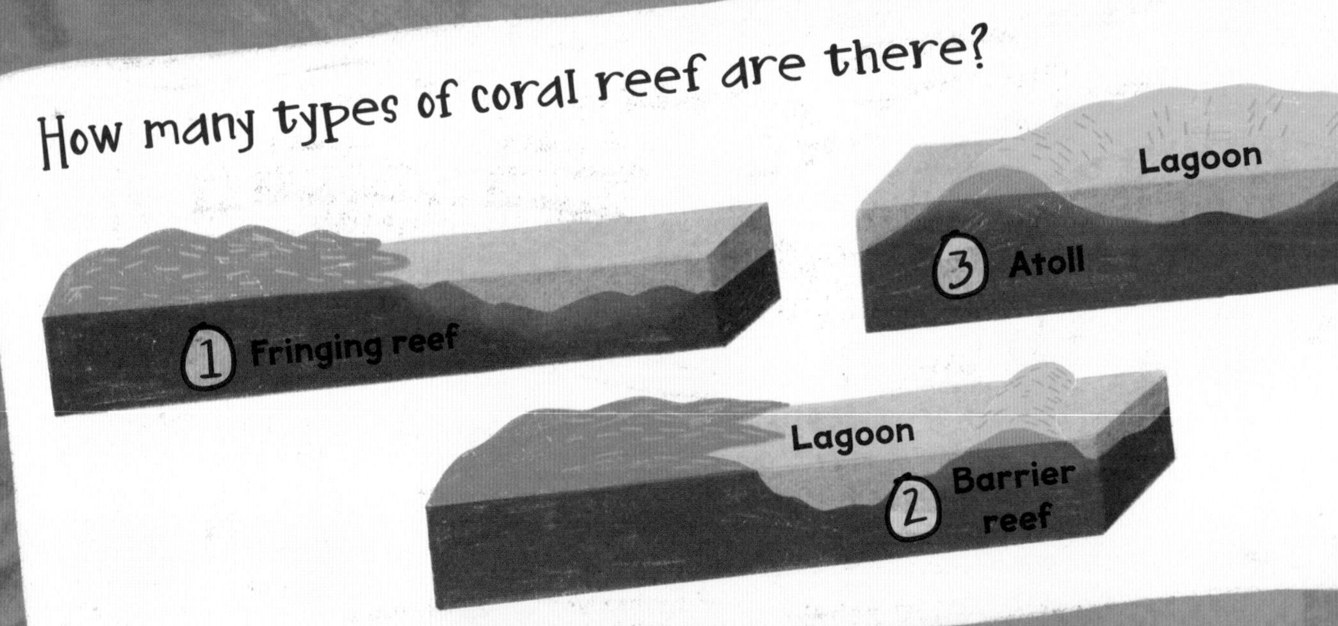

Brown pelican
Yum!
Bird droppings are good for the reef and help it to grow!
Fore reef
Finger coral
Manta ray
Reefs grow slowly – about 10 centimetres a year if conditions are just right.
Caribbean reef shark

There are three main types.
1. A **fringing reef** grows close to the coast;
2. A **barrier reef** also follows the coast but is separated from it by a lagoon;
3. An **atoll** is ring-shaped and surrounds a sunken island.
Also, small blobs of reef called **patch reefs** can sometimes form in lagoons.

Is a reef busy at night?

Lots of reef creatures – including coral – are nocturnal, which means they are most active at night. The coral turns frilly as the polyps peep out from their stony homes to feed after dark.

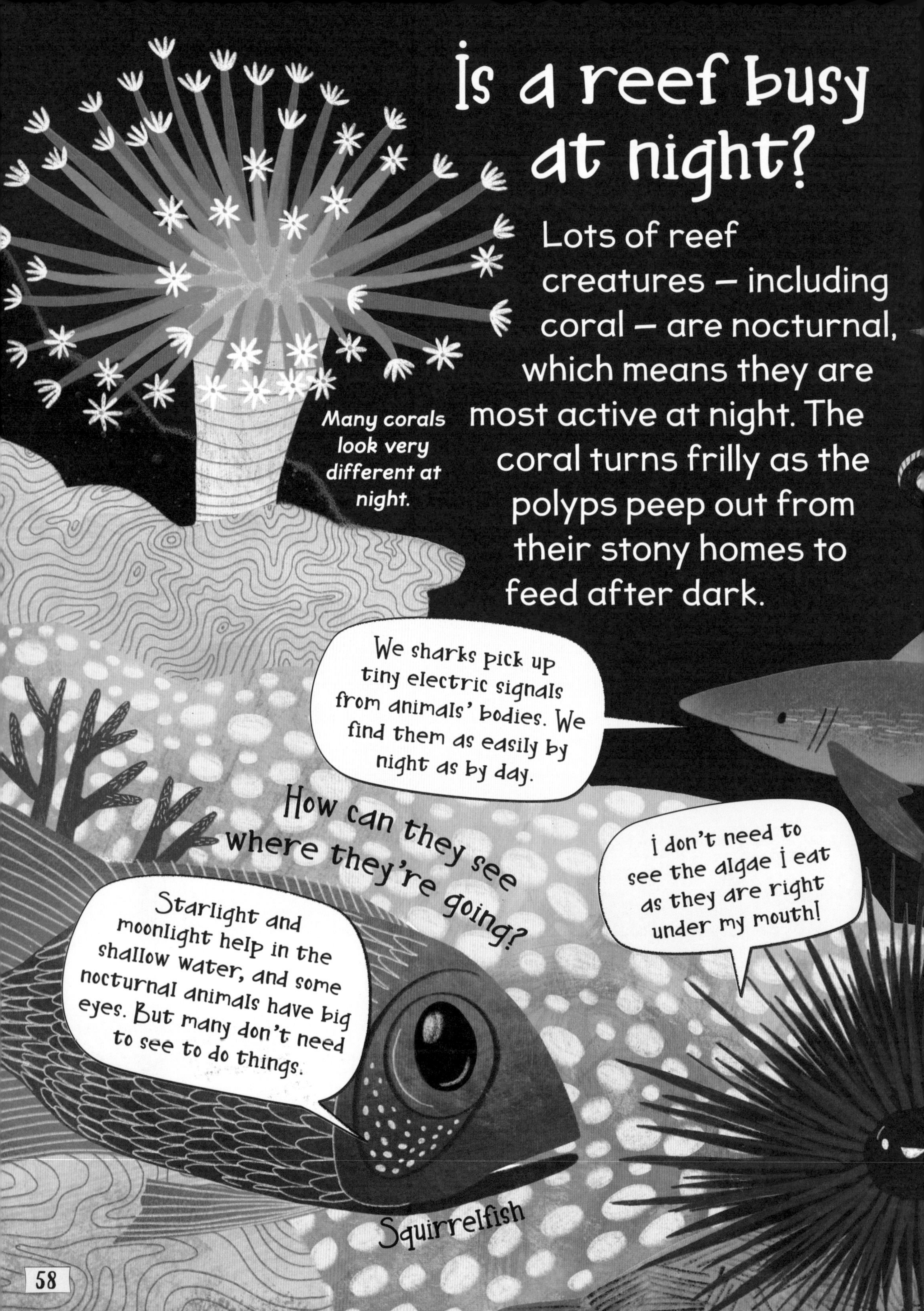

Many corals look very different at night.
We sharks pick up tiny electric signals from animals' bodies. We find them as easily by night as by day.
How can they see where they're going?
I don't need to see the algae I eat as they are right under my mouth!
Starlight and moonlight help in the shallow water, and some nocturnal animals have big eyes. But many don't need to see to do things.
Squirrelfish

Are there midnight snacks?

Yes! Lots of tiny plankton rise to the surface at night to feed – and other animals rush to gobble them up.

Reef octopus
I have great night vision and can also taste what I'm touching with my eight arms.
Spotted drum fish
You're not going out dressed like that!

Are night-time fish dressed to party?

No, not really. Many nocturnal fish have colours and patterns that help them blend into the shadows so it is harder for predators to find them at night.

Who stays in and who goes out?

At night, nocturnal animals go out, and daytime animals hide away. Some even share their homes, with one resting in it by day and another at night.

Australia

Great Barrier Reef

The GBR is 2600 kilometres long!

Can a reef be seen from space?

The Great Barrier Reef (GBR) near Australia can! It's the largest living thing on the planet and the biggest structure ever built by animals.

Staghorn coral

Cauliflower coral

How many types of coral are there?

Brain coral

Around 100 different species (types) of coral live on the GBR. There are inhabitants of all colours, sizes and shapes.

Is it just one giant reef?

No. There are 3000 individual reefs and 900 islands all running into each other. They make up about a tenth of the world's reefs.

Which cows graze on the reef?

Dugongs – a type of sea cow – like to feed on the reef. They hoover up seagrass with their funny snouts.

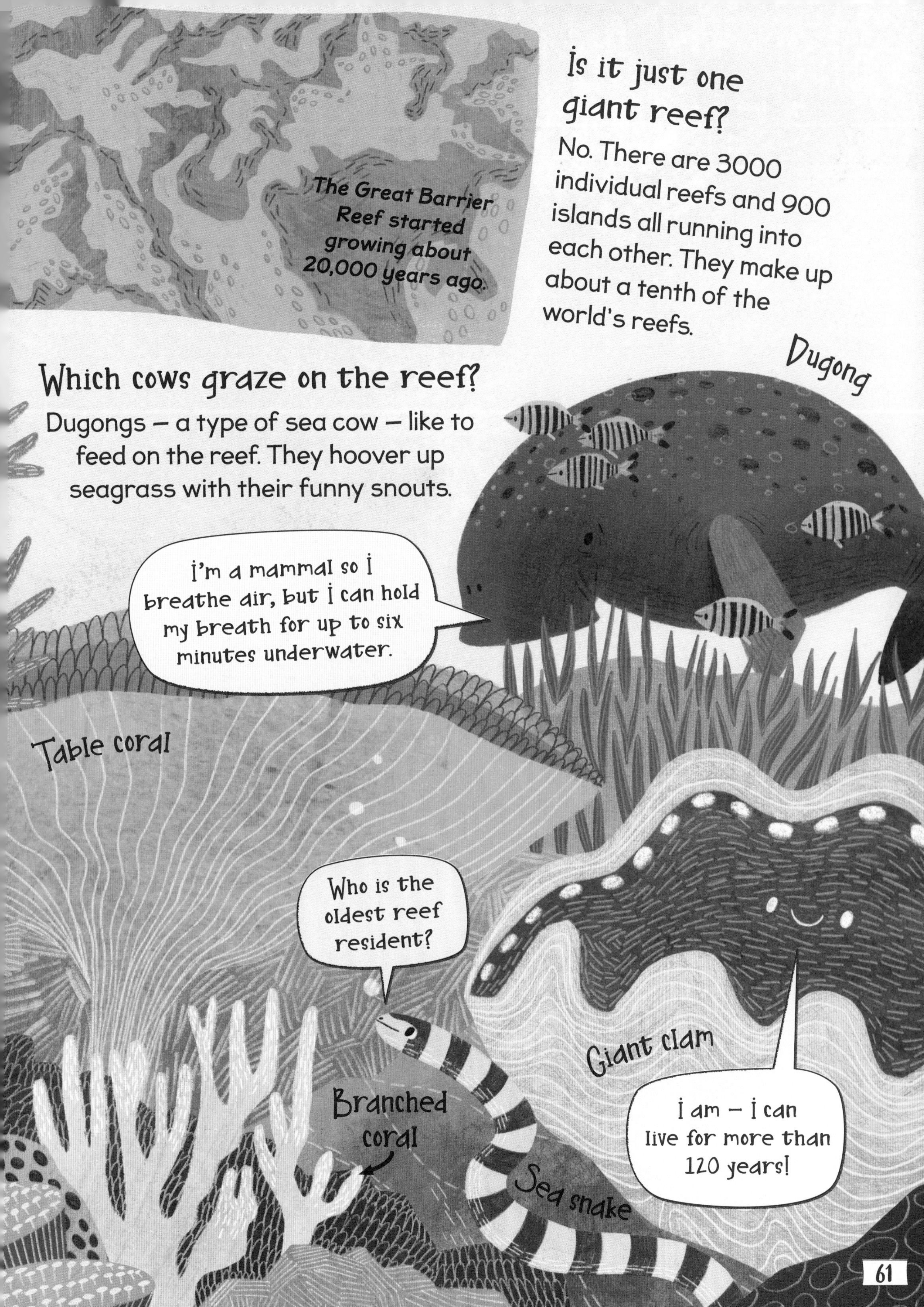

The Great Barrier Reef started growing about 20,000 years ago.
Dugong
I'm a mammal so I breathe air, but I can hold my breath for up to six minutes underwater.
Table coral
Who is the oldest reef resident?
Giant clam
I am – I can live for more than 120 years!
Branched coral
Sea snake

Would you rather?

Go diving around a coral reef...
...or look at it through a glass-bottomed boat?
We knock out our prey with one super-strong punch!
Be friends with a slippery sea cucumber or a bristly sea star?
Have a boxing match with a mantis shrimp or...
...a swimming race with a dolphin?

Be a **sea slug** with its crazy colours... or a **Caribbean reef octopus** that can change its colour when it pleases?
Hey – watch where you're crawling!
Get your food while staying in one place like a **coral polyp**... or roam around the reef gobbling up mouthfuls like a **crown of thorns starfish**?
Live on a **real** coral reef or...
an **artificial** one?
I love what you've done with the place!

Which coral reef creature is the...

Scariest

It depends what you are! For humans, a shark is probably the scariest, even though very few types are actually dangerous to people.

Coolest at camouflage

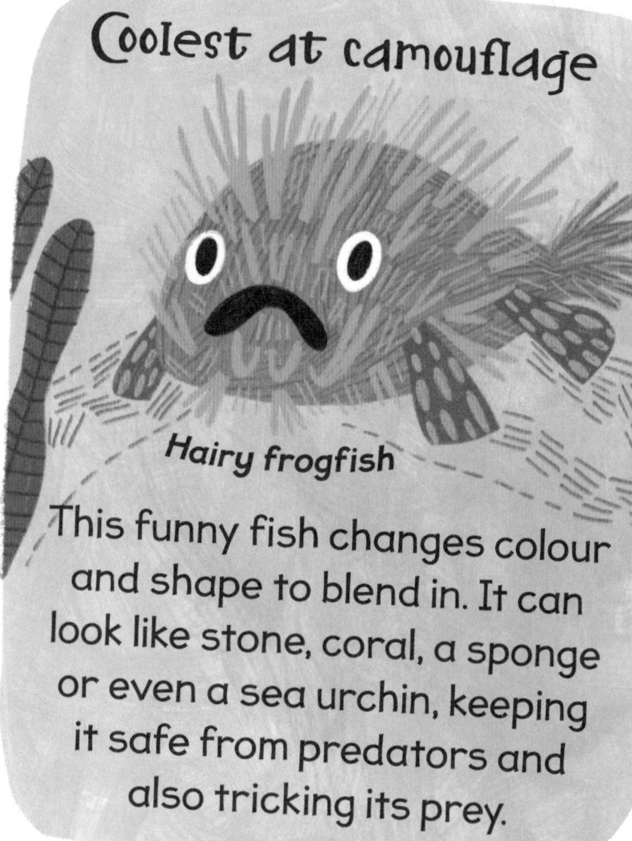

This funny fish changes colour and shape to blend in. It can look like stone, coral, a sponge or even a sea urchin, keeping it safe from predators and also tricking its prey.

Best communicator

A cuttlefish changes colour all the time. It uses colour to communicate, so different colours ripple over its skin as it chats to its friends.

Most poisonous

This small and pretty octopus contains enough venom to kill 26 adult humans.

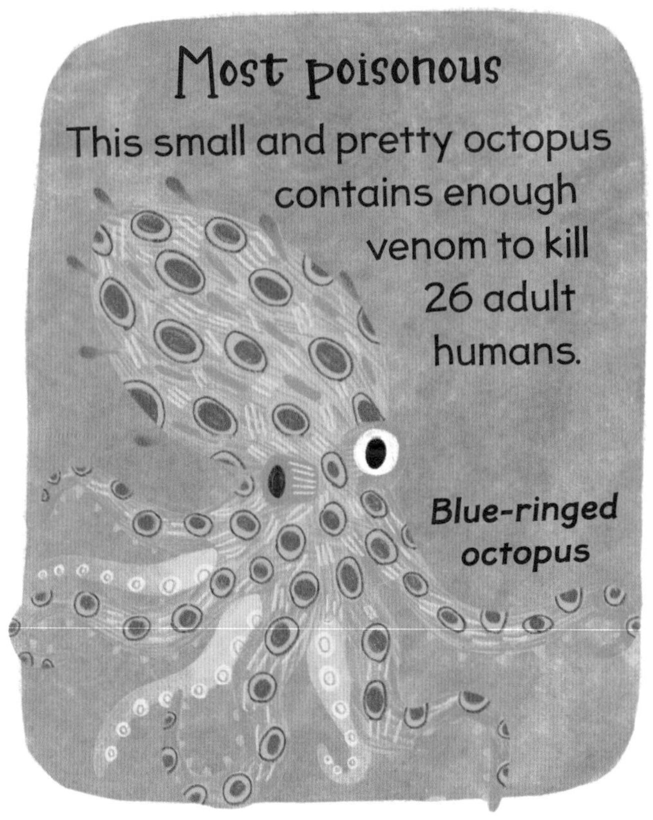

Best at boxing

One of the world's strongest animals for its size, this shrimp uses its club-like legs to throw a super-fast punch at its prey.

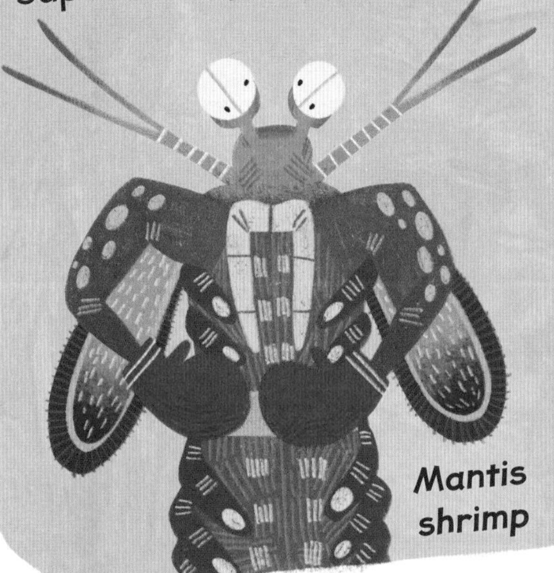

Best at growing new arms

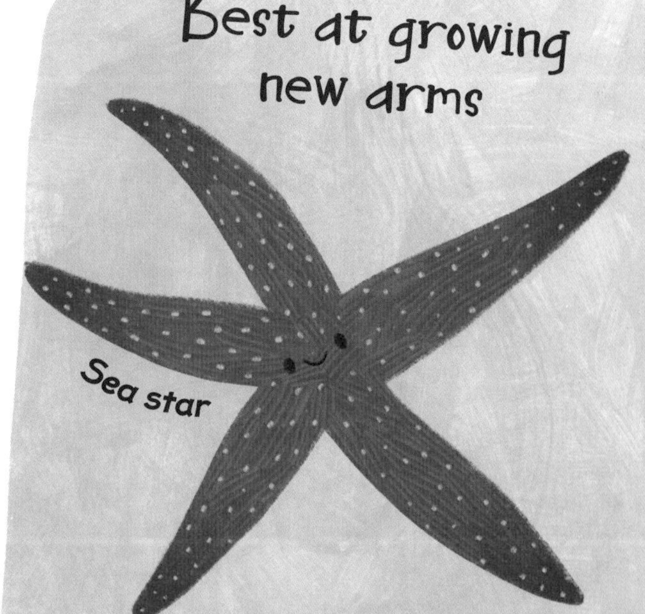

Sea stars and brittlestars can grow a new arm if they lose one. In some types, a lone arm can grow a whole new sea star!

Cleverest at disguise

These guys pick up anything to hand to help them hide from predators. They can stick bits of seaweed to their backs or wave pieces of coral around to trick other reef creatures.

Most bizarre

Sea slugs are soft, slithery creatures that often have feathery gills or frills.

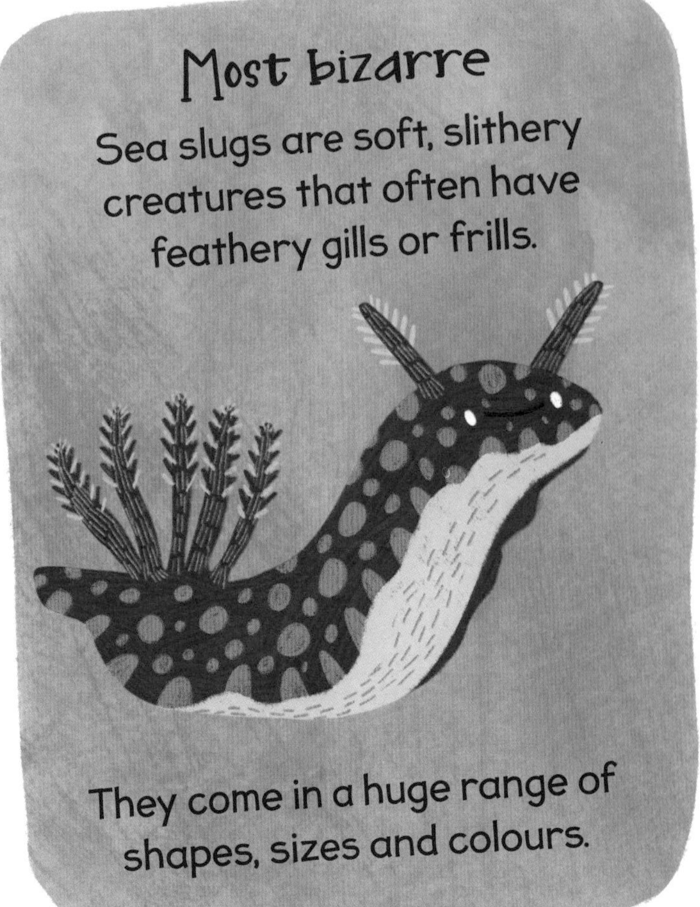

They come in a huge range of shapes, sizes and colours.

Can reefs live forever?

As long as new coral polyps keep building them, reefs can go on for thousands of years. But, if the polyps die, the reef dies, too.

Dirty, polluted water and seas heating up due to climate change stress polyps out!
When a reef turns white, we say it has been 'bleached'.
Crown of thorns starfish
I love to munch on coral polyps. A whole bunch of us can kill a reef in a year.

Has it gone white with fright?

When coral is stressed, it throws out the colourful algae living in it and turns white. Without algae making most of its food, the polyp can go hungry and die.

Are humans kind to coral?

Not always. We damage reefs with boats and fishing equipment, and mess up their ecosystems by taking fish and even lumps of coral. Man-made pollution and climate change hurt coral, too.

We grow when the ocean water gets warmer or becomes polluted.
I poo out crunched up coral as sand!
Algae

Does coral have any other problems?

Yes, algae. Not the helpful kind inside a polyp, but unhelpful algae that can grow wild and cover a reef. They block out the sunlight that the coral needs to live.

Some parrotfish munch coral with their strong beaks and teeth, but it's the polyps they're after.

Can coral just move house?

Not on its own. But we can help by moving coral to a new frame somewhere safe so it can start building a new reef.

We live on an old tank!

All kinds of things have been placed on the seabed to make new reefs.

Do reef creatures help each other?

Sometimes. Some live or work together – it's called mutualism. Algae that live inside a coral polyp make its food and get a home in return. There are other top teams on the reef, too.

Moray eels are kept free from parasites by cleaner shrimps.

And I promise not to eat you!

I get to eat bugs and dead skin. Yum!

Moray eel

Cleaner shrimp

Clownfish are protected by anemones and help find them food in return.

My stinging tentacles keep fierce fish away from the clownfish.

Anemone

Clownfish

I catch food and share it with the anemone. Its tentacles don't hurt me.

Who carries someone else as a weapon?

The pom-pom crab carries two anemones in its claws and uses them to sting animals it wants to eat! The anemones don't mind as they get lots of food from the sea around them.

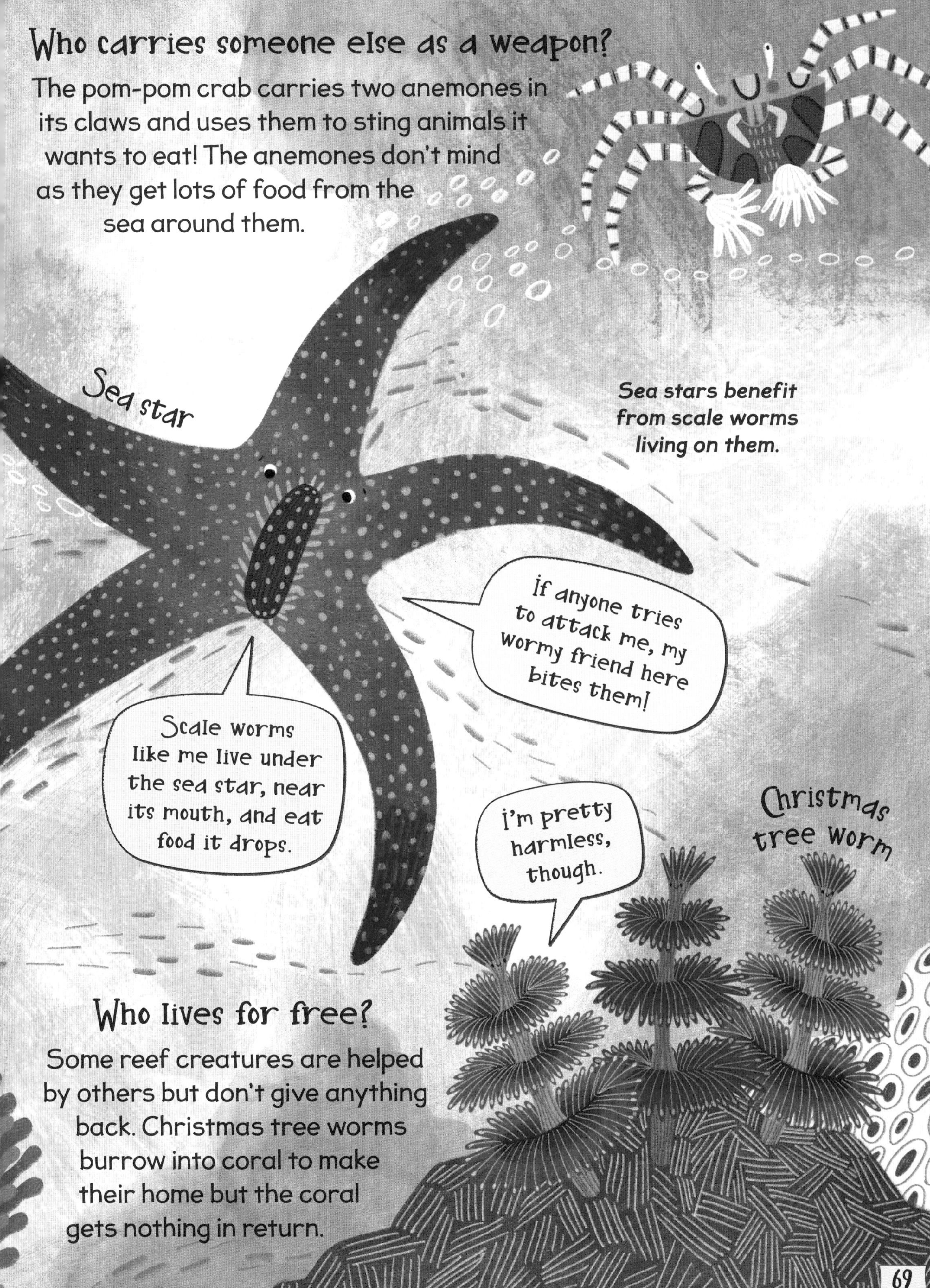

Sea star
Sea stars benefit from scale worms living on them.
If anyone tries to attack me, my wormy friend here bites them!
Scale worms like me live under the sea star, near its mouth, and eat food it drops.
I'm pretty harmless, though.
Christmas tree worm

Who lives for free?

Some reef creatures are helped by others but don't give anything back. Christmas tree worms burrow into coral to make their home but the coral gets nothing in return.

A compendium of questions

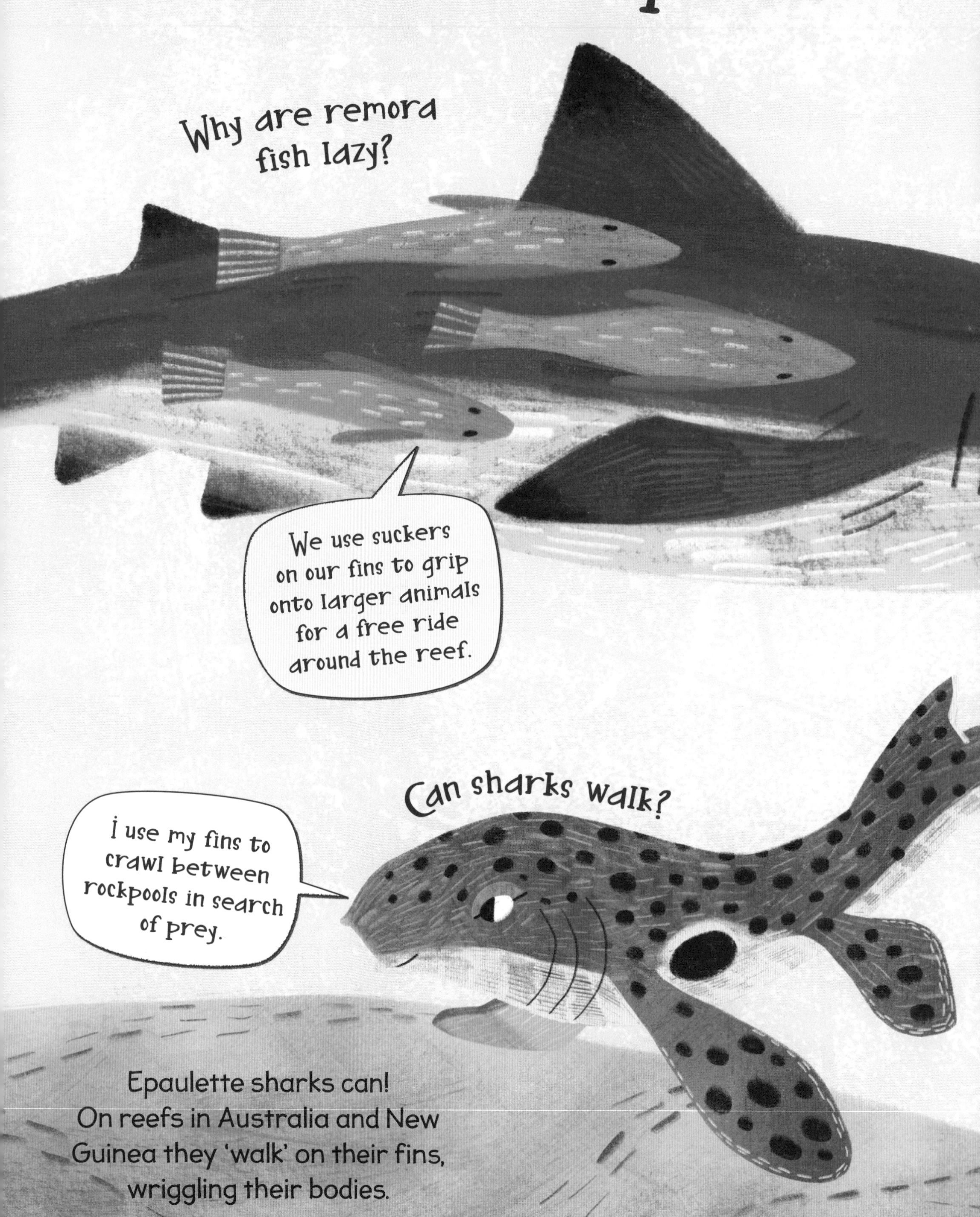

Why are remora fish lazy?
We use suckers on our fins to grip onto larger animals for a free ride around the reef.
Can sharks walk?
I use my fins to crawl between rockpools in search of prey.

Epaulette sharks can! On reefs in Australia and New Guinea they 'walk' on their fins, wriggling their bodies.

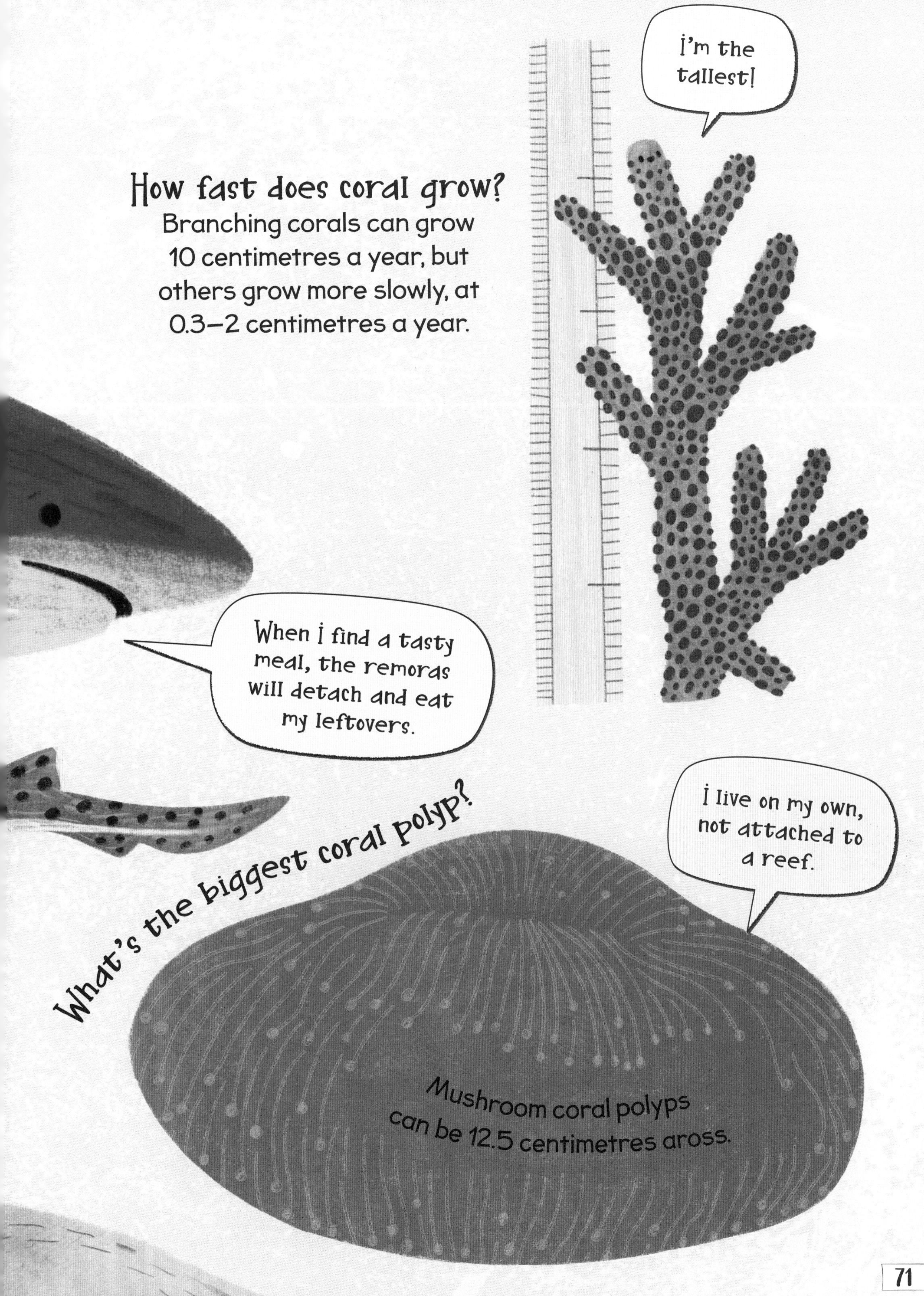
I'm the tallest!
How fast does coral grow?
Branching corals can grow 10 centimetres a year, but others grow more slowly, at 0.3–2 centimetres a year.
When I find a tasty meal, the remoras will detach and eat my leftovers.
I live on my own, not attached to a reef.
What's the biggest coral polyp?
Mushroom coral polyps can be 12.5 centimetres aross.

Which turtle is a friend to coral?

The endangered hawksbill turtle loves to eat sea sponges that compete with coral for space on the reef. Without them, the sponges could take over!

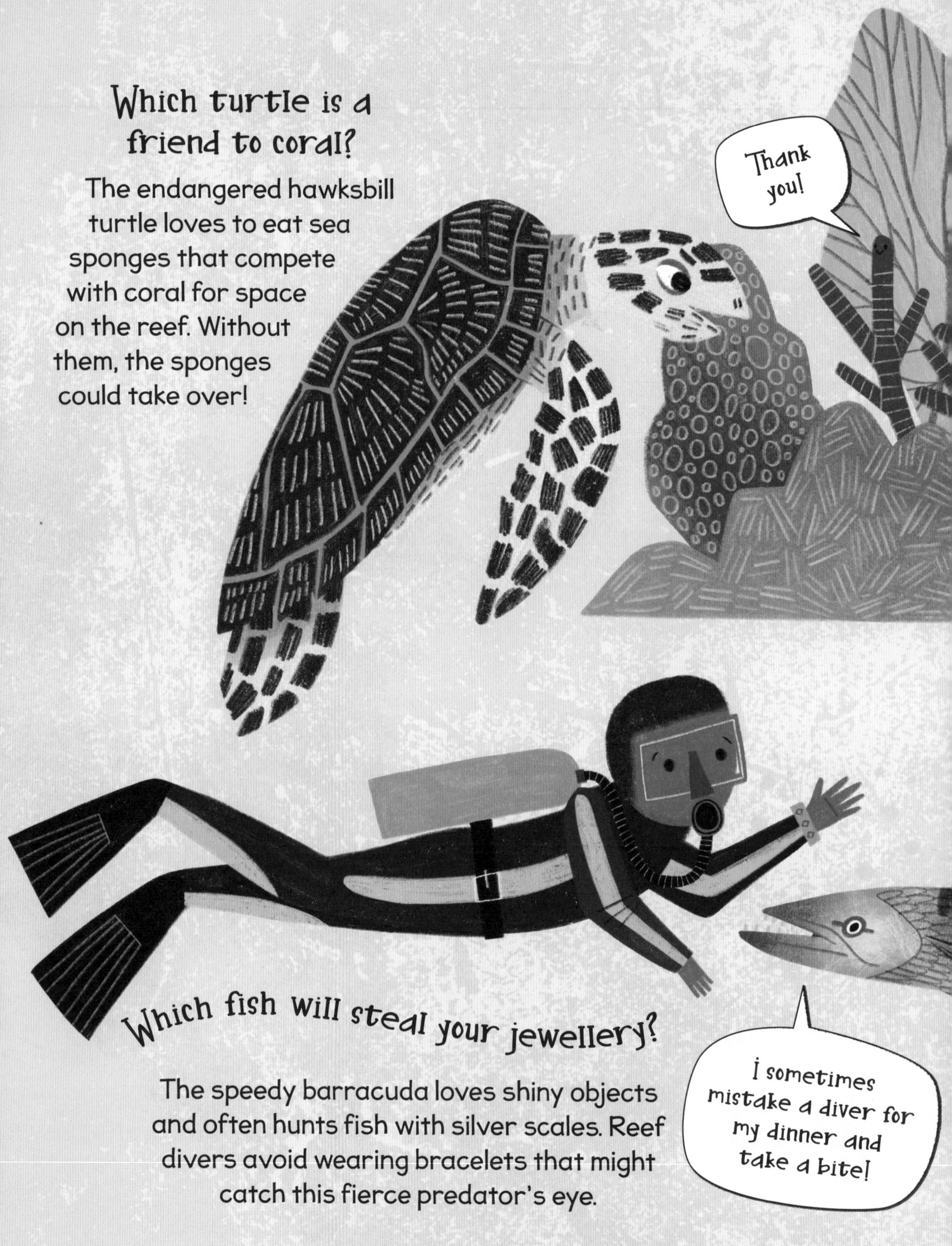

Thank you!
I sometimes mistake a diver for my dinner and take a bite!

Which fish will steal your jewellery?

The speedy barracuda loves shiny objects and often hunts fish with silver scales. Reef divers avoid wearing bracelets that might catch this fierce predator's eye.

Potato cod
Thank you so much – i'll be back next week!
i swallow water to inflate my body when i need to. It's a useful trick!

Which fish dance for their supper?

Wrasse fish dance to attract bigger fish to their 'cleaning stations' on the reef, where they gobble up yummy parasites on the bigger fish.

Which fish blows up like a balloon?

A porcupine fish inflates like a spiky balloon if it is surprised or frightened. This makes it hard to swallow, so predators give up.

Do you prefer winter or summer?
What's your favourite flavour of ice cream?
If you were a polar scientist, would you rather study animals or weather?

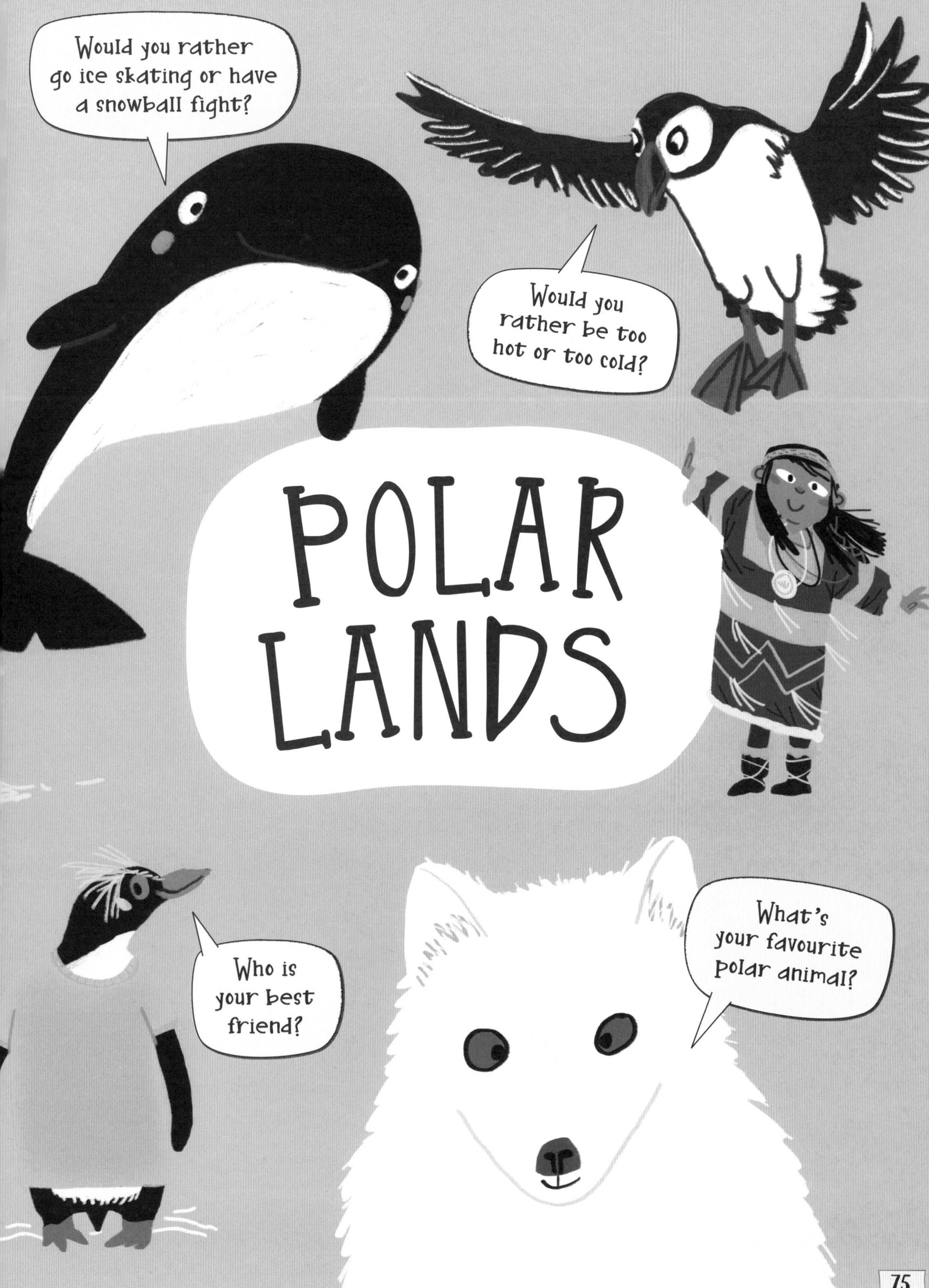
Would you rather go ice skating or have a snowball fight?
Would you rather be too hot or too cold?
POLAR LANDS
Who is your best friend?
What's your favourite polar animal?

How do i get to the polar lands?

Head north, to the icy Arctic around the Earth's North Pole, or travel south to the freezing Antarctic, at the Earth's South Pole.

Welcome to the Arctic!
Polar bear
Sunlight strikes the Earth at a slant near the Poles.
Narwhal
Sun
Sunlight strikes the Earth's surface most directly in the tropical regions north and south of the Equator.
Hello, i'm Earth. i'm tilted at an angle so my top and bottom (my polar regions) don't get the Sun's direct rays.
Sunlight strikes the Earth at a slant near the Poles.
Leopard seal

Beluga whale
The Arctic is a mostly frozen ocean surrounded by icy lands called the tundra.
Arctic wolf
Musk ox
Equator
South polar skua
The Antarctic includes a frozen continent called Antarctica, several islands, and the wild and stormy Southern Ocean.
Adélie penguin
The polar lands are the coldest, iciest places on Earth. I'm an orca, and my thick layer of blubber (fat) keeps me warm.
Welcome to the Antarctic!

What's under the Arctic ice?

Water! It's so cold, the top part of the sea surrounding the North Pole is always frozen into a huge, floating mass of ice.

Can you drink melted Antarctic ice?

Yes! The ice covering Antarctica is made from fallen snow, not salty seawater – but you have to melt it first!

Why are the Poles so cold?

Polar lands don't get direct light and heat from the Sun like other places on Earth. This means they never get warm enough for all their ice to melt.

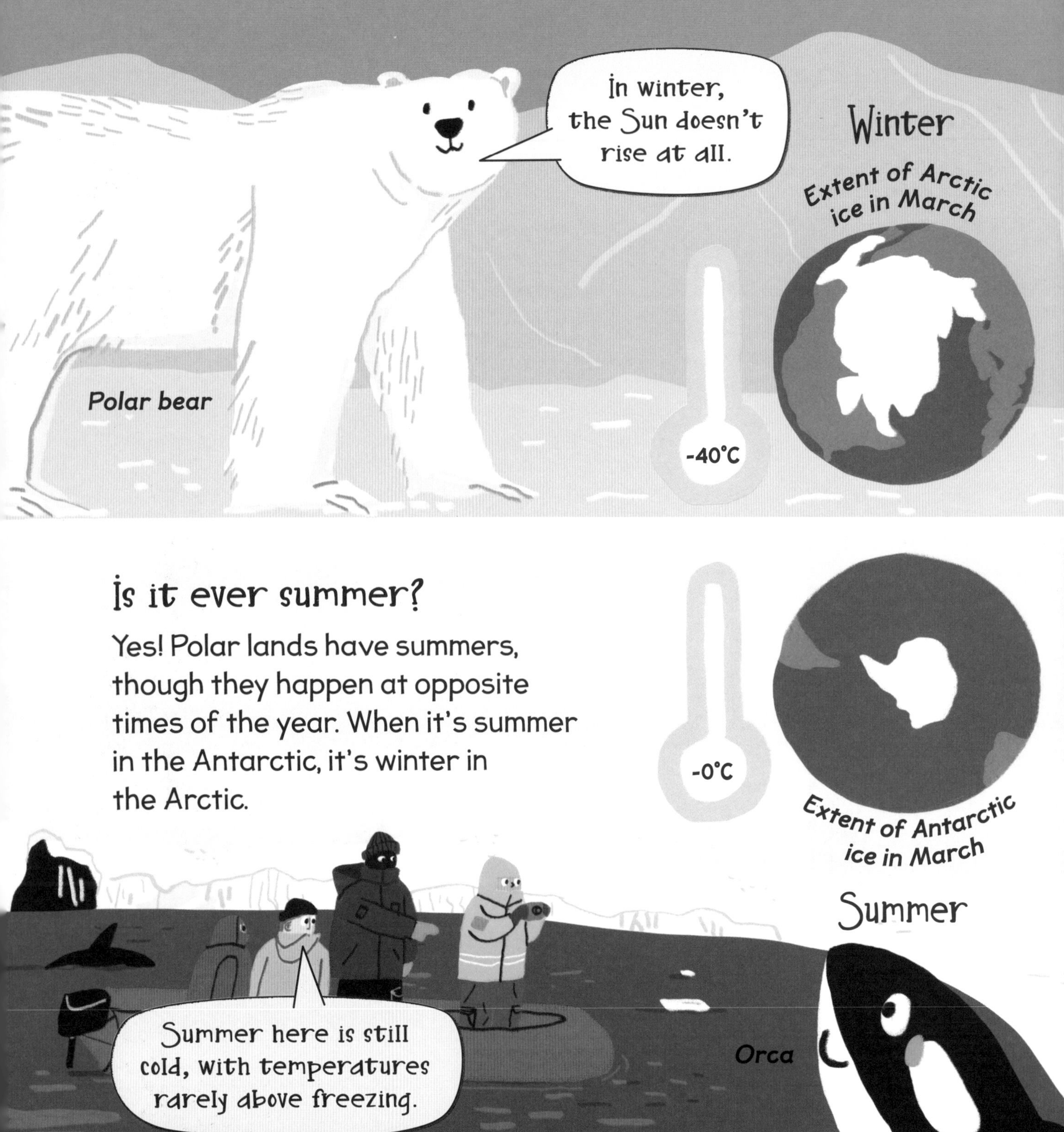

Is it ever summer?

Yes! Polar lands have summers, though they happen at opposite times of the year. When it's summer in the Antarctic, it's winter in the Arctic.

What is the midnight Sun?

During the Poles' short summers, the Sun does not set, so it's light all day and all night. This is called the midnight Sun.

We are snow geese. Like many animals, we return to the Arctic in spring, when some of the ice melts, to raise our young.

Summer
Extent of Arctic ice in September
13°C
Reindeer
NORTH POLE

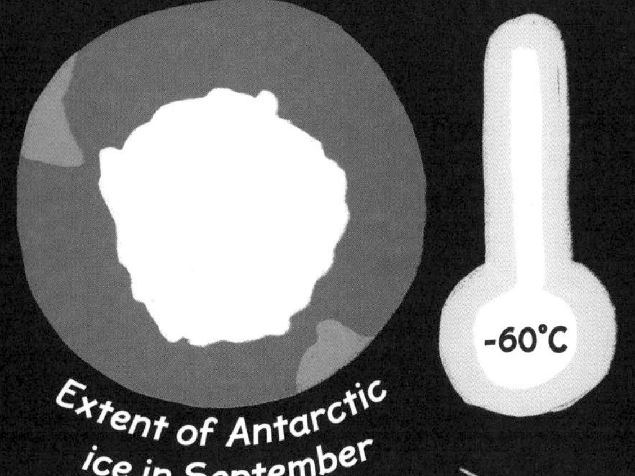

Which Pole is the coldest?

The South Pole is the coldest. In the Antarctic winter, the temperature drops to -60°C. That's three times colder than your freezer!

-60°C
Extent of Antarctic ice in September
SOUTH POLE
Winter
Emperor penguins
Winds rage and blow and it's dark for most of the day and night. We're huddling together to keep warm!

Are there people near the Poles?

Yes – people settled in the Arctic thousands of years ago. They include the Saami of northern Scandinavia, the Aleut of Alaska and the Inuit of Canada, Alaska and Greenland.

If we are a long way from home, a few Inuit hunters still build a shelter called an igloo from slabs of ice and loose snow.

Igloo

Inuit

I'm wearing traditional Aleut clothes, which are made from sealskin and fur.

Aleut

Some Saami still travel across the snow on sleds pulled by reindeer.

Saami

I'm the captain of an ice-breaker ship. Icebreakers smash through sea ice, clearing the way for other ships to follow close behind.
Does anyone live at the South Pole?
Yes. Scientists live on research stations in Antarctica. Most scientists usually stay for only a few months each year, and leave during the freezing, dark Antarctic winter.
Meteorologists, like me, study the weather.
I'm a geologist. I'm studying long cores (tubes) of ice to learn about Earth's past climate.
I'm a biologist. I study animals, like these penguins!

Did you know?

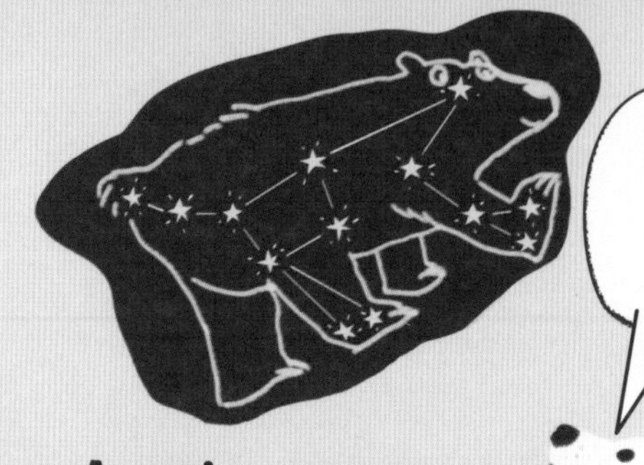

I thought it was named after ME!

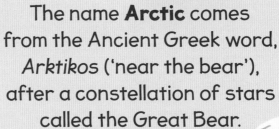

A baby puffin is called a **puffling**.

The name **Arctic** comes from the Ancient Greek word, *Arktikos* ('near the bear'), after a constellation of stars called the Great Bear.

If a male grizzly bear and a female polar bear have a cub together, it is called a **pizzly bear** or a **grolar bear**.

Giant petrels are nicknamed **stinkers** because they smell so bad!

A male elephant seal can inflate its bulbous nose like a **balloon**. This makes its grunts and bellows REALLY loud!

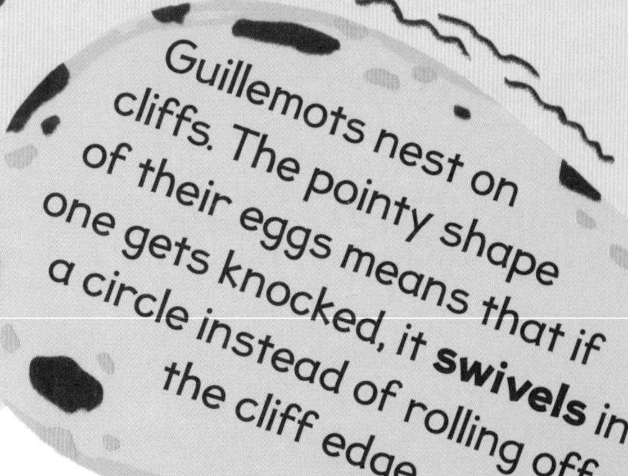

Guillemots nest on cliffs. The pointy shape of their eggs means that if one gets knocked, it **swivels** in a circle instead of rolling off the cliff edge.

A narwhal's **spiral tooth** can grow to 3 metres in length! People sold them long ago, pretending they were **unicorn horns**.

The biggest part of an iceberg lies **below** the water's surface.

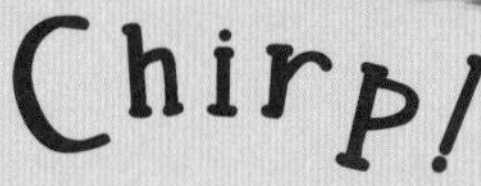

Beluga whales are sometimes called 'sea canaries' because they like to **chirp**, **whistle** and '**sing**'.

Greenland isn't **green**. Over 80 percent of the island is covered in a thick, white ice sheet.

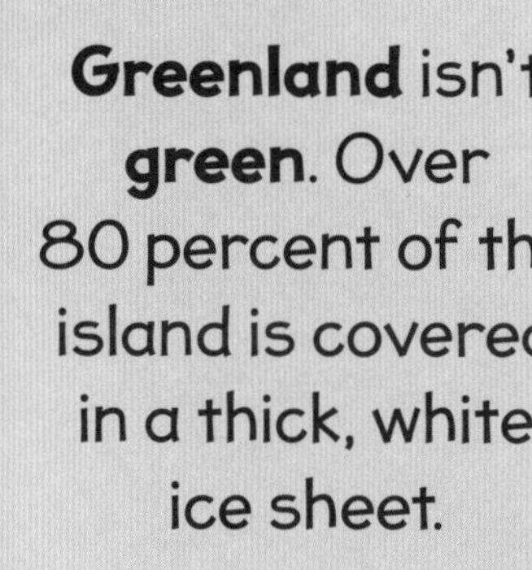

Polar bears keep their **eyes open** when swimming (though they do close their nostrils!).

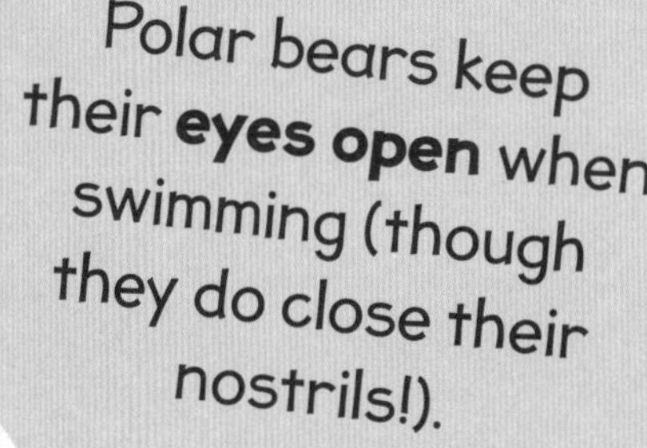

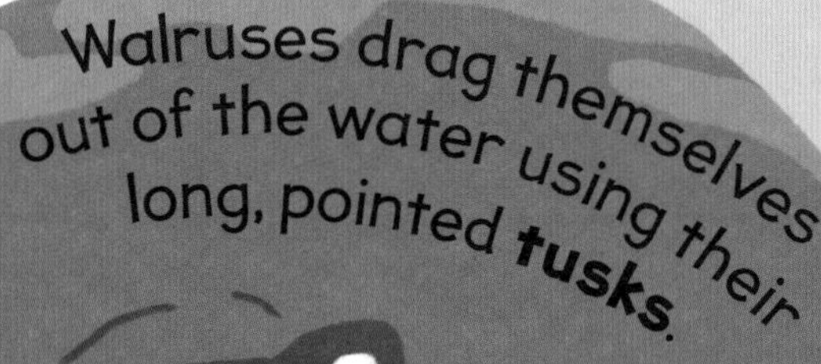

Walruses drag themselves out of the water using their long, pointed **tusks**.

What is a glacier?

A glacier is a huge river of slow-moving ice that creeps outwards or flows downhill over land until it reaches the sea.

①

1 Glaciers form when snow falls and doesn't melt. If this happens over many years, the snow is squashed down into ice. Then what happens?

②

2 The ice builds up, layer by layer, until it's so heavy it starts to move.

How thick is Antarctic ice?

It's mostly 2 kilometres thick but in some places it's much deeper. The ice sheet has built up in layers over thousands of years.

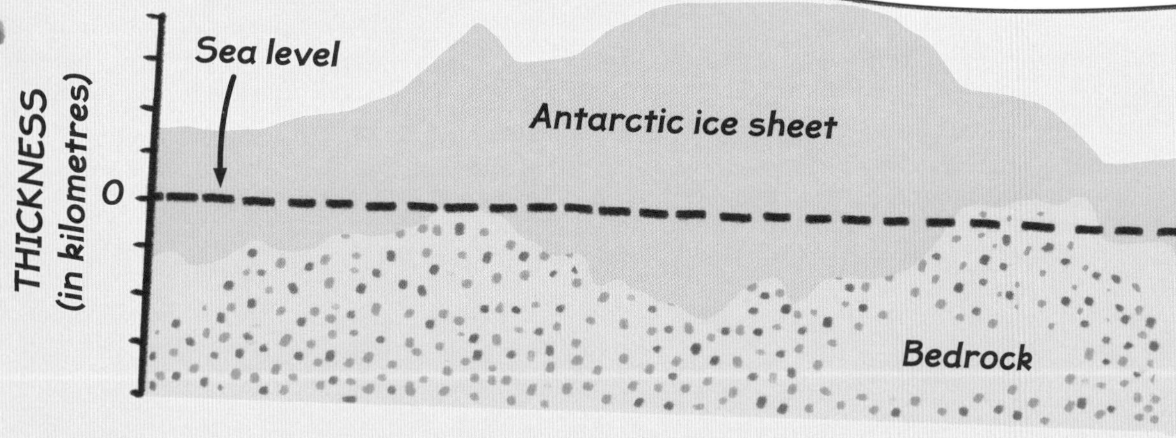

How are icebergs made?

Icebergs are giant slabs of ice that break off the edge of an ice sheet or glacier and float out to sea.

Some icebergs have jagged edges. Others are worn smooth by the waves.

Why are some icebergs blue?

Because they're old! Over time, tiny air bubbles inside, which made them look white, get squashed out and they look blue.

POLAR NEWS

ARE THE POLES IN PERIL?

YES! These special places are facing many challenges. It is important we protect our polar regions because they are home to many animals. Their ice also reflects the Sun's light and heat, helping to keep our planet cool.

Long pipelines carrying oil from Arctic oil fields sometimes leak. The oil can harm or even kill wildlife.

Mining for minerals (such as copper and iron ore) in the Arctic causes air and land pollution.

Some countries want to mine for minerals and oil in the Antarctic, too.

Luckily, the Antarctic is protected by the Antarctic Treaty, to keep it safe.

"Animals like me don't have enough ice on which to hunt!"
Mr P. Bear, Greenland

The Earth's **climate** is **getting warmer**, so the ice at the Poles melts earlier and freezes later each year.

"Stop polluting our home!"
Ms Chinstrap, Antarctica

Animals sometimes get tangled in **plastic pollution** floating in the polar oceans. Fish, seabirds and other wildlife are also harmed when they swallow tiny bits of plastic.

More and more tourists want to visit Earth's polar lands to see the wildlife. **Waste and litter** from tourist ships can pollute the landscape.

Who flies the farthest?

The Arctic tern migrates north for the Arctic summer, then flies all the way around the world to spend summer in the Antarctic. That's a round trip of up to 40,000 kilometres every year!

Why are reindeer always on the move?

Huge reindeer herds migrate north each year, to feed on the tundra during the Arctic summer. They head south again in Autumn, when the weather turns colder.

Who sings as they swim?

Humpback whales sing to each other as they migrate to and from their summer feeding grounds in the polar oceans. The whales may sing the same song together for several hours.

Humpback whale

Arctic terns
We can sleep when we're gliding!
ZZZZZZ
We tuck in our feet to make us more streamlined as we fly.
Reindeer
I have sharp hooves to scrape away ice and snow and reach the tasty lichen growing underneath. Yum!
Lots of animals migrate to polar lands for the summer, when some of the ice melts.
It makes my skin feel lovely and clean!
Beluga whale

Who likes a skin scrub?

Beluga whales love a spa treatment skin scrub! In Autumn, they swim to shallow, ice-free river mouths in the Canadian Arctic and scrub their bodies clean along the gravelly seabed.

Who wears two coats to keep out the cold?

The musk ox has a layer of soft wool growing close to its skin AND a really long shaggy outer coat to keep it warm in the icy Arctic.

Musk ox

Snowy owl

Who has very hairy ears?

The Arctic fox's small, round ears are hairy inside as well as out, to keep it nice and warm.

Lots of polar animals have extra hair or thick fur to keep warm. My outer coat can grow to one metre in length!

Arctic fox

I have thick, warm feathers all over my feet. I have a feathery beak, too!
Harp seal
Blubber is also a store of energy when I can't find enough to eat. It helps me float, too!
I may freeze and thaw seven times before I change into a moth!
Woolly bear moth

What is blubber?

Blubber is a thick layer of fat growing under an animal's skin. It keeps the animal warm in the freezing polar oceans.

Who turns into an icicle in winter?

The caterpillar of the Arctic woolly bear moth freezes in winter. It thaws out during the summer, to feed and grow.

How many?

There are more of us than any other seal!

20 million

The world's population of crabeater seals.

A snowy owl might feed her chicks more than **1000** lemmings in one summer!

6

The number of branches on every single snowflake. No two have ever been found the same.

A Weddell seal's breathing hole through thick Antarctic ice may be **2** metres deep.

A moose's antlers can grow **2** centimetres in a single day!

12

The number of countries signing the Antarctic Treaty (a promise to protect the Antarctic) in 1959.

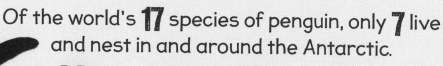

Of the world's **17** species of penguin, only **7** live and nest in and around the Antarctic.

Emperor King Gentoo Macaroni Adélie Chinstrap Rockhopper

Greenland sharks can live for more than **270** years!

The wingspan of a fully grown wandering albatross is **3.5** metres.

Caribou make the longest land migration on Earth each year!

9000 kilometres

-89.2°C

The coldest temperature ever recorded, at Vostok Station in Antarctica, in 1983.

60

The amount, in metres, that global sea levels would rise if the Antarctic ice sheet melted.

Who turns white in winter?

Some Arctic animals do! Their grey or brown fur or speckled feathers turn white, to camouflage them against the ice and snow. A white coat hides an animal from predators – and hides predators out hunting prey!

My white fur helps me sneak up on my prey in the snow!

Arctic fox

Are white coats warm?

Yes! White fur is made up of hollow hairs. The hairs trap heat near an animal's skin, helping to keep it warm.

Arctic hare

Collared lemming

My winter coat is silvery grey!

Weasel

Only the tip of my tail stays black in winter!

Who keeps their white coat all year?

Polar bears and some Arctic wolves! They live in the far North, which is covered in snow and ice for most of the year.

A polar bear has creamy white outer fur, made up of hollow guard hairs (1) and dense underfur (2). Beneath the fur, its skin is black (3).

What happens in summer?

In summer, when the snow melts, many animals shed their white winter fur and feathers.

My summer coat is half as thick as my winter coat!
Our summer fur is dusty brown or grey-brown, so we can hide among the rocks and plants!

Who grows up fast?

A ringed seal pup guzzles so much of its mother's rich, fatty milk, it doubles in size in just a few days.

My pup stays with me for about six weeks, learning how to hunt and dive.

My mum teaches me to watch out for predators, like walruses and polar bears.

Who is born on the move?

Reindeer babies! The calves must run to keep up with their migrating herd when they're just one or two days old.

I'm coming!

3. The females return 10 days after the eggs hatch
Right, it's your turn to look after our chick. I'm off to hunt some fish! See you soon!
2. A flap of skin provides warmth
1. The egg is balanced on top of the male's feet
I teach my pup how to root for food on the ocean floor.
The walrus squirts jets of water from her mouth to dig up shellfish, sea snails and shrimps.

Who's the best dad?

The prize for the best polar dad goes to the emperor penguin, who spends around two months without food, in the freezing winter darkness, looking after the egg laid by his mate.

Who's a good mum?

Walrus mums take good care of their pups for two years, until the pups can look after themselves.

Would you rather?

Swim like a penguin or **soar** like an albatross?
We can't fly but we're GREAT at swimming, surfing and diving.
Be friends with an **Arctic fox**...
...or an **Arctic hare**?
Live on a crowded cliff face, like a **guillemot**, or have your own nest, like an **albatross chick**?
Have **horns** like a musk ox, or **antlers** like a moose?
I grow a new pair every year!

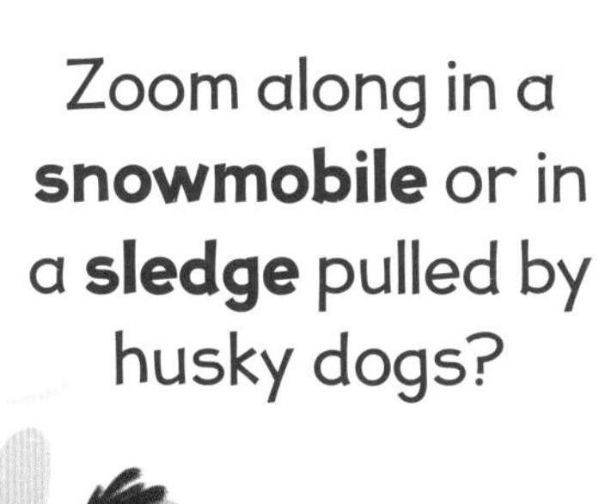

Zoom along in a **snowmobile** or in a **sledge** pulled by husky dogs?

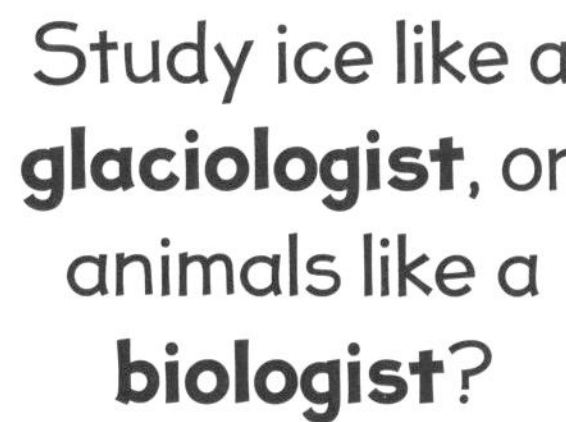

Study ice like a **glaciologist**, or animals like a **biologist**?

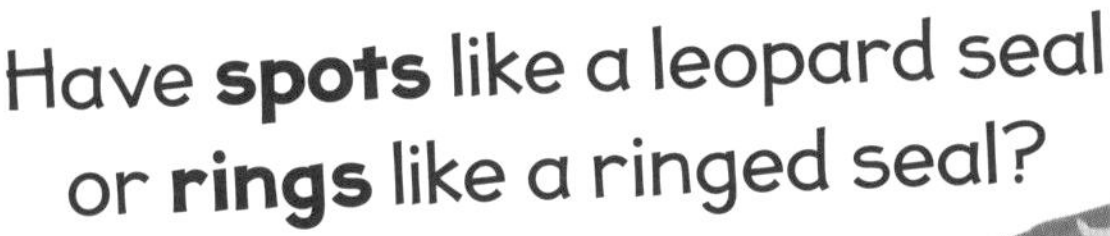

Have **spots** like a leopard seal or **rings** like a ringed seal?

You're a hungry snowy sheathbill. Would you rather eat **penguin sick** or **seal poo**?

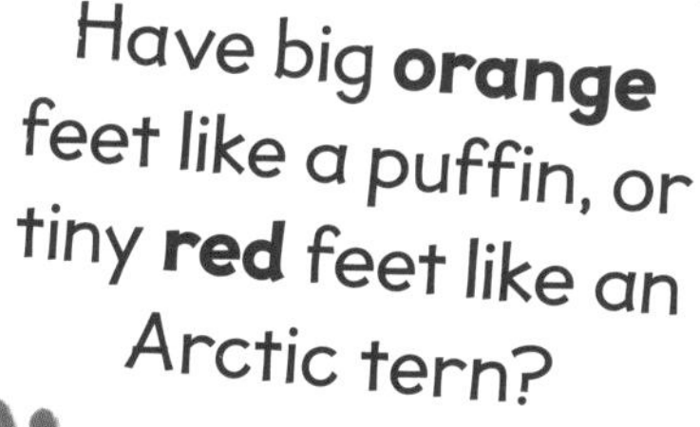

Have big **orange** feet like a puffin, or tiny **red** feet like an Arctic tern?

I'm a scavenger, so I'll eat either – or both!

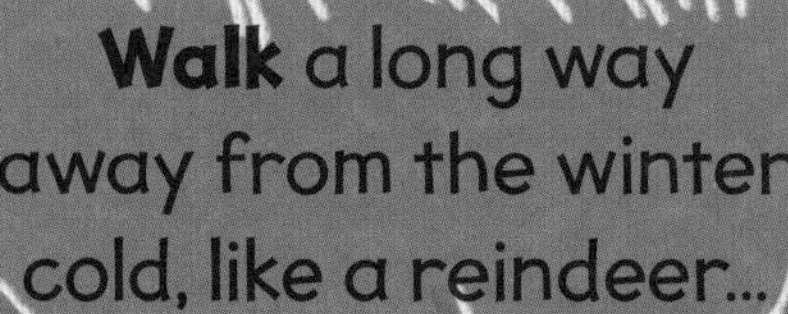

Walk a long way away from the winter cold, like a reindeer...

...or **huddle** in a snow tunnel like a lemming?

What do penguins eat?

Penguins love fish, squid and tiny, shrimp-like krill. Food is scarce in the polar lands. Animals need to eat as much as possible during the summer to build up a store of fat, to last them through the winter months.

Gentoo penguins
Krill
Krill like me are only as long as your finger but we live in such huge swarms, we turn the sea pink!

Leopard seal
Who hunts alone?
Fierce leopard seals chase after penguins and grab them off the ice! They also hunt smaller seals, squid and seabirds.
Musk ox
Arctic wolves
We form a line or a circle with our horns pointing out, to protect our babies.
Who hunts in a pack?
Arctic wolves hunt together. That way, they can bring down a much larger animal, such as a musk ox or a reindeer.

A compendium of questions

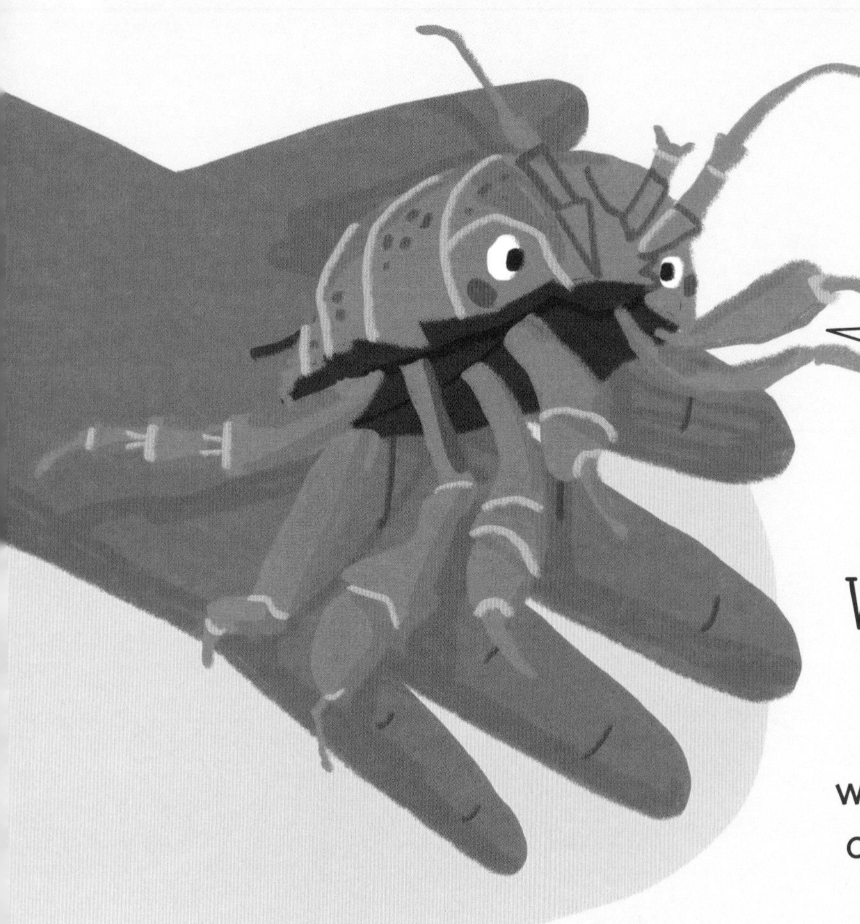

I have four antennae (feelers) to help me find my way in the gloomy ocean depths.

Which sea creature looks like a giant woodlouse?

An isopod looks a bit like a woodlouse, but it's as big as your outstretched hand! Isopods live on the Antarctic seabed.

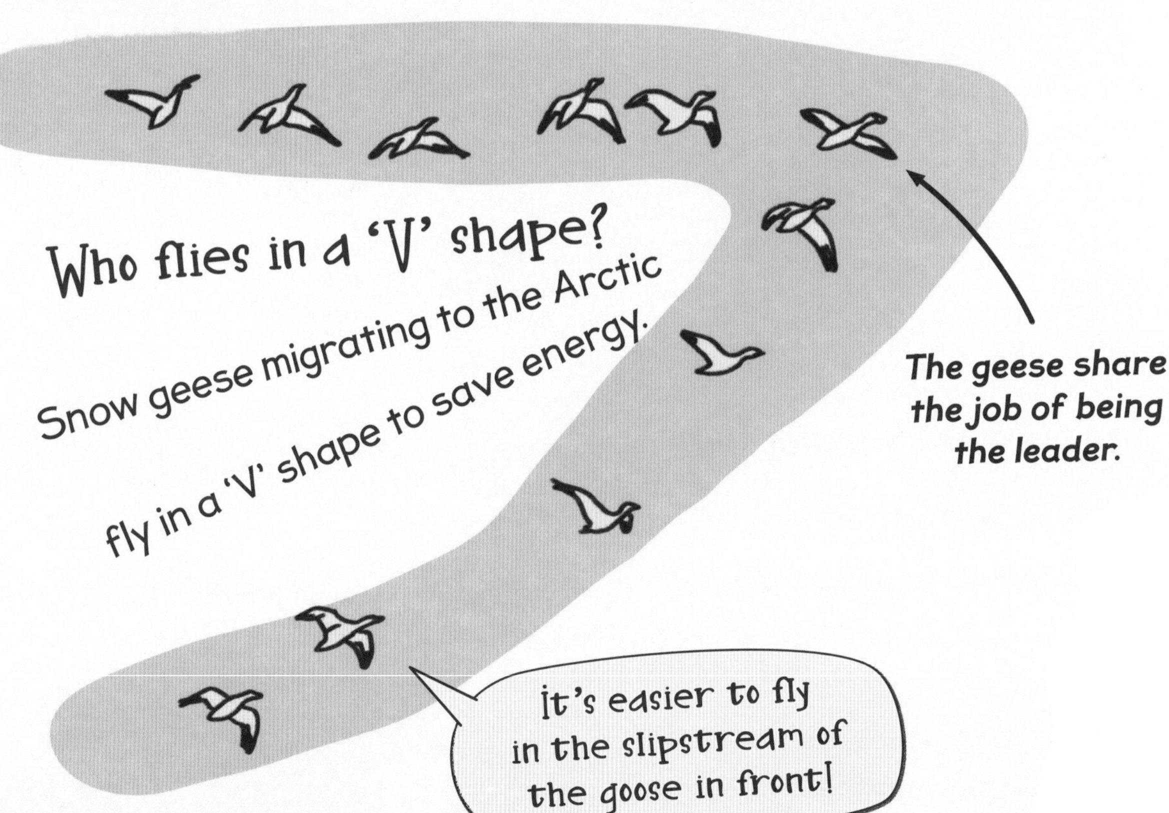

The geese share the job of being the leader.
It's easier to fly in the slipstream of the goose in front!

Who flies in a 'V' shape?

Snow geese migrating to the Arctic fly in a 'V' shape to save energy.

I'm protecting my chick from predators!

Why shouldn't you get close to a snow petrel?

It may squirt a stream of sticky, smelly sick at you to warn you away from its nest!

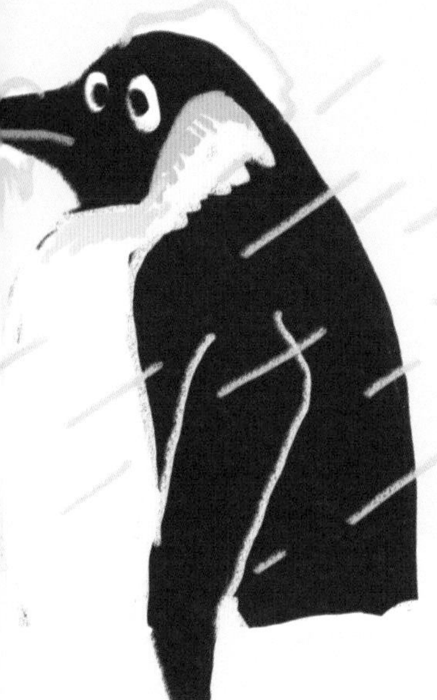

It doesn't mean I'm friendly! I'm a fierce predator.

Who has a big cheesy grin?

The sides of a leopard seal's mouth curve upwards, so it always looks like it's smiling.

Whose home is colder than a polar bear's?

An emperor penguin's! The average winter temperature at the South Pole is -60°C. Winter at the North Pole is a mere -40°C!

Which birds are pirates?

Skuas are sometimes called pirate birds because they steal most of their food from other birds.

Why don't polar fish freeze?

Some fish living in polar waters have a kind of antifreeze in their blood so they don't turn to ice in polar seas.

NORTH POLE

Why does a walrus have whiskers?

To help it feel its way along the dark seabed when searching for shellfish and other food.

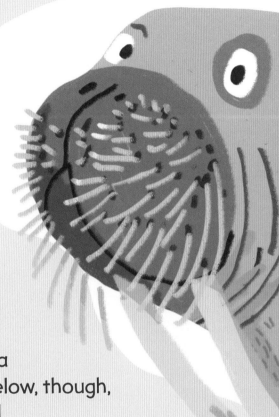

Where do i put this?

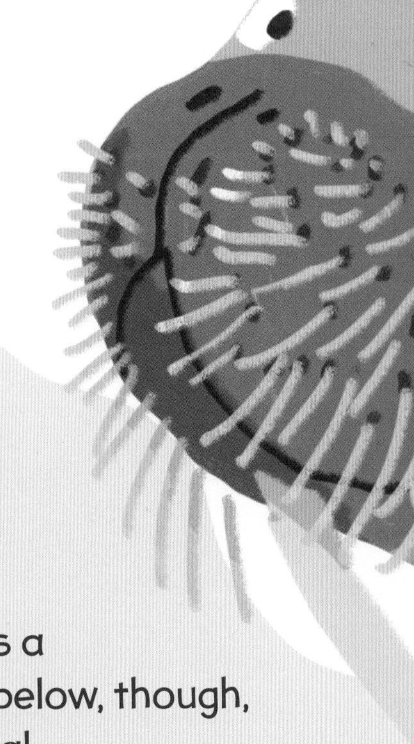

Is there a marker at the North Pole?

No, because the ice is always moving. There is a marker on the seabed below, though, made of rustproof metal.

Who raced to the South Pole?

Two expeditions – Roald Amundsen's team arrived first in December, 1911. Robert Scott's team got there a month later, but died on the return journey.

What's your favourite rainforest animal?
Do you prefer dancing or running around?
What is the best thing about where you live?

RAINFORESTS

What is a rainforest?

It's a MASSIVE crowd of trees and animals all living together! And it's very, very wet and usually hot. The rainforest is teeming with life.

We spend most of our time in trees and build big nests in the branches to sleep in.

Malayan tapirs

Orangutans

How much does it rain?

A lot! Most rainforests get at least two metres of rain a year. Water drips from all the leaves, high up and low down. The hot, wet air makes you feel sticky.

Like many rainforest animals, we are at risk of extinction (dying out) and need protection.

When i'm a baby i'm stripy to help me hide from predators.

Sometimes i use a large leaf as an umbrella!

Epiphyte
Fire-tufted barbet
Hornbill
Most bird species in the rainforests aren't found anywhere else in the world.
Sumatran tiger
Sumatran elephant

Is it all just trees?

No – there are lots of different kinds of plants packed into a rainforest, from soaring trees to tiny mosses. Some plants, such as epiphytes, even grow on others.

Do lots of animals live there?

Yes! Rainforests have the greatest variety of living things of any places on Earth, from tiny insects to bigger animals such as tigers and elephants.

Are there rivers in a rainforest?

Many rainforests have lots of rivers, fed by all the rain. The rivers of the Amazon rainforest contain a fifth of all the world's fresh water.

Where are the rainforests?

Rainforests grow where there is plenty of rain, all year. Many lie in a region called the tropics where it's hot and sunny as well as wet.

Mountain gorillas

Elk

Elk like me are large deer that live in temperate rainforests in North America.

Temperate rainforests have huge evergreen trees. Some have bears, mountain lions and elk.

Are there different types?

Yes. As well as hot **tropical rainforests**, there are **temperate rainforests** in cooler rainy areas and misty **cloud forests** in the mountains.

The cloud forests of Africa are our home. We live in family groups and eat plants and insects.
Asia
Oceania
frica
We live in Madagascar.
We like sunbathing in the morning to warm up after the cool night.
Ring-tailed lemurs

Can a forest grow in the clouds?

Yes! Cloud forests grow on mountains where air carrying moisture cools. Tiny water droplets form, making clouds at the level of the treetops.

Do the same animals live in each one?

Not at all. Most rainforests have a lot of species (kinds of plant or animal) found nowhere else, such as the lemurs of Madagascar.

Did you know?

HISS!

The enormous **atlas moth** has a wingspan of 30 centimetres. Its wing tips look like the head of a snake to ward off predators.

Piranhas are fierce fish of the Amazon that can make a barking sound and gnash their teeth.

WOOF!

The **hoatzin** bird of South America is also called the stink bird because its whole body smells like manure.

Bromeliad plants store their own water. Rain collects in the middle of the plant. A large bromeliad can hold up to 8 litres of water.

The Amazon's **anaconda** is the biggest snake in the world. It can be over 5 metres long and weigh almost 100 kilograms.
A **jaguar** can bite through the skull of a crocodile or the shell of a turtle. It likes to swim, so nowhere is safe!
Green iguanas can run up to 34 kilometres per hour!
Leafcutter ants are some of the strongest creatures on Earth.
They can carry leaves 50 times as heavy as themselves!
South American **emerald boas** are born red, yellow or orange and turn green when about a year old.
One **poison dart frog** has enough poison on its skin to kill 10 people.

What is it like in the rainforest?

It's hot and sticky, teeming with life and very green! At ground level, you can hardly see the sky as the millions of plants and trees block out most of the sunlight.

HOWL
SNARL
HOOT
GROW
I need to sleep in the day – but it's so noisy!
Bushbaby

What can you hear?

There are strange noises coming from every corner with chattering and chirping, howls, hoots, growls and hisses. You can hear the patter of rain, the rustling of leaves and animals' footsteps.

I feed on fruit and sugary tree sap and grow up to 11 centimetres long!
Goliath beetle

Chimpanzee
How does the forest pack in so many plants?
Many plants grow on top of others. Vines called lianas grow up and around tall trees and epiphytes grow on branches and in cracks.
We chimps use the rainforest's hanging vines to swing from tree to tree.
Grey parrot
The air is hot and still all the time. Wind doesn't reach the ground.
Hiss
African bush viper
Is it crowded?
Plants block every step of the way. Although trees don't have branches low down, fallen branches, dead leaves, bushes, ferns, vines and tree roots cover most of the ground.

Is it all a big tangle?

No. Rainforests have four layers. At the top is the overstorey, followed by the canopy, full of trees and vines. The understorey grows around the giant tree trunks, and the forest floor is where the plants are rooted.

Harpy eagle
I perch at the tops of trees looking for animals to eat.
The overstorey is windy, with more direct sunlight and rain than lower down.
Scarlet macaw
I eat seeds and fruit in the treetops.
The canopy is a continuous blanket of tall trees all fighting for sunlight.
Howler monkey
I make one of the loudest noises of any animal. You can hear me from miles away!
Sloth
I only come down to the forest floor once every week or two to poo.

Which is the busiest layer?

Probably the canopy. About 40 percent of the world's land-based species live here. Some of these animals never visit the ground.

Young trees, shorter trees and shrubs make up the understorey.
My spots help me blend in with the understorey's dappled light.
Jaguar
Blue morpho butterfly
I have a wingspan of up to 20 centimetres.
The forest floor is a mass of rotting plants, fallen trees, ferns and tangled roots.
Poison dart frog
I find plenty of insects to eat down here. The moist air keeps my skin damp.

How many?
11.9 Annual rainfall in metres in the wettest rainforest on Earth, in India. That's 12 times as deep as the shallow end of a swimming pool.
80
Wingbeats per second of the bee hummingbird – the smallest bird in the world.
89.5
Height in metres of the largest tropical tree in the world, a Yellow Meranti in the Malaysian rainforest.
The number of extra plants that can live on a single rainforest tree, making up a third of the tree's weight is
2000
Hey, what's it like up there?

We are actually a species of black bear with a white coat.

100

The approximate number of white 'spirit bears' still living in the Great Bear Rainforest, Canada.

10

The time in minutes it can take a raindrop to fall from the overstorey to the ground as it drips from leaf to leaf.

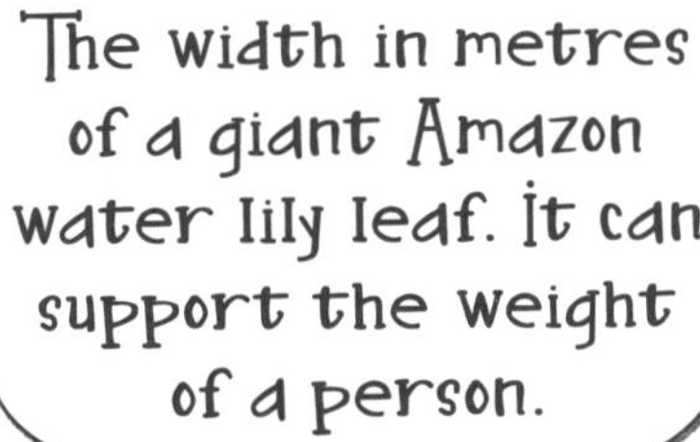

The width in metres of a giant Amazon water lily leaf. It can support the weight of a person.

3

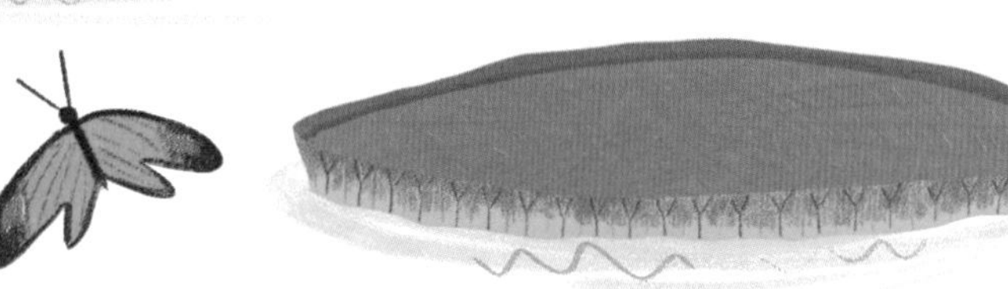

2/3

of all known flowering plants live in rainforests.

1300

The number of different types of butterfly in a single forest park in Peru.

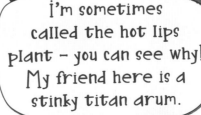

I'm sometimes called the hot lips plant – you can see why! My friend here is a stinky titan arum.

What do the trees eat for dinner?

Trees make their own food by using the energy from sunlight, chemicals in the air, and water. This is called photosynthesis. Tree roots also take chemicals from the soil to help them grow big and strong.

We birds eat insects, grubs, seeds, fruit and nectar.

Sri Lankan blue magpie

Sri Lankan grey hornbill

Purple-faced leaf monkey

Hey, watch out!

Does anything eat the giant trees?

Nothing eats a whole tree! But everything from tiny insects to large animals like monkeys and elephants eat leaves, fruit, seeds and nectar. Many eat tiny plants, too.

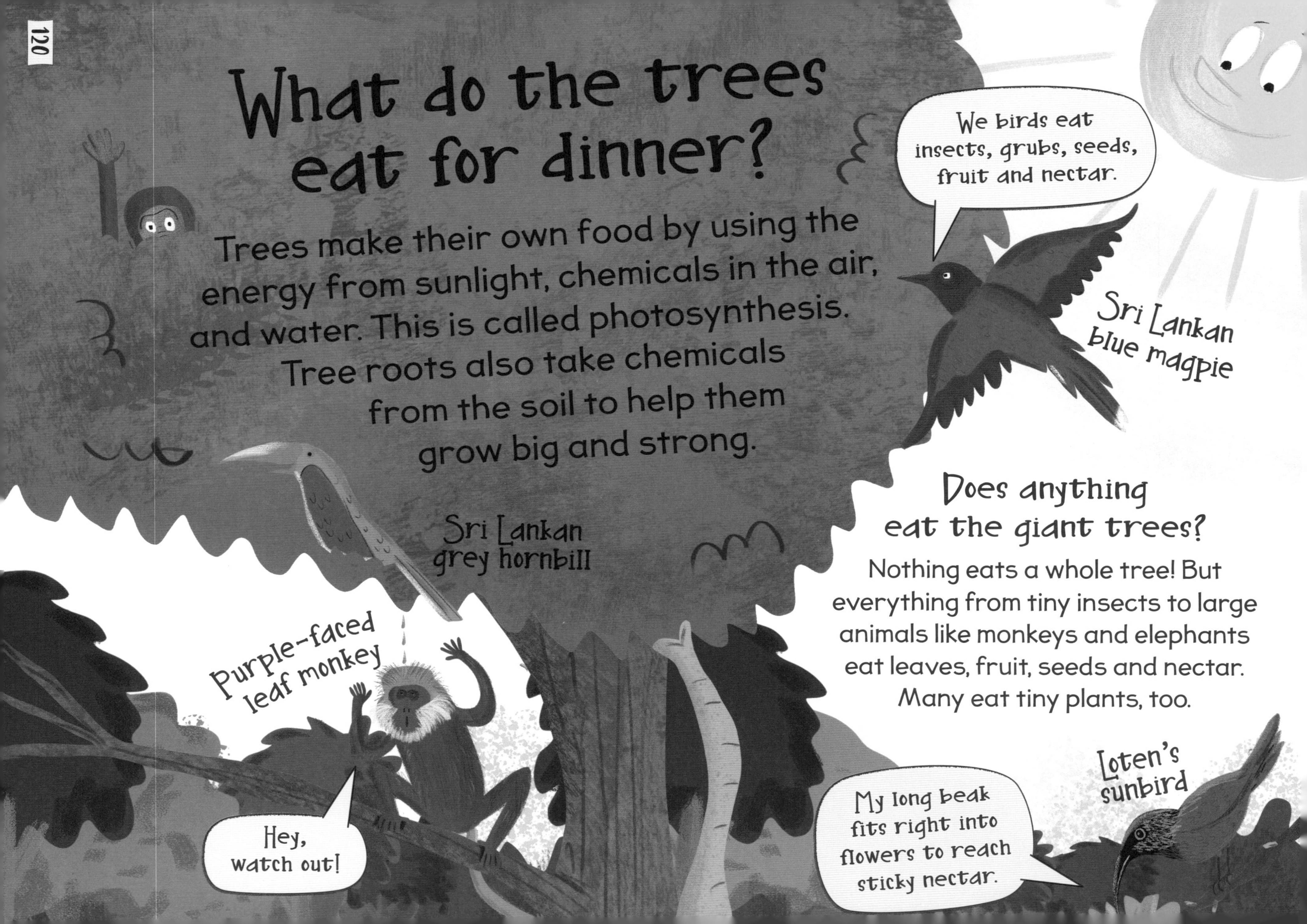

My long beak fits right into flowers to reach sticky nectar.

Loten's sunbird

What eats the animals that eat the trees?

Lots of things – large animals like me are fierce predators, and tiny insects suck the blood of bigger animals, too.
I can eat 100 kilograms of plants every day!
Elephant
Leopard
Beetle
Roots
Poo
Fungus
Worm
The rich soil we make feeds the growing plants.

Where does all the poo go?

There's a lot of poo and other waste in a rainforest! It's all broken down by decomposers – beetles, worms, maggots, fungi and microbes that get to work turning waste into soil.

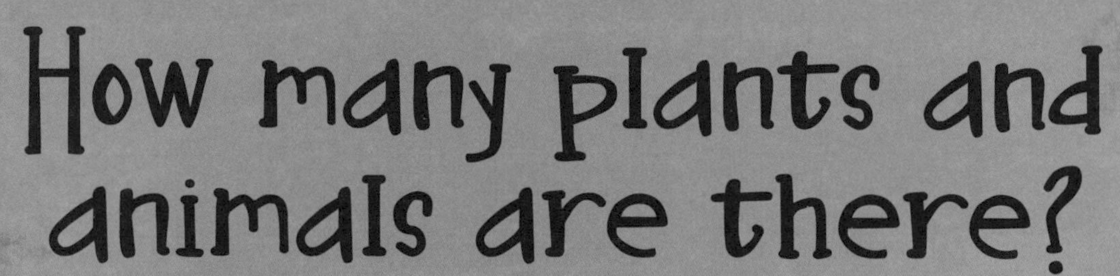

How many plants and animals are there?

A lot! Rainforests have the biggest range of living things on Earth. Although they cover just 6 percent of the land, more than 50 percent of all plant and animal species live here.

Scientists first saw me in 2010...

Fire-tailed titi monkey

...and they first heard me singing my sweet song in 2009.

Chico's tyrannulet

Have we found everything yet?

Not by a long way. Scientists have studied only a small portion of rainforest species. After just one expedition to the Amazon in 2014–15, a total of 381 new species were named.

Are there any dragons?

Yes! Boyd's forest dragons live in Australia's rainforest. They aren't real dragons but are a type of lizard that lives in trees and feasts on rainforest insects.

Boyd's forest dragon
I live in the Daintree and have spines on my legs that can puncture skin!
Spiny leaf insect
Rosy periwinkle

Which is the oldest rainforest?

The Daintree rainforest in Australia is over 100 million years old. It has 3000 species of plant and 12,000 species of insect.

Which plants are the most powerful?

Many rainforest plants help make medicines that fight disease. I'm from Madagascar and contain chemicals that are used in drugs to treat cancer.

What's the weirdest thing in the rainforest?

Maybe plants that eat animals! Carnivorous plants found in some cloud forests can trap small animals and dissolve them for their dinner!

Sundew plant

Eek! I'm caught in the sundew's sticky blobs and need to escape before I become lunch.

Can a spider eat a bird?

Yes, if it's a South American Goliath bird-eating spider. It's the world's heaviest spider at 170 grams and is as big as a dinner plate! It usually eats insects, small mammals (like mice) and lizards.

Pretend I'm not here.
Potoo
Hey, get off! This is my neck of the woods!
Flies love this awful smell because they like to lay their eggs in rotting meat.

When is a tree stump not a tree stump?

When it's a potoo bird in the Amazon! These insect-eaters hunt at night and perch camouflaged on tree stumps during the day.

Do strawberries fight each other?

No, but tiny strawberry poison-dart frogs do! Like many similar frogs, they wrestle each other for the best nest sites and territories.

Which flower smells of rotting meat?

The giant rafflesia flower in Indonesia! It's one metre wide, and its nasty pong attracts flies that pollinate the flower.

Would you rather?

Swing from vines with the **monkeys**...
...or climb a tall tree with a **spectacled bear**?
Be a super-strong **titan beetle** that can snap pencils with its jaws...
...or a pretty **firefly beetle** with a glow-in-the-dark tummy?
Eat a fresh tropical **pineapple** or make your own chocolate from hand-picked **cocoa beans**?

Be a beautiful **bird-of-paradise** with cool dance moves that attract a mate...
...or a speedy **cassowary** that can run through the rainforest at 50 kilometres an hour?
When trekking through the rainforest, would you rather come across a **blood-sucking leech** or a **giant hairy spider**?
Get up close to a **jaguar** in the Amazon or a **gorilla** in the Congo?
Visit a hot and steamy **tropical rainforest**...
...or a cool and rainy **cloud forest**?

Do people live in the rainforest?

Yes. Some tribes (groups of people) have lived in rainforests for thousands of years and still do. Some live in much the same way as their ancestors.

We catch fish from the river and find food in the forest.

Are there any cities there?

Not now – but up to 10 million people once lived in cities now buried in the Amazon rainforest. In Cambodia, trees grow through the ruins of the ancient city of Angkor Wat.

Angkor Wat

I'm helping us learn more about the different species in the rainforest.
Sloth
Amazon tree boa
Tiny mosquitoes carry deadly diseases and cause more deaths than any other animal in the world.
Mosquito

Who works in the rainforest?

Scientists track and investigate the plants and animals that live there. Also, some people are farmers, growing and collecting cocoa, coffee, rubber and other rainforest crops.

Is it dangerous?

It can be. There are some large animals that could attack you, like jaguars or crocodiles. There are lots of poisonous animals that could sting or bite you, including snakes, spiders and insects. It's also very easy to get lost!

What happens at night?

Lots of things – all the nocturnal animals come out. These creatures hunt or feed in the rainforest by night to keep safe from predators or to stay out of the daytime heat.

Madagascar long-eared owl

i hunt at night to grab small animals that are out looking for their own food.

Flying fox

i'm a type of bat. i come out after dark to feast on fruit.

Aye-aye

i tap tree bark and listen for grubs inside, then i wiggle them out with my freaky long finger.

Mouse lemur

There are lots of different types of lemurs in Madagascar and some of us come out at night.

i only live for five days so have to find a mate quickly so we can lay eggs.

Comet moth

Fossa

I'm a large cat-like mammal and I'll eat almost anything. I hunt by day or night.

Most of us frogs are nocturnal. You can hear us croaking at night-time.

Tree frog

Tufted-tail rat

I'm spiky, like a hedgehog, and hunt for grubs and insects on the forest floor.

When frightened, I blow myself up full of air, looking even more like a tomato!

Tomato frog

It's dangerous on the forest floor, even at night. I eat plants, but lots of animals want to eat me!

Tenrec

Are rainforests in danger?

Yes, and we need to look after them. Rainforests around the world are threatened by people.

There used to be lots more rainforest. It's being cut down all the time, making animals homeless.

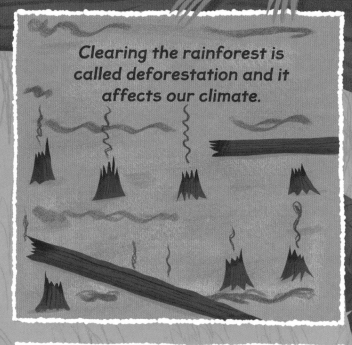

Clearing the rainforest is called deforestation and it affects our climate.

Large areas are also burned down to clear land for crops or beef cattle.

Around one-sixth of the Amazon rainforest has been destroyed.

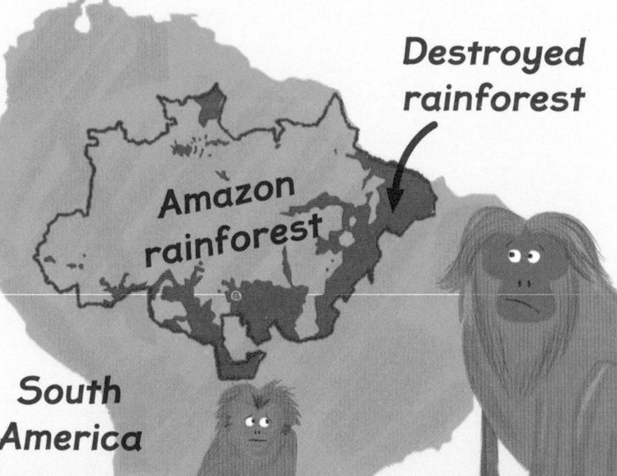

Why do we need rainforests?

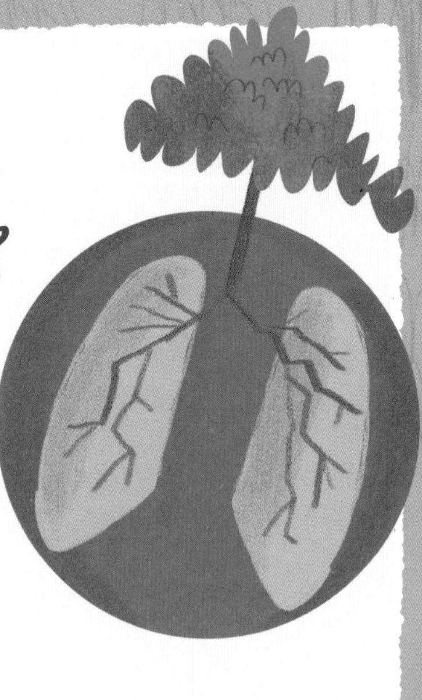

Life on Earth needs the right balance of oxygen and carbon dioxide in the atmosphere.

The plants and trees of the rainforest take carbon dioxide in and put oxygen back into the air, which all animals need.

How can we save the rainforests?

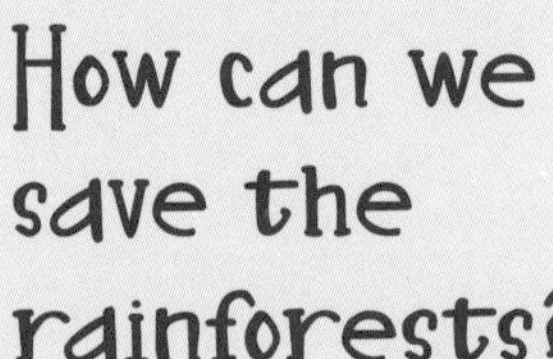

Everyone can make a difference. You can avoid beef from areas where rainforest has been cleared...

...and can ask your government to protect these areas and the people and wildlife that live there.

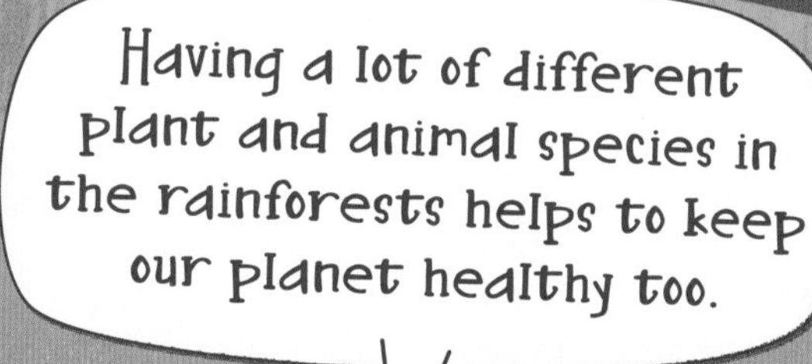

Having a lot of different plant and animal species in the rainforests helps to keep our planet healthy too.

A compendium of questions

Which animal smells like hot popcorn?

I do! I'm a binturong, from Southeast Asia. I have a gland under my tail that makes a popcorn smell.

Can we eat rainforest plants?

Yes, some of them. Lots of fruit and nuts first came from the rainforest, including tomatoes, pineapples, Brazil nuts and potatoes.

Happy birthday to us!
2000

What's the oldest thing in the rainforest?

Some trees in the temperate rainforest of Tasmania are 2000 years old.

Does an anteater only eat ants?

It eats ants or termites with its super-long tongue. A giant anteater can eat up to 35,000 in a single day!

My tongue is covered in sticky saliva, which helps me grab ants and termites.

Why are some sloths green?

Because tiny plants called algae grow in our fur!

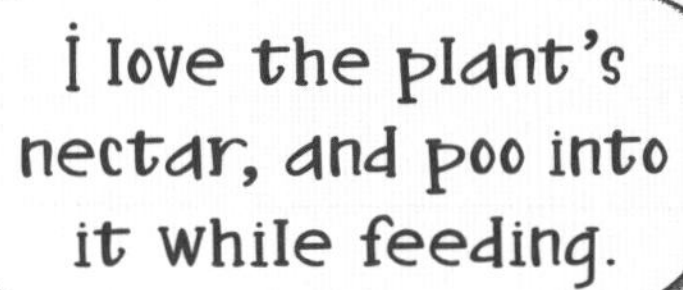

I love the plant's nectar, and poo into it while feeding.

Strangler figs begin as a seed on a tree branch, left by an animal. Its long roots slowly grow down the tree.

Is a strangler fig dangerous?

Only if you're a tree! It wraps so many roots and stems around a tree it eventually kills it.

Where does a tree shrew poo?

In a pitcher plant in the Borneo rainforest! The plant then digests the shrew poo, which helps it to grow!

Help!

The plant eats the shrew's poo! Yum!

When the strangler fig's roots reach the ground, they spread out through the soil. They can cut off nutrients and water to the tree's roots.

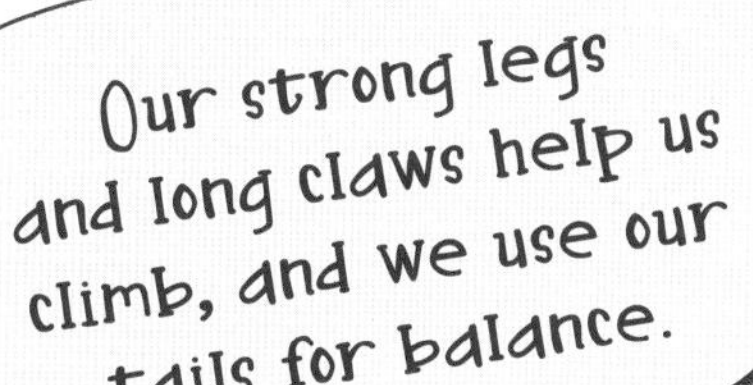

Our strong legs and long claws help us climb, and we use our tails for balance.

Do kangaroos live in the rainforest?

Not regular kangaroos, but tree kangaroos live in the rainforest of Papua New Guinea. They're smaller than their kangaroo cousins and have a longer tail.

Which creature has the longest claws?

My big third claw is also very useful when I'm digging a burrow!

Giant armadillos have a super-long third claw up to 20 centimetres long that they use to tear open tasty termite mounds for food.

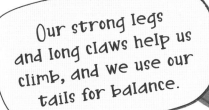

index